THE NEW GLOBAL MARKETING

Local Adaptation for Sustainability and Profit

Second Edition

Written by

Johny K. Johansson and Michael T. Furick

with Contributed Case Studies

cognella® | ACADEMIC PUBLISHING

Bassim Hamadeh, CEO and Publisher
Carrie Montoya, Manager, Revisions and Author Care
Kaela Martin, Project Editor
Abbey Hastings, Associate Production Editor
Miguel Macias, Senior Graphic Designer
Natalie Lakosil, Licensing Manager
Kat Ragudos, Interior Designer
Natalie Piccotti, Senior Marketing Manager
Kassie Graves, Director of Acquisitions and Sales
Jamie Giganti, Senior Managing Editor

DEDICATION

To my brave parents-in-law in Tokyo,
Katsuji and Tokie Kubota.

—JKJ

To the memory of Susan Furick.

—MTF

PREFACE

The last few years have witnessed dramatic changes in the global environment. Long-held assumptions about governments, political allies and economic collaboration have been upturned, as rulers and people in different countries have soured on globalization. President Trump's emphasis on "America First" in his 2017 inauguration address was foreshadowed by the 2016 Brexit vote, severing the ties between Britain and the European Union. Other Western countries have encountered popular opposition to their established liberal economic agenda. In an unlikely scenario, emerging markets such as China and India have become the major champions of global trade regimes and multinational business expansion.

The pro-democratic uprisings in the Middle East starting with Tunisia in 2011 and spreading from there have fizzled. As authoritarian governments re-captured power and meted out punishment, millions left for Europe, creating a huge immigration crisis. The result has been a populist revolt from Western natives, an increase in nationalism and a questioning of the open borders of the globalization movement. For many countries and people the promise of globalization—"economic growth lifting all boats"—has not been fulfilled. Statistically gross domestic incomes have grown, but most of the gains have gone to the top earners, including corporate leaders, while the middle income earners have been squeezed by the influx of immigrants.

How does this overall picture of the global economy affect global marketing? Global marketing is no longer the same.

First, the company today needs to be a good citizen and operate with "sustainability" as a primary guiding principle. Marketing has long been more than just "selling the product." By providing customer satisfaction, marketers were told that the bottom line result will be fine. But now global marketers cannot simply look at profit opportunities in a foreign market. The profit motive has to be expanded to the so-called triple bottom line: Economic, Social, and Environmental impact. Similar sentiments have surfaced in many places. For example, one recent newspaper article proclaimed that ESG (stands for "environmental, social, and governance") are "the 3 letters investors take seriously" (Andrew Ross Sorkin, *The New York Times*, June 27, 2017, B1). This text will show how these broader objectives of global marketing can be met.

This means that while the fundamental logic of economic globalization benefits is still valid, now the entering companies have to be much more cognizant of the local environment. "Global localization"—meaning that multinationals might have global strategies ("think global") but must be sensitive to local concerns ("act locally") is not new, but it is intensified. "Acting locally" today means not just adapting products and services to the local consumers. Today it means that the company must be socially active and play a "good citizen's" role in the local community. The United Nations' Millennium Development Goals have become the new global company mantra, emphasizing "sustainable operations" in each local market.

Second, global marketing has to accommodate the vast potential of the Internet very carefully. Today, all marketing plans involve some role for Internet-powered communication tools—from emails and banner ads to Facebook and Twitter. Since the Internet is global in reach, all marketing is potentially global. As the Internet connections reach ever more countries, towns, and villages, global communication is now an almost free good. An English-language Web-site can be accessed and read by millions of people around the world. With the ease of adding alternative languages—at worst, freely available translation software—even the most local brands can become household names in far-away countries.

It is easy to get excited about the opportunities raised by the Internet—as many observers are. But before getting too excited, it is sobering to realize that today many of the 192 countries around the globe are not always such welcoming places. In addition to political, economic and military conflicts, many of the more authoritarian governments—and even many run-of-the-mill democratic governments—often put stringent controls on Internet-related usage. For the fact is that this new global communication medium easily becomes a threat to the established order. While a marketer will hail the idea that it is possible to communicate freely to existing and potential customers around the globe, governments have come to realize that such a communication tool can be very disruptive.

Multinational companies have too much at stake in foreign markets to let go of existing investments and already nurtured customer allegiance. For their part, the citizens of countries around the world have grown increasingly fond of access to goods and services from around the world. Companies still find their fastest growth in foreign countries and each country's producers can specialize in those products for which they have sustainable advantages, and where they can contribute positively to the local environment and social cohesion.

A GUIDE TO THE CHAPTERS

In Part I, the book will introduce what it takes to do global marketing and how to assess whether a company is ready or not. In the first chapter the basics of global marketing are covered, and the task ahead of the global marketer is described. Chapter 2 discusses whether the company's strengths are sufficient for the task. The assessment of a company's strengths and weaknesses represents what is usually called "Internal evaluation" among market strategists.

The following three chapters in Part II lay out the opportunities and threats in the foreign environment faced by the global marketer. They cover the economic development in various countries (ch.3), the political and regulatory obstacles to do marketing there (ch.4), and the impact of cultural differences on the degree to which standardized global strategies can succeed (ch.5). These chapters represent the "external evaluation" parts for the market strategists.

In Part III, Chapter 6 discusses how to do market research and how data can be pulled together for country selection, to find the best country or countries to enter first. Chapter 7 then discusses the various modes of entry into foreign markets, comparing options such as exporting, franchising, and joint ventures. Chapter 8 covers global segmentation and positioning.

The chapters in Part IV deal with the global localization of the various marketing tools. Chapter 9 discusses global products and brands, and Chapter 10 deals with global services. Chapter 11 discusses global pricing, and Chapter 12 covers global distribution and e-commerce. Chapter 13 deals with global advertising and promotion, including online advertising. Chapter 14 is devoted entirely to digital global marketing, focusing on how global marketing is changing as Internet access, especially mobile access, is rapidly penetrating even the most distant countries.

FEATURES OF THE BOOK

Intended audience

This textbook is aimed at upper-level business undergraduates and MBAs. It is written with the expectation that the reader will have had some marketing education and also some exposure to international business. The material is in itself not particularly advanced, and the necessary background does not necessarily come only through formal coursework, but some acquaintance with the basic marketing and international business concepts is assumed.

Teaching method

The text is built around the now-common methodology in business schools of lectures plus case discussions. In addition, it is strongly recommended that students be assigned a semester or term-long field project, if possible in teams of 3–5 members. This team project should involve some actual product or service considering expansion into one or more foreign countries. More about this will be discussed in the Instructor's Manual.

The 22 cases in the book are divided into the four separate Parts of the book on the basis of their fit with the chapters just covered. At the same time, many are suitable for discussion in several places throughout the text, and the Instructor can make his or her own choice of case sequence to be discussed. The cases come from a variety of countries and show the quite remarkable variety of businesses in the world today. They are written by local authors in the different countries and help show how the case discussion style of business school education has spread decisively around the world.

We have kept the cases in the book deliberately shorter than the typical Harvard cases, even breaking up some longer cases into parts (A) and (B). This is to facilitate case discussions as part of a two-hour class session. Although some of the cases in the text are long and detailed enough for a whole session, where the sessions are devoted entirely to one case, as in some MBA classes, the Instructor is free to add longer cases as needed. In the Instructor's Manual we have indicated suitable longer cases for each chapter.

In addition to the common end-of-chapter discussion questions, we have also added Team Challenge Projects. These projects are focused on issues where contrasting views naturally clash—such as whether Internet privacy should be protected by the government. We have found it very useful to use two teams to argue for one or the other viewpoint. It energizes the class, and the participation stimulates students' thinking about important issues affecting global marketing.

Additional materials

PP Slides: We provide a full set of PowerPoint slides available to the Instructor upon adoption of the text.
Video: We also provide a list of suitable videos for each chapter in the book. These videos are downloadable, or, where convenient, available on the web.

Test Bank: A full set of multiple-choice questions for each chapter is available to the Instructor. Answers are also provided in the Instructor's Manual.

Instructor's Manual (IM): In addition to answers to the multiple-choice questions, the IM contains answers to chapter questions. The IM also provides suggestions about what longer cases are suitable for each chapter and suggestions about teaching methodology. The IM also provides additional readings and references for each chapter, and, crucially, suggested Course Outlines, for a full-length (14 weeks) semester and for a shorter, module-style 6–7 week class.

Case Teaching Notes: Each case has a separate teaching note written by the case authors, with answers to the end-of-case questions, suggestions about teaching the case, and, where available, information about the ultimate progress of the case company.

TO THE STUDENT

It is not unusual for students taking a Global Marketing course to feel bewildered and encounter several challenges. While many students may have been exposed to some type of International Business course, these courses usually have only a small focus on marketing. And marketing majors may be taking an International Marketing course as their first (or only) exposure to marketing in the international environment.

Some of their challenge comes first from a natural tendency to be ethnocentric or self-referencing. When you have limited frame of reference, you naturally use the only cultural basis you have (your own) to form opinions and ideas. This text has many examples in both cases and opening vignettes that attempt to have students look beyond their home country and try to understand viewpoints from another country. This might make some students uncomfortable, but the intent is to have the student understand and accept whatever business practices are in use in other countries (within ethical reason). For international marketers to be successful in the many new environments they may encounter throughout their careers, understanding other viewpoints and cultures is important, and we want the student to learn this.

The second challenge for students is to integrate what they may have learned in other international business courses with the requirements for success in international marketing. The textbook tries to merge the different material together by constantly applying previously learned techniques to solve marketing problems. For example, the student may have learned the financial specifics of letters of credit in their other business courses, and this text applies them to solve the marketing problem of "getting paid" in a country with a risky environment. Essentially learning when to use a letter of credit and why and what impact this will have on your customer.

Lastly, unlike domestic marketing where a focus on the 4Ps is many times sufficient for a measure of success (or at least a decent grade in a class), international marketing is much more complex, involving economics, trade barriers, politics, legal issues, etc. in addition to the 4Ps. There are many more "moving parts" for a student to consider in their analysis of a situation and/or a case study. To try to keep the student organized, the text revolves around three key questions that the student can come back to:

1. Is this a good product or company to expand internationally? (Chapters 1 and 2)
2. Is this a good country for expansion and why? (Chapters 3 through 8)
3. What are the details of the in-country marketing plan for success? (Chapters 9 through 14)

Early comments from students is that the text is easy to read and easy to understand and we hope that is the case.

ACKNOWLEDGMENTS

We want to thank all the many present and former colleagues who have been very influential in much of the material, but who should not at all be held responsible for the final product. In particular we want to thank a few special reviewers who helped form the book's structure and content at various stages.

They include:

Gary Bamossy, Clinical Professor of Marketing, Georgetown University, a former colleague who helped out with great feedback especially on the new material on digital global marketing.

Dale Tzeng, a former Georgetown MBA who is now Director, Digital Analytics at Horizon Media in New York, shared generously of his up-to-date digital advertising know-how.

Larry Cunningham, Professor of Marketing at the University of Colorado, Denver, a longtime colleague and friend and an adopter of previous versions of the text, who has done yeoman work on ideas for the book.

Mohamed Ezz, Professor at the University of Maryland University College, a previous adopter who has continued to give valuable feedback over the years and served as an intrepid reviewer.

Bill Evans, Professor & Head of Marketing, Groupe INSEEC/MBA Institute, Paris, France, for great reviews and European students' feedback.

We also want to thank Dr. Kay Heath, Professor of English, Georgia Gwinnett College, who viewed the content and provided feedback on ways to make the material easier for the student to learn.

Dr. Victoria Johnson, Dean School of Business, Georgia Gwinnett College, and Dr. Tyler Yu, Associate Dean, School of Business, Georgia Gwinnett College lead the School of Business and provided encouragement and funding as needed for longer term writing projects such as this one.

We also had great assistance from Nicole Moody, writer assistant, for her help with proofing copy, assembling lists, and formatting data.

Dr. Lynn Foil DMV provided help with the cover design and formatting and color coordination of slides and student materials.

Carrie Montoya and Kaela Martin at Cognella were particularly helpful in guiding the second edition. A very special "Thank you" goes out to our case writers. They have made very important contributions to the book for which we are deeply grateful. They come from virtually all over the world as you can see in the list below:

Professors Suresh George and Neil Pyper at the Coventry Business School, Coventry University, England.

Stephan Gerschewski, Assistant Professor of International Business at Linton School of Global Business, Hannam University, Daejeon, South Korea.

Don Sexton, Professor of Marketing, Director, Center for International Business Education and Research, Columbia Business School, Columbia University, New York, USA.

Dr. Mehran Nejati, Graduate School of Business, Universiti Sains Malaysia (USM), Penang, Malaysia.

Dr. Miguel A. Montoya, Tecnológico de Monterrey, campus Guadalajara, Mexico.

Professor Louise Curran, Université de Toulouse, Toulouse Business School, Toulouse, France.

Lianti Raharjo and Dahlia Darmayanti, Binus Business School, Bina Nusantara University, Indonesia.

Professor Philip Rosson of Dalhousie University, Nova Scotia, Canada.

Susana Costa e Silva at Católica Porto Business School, Portugal and Tássia Hanna Frade at Pontifícia Universidade Católica de São Paulo, Brazil.

Dr. Marina Apaydin and Hend Mostafa at the American University in Cairo, Egypt.

Dr. Cüneyt Evirgen and Yüksel Kaplancık at Sabanci University, Istanbul, Turkey.

Dr. Azhar Kazmi, Visiting Professor of Management at King Fahd University of Petroleum & Minerals, Dhahran, Saudi Arabia and Dr. Adela Kazmi, Lecturer in Management at Sophia College, Ajmer, India.

Laurence Leigh, Professor at the Suliman S. Olayan School of Business, American University of Beirut.

Masoud Kavoossi, Professor of International Business, School of Business, Howard University, Washington D.C., USA and Yuanyuan Li from the College of Economics, Jinan University, Guangzhou, China. and Ph.D. student at the School of Business, Rutgers University, NJ., USA.

ViireTäks, Ph.D. student, University of Tartu, Faculty of Economics and Business Administration, and Ph.D. Ermo Täks, Tallinn University of Technology, Faculty of Information Technology.

Kenneth A. Grossberg, Professor at Waseda Business School, Waseda University, Tokyo, Japan.

A special thank you also to the colleagues who prepared special topics for the book: Professors Jose De la Torre, Florida International University, and Ingo Walter, New York University, on Cuba, Nick Lugansky of Fluor Corporation on Russia, and Professor Masoud Kavoossi, Howard University, on Iran.

To all these great people, our heartfelt thanks!

Johny K. Johansson and Michael T. Furick
New York, NY and Lawrenceville, Georgia
August 2017

PREPARING TO GO GLOBAL

THE TWO CHAPTERS IN THIS first part set the stage for the global expansion. We first discuss the major changes in today's global environment, and then the skills and assets required for the company that goes abroad.

The first chapter spells out the new global marketing challenges today. Where globalization was accepted by most and became an "imperative" for companies, today free and open markets is a much more contested issue. Political and military conflicts also shadow the liberalization process. Still, globalization is proceeding further, partly with the help of the digital revolution. The rise of the Internet and the penetration of online access in the most far-off markets have enabled unprecedented reach for both customers and companies.

The second chapter discusses what it takes for a company to go global. It focuses on the strengths and weaknesses section of the standard SWOT strategic framework. The chapter presents the basic drivers of competitive advantages, separating the country-specific factors of international trade theory from firm-specific advantages. Country-specific factors are advantages that can be used by any company from the same country, while the firm-specific factors, such as strong brands, are unique to each firm. For global expansion, the firm-specific advantages are usually more important, since they are harder for competitors to imitate. A critical factor in the effort to go global is whether these advantages can be effectively transferred abroad.

" Brave new digital world "

In this chapter you will learn about:
1. The forces that drive localization and the potential at the bottom of the pyramid
2. What makes for competitive advantages and how they can be transferred abroad
3. The new technological developments that make global marketing different today
4. The concepts and tools that help global marketing decision-making

In what one might call "pre-historic" time, or the mid-1990s, global marketing was just beginning to get its feet on the ground. Companies had begun to recognize that not all foreign markets were so very "foreign." The removal of the Berlin Wall had opened up Soviet Russia, China's pro-market reforms were proceeding on schedule, and as it turned out, there seemed to be similar market segments in almost every country.

- Young people worldwide liked Madonna, wore Levi's jeans, ran in Nike or adidas shoes, and the kids went to McDonald's and drank Coca-Cola.
- A bit older young people drove a BMW or wanted one, were experimenting with the pocket-size mobile phone models, and had started using the dotcoms for e-commerce and the Internet to communicate across borders.
- And really older people—first those over 30 and later those above 40 years of age—were rediscovering some of the excitement of young age, with aging baby boomers acquiring tastes for finer wines, international travel, spas, and good food.

Global Marketing in a New Era

CHAPTER 1

Some 20 years later, the picture is not the same. Things have changed, and not only for the better. The trend is no longer so uniform, no longer pointing to further integration and international harmony. Global communication technology has been developed further, and has continued to drive the global convergence, with the Internet and Skype and travel and World Cup sports bringing people together. But political and religious differences, terrorism, and military conflicts have reversed the trend and lead to increased separation between people. Twenty years ago, many young students and professionals were interested in foreign cultures, learning a foreign language and meeting different people. Today, many countries and many peoples tend to prefer less involvement with foreign countries and strange people. Even within countries, political, ethnic, and racial differences have been allowed to surface and to dominate the daily discourse, threatening political instability and government paralysis. Even if consumers can still find many of the major brands in stores around the world or available through e-commerce over the Internet, globalization has peaked and national identity counts for more than international renown. Not all country leaders have retreated from the world stage, but global presence is no longer an unquestioned mark of excellence.

But global marketers are still positive on the situation. What can be called "the fundamentals" of global marketing are still the same. For the global marketer, there are three basic questions:

- The first question is still whether the company's product or service is strong enough to be successful internationally.
- The second question is how to assess the potential in various market countries.
- The third question is how to develop a market plan for a successful launch into the new country.

These are the fundamentals that this text is focused on. As we will see, the task of implementing these fundamentals has changed in the new circumstances of today's uncertain and often unpredictable global environment. Global marketing is not simply a matter of selling products to needy foreign consumers—the company needs to provide adapted products, sustainability, and local sales support in all of their markets.

Twenty or so years ago globalization was touted as an "imperative" for business. Today, globalization has reached its saturation. Globalization will not disappear—globalization is with us whether we like it or not. But the imperative for business today is "localization, sustainability, and social responsibility." Today, global marketing strategy necessarily involves "global localization." More and more companies have global reach and presence—with the Internet, international express shipments, and inexpensive global communications, "being global" requires fewer resources than ever—but they also face the increased threat that national governments implement stringent import controls, new business regulations, and increased support for domestic products and services. "Be a good local citizen" is the new global mindset.

OPENING VIGNETTE

MCDONALD'S IN RUSSIA: MIXING BUSINESS AND POLITICS[1]

In 1989, the "Anti-Fascist Protection Rampart" fell (what the West knew as "The Berlin Wall"), ushering in the eventual fall of communism, the demise of the Soviet Union, and the beginning of Russia as a Newly Democratized Country (NDC). McDonald's had been negotiating for 14 years to open stores in Russia and the company now saw its chance. The first McDonald's opened on Pushkin Square, Moscow, in 1990, and a two hour-long queue snaked out the door. Serving over 30,000 customers, this first day of sales in the Moscow location remains the record for opening day at any McDonald's. In a recently communist country with frequent food shortages, the Russians marveled at the fact that McDonald's always had food: "If you order a burger, you actually get a burger."

EXHIBIT 1.1.
A McDonald's restaurant on Nevsky Avenue, St. Petersburg, Russia

Copyright © 2011 by Shutterstock/ withGod.

Because of the chaotic distribution system in Russia, McDonald's had planned well with their McComplex that grew their own lettuce and tomatoes, baked their own buns, and helped local farmers raise their cattle. Even today all of McDonald's food supply comes from local Russian farmers. McDonald's in Russia (see Exhibit 1.1.) has grown to over 609 stores in over 60 cities and townships and some estimate that it has captured 70 percent of the Russian fast-food market. McDonald's Russia added 73 stores in 2016 and another 50 more in 2017 after expanding to the far-flung regions of the Urals and Siberia.

But in Global Marketing, times are constantly changing and the Russians (at least the Russian government) may have a different view now about McDonald's. Russia's annexation of Crimea and its support of the rebels in the Ukraine have led to U.S. and E.U. sanctions that have seriously affected the Russian economy and was still in effect as of mid-2017. In response, the Russian government has begun a campaign of anti-Westernization that is affecting American companies in Russia.

In 2012, Russia's Chief Sanitary Inspector said that Russians should stick to "Russian patriotic foods" and avoid exotic foods from McDonald's. In 2014, a leader of a Russian political party (Liberal Democrats) said that Russia should close all of America's McDonald's in Russia. When Russia imposed a ban on the importation of all food from Western countries, McDonald's was unaffected since they use local Russian suppliers. However, to make sure their point was made, in August 2014, a consumer-safety regulator temporarily closed four McDonald's stores for "sanitary violations" including the flagship store on Pushkin Square. Since McDonald's seems to remain very popular with Russian diners, the government left the remaining McDonald's operating. By November the first Moscow McDonald's was up and running again, and a month later the others did too, except two that were being remodeled.[2] To try to shield itself from politics in a world of "America First," McDonald's has attempted to become a Russian company: its suppliers are Russian, its executives are all Russian, and the familiar McDonald's logo outside the restaurants is only in Russia's Cyrillic script.

A GLOBAL MARKETPLACE

Despite recent political clamor for protectionism and against trade, a lot of businesses are global today. Ten or 20 years ago, global business was mainly in the hands of a select number of multinational giants. Small and medium-sized businesses concentrated on their home markets and perhaps one or two neighboring countries. Not so any longer. Even the smallest businesses have realized that they have something to market in faraway countries, many of which have recently opened to foreign competition. Today, companies of all sizes in various industries from many countries are actively competing in the world's markets (see Exhibit 1.2).

THE GLOBALIZING FORCE OF TECHNOLOGY

Behind the development toward a more global marketplace lies a revolution in **global communications** and **transportation**. Satellite television broadcasts have eliminated national borders in mass media. Advances in electronic telecommunications have made it possible to develop company information networks that rival government intelligence operations. Transportation networks developed by express carriers and company subsidiaries can rely on efficient supply chains and cheap air transport across long distances. Today it is possible for headquarters to participate directly in decision making in any subsidiary. Managers can direct operations any place on earth from airplanes and automobiles; even when they're on vacation they can be seen on the beach talking on their mobile phones.

	Country	Product exports 2016 (billions $$)	Percentage of world product export trade
1	China	2,098.0	13.3%
2	United States	1,471.0	9.4%
3	Germany	1,283.0	8.2%
4	Japan	641.4	4.1%
5	Korea, South	509.0	3.2%
6	France	489.1	3.1%
7	Hong Kong	487.7	3.1%
8	Netherlands	480.1	3.1%
9	Italy	436.3	2.8%
10	United Kingdom	412.1	2.6%
11	Canada	390.1	2.5%
12	Mexico	373.7	2.4%
13	Singapore	353.3	2.2%
14	United Arab Emirates	316.0	2.0%
15	Taiwan/Chinese Taipei	314.8	2.0%

Source: International Trade Center.

EXHIBIT 1.2.
Exports of the top 15 countries (2016). The top 15 exporting countries represent over 60 percent of the world's total exports. China's dramatic rise in the last couple of decades has given hope to the 4 billion people at the bottom of the economic pyramid who struggle to be part of the world of international trade.

Technological innovations in logistics and communications have made global expansion of multinationals both possible and desirable. The **Internet** is inherently global. The World Wide Web and its home pages can be accessed from anywhere by anyone (see Exhibit 1.3).

Businesses can establish presence in foreign markets without ever setting foot there. The costs of business transactions across borders in industries such as transportation, hotel and travel, and financial services have been substantially reduced. Entrepreneurial start-up firms can create an online presence, receive orders from abroad, get paid via PayPal, and ship products instantly and without financial risks. E-commerce allows one-to-one marketing across countries, with customization and personal attention at minimum cost.

These developments have enabled consumers around the world to learn much more about people elsewhere and about the products and brands available in foreign markets. In particular, the recent emergence of social media has allowed consumers an unparalleled access to information about companies and products—from their own friends and fellow consumers. Many people around the world know a lot about other countries, have friends there, and travel there frequently. Global marketing has become not only more attractive as a business opportunity but it has also allowed many people around the world to share in the fruits of globalization.

OTHER FACTORS FAVORING GLOBAL MARKETING

Globalization has been driven by other factors as well. **Global competitors** can provide a strong incentive for local firms to follow suit. On the home front, the presence of foreign competitors in a firm's domestic market increases the need for the firm to venture abroad, if for no other reason than to counterattack in foreign markets. Zara's and H&M's success in the United States has led The Gap, their U.S. competitor, to go abroad.

Economies of scale can be gained by globalization. To achieve lower unit manufacturing costs one plant often needs to supply more than one foreign market. Toyota's Kentucky plant, for example, produces the Camry model for the NAFTA market, and the BMW plant in South Carolina focuses on the 325 model, supplying the North American market. Global advertising can be cost efficient because it uses the same commercial

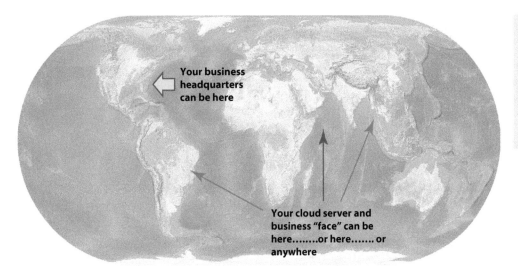

EXHIBIT 1.3.
International networks based on the "cloud" have enabled even small companies to operate locally while achieving global reach.

Source: https://commons.wikimedia.org/wiki/File:Eckert4.jpg

across countries with voiceovers in the native language. An ad with Ronaldo as a spokesperson can be used virtually everywhere.

Even where there are no scale economies, **economies of scope** (gains from spreading activities across multiple product lines or businesses) can push businesses to globalize. Thus, in consumer packaged goods, because the dominant global firms have small plants in many countries, they gain scope economies by marketing a wide selection of products. Unilever, Colgate-Palmolive, and Procter & Gamble have mostly uniform product lines and brand names across the EU, but have manufacturing plants in all the major European countries.

There are also **sourcing advantages**, such as supply from a low-wage country, improved logistics and distribution systems, and the growth of inexpensive global telecommunications. With the help of real-time and low-cost global communications, more companies have created complex global supply chains for products as well as components and parts (see Exhibit 1.4).

EXHIBIT 1.4.
Globalized supply chains are increasingly efficient (to lower costs) but also complex. For example, the Ford Motor Company uses over 1200 vendors in 60 countries to supply 8 U.S. assembly plants and 23 international assembly plants to fill orders from 11,900 dealers worldwide. Transmissions for U.S. vehicles could be made in any of seven countries. One can see, therefore, that implementing President Trump's demand for "America First" policies can be difficult.

Ex. 1.4a: Copyright © Depositphotos/soleilc.

Ex. 1.4b: Copyright © 2004 Caihua, (GNU Lesser General Public License 2.1) at: https://commons.wikimedia.org/wiki/File:Fairytale_bookmark_gold.png. A copy of the license can be found here: https://www.gnu.org/licenses/old-licenses/lgpl-2.1.html

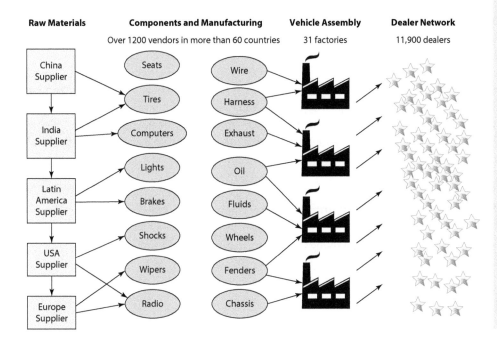

Many companies have global supply networks that help break down barriers between countries and increase management knowledge of foreign markets. The learning is mutual, as local suppliers develop skills and know-how and get ready to stand on their own. As foreign suppliers have become partners in the global network, the understanding of local culture, language, and managerial style is enhanced, and over time visitors gain insight into the habits and preferences of consumers in foreign countries.

OBSTACLES TO GLOBAL MARKETING

But "Going Global" has never been an obvious strategy choice for most marketers. In fact, most companies have always faced certain obstacles when contemplating global marketing. The two main factors are lack of knowledge and lack of resources.

- Management knowledge of the potential in foreign markets has often been lacking. Most managers focus on the home market and feel uncertain about conditions in foreign markets.
- Even when the foreign opportunities are recognized, there are limited resources for capturing them. Lack of financial strength is a typical problem, but the more critical obstacle is often a lack of managerial attention. Management is often stretched too thin for an effective global marketing effort.

But today there are new and unprecedented obstacles to globalization. The political turmoil and the rise of terrorism in recent years have added to the usual obstacles:

- The increased risk of terrorism has meant that many companies avoid some countries and regions altogether. Managers are reluctant to move to markets where they risk lives and also risk having the company and brands compromised.
- Increased protectionist policies in some countries have raised entry barriers against foreign entrants. The U.S. push towards an "America First" strategy under President Trump and the shift away from global trade is reflected also in the British turn away from the EU (the so-called Brexit) and the rise of national-first movements in other countries (see Exhibit 1.5).
- The political shift away from globalization towards more populist national policies has also made some foreign markets less receptive to global brands and multinational companies.

The fundamental factors that drive companies towards globalization have to be balanced against these new realities. Political uncertainty has made some companies put big global plans on the back burner for the time being. Many companies still maintain global operations but with a lower profile. They do not advertise their global presence, but emphasize their local adaptations. At home they highlight their roots and make sure that the local economy stands to gain with their presence regardless of country of origin.

RECENT DEVELOPMENTS IN GLOBAL MARKETING

There are several recent developments in global marketing that will be important in the rest of the book.

E-commerce

Electronic commerce (**e-commerce**) refers to the business transactions that take place entirely online, from the search for information about products and services to final purchase and delivery.

E-commerce has become a major factor in many countries around the world, growing especially fast in emerging countries where the retail network is weak and often nonexistent. It has grown also because of the increased penetration of smartphones which make mobile e-commerce feasible, another advantage in countries where PCs are less common.

E-commerce is still not the major form of commerce in any one country. It is still less than 10 percent in the U.S., and even though other countries show higher figures (see Exhibit 1.6), e-commerce is still a small part of total retail sales.

But e-commerce is growing faster than spending in total in all countries. In addition, e-commerce is very big for business-to-business (B2B) transactions, helping to establish efficient supply chains with global reach.

Because of the global reach of the Internet and online business, global marketers will have to incorporate e-commerce into their strategic plans. There are obstacles, but technology is developing rapidly and promises to make e-commerce a viable option for cross-border trade as well. Payment systems are developed that can handle currency exchanges for example. American PayPal (owned by eBay) and Chinese Alipay (owned by Alibaba) are already active in this area. Efficient delivery systems and computerized distribution centers are reducing transportation and warehousing costs. Large e-commerce companies such as Amazon.com have established facilities in foreign countries to speed up deliveries

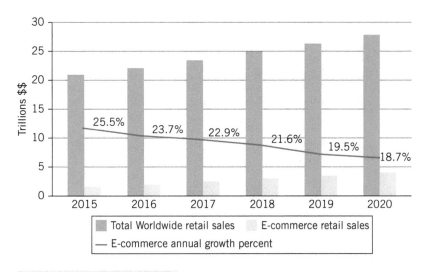

and lower costs, and air-express carriers such as DHL and FedEx already operate globally.

E-commerce will grow even further in the future (see Exhibit 1.6), and in this book we will keep coming back to the question of how to combine traditional global marketing principles with this new strategic opportunity.

Social Media

The emergence of social media has profoundly changed our modern world. Social media vehicles such as Facebook and Twitter are increasingly becoming communication vehicles not only between individual and groups, but also for companies, news media, and public policy makers. Companies large and small connect with customers through Facebook, as do elected legislators. The U.S. President Trump has taken "Policy by Twitter" to a whole different level, and the new French President Macron used social media to engineer an upset win in the 2017 French election. Social media is also changing marketing in revolutionary ways. It is also set to change global marketing dramatically.

The emergence of Facebook, Twitter, Instagram, Snapchat, and other social media platforms have introduced major changes in marketing communications:

- Consumers are always reachable—mobile communications make it possible to reach customers at any time.
- Communication is two-way—consumers can act on their own or react to marketing communications, offering comments and assessments about products and services.
- In sharp contrast to traditional media messages, the message emerging in online media cannot be controlled by the firm. The social media "buzz" can be negative or positive.
- Media costs are minimal in social media—another sharp contrast to traditional advertising media where especially television is a high-cost medium.
- Marketing communications in social media require constant updating, responding to the ever-changing buzz evolving in online discussions. Resources have to be allocated to monitor discussions and keep websites up-to-date.

Online communications are inherently global—and even if English is not necessarily the language spoken, many of the vehicles have translated their services and apps into foreign languages. In addition, local entrepreneurs have also started their own networks. For example, while Twitter has been translated into Japanese and found success, a local platform named Line has since taken the lead among young Japanese consumers.[3] Domestic competitors often have advantage in adapting to local preferences. For example, the Facebook emphasis on identity and friends is not very attractive to individuals favoring privacy and anonymity, as tends to be the norm outside of the United States.

The marketing impact from social media involves more than communications. An incomplete list includes at least the following items related to what *consumers can do.*

- Collect information on brands and firms
- Easily compare prices of a brand in different outlets
- Share brand opinions with others
- Interact directly with firms, giving more brand feedback over and above satisfaction

Similarly, *firm capabilities* are also greater. Firms can do the following:

- Send targeted ads, coupons, samples, and brand information to customers
- Increase word-of-mouth brand communication among customers
- Collect competitive brand information about customers and markets

The most fundamental shift due to social media is the increased power of the consumer. It has become increasingly difficult to communicate top-down in the manner of old-style advertising. Friends and peers are more trusted and responsive, as always, but now they are also reachable anytime, anywhere. Still, some information may be communicated through traditional media—for example, exposing consumers to new products and new features that they would not otherwise be aware of. It is also possible to use traditional media as a reminding tool, keeping the brand actively in the mind of the consumer. Traditional media allows a control of the message, which can be very useful for product positioning purposes, where specific benefits are communicated.

But in social media, the initiative lies with the individual consumer. Advertising might have planted some seeds of awareness, but any subsequent processing of the information is likely to depend on its value as social media "**buzz.**" This means that any communication from the firm will have to offer something newsworthy, something worthwhile to discuss, something interesting and perhaps surprising. In other words, in social media marketers need to behave as contributors to the discussion, and any brand messages should best take the form of newscasts of valuable discussion points. Some firms establish discussion forums, chat rooms, and consumer panels to interact directly with consumers for feedback and suggestions. Others become members of brand communities or opt to "follow" some bloggers. Most firms encourage consumers to "follow" their brand and offer special deals for the more loyal followers.

One result from the two-way global communications made possible by the Internet and social media is the empowerment of customers over producers. The power of the consumers has pulled marketers even closer to them, and the mindset of the marketer today has shifted from a focus on the brand choice and purchase occasion to the consumer shopping and **usage experience.** Marketers have become more attuned to how their products and services help the consumer in her daily chores, and how the products and services add value to people's lives.

To make this perspective more concrete, it is useful to view products and services as "doing a job" for the consumer.[4] That is, people buy products not only because they "solve a problem" or because they make lives more productive.[5] They acquire products in order to help them to do something.

This "a product is doing a job" perspective is particularly useful when trying to understand consumer behavior in foreign countries. It helps explain what might seem an irrational purchase, such as a poor farmer buying a flat-screen TV or a newly rich Chinese businessman spending a fortune at the roulette tables. It is good to remember that any purchase or particular practice might well seem rational to the individual person. Many foreigners are aghast to find how much redundant "stuff" the average American household stores up (coined **Affluenza** in an influential book),[6] how quickly Americans jettison perfectly good products in favor of a new model, and how

Annual Paid Vacation Days Per Worker	
France	30
UK	28
Austria	25
Finland	25
Spain	22
Italy	20
Germany	20
Australia	20
Switzerland	20
Canada	10
Japan	10
U.S.	10

Sources: Center for Economic and Policy Research (2014) and ETUI-REHS (2007).

EXHIBIT 1.7.
In Europe, a vacation does not mean "no pay."[7]

few vacation days the average American takes despite the apparent affluence. For many of us, these practices are easily explained as rational because of how much room is available in the average home, how "much better" the new model is, or how much money one would lose by not working (see Exhibit 1.7). The experienced global marketer knows how culturally contingent all our rational behavior really is. What makes sense to a Californian might not make sense to many others.

For the global market today, local adaptation is more than just tweaking product features and service characteristics. It means adapting the product to the way the customer actually uses the product, not how the product "should be used." Experienced marketers who think they "know the customer" often resist this level of adaptation. A good example is the reluctance with which the cup-holders in automobiles were greeted when the Japanese automakers first introduced them in the United States. The first Toyota models with cup-holders did not come from the models in Japan, where coffee drinking while driving was not common. Rather, it was the Japanese observations that California drivers drank coffee during their long freeway commutes that suggested to them that cup-holders might be a good idea. The Western automakers did not observe any need for this—as one executive dismissively said, "People should not drink coffee while driving."

The "Bottom of the Pyramid" (BOP)

Demand creation is not a one-way street from advanced to emerging countries. For example, today innovations in products can come from any country. As suggested by early accounts such as *Small is Beautiful*, the 1973 book by Fritz Schumacher, there are innovation lessons from less developed countries for the advanced world.[8] The appropriate technology for social and economic problems in countries such as India requires intermediate rather than advanced technology for sustainability. In fact, if companies are willing to adapt products to the needs of the poorest in many countries, there is money to be made "at the bottom of the pyramid." In a path-breaking 2002 article, Prahalad and Hart argued that there is a "fortune" to be made among the 4 billion poor people in the world (see Exhibit 1.8).

The notion has become known as "**B24b**," "Business to 4 billion," or simply **B-O-P marketing**. More recent books have expanded on this vision and demonstrated how such technology can then be introduced profitably in advanced economies.[8] Other authors have taken this theme even further, coining "reverse innovation" as the new way of multinationals to innovate globally while staying true to local needs and different cultures.[9] A striking illustration is the development of a low-cost, portable ultrasound machine by GE for use in rural China, an innovation then diffused to other countries with great success.

The notion that markets are potentially global reflects the reality that many of the conditions in advanced markets mirror those elsewhere once user requirements are properly understood. Not all consumers in advanced markets need "advanced" products. Not all consumers are "advanced" in their preferences all the time. Not all emerging countries' consumers need "basic" products only. Not all consumers in emerging countries prefer global brands all the time. The truth is, to an increasing extent, that there are characteristics of demand in all local markets that are a mixture of preferences for global and local brands—across consumers, and across purchase occasions.

As Indra Nooyi, chairperson and CEO of PepsiCo, writes in the Foreword to Govindarajan and Trimble's 2012 book about her experiences as the head of a global company:

"First, we have learned better to appreciate the differences of people from place to place. Second, we have learned that a market wants to have its culture, values, and tastes reflected back to it in the product it chooses to consume. And third, we have learned that people around the world—even for all their differences—still have some desires in common."[10]

Markets are increasingly global, not because they are the same everywhere—they are not—but because there are common desires among segments of consumers in different countries.

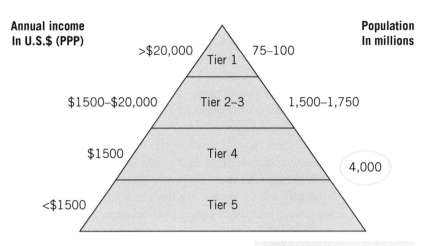

EXHIBIT 1.8.
The 4 Billion people at the bottom of the economic pyramid living on an income of a few dollars per day. According to the World Bank, about 1.1 billion people have risen out of extreme poverty since 1990. Still, more than 1 billion live on less than $2 a day, the definition of "extreme poverty."

Source: Prahalad and Hart, 2002.

Branding Advantage

As supply chains and products get globalized, they also get standardized. That is, many companies use the same suppliers for basic components and parts, and many of the manufacturing and assembly contractors work for more than one company (although some companies, like Nike, use exclusive contractors). These standardized components and parts make for sameness in the product lines of many competitors, something aided and abetted also by the common practice of monitoring and imitating ("benchmarking") competitors' new products.

One consequence of the standardization has been that competitive advantage increasingly relies on advantages on the marketing side.[11] This is perhaps good news for marketers, but it also means that there is more stress on marketing advantages than before. Since now competing products have quite similar technical and functional characteristics, there is often not much to clearly distinguish the offerings from different makers. One result of this is the increasing stress on branding. The brand is one of the few things that can still be kept away from competitors. A brand is unique to a firm and legally protected. A strong brand—that is a brand is widely known and highly respected—is for many companies today their most valuable (and sustainable) asset. Global brands have become more important than ever.

Country of Origin

In global marketing, the country of origin of a product has long been an important issue. Over the years, research has shown that certain countries have an advantage in certain products—for example, Germany in cars, Japan in consumer electronics, and France in wines. But today because of outsourcing and offshoring, the "made-in" label is today quite meaningless. The German car might be made in South Carolina, the patriotic American buyer of a Samsonite suitcase might find that the luggage was made in India, and, as most people know by now, even the iconic iPhone is assembled in China (with parts from a number of other Asian countries).

But there can still be a country-of-origin effect. In *luxury* brands, for example, some consumers feel cheated when they discover that their purchase is not what they thought it was. It is not good to find that your Louis Vuitton bag is not made in France. Luxury brands, as a result, try very hard to avoid outsourcing and offshoring, especially since a Vuitton bag made in China surely is counterfeit. And there is often a country-of-origin effect for *brands*, regardless of production location. The brand identity assumes the country identity. A BMW made in South Carolina is still a "German" car to consumers. The iPhone is from the United States—actually, more like "from California." A Honda Civic built in Ohio is still a "Japanese" car. This is not simply a mistake on the part of the consumers—these multinational companies make very sure that their production sites adhere to the stringent quality controls of the brand's origin.

All Marketing is Potentially Global Marketing

As a result of these forces, virtually all marketing today can become global marketing. Even the most local of brands in a faraway marketplace—such as the Kefraya brand of arak from Lebanon—will potentially have global reach into even the most distant countries. To find an arak brand, Google "arak" and go to Wikipedia to find a listing of brands, then go to the brand's website or its distributor's site (Kefraya is listed by several distributors, including the UK arm of Amazon.com). But the global reach is not just one-way. A local brand such as Kefraya also faces global competitors in their home market. Its presumably loyal customers are tempted not only by other local arak brands, and also by foreign brands of alternative drinks, available locally. You can have your Lebanese mezze meal with arak from Syria, or ouzo from Greece, or Yellow Tail wine from Australia and Castle beer from South Africa's SABMiller.

There are three globalizing factors at work in this: the Internet, improved logistics, and the global diffusion of marketing management skills.

- The biggest reason is that virtually all companies today can be reached via the Internet. A brand's website—or its distributors' websites—makes communication global and instantaneous. This is the main driver of the need for marketers to think globally from the start. But there are strong reasons beyond the ease of communications and reach of most brands. One reason is that, despite some temporary and local setbacks, economic growth in emerging countries has been strong and resilient over the last decade. With economic growth many emerging markets are beginning to look pretty similar to the traditional advanced markets.
- Furthermore, with innovations in logistics such as uniform shipping codes, express services, and streamlined customs procedures, transportation costs have decreased and have become a minor part of total product cost. Delivery times have been reduced dramatically with the introduction of airborne shipping and streamlined processing. Trade barriers such as tariffs still exist, but are gradually coming down. Transfer of technology due to offshoring and outsourcing has made many countries capable of manufacturing state-of-the-art products with quality levels on par or better than those of traditional producers. Geographical distances between markets have become less of a trade barrier than before.

- A third important driver for the convergence of domestic and global marketing is that management experience and skills are no longer confined to the more developed countries. While the depth of the managerial cadre is not yet as great in some of the new countries, the number of top managers and corporate leaders of the largest global companies who hail from emerging countries is increasing. One is perhaps not surprised to find a Korean, Mr. Lee Kun-hee, as the Chairman of Samsung Electronics, the world's largest information technology company. The same is true for Yang Yuanqing, a Chinese native who is the CEO of Lenovo, the large computer maker from China that acquired IBM's ThinkPad. But others are managing some of the leading Western companies. The most prominent is perhaps Carlos Ghosn from Brazil, head of two renowned automobile marquees, Renault and Nissan. But there are others, including Indra Nooyi, at the helm of PepsiCo, and Omar Ishrak, from Bangladesh, the CEO of Medtronic, the world's largest medical-device company.

GLOBAL MARKETING CONCEPTS

There are some key concepts we need to define clearly before going further.

Global Marketing Defined

Global marketing refers to marketing activities coordinated and integrated across multiple country markets. The integration can involve **standardized products,** uniform packaging, identical brand names, synchronized product introductions, similar advertising messages, or coordinated sales campaigns across markets in several countries. Despite the term "global," it is not necessary that all or most of the countries of the world be included. Even regional marketing efforts, such as pan-European operations, can be viewed as examples of global marketing. The point is an integrated effort across several countries—and the principles are roughly similar whether one talks about 5 or 50 countries.

Regionalization

Although in this book we will treat globalization and regionalization as relatively similar, there is growing awareness among marketers that regionalization is much more common than complete globalization. **Regionalization** means treating regions of the world as the new standardization unit. While domestic or national marketing strategies are adapted to the particular country market, and global strategies are standardized and implemented for the global market as a whole, regionalization means that similar marketing strategies are applied for regions—such as Pan-European, North American, or Asian strategies.

Many multinational companies have long organized along regional lines. As a typical example, the Hewlett-Packard Company breaks down its global organization into three regional sectors: Europe, Asia-Pacific, and the Americas. Similar structures can be found for Japanese companies such as Honda and Korean Samsung and European companies such as Dutch Philips. A completely globalized organizational design is simply too unwieldy to manage, and customer needs and preferences sometimes differ markedly between regions.

A new factor that has encouraged regionalization is the insight that even in the age of the Internet and global communications, distance still matters. Understanding customers in different parts of the world requires some face-to-face contacts and personal experience. The same is true for managing employees and dealing with local subsidiary managers. These and related distance factors were first categorized by Ghemawat as the four dimensions of a **CAGE** concept:[12]

1. Cultural distance—religious and language differences are still barriers.
2. Administrative distance—regulatory differences between countries pose problems.
3. Geographic distance—far-away markets are difficult to manage from home.
4. Economic distance—low development means weak infrastructure, payment ability, etc.

Ghemawat develops the strategic concept of "semi-globalization" which is akin to regionalization. He argues that the multinational firm can adopt a semi-globalized strategy by adapting to each region and standardizing within each region. He then suggests that the firm deals with the differences between regions by "arbitrage," that is exploiting differences between regions to moving operations to where they are best performed.

The regionalization strategy is also supported by empirical findings that show how unevenly the multinational firms' sales are spread over the world markets. By far the majority of sales for any multinational are in one or two regions, often close to home. An analysis by Rugman of the largest multinationals in the world ("The Fortune Global 500") found that 64 percent of the firms derived more than 50 percent of their sales from their home region, close to 10 percent of the firms drew most sales from only two regions, and only nine multinationals were truly global with significant sales from three regions or more.[13] Three of these global firms were American (IBM, Intel, and Coca-Cola), three were Asian (Sony, Canon, and Flextronics, an electronics manufacturer headquartered in Singapore), and three European (Finnish Nokia, Dutch electronics maker Philips, and LVMH, the French luxury-goods company whose brands include Louis Vuitton and Dior).

Rugman and Ghemawat both propose that corporate strategies be conceived in terms of regions rather than worldwide. Their analysis shows that in fact, this is what companies already do. Actually, many multinationals have product lines with a large number of brands, and they can treat some as "global," some as "regional," and some as "local." One example is Nestlé (see illustration in Exhibit 1.9).

The assumption that all countries can be treated the same way and that distance between countries does not matter is erroneous. It also means that when competitive advantages are analyzed, the proper market to look at might well be the region, not the country or the world. According to Rugman, one typical strategy is to choose being present in the "**Triad**" regions of Western Europe, North America, and East Asia (initially only Japan, now with China added).[14]

For many of the principles of global marketing discussed in what follows, however, the distinction between regions and worldwide is less of a concern. The validity of the principles is not a matter of kind, but of degree. Just like globalization, regionalization still needs an analysis across countries that tells whether customers are similar or not, cultures are similar or not, and business is similar or not. The standardization of marketing within a region can run into the same problems as standardizing across several regions. Yes, the chances are less, and the problems might be easier to spot, but the principles and the problems are the same. The big question, as we will see over and over again, is the degree to which the marketing can be adapted and fine-tuned to the local consumer, or whether standardization and offering the same as elsewhere is good enough.

Multi-Domestic Markets

Multi-domestic markets are defined as product markets in which local consumers have preferences and functional requirements widely different from one another's and others' elsewhere. The typical market categories include products and services such as foods, drinks, clothing, and entertainment, which tend to vary considerably between countries and in which many consumers prefer the local variants.

The firm selling into multi-domestic markets needs to localize and adapt its products and services to the different requirements and preferences in the several markets. Levels of salt and sugar in food products might need to change, and color patterns and sizes of packaging might be redesigned for attractiveness and taste. Drinks need to be taste-tested and perhaps given strong communication support, educating the local consumers and trying to change their preferences, as 7-Up has tried to do in the United States. In clothing, redesigning jeans to fit the different bodies of Asian people, widening the shoes, and shortening the sleeves are necessary steps, but the multi-domestic marketer may also have to create new colors, different styles, and alternative materials. Before globalization, firms were generally multinational for a reason: The products had to be adapted to each country's preferences. Marketing could not be uniform.

Global Markets

Global markets are defined as those markets in which buyer preferences are similar across countries. Within each country, several segments with differing preferences may exist, but the country borders are not important segment limits. In some cases the "global" market is more like a "regional" market, encompassing a trade area such as the EU, NAFTA, or Mercosur. Since the principal features of global marketing apply equally to regional and to truly global markets, this book will not make much of this distinction. However, it should be recognized that much of international trade takes place within such regions.

The typical characteristics of a global market have both customer and competitive aspects. The major global features to look for are the following:

Customer globalization:

- Increasingly common requirements and preferences across borders for specific market segments
- Global networks, as the purchasing function for multinational companies is centralized
- Disappearing national boundaries as customers travel across borders to buy wherever the best products and/or prices are found
- Increasing agreement among customers across the globe about how to evaluate products and services and recognition of which brands are the best

EXHIBIT 1.9.
Perrier water at the French Open tennis tournament and the Vittel water truck at Tour de France. *Perrier* is one of Nestlé's global brands, sponsoring tennis, a global sport. *Vittel* is one of Nestlé's regional brands, sponsoring bicycle races, a more regional sport. Nestlé has 64 water brands, with the majority of brands local.

Ex. 1.9a: Copyright © 2015 by Shutterstock/Leonard Zhukovsky.

Ex. 1.9b: Copyright © 2014 by Shutterstock/ NeydtStock.

Competitor globalization:

- Competition among the same world-class players in every major national market
- Declining numbers of competitors in the core of the market as domestic companies defend their turf by specialization or merge with larger firms
- Increasing use of national markets as a strategic tool for the benefit of the firm's global network

With global communications and spreading affluence, many previously multi-domestic markets are becoming more susceptible to globalization. People all around the world now know and like ethnic foods, such as Middle-Eastern hummus, Spanish paella, and Beijing duck. Apparel from Spain's Zara, Sweden's H&M, and Japan's Uniqlo are bought worldwide. Japanese sake, German beer, and French wine compete directly as dinner drinks in many local places. Al Jazeera, the BBC, CNN, and many others broadcast their version of the news to a worldwide audience. As multi-domestic markets open up and become more global, the rest of the world is able to pick and choose among the best that the multi-domestic markets offer. Increasing affluence generates a desire for variety and creates opportunities for local specialties from foreign countries in leading countries.

Global Products

Although local preferences have sometimes demanded product adaptation, there have been many surprising successes for firms with standardized **global products.** Markets once thought to be very different across countries have been impacted by global brands. Consumer goods such as beer, food, and apparel and service providers such as accountants, lawyers, and even retailers are some of the categories in which global firms have been successful against locals in many countries. Add to this the typically global markets in many industrial B2B products in high-tech products (Apple's iPhone), consumer durables (Bosch appliances), and sports apparel (Nike athletic shoes) and in many ways the markets have grown more homogeneous. Increasing similarity of preferences has led to the success of global products, which in turn has fostered further homogeneity of markets.

The key to success of the globally standardized products is not that they are especially cheap or that every consumer wants the same thing as everyone else. They are often the best-value products because they offer higher quality and more advanced features at better prices. They also tend to be stronger on the intangible extras such as status and brand image. But mostly they embody the best in technology with designs from leading markets and are manufactured to the highest standards. As much as they satisfy customers, they as often create new desires. In terms of the product life cycle, global products will often generate new growth in mature markets, as customers return sooner for upgrades and more modern features.

In global product markets, the firm needs to develop technological capabilities to be able to compete by introducing new products. As the speed of technological development has increased, intense competitive rivalries have led to a proliferation of new products in many markets, many of them "me-too" variants from lead markets. This reinforces competitive rivalry further. Rather than uniqueness and differentiation, which place a premium on superior segmentation and positioning strategies, the key for success is speed and flexibility in new product development—and a well-known and highly regarded global brand.

Global and Local Brands

Global brands are brands that are available and well-known throughout the world's markets. Examples include Swatch, Mercedes, Nestlé, Coca-Cola, Nike, McDonald's, Sony, and Honda. By contrast, a brand that is well-known and strong in some particular market, but unknown in other markets, is a local brand. Examples include food retailer Giant in the United States; Luxor TVs in Sweden (now owned by Turkey's Vestel company); Morinaga, a food processor, in Japan; and AEG appliances in Germany (now owned by Electrolux).

Exactly how many countries a brand should cover to be "global" cannot be precisely defined, but the brand should be available in major markets.

In this book "global" and "regional" brands are treated much the same, as long as the brand name is identical and the region is large. Some observers even argue that a global brand does not have to be the same everywhere, but this is going too far. For example, the chocolate bar "Marathon" in some European countries was called "Snickers" elsewhere—and the company renamed Marathon to Snickers in order to have exactly that, a "global" brand name. Similarly, when the Nissan company changed its Datsun car marquee in the West to Nissan, it wanted to make its Japanese name the global name. These are major decisions by companies. So, in this text, a global brand may not be found in precisely every corner of the world—but it should have the same name.

In global markets, with standardized global products, a global brand name is necessary for success—which is why many firms consolidate their brand portfolios around a few major brands as globalization proceeds. Nevertheless, because local brands often have their own special market niche and devout adherents, many multinationals maintain a number of acquired local brands as well in their portfolio.

Global Marketing Objectives

The benefits to doing global marketing today go beyond pure marketing considerations. There are at least six possible objectives for the firm going abroad:

1. **Exploiting market potential and growth.** This is the typical marketing objective.
2. **Gaining scale and scope returns at home.** Longer production series cut costs and capital investment increases productivity.
3. **Learning from a leading market.** Many small-market shareholders make no money in very competitive markets, but learn about new technology and about competition.
4. **Pressuring competitors.** Increasing the competitive pressure in a competitor's home market might help divert the competitor's attention from other markets.
5. **Diversifying markets.** By adding new countries and markets to the company portfolio, the firm's dependence on any one market will be lessened.
6. **Learning how to do business abroad.** For example, to learn how to deal with former communist countries, entering Poland may be a first step to entering Russia.

The potential diversity of objectives is one reason why global marketing involves more than the traditional one product-one market case typically treated in marketing textbooks.

USEFUL MARKETING CONCEPTS

Several basic marketing concepts that you probably already learned will be useful to the global marketer. Here are the most important ones.

The Product Life Cycle

One well-known and basic marketing concept must be briefly introduced here because we will make extensive use of it throughout this book. Country markets are often in greatly different stages of the **product life cycle (PLC),** the S-curve that depicts how the sales of a product category (or a brand, since brands also tend to have a life cycle) progress over time. The stages typically involve Introduction, Growth, Maturity, Saturation, and possibly Decline (see Exhibit 1.10).

For a given product such as mobile phones, some countries (Scandinavia) will be in the saturation stage while others (India) are in the introductory stage. The optimal marketing strategies will vary considerably between these markets.

As Exhibit 1.11 shows, the **diffusion process** that new innovations pass through underlies the shape of the PLC.

The first adopters are innovators or "pioneers," followed by early adopters (usually the opinion leaders), early majority, late majority, late adopters, and finally, laggards. In the beginning what matters for a company is usually the size and growth rate of the total market. As the market matures, market share and profitability become typically more important objectives.

The PLC is also relevant for market segmentation and product positioning, two other prominent marketing concepts. **Market segmentation** involves partitioning a given market into similar customer groupings for which uniform marketing strategies can be used. **Product positioning** refers to the perceptions or image that target customers have of a product or service—or, rather, the image that the firm would like the customers to have. Both market segmentation and product positioning are typically more important in the later stages of the PLC when customers are good at evaluating competing offerings.

In the early stages of the PLC, the pioneer target segment for the product is usually easy to identify. The pioneers are the buyers who have most interest in the product category and who are willing to take a chance on a new product. An example is "computer nerds" in the PC category. Later in the majority stages of the PLC, the buyers are much more heterogeneous. They can come from many different strata of society, and they do not all want exactly the same thing in the product because their needs differ. This means that the marketing mix (the product, the pricing, the promotions and the advertising media, and so on) all have to be tailored to different segments of the total market. The PC for the home user will be configured, priced, and sold quite differently from the PC used by a financial analyst. This is where it becomes important for the marketer to make sure which of the several potential segments to target and how to communicate to the selected segment(s). This is also where product positioning becomes important. [15]

The transition from the growth among the early adopters to the more mature stage of the early majority is not always smooth. As first

EXHIBIT 1.10.
The product life cycle (PLC)

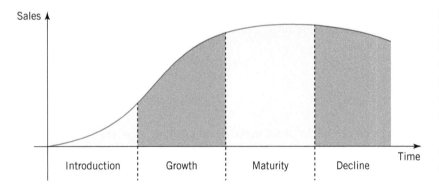

discovered by Geoffrey Moore, for high-technology products there is typically a gap or **"chasm"** opening up, creating difficulty for the diffusion of new products (see Exhibit 1.12).[16]

The reason for the chasm is typically that the motivations behind the purchase have shifted. While early adopters are still enamored by the newness and the technology, and are basically product-oriented, the early majority's basic motivation concerns usage benefits, such as saving time, ease of use, and acceptable prices. To overcome this chasm, it is important for the manufacturers' promotional language to shift from technology specifications—gigabytes, screen pixels, etc.—to customer benefits—number of songs stored, colorful images, etc. In emerging foreign markets, this kind of chasm can be seen not only for high-technology products. Introducing a new toothbrush brand or a new shampoo can involve a similar kind of newness that can stop a surprised potential adopter from trying the new product. Understanding this is important when entering a new foreign market, something we will return to several times in this book.

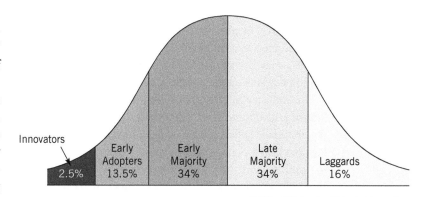

EXHIBIT 1.11.
The New Product Diffusion Process

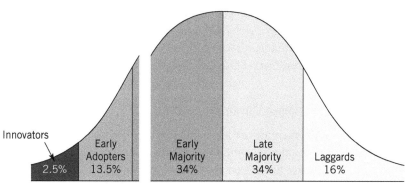

EXHIBIT 1.12.
The "chasm" in technology products' PLC

Source: Geoffrey Moore, Crossing the Chasm: Marketing and Selling High-Tech Products to Mainstream Customers. HarperBusiness, 2002.

Leading Markets

There are certain country markets where a global firm wants to be present even if competition is fierce and profitability is uncertain. These are **leading (or lead) markets.**

Leading markets are characterized by strong competitors and demanding customers; they are free from government regulation and protective measures; products and services incorporate the latest technology; and companies are strong at the high end of the product line. They are not necessarily the largest markets, although they often are.

Leading markets are generally found in different countries for different products. Strong domestic competitors emerge because of a country's location-specific advantages, such as natural resource endowments, technological know-how, and labor skills. Over time, these advantages enable domestic firms to accumulate experience. The customers of these firms are sophisticated and demanding, making these markets bellwethers for follower markets. For example, BMW responded to the preferences of the local German driver and the Autobahn with no speed limits (although 81 mph is suggested) by creating high performance cars. The U.S. consumers' preference for advanced technology and U.S. business' need to reduce labor costs through technology has kept the U.S. on the cutting edge of chip development.

The actual location of a leading market in an industry may also change over time. As follower markets mature and customers become more sophisticated, and as domestic producers develop new competitive skills, the follower markets may become the new leading markets. A good example is Japan in consumer electronics. Conversely, leading markets may lose their status, for as Japan rose, the United States lost its lead in consumer electronics.

An industry can have several leading markets for different segments of the total market, as in the automobile industry. In automobiles, in this sense, Germany, Japan, Italy, and perhaps even the United States can lay claims to preeminence. Different leading markets feature some market segmentation and product differentiation. German buyers place a premium on advanced auto technology, which is why other automakers have located engineering centers there. Italy has a well-developed luxury sports car market, and even German firms such as Porsche hire Italian designers. The Japanese provide mass manufacturing state-of-the-art knowledge, and their domestic customers get perhaps the best value for the money. The United States still provides a sophisticated market for large luxury cars, even if the domestic producers have not performed particularly well.

The existence of lead markets and the need for the firm to be in such markets push the firm toward global strategies in order to take full advantage of the benefits gained from being in lead markets. The firm can draw on lessons from competitors and customers in leading markets to design marketing strategies elsewhere. Product and technology developments in leading markets signal what is likely to happen in other countries. For example, while a semiconductor firm such as Texas Instruments has trouble making money in Japan, the lessons it learns in that difficult market help it to design entry strategies and service support elsewhere in the Asian region.

First-Mover Advantages

An emerging market that has just opened up offers the opportunity to be a first mover and create demand. Since domestic competition is often weak or nonexistent, the marketing tasks are to demonstrate how the product or service fills a need and to educate potential customers in its use. This generic marketing task can be challenging and expensive, with reluctant learners and a need for special promotional material and personal selling. But the brand has a chance to develop brand loyalty before competitors enter.

Being a first mover can create advantages but can also be hazardous. **The first-mover advantages** relative to followers include[17]:

- Higher brand recognition
- More positive brand image
- More customer loyalty
- More distribution
- Longer market experience

The drawback for a first mover is that the market is not yet developed, which means that:

- Channel members may need training.
- Customers might have to be educated.
- Advertising has to be more generic.
- Tastes and standards are unknown and perhaps unformed.

Because of the uncertainties involved, some firms decide to become followers, waiting to see how the first entrant does before entering a new market. When they then enter, it is usually with a kind of me-too approach, trying to capture some of the first mover's customers and also help grow the new market. The leading French beer, Kronenbourg, attacked the U.S. market through a campaign slogan that claimed it was "Europe's largest-selling beer," trying to capitalize on Dutch Heineken's, Belgian Stella Artois' and German Beck's popularity. By comparison, Efes, the up-and-coming Turkish beer, has positioned itself optimistically as "the number one Mediterranean beer in the world."

GLOBAL LOCALIZATION

Today, a global marketing strategy that globalizes all marketing activities is not desirable or even achievable. At the minimum, even if a company standardizes its product strategy by marketing the same product lines, product designs, and brand name, it has to localize distribution and marketing communications. This used to be the standard approach in consumer durables such as automobiles, cameras, and electronics. Today, many product lines include designs and models adapted to the local market needs. In consumer-packaged goods, companies came to localization earlier, and have now gone farther in their localization efforts, with country-specific product lines and local brands, adapted worldwide ad campaigns, and in-store promotions fitted to the local channel requirements.

Basic Factors Driving Adaptation:

- *Multi-domestic markets.* The most obvious case when to adapt is when the market is multi-domestic, which is when product preferences differ significantly between markets. Of course, in such cases the global potential is lower—"going global" for a firm selling peanut butter or frozen eel may not be a promising option. On the other hand, there could be pockets of consumers in some markets, and the firm could also try to persuade consumers to try something new (like peanut butter-and-jelly sandwiches or unami (grilled eel) on rice). It has worked in the past—hamburgers and sushi are good examples. It is often the standardized version with some adapted twist—falafel burger, for example—that could do the trick.
- *Market maturity.* When the host country market is in the early stage of the product life cycle, firms sometimes decide to avoid adaptation. One reason is that the market preferences are still unclear, so adaptation would be like trying to hit a moving target. Also, by not incurring adaptation costs, the firm is less exposed if the market does not take off. On the other hand, of course, by offering only an unadapted version, the chance of failure is greater.

    When the market is mature, adaptation is not only more feasible it is also more desirable. In the mature markets, consumer preferences are typically well-established and loyalty to the existing brands can be high. The objective is typically capturing market share, which requires some differentiating feature and adaptation.
- *Market size.* The economies of large scale are tied closely to the "efficient size" of a plant. The efficient scale is the minimum capacity limit on the number of units produced where all scale economies have been realized. The same logic can be applied to the marketing effort. In large markets such as the U.S. and China, the efficient scale can be reached more easily. Then it becomes efficient to develop an adapted version of the product and a marketing program localized for that market alone. By contrast, adapting to a small country, such as Switzerland or Chile, is rarely cost-efficient—but might still be necessary for other reasons, such as channel requirements.

SUMMARY

Increasingly today, marketing is encountering obstacles to globalization. The basic requirement for global marketing is that world markets are open and free and thus available for entry. As political risk rises and free trade is coming under pressure, entry barriers will lower the attractiveness of foreign markets. Furthermore, as populist arguments and nationalist sentiments become more mainstream, potential customers in foreign markets will shift their demand towards local home products and services.

However, economic fundamentals suggest that global marketing is still very potent. The most powerful global driver has been the way technology has facilitated inexpensive and fast worldwide communications and electronic commerce. Any brand is potentially global once up on the Web, and anybody anywhere can examine the offerings from various producers, be it B2C (business-to-consumers) or B2B (business-to-business).

Many of the well-established concepts and tools in marketing and international business can be useful in the new global marketing arena. This chapter has presented some of them, partly as a refresher. But in addition, the "new global marketing" draws on the new social media in promotion, big data for market research, global branding for goods and services, and global supply chains to standardize global products. The new global marketing effort depends on Internet communication networks and a wired world market. Global marketing is becoming a 24/7 effort with always-connected customers and never off-line customer service.

But with an always-connected consumer and instant global communications, and demanding consumers everywhere, globalization has gradually given way to global localization. Even large multinational companies today can be found with completely localized product lines. The imperative for global marketing today is "localization, sustainability, and social responsibility."

KEY TERMS

affluenza	global marketing
anti-globalization	global markets
bottom of the pyramid	global products
b-o-p marketing	globalization drivers
B24B	government globalization drivers
Buzz	lead(ing) markets
CAGE	local brands
competitive drivers	market drivers
cost drivers	market segmentation
chasm, the	mass customization
diffusion process	multi-domestic markets
e-commerce	observational marketing research
economies of scale	product life cycle (PLC)
economies of scope	product positioning
first-mover advantages	regionalization
global brands	social media
global channels	sourcing advantages
global communications	technology drivers
global customers	TRIAD
global localization	usage experience

DISCUSSION QUESTIONS

1. What are the factors that seem to drive the globalization of the automobile industry? Why is the computer industry not spread more evenly around the globe?
2. Identify three product categories for which you think the markets are global. Can you find three that are multi-domestic? What market data would you need to support your assertion?
3. What would a marketing manager learn in the U.S. market that could be useful in Europe?
4. After graduation, many students would like to work in a certain country, and often for a particular multinational. Using one of the Internet search machines (such as www.yahoo.com or www.google.com), see how much information you can gather about a multinational company's organization and marketing in a country of your choice to help you decide whether it would be a good company to work for in that country.
5. Some observers argue that the coming of electronic commerce on the Internet signals the arrival of a new era of global marketing. Assess how far this development has come by visiting a website for a retailer offering online shopping and see what the limits are on which countries they can ship to.

TEAM CHALLENGE PROJECTS

1. Team 1: Identify examples of two companies that have expanded internationally in the past two years. What were the drivers that caused them to expand? Team 2: Identify two companies that have not expanded. What were the drivers that caused them to stay domestic?
2. Foreign Direct Investment (FDI) in the U.S. exceeds $2 trillion. Firestone Tires, Sara Lee, *The Wall Street Journal*, and Smith & Wesson handguns (the gun that "won the Old West") are now owned by non-U.S. owners. Identify five "American" companies or brands that are owned by foreign companies. Team 1: Argue that this type of global diversification/ownership decreases value for Americans. Team 2: Argue that this type of diversification/ownership increases value for Americans.
3. Fisher-Price is an American company that produces toys for infants and children. The company had 2014 revenue of over $1.8B and operated in several dozen countries. Visit the website of Fisher Price Inc. (www.fisherprice.com) and click on/view several of the international website links. Team 1: Does this company use a local, regional, or global strategy? Argue that the company should extend its global strategy further. Team 2: Does this company use a local, regional, or global strategy? Argue that it should increase its focus on the home country rather than extending further outside.

SELECTED REFERENCES

Barta, Thomas, Markus Kleiner, and Tilo Neuman, "Is There a Payoff from Top Team Diversity," *McKinsey Quarterly*, April, 2012.

Christensen, Clayton M., Scott Cook, and Taddy Hall, "What Customers Want from Your Products," *Harvard Business* Review, January 16, 2006.

Dau, Luis Alfonso, "Learning across geographic space: Pro-market reforms, multinationalization strategy, and profitability," *Journal of International Business Studies*, Vol. 44, No. 3, April 2013, pp. 235–262.

Dawar, Niraj. "When Marketing is Strategy," *Harvard Business Review*, December 2013, pp. 101–08.

De Graaf, John, David Wann, and Thomas H. Naylor. *Affluenza: How Overconsumption Is Killing Us-and How to Fight Back*, 3rd edition. New York: Berrett-Koehler Publishers, 2014.

Friedman, Thomas L. *The World is Flat*. New York: Farrar, Straus & Giroux, 2005.

Ghemawat, Pankaj. *Redefining Global Strategy. Crossing Borders in a World Where Differences Still Matter.* Boston, MA: Harvard University Press, 2007.

Govindarajan, Vijay, and Chris Trimble. *Reverse Innovation: Create Far From Home, Win Everywhere.* Boston: Harvard Business Review Press, 2012.

Klein, Naomi. *No Logo.* London: Flamingo, 2000.

Kotler, Philip, and Kevin Keller. *Marketing Management.* 14th Edition. Upper Saddle River, NJ: Prentice Hall, 2012.

Levitt, Ted. "The Globalization of Markets." *Harvard Business Review,* May–June 1983, pp. 92–102.

Lieberman, Marvin, and David Montgomery. "First-Mover Advantages." *Strategic Management Journal, Summer* 1988, pp. 41–58.

McCracken, Harry. "How Japan's Line App Became A Culture-Changing, Revenue-Generating Phenomenon," *Fast Company,* March 2015.

Moore, Geoffrey. *Crossing the Chasm. Marketing and Selling High-Tech Products to Mainstream Customers.* New York: Harper Business, 2002.

Prahalad, C.K. *The Fortune at the Bottom of the Pyramid.* Revised and Updated 5th Anniversary Edition. Wharton School Publishing, 2009.

_____ and Stuart L. Hart. "The Fortune at the Bottom of the Pyramid," *Strategy + Business,* Issue 26, First quarter 2002.

Rugman, Alan. *The Regional Multinationals. MNEs and "Global" Strategic Management.* Cambridge: Cambridge University Press, 2005.

Schumacher, Fritz. *Small is Beautiful.* New York: Harper Perennial, Reprint edition, 2010.

Vahlne, Jan-Erik, and Inge Ivarsson, "The globalization of Swedish MNEs: Empirical evidence and theoretical explanations," *Journal of International Business Studies,* Vol. 45, No. 3, April 2014, pp. 227–247.

Wohl, Jessica, "Most McDonald's in Russia Reopen," *Chicago Tribune,* Dec 9, 2014.

Yip, George S., and G. Tomas M. Hult. *Total Global Strategy II.* Upper Saddle River, NJ: Prentice Hall, 2011.

ENDNOTES

1. Sources: Bloomberg 2014; Business Insider, 2015; Wall Street Journal, 2014.
2. From Wohl, 2014.
3. Suggested by Christensen, Cook, and Hall, 2006.
4. The problem-solving notion was proposed by Levitt 1983.
5. In De Graaf, Wann, and Naylor, 2014.
6. Source: Center for Economic and Policy Research (2014).
7. See Schumacher, 2010.
8. See Prahalad, 2005, for example.
9. Govindarajan and Trimble, 2012.
10. (Ibid, p.iii).
11. See Dawar, 2013.
12. The CAGE concept is discussed at length in Ghemawat, 2007.
13. From Rugman, 2005. Vahlne and Ivarsson (2014) find the same "triad" pattern for Swedish MNCs.
14. Rugman, 2005.
15. For more on the PLC, see e.g. Kotler and Kelley, 2012, ch.11.
16. See Moore, 2002.
17. First proposed by Lieberman and Montgomery, 1988.

" What does your firm have to offer? "

In this chapter you will learn about:

1. The underlying concepts and tools that are important in international trade and global strategy
2. A framework for analyzing a company's readiness for going abroad, and whether it is likely to have a competitive advantage there
3. How to assess the transferability of its advantages to a foreign location
4. The importance of the "triple bottom line" and what it requires in terms of adaptation to the foreign environment

For the global marketing manager, it is natural to think about overseas opportunities in terms of customer needs and wants. It suggests that the main issue for global marketing is whether there is a demand for the product. But this is not the best question to start with. The best first questions are what exactly the firm's strengths and weaknesses are, what it has to offer abroad, and whether the offering can be transferred successfully to a foreign market. What is the company good at—and not good at? What exactly are we offering our customers that might explain our success at home? Is the success due to internal strengths or simply due to some fortunate conditions in the environment?

Here companies should be careful. For example, companies often tout their "high-quality product." Does Starbucks offer "high-quality coffee?" Is that the reason for their success? Does Nike succeed because of "high-quality running shoes?" With brands, organizations are often myopic and nearsighted, thinking that a key advantage is that "everybody knows our brand." Can even a brand such as Oreo cookies be sure? Even if the current customers do, is that a key strength that Oreo can use in a completely different country?

Company Strengths and Weaknesses

CHAPTER 2

This kind of "internal analysis" of a company's strengths and weaknesses has been discussed at length by economists, competitive strategy analysts, as well as marketers over a long period of time. It will be useful to go through some of the insights, theories, and concepts they have developed, to equip ourselves with some established techniques and tools before doing our internal company analysis.

OPENING VIGNETTE

CAN TESLA GET IT DONE IN CHINA?[1]

The electric car-maker Tesla, founded in 2004, is the only successful car manufacturing start-up in America since the early 1900s. Its focus is to build high-performance electric-only vehicles; specifically, cars that will accelerate from 0 to 60 mph in under four seconds (faster than most BMW and Mercedes vehicles) with zero tailpipe emissions, and a 300-mile range with zero maintenance for 100,000 miles. Tesla accomplished this by applying the latest technologies and innovations in car design while others before them had tried and failed (GM had invested over $1 billion in its all-electric EV-1 only to buy them all back and crush them in 2006). But Tesla also struggled to bring a product to market, finally shipping its first production car, the Roadster (purchase price of $100,000 U.S.), in March 2008, two years later than planned. They then spent the next year recalling 75 percent of their vehicles to fix loosened bolts and handling issues. George

Clooney (the American movie star) summed up Tesla's problems at the time when he said, "I sold my Tesla. I've been left on the side of the road a while in that thing."

But Tesla has continued on, helped by the proceeds of their initial public stock offering in 2010 and the fact that they have made good on their ability to deliver a supercar that changed minds about electric vehicles. An increase in the number of charging stations has also helped (see Exhibit 2.1).

With the release of a lower-cost Model S Roadster ($70,000 purchase price) Tesla was able to sell over 30,000 vehicles in 2014. A Model X SUV was released in late 2015, and in total Tesla sold 76,230 vehicles in 2016 (60% in the U.S. market).

The Chinese car market has grown to become the largest car market in the world with 29.4 million vehicles sold in 2017 (35 percent of the global total). Seeing opportunity, Tesla decided to enter that market in 2013 and immediately ran into a number of cultural and commercial hurdles.

- 74 percent of urban Chinese live in apartments, and without your own garage, it is difficult to recharge your Tesla vehicle on the street.
- There was a lack of charging stations around China in general.
- Lastly, China's new rich want to show off their wealth, and the Tesla is a rather plain vehicle (i.e., not conspicuous enough). By comparison, Porsche sold 65,249 vehicles in China in 2016 and now has five car models specifically developed for the China market including a 680 horsepower version of its Panamera Turbo.

As with any new technology, the early adopters buy immediately while the majority of the market waits to see the results. In China, the early adopters now already have their Tesla vehicles but the demand for Tesla's electric-only vehicles has generally not increased.

The first 100 cars sold in the U.S. were all bought by Hollywood stars, the governor of California, and celebrities. In contrast, Tesla's in China are being bought mostly by newly rich businessmen (the owner of an international trading company, chief marketing officer of an online media company, angel investor, director of brand sales). This difference in customer segment may help explain why Tesla sold only about 3,500 cars in China in 2014. But the trend turned. In 2016, Tesla tripled sales, with revenues over US $1 billion, as China accounted for a hefty 15% of total sales.

However, the Chinese government has committed to electric vehicles and offered cash incentives to buyers and free license plates. Additionally, it has invested heavily in charging infrastructure. There are now hundreds of Superchargers (one hour to charge) and thousands of Destination chargers (five hours to charge) scattered about the country. Tesla is also building dozens of its Superchargers in selected cities that can charge a Tesla in one hour instead of the usual four to five hours with a regular charging station. This may help solve the Chinese concern about charging the vehicle. Tesla also introduced its new Model X into China and thus 2016 became a "break through" year for the company with sales of over 11,000 vehicles in China. China is still only 14% of Tesla's sales and represents less than .04% market share in China.

It remains to be seen whether government support can help Tesla can find a way to crack the secret of the world's largest car market. So far, so good.

One major distinction in what follows will be whether any competitive advantage derives from favorable *country factors* or are specific to a firm. Is our company successful because of where we are located? Or is it because it does something no other company can do? Economists have been active mostly on country factors. Business strategists, by contrast, focus on competitive advantages that are *firm-specific*. For the international marketer, as we will see, both factors can be instrumental in deciding to go abroad and to select a certain country market. A third factor of major importance will be *transferability*—can you transfer your strengths across borders without compromising them?

COUNTRY-SPECIFIC ADVANTAGES (CSAs)

The theory starts with the well-known concept of comparative advantage.

Comparative and Absolute Advantages

The principle of **comparative advantage** provides the fundamental rationale for the existence of international trade. Free trade between two countries yields economic payoffs to the countries (in terms of higher welfare) provided the countries have different endowments of resources, that is, different advantages. It is not important if one country is better than another in producing all kinds of products, that is, that producers there have an **absolute advantage.** One country might have an absolute advantage (that is, its resource inputs show higher productivity) for all the products involved and trade will still yield positive benefits to both countries. The requirement is simply that in one country production involves less of a sacrifice in the output of alternative products than it does in the other country—which will be the case unless the mix of resources is exactly the same in both countries—so that there is a relative advantage in production.

For comparative advantages to be determining of international trade patterns trade has to be *free*. The production factors have to be actually fixed to a particular *location*. In the absence of free trade, each country has to be more self-sufficient, and less specialization is possible. As for production factors, the increased mobility of labor (the "importation" of south European workers to the northern European countries, and the use of Indian laborers in the Middle East oil fields, for example) has made labor less of a country-specific factor.

The theory makes a clear distinction between strengths that are specific to the firm and those a firm possesses because of the country it is from or where it produces. To illustrate, producing in a low-cost European country such as Portugal—as Volkswagen does, for example—may give a cost advantage over a competitor producing in Spain—as Nissan does. But this is really a **country-specific advantage (CSA)** that can be captured by any producer in Portugal. By contrast, Volkswagen's image and brand name are assets that are unique to the company, **firm-specific advantages (FSAs)** that cannot be duplicated by other firms. A competitive analysis in the global context needs to identify whether a company's strength is firm-specific or not. If it is not firm-specific, the competitive advantage is usually less sustainable since the company cannot prevent imitation.

Potentially, all the factors that create differences in the countries' comparative advantages also create differences in absolute advantages. When formulating competitive strategy at the firm level, it is the absolute advantages that count. Countries as trade partners are just that, partners, and for the countries the comparative advantage principles apply—an "I win-you win" situation. But at the firm level, the successful company needs to have an edge on competitors such as higher quality or lower cost. This is an "I win-you lose" situation, determined by absolute advantages. A country's absolute advantages can be erased by emerging foreign countries with lower wages or other advantages. This is the working of the **international product cycle (IPC).**

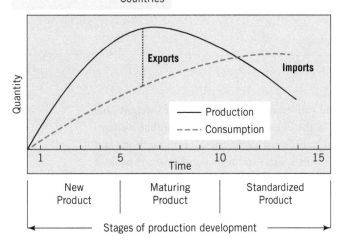

EXHIBIT 2.2.
The IPC for Advanced Countries

The International Product Cycle (IPC)

The IPC was initially proposed by Raymond Vernon.[2] He demonstrated how the invention and manufacturing of new products in the United States shifted over time to new locations overseas and in the process affected trade patterns. The process is depicted in Exhibit 2.2.

In the initial stage, the innovator produces and markets the product at home to a growing home market. As production increases above the home market demands, the firm turns to exports and develops markets in other developed countries. Then, as these new markets grow and their domestic production of the product gets underway, trade shifts again to third-world markets. As the production know-how gets more widespread, however, these countries gradually develop their own manufacturing capability, helped by the processes and the technology by now standardized. As low-cost production in these third-world (or newly industrialized) countries gets underway, their imports give way to exports back to the original country's market. The cycle has come full circle, and the original inventor now imports the product (see Exhibit 2.3).

As many countries other than the United States have become adept at inventing new products and services, the international product cycle as originally developed has become outdated, and Vernon and others have amended it.[3] Today, for example, it is not uncommon to find that a country that started production of a certain innovative product continues as the foremost manufacturing site. The American supremacy in computer design is a good example. This process has been documented in detail by Porter.

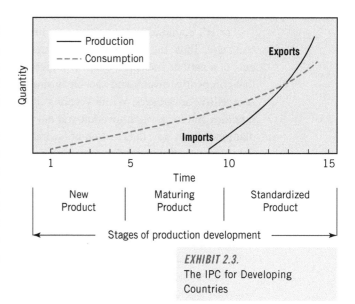

EXHIBIT 2.3.
The IPC for Developing Countries

Porter's National Diamond

In an important extension of the theory of comparative advantage, Porter introduced the **diamond of national advantage.**[4] The diamond comprises four factors that determine the competitive advantage (or disadvantage) of a country:

1. *Factor conditions.* The nation's position in factors of production, such as skilled labor or infrastructure, necessary to compete in a given industry.
2. *Demand conditions.* The nature of the home demand for the industry's product or service.
3. *Related and supporting industries.* The presence or absence in the nation of supplier industries and related industries that are internationally competitive.
4. *Firm strategy, structure, and rivalry.* The conditions in the nation governing how companies are created, organized, and managed, and the nature of domestic rivalry.

Exhibit 2.4 shows how these factors interrelate.

A nation's competitive advantage—and, consequently, the country-specific advantages for firms from that country—depends on the strength of each of these factors. Favorable factor conditions include the traditional endowment of natural resources that was the basis of the original theory of comparative advantage. Porter argues that, over time, vigorous competition in the industry will help develop stronger firms and support growth and improvement among supplier firms. Furthermore, sophisticated and demanding customers at home help hone the competitive skills of the industry further. If a country offers higher labor skills or lower wages, the multinational firm will locate production there.

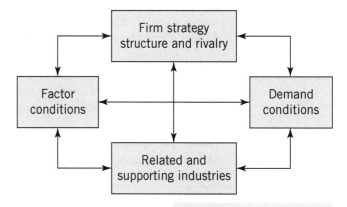

EXHIBIT 2.4.
Porter's National Diamond

Adapted from Michael E. Porter, The Competitive Advantage of Nations. Free Press, 1990.

Porter's diamond implies that a country can remain competitive in an industry even as its manufacturing costs rise. Thus, the diamond goes counter to the original IPC theory. While the IPC explains the "hollowing out" of a nation's industrial base, with manufacturing moving to low-wage countries, Porter's diamond suggests that competitive rivalry and capable business management can help nations develop new skills and renew their competitive advantages. While Vernon's IPC concludes that advanced nations will trade for standardized commodities and focus on innovation and new industries ("get out of televisions and focus on computers"), Porter's diamond shows how the creation of favorable conditions can make a nation stay competitive in a given industry for a long time ("automobiles is what we do best"). Actually, in most economies of the world, both tendencies are at work simultaneously.

Krugman's New Trade Theory

Krugman and other "new trade" theorists have pointed out that international trade patterns will not necessarily follow the original theory's predictions.[5] The reason is that the products traded are generally differentiated and not homogeneous. For example, a country such as Germany both exports and imports a large number of cars. If Germany is good at cars, why would Germany not produce all the cars demanded domestically and then trade for other products or services? The answer is differentiation and specialization.

Differentiation leads to specialization and the creation of firm-specific advantages that come from learning by doing. German automakers become good at producing certain types of cars, not others. Similarly, as advanced technology centers arise around strong research universities and innovative new firms, the local workers develop skills unique to specific industries. This explains the development of high-technology areas such as Silicon Valley south of San Francisco, Bangalore in India, and the Stuttgart-Munich area in Germany.

These ideas suggest that a country can become efficient in the production of goods in which it starts with little or no competitive advantage. It also represents the process by which companies develop new resources. This learning of new skills is of course very much a theme of this text, since the global marketing manager's experiences with foreign countries serve to expand marketing know-how.

Country-of-Origin Effects

One particular country-specific advantage (that can also be a disadvantage) is the so-called **country-of-origin (COO) effect.** The effect referred originally to the impact on customers of the "made-in" label, signifying the country of manufacture. With off-shoring and outsourcing the effect has been extended to assembly locations and even to the brand itself. An Apple iPhone assembled in Taiwan from components sourced in China is still perceived as "American." That is, the COO effect refers to the perceived home country of a branded product or service. The effects can be several, and they can change over time.

- **Quality perceptions**. The original finding about COO effects was on quality. The quality of products or services from countries with a positive image tend to be favorably evaluated, while products from less positively perceived countries tend to be downgraded.[6]

  A number of research studies have been conducted on the effect of "made-in" labels. In general, the studies show a pronounced effect on the quality perceptions of products, with country stereotypes coloring consumers' evaluative judgments of brands. It translates into sales as well. The purchase of automobiles is a case in point. Since published driving tests of new models tend to consider what country the marque comes from, country of origin naturally becomes a key buying criterion. In one study it was found that the Japanese automakers' strong penetration in the U.S. market in the 1970s was based more on country advantages than on firm-specific advantages. American auto buyers bought "a Japanese car," not necessarily a Nissan or Toyota specifically.[7]

- **Variable quality**. One complicating factor is whether a country produces at widely different quality levels. If companies in a country tend to adhere to strict quality standards, all in that country stand to gain from country-of-origin effect, just as a global brand name means the company "guarantees" a certain performance level. Consumers come to trust imported products from countries such as Germany, Japan, and Sweden, because they show relatively low quality variation. On the other hand, products from Britain, the United States, and Italy may or may not be high quality because these countries feature producers at widely different quality levels. This renders the made-in label useless for quality judgments (just as inconsistent quality would ruin a brand name). One illustrative study assessed the influence of country of origin on the choice of certified *halal* food.[8] Halal denotes foods that are permissible for Muslims to eat or drink under Islamic Shari'ah (law). The criteria specifies both what foods are allowed, and how the food must be prepared. The assumption was that Muslim consumers would prefer halal food from Muslim countries rather than non-muslim countries. The results showed no effect from country of origin. One reason was that consumers perceived quality differences within Muslim countries, and also within non-Muslim countries, making country-of-origin an uninformative cue. The authors suggest that some countries need to pay more attention to the *halal* not only as a commercial activity but also as a spiritual need of Muslim consumers, and to establish their credibility in the marketplace.

- **Persistence**. Contrary to what one might expect, there is also evidence that these effects do not easily go away over time. Because of increased global communication consumers learn more about foreign countries, and they learn what technologies and products firms in the countries are good at.

   But country perceptions do change over time. For example, while American products enjoyed a reputation for high quality after World War II, they slipped badly in the 1970s and 1980s as superior foreign products raised customer expectations. British quality perceptions largely followed the same path, only earlier and quicker, while Japanese products showed the opposite trend and the German quality image remained strong.[9] South Korean cars have followed an upward trend in the quality of their vehicles since their introduction in the 1980s, and both Kia and Hyundai now offer a warranty of 10 years and 100,000 miles, the longest of any car manufacturer.[10]

   Given the intense global competition in many markets, however, there has been evidence of a convergence of quality ratings in the new millennium. Today, even products and brands for the new emerging countries stand a good chance of being seen as equal in functional quality as their peers from advanced countries—although their brands do not usually carry the same prestige.

- **Brand effects**. With the growth of multinational production, the original emphasis on "made-in" labels seemed pointless. Initial beliefs were that the COO effect would disappear as no one really cared anymore where the product was made. But two things happened. First, many consumers became confused and angry—Chrysler customers who had decided to "Buy American" found out the car was made in Mexico, causing an outcry. VW buyers searched for models that were not made in Pennsylvania. The Corolla built by Toyota and GM's joint venture in California were sold at a discount relative to its identical model from Japan.

   Gradually, as production location became less important, the COO effect became associated with the brand rather than the product. Research showed that brands have "home countries" as well, making Sony a Japanese brand anywhere, regardless of where it was produced. The Sony label is taken by the consumer as a sign of insurance that the product will function as a "real" Sony just like the Apple Mac assembled in Taiwan.[11]

- **Category differences.** Country-of-origin effects differ by product category (Exhibit 2.5). Not surprisingly, they are less pronounced in products for which technology is widely diffused across the globe (the international product cycle at work), and products from different countries consequently are of similar quality. In apparel, for example, made-in labels ("made in" Malaysia, China, Portugal, Hungary, and so on) tend to have less effect because consumers are becoming accustomed to seeing clothes of similar quality from various places. By contrast, in advanced medical equipment, electronics, cosmetics, and wine, country of origin still counts for a great deal.

  Country-of-origin effects are also less pronounced in more mundane and "utilitarian" products such as paper products and detergent as compared to more fanciful or "hedonic" products such as drink, luxuries, and entertainment.[12]

- **Positive *and* negative?** A product's country-of-origin advantage can be positive in one market, negative in another. Thus, for example, what may be an advantage to being an American brand in Asia may be a disadvantage in Europe. Marketers recognize this, and many change strategies accordingly. To illustrate, while Levi's may be positioned as the original American jeans in Japan, its American roots are now downplayed in the European Union. Similarly, carmakers Audi and Mercedes' German roots are emphasized in the United States and elsewhere but not at home where the German roots are taken for granted. Korean brand names are much appreciated in Asia, but being from Korea had not yet translated into a strong positive country-of-origin effect for Korean brands elsewhere until lately with Samsung, LG, Hyundai, and others gaining increasing respect for Korean-made functional quality. Samsung's brand has even surpassed Japanese rival Sony's for value, if not yet for status.[13]

CSAs and Nation Branding

Many nations have now become aware of the impact a positive nation image has not only to attract tourists and gain a country-of-origin advantage for its products, but also to attract foreign direct investment, skilled immigrants from other countries, and political credibility. Emerging nations take out advertising pages in daily newspapers to acquaint readers with their resources, and most nations train their diplomats in sales and marketing techniques.

"**Nation Branding,**" as it is called, was developed by Simon Anholt.[14] His framework identifies six dimensions that together constitute the image of a country. The dimensions are Culture & Heritage, Exports, Governance, Immigration & Investment, People, and Tourism.

The results are typically presented in illustrative diagrams that visually capture and contrast the images of different nations. The diagrams reveal how different people can perceive the same country differently.[15]

In Exhibit 2.6 Americans seem quite lukewarm about France, even though they appreciate its culture and heritage. These perceptions are not shared equally by the Japanese (see Exhibit 2.7): The Japanese are clearly more impressed by France. Stressing a French country-of-origin would be much more promising in Japan than in the United States.

The profiles are useful to identify where two different nations may have quite different image of a given market country. This is helpful in identifying whether a country-of-origin effect will be positive or negative. The maps can also be useful to identify where our own perceptions of our own country differs from that of outsiders. We ourselves might not be the best judges of what is unique about our own country. In either case, an ethnocentric perspective can easily be misleading for a company developing strategies for marketing its products.

In the end, it is important to emphasize that country-specific advantages may not be constant over time, as new countries move up and develop new skills. Also, it is important to recognize that a country's advantages do not always look the same to all observers. Different people will have different perceptions of a country's eminence in manufacturing or design or general attractiveness. The way we see others is not necessarily the way others view them, and the way we view ourselves is not always the way others view us—and if they are the customers, their perceptions count for more.

FIRM-SPECIFIC ADVANTAGES (FSAs)

The fundamental premise of any enterprise is that it can transform valuable inputs into even more valuable outputs. The rule for survival of a company is that it provide some desired benefit to the customer better than other enterprises do—it has a sustainable competitive advantage. Similarly, the company entering markets abroad must have advantages that outweigh the increased costs of doing business in another country in competition with domestic firms. These advantages should not be available to competitors and are, therefore, to some degree monopolistic. These are firm-specific advantages (FSAs) to emphasize that they are unique to a particular enterprise. (Since different writers sometimes use different terms, Exhibit 2.8 gives some alternative synonyms for FSAs and CSAs.)

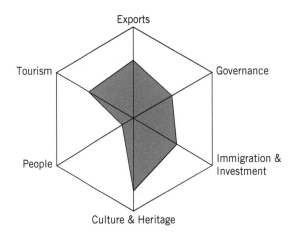

EXHIBIT 2.6.
One's own culture can change the perspective of another culture. How Americans see Brand France

Copyright © 2015 by Simon Anholt/ Anholt-GfK Roper Nation Brands Index. Reprinted with permission.

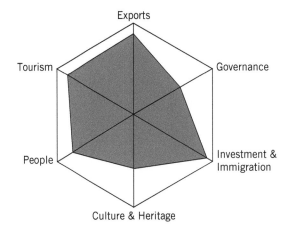

EXHIBIT 2.7.
How Japanese See Brand France

Copyright © 2015 by Simon Anholt/ Anholt-GfK Roper Nation Brands Index. Reprinted with permission.

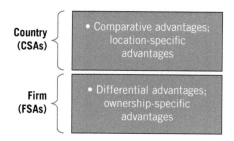

Country
(CSAs)

- Comparative advantages; location-specific advantages

Firm
(FSAs)

- Differential advantages; ownership-specific advantages

EXHIBIT 2.8.
Two Sets of Synonyms for
FSAs and CSAs

Firm-specific advantages may be of several kinds. They might be a patent, trademark, or brand name or be the control of raw materials required for the manufacturing of the product, access to know-how essential to the development of a service, or simply control of distribution outlets. These advantages could also include process technology, managerial capacity, or marketing skills. They might well have their source in country-specific variables, but the essential point about them is that they can be used by the company alone.

Marketing FSAs

From a marketing perspective it is important to recognize that the source of a firm-specific advantage can lie in specific market know-how. For example, large consumer goods manufacturers (Nestlé, Unilever, Procter & Gamble) have accumulated experience and skills in many foreign markets that give them an edge over competition. These skills include techniques for analyzing and segmenting markets, developing promotional programs and advertising campaigns, and administering massive introductory campaigns for new products and services. Similar skills in the marketing area might be said to lie behind some of Caterpillar's and IBM's successes in many markets (Caterpillar, the American heavy-machinery company, has a policy that a serviceman should be able reach any construction site within 48 hours, for example), and also the close relationship with distributors nurtured by many companies in Japan (see box, "Marketing FSAs").

BOX: Marketing FSAs

Most companies have several marketing strengths, but are sometimes characterized by one or two major FSAs. Among global companies with strong marketing, the following FSAs stand out:

Strong brand names—	*Rolex, BMW, Coca-Cola*
State-of-the-art technology—	*Nikon, Audi, Apple*
Good corporate citizen—	*Unilever, IBM, P&G*
Distribution strength—	*Samsung, H&M, Starbucks*
Advertising strength—	*Nike, L'Oreal, Corona*
Good value—	*Uniqlo, IKEA, LG*

Other companies have marketing FSAs not easily exploited overseas:

German Henkel's (detergents) strong presence in the European market has been difficult to leverage elsewhere, as it depends on strong distribution and brand loyalty based on special washing traditions with respect to water hardness and temperatures used, less use of tumble dryers, and frequency of washing.

Kao's (detergents) and Shiseido's (cosmetics) strengths in distribution at home in Japan, where they have control at both wholesale and retail levels, cannot easily be duplicated elsewhere.

A clear understanding of what the FSAs are is a key to the formulation of a successful marketing strategy in a country, especially for market segmentation and product positioning. Note that the firm-specific advantage might well vary across countries. In other words, the differential advantage that products and services enjoy over competition might be different for customers in different country markets. Samuel Adams' Boston Ale might be a strong beer brand in Boston and other U.S. markets, but cannot trade on its brand in England where it has to prove its worth against a number of local competitors with stronger brands.

TRANSFERABILITY

An important question that arises often in global marketing is the **transferability** of company strengths to other countries. Usually not all of them can be transferred.

The firm establishing manufacturing in a market country can both gain and lose some advantages in the process. Being closer to the customer is always a gain for a firm. For example, distributors can feel more secure about supplies, and customers can rely on after-sales service. The firm becomes more of an insider because it is able to hire a domestic workforce and create goodwill by being a good citizen. Company managers become more attuned to the way of doing business in the country and come to understand the market better.

But there can be drawbacks. If the company is seen as an intruder, replacing a former domestic competitor, there may be more ill will than goodwill. Domestic competitors may mount a campaign against the newcomer, and since it is unlikely that all former employees can be hired, media can come to focus on the fate of some displaced workers. These are typical negatives for most countries, and the firm needs to conduct itself with care to minimize the potentially negative market reaction.

There is also a possibility that a country-of-origin quality effect comes into play. The exported products embody the production know-how and skills, including the country-specific advantages of the company at home. Some customers will question whether these can be transferred successfully to the plant in the new country. When Volkswagen started to build its Rabbit model in Pennsylvania in the 1970s, customers rushed to buy the last imports of the model from Germany.[16] The typical strategy to overcome such consumer doubts has been to avoid emphasizing where the product was made. BMW advertises the "German Engineering" and performance of its four types of luxury Sport Utility Vehicles but does not mention that these are all made in Spartanburg, South Carolina. Of course, this approach forgoes some of the positive benefits of manufacturing within a country, and so a more constructive approach is to re-export the product back home. Honda, the Japanese car company, exports its Honda Accord coupe made in Marysville, Ohio, to Japan, thereby assuring the American consumers that the quality of the car is up to Japanese standards.

Various factors might make the employment of marketing FSAs difficult in other countries. Where commercial TV is not available, it is difficult to leverage the skills developed in the area of TV advertising. Procter and Gamble's reluctance to enter the Scandinavian markets is one illustration of this, now partly alleviated as satellite TV and new channels open up the market to TV advertising. When the FSAs are in distribution channels (as in the Electrolux case—see box, "A Marketing Skill Transferred"), going abroad might involve having to create new channels in the local market.

INTERNAL ASSESSMENT: STRENGTHS AND WEAKNESSES

These traditional concepts are necessary to properly analyze the **internal factors** that help explain success at home and might be transferable to other country markets. As said at the outset, only if there are good reasons to believe that some strengths are applicable in other countries is it really worthwhile to start examining markets abroad.

A SWOT Analysis

The first phase of the internal "self-analysis" is similar to the SW part of what is often called a SWOT (Strengths, Weaknesses, Opportunities, and Threats) analysis in business strategy.[17] The strengths and weaknesses will then be matched against the requirements of the global marketing tasks.

In the general case, an SW analysis covers broad topics including:

- *Financial resources*, such as funding, sources of income, and investment opportunities.
- *Physical resources*, such as your company's location, facilities, and equipment.
- *Human resources*, such as employees, volunteers, and target audiences.
- *Current processes*, such as employee programs, department hierarchies, and software systems.

For global marketing purposes, it is common to narrow the SWOT scope down to more market-oriented topics:

- *Strengths*: characteristics of the company that give it an advantage over actual or potential competitors in the marketplace.
- *Weaknesses*: characteristics that place the business at a disadvantage relative to competitors in the marketplace.
- *Opportunities*: environmental factors that the firm could exploit to its advantage in the marketplace.
- *Threats*: elements in the environment that could cause trouble for the business in the marketplace.

A typical **representation** of the SWOT matrix is given in Exhibit 2.9:

The Opportunities and Threats (OT) part of the framework involves the external environment. Here we will focus on the SW part.

The basic issue in a global marketing SW analysis is whether the company has something valuable to offer in foreign markets. The answer requires that the company management makes an honest attempt to assess whether their strengths in the home market can be leveraged abroad and whether the company has sufficient resources.

A typical "strength" question is "What benefits do our products and services offer consumers over and above what competitors can do?" The benefit attributes are typically called "points of advantage"—it could be the superior reliability or better value, for example, typical of Hyundai cars. Or it could be better design (the iPad?) or more stylish (Italian suits?).

The "weaknesses" part involves the contrasting "**points of disadvantage**." Korean cars may have lower status, the iPhone is expensive, and an Italian suit might not have the

EXHIBIT 2.9.
The SWOT framework

durability required for an everyday office suit. Of course, for some consumer segments these drawbacks may not be important—for them the strengths overcome the weaknesses. Nevertheless, it is important for the firm to be clear about how their products and services are viewed in the marketplace. It is usually not enough to do the SW evaluation with only internal input. The way the executives of a firm view the company's products is rarely the same as consumers see them.

Walmart's international experience can be used to illustrate these points. As the world's largest retailer, Walmart would seem to have an advantage over most competitive stores. But its international record is mixed—very successful in China, not at all successful in Germany, for example.

Walmart's strengths are several:

- Low cost and low price
- Extensive and efficient supply chain
- Large stores with a large variety of products and services
- Rapid adjustment to new products and competitive moves

It is less obvious what its weaknesses are, but two might be:

- The need for cheap land keeps store locations outside main urban centers
- A brand image of cheap prices and poor customers

In the United States, still the main market for the company, the strengths served very well as Walmart expanded by opening stores in rural areas of the country. Expanding into the urban areas has been more difficult as the need for cheap locations becomes a limiting weakness.

Walmart has been successful in China where its strengths work very well. China suppliers were already a big part of the Walmart system, so expanding there was readily facilitated. The low price points and the wide assortment of products played into the newly richer consumer in China. The need for cheap land was no longer such a hindrance, since government zoning laws were relaxed to allow new urban centers to be established in prime locations. One of Walmart's most successful stores was established in Shanghai's upscale Pudong district.

Walmart's experience in Germany was less successful, lasting only the eight years between 1998 and 2006. Entering a very competitive German market, Walmart tried to establish their vaunted supply system by acquiring two existing discount chains, Wertkauf and Interspar. But the attempt to reproduce their existing system failed as suppliers and store clerks were unwilling to change traditional work procedures in favor of Walmart's efficiency oriented norms. Workers were discouraged from flirting with one another and forbidden to date colleagues in positions of power. As for the German consumers, lower price by itself was not enough of an attraction for people who pride themselves on an eye for quality. And the so-called "Walmart greeters" positioned inside the entrance doors were ignored or even pushed aside by customers who felt no need for such politeness.

Walmart's experience shows that what a firm might think of as its "strengths" can sometimes become unimportant or even a weakness in a foreign market. Economic, social, and cultural differences make for different kinds of consumers, and adaptation becomes necessary for success.

Some firm-specific advantages (such as brands and patents) can be considered company "assets." A strong brand, for example, is worth money. Seen as assets, the company can also consider selling the assets—the British Jaguar brand is today owned by Tata, the Indian conglomerate. In general, companies can use their assets (strengths) themselves, or they can sell (or license) them if there is a market for them. The former case is sometimes called **"internalization,"** the latter is called **"externalization."**[18] Outsourcing is equivalent to externalization.

There is more to speak about concerning strengths and weaknesses, but first a word about the OT (Opportunities and Threats) part of the matrix. While strengths and weaknesses are "internal factors," the OTs reflect "**external factors**." The "internal factors" usually are "firm-specific advantages," while the external factors include "country-specific advantage." The opportunities and threats are environmental factors which may help or hinder the business, and they are typically not under the firm's control.

Value Chain Analysis

When assessing strengths and weaknesses, it is important to be very specific about exactly where the strength lies. To get a more in-depth understanding of where their strengths really lie, companies often try to identify where in the so-called value chain their unique competence and capability lies.[19]

The **value chain** refers to the process by which raw materials and other inputs are transformed into final goods.[20] This process can be viewed as a chain of sequential tasks, each adding value to the product. Some tasks are in operations (purchasing, design, manufacturing, and marketing), others are support activities (finance, personnel).

An integrated firm has a long value chain, while a less integrated firm focuses only on some of the operations. The way McDonald's, the American fast-food restaurant chain, operates in different countries is instructive. In the United States the company has outsourced major activities by hiring independent firms to supply the beef, potatoes, bread, and other ingredients and by allowing independent entrepreneurs to open franchised outlets. Its value chain is comparatively short. However,

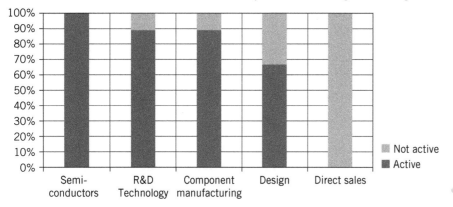

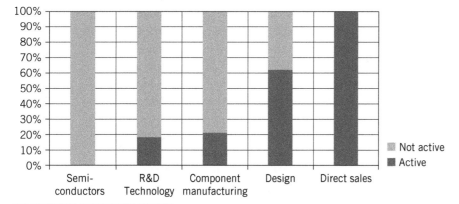

EXHIBIT 2.10.
Two electronic firms' value chains, Samsung (top), Dell (bottom) Samsung's FSA is in the early stages while Dell's FSA is in the later stages. As a result of differing FSAs, these two firms rarely compete with one another.

McDonald's inspects operations and keeps tight quality controls on all phases of business. In Europe, suppliers are also independent local producers, but some key franchised locations (including one on Paris's Champs Elysees) are owned by McDonald's itself, mainly for purposes of quality maintenance. In Moscow, McDonald's found it necessary to develop its own suppliers, since the local suppliers could not provide the necessary quality. Its value chain in Russia is longer.

Exhibit 2.10 shows how two companies, Samsung and Dell, have configured their value chains in consumer electronics differently.

While giant manufacturer Samsung has no direct involvement at the retail level, Dell works primarily in design and direct sales and does little technology development and component manufacturing of its own. This shows how the firms' strengths and weaknesses (FSAs) can be found at different stages in the value chain for electronic consumer goods. The stage of the value chain that can best be leveraged—and where the strengths lodge—might vary by country. For example, in markets in which the firm has limited experience or in which products are at a different stage in the life cycle, licensing a technology to a local manufacturer might be preferable to making and selling the product.

The value chain can also be changed as new ways of combining activities appear and entrepreneurs grasp opportunities to simplify the entire flow. This is how the Swedish furniture retailer IKEA developed a new formula for selling home furniture. Instead of showcasing finished furniture in downtown stores and later shipping merchandise to buyers' homes as traditional furniture retailers did, IKEA created a self-service store from which purchasers could bring home their furniture the same day. IKEA has in fact developed a new value chain (or a new "business model"), in which the customer does more work than before. In return, the prices are much lower. IKEA soon ventured abroad and has become the first successful furniture retailer on a global scale.

Another good example of how a value chain approach works is the strategy adopted by Virgin Atlantic Airways under Richard Branson. It was not possible to compete via aircraft choice—Boeing and Airbus jointly dominate the industry. Available routes were limited and landing rights were expensive and difficult to get. Branson turned to customer service and beautiful stewardesses, but other airlines (Singapore, Thai, Cathay) had already preempted that strategy. Pushing further down the value chain, Branson decided to focus on pre-flight and in-flight entertainment, creating outstanding airport lounges and a fun and exciting in-flight atmosphere.[21] To cover the extra costs involved, Barnson concentrated the effort on a few large high-traffic routes and airports: London's Heathrow, New York's JFK, and Hong Kong's Chek Lap Kok. Traveling on Virgin is an "experience"—but as Virgin's strategy proved successful, other airlines have joined in, including newcomer Emirates out of Dubai.

COMPETITIVE ANALYSIS: EXTENDING PORTER'S "FIVE FORCES" MODEL

Since the competitive advantages lodged in a firm's CSAs and FSAs generally vary across country markets, there is a need to analyze the competitive environment in each country market. This analysis is best based on **Porter's "Five Forces" Model**. The model identifies five sources of competitive pressures on the firm in a given industry: rivalry, new entrants, substitutes, buyer power, and supplier power (see Exhibit 2.11).

BOX: A Marketing Skill Transferred: Electrolux in Japan[22]

The Electrolux Group is today the world's largest producer of powered appliances for kitchen, cleaning, and outdoor use. More than 55 million Electrolux Group products (such as refrigerators, cookers, washing machines, vacuum cleaners, chain saws, and lawn mowers) are sold each year to a value of approximately U.S. $14 billion in more than 150 countries around the world.

Electrolux has long sold its product through door-to-door salesmen demonstrating the virtues of the product in the home of a prospective customer. Over the years considerable refinement in the sales approach was developed and taught to new salesmen. The sales technique became one of the company's distinctive skills.

When entering Japan, Electrolux found initial reactions among the trade people toward this type of selling approach negative. It was said that the Japanese were not used to having unknown people enter their homes and would not allow the salesmen's entrance. Electrolux first decided to follow the standard Japanese approach of selling through department stores and specialty shops. For a period of several years the company attempted several variations on this approach, all with the same result: sales were too small to cover costs, and the higher price of their product (because of transportation costs, tariffs, and distributors' markups) was not considered sufficiently offset by better performance. Competitors among the domestic producers (Toshiba, Hitachi, and others) continued to dominate the market.

Believing that with a proper demonstration of performance the price differential could be justified, management of Electrolux decided against all odds to introduce their particular selling method in Japan. After extensive training of their Japanese salesmen, the door-to-door approach was introduced. The result was an immediate success. Electrolux became a market leader at the upper end of the market.

Electrolux's experience vindicates the idea that we should concentrate on doing what we do best. It also demonstrates the fact that in a new country one does not necessarily have to do things the way they have always been done, not even in a relatively homogeneous or isolated country such as Japan.

Here we will extend the Porter strategy analysis to deal with global competition across several country markets.

Market Rivalry

The intensity of competitive rivalry between firms competing directly in a country market is the most obvious competitive force. This is the mode of competition focused on in economic theory. In global marketing it is useful to separate the competitors into domestic and foreign companies. In many industries, such as autos, this division comes close to a division into what Porter calls strategic groups.

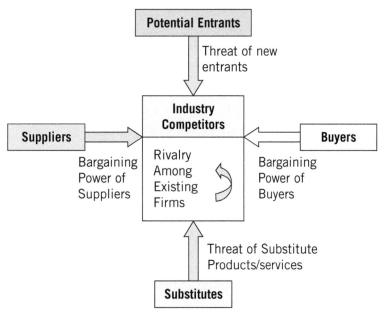

Strategic Groups

A strategic group consists of competitors of similar size and similar target markets. In autos, the three American automakers (GM, Ford, and Chrysler) tend to form one group, as do the Japanese (Toyota, Nissan, Honda, and Mazda). The two German makers BMW and Mercedes also form a natural group, but Volkswagen is different, perhaps in a group with the Japanese.

Strategic groups are useful for competitive analysis since they suggest the likely strategic direction the companies may take. When Apple introduces a new iPhone, Samsung follows with its Galaxy. When Samsung's big size becomes popular, Apple also introduces bigger size. In the ongoing global battle between Coca-Cola and Pepsi-Cola, when Pepsi bought Tropicana, the juice maker, Coke responded by trying to buy France's Orangina, only to be blocked by a French judge alerted by Pepsi lawyers.

Domestic Competitors

In most country markets there will be a group of domestic companies that has traditionally served the home market. For example, most governments in the past controlled telecommunications and air transportation and subsidized farmers. With similar effect, regulations in support of small businesses and retailers against foreign ownership and customer sentiments in favor of local goods have in the past combined to create entry barriers for foreign firms and advantages for domestic producers.

Today, as protectionism is on the rise, these factors are gradually increasing in importance. The backlash against free markets and economic integration means that domestic competitors often have special advantages. The notorious "Reinheitsgebot" ("Purity law") in Germany, an old, now amended regulation that prohibited the use of artificial conservation ingredients in beer, effectively blocked foreign entry and made local production a necessity (which is why many in Germany still prefer their local fresh beer). Nor do the domestic companies simply stand back and watch as foreign competitors enter. At one point the three large American auto companies jointly sponsored an advertising campaign encouraging car buyers to show loyalty to their fellow citizens by buying American makes.

Foreign Competitors

The foreign companies can often be analyzed as separate strategic groups, broken down by home country. For example, the large Korean conglomerates, such as Samsung, LG, and Daewoo, have followed the same initial OEM (original equipment manufacturing) strategy in Western consumer electronics markets to gain access without much knowledge of customer preferences.

Regional trade blocs also play a role in determining advantages and disadvantages of foreign competitors. Foreign companies from inside a trading area have an advantage over other foreign competitors. Although the European Union is not trying to become a fortress, the advantages of manufacturing inside Europe are such that many North American and Asian companies invest in production inside the EU. For example, Ireland's generous tax benefits (today increasingly questioned by other EU members) have induced many companies to locate there, including Apple.

New Entrants

While Porter was mainly concerned with new entrants into an industry—such as Disney buying the ABC television network, or banks entering the securities business—the threat applies equally, if not more, to potential competitors entering into a new foreign market. In particular, it is important that the global marketer realizes that other global companies may also enter a country market under consideration, and that the order of entry can directly affect the sales and market shares gained.

An emerging market that has just opened up offers the opportunity to be a first mover and create demand. Procter & Gamble succeeded with its Head & Shoulders shampoo in China, offering consumers a shampoo that provides both dandruff protection and beautiful hair.

Substitutes

In food products and drinks where markets are multi-domestic, the globalized product or service not only must be adapted to local customs and preferences—it is also likely to encounter different substitutes. When

McDonald's opened its first outlets in Russia, the Russians responded with a chain of fast-food stores serving blinis and other Russian specialties. Kellogg's is still trying to convince people around the world to switch from hot breakfast meals to cold breakfast cereals. KFC in Japan successfully fought the habit of mothers serving hot ramen, a noodle dish, getting many to switch to fried chicken on the premise that it helps build strong bodies in young children.

Buyer Power

In countries with large government ownership of businesses, the only customer may be a government agency. Other industries can also be affected. For example, liquor sales and advertising are highly regulated in many countries, with public monopolies as the buying agent, virtually eliminating the ability of companies to create meaningful product or service differentiation and competitive advantages.

Supplier Power

In some countries where there is widespread cooperation between firms, an entrant may find it difficult to establish the required network of distributors and other intermediaries. Domestic competitors with established networks will have a decided advantage.

THE TRIPLE BOTTOM LINE

So far in this chapter we have dealt with the underlying factors from economics and competitive theory determining the success of the global company. The perspective has been limited to the "financial" or "profit" part of the triple bottom line. That is because of the tradition in economics and strategy: companies exist to make money for the shareholders, pure and simple.

This tradition is not misguided in and of itself—in the free market system, companies will only succeed and survive if they can earn enough profits. But in the global marketplace today, the local communities demand a share of benefits for their own people and a sustainable operation so that the foreign presence does not deplete the local resources and environment. In the past, many global companies consider themselves doing good simply by offering local jobs and by not polluting the environment. Today the companies have to be much more proactive, offering not just jobs and doing no harm.

The "**triple bottom line**" is the name given to the three-way goal that today's global competitors try to achieve: **social, environmental, and financial**. These three divisions are also called the **three Ps: people, planet, and profit.**[24] For example, in emerging markets global companies have started providing educational and family services and have sponsored sports programs and improved healthcare. They have also helped upgrade the environment by cleaning up drinking water, combating global warming by measuring and controlling their carbon footprints, and reducing smoke and other pollutants from their plants.

The reason why companies now increasingly do these things is not simply that it ultimately leads to higher profits.[25] In many cases the goodwill created by the CSR (corporate social responsibility) measures and environmental actions does help the acceptance of the company's products by consumers and thus perhaps to higher profits. But the more fundamental reason is that many of today's global competitors have understood the long-term importance of a commitment to the people they touch and the planet they inhabit. More than simply a profit motive, it is the sustainability of any corporate activity on this planet that is at stake.

The most important challenge today for any global competitor is to clearly exhibit a commitment to the local market. The global competitor may be stronger financially, and have greater repertory to create synergies across markets than local companies. But what is most important is to make sure that the company is intent on becoming a positive force for the local market and community. This is where the philosophy of the "triple bottom line" really comes into play.

We will cover more of this later in this chapter and throughout this text. As we will see, it means that assessing strengths and weaknesses for the firm contemplating going overseas, involves more than simply assessing its current operations, its managerial competence, financial strength and product superiority. It also means facing the question of operating according to the triple bottom line in a foreign country, where the local population's living conditions and environment are completely new and different. Can the company make it there?

The key, today more than ever, for the global marketer is the commitment to local adaptation and how their presence benefits the local community.

THE NEW GLOBAL MARKETER

As a company venturing abroad, we need to match our strengths to the requirements involved in "going international." This requires an understanding of what it takes to be a successful global marketer. Since that task has changed significantly in the last few years, it is useful to spell out what today's global marketer needs to do.

At the beginning of globalization some 30 years ago, "global marketing" strategies were typically based on the following assumptions:

1. A company has entered, or is planning to enter, many of the world's different markets—"going global" is an "imperative";
2. The company is marketing the same or similar products and services everywhere—it stays true to its core competency and its FSAs;
3. Its customers are the same or similar everywhere—whether they are consumers or businesses, they buy the product or service for same or similar reasons and usage;
4. There are significant cost savings in coordinating company strategies across countries—using the same marketing mix everywhere lowers costs, for example;
5. Coordination limits local managers' independence—global marketing strategies tend to be top-down, but country managers have to accept that;
6. Global marketing potentially results in mis-positioned products and services but can be overcome with state-of-the-art products and a strong brand.

Gradually, even at early stages of globalization, some of these assumptions proved questionable. The expected cost savings (no. 4) did not always materialize because coordination costs turned out to be higher than expected. This happened sometimes because local country managers (no. 5) opposed the global strategy. Usage (no. 3) was not always the same—in some countries ice cream is a health food, for example. A strong brand (no. 6) might not be enough to overcome loyalties to domestic producers.

Today, with "localization" getting increasingly important, all of these conditions have become even more questionable. It is not that "global marketing" has disappeared, quite the contrary. Global companies from advanced markets are getting a larger share than ever of their revenues and profits from foreign markets, and many new companies from emerging markets are expanding and building strong brands in advanced foreign markets. But in doing so they all have had to re-think what successful global marketing can do and how a global marketing strategy should look.

Starting in reverse order, successful companies have had to fix mis-positioning (no. 6) by adapting products more for local conditions, and, in several cases, even introducing new products specifically targeting some local market. To do this it has been necessary to empower local managers more (no. 5), and allow them to participate in and tweak the formulation of the global strategy. This has meant that some of the cost savings (no. 4) of a global strategy have been lost. As a result, today a global marketing strategy is often promoted internally as a way to increase revenues (by increasing brand reach), less to lower costs.

The notion that consumers around the world all want the same product and for the same reasons (no. 3) was controversial when it first appeared. It has proved largely wrong. As emerging countries move up the economic ladder, its consumers become as diverse as anywhere. We may want the same *new* features (in a new smartphone, say) but technology diffusion has been so fast that a large number of competitors can quickly offer similar state-of-the-art options and we can then stick to "our brand." Consumers demand adaptation to their situation. What matters is how good the product is for the "here and now" and how it fits into the consumer's life.

What about no. 1 and no. 2? Successful companies today do much more than produce products and services. The need to pay attention to the environment, the company's "carbon footprint," the sustainability of its operations and the company's role in the global and local community are no longer idle issues. "Conscious capitalism" is not just a fad, but a necessary broadening of management's vision whether global or local. Managers have to think outside the box—and operate outside the "core competence" and narrowly focused FSAs of the company (no. 2). As a necessary consequence, going into foreign markets is a much more serious step than before (no. 1). It requires commitment.

IBM allows its employees to teach in local schools and universities, P&G has opened schools in India, Unilever's Project Sunlight teaches conservation in day-to-day activities, and more. Whether one likes it or not, the wider responsibilities that companies are taking on, or forced to take on, challenge companies as well as their shareholders. "Going global" is no longer an "imperative," and any entry needs to be viewed as a long-term commitment.

The New Global Marketing Tasks

What this means is that there are two parallel tasks for today's global marketer. On the one hand, nothing has changed about global marketing fundamentals. Once the firm is committed to a global marketing strategy, it will have to be based on sound fundamentals. There has to be some target segments inside different countries and across different countries. Product positioning should account for the critical benefits that are salient for each specific market. The 4Ps of the marketing mix still have to be decided upon and be integrated into a coherent marketing strategy. Much more on this will follow in the next several chapters.

But in addition there has to a stronger recognition of local conditions than was thought necessary before. Whether rich, middle class, or poor, consumers' reasons for purchase and intended product usage need more adaption to than was expected before. Short-term cost savings might to be let go in favor of more fine-tuned localization in order to be successful against local competitors. Local country managers need to be consulted in advance of any global strategy formulation, and listened to carefully. Overall, the tradeoff between globally coordinated top-down uniform strategies and localized but costly variety needs to swing in the local direction.

The new assumptions to guide global marketers are the following:

1. "Going global" is no longer an "imperative"—each foreign entry has to be carefully considered;
2. The company may have to develop new products for specific foreign markets—and even go beyond its core competence;

3. The potential customers in each market might have different reasons for buying a product and how to use it;
4. Many expected cost savings do not come automatically and some may not materialize;
5. Local managers should have a strong say in the formulation and implementation of any global strategy;
6. Mis-positioned products may have to be completely redesigned—a strong brand will often not be enough in any one local market.

These changes reflect similar changes among customers across domestic markets as well, not only foreign markets. They reflect a profound shift among consumers toward greater control over their own buying and consumption behavior.

The international political, economic, and cultural environment today does not favor globalization as such. It favors economic growth that is helping each local community move toward a better life for all its members—and not all people are convinced that free markets and corporate capitalism are the best solutions. It is up to the global marketer and his or her company to prove them wrong.

The New Tools

As should now be clear, global marketing requires more skills than before and also additional tools. First of all, the application of existing marketing tools needs to be more skillful.

- Market segmentation should be more detailed, uncovering the usage differences in addition to demand differences. This will usually mean that marketers have to get closer to the user and observe the product in action (does our cell phone have to be waterproof, for example?).
- Product positioning needs to be more relevant to the targeted segments, something that requires fine judgment and strong market research uncovering aspects not even clear to consumers themselves (in shampoo, will "shiny" hair make some consumers think of "oily" hair—and is that bad?).
- The 4Ps have to be imaginatively applied. How can a high price become affordable—installments or credit? Will people buy this online? How attractive does the packaging look on a cell-phone screen? A full-color coupon for a 20 percent discount might look good but will not be printed out because it will use up a lot of ink. How can we as foreigners build customer relationships and loyalties? And so on.

Those are the new demands on the traditional tools which are still useful. But two new areas of management need also be mastered by today's global marketer: **sustainability management** and **Corporate Social Responsibility (CSR),** the planet and people parts of the triple bottom line.

Firms who have accepted these new responsibilities and tasks typically try to relate their efforts to their existing core competencies.[26] Sustainability management typically involve broad issues such as global warming and environmental degradation, but in taking on the new tasks, management will generally focus on its company's carbon footprint and the waste produced by its manufacturing processes. CSR can also involve human-rights issues and community outreach, but management will typically focus on discrimination in its own foreign subsidiaries and support for towns in which it operates.

Consultants help companies to integrate their efforts with their business strategy to the extent possible. Nevertheless, the new tasks require new skills, and demand new resources. Sustainable operations often require a re-thinking about a number of processes in a firm's value chain. CSR management demands that resources are set aside for activities whose effect on the bottom line are difficult to track. While sustainability management forces a reformation of how the firm operates, often leading to leaner and cost savings measures, CSR adds costs for seemingly peripheral matters.

Sustainability and CSR: The NIKE Example

To recognize what sustainability management involves and how it relates to CSR, it is useful to examine how one major global company, Nike, has implemented its sustainability program and CSR effort. In some ways Nike is prototypical of today's global company, with outsourced manufacturing, home-based design and marketing, and a global brand. The following description is drawn mainly from its 2013 special report.[27]

Nike's sustainability program starts by analyzing the company's "carbon footprint," the degree to which its operations cause greenhouse gas emissions. To accomplish this, the company disaggregates its value chain to specify exactly where the footprint is particularly great. Nike's value chain is given in Exhibit 2.12.

As can be seen in the exhibit, the major contribution to its carbon footprint comes in the "Design" stage, where the materials to be used are decided on. A significant second source of carbon comes in the Make stage, when the shoes are manufactured. The "Use" stage also contributes to the carbon footprint, but the company has less power to effect changes in that stage.

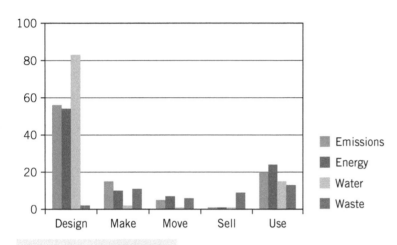

EXHIBIT 2.12.
Nike's Value Chain and Carbon Footprint (%)[28]

Adapted from Nike, "Our Sustainability Strategy" (2013).

It takes time and resources to properly identify key activities and quantify the amounts of spillover and waste they produce. Consulting organizations have sprung up to help companies in this process, precisely because the skills and expertise involved are usually not within the company domain.

The link between sustainability and CSR can be seen in Nike's way with the contract factories used in outsourcing. Factories are rated using a Sourcing & Manufacturing Sustainability Index (SMSI), which puts sustainability considerations on equal footing with quality, cost, and delivery. Also, Nike provides leadership and instruction in fitness, coaching, and training services, including a study on the effects of physical inactivity in childhood and the need to build physical activity into the daily life of children.

The New Bottom Line

In the triple bottom line profitability has been joined by CSR and environment—people and planet. Sustainability and CSR are basically efforts to help stop environmental degradation and gain goodwill in local communities. The Nike example demonstrates how focusing on sustainability and CSR can actually help also to drive costs down. But for most companies, cost reductions and revenue increases will not be very easy to achieve— and Nike's gains were not easily achieved either.

Regardless, there is today no need to appeal to altruism or societal-welfare arguments to convince companies to do more CSR or operate sustainably. As consumers increasingly buy from companies they admire and respect, and even pay more for some products just because they are green, not being part of the movement toward global responsibility and environmental sensitivity will make companies lose both customers and investors. "Going global" may no longer be an imperative—but "going sustainable" surely is an imperative.

SUMMARY

The first step in a "going global" marketing strategy is whether the available resources are sufficient and whether the company has products and services that can compete in foreign markets. The firm has to recognize the distinction between country-specific and firm-specific advantages. Country-specific advantages can be beneficial to any firm from the home country and will be difficult to protect from imitation. They will also be a potentially negative in some markets where country of origin has a low standing. An automobile from Germany will usually get benefits, but perhaps not in Israel.

Firm-specific advantages such as a strong brand name or copyrighted software belong to the firm and can usually be sustained and protected from imitation. But like country advantages they can be less valuable in some markets where the name is less known or the software pirated. In general, global expansion tends to be more attractive for firms with firm-specific advantages than just country-specific advantages, but in either case, the transferability of the advantages can be a major issue. In personal services, where language skills become necessary, the training of local service delivery personnel can be very costly. High-service department stores have always had difficulties expanding abroad.

Assessing the potential of an international expansion should draw on the economic fundamentals of comparative advantage and competitive strategy. Using concepts and tools that have been well-established in the basic disciplines, the firm can use a SWOT type of analysis to start analyzing the Strengths and Weaknesses of the firm. Even before a certain target country market is identified, the assessment helps to identify critical issues and variables to research. The selection of the most promising target market can only proceed once the environmental variables have been considered, but a preliminary internal "self-analysis" helps to formulate what the critical areas are.

In the end, the company also has to recognize that becoming a "good local citizen" and also a company with environmentally sustainable operations is necessary not only in terms of brand or corporate image. The new demands from consumers mean that managers have to accept much more involvement not only with customers but with all stakeholders in the society and local community.

KEY TERMS

absolute advantage

comparative advantage

competitive advantage

competitive repertoire

country-of-origin effect

country-specific advantage (CSA)

diamond of national advantage

firm-specific advantage (FSA) internalization

international product cycle (IPC)

nation branding

new trade theory

Porter's five forces model

strategic intent

technology transfer

transferability

value chain

DISCUSSION QUESTIONS

1. Identify the competitive advantages of some market leaders such as McDonald's, Nike, Swatch, and Sony. Are these country-specific or firm-specific advantages?
2. Use Porter's five forces model to analyze the competitive environment of a country of your choice (pick a product category that you are familiar with).
3. Discuss how the transferability of competitive advantages of a service differs from that of a product.
4. Visit an Internet vehicle-buying service (such as AutoVantage) and compare the various makes offered. Discuss how the close comparisons possible online makes competitive advantages easier to identify. What role is played by a strong brand?
5. On the vehicle website, keep track of your own comparisons to create a flow diagram that shows what features were accessed and at what stage (for example, price and engine power). Then compare with others in the class. What does this tell you about how potential buyers arrive at a decision on the Internet?

TEAM CHALLENGE PROJECTS

1. In 2016, the U.S. manufacturing sector contributed over $2.2 trillion to the U.S. economy, directly hired 12.3 workers with millions more in support industries, and provided an average wage of $26.00 per hour. Team 1: Develop a list of products that are best manufactured in the U.S. rather than manufactured in other countries. What was your decision criteria? Team 2: Develop a list of products that are best manufactured outside the U.S. What was your decision criteria?
2. Pick four countries that you believe have a clear Country Specific Advantage (CSA) and list each country and its product(s). (Italy with fashion clothing could be an example.) Team 1: Visit the tourism website of the four countries and determine if the country does or does not advertise its CSA competitive advantage. Explain why the current approach is best. Team 2: Visit the tourism website of a different set of four countries and determine if the country does or does not advertise its CSA competitive advantage. Explain why these countries need to change.
3. Identify two U.S.-headquartered companies that have more than 50 percent of their revenue from international sales. Team 1: Do a SWOT analysis to explain the company's success in international markets. Team 2: Do a SWOT analysis to position the company to further expand sales in the U.S. market instead.

SELECTED REFERENCES

Anholt, Simon. *Brand New Justice: The Upside of Global Branding*, Oxford: Butterman and Heinemann, 2003.

Baer, Drake, "5 Reasons Why Tesla Is Struggling In China," *Business Insider*, Jan. 15, 2015.

Balabanis, George and Adamantios Diamantopoulos, "Domestic Country Bias, Country-of-Origin Effects, and Consumer Ethnocentrism: A Multidimensional Unfolding Approach," *Journal of the Academy of Marketing Science*, Winter 2004, Volume 32, Issue 1, pp. 80–95.

Bhanji, Zarah and Joanne E. Oxley, "Overcoming the dual liability of foreignness and privateness in international corporate citizenship partnerships," *Journal of International Business Studies*, Vol. 44, No. 1, May 2013, pp. 290–311.

Bilkey, Warren J. and Eric Nes. "Country-of-Origin Effects on Product Evaluations." *Journal of International Business Studies* 8, no. 1 (Spring–Summer 1982), pp. 89–99.

Borzooei, Mahdi and Maryam Asgari, "Country-of-Origin Effect on Consumer Purchase Intention of Halal Brands," *American Journal of Economics, Finance and Management*, Vol. 1, No. 2, 2015, pp. 25–34.

Buckley, Peter J. "Forty Years of Internalization Theory and the Multinational Enterprise," *Multinational Business Review*, Vol. 22, No. 3, 2014, pp. 227–245.

Clarkson, Natalie, "Why Did Richard Branson Start an Airline?" *Virgin Travel*, October 1, 2014.

Fine, Lawrence G. *The SWOT Analysis: Using your Strength to overcome Weaknesses, Using Opportunities to overcome Threats*, CreateSpace Independent Publishing Platform; 1 edition, 2009.

Fischer, M., Voelckner, F. & Sattler, H., How Important are Brands? A Cross-Category, Cross-Country Study. *Journal of Marketing Research*, 47 (5), 2010, pp. 823–839.

Grant, Robert M. *Contemporary Strategy Analysis*, 8th ed. New York: Wiley, 2013.

Hanaysha, Jalal and Haim Hilman, "Advertising and Country of Origin as Key Success Factors for Creating Sustainable Brand Equity," *Journal of Asian Business Strategy*, Volume 5(7) 2015, pp. 141–152.

Hanssens, Dominique M. and Johny K. Johansson. "Rivalry as Synergy? The Japanese Automobile Companies' Export Expansion," *Journal of International* Business Studies, Vol. 22, No. 3 (1992) pp. 503–527.

Interbrand Best Global Brands 2014 (http://www.bestglobalbrands.com/2014/ranking/), accessed 2/28/2015.

Johansson, Johny K. "Missing a Strategic Opportunity: Managers' Denial of Country-of-Origin Effects," in Papadopoulos and Heslop (1993).

_____ and Hans B. Thorelli. "International Product Positioning," *Journal of International Business Studies*, Vol. XVI, No. 3 (Fall 1985), pp. 57–76.

Kogut, Bruce. "Designing Global Strategies: Comparative and Competitive Value Chains." *Sloan Management Review*, Summer 1985, pp. 27–38.

_____ and Udo Zander. "Knowledge of the Firm and the Evolutionary Theory of the Multinational Corporation." *Journal of International Business Studies* 24, no. 4 (1993), pp. 625–46.

Krugman, Paul R. *Geography and Trade*. Cambridge, MA: MIT Press, 1988.

Levin, Dan, "Lurching Start for Tesla in China," *The New York Times*, Feb. 11, 2015, B1.

Nike, *Our Sustainability Strategy, 2013* (http://www.nikeresponsibility.com/report/content/chapter/our-sustainability-strategy), accessed 3/1/2015.

Papadopoulos, Nicolas and Louise A. Heslop, eds. *Product-Country Images: Impact and Role in International Marketing*. New York: International Business Press, 1993.

Porter, Michael E. *Competitive Advantage*. New York: Free Press, 1985.

_____. *The Competitive Advantage of Nations*. New York: Free Press, 1990.

Savitz, Andrew with Karl Weber. *The Triple Bottom Line: How Today's Best-Run Companies Are Achieving Economic, Social and Environmental Success—and How You Can Too*, 2nd ed. San Francisco: Jossey-Bass, 2013.

Teece, David J., "A dynamic capabilities-based entrepreneurial theory of the multinational enterprise," *Journal of International Business Studies*, Vol. 45, No. 1, Jan. 2014, pp. 8–37.

Vernon, Raymond. "International Investment and International Trade in the Product Cycle." *Quarterly Journal of Economics* 80 (May 1966).

_____. "The Product Cycle in a New International Environment." *Oxford Bulletin of Economics and Statistics* 41 (November 1979).

Wells, Louis T. "A Product Life Cycle for International Trade?" *Journal of Marketing*, July 1968, pp. 1–6.

Young, Susan L. and Mona V. Makhija, "Firm's corporate social responsibility behavior: An integration of institutional and profit maximization approaches," *Journal of International Business Studies*, Vol. 45, No. 6, Aug. 2014, pp. 670–698.

ENDNOTES

1. Sources: Baer, 2015; Levin, 2015.
2. See Vernon, 1966.
3. Including Wells, 1968, and Vernon 1979.
4. From Porter, 1990.
5. See Krugman, 1988.
6. See Bilkey and Nes, 1982, for an early overview of the effect of made-in labels. Hanaysha and Hilman (2015) link the effects to brands. Balabounis and Diamantopoulos, 2004, show the effect of consumer ethnocentrism.
7. See Hanssens and Johansson, 1992, and Almeida, Armaan, "The 6 Most Reliable Used Cars 2013," www.CarsDirect. com.
8. See Borzooei and Asgari, 2015.
9. Papadopoulos and Heslop, 1993.
10. See Almeida, 2013.
11. These examples come from Johansson, 1993, and Hanyasha and Hilman, 2015.
12. See Balabanis and Diamantopoulos, 2004, and also Fischer, Voelckner and Sattler, 2010.
13. Reported in Interbrand: Best Global Brands 2014, www.interbrand.com.
14. See Anholt, 2003.
15. Source: Exhibits provided by Anholt and GMI, Global Market Insite.
16. From Johansson and Thorelli, 1985.
17. See, for example, Fine, 2009; also Grant, 2013.
18. Following Buckley, 2014.
19. In business strategy theory, the capabilities of a company are the source of sustainable competitive advantages. See Teece, 2014.
20. From Kogut, 1985.
21. See Clarkson, 2014.
22. Sources: Annual reports; www.electrolux.com, personal interview.
23. Adapted from Porter, 1985.
24. From Savitz, 2013.
25. As Young and Makhija (2014) argue, profit maximization is not necessarily counter to more benevolent or "institutional" justifications for CSR.
26. One example is Microsoft's PiL (Partners in Learning) program, which aims to raise educational attainment and supports schools and teachers in about 100 mostly developing countries. See Bhanji and Oxley, 2014.
27. See Nike, 2013.
28. Adapted from Nike, 2013.

DAN CATHY, CHAIRMAN AND PRESIDENT OF CHICK-FIL-A sat in his office looking at the Atlanta skyline. Since the death of his father last year (the founder of Chick-fil-A), he had struggled with the correct expansion strategy to continue the company's 46 years of financial success. On the one hand, with only 2100 restaurants in 42 states, there was plenty of expansion room in the U.S. but with an obvious saturation point down the road.[1] Expanding into international markets was the alternative but would the company's competitive advantages work internationally? Changing the company's successful business model for the international markets was very risky but not changing it might mean failure. The recent dramatic failure of the Target Department Stores in their first international expansion (into Canada) weighed heavily on his mind. What to do?

BACKGROUND

Chick-fil-A is a privately held American fast-food restaurant chain headquartered near Atlanta, Georgia, that specializes in chicken fast-food items such as sandwiches, chicken salads, chicken soup, fries, etc. It only serves chicken. (Company's current slogan: "We did not invent the chicken … just the chicken sandwich.") The company's name Chick-fil-A was registered in 1961 and is a "cute" spelling of how Americans pronounce "chick-fillet."

It has grown rapidly since its start in 1946 with revenue of over $7.9 billion in 2016. Its annual growth rate has exceeded 12 percent in eight of the past 10 years, continuing a string of 48 years of continuous sales growth.[2]

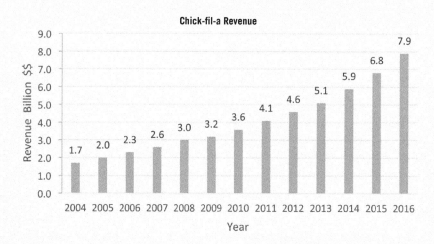

Chick-fil-a Revenue

---
[1] *This case was prepared by Michael T. Furick.*

Chick-fil-A is now the largest fast-food chicken company in the U.S. in terms of market share, growing larger than KFC for the top spot in 2013.[3] This is particularly striking since KFC has over 4,400 U.S. restaurants, more than double Chick-fil-A's restaurant count of 2,100.[4]

Chick-fil-a now the U.S. Market Share Leader

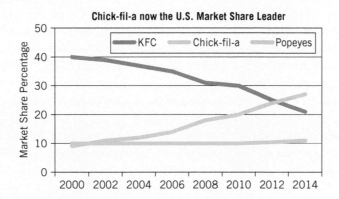

In addition, in 2010 Chick-fil-A took the fast-food industry lead in average sales per restaurant, with $4.4 million, and continues to hold that lead. WhataBurger is second with $2.7 million per restaurant and McDonald's is fifth with $2.50 million.[5]

A Chick-fil-A restaurant in Atlanta and its main offering

Copyright © 2014 by Bigstock/Wolterk.   Copyright © 2015 by Bigstock/dbvirago.

Most Chick-fil-A restaurants are stand-alone surburban locations. The highest-volume chicken sandwich comes plain except for "two crucial pickles." Smaller versions are even served for breakfast as seen here.

SUCCESS FACTORS

Chick-fil-A's success has been driven primarily by the higher quality (actual and customer perceived) of its chicken food items. The company emphasizes fresh ingredients rather than frozen ingredients in all its items. While the chicken is shipped frozen, it is thawed out by each store up to 48 hours before needed and then coated with breading by hand in small batches. While this focus on "fresh" is not a business constraint for some items like lettuce for salads, potatoes for fries, and drinks, the handling of raw chicken requires the company to strictly maintain its logistics and a high level of store cleanliness and employee training to ensure safety of its products.

The company's focus on fresh seems to have hit the mark with consumers. Readers of *Consumer Reports Magazine* rated Chick-fil-A the highest for taste in its 2014 survey about the nation's best and worst fast foods. In the same survey on taste, which compared eight major chicken brands, KFC came in last.[6] In addition, Chick-fil-A seems to have a menu that has a wider appeal among diverse customers, especially families. The menu includes the signature chicken sandwich but also chicken nuggets, strips, waffle fries, a selection of wraps and salads, plus desserts such as specialty milkshakes and ice cream treats.[7]

The company has also focused on providing meals specifically for children and its "toy" in the kids meal is always of an educational nature (globe, book, etc.). In 2014, McDonald's lost its perennial first-place position as the chain with the most "kid appeal," according to Sandman & Associates Inc., a restaurant market research firm. For the first time in 25 years the top spot went to Chick-fil-A Inc. for kid meals and "kid appeal."[8]

To continue to foster a "healthy" food image, the company plans to use only chickens raised without antibiotics. Other changes being considered include removing yellow coloring dye from its chicken soup and taking out food additives such as high-fructose corn syrup in dressings and sauces.

"Healthy" of course is relative: Chick-fil-A's chicken sandwich meal includes a fried chicken sandwich, medium fries, and a Diet Coke, with no condiments and contains 830 calories and 36 grams of fat. McDonald's comparable chicken sandwich meal contains 870 calories and 38 grams of fat.

CUSTOMER SERVICE

Unusual for a fast-food restaurant, the company attempts to provide a higher level of customer service in its restaurants, such as employees bringing free drink refills out to customer tables plus other employees roaming the dining floor to help customers. The company refers to this as its "second-level service," beyond the usual first-level service of clean restaurants and properly prepared food offered by all its competitors. It spends a lot of time training new employees on this "second-level service" concept. Chick-fil-A holds the lead in customer satisfaction for overall dining experience among limited-service restaurants for 2015. The company's score of 86 (out of 100) is the highest ever recorded for a fast-food restaurant (KFC scored 73 and McDonald's scored 67).[9]

Maintaining this high level of customer service is one of the reasons that Chick-fil-A uses a franchising model significantly different from other restaurant franchises, notably in retaining ownership of each restaurant. Chick-fil-A pays for the land, the construction, and the equipment. It then rents everything back to the franchisee for 15 percent of the restaurant's sales plus 50 percent of the pretax profit remaining. This arrangement requires low upfront investment on the part of the franchisee and Chick-Fil-A franchisees need only as small as a $5,000 initial investment to become an operator.[10]

Competing fast-food chains on the other hand require significant upfront investments. McDonald's as an example: "Generally, we require a minimum of $750,000 of non-borrowed personal resources to consider you for a franchise."[11] Chick-fil-A gets as many as 25,000 applications from potential franchise operators for the few hundred new restaurant slots that open each year. The formula works well for operators with the company's roughly 1100 operators taking home operating profits of about $210 million in 2011, or an average of $190,000 each.[12] Chick-fil-A franchisees are a very hard-working group, using "sweat equity" and high customer satisfaction to build successful businesses starting with very little investment.

Unique Promotional Efforts

"Eat mor Chickin," intentionally misspelled, is the chain's most prominent advertising slogan, created in 1995. The slogan is seen in advertisements featuring cows that are wearing signs that read: "Eat mor Chickin." The most prominent version of this is on highway billboards where a black-and-white cow sits atop the back of another cow painting the words "Eat mor Chickin" on the billboard. This advertising strategy has the cows uniting in an effort to reform American food by reducing the amount of beef that is eaten. Essentially the cows want Americans to eat fewer hamburgers at their competitors and instead focus on eating chicken. To everyone's surprise, the cows' clever self-preservation message would be the beginning of a campaign still running strong 20 years later.

The campaign has now grown to include cow calendars with discount coupons, stuffed animals, cow clothing, cow board games, etc.

The "Cows" doing a local promotion event.

photo purchased as follows:

Copyright © 2012 by Shutterstock/Paul Brennan.

The "Cow" campaigns have won a number of awards, including most popular campaign by Advertising Week, inducted into New York's Advertising Hall of Fame, inducted into Outdoor Advertising Hall of Fame, a Silver Lion award at the Cannes Advertising Festival, the OBIE award for outdoor advertising, and two "Effie" awards. The "Cow" campaign is considered by the advertising industry to be one of the most effective advertising campaigns in recent history and has been a major driver of the company's success.[13]

CHRISTIAN CULTURE[14]

The company's culture is strongly influenced by the Southern Baptist religious beliefs, a branch of Christianity that preaches overt expressions of faith, including public singing and praying. The company's official statement of corporate purpose says that the business exists "To glorify God by being a faithful steward of all that is entrusted to us. To have a positive influence on all who come in contact with Chick-fil-A."[15] McDonald's mission on the other hand is "to be our customers' favorite place and way to eat and drink."[16] Chick-fil-A's efforts to stop gay marriage legislation has led to boycotts in Boston and Chicago and The Jim Henson Co. pulling its Muppet toys from the company's kids' meals. The controversy has since died down.[17]

The chain has gained prominence (and a measure of customer preference) for the fact that none of its restaurants are open on Sunday. Its executives often say the chain makes as much money in six days as its competitors make in seven.[18]

Expansion Abroad?

As Dan Cathy thought about his company's competitive advantages, he wondered which ones would transfer internationally. U.S. fast-food companies had expanded aggressively internationally: McDonald's had over 17,000 locations, KFC could be found in 13,000 locations with 4,000 in China, and Subway had over 15,000 locations in 90 countries. Chick-fil-A, on the other hand, had no international locations. Maybe following in their footsteps was the way to go?

1. What are the strengths and weaknesses of Chick-fil-A?
2. Which strengths would transfer abroad—and which ones would likely not?
3. Should Chick-fil-A expand internationally? Explain fully.
4. What countries would you recommend and what characteristics of the country would be important?

REFERENCES

"Acquiring a Franchise," *McDonald's website*, 2015.

Bertagnoli, Lisa, "McDonald's has a new generational problem: kids," *Crain's Chicago Business*, September 6, 2014.

Bixler, Brain, "Battle of the Brands: Compared to KFC, Chick-fil-A Rules the Roost in Limited-Service Chicken Segment," *Franchise Chatter*, 2014.

Cathy, Truett, "How Did You Do It, Truett?" *Looking Glass Press*, 2007.

"Chick-fil-A 'Eat mor Chickin' Cows Take Silver Effie Award for Sustained Success Campaign," *PRNewswire*, 2009.

"Chicken from Farm to Table," USDA Food Safety Information Brochure, 2010.

"Company Fact Sheet," *Chick-fil-A website*, 2015.

"Consumer Reports' fast-food restaurant ratings: Chicken," *Atlanta Journal Constitution*, March 30, 2015.

Grantham, Russell, "Chick-fil-A model helps it lead," *Atlanta Journal Constitution*, December 28, 2011.

Industry Results for Limited Service Restaurants, *ACSI Restaurant Report 2015*, American Customer Satisfaction Index (ACSI) Inc., 2015.

Kalinowski, Mark, "Chick-fil-A a Serious and Growing Competitive Threat," *Janney Capital Markets*, 2013.

"Mission & Values," *McDonald's website*, 2015.

McGhee Bernard, "Chick-fil-A Founder S. Truett Cathy Dies," *Associated Press*, September 8, 2014.

Schmall, Emily, "The Cult of Chick-fil-A," *Forbes Magazine*, July 6, 2007.

Tice, Carol, "7 Fast-Food Restaurant Chains That Rake in $2M+ Per Store," *Forbes Magazine*, August 14, 2014.

ENDNOTES

1. See "Company factsheet," 2015.
2. Source data from Technomic and Janney Capital Markets.
3. Source data from Technomic and Janney Capital Markets.
4. See Kalinowski, 2013.
5. See Tice, 2014, and QSR50, 2017.
6. See "Consumer Reports fast food ratings: Chicken," 2015.
7. See Bixler, 2014.
8. See Bertagnoli, 2014.
9. See "Industry results for Limited Service Restaurants," 2015.
10. See Schmall, 2007.
11. See "Acquiring a franchise," 2015.
12. See Grantham, 2011.
13. See "Eat mor Chickin Cows take … " 2009.
14. See Schmall, 2007.
15. See Schmall, 2007.
16. See "Missions and Values," 2015.
17. See McGhee, 2014.
18. See Cathy, 2007.

KFC, THE FRIED CHICKEN FAST-FOOD CHAIN, IS attempting to go from fast food to "fast casual" with new upscale concepts in three countries. In Louisville, Kentucky, the concept outlet is called "KFC eleven," in Toronto Canada it is "KFC Fresh," and in Australia it is "KFC Urban." All three concepts are aimed at a younger, more stylish millennial set, and Colonel Sanders is not invited. One major difference between the three locations is that in Canada and Australia, the new restaurants serve alcohol and beer (and cider in Australia). Not so in Kentucky.

Actually, although the no-alcohol policy is standard for the fast-food industry, one KFC outlet has already introduced alcohol. Since 2012, KFC in Japan has one outlet in Tokyo, "KFC Route 25," that serves whisky after 5 PM on a third-floor extension.

BACKGROUND

To many people, Kentucky Fried Chicken (KFC) is more than just a fast-food restaurant chain. It represents traditional values, responsibility, and a great-tasting meal for the whole family. Founded by Harland Sanders in 1930, KFC has experienced decades of success and innovation. It considers itself the world's most popular chicken restaurant chain (KFC, 2014), with over 18,000 outlets across 115 countries and territories around the globe.

This family fast-food chain has shown a balanced approach toward business by committing to its social and environmental responsibilities. The company states that, "There's more to KFC than great food. We promote education, diversity and animal welfare in a number of positive ways." Through its non-profit wing known as KFC Foundation, it provides educational opportunities for people. This has caused KFC's brand to be known as responsible and community-oriented in the minds of consumers.

KFC AUSTRALIA

In January 2015, KFC Australia applied for liquor licence for a new outlet in Parramatta, Sydney. Located 23 kilometres west of the Sydney central business district on the banks of the Parramatta River, Parramatta is a suburb and major business district in the metropolitan area of Sydney, New South Wales, Australia. In a statement the company indicated that it "hopes to introduce a new KFC experience in Parramatta's CBD in the near future, serving beer and cider as part of its menu."

---

[1] This case was prepared by Dr. Mehran Nejati, Graduate School of Business, Universiti Sains Malaysia (USM), Penang, Malaysia, as a basis for class discussion rather than to illustrate either the correct or incorrect handling of an administrative situation.

KFC in Melbourne, Australia

The announcement seemed to have come as a shock for many consumers in Australia. It attracted strong criticism from various organizations throughout Australia, indicating that serving alcohol by KFC was wrong. Mike Daube, Professor of Health Policy at Curtin University, condemned the move and encouraged authorities to refuse granting a licence to the company. "KFC is the last place where alcohol should be sold," he said. "This is a company that markets to kids and families. This comes at a time when kids around the country are watching the KFC Big Bash on TV and at grounds every day. Now they will associate KFC and its marketing not only with junk food but with alcohol" (Cheer, 2015).

While other fast-food competitors in Australia serve beer and alcoholic apple cider in their outlets, they are much smaller and are regarded as niche operations compared to KFC which has over 600 Australian restaurant operations. Thus, the social implications of this decision and its potential practice by KFC could be significant on the community.

KFC was taken aback, since the two Canadian concept restaurants in Toronto introduced just a few months earlier had not met any resistance. The company defended its decision, stating that the restaurant in Sydney's west would be targeted to people older than 25 years. Moreover, a KFC spokesman said that no family or children's meals would be served in that restaurant, distancing the concept of alcoholic drink from KFC's family meal format.

THE UPSHOT

The announcement created heated debate among consumers. Supporters of this decision regarded it as an additional way to ensure freedom of choice for consumers, whereas others found it to be another way to expose more Australians to alcoholic drinks. The dilemma comes at a time where according to the Australian Bureau of Statistics, Australians are drinking less alcohol overall than any time in the previous 15 years. The reduction in alcohol consumption is mainly caused by the ongoing downward trend in apparent consumption of beer, and a flattening out in the consumption of wine. Hence, the introduction of new drinking opportunities at KFC outlets puts a questionable shadow on how the trend will turn out to be, if the licence to serve alcohol is granted to KFC.

A spokesman for the Liquor and Gaming Authority said it had asked KFC to provide a statement showing its proposal would not be detrimental to the community's wellbeing, and that the statement had not yet been received.

DISCUSSION QUESTIONS

1. What cultural factors lie behind KFC's decision? First, why not serve alcohol in the U.S. concept store? Second, why would Canada and Australia differ in their reaction to the decision? Third, why were these two countries picked by KFC as the first markets to test alcohol? Fourth, if successful in Canada and Australia, which other country or countries should be tried next?
2. Evaluate KFC's decision to serve beer and alcoholic apple cider in its outlets from the perspective of triple bottom line. What are the economic, social, and environmental consequences of this decision?
3. Is KFC's decision to serve alcoholic drink in its restaurants morally wrong? If you were in charge of granting the liquor licence, would you grant or deny a licence to KFC? Explain the justification for your decision.

REFERENCES

Cheer, Louise. (2015, 6 January 2015). Sydney KFC is opening a restaurant serving BEER. Retrieved 15 January, 2015, from http://www.dailymail.co.uk/news/article-2897856/First-Maccas-built-hipster-inner-city-cafe-KFC-opening-restaurant-serving-BEER.html.

KFC. (2014). What made us great is still what makes us great. Retrieved 15 January, 2015, from http://www.kfc.com/about/.

"Two KFC Locations Will Now Serve Beer In Toronto," *The Huffington Post Canada*, July 24, 2014. Retrieved 6 February, 2015, from http://www.huffingtonpost.ca/2014/07/24/kfc-beer-toronto_n_5618329.html.

HOW AN INNOVATIVE PET PRODUCT FROM AUSTRALIA TOOK ON THE WORLD[1]

Looking out of his office in Los Angeles, Tobi Skovron, the CEO and co-founder of Pup-Pee Solutions, reflected on the last 10 years since building his venture and pondered how to move the company forward to a bright future.

The Beginnings

Pup-Pee Solutions was established in 2003 by Australian entrepreneur Tobi Skovron and his wife Simone Skovron. The idea for the business emerged from finding a solution for living in an apartment with a pet that did not involve cleaning stains on the carpet or early Sunday morning walks. Thus, the idea of the Pet Loo was born. The Pet Loo, also known as the "backyard in a box," is a lawn toilet on a square synthetic grass area (measuring approximately 80cm × 80cm) with a patented drainage system that allows pets to do "their business."

It is ideal for pet owners living in apartments, condos, houses, offices, boats, or anywhere that does not have an easy option for taking a pet outside. Using 100 percent chemical-free, hygienic and odorless materials, the Pet Loo is an indoor potty option for pets.

---

1 *This case was prepared by Stephan Gerschewski, Assistant Professor of International Business at Linton School of Global Business, Hannam University, Daejeon, South Korea.*

The Pet Loo has received numerous awards, such as the People's Choice Award on *The New Inventors* on ABC Television Australia and the Australian Pet Product of the Year from the Pet Industry Association of Australia (PIIA), and it is listed in the top 50 favorite Australian exports. The product portfolio of Pup-Pee Solutions consists of the flagship product Pet Loo as well as other waste-management products, such as Pee Pods and Liquid Ate, which are cleaning products for pets. Today, Pup-Pee Solutions is selling its products in about 84 countries around the world.

The Entrepreneur

Tobi Skovron describes himself as an entrepreneur at heart, and he was strongly influenced by his father, who was also an entrepreneur and who taught him two important things: 1) "If you want something done right, do it yourself" and 2) "Don't wonder why or how, go in there and make it happen." According to Mr. Skovron, "entrepreneurship is in my blood, I am following a dream and it is coming to me naturally. I see an opportunity and jump on it and I execute it and make it happen. I don't sit here and think about what could have been? I don't ever want to die wondering." Tobi Skovron won the Australian Entrepreneur of the Year under 30 award in 2008. His wife and co-founder of Pup-Pee Solutions, Simone Skovron, is a qualified social worker and vet nurse and deals mostly with the people and pet side of Pup-Pee Solutions, while Tobi Skovron is primarily responsible for the major business decisions. Both Tobi and Simone Skovron are extremely passionate about pets and their business and they have turned their passion into a venture of global scale.

Internationalization

Pup-Pee Solutions started to go global in 2006. Prior to entering its first overseas markets, from 2003 to 2006, the company set all the intellectual property rights, patents, trademarks, and copyrights and prototyped and tested everything to make sure that the product to bring to the market was second to none. Currently, Pup-Pee solutions has published patents in the USA, New Zealand, Canada, UK, Europe, Australia, and Asia.

From the outset of establishing the company, Tobi Skovron displayed a strong global mindset and this was characterized by the attitude "If I can sell this in Australia, I can sell it anywhere in the world." Tobi Skovron developed a successful program in Australia first and then replicated it in overseas markets. As the Australian market is relatively small, it was going to reach its saturation point. Therefore, internationalization was a viable solution to survival for Pup-Pee Solutions. In essence, the company was carefully set up in its own backyard and then rolled out to global markets. According to Mr. Skovron, the "game" for various countries in Asia or Europe is essentially the same, only the "language" of the game is different with mild product adaptations for the respective markets. Pup-Pee Solutions entered Hong Kong, Singapore, Taiwan, UK, Ireland, Australia, New Zealand, USA, and Canada within the first 12 months of going global in 2006. The first overseas market was the USA due to the attractiveness and size of the market with around 200 million cats and dogs combined and the biggest and most advanced market for pet waste-management products. As Mr. Skovron explained, Australia is just 6–7 percent of the U.S. market and, using a sports metaphor, USA is the "NBA" for pet products, while Australia is on "college basketball" level.

Currently, the sales ratio of Pup-Pee Solutions amounts to 60 percent Australian and 40 percent international sales. The early and rapid internationalization of Pup-Pee Solutions is a prime example of a so-called "born global company." Born global firms are young and innovative companies that derive their competitive advantage from doing business in multiple countries right from the establishment of the company. A born global firm is generally defined as a company that achieves at least 25 percent international sales within the first three years of operation.

Foreign Market Entry Mode and Strategy

Pup-Pee Solutions focused mainly on distribution when expanding overseas by forming relationships with third-party distributors. The company is supplying people that are involved in distribution and they add Pup-Pee Solutions' products to their portfolio and sell them through to their retail outlets or directly to their customers. When choosing distributors, Pup-Pee Solutions is thoroughly evaluating the skills of the distributors and is focused on developing long-term relationships rather than a "quick fix." In addition, Pup-Pee Solutions is selling its products through its online shop on the company website to countries, such as Russia, Ukraine, and Bulgaria where there are currently no third-party distributors. Pup-Pee Solutions has also set up three manufacturing warehouses. The liquid range is produced in Australia for markets in the Southern Hemisphere, while the liquid range for the Northern Hemisphere is made in New York and the hardware is manufactured in China. In terms of distribution, Pup-Pee Solutions has three sales subsidiaries in Melbourne, New York, and Los Angeles.

An important mechanism of finding new customers was by attending international tradeshows which enabled Pup-Pee Solutions to increase its reputation in the industry and get referrals to customers via word-of-mouth. For example, Tobi Skovron attended a global tradeshow in Orlando which landed him a very large customer which, in turn, let him made bigger things in the U.S. market. The Australian government export agency Austrade also provided valuable support by developing market analysis reports that facilitated internationalization.

Importantly, Pup-Pee Solutions focused on entering foreign markets one-by-one rather than entering several countries simultaneously. Thus, Pup-Pee Solutions adopted a "sprinkler" rather than a "waterfall" approach to global strategy. According to Tobi Skovron, it is crucial to set up your business in your own backyard first and carefully prepare your business plan and iron out any discrepancies. Mr. Skovron recommends "don't sprint a marathon" and cautions that "there is no such thing as an overnight success" and "don't let perception deceive you." In addition, it takes a lot of determination and perseverance to succeed and "your product has to stick because easy come, easy go."

Another key success factor of Pup-Pee Solutions related to the Pet Loo brand which attracted a large and loyal customer base. Pup-Pee Solutions made extensive use of social media channels, such as Facebook, Twitter, and Internet blogs to promote the company and build the brand. In addition, public relations (PR), advertising, search engine optimization (SEO), YouTube, and a "sheer hunger for success" spurred the development of Pup-Pee Solutions.

In growing the company, Tobi Skovron focused deliberately on achieving healthy financial performance of the firm, as it all comes down to finances. If the sale has not been made, Pup-Pee Solutions is not able to grow. This means that distributors are selected carefully with a long-term outlook and the employees of Pup-Pee Solutions are "hungry to make a difference" and work hard to move the company forward.

How was Pup-Pee Solutions able to compete against the established and leading "big players" in the industry, such as PetSafe? Pup-Pee Solutions focused strongly on its innovative product portfolio, protecting its numerous intellectual property and leveraging the Pet Loo brand. Tobi Skovron used the metaphor that "the size of the dog does not really reflect the bite of the dog" to describe the successful global strategy of Pup-Pee Solutions.

Barriers to Internationalization

Despite its worldwide success, Pup-Pee Solution's global market entry was characterized by several key barriers. One major barrier was protecting the intellectual property of the company. As Tobi Skovron explained, "If you would like to sell your products at major retail outlets, such as Petco, Petsmart or Dr. Fosters, you have to sign a waiver that states that your product is registered, patented, and you are not infringing on somebody else's rights." However, it happened that competitors in other countries infringed on Pup-Pee Solutions' patents and copyrights. For example, one competitor in Canada blatantly copied the design of Pet Loo and was later forced to withdraw the products from the shelves of its retail stores after Tobi Skovron found out about the infringement.

In addition, Pup-Pee Solutions faced some cultural barriers, such as language and misinterpretations of the product use. For instance, in Germany, the company had to put a large, red disclaimer on the Pet Loo product which stated that the Pet Loo is not an excuse not to walk your dog as some German customers interpreted the purpose of the Pet Loo in this way.

Looking Ahead to the Future

One afternoon in late 2013, Tobi Skovron received an invitation from Randy Boyd, CEO of PetSafe, to visit the company's headquarters in Knoxville, Tennessee. PetSafe is the industry leader and prime innovator in the development of safe, reliable, and technologically superior pet products. During the meeting, Randy Boyd showed an active interest in the Pet Loo and submitted an offer to Tobi Skovron to acquire Pup-Pee Solutions.

Pup-Pee Solutions had rapidly developed over the past 10 years and had successfully exported its products to more than 80 countries. The company was at a crossroads now and important questions were emerging: How could the company further expand and grow? Should Tobi Skovron sell Pup-Pee Solutions to PetSafe or should he keep ownership of his venture? How would a potential sale to PetSafe affect his family and current employees of Pup-Pee Solutions? A difficult decision loomed on Tobi Skovron's mind …

QUESTIONS

1. Why and how was Pup-Pee Solutions established? Briefly describe the history of Pup-Pee Solutions.
2. Describe the foreign market entry strategy of Pup-Pee Solutions. What were the key factors in the entry mode process? What were some of the barriers to internationalization?
3. What is the competitive advantage of Pup-Pee Solutions?
4. Imagine you are in the shoes of Tobi Skovron. What would you do now? Would you sell the company to PetSafe or would you keep ownership of Pup-Pee Solutions? Explain your decision.

ABSTRACT

In 1986 the Hyundai Excel became the most successful foreign car launch in U.S. history; by year three, U.S. sales had dropped dramatically. How could Hyundai regain its momentum in capturing a major share of the global auto market?

Hyundai (A) is the first part of a four-part Hyundai case study.

INTRODUCTION

Hyundai's Excel—priced at $6,000—was the most successful launch of a foreign-made car in the United States ever.[1] In its second year—1987—overseas sales (largely to U.S. customers) were 264,000 cars, followed by 405,000 in 1988. Advertising was built on the slogan, "Cars That Make Sense." However in 1989 volume fell to 215,000 cars and was projected to decline to 138,000 in 1990. What happened?

BACKGROUND

During a three-year period, Hyundai's labor costs doubled and, with the rise in value of the Korean won and fall in value of the Japanese yen, Hyundai's price advantage over such Japanese automobiles as the Toyota Tercel nearly vanished. Observed Lee Soo II, Hyundai's managing director of planning, "We have some problems to compete with the Japanese products. … We are not so optimistic for our future exports because of the severe competition."[2]

Uneven quality control produced automobiles with a shaky reputation among U.S. buyers. The U.S. National Highway Traffic Safety Administration reported that the manual transmission on 1986–1989 Excels locked up while the car was moving,[3] prompting comedian David Letterman to joke, "Want to frighten astronauts in space? Place a Hyundai logo on the spacecraft's control panel."[4]

Hyundai's executive vice president admitted that, after three years and 40,000 miles, Excel owners were likely to find their cars had "… no major mechanical problems, just a lot of little annoying

---

1   *This case was prepared by Don Sexton, Professor of Marketing, Director, Center for International Business Education and Research, Columbia Business School. This case was sponsored by the Chazen Institute and the Columbia University Center for International Business Education and Research (CIBER).*

ones."[5] Many potential Hyundai purchasers believed that, whatever they saved on the price of the automobile in the showroom, they would later lose paying for repairs in the shop.

These quality issues were especially damaging to the potential sales of the new Sonata model, positioned to compete against the Honda Accord but late to market.[6]

Hyundai's problems seemed to be shared by other South Korean companies. Trade and Industry Minister Park Pil Soo commented that from 1986 to 1988 Korean companies "didn't acquire new technology and they didn't automate their facilities … Now they have few things to sell."[7]

GROWTH AT HOME

Meanwhile, Hyundai benefited from huge increases in the demand for cars in South Korea. In 1989 Hyundai's domestic passenger car sales increased by 63 percent. However domestic demand alone was not expected to be sufficient to support the long-term growth objectives of Hyundai. One industry analyst commented, "They may prefer to stay in the minor leagues, but other countries are coming up behind them. They can't afford not to go ahead."

To grow Hyundai needed to develop the global market, but where, when, and how?

DISCUSSION QUESTIONS

1. What strengths and weaknesses did Hyundai have in the U.S. market?
2. How did Hyundai enter the U.S. market? What were the key components of its strategy?
3. What options should Hyundai consider?

ENDNOTES

1. David Bank and Peter Leyden, "The Once-Hot Hyundai Takes a Dive in Sales," *St. Petersburg Times*, June 10, 1990.
2. Bank and Leyden, "Once Hot Hyundai."
3. Micheline Maynard, "Hyundai Sales Are Skidding," *USA Today*, Oct. 1, 1992.
4. Warren Brown, "Hyundai's Mission Possible: Beat the Luxury Brands," *The Washington Post*, April 1, 2007.
5. David Kiley, "Hyundai. Maybe Htundai," *Adweek*, September 17, 1990.
6. Bank and Leyden, "Once Hot Hyundai."
7. Bank and Leyden, "Once Hot Hyundai."

PART TWO
INTERNATIONAL OPPORTUNITIES AND THREATS

IN THE NEXT THREE CHAPTERS we will discuss the new global environment, the opportunities and threats facing the global marketer. We will use a mini-version of the standard **PESTEL** (or **PESTLE** in British English) formula to cover the range of environmental forces involved.

THE PESTEL FRAMEWORK

PESTEL stands for Political, Economic, Social, Technological, Environmental, and Legal factors that together make up the global market environment (see Exhibit II.1).[1]

- *Political factors* basically cover the degree to which the government intervenes in the economy. They could include areas such as tax policy, labor law, and environmental law, but for global marketing the emphasis is on trade restrictions, tariffs, and political stability.
- *Economic factors* include level of economic development, per-capita income growth, population size and growth rates, and exchange rates. Exchange rates affect the costs of exporting goods and the supply and price of imported goods in an economy.
- *Social factors* include the cultural aspects such as religion, social norms, and ethnicity. They also include attitudes toward work and leisure, individual-

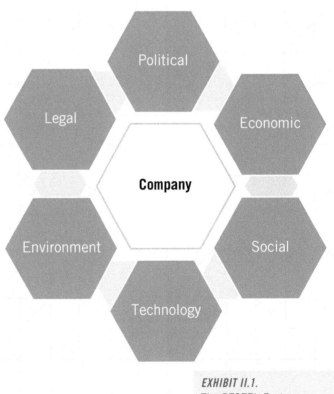

EXHIBIT II.1.
The PESTEL Factors

ism versus groups, and family relationships. Trends in social factors often affect the demand for a company's products and also how a subsidiary is managed.

- *Technological factors* include a country's level of infrastructure in communications and transportation, level of R&D activity, and rate of technological change. They can be barriers to entry, especially to services, and help determine transportation costs and foreign direct investments for outsourcing.

- *Environmental factors* involve sustainability issues such as environmental deterioration in water and air quality and the potential impact of climate change. Sustainability issues affect how companies operate and the products they offer, both creating new markets and diminishing or destroying existing ones.

- *Legal factors* include discrimination law, consumer law, antitrust law, employment law, and health and safety law. These factors directly affect how a company operates abroad and the efforts it makes to be a good corporate citizen in the local environment.

Focusing on global marketing factors, we have combined these and related issues into three chapters. We start with the *economic* environment in the present chapter. The following chapter will deal with the *political and legal* environment, and then in Chapter 5 we will cover the *cultural* environment.

Relating back to the SWOT framework, the economic environment can be seen as part of "**opportunities**," broadly speaking. The following two chapters involving political, legal, and cultural factors work mainly as constraints on the global marketer and can therefore be viewed as "**threats**."

In this chapter you will learn about:

1. How economic growth has helped to raise people out of poverty and made many countries join the ranks of more affluent countries
2. The powerful role of population and income per capita to drive market attractiveness provided trade barriers are low
3. The importance of fair trade, sustainable operations, and attention to the bottom of the pyramid in spreading the created wealth more evenly
4. How trade blocs have helped create a more attractive investment climate and increased market size

One main driver of globalization and international expansion has been the increasing economic activity, affluence, and demand in new foreign markets. After World War II, international expansion focused on developed markets in Europe and Asia. Those markets are still large, but growth has slowed and in more recent years the economic growth in new emerging markets has been more attractive to international marketers. In particular, the recently emerging countries with large populations—including the so-called BRICS (Brazil, Russia, India, China, and South Africa)—have become important markets.

This chapter will deal with two dominant economic factors in a country's economic success. First is the economic growth in the country, which explains how countries are able to produce things at home and to pay for domestic and foreign products. The second factor involves international trade, the volume of exports and imports, and the ease of trade. Open country markets help citizens of different countries to get access to foreign goods. Economic growth enables people to pay for the goods. Economic growth and international trade go hand-in-hand.

Economic and Trade Environment

CHAPTER 3

OPENING VIGNETTE

LARGE COMPANIES NOW COME FROM ALL OVER

Forbes Magazine annually publishes a list of the 2000 largest public companies as measured by revenues, profits, assets, and market value (weighted equally). An examination of these largest 2000 companies in the world over the past 11 years vividly shows the rapid pace of change occurring in the competitive landscape and provides a window into broader economic trends happening worldwide.

In 2003, the top 10 largest companies in the world were all European or American with one Japanese company. By 2017 four of the top 10 spots were held by Chinese companies, while the U.S. claimed five top spots. The list shows the dramatic shift (in the number of companies) between East and West that has occurred in the business environment. (see Exhibit 3.1)

	2003	2017	Growth
North America	836	608	-27%
Asia	532	674	27%
Oceania(Australia)	38	65	71%
Africa	19	17	-11%
Central-South America	34	40	18%
Europe	521	474	-9%
Middle East	20	82	310%

Source: Fortune Global 2000. www.forbes.com

EXHIBIT 3.1.
Location of the largest 2000 companies.[2]

Source: www.forbes.com.

It should be noted that banks and diversified financials dominate the list thanks to their outsized revenues and massive total assets. Many of the banks, especially in the case of China, have significant government involvement and backing. Also, the fact that some regions lost percentagewise does not mean their companies' performance went down. The decade showed unprecedented economic growth, and the winners simply gained more. Nevertheless, as the figures show, the East and the South are on the march.

MARKET SIZE AND GROWTH

There are several factors that drive market demand in most countries, but two stand out: size of population and growth of per-capita income. A simple economic metric is that potential market demand equals population multiplied by per-capita income. A country with a large population and a high rate of per-capita income growth is generally a very attractive market.

Population

The world **population** in 2017 was estimated to be 7.5 billion by the United States Census Bureau (USCB). Approximately 4.4 billion people live in the top 10 countries, representing around 58 percent of the world's population (see Exhibit 3.2).

EXHIBIT 3.2.
Population in the world's largest countries China and India together account for one third of the world's population.[3]

Source: United Nations Population Division, 2017.

Rank	Country (or Area)	Population 2017 Millions of People	World Share
1	China	1,388.2	18.50%
2	India	1,342.5	17.90%
3	U.S.	326.5	4.30%
4	Indonesia	263.5	3.50%
5	Brazil	211.2	2.80%
6	Pakistan	196.7	2.60%
7	Nigeria	191.8	2.60%
8	Bangladesh	164.8	2.20%
9	Russia	143.4	1.90%
10	Mexico	130.2	1.70%
	Total	4358.9	58.00%

Source: United Nations Population Division, 2017

Population figures might seem dry, but they really do have marketing significance, even when income per capita might be low. Three illustrations:

- *Product adaptation.* With enough people, it often pays for a company to adapt products. Countries with smaller populations do not usually get products and services adapted, even when incomes are relatively high. Adapting automobile suspensions for poor Indian roads will be more economically justified than adding engine heaters for cold Scandinavian winter weather.
- *Network effects.* Another example is the so-called network effect often assumed to especially affect consumer electronic products. When potentially there are many people that can acquire the same products and technology, company investments in service and support will be greater and complementary products are more likely to come into the market.
- *Economies of scale.* With a small population base, manufacturing plants may not reach efficient scale. This means cost of production will be higher than elsewhere. In this case the solution is either to produce for export or to move production elsewhere. With a larger population, factories are more likely to reach efficient scale.

Understanding the marketing environment in some of these countries necessarily includes simple but important comparisons of population size. What might be seen as very similar countries can have widely different population numbers. Indonesia's 264 million people are almost 10 times greater than neighboring Malaysia's 31 million, a big difference for economic policy makers but also for marketers. According to U.S. Census Bureau data, the unified Germany has about 81 million people, biggest in Europe (not counting Russia's 143 million), much bigger than another country with a Germanic culture, Austria, at 8.6 million. France and the United Kingdom have about 65 and 66 million, respectively, while Sweden has 9.9 and Denmark 5.7 million people, much smaller markets. Hungary at 10 million is small compared to Poland's 39 million, but both countries have seen their numbers go down. In Latin America, Chile at 18 million is small compared to Brazil at around 211 million. Japan is 2.5 times as large as South Korea's 50 million, but Japan has a rapidly aging population. The younger "tiger" Hong Kong has a limited home market of 7.4 million people.

Rank	City/Urban Area	Country	Population Millions of people
1	Tokyo–Yokohama	Japan	37.8
2	Jakarta (Jabodetabek)	Indonesia	30.5
3	Delhi	India	25.0
4	Manila (Metro Manila)	Philippines	24.1
5	Seoul–Gyeonggi–Incheon (Sudogwon)	South Korea	23.5
6	Shanghai	China	23.4
7	Karachi	Pakistan	22.1
8	Beijing	China	21.0
9	New York City	United States of America	20.7
10	Guangzhou–Foshan (Guangfo)	China	20.6

Numbers include population within the city and the surrounding suburbs.
Source: World's Largest Cities (2016) www.worldatlas.com/citypops.htm

Mega-Cities

In many cases, the most common entry point of international marketers are the big cities—often capitals—where the majority of purchasing power can be found. The 10 biggest cities in the world are shown in Exhibit 3.3.

EXHIBIT 3.3.
The top 10 cities in the world 2016.[4] Mega size cities are not unusual. It is possible for a successful marketing plan to just focus on one major city.

Source: http://www.worldatlas.com/citypops.htm.

The reason these large **"mega-cities"** are used as entry points is not only because of the large population. They typically have other features attractive to many entering companies:[5]

- *Distribution and communication networks* are most developed here.
- *Urban people* are the most cosmopolitan and typically well-off. They become the natural targets for many foreign brands.
- The large cities are *trend-setters* for the rest of the country.
- The main city is often the *capital* where the central government is located (in this respect the United States is an exception and unusual).

These cities are often very crowded.[6] Exhibit 3.4 shows the notorious crossing at Tokyo's Shibuya station.

In addition to crowded streets, Tokyo is routinely ranked as having the world's most crowded subways.[7] It is sometimes hard to imagine how many people can actually be in the same place at the same time. In Tokyo, there is a saying that the government does not want to count how many people are actually within the city proper on a given day, since the number per square meter is too high to be credible.

Per-Capita Income

The level and **growth** of **income per capita** is the other part of the fundamental economic metric of a country's attractiveness as a market. The level of economic development in a country is not only determined by income per capita—what matters is also infrastructure development, literacy rates, income inequality, and other factors. But the basic income-per-capita figures provide a quick and important indicator of how developed a country is.

The calculation of income per capita starts with the country's **GDP or gross domestic product.** The GDP is the market value of all final goods and services from a nation in a given year. It is typically a measure of the total economic output of a country calculated at government official exchange rates. The top 10 economies in 2015, according to the IMF World Economic Outlook, are given in Exhibit 3.5.

These figures do not take into account differences in the cost of living in different countries, and the results vary with changes in the exchange rates of the country's currency. Most of us have probably seen this problem first-hand. It means that in some years American tourists with a strong dollar can easily travel in Europe and eat at the best restaurants, while in other years a stronger euro entices Europeans to come to New York to buy luxury brands they cannot afford at home. To compensate for these effects, it is common to adjust the raw figures with a so-called **Purchasing Power Parity (PPP)** index which reflects the amount of goods a consumer can buy locally with a certain income.

When comparing per-capita incomes, the PPP-adjusted figures are typically used since they reflect individual purchasing power and cost of living. The top 10 countries are as follows (Exhibit 3.6).

Rank	Country	GDP (millions $$)
1	United States	18,569
2	China	11,218
3	Japan	4,939
4	Germany	3,467
5	United Kingdom	2,629
6	France	2,463
7	India	2,256
8	Italy	1,851
9	Brazil	1,799
10	Canada	1,529

Source: International Monetary Fund, World Economic Outlook Database, 2017

EXHIBIT 3.5.
The 10 biggest world economies 2016.[8]

Ex. 3.5: Source: International Monetary Fund, World Economic Outlook Database.

Rank	Country	Adjusted PPP International Dollars $$
1	Qatar	127,660
2	Luxembourg	104,003
3	Macao SAR	95,151
4	Singapore	87,855
5	Brunei Darussalam	76,884
6	Kuwait	71,887
7	Norway	69,249
8	Ireland	69,231
9	United Arab Emirates	67,871
10	Switzerland	59,561
11	San Marino	59,058
12	Hong Kong SAR	58,322
13	United States	57,436
14	Saudi Arabia	55,158
15	Netherlands	51,049
16	Bahrain	50,704
17	Sweden	49,836
18	Iceland	49,136
19	Australia	48,899
20	Germany	48,111

Source: International Monetary Fund, World Economic Outlook (2017), GDP based on PPP per capita. The International Dollar Int$ is a hypothetical unit of currency that has the same purchasing power parity that the U.S dollar had in the United States at a given point in time, here 2016.

EXHIBIT 3.6.
Top 20 Income-per capita countries in 2016.[9]

Source: International Monetary Fund.

The relatively small population of some of these countries clearly shows up in the ranking. To get a simple economic index of the potential demand we multiply the population size with the per-capita income:

Potential demand = Population size x Income per capita.
The top markets according to this metric are shown in Exhibit 3.7.

EXHIBIT 3.7.
Potential demand. Top 15 markets (2016)
Ex. 3.7: Source: International Monetary Fund, World Economic Outlook Database, 2017.

Rank	Country-Region	PPP$$	Population millions	Total Calculated Potential Market (billion int$)
1	China	15,398	1,383	$ 21.29
2	United States	57,436	323	$ 18.56
3	India	6,615	1,309	$ 8.66
4	Japan	41,274	127	$ 5.23
5	Germany	48,110	83	$ 3.98
6	Russia	26,489	143	$ 3.79
7	Brazil	15,241	206	$ 3.14
8	Indonesia	11,720	259	$ 3.03
9	United Kingdom	42,480	66	$ 2.78
10	France	42,313	65	$ 2.73
11	Mexico	18,938	122	$ 2.31
12	Italy	36,833	61	$ 2.23
13	Turkey	24,911	80	$ 1.98
14	South Korea	37,740	51	$ 1.93
15	Saudi Arabia	55,158	32	$ 1.75

The importance of population size shows up clearly in Exhibit 3.7. The corresponding figures for per-capita leader Qatar is $314 billion, not a very large market. Switzerland, also a "rich" country, with about 8 million people, is a $471 billion potential market, still quite small. But population is not everything. Indonesia's huge population of 259 million yields a market of $3.03 billion, about the same size market as France which has one-fourth of the population.

Economic Growth

An attractive country market is not simply one with a large potential. Also important is the rate of **economic growth**. A market that is growing fast makes entry easier. Since all competitors can gain in a growth market, competitive rivalry is often less intense. In addition, entry barriers are lower as new and not-yet-loyal consumers come into the market.

Economic growth is often measured as the percent rate of increase in real gross domestic product, or **real GDP**. "Real" means inflation-adjusted figures, to avoid the distorting effect of inflation on the price of goods produced. For marketing purposes, the more important figure can be the per-capita growth of GDP, but the two numbers are usually highly correlated.

The growth in per-capita income in selected countries during the last four years is shown in Exhibit 3.8.

Country Name	2010	2011	2012	2013	2014	2015	2016
World	3.1	1.9	1.2	1.4	1.6	1.5	1.2
South Asia	7.5	4.8	4.1	4.6	5.7	6.1	5.5
North America	1.7	1.0	1.4	1.0	1.6	1.7	0.8
European Union	1.9	1.7	(0.7)	(0.1)	1.4	1.9	1.5
Sub-Saharan Africa (excluding high income)	2.6	1.5	0.9	2.0	1.8	0.3	(1.5)
Germany	4.2	5.6	0.3	0.2	1.2	0.8	0.7
Japan	4.2	0.1	1.7	2.1	0.5	1.3	1.1
Korea, Rep.	6.0	2.9	1.8	2.4	2.7	2.2	2.4
Turkey	7.0	9.5	3.2	6.7	3.5	4.4	1.3
United Kingdom	1.1	0.7	0.6	1.2	2.3	1.4	1.0
United States	1.7	0.8	1.5	1.0	1.6	1.9	0.9
Saudi Arabia	2.1	6.8	2.3	(0.2)	0.8	1.5	(0.5)
Brazil	6.5	3.0	1.0	2.1	(0.4)	(4.6)	(4.4)
China	10.1	9.0	7.3	7.2	6.8	6.4	6.1
India	8.8	5.2	4.1	5.1	6.2	6.8	5.9
Russian Federation	4.5	4.2	3.3	1.1	(1.1)	(3.0)	(0.4)
South Africa	1.6	1.8	0.7	0.9	0.1	(0.3)	(1.3)

Source: The World Bank database: World Development Indicators.

EXHIBIT 3.8.
GDP per-capita income growth (percentage change) in selected countries.[10] The world's growth continues driven primarily by rapid growth in China and India. The other members of the BRICS countries have lost some of their "shine."

Source: The World Bank database.

The table clearly shows the superior growth records of China and India, and the somewhat more uneven records in the other members of the BRICS group (Brazil, Russia, and South Africa). The Russian economy is heavily reliant on oil and gas, so its growth figures reflect the significant price changes on the energy markets in recent years. Brazil and South Africa had some difficulties because of slowing demand for their raw materials exports after the 2008 financial crisis. The large populations in the BRICS countries—and in Turkey as well—clearly point to very promising markets. The table also documents the relatively slow growth rate in the developed Western markets and the United States. Japan, it should be noted, has been a large but less attractive market with low or negative growth since the beginning of the 1990s.

DEVELOPING COUNTRIES

So far we have dealt with the economic strength of the countries using the traditional metrics of demand size and growth—the larger the size and the higher the growth rate the more attractive the market. But today's global marketing has to go beyond the metrics of size and growth and face the developing world, the triple bottom line, and selling to the bottom of the pyramid.

Developed vs. Developing Countries

The World Bank classifies countries into four groups according to the gross national income (GNI) per capita. GNI is gross domestic product (GDP) plus net receipts of income from abroad. In some countries, the payments from abroad can be substantial. An example is Pakistan, where many families receive payments from relatives working in the Middle East. Similarly, Mexican workers often send money transfers back home from the United States.

The following are the income divisions currently used by the World Bank:

- *Low-income countries* with GNI per capita of $1,035 or less
- *Lower-middle-income countries* with GNI per capita between $1,036 and $4,085
- *Upper-middle-income countries* with GNI per capita between $4,086 and $12,615
- *High-income countries* with GNI above $12,616

There are 195 countries in the world (196 if Taiwan is counted separately from China) and of these, 188 belong to the World Bank and the International Monetary Fund (IMF). In its lending, the World Bank also distinguishes an additional 26 territories (such as Guam and Isle of Man). Of these 214 countries and territories, there are 75 high-income countries in the World Bank, 55 upper-middle-income countries, 48 lower-middle-income countries, and 36 low-income countries.[11]

The World Bank suggests that low- and middle-income countries and regions are "**developing**" while high-income countries and regions are "**advanced**." The World Bank has now stopped using the "**emerging**" concept. Using old definitions, an "emerging" market would be an intermediate category of countries that haven't yet reached the minimum Gross National Product (GNP) per capita of $9,656.[12] That cutoff would mean Russia and Brazil are no longer "emerging," China is very close to passing the emerging market threshold, while India is still lagging behind. For marketing purposes, it can still be useful to think of the four BRIC countries as "emerging" rather than "advanced."

Over time, as economic development occurs, countries "graduate" from one level to the next. The following, including four Asian Tigers and new Euro countries, were considered developing countries until recently, and are now listed as advanced economies by the IMF (see Exhibit 3.9):

The Bottom of the Pyramid

It is easy to assume that the marketing opportunities are clustered in the advanced grouping of 75 countries. After all, in traditional economics one common "demand" metric is usually defined as (**Willingness to buy**) multiplied by (**Ability to buy**). Countries and territories in the "developing" category might certainly have willing buyers, but not many with the ability to buy.

This was long the commonly accepted wisdom. But the bottom-of-the-pyramid (B-O-P) development changed that.

The 4 billion-strong B-O-P market naturally includes the countries classified as "low income" by the World Bank. But even in advanced countries there are pockets of low income which are part of the bottom of the pyramid. This means that once products and services are scaled down, simplified, and adapted to the specific needs of the poor, there is also demand in other countries that companies can tap into.

The key ideas from B-O-P markets involve, for example, arranging for shared ownership of appliances and equipment, offering credit for even minor purchases, and simplifying parts and components so that repairs become easier. What is required is that the company decentralizes authority. It needs to train and then empower low-level employees, so they can make decisions about product alterations, service support, and customer follow-up on the spot. Nothing revolutionary in this—it's actually similar to the "stay-close-to-the-customer" idea, but striking in that these customers have long been ignored.

For many businesses this kind of re-thinking is best seen in terms of **corporate social responsibility (CSR),** creating goodwill and helping the local economy. The profits may not be very great and can be long in coming. But the B-O-P markets offer an entrant a good opportunity to do well by doing good. Rather than trying to treat marketing to the poor as a free-standing profit-and-loss center, the more important payoff may well be the good will from other stakeholders that comes with a presence in B-O-P.[14]

As Prahalad and Hart say: "Countries that still don't have a modern infrastructure or products to meet basic human needs are an ideal testing ground for developing environmentally sustainable technologies and products for the entire world. Furthermore, MNC investment at the bottom of the pyramid means lifting billions of people out of poverty and desperation, averting the social decay, political chaos, terrorism and social meltdown that is certain to continue if the gap between rich and poor continues to widen."[15]

Sustainable Development

The Prahalad and Hart work was in a way a "wake-up" call to established international development economists. Early on, a country's "development" level usually meant the per-capita income level. This is what the World Bank figures capture. Traditionally, richer

Hong Kong (since 1997)

Israel (since 1997)

Singapore (since 1997)

South Korea (since 1997)

Taiwan (since 1997)

Cyprus (since 2001)

Slovenia (since 2007)

Malta (since 2008)

Czech Republic (since 2009)

Slovakia (since 2009)

Estonia (since 2011)

San Marino (since 2012)

EXHIBIT 3.9.
New "advanced" economies[13]

Ex. 3.9: Sources: http://www.imf.org/external/np/exr/key/advanced.htm and http://www.investopedia.com/terms/a/advanced-economies.asp.

countries were considered "developed," while poorer countries were "developing" or, if really poor, "underdeveloped." Since most developed countries could be found in the Northern Hemisphere and the developing countries below the Equator, it was common to talk about the debilitating and unfair "Rich North versus Poor South" economic and political division.

In more recent years, there has been a significant move toward defining a broader concept of development. The impetus has come from the recognition that economics is not everything, and that the inequality of incomes in a country can create pockets of poverty in even highly developed countries. Here is how one World Bank report phrases the issue:

"Countries with similar average incomes can differ substantially when it comes to people's quality of life: access to education and healthcare, employment opportunities, availability of clean air and safe drinking water, the threat of crime, and so on."[16]

The report goes on to say that economic growth has often been achieved at the cost of greater inequality, weakened democracy, loss of cultural identity, and overconsumption of natural resources needed by future generations.[17]

As a result of the pressures from World Bank, the United Nations, and various national agencies, a new concept of **"sustainable" development** has gained currency among politicians and economists. A development is "sustainable" when it "meets the needs of the present without compromising the ability of future generations to meet their own needs."

In many countries today, developed and developing, the governments are increasingly focused in such sustainable development. This thrust is of significance to many global marketers. In the big picture, the expanding international firm brings new goods and services to the country markets entered. In many cases these goods and services have to rely on existing and available infrastructure, resources, and local hires. When the national resources are lacking, it is important that the new entrant be willing to shoulder some of the costs involved in improvement. When McDonald's entered Russia by opening in Moscow in 1990, the company found it necessary to also establish a potato farm that could supply the store with quality french fries. Similarly, when P&G targeted Russia after the 1989 opening of the post-Soviet markets, it helped to expand the port in Leningrad (now St. Petersburg) in order to avoid the cumbersome border crossings for trucks carrying products from its European plants.

The international marketer can certainly be a force for positive growth as well as sustainable development. But to help with sustainable development, the company has to define the business opportunity broader than just "selling more product." This has led to the **triple bottom line** concept involving social, environmental, and financial metrics. We will get back to the triple bottom line repeatedly throughout this text. In this chapter we will discuss one part of the "social" concerns, "Fair Trade," and then the environmental issues relating to Global Warming and "Green Trade."

INTERNATIONAL TRADE

The most obvious manifestation of global marketing in terms of hard data is **international trade**. The **export** and **import** trade figures reveal the extent to which goods in one country are bought by the citizens in another country.

When the volume of the bilateral trade between two countries is high (whether in terms of units shipped or value in dollars), the two countries tend to have close ties in other ways as well, cultural, economic, and political. The companies in the two countries are likely to have good knowledge of each other's markets and have executives with experience in both markets. Conversely, when trade is minimal, the companies will not only have trouble understanding the foreign market, they will also lack experienced management in such markets. This means the entry barriers are higher, and companies usually have to rely on insiders and gatekeepers who have special access to government and other institutions. International trade figures can be useful to quickly gauge the degree to which a country is open to foreign companies.

Exports and Imports

Exhibit 3.10 shows the world exports and imports for the 20 largest exporting countries.

	Country	Exports (billion$)	Imports (billion $)	Trade Surplus or (Deficit)
1	China	$2,011	$1,437	$574
2	United States	$1,471	$2,205	($734)
3	Germany	$1,283	$987	$296
4	Japan	$641	$629	$12
5	South Korea	$509	$405	$104
6	France	$505	$525	($20)
7	Hong Kong	$487	$509	($22)
8	Netherlands	$460	$376	$84
9	Italy	$436	$372	$64
10	United Kingdom	$412	$581	($169)
11	Canada	$402	$419	($17)
12	Mexico	$359	$372	($13)
13	Singapore	$353	$271	$82
14	United Arab Emirates	$316	$246	$70
15	Taiwan	$314	$248	$66
16	Switzerland	$301	$243	$58
17	India	$271	$402	($131)
18	Spain	$266	$287	($21)
19	Russia	$259	$165	$94
20	Belgium	$250	$251	($1)

EXHIBIT 3.10.
Country Imports and Exports 2016 (deficits in parentheses).[18] In 1970, 26% of the world GDP depended on free international trade. As of 2015 that number had increased to 58%. However, the huge trade surplus of China and the huge trade deficit of the U.S. is a source of friction between these countries.

As the exhibit shows, the developed economies still account for the majority of international trade. There is a significant change, however, in the last few years, with developing economies rising from 29 percent in 2005 to 44 percent in 2013 according to the WTO (International Trade Statistics, 2014). This is mainly due to the emerging economies of Asia. The least-developed countries still lag far behind.

Trade figures do not show the complete picture of the interactions between regions or countries. The actual exchanges between the two countries may be greater but could also be less. There are four main complicating issues:

- *Services* are notoriously hard to track
- Trade is often between *subsidiaries* of multinationals
- *Tax dodges*—including transfer pricing, i.e., pricing of goods traded between company subsidiaries so as to minimize taxes paid
- *Non-exporting modes* of entry

First, export and import figures only cover physical goods, not services. Services do play an increasing role in international trade, but are very hard to get hard data on. The reason is that much of the trade in services involves people traveling between countries—consultants, lawyers, doctors and nurses, and so on. Such trade is difficult to track, although they do show up in a nation's balance of payments and transfers. Thus, international trade figures can be understating the actual trade involved.

Second, trade figures reflect shipments between different subsidiaries of the same firm. For example, parts manufacturers for Ford in South Korea might ship automobile components to a Ford plant in England that build cars for the European market. This means that the official trade figures for South Korea to England are inflated, and overstate the actual relationship. Some writers claim that as much as one-third of American international trade consists of such intra-company transfers.

A third problem is that not all trade gets reported. Trade figures in value terms are probably understated because people simply do not report transfers and money made in a foreign country. People's travel is difficult to track and personal services are likely considerably underreported for tax reasons. Some may also smuggle merchandise into a country, avoiding patrols and inspections where borders are porous (see Exhibit 3.11).

Fourth, it is important to recognize that global marketing involves more than just exports and imports. Exporting is only one way to enter a foreign market. Much of global marketing is done by subsidiaries in the market countries. These are established via direct foreign investments. Other ways of entering a foreign market involve licensing

EXHIBIT 3.11.
Smuggling Polish products with a minibus into Kaliningrad, Russia. It is highly unlikely that this trade will show up in official data.

of technology and alliances, not reported in trade figures.

Overall, however, the trade volume (exports plus imports) as a percentage of GDP does represent an imperfect but still valuable snapshot of the level to which a country's companies engage in international markets. A common measure to show involvement is to calculate total foreign trade (exports + imports) as a percentage of a country's GDP. The 2014 figures for the largest exporting countries are given in Exhibit 3.10.

The disparity of the figures is noteworthy. It depends largely on the size of the population. Smaller countries like Estonia and The Netherlands clearly are very involved in foreign trade. Larger countries

EXHIBIT 3.12.
The WTO headquarters in Geneva, Switzerland. The WTO is housed in a massive building with a somewhat intimidating front entrance and a sprawling five-story structure that is reminiscent of the Pentagon (the building housing the U.S. Department of Defense in Arlington, Virginia). The WTO is the supra-national institution that oversees international trade.[19]

Copyright © 2014 by Shutterstock/ Martin Good.

are less so, and the United States and Japan's relatively low figures are often surprising to observers. Foreign trade is simply not such a big part of their economies. New, emerging countries show a different pattern, and it is difficult to overemphasize the role exports in particular play in their economies. Brazil, Russia, and China—less so India—have consistently had great export surpluses each year that are important drivers of their economic growth (Russia exports oil and gas, and with prices coming down, its growth slackens).

The World Trade Organization (WTO)

International trade unavoidably raises a number of contested issues between countries—about dumping (that is, pricing below cost), about unfair protection of domestic companies, about preferential tariffs, and so on. Many of these issues sooner or later will get to the WTO, the global arbiter of trade disputes (see Exhibit 3.12).

The WTO consists of 159 member countries. This means the organization comprises most of the world's 195 countries. Its aim is to lower trade barriers around the world, reduce tariffs on goods in particular, and to encourage multi-lateral agreements that allow deficits and surpluses to be balanced between several partners. Bilateral trade, that is trade between two country partners, is generally viewed as less efficient, and in terms of economic theory "second-best solutions."

The non-members are not simply insignificant smaller countries. Some of the major emerging markets discussed in this book have just become members—mainland China in 2001 and Russia in 2012. Taiwan, renamed Chinese Taipei, was admitted separately in 2002.

WTO requirements. There are quite stringent commitments requested of members. Four main requirements in particular can seem daunting to some emerging countries:

- Institute a comprehensive plan for the lowering of tariffs and **trade barriers** in general (meaning the new member's internal markets have to open up)
- Eliminate special protection or **subsidies** for certain domestic producers (such as American cotton growers and Japan's rice farmers)

- Do not offer **preferential treatment** of trade from certain countries (such treatment might have to be extended to all members)
- Enforce **intellectual property rights** (meaning that product counterfeits and pirated software should be stopped)

The success of the WTO in each of these areas has been mixed.

Opening up markets. The WTO has made most progress on the first item, which is perhaps the biggest issue for world trade. Opening up the markets around the world has been an accomplishment several years in the making—it is the foundation of the globalization process, and, by extension, the source of the increased international marketing activities.

Protective policies. The protection of industries issue is actually a complicated issue. There is a strong economic argument for allowing protection for so-called "**infant industries**" in emerging markets. Without the protection of high import tariffs, local content requirements, and import quota limits, a new business might never get off the ground. For example, Russia is now seeing some home-grown fashion designers appear, and shoemakers in China are starting to sell women's styles abroad. The entrepreneurs behind such ventures can be protected by the high prices demanded for competing imports—prices that go so high precisely because of various import barriers. Imported cars in India face very high import barriers, and are very expensive. This offers the domestic car industry a chance, and even if India (a WTO member since 1995) has pledged to lower barriers, the progress has been slow.

Equal treatment. Enforcing equal treatments of trading partners has met with some difficulty because of historical ties and preferential and bilateral trade. It is often a matter of familiarity. A new exporter from an emerging country can expect to meet some suspicious resistance from customs officials in the West. Sometimes the officials react to political conflicts and popular opinion. Early shipments of Japanese electronics into France were routed through one small and understaffed clearing point, delaying processing.

Intellectual property rights. The intellectual property rights enforcement has been a contentious issue for years. Intellectual property refers to things that individuals create, including new inventions; literary and artistic works; special designs; and logos, brand names, and images used in commerce. Intellectual property rights are typically protected in law by, for example, patents, **copyright**, **and trademarks** so that people can earn recognition or financial benefit from what they create. By balancing the interests of the creator and the public consumer of the work, the protection aims to foster an environment in which creativity and innovation can flourish.

Under the WTO umbrella, an agreement called **TRIPS (Trade-Related Aspects of Intellectual Property Rights)** was issued in Doha in 2008.[20] Among the several items covered, four stand out as especially important for international marketers.

- *Copyright and Related Rights.* Copyright protection shall extend to books, films, and similar expressions of ideas, but not to ideas as such.
- *Trademarks.* Any sign, or any combination of signs, distinguishing the goods or services of an enterprise can be registered as a trademark (brand). Actual use of a trademark shall not be a condition for registration.
- *Geographical Indications.* Prevent the designation (e.g., the "made-in" label) of a good suggesting that the good in question originates in a geographical area other than the true place of origin.
- *Patents.* Patents shall be available for any inventions, whether products or processes, in all fields of technology, provided that they are new, involve an inventive step, and are capable of industrial application.

Intellectual property rights were not universally recognized before this agreement. Some emerging countries especially had a difficult time understanding why one could not simply Xerox some bestselling book and re-sell it much cheaper, or videotape a new Hollywood blockbuster film and sell a cheap version, or download and copy a software program from the computer. The piracy was especially rampant in China, partly because its vast domestic population provided a natural market for cheap knockoffs (Chapter 4 will cover the counterfeit problem in more detail). The TRIPS is an important step forward, with global brands and new technology more crucial than ever in international marketing.

The WTO and Emerging markets. A long-standing conflict within the WTO has stymied its effectiveness. There is a basic disagreement between emerging markets such as Brazil and India (who resist opening their markets to some foreign-manufactured products and services) and the U.S. and Europe, which are reluctant to free their agricultural markets for political reasons.

In response, a group of developing countries have agreed to form a bloc within the WTO. The G20, also known as the Group of 20, is a bloc of developing nations established on 20 August 2003. Distinct and separate from the G-20 major economies, the group emerged at the 5th Ministerial WTO conference, held in Cancún, Mexico, in 2003. The G-20 accounts for 60 percent of the world's population, 70 percent of its farmers, and 26 percent of world's agricultural exports.[21]

The *Brasilia Declaration* from June 6, 2003, signed by Ministers of Brazil, South Africa, and India state that "major trading partners are still moved by protectionist concerns in their countries' less competitive sectors," meaning agriculture. The declaration demanded a reversal of protectionist policies and trade-distorting practices by developed nations.

It is not clear how the conflict will be resolved. However, one positive indication of the groups influence (and the influence of emerging markets generally) is that the WTO Director General since 2013 is a Brazilian, Roberto Azevedo. And the WTO has ramped up its PR effort.

Fair Trade

One of the issues in international trade which has become part of the "sustainability" movement is the notion of fair trade. **Fair trade** can be described as international trade that ensures that producers in poor nations get a fair share of the gains from trade. Fair-trade products include some of the basic commodities from third-world nations such as coffee, bananas, and chocolate, but also crafts, clothing, and jewelry. The driving motivation is that world-market prices for coffee, rice, and other commodities are highly volatile and often below the costs of production.[22] A stable price that covers at least production and living costs is an essential requirement for farmers to escape from poverty and provide themselves and their families with a decent standard of living.

The original proponents of fair trade were Non-Governmental Organizations (NGOs) objecting to the relatively low percentage of the final product price that went to the original producer. These NGOs included a wide array of social and environmental organizations such as Oxfam, Amnesty International, and Caritas International. The flag bearer today is FLO, the Fair Labeling Organization. FLO International is a non-profit, multi-stakeholder association involving 23 member organizations, traders, and external experts. The organization develops and reviews fair-trade standards and assists producers in gaining and maintaining fair-trade certification and capitalizing on market opportunities.

The farmers have to pay FLO an annual fee for participating and in return are guaranteed a "fair price" for their products, more stable and usually above the going commodity price in the world market. In the typical case the farmers join as a coop collective, and the community receives the extra price premium as a way to further build schools, improve water supply, and generally improve living conditions for the community. The FLO certification is often perceived as an empowerment tool for the local farming community.

EXHIBIT 3.13.
The Fair Trade logo. Coffee is
one of the most common Fair
Trade commodities, with funds
going to support small
independent producers.

wavebreakmedia/Shutterstock.com

FLO certification standards for small farmers' organizations include requirements for democratic decision-making, ensuring that producers have a say in how the fair-trade premiums are invested and fair-trade standards for hired labor to ensure that workers receive decent wages and enjoy the freedom to join unions and bargain collectively. FLO certified plantations must also ensure that there is no forced or child labor and that health and safety requirements are met. The certified FLO business is given the right to advertise that its products meet FLO standards.

The basic weapon in forcing multinationals to adopt fair-trade purchasing practices has been the development of the formal certification program for fair-trade businesses. Featuring the "Fair Trade" logo allows the business to advertise its fair-trade allegiance (see Exhibit 3.13).

As fair-trade standards have come to be accepted in the markets around the world, more and more consumers demand that companies sell certified products.[23] As always in free markets, this means the companies sooner or later come to realize the advantages of doing just that.

Fair trade has grown fast. In 2006, FLO certified sales amounted to approximately $2.3 billion worldwide, and by 2014 had increased to over $7 billion.[24] More than 1.4 million farmers and workers in 74 countries benefit from fair trade. Fair-trade products generally account for less than 5 percent of all sales in their product categories in Europe and North America but span a wide range of product types and even have certified gold mines (see Exhibit 3.14).

EXHIBIT 3.14.
Fair-trade product categories[25]

Source: Fairtrade.net.

Product	Annual Growth Rate in Fair Trade (percent)
Bananas	12
Cocoa	na
Coffee	8
Cotton	−13
Dried fruits	−5
Flowers	16
Fresh fruit	10
Fruit juice	15
Gold	na
Herbs	182
Honey	44
Quinoa	11
Rice	−3
Sports balls	−28
Sugar	22
Tea	−2
Vegetables	62
Wine	27

Like most developmental efforts, fair trade has proven controversial and has drawn criticism from both ends of the political spectrum.[26] Free-market economists abhor fixed and set prices for producers, since prices serve as a signal as to what should (and what should not) be produced by free entrepreneurs. The counter-point is that since many agricultural commodities in advanced countries also have price guarantees, the argument is hypocritical and unrealistic, especially since many of these poor producers have no viable alternative occupation. More left-leaning economists argue that fair trade does not adequately challenge the current trading system, because as long as advanced nations protect their workers poorer countries need more help than just stable prices. The counter-point to this is that globalization and free markets can be of benefit to all, and the World Trade Organization (WTO) is attempting to reduce protective tariffs among advanced nations.

Global Warming and Green Trade

Two environmental factors which have recently become issues in international trade and development are global warming and green trade. **Global warming** refers to the increased temperatures around the world, due to the weakening of the ozone layer in the earth's upper atmosphere. Although the precise reasons for this are still debated, the evidence suggests that deforestation and the burning of fossil fuel by humans are the main culprits. **Green trade** comprises the trade in products that are environmentally benign and not resource depleting.

According to NASA's "Vital Signs of the Planet" (https://climate.nasa.gov/) several indicators demonstrate the extent of global warming:

Temperature: Sixteen of the seventeen warmest years on record have occurred since 2001.

Ice melting: Satellite data show that the Earth's polar ice sheets are losing mass.

Water rising: Global sea levels have risen nearly 7 inches (177 mm) in the last 100 years.

Carbon: Carbon dioxide levels in the air are at their highest in the last 650,000 years.

Extreme weather: The number of record high temperature events in the United States has been increasing since 1950 as has the number of intense rainfall events.

There are naysayers, especially prominent in the United States. A representative example is the headline in *The Sentinel* of Kansas City on May 26, 2017: "Global Cooling? No Day Above 83F in KC Forecast Through June 9." Deciding to pull out of the multinational Paris accord in 2017, President Trump put himself in the camp of naysayers. For many U.S. businesses, however, the global warming poses a serious threat. Bill Gates, founder of Microsoft, says that to avoid the most catastrophic impacts of climate change, "We need a massive amount of research into thousands of new ideas—even ones that might sound a little crazy—if we want to get to zero emissions by the end of this century."[27]

Clean energy practices are becoming standard procedures for some of the largest and most profitable companies in the world, including AT&T, DuPont, General Motors, HP, Sprint, and Walmart. Fifty-six percent of the combined 173 companies in the Fortune 100 and Global 100 have set greenhouse gas reduction goals. Gates has launched the "Breakthrough Energy Coalition" along with 27 of the world's richest billionaires, including Jeff Bezos (Amazon), Richard Branson (Virgin Group), and Jack Ma (Alibaba), all of whom have pledged billions of dollars to be invested into researching new energy technologies. They will work in tandem with "Mission Innovation," a consortium of 20 countries including the United States, that have pledged to double their investments in clean energy to $20 billion over the next five years. The investment model will be a public-private partnership between governments, research institutions, and investors.

Closely related to the global warming problem is the emergence of green business. **Green trade** refers to the process of selling products and/or services based on their environmental benefits. Such a product or service may be environmentally friendly in itself or produced in an environmentally friendly way, including:

- Being manufactured in a sustainable fashion
- Not containing toxic materials or ozone-depleting substances
- Able to be recycled and/or is produced from recycled materials
- Being made from renewable materials (such as bamboo, etc.)
- Not making use of excessive packaging
- Being designed to be repairable and not "throwaway"

Green trade is typically practiced by companies that are committed to sustainable development and corporate social responsibility. More organizations are making an effort to implement sustainable business practices as they recognize that in doing so they can make their products more attractive to consumers and also reduce expenses, including packaging, transportation, energy/water usage, etc. Businesses are increasingly discovering that demonstrating a high level of social responsibility can increase brand loyalty among socially conscious consumers.

The global warming problem is being attacked with increasing intensity. The deforestation in many poor countries (including the Amazonas in South America) will probably slow down as incentives are developed to maintain and not harvest existing forest stands. This means that existing measures of GDP have to be adjusted to compute a sustainable GDP growth rate—the "environment" part of the triple bottom line. The outcome is likely to be an increase in the number of enterprises focusing on more organic products, and thus an increase in green trade. But they do have to be transparent and honest about it. According to watchdogs, there are apparently many instances of "green" labels used for not-so-green products and the color green has become a popular packaging choice to suggest a "green" product to unwary consumers.[28]

Related to this development is the increased consciousness of the "**carbon footprints**" of various products shipped long distances around the world. The energy expended on shipping products such as water bottles from faraway destinations to consumer markets around the world has gained attention in this respect. Not only does the use of plastic bottles involve a considerable energy cost, the viability of shipping water from abroad into perfectly well-served local markets is now questioned. As long as no charge is leveled on carbon footprints and the externality costs of global warming, such shipments can be very profitable—we might all prefer to drink Evian. However, if global warming increases and gets media attention, consumers around the world will most likely change behavior. Given how free markets work, the firms will then find it more profitable to avoid transportation, lower their carbon footprints, and stress their local roots.

It seems quite clear that global warming will have an increasing impact on economic development, including company outsourcing and close-to-market production. Very soon one of the most compelling reasons for a multinational firm to avoid **outsourcing** will be to limit the costs involved in justifying its large carbon footprint in poorer countries.

MAJOR TRADE BLOCS

For international trade and investment, membership in a **trade bloc** plays a very important role. There are two basic reasons for this.

One, it makes the country more attractive to foreign investors, since manufacturing plants can be located there and receive **preferential treatment** for exports to other member countries. This is a key factor behind Malaysia's and Thailand's economic growth, fueled by membership in the ASEAN grouping. It helps in particular where components and parts need to be shipped between different assembly plants of a multinational. The large Toyota automobile plant in Indonesia exports to other ASEAN markets but also receives parts and supplies from its subsidiary operations in other ASEAN countries. Separating its manufacturing of engines, transmissions, and components between the different ASEAN countries to gain scale advantages, Toyota manages to obtain a preferential treatment for cross-shipments at half the regular tariff rates.

A second factor increasing the importance of trade blocs for the new growth countries is the **enlarged market potential**. Mercosur membership allows Argentina, a country with a population of about 41 million, to boost its market size to close to 250 million, adding Brazil, Paraguay, and Uruguay. Market entries and foreign investment that could not be justified with a smaller population can be attracted much more easily. Conversely, the lack of a trade bloc among geographically close neighbors will be a drawback for a region. In the Middle East, for example, the Arab request that entering multinationals not deal with Israel has made it difficult to realize the full growth potential for the small Israeli economy. Trade blocs do tend to reduce **political risk**.

In what follows we will discuss the major regional trade blocks separately and also cover the economic environment in some of the largest individual countries.

Africa

Africa is a very fragmented continent, with 53 or 54 countries counting the islands outside the mainland. Many of these are small, but Nigeria at 174 million and South Africa at 52 million are major countries. There are multiple regional blocs in Africa, also known as **Regional Economic Communities (RECs).** Typically they have overlapping memberships, with a country participating in several RECs.

It is common to identify six key trading blocs in Africa:[29]

- SADC. Southern African Development Community. Its 14 member states are Angola, Botswana, Democratic Republic of Congo (DRC), Lesotho, Malawi, Mauritius, Mozambique, Namibia, Seychelles, South Africa, Swaziland, Tanzania, Zambia, and Zimbabwe. South Africa accounts for 13 percent of the total land area of SADC, 22 percent of the total population, and 73 percent of the total GNP.
- SACU. Southern African Customs Union. SACU is a customs union comprising Botswana, Lesotho, Namibia, Swaziland (the BLNS states), and South Africa. The agreement includes, among other things, the levying of uniform customs and excise duties, free interchange of duty-paid goods imported from outside member countries, imposition of additional protective duties by BLNS states, and regulation of the marketing of agricultural produce. There are no duties payable on goods traded between SACU members.
- COMESA. Common Market for Eastern and Southern Africa. A large organization of 21 states, including Egypt, Kenya, and Zambia, but not South Africa.
- ECOWAS. Economic Community of West African States. The organization aims to create a common external tariff with the elimination of all tariff and non-tariff barriers between the 16 member states, including Ghana, Nigeria, and Togo.
- UDEAC. Union Douaniere et Economique de l'Afrique Centrale. A customs and economic Union of Central Africa. The members are Cameroon, Central Africa Republic, Chad, Congo, Equatorial Guinea, and Gabon.
- EAC. An East African Community, created by Kenya, Uganda, and Tanzania. Later Burundi and Rwanda joined.

Once the African economies achieve more substantial economic growth and take off—like South Africa— these countries are poised to become much bigger players on the global stage. While presently their endowment of raw materials—minerals and oil in particular—form the industrial base, if political and ethnic turmoil can be harnessed, these countries are potentially rich.

Asia

Asia has shown enormous progress after the opening up of the two large population behemoths, China and India. There are several regional trade agreements among these countries that offer good starting points for global and even pan-regional strategies for an international marketer.

ASEAN—Association of South East Asian Nations[30]

ASEAN was created in 1967. It includes Indonesia, Malaysia, the Philippines, Singapore, and Thailand, with Brunei Darussalam added in 1967, Vietnam in 1995, Myanmar and Lao PDR in 1997, and Cambodia in 1999. Originally a political union, it has evolved into a free-trade area.

AFTA—ASEAN Free-Trade Area

In 1992, ASEAN countries met to formalize a far-reaching trade agreement, forming AFTA. Created to match the emergence of the European Union, the principal result was a preferential tariff rate no higher than 5 percent between member nations (with the ultimate aim of reducing tariffs to 0 percent), reduction of non-tariff barriers, and a common external tariff rate. The AFTA development is a significant step toward creating the kind of common market one finds in Europe's EU and Latin America's Mercosur, and it is likely that "pan-AFTA" products and marketing campaigns will gradually emerge.

APEC—Asia-Pacific Economic Cooperation[31]

APEC is a large association of 22 countries that spans both sides of the Pacific from Canada and Chile to Australia, and includes Japan, Chinese Taipei (Taiwan), and Hong Kong, but not mainland China or India.

ARF—ASEAN Regional Forum

The ASEAN Regional Forum (ARF) was established in 1994. It comprises 27 countries: the 10 ASEAN member states (Brunei, Cambodia, Indonesia, Laos, Malaysia, Myanmar, Philippines, Singapore, Thailand, and Vietnam), the 10 ASEAN dialogue partners (Australia, Canada, China, the EU, India, Japan, New Zealand, ROK, Russia, and the United States), one ASEAN observer (PNG) as well as the DPRK, Mongolia, Pakistan, Timor-Leste, Bangladesh, and Sri Lanka. It is primarily focused on security.

With China's size and rapid growth, experts predict the next agreement is likely to be an ASEAN-China Free Trade Area. China is in many ways a special case. The Chinese government early on designated several major areas as **Special Economic Zones (SEZs)**. The five original SEZs are Shenzhen, Zhuhai, Shantou (all in the Guangdong province in the South), Xiamen (in Fujian province), and Hainan (in Hainan province). Other areas and provinces have been gradually added. To attract investment, the corporate tax rate within SEZs is lower and enterprises within the zones enjoy tariff exemptions and reductions.

The SEZs serve to bring in foreign manufacturing jobs, with Chinese workers staffing the assembly lines. The products are intended for reexport, helping the government to generate hard foreign currency. But it has also meant increased penetration by foreign products in China. Although the products imported into those areas are not allowed outside the zones' borders, many are smuggled into China, copied, and sold. The difficulty of controlling this black or gray trade and the widespread copyright infringement practices means that the authorized distributors find themselves competing with local counterfeits and pirated copies.

Latin America

Several regional trade agreements affect marketing in Latin America directly by enhancing the opportunities for region-wide marketing strategies. The major agreements are as follows:

LAIA—Latin American Integration Association

This agreement between all South American countries and Mexico expands a previous free-trade agreement (LAFTA) into a customs union with free flow of goods and a common tariff rate toward nonmembers.

ANCOM—Andean Common Market

In February 1993, Bolivia, Colombia, Ecuador, and Venezuela began operating the Andean common market. Since then Peru has been added. ANCOM means reduced tariffs, increased intraregional trade, free factor mobility, and a political climate more favorable to foreigners. Peru has now also been added to the group.

MERCOSUR—Southern Cone Common Market[32]

A common market consisting of Argentina, Brazil, Paraguay, and Uruguay, with Venezuela added in 2012 (when Paraguay suspended participation). Six other Latin American countries are associated members, with Bolivia close to full membership. With the economies of Brazil and Argentina performing well, this has become perhaps the strongest grouping in Latin America. The member countries have agreed to establish a common external tariff and lower tariffs for intraregional trade. There have been problems in adjusting internal tariffs on a smooth schedule (in 1995, for example, Uruguay had 950 products listed as "exceptions" to the common agreement), but the sheer growth of the countries has generated a strong momentum in internal trade. For example, the Brazilian shoe industry benefits from the supply of less expensive Argentine leather, while competition from Argentine wheat has reduced Brazilian wheat production by a third compared with levels before the agreement.

NAFTA—North American Free Trade Area

The 1994 ratification of NAFTA has meant that Mexico has moved closer to its northern neighbors. The agreement has created increased exchange between Canada, the United States, and Mexico.[33] But rather than seeing this as a step away from the Latin-American region, from a marketing viewpoint Mexico has become a natural entry gate to the larger Latin-American market for North American businesses. While President Trump denounced NAFTA during his campaign, he has now softened his criticism, and NAFTA is likely to remain strong.

European Union (EU)

Even with the 2016 Brexit vote by the UK to leave the union, the EU still is a very viable large market. Despite being characterized as "in trouble" by some American observers, the EU completed two free trade agreements in 2017: one with Canada and one with Japan. The EU is a single market with upward of 450 million consumers, the biggest mature market in the world.

The decision in 1986 to establish a single European market within the EU by 1992 led to a completely changed strategic environment for most businesses, European and others. Tariff barriers and customs duties were scrapped, and goods and labor were to move freely between countries. Product standards were harmonized. One example is the EU opposition to **Genetically Modified Organisms** (GMOs), a contrast to the U.S. standards. Cumbersome border controls were abolished, and a common European passport was created. National price controls were eliminated, helping to create a large and unified market with competitive prices. A single currency, the "euro," was introduced in 1999, simplifying payments and equalizing prices (although not all countries joined the "euro," with the United Kingdom holding on to its pound, for example).

The original six countries (France, Germany, Italy, and the Benelux countries) became nine in 1973 with the addition of Ireland, Denmark, and the United Kingdom. Greece followed in 1981; Portugal and Spain in 1986, when the EU flag was designed (see Exhibit 3.15). Austria, Sweden, and Finland made it 15 members in 1995.

When the Soviet bloc broke up, the promise of being able to live, work, and do business throughout the European Union resulted in a host of applicants for membership from former Soviet members. Admitted in 2004 were the central European countries Poland, the Czech Republic, Slovakia, and the three Baltic States: Estonia, Latvia, and Lithuania. Further down were Romania and Bulgaria, which were admitted in 2007. Croatia, admitted in 2013, is the first of the war-torn former Yugoslavian countries to join. Ukraine was poised to join the EU when Russia intervened, occupied Crimea, and threatened Ukraine's move towards the EU. Russian President Putin has taken a strong stand against further alignment with the West among the former Soviet republics in Eastern Europe.

As of 2017, there were 28 members (counting the UK whose exit is still being negotiated) of the EU, 19 within the euro currency union (see Exhibit 3.16).

The per capita incomes varied widely. At the upper end is tiny Luxembourg, followed by the Scandinavian countries and the larger and established European members. At the lower end are several of the newly admitted central European countries, and also some historical stalwarts like Greece and Portugal, whose weak economies now strain the limits of the euro currency union. As of mid-2017, the United Kingdom remains a full member of the EU and rights and obligations continue to fully apply in and to the UK despite the Brexit vote.

EXHIBIT 3.15.
The Flag of the European Union. Even though the EU has expanded further after the 12 members in 1986, the original circle of 12 stars has been kept for the flag.
Copyright © Depositphotos/ denisismagilov.

EXHIBIT 3.16.
Member countries in the European Union[32]. In 2016 Great Britain voted to exit the EU (the so-called BREXIT).

Source: http://europa.eu/ about-eu/countries/index_en.htm.

	Capital	Acceded	Population	GDP Per Cap. (PPP $)	Currency	Languages
Austria	Vienna	1995	8,451,900	42,409	Euro	German
Belgium	Brussels	1957	11,161,600	37,883	Euro	Dutch French German
Bulgaria	Sofia	2007	7,284,600	14,312	Lev	Bulgarian
Croatia	Zagreb	2013	4,262,100	18,314	Kuna	Croatian
Cyprus	Nicosia	2004	865,900	27,086	Euro	Greek Turkish[a]
Czech Republic	Prague	2004	10,516,100	27,191	Koruna	Czech[d]
Denmark	Copenhagen	1973	5,602,600	37,657	Krone	Danish
Estonia	Tallinn	2004	1,324,800	21,713	Euro	Estonian

	Capital	Acceded	Population	GDP Per Cap. (PPP $)	Currency	Languages
Finland	Helsinki	1995	5,426,700	36,395	Euro	Finnish Swedish
France	Paris	1957	65,633,200	35,548	Euro	French
Germany	Berlin	1957	80,523,700	39,028	Euro	German
Greece	Athens	1981	11,062,500	24,505	Euro	Greek
Hungary	Budapest	2004	9,908,800	19,638	Forint	Hungarian
Ireland	Dublin	1973	4,591,100	41,921	Euro	Irish English
Italy	Rome	1957	59,685,200	30,136	Euro	Italian
Latvia	Riga	2004	2,023,800	18,255	Euro	Latvian
Lithuania	Vilnius	2004	2,971,900	21,615	Euro	Lithuanian
Luxembourg	Luxembourg	1957	537,000	79,785	Euro	French German Luxembourgish
Malta	Valletta	2004	421,400	27,022	Euro	Maltese English
Netherlands	Amsterdam	1957	16,779,600	42,194	Euro	Dutch
Poland	Warsaw	2004	38,533,300	20,592	Złoty	Polish
Portugal	Lisbon	1986	10,487,300	23,385	Euro	Portuguese
Romania	Bucharest	2007	20,057,500	12,808	Leu	Romanian
Slovakia	Bratislava	2004	5,410,800	24,249	Euro	Slovak
Slovenia	Ljubljana	2004	2,058,800	28,195	Euro	Slovene
Spain	Madrid	1986	46,704,300	30,557	Euro	Spanish
Sweden	Stockholm	1995	9,555,900	41,191	Krona	Swedish
United Kingdom	London	1973	63,730,100	36,941	Pound Sterling	English

Australia and New Zealand

Australia and New Zealand have traditional ties to the British Commonwealth, which gave the countries preferred trading status with the United Kingdom. When the United Kingdom joined the European Common Market in 1973, however, the favored trading status was lost, which led to severe economic strains and ultimately new open-market policies in both countries. They have since reoriented their economies toward Asia.

The countries are both members of the APEC (Asia-Pacific Economic Cooperation) grouping and also participate in the ARF (ASEAN Regional Forum). These are still very heterogeneous associations, far from the integrated-trade-area concept of ASEAN proper, but nevertheless instrumental in the trade growth with Asia.

The two countries have close trade ties with each other, manifested in the ANZCERTA pact (Australia New Zealand Closer Economic Relations Trade Agreement). For most global marketers, the two countries can be approached as one regional market.

Trans-Pacific Partnership (TPP)[34]

The **TPP** was an ambitious, comprehensive trade agreement negotiated under President Obama of the United States and jettisoned by President Trump. The aim was regional integration and strengthening of the multilateral trading system among the participating countries. The participant countries are Australia, Brunei Darussalam, Canada, Chile, Japan, Malaysia, Mexico, New Zealand, Peru, Singapore, the United States, and Vietnam. Some of these countries still pursue the agreement, and it might still succeed.

Transatlantic Trade and Investment Partnership (TTIP)

The **TTIP** is a new trade agreement that has been under discussion since 2011 between the European Union and the United States. The negotiations aim at removing trade barriers (tariffs, unnecessary regulations, restrictions on investment etc.) in a wide range of economic sectors so as to make it easier to buy and sell goods and services between the EU and the US. While President Trump has not specifically denounced the agreement, as of 2017 the negotiations are at a stalemate.

THE BRICS BLOC

The acronym BRICS stands for Brazil, Russia, India, China, and South Africa. First coined as **BRIC** in 2001 by Jim O'Neill, then chief economist for Goldman Sachs in London, South Africa was added in 2010. The idea behind BRIC was that much of the future economic global growth would come from those four large countries. Together they accounted for about 2.8 billion people or 40% of the world's total population. Their economies were still underdeveloped, but their governments embraced globalization and open markets. O'Neill predicted that by 2041 the four BRICs would overtake the six largest western economies in terms of economic power.[35]

BRICS has become the rallying term for an alternative grouping of emerging countries as a counterweight to the dominant advanced countries. The first formal summit of the BRIC countries was held in 2009 in Yekaterinburg, Russia, with the four leaders (Lula, Medvedev, Singh, and Hu Jintao, respectively). A year later South Africa was invited to join, creating the 5 member BRICS group (Exhibit 3.17). In 2014 a BRICS development bank was established.[36]

Since the inception of BRIC in 2001, China has had the leading growth rate of GDP averaging 10.0% annually, followed by India with 7.1%, Russia with 4.5%, Brazil and South Africa at 3.4%.[37] The United States averaged 1.8%

over the same period and the European economies languished around 1% growth. After the 2008 financial crisis the economic growth in the BRICS countries has been uneven. All BRICS economies have also been plagued by corruption charges, leading to political and government crises. Especially hard hit have been Brazil and South Africa, with negative economic growth in some years.

DATA SOURCES

When doing research on economic and trade issues start with the easily available secondary data sources, such as the World Bank, International Monetary Fund (IMF), and WTO reports. For the major developed countries, OECD (Organization for Economic Co-operation and Development) reports are useful, covering the 34 member countries. A large number of organizations—consulates, commerce departments, newspaper and magazine affiliates, information agencies—can be helpful. The data are today often accessible through their websites. Some of the more prominent sources are given in Exhibit 3.18.

Actually, with the globalization of markets and Internet growth, the availability of secondary data (data already collected for some other purpose and readily available) has grown exponentially. Internet and online search machines such as Google have made it easy to access basic economic and demographic data as well as newsworthy developments. Basic data availability online continues to improve for companies (annual reports, for example) and for people in various regions or trade blocs (the Eurostat, for instance).

EXHIBIT 3.17.
The BRICS national flags in order. Given the great differences between the member countries, it is unlikely that we will see the kind of common flag that was developed for the European Union.

Copyright © by Shutterstock/Gil C.

SUMMARY

This chapter has explored the level of economic growth and discussed the major trade blocs that guide international trade between the world's regions and countries. The aim has been to establish the economic fundamentals of the opportunity facing international marketers.

The market potential of global markets involves fundamentally the population size and per-capita incomes. The opportunity is greater in countries with large populations and high per-capita incomes, in particular if economic growth is rapid. But recent expert writings and business experiences have shown that also the countries and people at "the bottom of the pyramid" can provide viable markets for many goods and services, provided companies can invest in adaptation to different usage conditions.

Also important, economic growth has to be sustainable. Income inequality in the country should not be too high, and other-than-income variables need to be considered. Such variables include air quality, environmental degradation, healthcare, and other variables that affect the quality of life in the country. The entering firm needs to consider the degree to which its products and services contribute not just to more material possessions but to the consumers' well-being in general.

EIU Country Data
Economic indicators and forecasts providing data series on economic structure, foreign payments, external debt stock, external debt service, external trade, trends in foreign trade, and quarterly indicators.

Council of European Social Science Data Archives (CESSDA)
Listing of European macroeconomics data archives.

CIA World Factbook 2002
Economic and political profiles of countries worldwide.

Economist Intelligence Unit (EIU)
Analysis and forecast of economic, political, and business environment for over 180 countries.

EIU Country Reports
Provides quarterly analyses and forecasts of the political, economic and business environment in more than 180 countries.

Eurostat
Economic data for the European Union (EU).

Global Prospectus LLC
Global market and industry data.

IMF: Direction of Trade

World Bank Country Data: Contains profiles on 206 countries.

EXHIBIT 3.18.
Economic and Trade Data
Sources

One big factor that affects whether a country of region has strong potential is the difficulty or ease of market entry. High trade barriers such as tariffs and custom duties will escalate the entry costs and thus price. Countries belonging to the WTO are preferable—lower tariffs—as are those that belong to regional trade groups. Membership in a trade bloc not only eases the entry, but it helps enlarge the local market. An otherwise less attractive market because of small size can often be a good entry point into a trade area, as has happened to Ireland as a gateway into the European Union.

Economic and trade factors are not the only one that determine country attractiveness, but they are fundamental factors.

KEY TERMS

ability to buy	gross domestic product (GDP)
advanced countries	growth
carbon footprints	import
copyright and trademarks	import substitution investments
corporate social responsibility (CSR)	income per capita
developing countries	infant industries
economic growth	intellectual property rights
emerging countries	international trade
enlarged market potential	mega-cities
export	opportunities
fair trade	outsourcing
Genetically Modified Organisms (GMOs)	PESTEL
global warming	political risk
globalization	population
green trade	preferential treatment
Regional Economic Communities (RECs)	Purchasing Power Parity (PPP)
Special Economic Zones (SEZs)	real GDP
subsidies	trade bloc
sustainable development	trade deficits
threats	triple bottom line
trade barriers	TRIPS (Trade-Related Aspects of Intellectual Property Rights)
	willingness to buy
	World Trade Organization (WTO)

DISCUSSION QUESTIONS

1. What are the new divisions by the World Bank among countries in terms of economic development? Access the

Bank's website to find out the rationale behind abandoning the "emerging country" concept. Are the new divisions better than the old ones?

2. Does the triple-bottom-line concept go against free-market principles? Does fair trade go against free-market principles? Does the "bottom-of-the-pyramid" idea go against free-market principles?

3. What are the main economic factors that determine attractiveness of a country for a global marketer? Why would economic *growth* be more attractive than simply the *level* of income per capita?

4. Have you consciously tried to buy fair trade or green products even though they may cost more? Access the websites of some brands that you like—do they seem to be paying attention to the *social* and *environmental* aspects of the triple bottom line or are they just trying to promote high quality, or low price, etc.?

5. What is the rationale behind the PPP (Purchasing Power Adjustment) to incomes per capita? Is this adjustment necessary when two countries are in the same currency regime (as the countries in the euro area). Why do people in Greece seem opposed to exiting the euro zone and instead go back to the drachma?

TEAM CHALLENGE PROJECTS

1. The bottom of the pyramid represents over 4 billion potential customers who traditionally have been underserved by the world's markets. Team 1: Pick a product that you think can be successfully sold to a worker in a developing country who earns $10 per day. Outline in detail the specific 4Ps of your marketing plan. Team 2: Pick a product in the same price range that would clearly fail if marketed to this worker. Explain what of the 4Ps would cause the failure and why you cannot fix this problem.

2. Fair trade can be described as international trade that ensures producers in poor nations get a fair share of the gains from trade. Essentially the buyer of a product or commodity agrees to pay a higher price in order to ensure that the seller has a reasonable quality of life and chance for success. Pick a product that you think fits with the fair-trade philosophy. Team 1: Develop the presentation to the VP of Purchasing to convince them to endorse the fair-trade philosophy for your company. Team 2: Develop a presentation to the VP of Purchasing urging them NOT to adopt the fair-trade philosophy.

3. Team 1: Use the PESTEL model and develop an analysis of the potential environment for the sale of solar panels in Saudi Arabia. On the one hand, the economy of Saudi Arabia is built on the sale of oil. On the other hand, compared to other countries, Saudi Arabia has among the highest number of sunny, cloudless days per year and maximum electricity demand occurs on the sunniest days because of air-conditioner usage. Team 2: Use the PESTEL model to develop an analysis that opposes the use of solar panels in Saudi Arabia.

4. Find a recent (within the last two years) example of a dispute presented before the WTO or another economic world dispute resolution organization. Outline the issues for each side. Team 1: Determine which side should "win" and explain why. Team 2: Determine what the losing side should do differently to "win" and why it will win next time.

SELECTED REFERENCES

Belcher, Mark, "Cleaning products recalled due to mislabeling," *News 4*, WIVB.com, January 22, 2015.

Castaldo, Sandro, Francesco Perrini, Nicola Misani and Antonio Tencati, "The Missing Link between Corporate Social Responsibility and Consumer Trust: The Case of Fair Trade Products," *Journal of Business Ethics*, Vol. 84, No. 1, 2008, pp. 1–15.

Cramer, Christopher, Deborah Johnston, Carlos Oya and John Sender, "Fair Trade, Employment and Poverty Reduction in Ethiopia and Uganda," *Research Report*, Department for International Development, United Kingdom, April 2014, 143.

"Data: GDP Growth (Annual %)," *The World Bank*, 2015.

De Pelsmacker, Patrick, Liesbeth Driesen and Glenn Rayp, "Do Consumers Care about Ethics? Willingness to Pay for Fair-Trade Coffee," *Journal of Consumer Affairs*, Vol. 39, Issue 2, (Winter), 2006, pp. 363–385.

"Eurostat Statistics Explained," *Eurostat,* April 28, 2015.

Hamel, Ian, "Fair Trade Firm Accused of Foul Play," *www.swissinfo.ch,* August 3, 2006.

"Marketing Theories—PESTEL," www.Professionalacademy.com, 2015.

Morrison, Sarah, "Fairtrade: Is it really fair?" *The Independent*, May 6, 2012.

Prahalad, C.K. *The Fortune at the Bottom of the Pyramid*. Wharton School Publishing: Pearson, 2005.

_____and Stuart L. Hart. "The Fortune at the Bottom of the Pyramid," *Strategy + Business*, Issue 26, First quarter 2002.

Riefler, Petra, Adamantios Diamantopoulos and Judy A. Siguaw, "Cosmopolitan consumers as a target group for segmentation," *Journal of International Business Studies*, Vol. 43, No. 3, 2012, pp. 285–305.

Savitz, Andrew with Karl Weber. *The Triple Bottom Line: How Today's Best-Run Companies Are Achieving Economic, Social and Environmental Success—and How You Can Too*, 2nd ed. San Francisco: Jossey-Bass, 2013.

Suominen, Kati, "Trade Deals Mark Positive Shift for U.S.," *U-T San Diego*, Jan. 1, 2015.

Tett, Gillian, "The Story of the BRICS," *Financial Times*, 2014. TerraChoice, "The 'Six Sins of Greenwashing' Study," *TerraChoice Environmental Marketing Inc.*, www.terrachoice.com, November 2007.

The Economist, "A Summary of the Livability Ranking and Overview," *The Economist Intelligence Unit*, August 2014.

TPP, "Statement of the Ministers and Heads of Delegation for the Trans-Pacific Partnership Countries," Singapore, December 10, 2013.

TTIP, The Transatlantic Trade Investment Partnership "http://ec.europa.eu/trade/policy/in-focus/ttip/", 2015 (accessed 3/14/2015).

"VI BRIC Summit," *Ministry of External Relations*, Brasilia, Brazil, 2014.

"Why Is South Africa Included in the BRICS?" *The Economist,* March 29, 2013.

Yüksel, Ihsan, "Developing a multi-criteria decision making model for PESTEL analysis," *International Journal of Business and Management*, Vol. 7, No. 24, 2012, pp. 52–66.

ENDNOTES

1. This draws on "Marketing Theories ..." 2015 and Yüksel, 2012.
2. Source: Forbes Global 2000 (2003 & 2014), www.forbes.com.
3. Source: United States Census Bureau (USCB) 2015.
4. Source: http://www.worldatlas.com/citypops.htm.
5. Riefler, Diamantopoulos and Siguaw, 2012 demonstrate the attractiveness of cosmopolitan segments.
6. See *The Economist*, 2014.
7. See, for example, https://www.youtube.com/watch?v=pRBLnth4oSg or https://www.youtube.com/watch?v=mMAkD5EvoFU.
8. Source: IMF World Economic Outlook.
9. Source: International Monetary Fund (2014). The international dollar, Int$, is a hypothetical unit of currency that has the same purchasing power parity that the U.S. dollar had in the United States at a given point in time, here 2014.
10. Source: The World Bank and IMF.
11. From http://data.worldbank.org/about/country-classifications.
12. From http://www.infoplease.com/finance/tips/money/moneyman_112299.html.

13. Source: International Monetary Fund.
14. See Savitz, 2013.
15. Prahalad and Hart, 2002, pp. 1–2.
16. Source: http://www.worldbank.org/depweb/english/beyond/beyondco/beg_01.pdf, p.7.
17. For more on sustainability, access the World Bank website at http://www.worldbank.org/en/topic/sustainabledevelopment.
18. Source: *CIA World Factbook* 2016.
19. This section draws on WTO website at https://www.wto.org/english/thewto_e/thewto_e.htm.
20. https://www.wto.org/english/tratop_e/trips_e/trips_e.htm.
21. From Suominen, 2015.
22. See Castaldo, et al., 2008.
23. See De Pelsmacker, Driesen, and Rayp, 2006.
24. These and the following figures from Fairtrade International's website, http://www.fairtrade.net.
25. From http://www.fairtrade.net.
26. Renee Cho, "What Five Tech Companies Are Doing About Climate Change," Harvard Business Review, March 4, 2016.
27. See, for example, Morrison, 2012; Cramer et al, 2014; Hamel, 2006.
28. From TerraChoice, 2007; Belcher, 2015.
29. Source: http://www.mbendi.com/land/af/p0010.htm.
30. See http://www.asean.org/.
31. See https://ustr.gov/trade-agreements/free-trade-agreements/north-american-free-trade-agreement-nafta/.
32. See http://www.internshipschina.com/community/chinainsights2/55-china-insights/
    669-the-development-of-china-s-special-economic-zones#.VVy1j03D9jo.
33. See https://ustr.gov/tpp.
34. See Tett, 2014.
35. See "VI BRIC Summit," 2014.
36. See "Data: GDP Growth (Annual %)," 2015.
37. See TTIP, 2015.
38. From http://www.atlanticcouncil.org/publications/reports/ttip-on-track-but-off-message.
39. See Tett, 2014.
40. See "VI BRIC Summit," 2014.
41. See "Why Is South Africa," 2013.
42. See "Data: GDP Growth (Annual %)," 2015.
43. See "Eurostat Statistics Explained," 2015.

In this chapter you will learn about:

1. How different economic-political systems impose different types of constraints on economic activity, usually favoring domestic companies
2. How the failure of centralized economic planning has moved most countries toward more open markets, often interrupted by corruption, political crises, and terrorism
3. How countries are rated in terms of political risk, economic freedom, and ease of doing business
4. How patent and copyright legal protection is not always effective against infringements and counterfeits

In foreign markets there are a variety of political and legal environments that a local marketer might encounter, and every national market is different. However, more *developed* markets typically have low political risk and a legal system that offers a certain level of assurance that contracts can be enforced and private ownership is recognized in law. By contrast, *emerging* countries are more typically characterized by political risk and legal uncertainties. As a result, an entrant is exposed to greater risks. Direct foreign investment can be especially unwise.

The Political and Legal Environment

CHAPTER 4

WHAT IS IN CUBA'S FUTURE?

In January 2015 U.S. President Barack Obama called on Congress to end the five-decade commercial, economic, and financial embargo imposed by the United States on communist Cuba. Nearly two years after the Batista regime was overthrown by the Cuban revolutionaries on January 1, 1959, Cuba nationalized American-owned oil refineries without compensation in response to their refusal to process Russian oil. An **embargo** prohibiting the movement of merchant ships into or out of Cuban ports except for food and medicine was imposed by the United States on October 19, 1960. In 1962 the embargo was extended to include virtually all trade. The Helms-Burton Act of 1996 further restricted United States citizens from doing business in or with Cuba, and restricted assistance to any government in Havana until certain claims against the Cuban government were met, free press and freedom of association were guaranteed, and free elections were held in Cuba. In 1999, President Bill Clinton expanded the trade embargo by also disallowing foreign subsidiaries of U.S. companies to trade with Cuba. Cuba's economy has stagnated, especially after its largest foreign trade partner, the Soviet Union, collapsed (see Exhibit 4.1).

President Trump's 2017 temporary suspension of lifting the embargo has increased the uncertainty in Cuba. Nevertheless, the reconciliation project is continuing with the American embassy still functioning in Havana. To help explain what a detente might entail for Cuba's economy and its 11 million people, two American experts recently agreed to share their perspective of what they see for Cuba in the near

future. They were Ingo Walter, Vice Dean of Faculty and Professor of Finance at the Stern School of Business, New York University, and José de la Torre, Former Dean and J.K. Batten Chair in Strategy (Emeritus) at Florida International University. Professor Walter had just returned from a trip to Cuba, and Professor de la Torre is a Cuban émigré, having left Cuba as a student in September 1960.

Below are excerpts from their discussion:

Professor Walter: (The Cuban) people are comparatively well-educated, with unusually strong extended family ties and sufficient entrepreneurial vigor to be explosive once preoccupation with working around the "dead hand" of the state gradually fades away. The few sectors already liberalized show plenty of sprouts, like a long-vacant lot after a spring rain, suggesting the latent power of lifting price and wage controls sometime down the road— there's a reason farmers, budding restaurateurs, and taxi drivers are among the best-off Cubans today.

Professor de la Torre: (Education) is an asset developed by the Revolutionary government that many in the exile community are unwilling to recognize. Cuba's literacy rate was second in Latin America (after Uruguay's) in 1958, but there was still a lot to be done in order to incorporate the countryside into a modern education system.

Professor Walter: Many old timers of Cuban origin (in the United States) have long memories and powerful resentments. Newer generations consider their seniors trapped on the wrong side of history and want to get on with change. Just about everyone feels strongly.

Professor de la Torre: The divide among the Cuban American population is not only about age, although that is important. It also depends on their U.S. arrival date. Recent immigrants are considerably more willing to engage the regime than those who came in the early waves.

Professor Walter: Capital formation, too, is restricted by an archaic banking system that executes transactions at a tenth the efficiency one might see in Botswana, and fails totally as a source of credit to incipient businesses and households. Cuban cooperatives and lending among family and friends are among the few forms of financial intermediation. Like everyone else, Cubans will borrow and lend, save and invest once the bottle is uncorked. Future tourists will be amazed how fast the overcrowded wrecks of old Havana buildings get restored or repurposed stretching far beyond the Old Havana tourist zone.

Professor de la Torre: One concern I have always had is what happens when the "cork is lifted" as you put it. Cubans are indeed very resourceful and entrepreneurial, a necessity to survive in this environment. But they are also used to operating at the margin of the law since that is often the only way to survive. In fact, there is a Cuban expression, "*resolver*" (roughly translated to "manage" or "work it out") that applies to this necessity to work around the system. Will they go the Russian way (i.e., mafias and other illicit activities) once the system is opened up, or will their energy be focused in legal entities?

Professor Walter: If labor and capital get moved closer to their growth potential, there's also plenty of know-how to work with. State-of-the-art technology will find its way into Cuba quickly through licensing or foreign direct investment once international companies decide government is serious about sensible development—and the institutional and legal framework it requires—just as it has in many other successful developing countries. And there will be plenty to work with, notably a decent educational and healthcare infrastructure and an impressive cohort of talented and motivated professionals.

Professor de la Torre: Biotechnology and health sciences are some of the brightest spots for future development. The head of the molecular biology department at UCLA used to travel to Cuba often and invited Cuban scientists to work at UCLA while I was there. She told me that they were "first rate" scientists and that they accomplished marvelous things with antiquated equipment and under very difficult circumstances. She always told me that she expected this industry to blossom after normal relations were reestablished.

Professor Walter: The Cuban diaspora is a unique potential asset that can be drawn upon if outstanding legal and property issues can be handled (as they have been in Europe) and as the irreconcilable advance to old age. Cuban immigrants to the U.S. during the decades of hostility have on average done very well indeed in the professions, skilled trades and as entrepreneurs. They and their progeny exist in large numbers, and as they say "… you can't take the Cuba out of a Cuban." Centrifugal force can work its magic in speeding things up if the playing field is laid out right.

Professor de la Torre: I am skeptical of the contribution of the Cuban diaspora. Many are simply not interested (the younger ones) while others may have a romantic and outdated view of the reality of the Island. Yes, they can contribute, but political resentment by those who stayed behind and competition from others may reduce their role.

Professor Walter: The decades-old American Cuba embargo has been called both an abject failure and the key blocker of an even worse outcome. Who knows? It's a reasonable guess, though, that the time has come for something new—something that can work its magic though the power of human nature, the invisible hand of the market, and sound economic development.

Professor de la Torre: Indeed very true. But it will take a lot of time and patience. See Raul Castro's conditions for reestablishing full commercial relations, which include the U.S. paying "reparations" for the damage done to Cuba through the embargo. And the Helms-Burton law has unacceptable conditions that must be met before we can lift the embargo. All of this will take a long time to work out. On my recent trip to Cuba in March 2017 I saw some progress in tourist-oriented businesses, but the domestic-oriented industries seemed not to have reached any significant take-off yet. Progress will be slow.

ECONOMIC-POLITICAL SYSTEMS

To understand a country's political and legal environment, it is useful to first study the economic-political system under which its producers and consumers operate. Two diametrically opposed systems are planned economies (socialist or communist) and capitalism.[1]

Planned Economies

The 1989 fall of the Berlin Wall signified a victory of free-market capitalism over the **planned command system**. In the utopian **communist** conception in Soviet Russia, the factors of production (machinery and plants) were owned by the government (as representative of the "people's collective"), and goods and services were produced and distributed according to a plan, typically five years long. The system was predicated on the assumption that the needs of the collective (the nation) were primary, and manufacturing focused on political, security, and military needs first. "Business" was basically B2B, with factories producing various inputs for other factories, according to plan. Consumer needs were secondary, and in any case individual needs and wants were very basic and well-known by the planners.

With some variations, and with significant assistance from the Soviet Union, this system was adopted by other communist-leaning countries, including China, Cuba, and a number of left-leaning countries in Asia, Africa, and Latin America. As an economic model, communism has largely failed. However, there are countries today, including China and Vietnam, which are still politically communist but have moved to a free-market system.

Free-Market Capitalism

The four main principles that distinguish **free-market capitalism** from communism are:

- *Capital.* Private ownership of capital.
- *Prices.* Market prices determined by demand and supply.
- *Risk.* There is business risk.
- *Allocation.* Resources are allocated according to the price mechanism.

Capital. Private ownership of capital means that factories and plants and stores and businesses in general are actually owned by private individuals. In incorporated businesses, these individual owners are "investors" in the shares of businesses listed on a stock exchange. If you own shares of the Coca-Cola company, you actually are one of the "owners" of the company, and you partake in the profits made by getting annual dividends from the company. Sounds simple, and it actually is. It is also somewhat difficult to "feel" like an owner, since there are often so many outstanding shares. But the fact is that under the system, legally, the CEO of Coca-Cola (who in 2015 was Mr. Muhtar Kent, a Turkish national) is working "for you." In economic terms, Mr. Kent is your "agent."

But private ownership can also be more private and closer to the initial meaning. In family-owned companies, the owners hold on to the business (or at least a majority portion of the shares) and run the business with an eye for keeping it in the family as the years go by. Family-owned businesses can be found in most places, but they are basically the norm in some countries. The Middle East, Latin America, and South Asia are regions where family businesses are prevalent (several of the cases in this book represent family-owned businesses).

The international marketer evaluating entry into countries where family-owned businesses are common (such as in Brazil and the Middle East) has to recognize the difference between family-owned and incorporated businesses. The typical incorporated business operates under strict economic rules. Presenting a "win-win" proposal to a potential distributor in a foreign market can be agreed to quite easily. In fact, the CEO as an agent of the shareholders cannot in principle raise any personal objections to an agreement. Personal preferences of the CEO cannot be decisive if the shareholders stand to lose. This is quite in contrast to a family business, where a relative who happen not to like some person can often derail a very promising deal.

Prices. The second principle, *market prices determined by supply and demand,* might seem quite obvious to anyone who has studied economics, but seems also not in accordance to reality. We go to the store and buy what is there—or don't buy it. How does our demand influence the price? We don't usually haggle with the store clerks.

But if you think about it, the theory still works. When enough people don't buy, it sends a signal to the store's owner. After a while, with unsold merchandise, the store will likely feature a "SALE," a discounted price for the product. After selling out, the store may re-order a new model, and put it up at a somewhat lower price than earlier—not discounted, necessarily, but simply as a reaction to what the demand seems to justify. This is, as indirectly as it sounds, exactly the way supply and demand help set the price. Generally speaking, when the private owner of a business realizes that the price is too high, it will have to come down for the owner to realize a profit. If it is too low to make a profit, the business will have a loss, and the owner may go out of business.

For many readers of this textbook, this explanation is self-evident and unnecessary. But in countries with a history of communism, this simple story will seem like a fairy tale. The adjustment simply seems too imperfect, slow, and wasteful. It is pure trial and error. One of the authors taught an executive seminar in St. Petersburg in early 2005, and remembers being confronted after a class by one of the best students, a prototypical former rocket scientist. Frustrated, he asked, "Why can't the firm simply correlate prices and quantity sold, and then set the right price?" "They try to do that," was the answer, "but preferences of consumers will change, and competitors will attempt to ruin your plans." It might be trial and error, but it works.

Risk. In the free-market system, running a business means taking risks. The business risk is the danger that what is produced in terms of goods and services will not find a buyer at prices that generate a normal profit. The risks happen because customer preferences are never completely known or static, and the action of competitors cannot be perfectly predicted. Communist managers never had to take such risks. The plan stated the production quota and to whom the output was to be distributed. As for consumers in communist countries, they had very little choice, so whatever was available could be chosen without much deliberation. Consumers did not have to make difficult choices between competing alternatives. No risks were taken. The international marketer should not be surprised to find that consumers in some of these countries are very much attracted to large global brands. They remove the functional risk and psychological uncertainty of choosing.

Allocation. A fourth principle of free-market capitalism is that resource allocation is guided by the price mechanism. When demand goes up, prices go up, initially, and profits rise. But this encourages more supply, because more resources will be invested in those goods and services by the private owners of capital. In this way, demand steers supply. This happens both for B2B and consumer goods. For this mechanism to work, it is important that prices are not manipulated, for example by government controls. Where prices are set artificially low, fewer resources will flow into the goods, unless the government mandates the resource allocation. This is what happens in the communist system, where the price mechanism is not working and resources are allocated by the plan. Since the B2B is prioritized, the consumers can be shortchanged. The entering international marketer needs to examine carefully whether the prices in the foreign market are manipulated by the government. In China, for example, the prices of basic hospital services are kept low, while prices of more high-tech treatments are allowed to vary freely. An entering medical equipment company needs to make sure how its particular product or service would be classified.[2]

The Social-Democratic Hybrid

The social-democratic system has significant government ownership of production factors in so-called "**public utilities**" (electricity, transportation, telecom, healthcare, and broadcasting) as well as "**national security**" industries (mining, steel production, oil imports), but free-market principles for consumer products and many B2B goods and services.

EXHIBIT 4.2.
Indicators of economic freedom[5]

Adapted from The Heritage Foundation.

- **Business Freedom**: The ability to start, operate, and close a business.
- **Trade Freedom**: Absence of tariff and non-tariff barriers.
- **Monetary Freedom**: Price stability and lack of price controls that distort market activity.
- **Government Size/Spending**: Level of government expenditures as a percentage of GDP.
- **Fiscal Freedom**: The tax burden imposed by government.
- **Property Rights**: The ability of individuals to accumulate private property.
- **Investment Freedom**: Ability to move resources into and out of specific activities internally and across the country's borders without restriction.
- **Financial Freedom**: Banking efficiency and independence from government control of the financial sector.
- **Freedom from Corruption**: Corruption introduces insecurity and uncertainty into economic relationships.
- **Labor Freedom**: Resilient legal and regulatory framework of a country's labor market.

While the communist model has been discredited, the middle-ground hybrid social-democratic model can still find proponents.[3] While the name really refers to the political system, the mix of public and private ownership economy that social-democratic nations often display is to some extent the more typical economic system today. Even the proto-capitalist United States economy has strong government controls if not ownership of some productive factors. If one accepts that subsidies and support from governmental agencies often comes with centralized oversight, industries such as oil and gas, as well as cotton, various food crops, and high-technology industries deemed crucial for national security are not free of government influence.

But generally the **social-democratic hybrid** involves a more significant level of government ownership of productive factors. In Sweden, with a classic hybrid model, government used to control close to half of total productive capacity. A more free-market-oriented government has lately privatized several properties, including alcohol sales, some healthcare providers, and hospitals. European governmental spending is generally a significant influence in the economy. Government spending as a percent of GDP in France was at 56 percent, in Denmark at 57 percent, while Sweden stood at 51 percent in 2014. The corresponding figure for the United States is about 42 percent, with a significant amount for military spending.[4] The hybrid model might be attractive to the new Cuba. With the recent opening of relations between the U.S. and Cuba, an easing of market regulations in Cuba seems likely to be similar to what we saw in the opening vignette.

Economic Freedom

With different economic systems, the end result is that economic freedom varies across countries. *The Heritage Foundation* and the *Wall Street Journal* have created an index that ranks countries in terms of **economic freedom**. The indicators used are not simply government involvement but more general factors. The 10 factors are given in Exhibit 4.2.

With such a large set of indicators, some countries score better than one might expect, while others do worse. The current top 10 countries in terms of economic freedom are shown in Exhibit 4.3.

EXHIBIT 4.3.
Top 10 countries in economic freedom[6]. What factors do you think moved the U.S. downward into the 17th position in the 2017 report?
Ex. 4.3: Source: http://www.heritage.org/index/ranking (2017 & 2012).

Country	2012 Rank	Score 2012	2017 Rank	Score 2017
Hong Kong	1	89.9	1	89.8
Singapore	2	87.5	2	88.6
New Zealand	4	82.1	3	83.7
Switzerland	5	81.1	4	81.5
Australia	3	83.1	5	81
Estonia	16	73.2	6	79.1
Canada	6	79.9	7	78.5
United Arab Emirates	28	71.1	8	76.9
Ireland	9	76.9	9	76.7
Chile	7	78.3	10	76.5
United States	10	76.3	17	75.1

Source: http://www.heritage.org/index/ranking (2017 & 2012).

As can be seen, the list includes a variety of economies. There is Estonia, the small country (population 1.3 million) formerly under Soviet control, and also Canada, where government plays a significant role. Hong Kong at number one seems quite curious, given that it is a Special Administrative Region of China, but so far mainland China (ranked at number 139) has allowed Hong Kong to forge its own path. The list helps demonstrate the fact that economic freedom is not simply a matter of capitalism or socialism.

POLITICAL RISK

"The world is a dangerous place." In many ways, this half-serious old adage is as apt today as ever. Political instability, government coups, and ethnic-religious clashes seem to be the new norm in the Post-Cold War world. Over time these risks can change quickly, of course, as new crises erupt, regions are realigned, and promises are cancelled as governments change.

For the company trying to decide how risky a region or country can be, there are fortunately a number of indicators of political risk available. Exhibit 4.4 shows a listing from the Marsh company:

Rank	Country	Score
1	Canada	93
1	Hong Kong	93
3	Norway	91
4	Singapore	90
4	Taiwan	90
6	Australia	88
6	Austria	88
8	Sweden	87
9	Czech Republic	86
9	Oman	86
9	Switzerland	86
9	United Arab Emirates	86

EXHIBIT 4.4.
Countries ranked in ascending order of political risk[7]
(Lowest political risk = 100)

Source: https://www.prsgroup.com/category/risk-index

The BRICS Countries

Rank	Country	Score
59	Brazil	71
84	Russia	59
79	India	66
62	China	70
75	South Africa	67

In addition to these broad indicators, companies also use survey techniques to get input from key informants with experience in the different countries. One survey by McKinsey measured how a global

Factors		Examples
Level 1:	*General Instability*	Revolution, external aggression, terrorism.
Level 2:	*Expropriation*	Nationalization, contract revocation.
Level 3:	*Operations*	Import restrictions, local content rules, taxes, export requirements.
Level 4:	*Finance*	Repatriation restrictions, exchange rates.

EXHIBIT 4.5.
Political Risk Factors[8]

Adapted from Kobrin (1979) and Toksöz (2014).

cross-section of international executives assessed the geopolitical situation in June 2017.[9] The survey showed on the whole upbeat sentiments, despite the political uncertainties with North Korea's nuclear ambitions, the Syrian civil war and President Trump's "America First" policy. A few selected findings:

- In every region, geopolitical instability was cited most often as a threat to global growth—and much more often than in previous surveys.
- Executives were more likely than ever to identify terrorist attacks as a threat to long-term global growth.
- Respondents remained more positive than negative about conditions in their home economies, especially in India and in Europe.
- Emerging-market respondents reported a brighter view on trade levels—and a more optimistic outlook—than their developed-market peers.
- Executives in emerging markets are as likely as their peers to expect increasing customer demand, but some remain about twice as likely to expect a decline demonstrating the higher volatility in emerging markets.

For most firms these kinds of broad indicators will be a starting point for decision—making. Firms then need to analyze more precisely what factors underlie the political instability observed.

Political Risk Factors

There are several factors that contribute to the level of political risk. The factors that need to be considered can be arranged in a descending order of importance. The seriousness of political risks generally decrease from the first to the fourth level in the list in Exhibit 4.5.

General instability. Political instability can change over time, but some regions and countries are prone to crises. In Africa, the Democratic Republic of the Congo (aka Congo Kinshasa), South Sudan, and Zimbabwe, and now Egypt and other Northern African countries have serious political instability issues. Other countries include Syria, Pakistan, and Afghanistan in Near Asia, as well as Ukraine and Georgia in the Russian interest sphere. North Korea is an extreme outlier with its belligerent foreign policy and because of its closed market is not a candidate for entry. Generally speaking, these and other countries with serious political disturbances do not provide very good opportunities for an entry.

Expropriation. When governments nationalize foreign capital it happens usually in mining and oil and similar extractive industries. "**Expropriation**" means takeover without compensation. The justification announced is typically that foreign investors "plunder" the riches of the country.

Fortunately, because of the international pressure and the negative fallout from expropriation, such actions have become less frequent. The fall of the communistic dogma has also played a role—the evidence against state ownership of productive resources has become greater and more convincing than before. Still, even if **privatization** of state properties has become more common, foreign ownership of domestic assets can ignite political flames even in advanced economies. In 2006, a Dubai-based company from the UAE was denied a proposed deal to take over the management of six major U.S. ports because "ports are vulnerable to the entry of terrorists or illicit weapons."[10]

Operations. Import restrictions, tariffs, and other trade impediments are in some ways lesser risks that do not necessarily terminate entry possibilities, but basically add costs. However, because they can change quickly in retaliation for political disagreements and perceived snubs, these trade impediments can change the plans laid down for an intended entry. Where there is a risk for such changes—as when rocket firings by North Korea lead to a conflict between the Japan and China, or when access to the Russian market is made risky by the Crimean annexation—most companies will opt to avoid direct investment and perhaps adopt a lower-profile entry into a neighboring country that is less at risk.

Finance. The difficulty of bringing foreign earnings home is a real problem in countries with a weak currency such as India where currency restrictions are still making it hard to exchange rupees. But the problem can also arise because of taxation issues. For example, many American companies keep earnings abroad tax-free to avoid taxes at home.

Exchange-rate manipulation can also become a problem. With floating exchange rates, foreign earnings become more uncertain, set by the open market. On the other hand, with fixed exchange rates there is room for unilateral intervention by a government. The 2015 devaluation of the renminbi sent shockwaves through the financial world.

Political risk is most critical for the firm intending to expand into a country via **foreign direct investment (FDI).** Investing in a country exposes the company to the risks of revolution, government takeovers, and expropriation of its assets. This level of risk is typically unacceptable, and if there is a high probability that this could happen, FDI will be ruled out. Still, with a strong market, the firm might be tempted to enter. Most entries into China have faced these kinds of political problems, and quite a few have found that the company has to wait a long time for net profits. Making money in China has not been easy for any Western companies.

Politically related measures can have an impact above and beyond investment decisions. For example, the 2003 Iraq war spawned a lot of negative fallout against the United States. Some of the stain may still be seen. In their annual end-of-year report 2014, the Gallup Company found that the United States was considered by far the greatest threat to world peace. Of the 66,000 people polled, just under a quarter named Uncle Sam as the greatest threat to world peace.[11] Analyzing the results, the company pointed to the prevalent negative view of America among the large Islamic populations, especially in Pakistan, the country that placed a distant second to the U.S.

The sources of information about political risk vary from very detailed statistical reports on the history of the country's political development to impressionistic tales by recent visitors to the country. The best data used will usually come from any one of the several firms offering **political risk analysis.** If at any of the levels the risk is deemed unacceptable, the investment project receives a "no-go" stamp and is discontinued in favor of foreign direct investment (FDI) elsewhere or simply export or licensing negotiations.

Internet Censorship

Since much of global business today involves Internet communications in some form or another, government constraints on **Internet access** and digital communications can pose serious problems. At different times authoritarian governments have imposed constraints and censorship on Facebook and Twitter communications. China is one notorious example, where digital communications are carefully monitored, messages intercepted, and access blocked by authorities. The governments of Iran and Turkey have at times revoked Twitter access and even imprisoned individuals. The Mid-East "democratic spring" of 2010 was largely initiated by the use of Twitter messages to coordinate mass protest actions.

Added to these constraints is the uncertainty of the degree to which **government spying** occurs. As was unearthed in 2013, many governments around the world, including the United States and European nations, maintain a quite comprehensive spy network, primarily focused on political developments but also veering over into strictly business networks. This is particularly the case for any firms selling products and services with possible ties to national security.

Today one could be fairly certain that some government or governments keep a close watch on companies such as Microsoft, Apple, and Bechtel, the large construction and engineering multinational. Similarly, non-U.S. companies such as China's Lenovo, Russia's Gazprom, the world's largest gas producer, and Samsung from South Korea are likely to also be closely watched by various governments. For example, in 2014 the *New York Times* revealed that the United States' National Security Agency had managed to infiltrate the servers of Chinese electronic giant Huawei.[12] In 2017 there were frequent reports about Russian meddling in the 2016 U.S. Presidential election.

In general, Internet censoring and related political constraints are often difficult to predict. They depend on the reaction of governments to events that are often unforeseen. Many Japanese companies encountered problems in China as a furor arose over the control of the Senkaku Islands (Diaoyu islands to the Chinese) off the Chinese coast. In 2014 the Turkish government tried to ban Twitter and Facebook because of anti-government protests guided by the social media.[13]

For many companies, these kinds of political risks are not worth taking and the company will simply avoid entry.

Russian Tit-for-Tat

The new and volatile Russia is a good illustration of how political risk affects business. After Russia's 2014 annexation of Crimea and the Russian-supported rebellion in Eastern Ukraine, Western powers agreed to impose broad economic sanctions on the Russian economy and on Russian businesses abroad. For example, Russia's state-owned banks were cut off from Europe's capital markets, while Russian defense and energy firms would no longer be able to import hi-tech Western equipment used for military purposes, fracking, or Arctic oil exploration.

Within weeks, Russia's Parliament decided to play tit-for-tat and impose its own restrictions of foreign businesses inside Russia. First Dmitri A. Medvedev, the prime minister, announced that Russia would ban all beef, pork, fish, fruit, vegetables, and dairy products from the European Union, the United States, Canada, Australia, and Norway for one year.

Then four of McDonald's popular restaurants in Moscow were closed for alleged food deficiencies and health concerns. When Visa and MasterCard cut services to several Russian banks banned from transactions with American companies, the Kremlin retaliated by passing a law forcing Visa and MasterCard to either deposit vast sums with the central bank or relocate their payment processing systems to Russia. New constraints on Russian operations by Ford, PepsiCo, IKEA, Carlsberg, and other Western companies active in Russia were said to be considered. Many companies deployed staff out of the region or were forced to put them on paid leave.

President Putin is working hard through diplomatic channels to get sanctions lifted, but as of mid-2017 Western powers have not yet been very forthcoming. To get a sense of what might happen in Russia, the authors asked a Russian specialist, Nicholas Lugansky of Fluor Corporation, to give his assessment of the likely scenario (see box, "Where is Russia heading?").

BOX: Where is Russia Heading? By Nicholas Lugansky*

With several others, I was one of the proponents of this early investment. I worked for a large U.S. corporation active in engineering and construction management, our business boomed with Western clients that were eager to build industrial facilities in Russia. We also supported Western government projects related to implementing international arms treaties with Russia.

The first alarm sounded in early 2000s, when newly elected President Putin jailed his political opponent Mikhail Khodorovsky and disassembled his Yukos company based on questionable charges. But most observers saw it as a single incident related to political rivalry. This turned out to be a mistake. Gradually, with Putin and his cronies concentrating power in oligarchical Russia, the market became more precarious. Still, the promise of investments into oil and gas-rich Russia and its vast consumer markets attracted foreign capital.

Everything changed when in 2014 Russia annexed Crimea and engaged in military efforts to destabilize Ukraine. With Western sanctions imposed, the deteriorating political climate led to a massive outflow of funds and restrictions on borrowing. First Russian companies lost access to capital to finance industrial and mining projects. Then the Western companies started postponing a number of multibillion-dollar projects. Most companies are now scaling down their Russian footprint.

Some business pragmatists suggest that situation will change again, as especially European investors have too much to lose. However unless structural changes take place in Russian politics, the climate of Russian investment will be precarious and will be exploited only by opportunistic (and not long term) investors. That said, we will continue to see European companies engaged in Russia as they have substantial industrial base in the country and will try to maintain their presence to recoup their investments until changing strategy completely. But U.S. companies are more likely to stay out.

Nicholas Lugansky is Director, Business Development-South America, for Fluor Corporation. Fluent in Russian, he occupied a similar position with American companies in Russia in the 1990s and the first decade of the millennium. His update on the current situation in Russia was prepared specifically for this book in March 2015. Fluor Corporation was not consulted in preparation of this article.

Corruption

One special form of political risk is the problem of **corruption**. When borders have to be crossed, there will always be a business opportunity for gate-keepers who can assist, at a price, in opening the gates. These are not necessarily corrupt people. The business opportunity for specialists with political, cultural, and linguistic experts who provide the kind of assistance needed to assess political risks before entry, and the legal assistance once an entry is underway, is perfectly sound. It goes hand in hand with globalization. Unfortunately, when entry barriers are high, governmental regulations are unclear, and a lot of money is at stake, the temptation for the gate-keepers to accept some side money "under the table" can sometimes be too strong.

Transparency.org is one agency that tracks corruption levels in different countries. Exhibit 4.6 shows the 2016 results.

Rank	Country	2016 score	2012 score
1	Denmark	90	90
2	New Zealand	90	90
3	Finland	89	90
4	Sweden	88	88
5	Switzerland	86	86
6	Norway	85	85
7	Singapore	84	87
8	Netherlands	83	84
9	Canada	82	84
10	Germany	81	79
10	Luxembourg	81	80
10	United Kingdom	81	74

EXHIBIT 4.6.
World Corruption Scores 2016. Countries at the top of the list tend to have higher degrees of press freedom, access to information about public expenditure, stronger standards of integrity for public officials, and independent judicial systems. The lower-ranked countries are plagued by untrustworthy and badly functioning public institutions especially the police and judiciary.

Source: https://www.transparency.org/news/feature/corruption_perceptions_index_2016.

The BRICS Countries

Rank	Country	2016 Score	2012 Score
79	Brazil	40	43
131	Russia	29	28
79	India	40	36
79	China	40	39
64	South Africa	45	43

Source: https://www.transparency.org/news/feature/corruption_perceptions_index_2016

For the fifth time, Marriott International, Inc. has been recognized by the Ethisphere Institute as one of the 2012 World's Most Ethical Companies. According to Ethisphere Marriott was selected for showing leadership in promoting ethical business standards.[14]

EXHIBIT 4.7.
Marriott is recognized as one of the World's Most Ethical Companies.

Source: https://ethisphere.com/ethisphere-announces-2017-worlds-most-ethical-companies/

Comparing Exhibits 4.4 and 4.6 we see that corruption and political instability show noticeable correlations. Russia, in particular, suffers from a great deal of corruption, but China is also afflicted.

The United States and a number of other countries have **anti-corruption laws** on their books. These laws significantly constrain the degree to which the countries; firms can engage in side-payments. It is not surprising to hear from the executives of many of these firms that they cannot conduct business very easily in some countries because of the legal constraints from home. At the same time, a company can use its anti-corruption stance as a mark of excellence. One example is the Marriott Hotels International, recognized as a leading ethical company (see Exhibit 4.7).

This kind of recognition shows how international marketers can help create a better business culture in countries with less ethical standards, and in the process gain goodwill and brand benefits over and above the bottom line of profits.

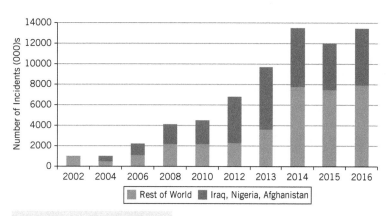

EXHIBIT 4.8.
Growth of Terrorism[15]
International terrorism rose again in 2016 after a slight dip in 2015.

Source: http://kosu.org/post/more-75-percent-terrorist-attacks-2016-took-place-just-10-countries.

International Terrorism

The rise of **international terrorism** is today the most virulent type of political risk. Even before the September 11, 2001, attacks on the twin towers of the World Trade Center in New York, and the Pentagon in Washington, D.C., terrorism was listed as a top concern among multinationals. The Iran revolution, politically motivated murders in South America, and the crime wave in newly capitalist Russia have made multinational companies and their expatriate managers very uneasy and eager to purchase insurance. Although terrorism's international reach can make almost any country unsafe, as the ISIS killing of two innocent Japanese in 2015 showed, terrorism and escalating crime have put an especially dark shadow on certain countries' and regions' attractiveness (see Exhibit 4.8).

As the exhibit shows, current trends are not encouraging. Recent years show a strong upward trend. What is also important to recognize is that the ideology behind the increase has shifted over the period. Early on, the most common rationale was *nationalist-separatist*, the ideology behind the guerilla movements in South America in particular, taking their inspiration from Cuba's Che Guevara (see Exhibit 4.9).

There were also *politically* motivated terrorist acts, exemplified by the so-called Red Brigades in various countries, including the Baader-Meinhof Gang in Germany, that attacked capitalists and corporations.[16]

But in recent years, the rising incidents of international terrorism have been largely due to *religious fundamentalism*, believers attacking non-believers. The data show a striking pattern (see Exhibit 4.10).

This shift of the ideology behind terrorism is significant for global marketers. While all three movements have obvious repercussions on corporate strategy at a country level (whether to enter, exit, and so on), religious conflicts are not necessarily limited to countries or regions. For example, both Muslims and Christians, at least among fundamentalists, tend to view the spreading of the gospel as a world mandate. This makes religious-based terrorism risks in any one location less predictable. Furthermore, in its efforts to sell products and services, marketing naturally tends to promote materialism. This goes counter to the emphasis on spirituality that one finds in almost all religions. Today, however difficult it is to predict terrorist attacks, the chance of religious-based pushback has to be factored into any global marketing endeavor.

Since governments change and new regimes come to power, it is important that the company makes sure to follow risk indicators closely and keep them updated. Where the risk index is high, scenario planning becomes necessary, with any proposed strategy tested against alternative political developments. It is time for the kind contingency discussion of "best case" versus "worst case" scenarios. Predicting political change in Russia may be difficult, but alternatives can be sketched out and the most robust strategy identified. Of course, "most robust" does not necessarily mean "very robust." Given the Russian scene at the start of 2015 it is not surprising if many firms have been pulling out—even the most robust strategy might not be attractive enough, given the risks involved.

What is particularly striking about the terrorism risks faced by a new entrant is that the company can do very little about it. However, according to research, some companies operating in areas with violent conflict actually attempt to actively resolve conflicts by speaking out and cut ties with perpetrators.[18] Political risk due to government instability, guerilla warfare or international terrorism is thus not strictly outside of managerial control but companies can help reduce violence. In addition, when locating subsidiary plants overseas, managers should assess zones within countries for the risk of violence. Many foreign subsidiaries tend to cluster together in foreign locations, partly to feel more protected. However, research shows that local indigenous operations in close proximity can help protect a foreign subsidiary from violence—the firm has become an "insider."[19]

There is also political risk insurance available for most incidents and accidents, but it is very expensive. For example, the Aon insurance company offers protection worldwide against kidnappings of senior executives by terrorists. But many companies decide against sending senior managers into dangerous zones, preferring instead to outsource necessary work to specialists with private security manpower, who are often former military personnel.

EXHIBIT 4.9.
Revolutionary icon Che Guevara pictured over a Cuban flag. Che Guevara, Cuba's Guerrillero Heroico ("Heroic Guerrilla Fighter"), remains a potent idol of revolutionary movements around the world.

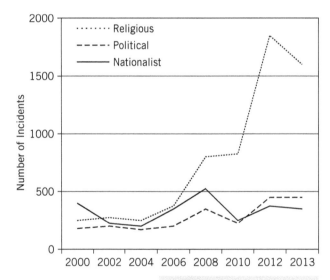

EXHIBIT 4.10.
Trends in Terrorist Group Ideology, 2000–2013[17]

Source: Institute for Economics and Peace (2014).

LEGAL AND REGULATORY ISSUES

Legal issues are always a problem in international expansion, and all companies need to employ lawyers to help with the legal paperwork involved. A short list includes the following items:

- *Export and import licenses*—especially important for technology and pharmaceuticals
- *Packaging* requirements, labeling and customs regulations
- *Quota* applications and tariff computations
- Local *health regulations*, product safety requirements
- *Copyright* infringements
- *Due diligence* concerning potential distributors' financials
- *Contract law* for agents and importers

Some of these issues will be covered in more detail in the later chapters. But at the early stage of country selection, it is also important to unearth more general potential issues in criminal and civil law.

Legal Systems

Many advanced countries have adopted one of two types of legal systems, Roman law and Anglo-Saxon law. In **Anglo-Saxon common law**, legal proceedings are based on previous decisions (precedents) and evolve according the common perceptions and opinions established, often by a **jury of peers**. **Roman law**, by contrast, involves more of an application of unchanging legal principles and statutes, with cases often decided by judges and legal scholars. In an Anglo-Saxon court, the major role of the attorney is to present his client's case in as favorable light as possible, and presumably the truth will emerge from the give-and-take of two sides in conflict. This means an attorney is free to attempt to derail a proceeding against his or her client without particular reference to right or wrong. By contrast, in Roman law the court and the judge attempt to establish the truth of a case based on the evidence presented, without reference to a common case jury. In either case, the foreign firm can only be represented by solicitors and attorneys admitted to the bar and court.

The communist legal system differs significantly from these two systems, as does the legal system adopted by Muslim countries. Exhibit 4.11 shows the main differences in the legal systems of the world.

EXHIBIT 4.11.
Legal systems of the world[20]

Adapted from World Bank (2015).

	Common Law	Civil Law	Socialist Law	Islamic Law
Names	Anglo-Saxon	Roman	Socialist	Sharia
Type of law	Case law	Statutes/legislation	Statutes/legislation	Religious documents, case law
Lawyers	Judges impartial referees; lawyers advocate for the case	Judges dominate trials	Judges dominate trials	Clerics dominate, Lawyers play minor role
Judges' qualifications	Experienced lawyers (appointed or elected)	Career judges	Career bureaucrats, Party members	Religious training

	Common Law	Civil Law	Socialist Law	Islamic Law
Degree of judicial independence	High	High; separate from the executive and the legislative branches of government	Very limited; arm of government	Limited but occasionally high
Jury of peers	Provided at trial level	May adjudicate in conjunction with judges in serious criminal matters	Used at lowest level	Allowed among some Sunnis, not Shiites
Examples	Australia, UK (except Scotland), India (except Goa), Ireland, Singapore, Hong Kong, USA (except Louisiana), Canada (except Québec), New Zealand, Pakistan, Malaysia, Bangladesh	All European Union states (except UK, Ireland and Cyprus), All of continental Latin America (except Guyana and Belize), Québec, All of East Asia (except Hong Kong), Congo, Azerbaijan, Iraq, Russia, Turkey, Egypt, Madagascar, Lebanon, Switzerland, Indonesia, Vietnam, Thailand	Soviet Union and other communist regimes	Many Muslim countries have adopted parts of Sharia Law. Saudi Arabia, Afghanistan, Iran, UAE, Oman, Sudan, Yemen

Beyond national law, there is also a level of international laws that guide certain supranational cases. One instance is **The International Court** in The Hague, a court used primarily for international crimes against humanity. However, the edict issued by international law proceedings and has always been difficult to implement, and in most relevant cases the parties will have recourse only to specific national courts.

Because of the differences between nations and their applications of laws, finding the proper domicile for the legal proceedings can be a sensitive and contentious issue. Many multinational companies try to avoid going to court in foreign countries, not always easy as Microsoft found out in its ongoing struggle with the European Union's Commissioner for Competition. Alerted by anti-trust lawsuits in the United States against Microsoft by Novell in 1993 and Sun Microsystems in 1998, the European Commissioner instigated anti-trust proceedings on its own turf. After years of legal wrangling, in March 2013 Microsoft was fined a staggering $732 million by the EU court.[21] The court then turned around and sued Google for similar anti-competitive behavior.[22]

Ease of Doing Business

Rules and regulations at the national level are often constraints on an entering business that need to be carefully identified before entering. Each nation has its own rules and regulations that will sometimes thwart an otherwise successful entry.

In recent years a World Bank team under the leadership of Dr. Simeon Djankov has produced an assessment of **business regulations** in a growing list of countries. In 2008 the initial report covered no fewer than 178 countries, each country showing updated regulatory requirements for 10 categories of business activities. The 10 categories are:

- Starting a business
- Getting licenses
- Hiring and firing workers
- Registering property
- Getting credit
- Protecting investors
- Paying taxes
- Trading across borders
- Enforcing contracts
- Closing a business

Available in one volume or by country, the "**ease of doing business**" annual reports update all 10 sets of indicators and rank countries on their overall ease of doing business. The reports identify which countries are improving their business environment the most and which ones have slipped. Economies are ranked on their ease of doing business, from 1–178, with first place being the best. A high ranking on the ease of doing business index means the regulatory environment is conducive to the operation of business. The list of the top 10 countries from the 2016 report is given in Exhibit 4.12:

EXHIBIT 4.12.
The top 10 countries for "Ease of Doing Business" (2016)[23]

Source: Ease of Doing Business 2015 database, The World Bank.

Country	2016 RAnk
New Zealand	1
Singapore	2
Denmark	3
Hong Kong SAR, China	4
Korea, Rep.	5
Norway	6
United Kingdom	7
United States	8
Sweden	9
Macedonia, FYR	10

Source: Ease of Doing Business 2016 Database, The World Bank

There is a surprise in this listing. Macedonia is not a country one would expect, and it goes to show how fast government liberalization can have an effect. The bottom 10 were, predictably but sadly, mainly developing countries, especially African countries, with the Democratic Republic of Congo in last place. Some of the more prominent countries did not fare all that well as old habits of protectionism and corruption have resurfaced in countries such as Russia and even Brazil (see Exhibit 4.13).

Three Regulatory Environments: China, India, and the EU

Since the regulatory environment differs considerably across countries, it is useful to analyze different countries separately. We will first examine China and India in more detail, large and important emerging markets. Then we will briefly discuss the European Union.

China

China is still a communist country, and although the market opening gradually initiated around 1980 by Deng Xiaoping has been enormously successful in economic terms, politically the country still exercises strong central controls.

Although the WTO entry gradually is changing the picture, the Chinese government is by most measures the greatest entry barrier into China. It still controls importation through various measures: import license controls, protective tariffs, foreign exchange control, and government-controlled foreign trading companies.

The WTO Effect. With the ongoing reform of China's foreign trade system and the WTO entry, the government-controlled trading companies have lost their monopoly to the mushrooming local trading companies and the industrial firms. The foreign-invested companies are automatically granted foreign trade rights. In general, China's foreign trade system is undergoing a big reform and most of the effort is geared toward the goal of satisfying the requirements of the new WTO status.

With WTO membership, China has gradually lifted the constraints on a wholly foreign-owned enterprise (WFOE, often pronounced "woofy"). WFOEs were originally conceived for encouraged manufacturing activities that were either export orientated or introduced advanced technology. However, the WFOE is increasingly being used for service providers such as a variety of consulting and management services, software development, and trading as well.[25]

India

The liberalization in India in the early 1990s eliminated the ceiling on the share of foreign ownership. The return of Coca-Cola, General Electric, and other Western companies that had left during the socialist regime was a great boost to the Indian economy. The country's **educated elite** has started to return. Although not all foreign investment efforts have been successful, improvements have been steady and India has been able to rack up strong growth figures for several years. India is a good poster case for what open markets can do.

India's great new industry is computer-software development. The Bengaluru (previously known as Bangalore) area in southern India is one where the climate and living conditions are sufficiently similar to California's Silicon Valley for a software engineer to thrive and for a software industry to flower now that the requisite level of economic freedom and political stability have been reached.

Many of the new software companies, to be sure, are funded by direct foreign investment from abroad. The typical firm is a supplier and possibly a subsidiary of large multinationals headquartered elsewhere. Still, there are enough indigenous entrepreneurs to proclaim Bengaluru the Indian Silicon Valley. The industry has set its sights on expansion into the world's largest markets and, drawing on its past colonial history, has already become a strong presence in the United Kingdom. Tata, Infosys, and Wipro are three large software companies whose brand names are well-known globally. In 2013, in a Euromoney Asia survey, Infosys was ranked no.1 among the best-managed companies in the Asia Pacific.[26]

COUNTRY	RANK
Japan	34
Mexico	47
Russia	40
China	78
Brazil	123
India	130
South Africa	74

Source: Ease of Doing Business 2016 Database, The World Bank

EXHIBIT 4.13.
Selected ranks on "Ease of Doing Business" 2016.[24] Many of the BRICS countries struggle to overcome old habits of protectionism and corruption.

Source: Ease of Doing Business 2015 database, The World Bank.

The growing economy offers its own concrete examples of the paradox that is India. As a foundation is prepared for the construction of another wired high-tech office building, the rubble is cleared not by bulldozers but by sari-clad women who carry it away in baskets on their heads (see Exhibit 4.14).

Sometimes, and more and more in India, the West and the East do meet.

European Union

The EU has now taken over the role as the primary trade negotiating entity for its 28 member countries. Still, the traditional bilateral and multilateral relationships at the national level are only gradually being replaced, and in some cases sustained indefinitely. Thus, for example, the 54 member nations in the Commonwealth—a regional grouping dating back to the British colonial domination in the 1900s—still pursue preferential trade among its members. But the main trade negotiating power rests with the EU.

The EU generally undertakes **trade negotiations** and **dispute resolution** with other regional groupings, often under the World Trade Organization (WTO) umbrella. For example, the EU deals directly with the NAFTA and the ASEAN groupings. At the same time, special task forces are created to work on specific issues. The Asia-Europe Meeting (ASEM) is a group of Asian and European countries (EU members) that meet regularly to discuss issues of trade and investment. There are similar groups dealing with Latin America (the EU-Andean Community, the EU-Mercosur, for example), with Africa (the Euro Mediterranean Partnership, focusing on North Africa, for example), and a cooperation agreement with the Gulf Cooperation Council focused on the Arab states in the Persian Gulf.

EXHIBIT 4.14.
Women construction workers in Pushkar, Rajasthan, India. Balancing buckets or pails of cement on their heads, these women workers have adapted their ancient agricultural skills to the modern world.

Copyright © 2009 by Shutterstock/ Cornfield.

The EU also takes the lead in conflict resolutions with other trade regions. For example, when the United States imposed higher tariffs on imported steel, the EU raised the issue in the WTO, where the tariffs were judged illegal. This set the stage for possible retaliation by the EU, forcing the Americans to back down. On the other hand, the EU has to cope with sometimes conflicting trade demands and practices from its own members. For example, the euro crisis in 2014, Greece's demand of a moratorium on its debts in 2015, and the new British government's desire for special exceptions have threatened the EU cohesiveness.[27] Nevertheless, in the big picture, the EU will continue to be an important player in the world's trade negotiations.

PATENTS AND COUNTERFEITS

Two issues that often arise in international expansion is, first, the protection of patents and copyrights, and, second and related, counterfeits, fake products, and pirated brands.

Patents

In many cases a company's competitive advantage is lodged in some particular technological advancement, often a patented innovation. When foreign expansion is contemplated, the risks involved in having foreign competitors infringe on patents have to be considered. This affects in particular entry into a market such as China, where legal enforcement of **copyrights** and **patents** is still weak, and where intrepid local manufacturers often have the requisite technological skills to copy and replicate advanced technology.

Patent registration in different countries is important and can be costly, but the more serious issue is monitoring and enforcing the patent protection. One prominent example is from Apple, notorious for its vigilance. The iPhone's original touchscreen patents, also called "Steve Jobs' patents," have been registered and enforced worldwide. In order to forestall imitators, Apple has instituted a number of lawsuits against alleged **infringements**. The company has gained some notable victories, especially one against Samsung's Galaxy models with fines of more than $500 million, later reduced.[28]

Most companies cannot afford the kind of legal proceedings engaged in by Apple and Samsung, and the risk of losing a patent fight discourages foreign expansion for many smaller companies. The issue is particularly significant in the case where import barriers force production to move to the market country. Moving into China was long a matter of establishing a joint venture with a Chinese company. No longer a legal requirement, the law allowed Chinese companies to learn and absorb new technology and management **know-how**. This helped the Chinese economy to grow quickly—but it also enabled the Chinese companies to copy the advanced technology of the foreign firms. As one Japanese executive for Honda wryly commented: "Honda may have the largest market share for motorcycles in China—only most of them are not made by Honda."[29] Microsoft is another company that has encountered piracy problems in China and has tried a novel way to combat it—by not playing tough (see box, "Chairman Bill?").

Counterfeits

One difficult regulatory problem particularly for global brand producers is the prevalence of **counterfeits**.

Counterfeits or **knockoffs** are fake products, imitations designed and branded so as to mislead the unwary customer into assuming that they are genuine brands. Counterfeit products should be distinguished from "gray trade" or parallel trade. Gray trade is parallel distribution of genuine goods by intermediaries other than authorized channel members (gray trade will be discussed further in the chapters dealing with price and distribution.)

Counterfeit products pose an ominous problem in the global marketplace. According to expert estimates, worldwide company losses due to counterfeit products are over $250 billion annually.[31] The traditional cases of counterfeit products involve luxury goods with global brand names. Gucci wallets, Louis Vuitton bags, Cartier watches, and Porsche sunglasses are typical examples (see Exhibit 4.15).

BOX: Chairman Bill?[30]

Since arriving in China in 1992, Bill Gates and Microsoft have established a network of business operations in China, from sales and marketing, to customer support and even research and development. Its size is second only to the operations at home in Redmond, Washington. But this does not mean doing business in China is easy: Microsoft is still dogged by piracy of its software.

Microsoft estimates that 90 percent of its software used in China is pirated. Outside the company's $80 million research center in Beijing, young Chinese line the sidewalk attempting to steer potential customers away from the authorized seller, down alleys to run-down apartments where bootleg copies are sold. A typical price is $1 for software that regularly sells for $200. Sure, not all the accompanying booklets are available with the diskettes, backup service might be questionable, and later upgrades are impossible to get, but isn't it worth a try?

Microsoft has been battling back with a mix of government appeals and consumer bullying, but with little success. The Chinese government actively has been promoting the Linux alternative, and its bureaucrats also find it distasteful to punish their own citizens just to add more funds to Bill Gates' already full coffer. Even China's accession to the WTO seems to have done little to dent this attitude. So Microsoft has lately decided on a new strategy. Thinking positively, the company has started to offer its top customers in government and business upgraded customer support, dedicated account managers, and even more sharing of the technology. The strategic notion is that with the added value of these services, top customers will be reluctant to endorse—and use—pirated software. Then, in turn, they will be more sympathetic to pursuing the bootleggers.

Good luck with that. Fast forward to today and software piracy is still a big problem for Microsoft with 77 percent of all software in China estimated to be pirated.

Microsoft's new approach? In a sign that might indicate defeat, Microsoft is offering a free upgrade to its latest iteration of Windows OS, named Windows 10, even to those Chinese users who have been running bootlegged or pirated versions of Windows 7 and Windows 8. By offering Windows 10 as a free upgrade Microsoft hopes to maintain its enormous market share in operating systems in China and position for "Software as a Service" or SaaS. As the world increasingly moves its productivity tools to the cloud, newer operating systems that optimally utilize paid subscription services will urge Chinese users to eventually pay to take advantage of software services. Video-game vendors in China are already using this type of business model (i.e., pay to play every day). At least, that's the idea.

But counterfeit products are no longer confined to designer jeans and watches. Items now routinely counterfeited include chemicals, computers, drugs, fertilizers, pesticides, medical devices, military hardware, and food—as well as parts for airplanes and automobiles.

There are several factors driving the explosion in counterfeit products:[32]

1. the low cost of high-technology manufacturing results in low investment costs and high profits;
2. globalization has lowered many trade barriers;
3. expansion of channels and markets particularly the retail sector in developing economies;
4. the growth of powerful and desirable worldwide brands;
5. weak international and national enforcement;
6. high tariffs and taxes that benefit lower-priced products;
7. consumer complicity.

A recent survey by Price Waterhouse Cooper of consumers in the UK found that over 40 percent of consumers were willing to purchase counterfeit films, music, clothing, and accessories, 18 percent were willing to purchase counterfeit alcohol, and even 16 percent were willing to purchase medicine.[33] According to the research, price differentials are only part of the explanation. For some, buying counterfeits can also enhance self-esteem, seeing themselves as "smart shoppers."[34]

Counterfeiting is truly a global phenomenon and counterfeiters operate at all levels of the economy. Over 750,000 counterfeit shirts, shoes, and soccer balls were confiscated at the 2014 FIFA World Cup in Brazil.[35] Asian and European customs agents worked together to seize over 1.2 million counterfeit goods and 130 million counterfeit cigarettes over a two-week period in October 2014. Many Internet sites are now selling fake luxury goods.

Not all counterfeits come from developing countries. For example, experts estimate that perhaps 20 percent of all fakes are made in the United States by producers who can't make a profit otherwise or who see the opportunity of a quick kill.[36]

Companies that rely mainly on their brand name are fighting back especially hard. To help identify fakes, some firms have resorted to various coding devices. Levi Strauss, the jeans maker, weaves into its fabric a microscopic fiber pattern visible only under a special light. For some firms, the counterattack has been a two-pronged "**search and destroy**" mission. Firms make an effort to find the factories that turn out the counterfeits, and they track down the fakes in the stores. Private investigation outfits have emerged to offer their services to multinational companies. Cartier is involved in 2,500 legal proceedings and devotes $3.8 million annually to its crusade; Louis Vuitton has more than 1000 active cases each year. Tiffany has also sued eBay, claiming the website has aided violations of the Tiffany trademark by allowing individuals to auction off fake Tiffany jewelry.

Global counterfeit trade is cutting into profits of companies that are successful because of their brands. But no amount of effort will ever completely eradicate the copycats. For as long as there is consumer demand, companies will find that imitation is the "severest form of flattery" rather than the "sincerest form of flattery."

DUMPING

Dumping is commonly defined as selling goods in some markets below cost. There is also a less common practice of selling products at home at prices below cost, referred to as "**reverse dumping**." Either case of dumping is typically illegal since it is destructive of trade, and competitors can take an offender to court to settle a dumping case. The usual penalty for manufacturers whose products are found to violate the antidumping laws is a countervailing duty, an assessment levied on the foreign producer that brings the prices back up over production costs, and also imposes a fine.

Dumping cases are initiated by the presumed victims of the dumping actions. The injured party files a complaint with the appropriate agencies, in the United States with the Department of Commerce and the International Trade Commission. The defending firms are then asked to appear and present their side of the case. After deliberations are finished, the government agency issues a verdict, finding the defendants guilty or not guilty as the case may be. Appeals can typically be made to a higher court, in the United States to the U.S. International Trade Commission. Once a verdict is upheld, the appropriate remedy is decided upon, **countervailing duties** (adding duties on the products for price to reach the proper level) and/or **antidumping fines** (an outright penalty). These proceedings all take place in the country of the complainants, consistent with the WTO rules and directives.

While some cases proceed rapidly through the process, most dumping cases are notorious for their protracted duration. The World Trade Organization's (WTO) case DS442 between the European Union and Indonesia concerning dumping and importation of fatty alcohols (used for detergents and cosmetics) was filed in 2012. So far a panel has been formed to discuss the case but no panel members have been selected. Case DS424 between the United States and Italy for dumping and importation of stainless steel was filed in 2011 and the current status is "in consultation."[37] Things have gotten better, even if time and costs are still high.

The manner in which the relevant costs are used to define dumping varies between countries, reflecting the fact that economists have difficulty agreeing on a common definition. Most countries and regional groupings have established their own particular version of antidumping regulations. Under the new WTO trade laws, the antidumping rules that are to apply to all members are more liberal than usual, making penalties more difficult to assign. The new rules, developed with the intent to support emerging countries' exports, feature: (1) stricter definitions of injury, (2) higher minimum dumping levels needed to trigger imposition of duties, (3) more rigorous petition requirements, and (4) dumping duty exemptions for new shippers.

China is an interesting special case. The country ranks first in the world for the number of antidumping suits lodged against it. One problem has been that without a true market economy, the cost basis for determining potential dumping practices does not exist. Foreign governments have used **third-country prices** to arrive at a proper cost figure. The argument is that in China, where state-owned exporters receive subsidies and bank loans they never have to repay, under a system that is largely secret, there is no basis to assess costs. Although the WTO entry has forced a change, experts suggest that it will be at least a decade before these practices are eliminated.

DATA SOURCES

A useful start when doing research on political and legal issues is to look at the easily available **secondary data sources**, such as the U.N. publications, the OECD and GATT/WTO reports, and the Department of Commerce reports in the United States. A large number of organizations—consulates, commerce departments, newspaper and magazine affiliates, information agencies—can be helpful. The data are today often accessible through their websites, and can easily be found with the help of an Internet search engine such as Google or Yahoo. Some of the more prominent organizations and sources are listed in Exhibit 4.16.

Political risk indicators and some data on the degree to which the market is open and free of government interference can be obtained from the *Political Risk Yearbook,* published annually by Political Risk Services in Syracuse, New York. These data provide expert assessments of political instability in a country, including the chances of a violent change in government and the degree of social unrest. They also contain summaries of restrictions on business, such as limitations on foreign ownership and constraints on the repatriation of funds. Countries that score high on political instability and restrictions on business can usually be eliminated from consideration early.

The best guide for entry barriers and regulatory obstacles is probably the annual **"Doing Business" reports** from the World Bank. They offer data on regulatory barriers to doing business in a wide variety of countries. The 2015 publication covers 178 countries.

SUMMARY

In some ways political risk is the simplest factor to avoid in international marketing. The basic rule would be to "avoid taking any political risk." The problem is that what looks at one point in time as a perfectly riskless entry can turn into a very difficult political and expensive nightmare. Not only can big political-military issues suddenly arise—which they do regularly—but even relatively minor conflicts can be blown out of proportion with economic repercussions. And terrorism is sometimes linked to economics: American business executives have been kidnapped and used for ransom by dissident groups such as the Shining Path guerrillas in Peru.

Two particular angles further complicate the picture. One is that economic sanctions will often be used when political conflicts erupt. That is, regardless of causes and effects, slapping some economic punishment on a country's business becomes often a very convenient and politically riskless option. The Russian annexation of Crimea has been met by economic sanctions from the United States, blocking assets of Russian businessmen in the United States and imposing travel restrictions. One might expect that American business men will be denied Russian visas in tit-for-tat retaliation by Putin.

The second problem is that countries allied to the "wronged" country might have to show solidarity, and join economic boycotts, for example. European countries are asked to join the U.S. sanctions against Russia, but hesitate because of their reliance on Russian gas exports. Also, the Europeans have major business interest in Russia, and fear they will lose their investments as well as goodwill.

The solution is for the potential entrant to analyze carefully the political risks involved, their likelihood but also severity and probable length. The fact is that every entry abroad faces some political risk and exposure to changes in regulations. If the risks are deemed too great, avoid entry. But if the opportunity is great enough, some risks may be worthwhile taken. And there is the solution of getting some political risk insurance, although the premiums tend to very high (in fact so high that companies sometime forego important trips for their top executives rather than putting them at risk).

The company can also find ways of minimizing its exposure to the risks by choosing less capital-intensive modes of entry. We will deal with the various modes of entry in a later chapter.

KEY TERMS

Anglo-Saxon common law
anti-corruption laws
antidumping fines
business regulations
business risk
communist
copyrights

Africa Briefings
Macroeconomic and economic sector data for African countries.

Business Environment Risk Intelligence (BERI)
Provides political risk ratings for 130 countries on a scale from 0 (greatest risk) to 100 (least risk).

CIA World Factbook 2002
Economic and political profiles of countries worldwide.

Economist Intelligence Unit (EIU)
Analysis and forecast of economic, political, and business environment for over 180 countries.

EIU Country Commerce
Provides operating conditions, commercial laws, and business regulations of approximately 60 countries worldwide.

EIU Country Reports
Provides quarterly analyses and forecasts of the political, economic and business environment in more than 180 countries.

Global Risk Assessment, Inc.
Analysis and research for political, investment, and trade risk.

Internet Center for Corruption Research
Country ranking according to level of corruption.

PRS Group
Data on country and political risk analysis.

Transparency International
Annual ranking of perceived corruption in 90 countries.

World Bank: Profiles on 206 countries.
World Bank: World Development Report.
World Bank. 2013. Doing Business 2014: Understanding Regulations for Small and Medium-Size Enterprises.

EXHIBIT 4.16.
Political and Legal Data Sources

corruption

counterfeits

countervailing duties

currency controls

democratic process

dispute resolution

"Doing Business" reports

dumping

ease of doing business

economic freedom

educated elite

embargo

export controls

expropriation

family-owned companies

foreign direct investment (FDI)

free market capitalism

government spying

guerilla warfare

import license controls

incorporated businesses

infringement

international institutions

international terrorism

Internet access

jury of peers

knockoffs

know-how national security

patent registration

patents

planned command system

political risk analysis

private ownership

privatization

public utilities

resource allocation

reverse dumping

Roman law

sanctions

search and destroy

secondary data sources

social-democratic hybrid

Soviet satellite countries

The International Court

third-country prices

tit-for-tat

trade negotiations

DISCUSSION QUESTIONS

1. Judging from the comments made by Professors Walter and de la Torre in the opening vignette, what do you think the market potential will be in Cuba in the next five years or so? Compare autos, apparel, cosmetics—which one(s) will have the greatest potential?

2. Some observers have argued that corruption is simply the price for doing business in emerging countries, and that "greasing the palm" in fact overcomes the lack of established channels in the countries. Argue for this position, and then against this position.

3. What makes counterfeits so difficult to eliminate? When a copier is used in one emerging country to make copies of a textbook for a class in a poor area, does it not just help the students without hurting anyone really? Why would the author complain?

4. Use the World Bank website to find more about the "doing business" ratings. What indicators are used to compile the index? Discuss the rationale behind each of them. Anything left out?

5. Why is establishing the proper cost basis such a problem with dumping allegations? Why not simply pick the price charged in the home market as a starting point, and then consider a "fair" profit margin in that price to arrive at the cost?

TEAM CHALLENGE PROJECTS

1. Argentina is one of the world's major agricultural countries and ranks as a top producer and exporter of beef, honey, wheat, citrus fruit, grapes, soybeans, squash, maize, and other crops. Additionally, because the country is in the Southern Hemisphere, summer in Argentina is winter in the U.S. and vice versa. You are the U.S. Congressperson representing a farm state whose economy is highly dependent on U.S. consumer purchases of food products. Team 1: Write the speech that you would give in Congress to convince your fellow Congressmen to vote YES to increase tariffs with the goal of limiting/reducing the importation of goods from Argentina. Team 2: Write the speech that you would give in Congress to convince your fellow Congressmen to vote NO to increase tariffs with the goal of expanding the importation of goods from Argentina.

2. Many countries have weak copyright and trademark laws or weak/no enforcement of laws already in place. Team 1: Develop a list of at least five tactics you can use from a marketing perspective to protect your products and company name from counterfeiting. Team 2: What would be the actions by the counterfeiters to get around your five tactics?

3. The American beer company Anheuser Busch (founded in 1852) uses the names Budweiser and Bud on its beer products and advertising. The Czech company Budweiser Budvar also uses the Budweiser name on its beer products arguing that its beer has been made in the Czech town of Budweis since 1892. Anheuser Busch has been fighting a legal battle for many years and lost in Columbia and Switzerland (the Czech company can use the name Budweiser) and won in France while the UK decided that both companies can use the name Budweiser. In 2005 the EU granted Protected Geographical Indication status (PGI) to the Czech company allowing it to freely use the Budweiser name in its traditional territories. This has caused confusion in the markets and hurt sales of the American company's products. You are the Vice President of Worldwide Marketing for Anheuser Busch and have to give an update to your Board of Directors on the strategy for dealing with Budweiser Budvar. Team 1: Write the presentation you will give to your Board for continuing the battle with Budweiser Budvar. Team 2: Write the presentation you will give to your Board for making "peace" with Budweiser Budvar. What are the "terms" of peace?

4. Identify three countries for which the U.S. State Department has recently issued travel advisories or outright travel bans. Team 1: Argue that these countries still represent good international targets/prospects. Team 2: Argue that travel restrictions represent a warning sign that these countries are no longer stable or desirable and these countries are no longer international business prospects now or in the future.

SELECTED REFERENCES

"Antidumping and Countervailing Duty Laws under the Tariff Act of 1930," United States International Trade Commission.

Bapuji, Hari, *Not Just China: The Rise of Recalls in the Age of Global Business.* New York: Palgrave Macmillan, 2011.

"Brazil: Thousands of Fake Sporting Goods Intercepted Ahead of World Cup," *just-style.com,* June 18, 2014.

Brown, Eric, "In Gallup Poll, The Biggest Threat To World Peace Is … America?" *International Business Times,* January 2, 2014.

Chaudhry, P. and A. Zimmerman, "Protecting Your Intellectual Property Rights," Chapter 2 in *Management for Professionals,* Springer Science and Business Media, New York, 2013.

Coskun, Orhan, "Turkey blocks Twitter days before vote as PM fights scandal," *Reuters,* March 21, 2014.

Dai, Li, Lorraine Eden and Paul W. Beamish, "Place, space, and geographical exposure: Foreign subsidiary survival in conflict zones," *Journal of International Business Studies,* Vol. 44, No. 6, Aug 2013, pp. 554–578.

Frohlich, Thomas C., Alexander E.M. Hess and Vince Calio, "9 Most Counterfeited Products in the USA," *USA Today,* March 29, 2014.

Judge, William Q., Stav Fainshmidt and J. Lee Brown III, "Which model of capitalism best delivers both wealth and equality?" *Journal of International Business Studies,* Vol. 45, No. 4, May 2014, pp. 363–386.

Kanter, James, "European Regulators Fine Microsoft, Then Promise to Do Better," *The New York Times,* March 7, 2013, B2.

King, Neil Jr. and Greg Hitt, "Dubai Ports World Sells U.S. Assets," *The Wall Street Journal,* Dec. 12, 2006.

Kobrin, Steven J. "Political Risk: A Review and Reconsideration," *Journal of International Business Studies* 10, no. 1 (1979), p. 67–80.

Kosman, Josh, "Microsoft the Big Winner in Google Antitrust Lawsuit," *New York Post,* Business, April 15, 2015.

Ku, Eunice, "Setting Up a Wholly Foreign-Owned Enterprise in China," *China Briefing,* Sep 11, 2013.

Liu, Xingzhu, Yuanli Liu and Ningshan Chen, "The Chinese experience of hospital price regulation," *Health Policy and Planning,* Volume 15, Issue 2, 2000, pp. 157–163.

Lowensohn, Josh, "Apple v. Samsung: Judge orders new trial on some damages, cuts award by $450M," *CNET.COM,* March 1, 2013.

Oetzel, Jennifer and Kathleen Getz, "Why and how might firms respond strategically to violent conflict?" *Journal of International Business Studies,* Vol. 43, No. 2, Feb/Mar 2012, pp. 166–186.

Penz, Elfriede, Bodo B. Schlegelmilch & Barbara Stöttinger "Voluntary Purchase of Counterfeit Products: Empirical Evidence From Four Countries," *Journal of International Consumer Marketing,* Volume 21, Issue 1, 2008, 67–84.

Pricewaterhouse Cooper, "Counterfeit goods in the UK: Who is buying what, and why?" *PWCIL Press,* October, 2013.

Sanger, David E. and Nicole Perlroth, "N.S.A. Breached Chinese Servers Seen as Security Threat," *The New York Times,* March 22, 2014.

Schafer, Sarah, "Microsoft's Cultural Revolution," *Newsweek,* June 28, 2004, pp. E10–12.

Sowell, Thomas, *Basic Economics,* 5th ed. New York: Basic Books, 2014.

Toksöz, Mina, *Guide to Country Risk: How to Identify, Manage and Mitigate the Risks of Doing Business across Borders.* London: *The Economist;* First Trade Paper Edition, 2014.

ENDNOTES

1. The economics text by Sowell, 2014, is a well-written guide to economic systems.
2. From Liu, Liu, and Chen, 2000.
3. Judge, Fainshmidt, and Brown III (2014) demonstrate how six "hybrid" capitalist systems produce both wealth and equality in various proportions.
4. According to the *2015 Index of Economic Freedom,* http://www.heritage.org/index/ranking.
5. Source: http://www.heritage.org/index/.
6. From http://www.heritage.org/index/.
7. From the risk index developed by the PRS Group: https://www.prsgroup.com/category/risk-index.
8. Source: Adapted from Kobrin, 1979, and Toksöz, 2014.
9. "Economic Conditions Snapshot, June 2017," McKinsey Global Survey.
10. King and Hitt, 2006.
11. Brown, 2014.
12. As reported by Sanger and Perlroth, 2014.

13. As reported by Coskun, 2014.

14. http://www.transparency.org/research/cpi/overview.

15. From Global Terrorism Index 2014, Institute for Economics and Peace, *www.visionofhumanity.org/*.

16. For further readings, see http://web.stanford.edu/group/mappingmilitants/cgi-bin/groups/view/77.

17. From Global Terrorism Index 2014, Institute for Economics and Peace.

18. See Oetzel and Getz, 2012.

19. See Dai, Eden, and Beamish, 2013.

20. Compiled from the World Bank data on their website, www.worldbank.org.

21. See Kanter, 2013.

22. See Kosman, 2015.

23. Source: Ease of Doing Business 2015 database, The World Bank.

24. Source: Ease of Doing Business 2015 database, The World Bank.

25. From Ku, 2013.

26. From the company website: see www.infosys.com/newsroom.

27. The Cameron government has promised to hold a referendum within two years of the 2015 election.

28. See Lowensohn, 2013. The amount that Samsung will in the end pay is not yet clear (as of March 2015) but is likely to be significantly lower than $500 million.

29. Personal interview.

30. Sources: Schafer, 2004; "Microsoft Makes New Effort to Expand in China," 2004; Hagerty and Ovide, 2014.

31. See Frohlich, Hess, and Caliol, 2014.

32. See Chaudhry, P. and A. Zimmerman, 2013.

33. See Price Waterhouse Cooper, 2013.

34. Penz and Stöttinger, 2005; Penz, Schlegelmilch, and Stöttinger, 2008.

35. See "Brazil: Thousands of fake …" 2014.

36. From Bapuji, 2011.

37. The WTO has a website dedicated to the listing of pending cases, see https://www.wto.org/english/tratop_e/dispu_e/dispu_status_e.htm.

"The Glory of Diversity"

In this chapter you will learn about:

1. How culture is a fundamental force that establishes the basic values in a society and also tells what kind of behavior is acceptable
2. How culture in different countries can be measured and distinguished
3. How culture affects the way to do business in different countries
4. How culture affects consumer choice via the social norms derived from culture and the willingness of people to comply with the norms

This third and last chapter on "opportunities and threats" will deal with the challenges in the cultural environment abroad. We will first discuss the meaning and manifestations of cultures around the world. The chapter will then deal directly with the three major aspects of cultural influence for marketing:

- Culture's influence on business negotiations
- Culture's role in Business-to-Business (B2B) marketing abroad
- Culture's impact on B2C and consumer choice

The last sections will deal with two recent cultural developments, religious fundamentalism and multiculturalism.

The Cultural Environment

CHAPTER 5

WHAT BOOKS DO PEOPLE IN DIFFERENT COUNTRIES READ?

For those who want to argue that the world has become more homogeneous as economic prosperity has increased, the book world would seem to offer strong support. Many of us still remember the global excitement stirred up by any release of a new Harry Potter book. J.K. Rowling does not write any more Potter books, but her sales of an estimated 400 million books places her close to a top-10 bestselling writer of all time. The lead is still held by Shakespeare and Agatha Christie, with an estimated total of around 3 billion books sold each.

Further evidence of growing homogeneity around the world is the success of some current writers, including E.L. James, British author of *Fifty Shades of Grey*, a hit in many countries and listed even by Amazon Japan as a 2015 bestseller. There is also Dan Brown with *The Da Vinci Code* and *Inferno*, big sellers around the world, and authors in the Scandinavian-style detective genre like Jo Nesbø, Stieg Larsson, and Henning Mankell are popular even in countries with less severe climates like Hungary and Australia.[1]

It is tempting to conclude that fiction has become a global market where local talent is suppressed and losing out to mass-marketed big writers. But this is a much too facile conclusion. The fact is that book writing has become an attractive industry where a number of local writers have done very well, not only at home but also with global success. The story is much more similar to that of the beer industry—fiction is a global market with a lot of diversity in local markets.

The evidence for the increasing global reach of local talent can be exemplified by writers like Khaled Hosseini of Afghanistan, whose *The Kite Runner* became a bestseller globally, and Haruki Murakami of Japan, a prolific writer and an often-cited candidate for the Nobel Prize. Then there is Susan Abulhawa, a Palestinian-American writer whose bestselling first novel *Mornings in Jenin* became a global success and in 2014 topped the Amazon.de bestseller list in its German translation. Canadian Yann Martel's *Life of Pi* has sold over 10 million copies worldwide.

But the more tantalizing evidence for diversity is the mix of local and global writers in most countries' top-10 lists. One overview suggests the variety across countries.[2]

In Indonesia, the number one book, selling around 5 million copies, is *The Rainbow Troops* by Andrea Hirata, a local writer still little known elsewhere. In India, a top seller is *2 States: The Story of My Marriage* by Chetan Bhagat, who *The New York Times* claimed as "the biggest selling English language novelist in India's history." Six of the most widely read novels in South Africa in 2017 were mostly about South Africa's political dysfunction, reflecting a country trying to make sense of a tumultuous political environment, high crime statistics, and an unreliable power grid.

The bestselling book in Brazil's history is *Agape*, a self-help volume written by Brazilian Catholic priest Marcelo Rossi, which sold 7.7 million copies in the first 21 months after its publication. In Russia, *The Green Tent* by Ludmila Ulitskaya and Viktor Pelevin's *Pineapple Water for the Fair Lady* sold well, continuing the Russian predilection for serious fiction rather than the "young adult" thrust of many global bestsellers.

Of course, some countries still were happiest with the global offerings. In the UK, Dan Brown's Robert Langdon seems to have a devoted following, and in France, where literary fiction has a long and proud tradition, *Harry Potter and the Cursed Child* topped the bestseller lists in 2016. As a counterpoint, in Norway, home of the new wave in detective fiction, a new "literary" translation of the Bible was the bestseller throughout the year. In China, *Anne of Green Gables* by L.M. Montgomery was voted "one of the most influential books" in 2012, showing the universal appeal of a story about a spirited girl growing up on a farm in Canada (see Exhibit 5.1).

In 2016, one in five books sold in China was by an international author. L.M. Montgomery's book about Anne was first published in 1908 and has been a perennial world bestseller since then. In 2015 it was the basis for a very successful TV miniseries in Japan, focusing on its Japanese translator.

The world's cultures are not becoming homogenized; they allow for a lot of local variation. Still, there is also room for books with universal appeal.

CULTURE DEFINED

"Culture" can be defined as the set of rules, values, and norms that guide an individual's upbringing, education, and "coming of age." Culture involves both *fundamental values* and *actual behavior*. An individual learns what values are important to people and what behavior is acceptable. "Values" include beliefs about the proper deference to parents, beliefs about what is important in life, beliefs about how one can and should help others, and so on. "Behavior" is what one does and how one does it—running to meet someone dear, "no talking while eating," smiling when taking pictures, and so on. Much of this learning comes from parents and peers and teachers, but also from religion, advertising, and participation in games and teams. Culture is not something that comes with one's genes; it is not something one is born with, and it is not something that is the same everywhere. As individuals, we "learn" our culture.

Culture can differ dramatically across countries. The differences that are more critical are those that are sustained over time. When it comes to *values*, the changes are slow, long in the making and hard to detect. Actual *behavior*, on the other hand, can change much faster. Getting people to drink coffee from a paper cup is easier than getting people to change religion.

Some behaviors of course are difficult to change if they have become an ingrained habit. Past habits die slowly and even the police might be called in by a complaining customer to set things right.[3] And judging from Russia's difficulty in controlling corruption, the efforts to instill a free-market spirit among its citizens, long used to government kickbacks and indoctrinated about the evils of the capitalist system, have had only limited success.[4]

For international marketers, it is important to distinguish whether their marketing campaigns are just asking for a change in preferences and choice behavior or whether they are actually challenging fundamental values.

Trying not to challenge any traditions can be a tricky balancing process, however. IKEA, the global furniture store, deleted a story about a lesbian couple from its Russian catalog because of legal fears stemming from Russia's new law against "non-traditional lifestyles." In response, Russian gays and lesbians met up at the Brooklyn IKEA in the U.S. for an impromptu photo shoot of a gay couple kissing on an IKEA showroom bed. IKEA has apologized to Western media, saying the edits did not align with its own values.[5]

So people in different cultures have different values and beliefs, they think differently, and they like different things. These preferences are not set in stone, however, although many of us will sometimes claim so. You can hear people say, "I will never eat raw fish" (meaning sushi) or "I will never wear suspenders" or "I will never watch women's basketball." These are tastes or preferences (you might even say prejudices) that are a result of years of indoctrination—which is how "culture" basically gets constructed.

As you would expect, all of this matters greatly for international marketers. For example, can a brand use the same spokesperson everywhere? Likely not, although for some transcultural segments it might work. In sports, David Beckham can be used everywhere perhaps—but not Derek Jeter or Tom Brady.

For international marketers, culture is more than just environment. Culture determines preferences and thus helps determine demand. It also determines behavior and thus ways to do business. Culture does not simply set new limits on the opportunities for buyers and sellers but also helps determine their goals, preferences, and aspirations.

CULTURAL DIMENSIONS

There are several useful ways of classifying cultures across countries. Actually, cultures and countries do not necessarily go together. Countries with large populations such as India, China, Russia, and the United States are really **multicultural,** meaning that they contain a wide variety of cultures within their borders. The same goes for some

smaller nations, such as Belgium, Canada, South Africa, and the former Yugoslavia. In other cases, several countries can be seen as one cultural grouping. Examples include Scandinavian countries (Denmark, Norway, Sweden) and Latin American countries (Venezuela, Colombia, Ecuador, but not necessarily Brazil).

High- vs. Low-Context Cultures

An important distinction between cultures is that between **high- and low-context cultures.** In high-context cultures the meaning of individual behavior and speech changes depending on the situation or context. Nonverbal messages are full of important—and intended—meanings. Even if no words are spoken, individuals communicate. Things are "understood." And when words are spoken, "reading between the lines" is important. High-context cultures have a similarity of backgrounds, a commonness of purpose, a homogeneity in society, careful enculturation and socialization starting at an early age in the family, often one religion, one language, centralized broadcast media, coordinated educational system, and so on.

In low-context cultures, by contrast, intentions are expressed verbally. One's meaning should be explicit, not taken for granted. Propositions have to be justified and opinions defended openly. In low-context cultures the situation is not allowed to change the meaning of words and behavior—the context conveys little or no extra information. This is quite useful and necessary in a country that is multicultural and where people's value systems and attitudes can be very different. The advertising use of a USP (Unique Selling Proposition)—for example, Head & Shoulders' "Up to 100 percent dandruff free"—works better in low-context cultures, while the advertising in high-context cultures such as Asia is more image-oriented (for example, Head & Shoulders emphasizes the luxuriant hair of a beautiful model with the dandruff differentiation secondary).

The differences between high- and low-context cultures can be quite subtle. Two researchers, Richard Nisbett and Takahiko Masuda from the United States and Japan, respectively, have shown that Westerners tend to attribute causation to objects and persons, while Asians attribute causation to social factors and context. In other words, the reason why something is done lies in the situation and not in the explicit desire of the individual. As a simple example, when experimenters asked students to take a picture of their fellow student, the results were revealing (see Exhibit 5.2).

High-context cultures can be found in most of the European countries, some of the Latin American countries (Chile, Mexico, perhaps Venezuela and Argentina), in Japan, and many of the newly industrializing Asian countries (including China and India). In countries with high-context cultures—such as Saudi Arabia and Japan—a written contract is not always enforceable if the situation changes or if new people move into executive positions.

Americans, because of their **diversity,** have a low-context culture. Low-context cultures can also be found in countries such as Australia and New Zealand with large immigrant populations. In such cultures, relying on "shared understandings" is risky.

Non-Verbal Communication

High-context cultures require a marketer to understand not only what is explicitly stated but also what is *not* being said. This is a pretty steep requirement when faced with a foreign language. Many new arrivals in a high-context culture can feel adrift. Finding it hard to decipher what people actually mean is a form of "culture shock." It helps to know what to look for and how to interpret non-verbal communication.

Hall identified five different categories of **silent languages**: space, material possessions, friendship patterns, agreements across cultures, and time.[7]

- *Space* relates to matters such as the distance between two people conversing. In the Middle East men will maintain an intimate distance, often too close for comfort for Western people. Moving away is impolite.
- *Material possessions* of course always speak volumes about one's station in life, particularly where social hierarchies are well-developed so that people learn what to look for. The emphasis on well-known brands in Asian markets, for example, reflects a need to clearly identify one's position with signals other people readily understand.
- *Friendship patterns* involve the degree to which friends can interact in business dealings and can be asked to do things, such as providing funds for investments. Family businesses are common in Arab and Latin countries, for example. By contrast, in some low-context cultures, even your best friend will refuse to lend you money for a taxi home—trust is low "on principle."
- *Agreements* across cultures affect the degree to which business can be transacted without a written legal document. Verbal contracts and a "handshake" are usually not sufficient in the United States, for example.
- *Time* is a confounding issue because different cultures consider punctuality a "must," while other cultures (Latin in particular) are very free about arrivals and departures. Punctuality itself is also different—a Japanese can come early and wait, while a German will not be seen before an appointed time.

More recently, non-verbal communication has expanded to include "body language." **Body language** is where attitudes and intentions are displayed without words, by body position, or by facial gestures such as a raised eyebrow, a smile, or a frown. It is one form of non-verbal communication that seems to be effective in both high- and low-context cultures.

One of the most prominent proponents of body language is Professor Amy Cuddy of Harvard University, whose TED presentation about her research on body language has been widely watched.[8] She suggests, for example, that if your body position is hunched, you signal submission and powerlessness. When you feel powerful, your body

EXHIBIT 5.3.
"The Scream" by Edvard Munch.
The iconic painting is a global image of expressionist art and of body language.

Edvard Munch, 1893.

position is more upright and alert, arms up to "dominate" another. The smile projects confidence, the crossed arms project determination, the raised hand conveys caution, and hesitation reveals uncertainty.

There is evidence that body language is universally understood. The expression of fear through screaming and holding the head with both hands, for example, is surely understood across cultures (see Exhibit 5.3).

Hofstede's Cultural Dimensions

The high- versus low-context distinction and the "silent languages" provide simple but useful concepts by which to think about various cultures. Hofstede's questionnaire study of IBM's employees around the globe in 1980 is a much more systematic assessment of cultures across countries.[9] It has also become the standard approach to cultural classification for global marketers.

According to Hofstede's survey findings, countries can be classified along four basic cultural dimensions. The first of **Hofstede's cultural dimensions** is **individualism versus collectivism.** In a collective society, the identity and worth of the individual is rooted in the social system, less in individual achievement. A second dimension is **high versus low power distance.** High power distance societies tend to be less egalitarian, while democratic countries exhibit low power distance.

Hofstede's third dimension, **masculine versus feminine,** captures the degree to which a culture reflects an assertive personality rather than a more relationship-oriented style and the corresponding values. Finally, weak versus strong **uncertainty avoidance** rates nations according to the level of risk tolerance or risk aversion among the people.

To display how countries and cultures score on the four dimensions, requires a four-dimensional graph. It is common to use simpler two-dimensional graphs. Exhibits 5.4 and 5.5 show how this works.

Exhibit 5.4 shows a graph of countries relatively high in Individualism, and how they score on small and large Power distance.

As can be seen from the "map," the Israelis and Spanish are both high on Individualism, but different from each other on the Power dimension. While Israelis are individualistic and egalitarian, Spanish are also individualistic but believers in formal authority. (Note that the distances between countries on the map represent the degree to which the countries differ culturally.)

But at the other end of the Individualism scale lies Collectivism. The lower half of the map in 5.4 is shown in Exhibit 5.5.

From this part of the map we see that the countries that are relatively Collectivist all score high on Power distance. Also striking in the map is perhaps that these countries belong to the "emerging" economies, where presumably individualist sentiments simply cannot be sustained. Being an Individualist requires a sufficient budget as we all know.

Looking at these kinds of maps, likely managerial difficulties can be uncovered. For example, Israeli and Indian scores are clearly diametrically opposed. While an

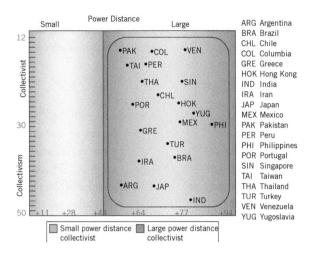

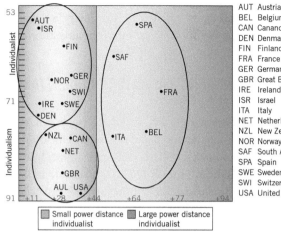

Israeli manager would act alone and treat others as equals, an Indian manager might be more successful first seeking support among peers and then imposing decisions on subordinates.

In some later applications Hofstede added a fifth dimension, **Confucian dynamics,** to distinguish the *long-term orientation* among Asian people, influenced by Confucius, the Chinese philosopher, from the more short-term outlook of Western people.[10] In 2010 he also added another dimension, **Indulgence versus Restraint.** *Indulgence* stands for a society that allows relatively free gratification of basic and natural human drives related to enjoying life and having fun. *Restraint* stands for a society that suppresses gratification of needs and regulates it by means of strict social norms.[11] An example of a simplified summary of cultural differences between three major regions is given in Exhibit 5.6.

EXHIBIT 5.4. (above right)
Individualist Countries

EXHIBIT 5.5. (above left)
Collectivist Countries

Source: Hofstede, 1980.

	Asia		Anglo-Saxon	W. Europe	
	Japan	China	(Canada, U.S., UK)	Northern	Continent
Individualism	Low	Low	High	High	High
Power distance	High	High	Low	Low	High
Masculinity	High	High	High	Low	High
Risk tolerance	Low	High	High	High	Low
Long-term view	High	High	Low	High	Low
Indulgence	Low	High	High	Low	High

EXHIBIT 5.6.

Hofstede's Classification of Triad Countries[12]

Adapted from G. J Hofstede and M. Minkov, Cultures and Organizations: Software of the Mind. McGraw-Hill, 2010.

The Hofstede mapping of countries is useful in that it offers a snapshot of the cultural distances between countries. Marketers can anticipate the degree to which marketing programs, especially communications and advertising or services, might need to be adapted to a new culture. For the multinational company with different product lines in different countries, a close look at these cultural distances can even help with choices about which line should be introduced in a new market.

Thinking along Hofstede's dimensions, managers can evaluate how difficult it may be to do business in a country culturally distant from their own and how severe a cultural shock they and their families are likely to get when moving to the country. The typical American manager going to run a subsidiary in a country whose culture is more risk-averse and less individualistic, with more power distance and reverence for authority than her or his own, might anticipate some difficulty adjusting.

ALTERNATIVE WAYS TO UNDERSTAND CULTURE

Several extensions of the Hofstede model have been proposed, some of which can be instructive and useful alternatives for global marketers. One direct extension is the ambitious GLOBE project, a more recent study of 62 countries that used measures drawn from Hofstede's work augmented by several additions.[13] GLOBE stands for "Global Leadership and Organizational Behavior Effectiveness." Perhaps not surprisingly, some of the extracted dimensions differed slightly from Hofstede's, and some counties were re-classified from collectivism to individualism.[14] Part of the explanation lies in the fact that cultures change as economic prosperity rises.

There are other alternatives to Hofstede, which also have found use among marketers. Here three versions will be briefly discussed.

Trompenaars and His Cultural Dilemmas[15]

The spiritual and intellectual heir to Hofstede is another Dutchman, Fons Trompenaars, a management scholar. Trompenaars' basic thrust is that culture is best viewed as "the way in which people solve cultural dilemmas." A few examples of such dilemmas:

Are people responsible for themselves only or do they take responsibility for a community?

Are people trying to do the "right" thing or are they pragmatic?

Do people judge an individual on the basis of achievement or on the basis of pedigree, status, connections?

Is a relationship "just business" or is "the whole person" involved?

These contrasts are in many ways an extension of Hofstede's dimensions.

Rapaille's Archetypes: Decoding Cultures[16]

Dr. G. Clotaire Rapaille is a French-born anthropologist living and working in the United States. He has more than 30 years of experience helping multinational businesses cope with cultural diversity. His experiences have been distilled into seven marketing "secrets" for understanding and, as he calls it, *decoding* cultures.

Rapaille's approach tends to treat culture as a person. The code is like the DNA of a person. Understanding a culture is similar to understanding a person. A striking illustration of the value of the approach is in his work on quality. Deciphering why the Japanese-inspired "Total Quality Control" programs had failed at AT&T, the giant telecommunications company, Rapaille found that "quality" had a different meaning for people from different cultures (see Exhibit 5.7).

In Japan, "quality" meant "perfection." In Germany, "quality" meant "according to standards." In France, "quality" meant "luxury." In the United States, "quality" meant simply "it works."

Gannon's Metaphors[17]

In practice, it is impossible for the global marketer to learn a great deal about all cultures. According to Gannon, a U.S. anthropologist, it is more effective to develop a holistic sense of a culture by creating an image (a metaphor) representing how the people think and behave.

Gannon suggests that the metaphor of American football captures many of the features of American culture, with its emphasis on competition, specialization of individual functions, strong leaders calling the plays, and the desire for individual recognition. By contrast, the German culture can be characterized by the classical symphony, with its strict discipline under a leader and skilled individuals performing together like a well-oiled machine. However simplified such metaphors are, Gannon argues, they give the manager the right mindset with which to approach customers, distribution middlemen, potential partners—and bureaucrats—in the foreign culture.

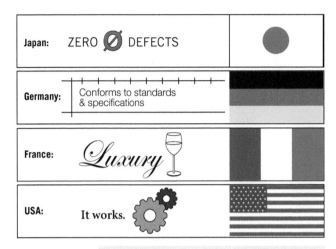

EXHIBIT 5.7.
The meaning of "Quality" in four countries

Source: Rapaille, 2001.

Ex. 5.7: Adapted from Rapaille (2001).

CULTURE AND CROSS-CULTURAL NEGOTIATIONS

Cross-cultural negotiations are a fact of life for the global marketer. Establishing a relationship with suppliers, distributors and other middlemen, and potential alliance partners invariably involves some kind of face-to-face negotiations. Foreign entry via licensing or a joint venture necessarily involves finding contract partners. Local marketing puts the marketer in direct contact with channel members who need to be convinced to carry the product. Global management involves trade-offs between local subsidiaries' autonomy and headquarters' need for standardization.

Researchers have analyzed negotiations in many cultures and identified four sequential stages that characterize information exchange in most business negotiations.[18]

1. *Non-task sounding.* This is an initial period when the conversation consists mainly of small talk, designed to get the partners to know each other better.
2. *Task-related exchange of information.* An extended period when the main issues are brought out, facts are presented, and positions clarified.
3. *Persuasion.* This is the stage when the parties attempt to make each other see the issues their way, when there is further explanation and elaboration of positions, and questioning of the other side's evidence.
4. *Concessions and agreements.* Toward the end of most negotiations is a period when mutual concessions might be made, when there is some yielding of fixed positions in order to reach an agreement. Agreements are usually confirmed with a handshake, regardless of cultures (see Exhibit 5.8).

Applying the framework to negotiations between Japanese and Americans, the significant cultural differences outlined in Exhibit 5.9 were identified. As can be seen, the length and the importance of the stages differ between the two countries. The Americans use less time for non-task soundings than the Japanese, and they are brief with explanations,

EXHIBIT 5.8.
Agreement is reached.
The end of a successful negotiation is usually accompanied by handshakes and smiles in most cultures. But getting there requires an understanding of how the negotiation stages are impacted by the cultural background of the participants.

while the Japanese are more thorough. The Japanese are likely to wait with concessions until the very end, while the Americans move toward an agreement by gradually yielding ground. Against this background it is hardly surprising if trade negotiators from Japan and the United

EXHIBIT 5.9.
Four stages of business negotiations[19]

Adapted from James Day Hodgson, Yoshihiro Sano, and John L. Graham, Doing Business with the New Japan: Succeeding in America's Richest International Market. Rowman & Littlefield, 2007.

STAGE

1. *Non-task sounding*
   Japanese: Considerable time and expense devoted to such efforts is the practice in Japan.
   Americans: Relatively shorter periods are typical.

2. *Task-related exchange of information*
   Japanese: This is the most important step—high first offers with long explanations and in-depth clarifications.
   Americans: Information is given briefly and directly. "Fair" first offers are more typical.

3. *Persuasion*
   Japanese: Persuasion is accomplished primarily behind the scenes. Vertical status relations dictate bargaining outcomes.
   Americans: The most important step: Minds are changed at the negotiation table and aggressive persuasive tactics are used.

4. *Concessions and agreement*
   Japanese: Concessions are made only toward the end of negotiations—holistic approach to decision-making. Progress is difficult to measure.
   Americans: Concessions and commitments are made throughout—a sequential approach to decision-making.

States sometimes seem to be in disagreement about how negotiations are progressing.

Negotiators from different cultures have also been classified as proactive "A" types (also called "hard" negotiators) or reactive "B" types ("soft" negotiators). Exhibit 5.10 identifies the major traits of three types of negotiators, where Type C (Chinese) has been added, based on the experience of a seasoned China negotiator, Ulf Andersson, CEO of iPlast in Sweden.

EXHIBIT 5.10.
Different types of negotiators[20]

Adapted from Jeswald W. Salacuse, The Global Negotiator: Making, Managing, and Mending Deals Around the World in the Twenty-First Century. Palgrave Macmillan Trade, 2015.

Trait	Type A (American) Negotiator	Type B (Japanese) Negotiator	Type C (Chinese) Negotiator
Goal	Contract	Relationship	Contract
Attitudes	Win/Lose	Win/Win	Win/Win
Personal styles	Informal	Formal	Formal
Communications	Direct	Indirect	Direct
Time sensitivity	High	Low	Low
Emotionalism	High	Low	Low
Agreement form	Specific	General	Specific
Agreement building	Bottom-up	Top-down	Top down
Team organization	One leader	Consensus	Consensus
Risk taking	High	Low	Low

The type A negotiator starts with the easily agreed-upon smaller details and works up, while the type B negotiator first wants to agree on the overall framework of the agreement. According to Andersson, "the Chinese are 70 percent Japanese and 30 percent American." Most of the traits in the list are self-explanatory. The "agreement building" trait refers to the process through which the agreement comes to its final form. As the list suggests, the type A negotiator is a more dynamic, energetic, and risk-taking entrepreneur while the B type is a slow, seasoned, mature individual who avoids risk. Either approach can work—which one is best depends on the cultures involved. It's when they clash that there may be trouble.

CULTURE, SALESMANSHIP, AND B2B MARKETING

Culture affects the "people skills" of the global marketer, the skills needed to deal with people and to be a good salesperson. Because of the importance of personal factors in selling, it is not surprising to find that good salesmanship varies across countries. Personal selling is usually the least global of all the marketing activities. As Percy Barnevik, former CEO of ABB (Asea Brown-Boveri), once put it: "When you are selling in Germany, your salesmen have to be German."[21]

Personal Salesmanship

Salesmanship is the art of making a sale to another person. There are some key personal characteristics of good salesmanship, such as appearance, enthusiasm, and self-confidence. These and other related factors all refer to the salesman as a person. He or she has to be a "good" person, someone one would like to do business with.

- *Appearance.* There is no doubt that appearance is a very important factor in international business dealings. The important features of a person's appearance are not the same everywhere. Asian nationals tend to be much less preoccupied with "good looks" and more concerned about appropriate clothing for the occasion than Westerners, whose individualism is usually given much more play. The astute salesperson will learn in-depth about the host country's particular customs.
- *Enthusiasm.* To the extent that enthusiasm reflects an interest in showing one's company and product in a positive light, it is certainly an asset in most countries. But excited delivery, a loud voice, and fast talking do not sit well in many cultures. The energy of enthusiasm needs to be carefully tempered abroad—it tends to go over best in "hard sell" situations of the kind typically encountered in New York, Mumbai, or Tel Aviv.
- *Self-confidence.* The same restraint is valid for self-confidence, that great asset of Western individualists. In cultures where group decisions are the norm, the role of self-confidence is appropriately reduced. A knowledgeable individual possessing confidence can make his or her voice heard, but self-confidence is no requirement for an influential presentation; the product and the company are what the individual has to sell, and the "self" should not get in the way.
- *"Good person."* Especially in high-context cultures, the objectives of the business transaction go beyond the immediate business proposition. In such cultures, the relationship can be so important that the "personal worth" of the salesperson becomes a much bigger issue than is customary in the American tradition.

The Western type of salespersons, enthusiastic and confident individuals asserting themselves as the "face" of their companies, can be unsuccessful in Eastern cultures, where individualism is subdued and the ultimate objective of the business transaction is more than just economic. But, as always, there are exceptions.

B2B Marketing

Marketing to local industrial buyers (business-to-business or B2B marketing) is strongly affected by culture. Not only does the purchasing agent's own cultural background play a role, but so does the culture of the organization.

A local B2B marketer with the appropriate customer orientation has to understand the local buyer's native culture and adjust the expectations and behavior accordingly. In addition, the buyer's position in the organization and which other players in the organization influence the buying decision are important factors to know. The proper perspective for the B2B marketer is to identify the role the product can play in making the buyer successful in his or her organizational role. In short, the local marketer should help the buying organization succeed and make the buyer look good—challenging tasks, especially in a foreign culture.

The buyer in an organization is usually only one of the actual decision-makers.

- *Buyers* are individuals with formal authority for selecting the supplier and arranging the terms of purchase.
- The *users* of the product or service—engineers, designers, manufacturing managers—often have more influence on the decision as to which supplier to choose.
- Higher-level *executives* might have to sign off on a purchase decision.

Apart from the line-and-staff linkages between these groups there can be other influencers—such as consultants—who can wield unseen authority. Informal organizational cultures—such as can be found in many young technology-driven organizations—are often more difficult to approach since lines of authority are not very clear.

The group decision-making in many industrial purchases means that cultural influences will be strong, both from the organizational culture and the culture at large. The **organizational culture** is defined by the routines and procedures for problem-solving and decision-making, "how we make decisions around here." Most organizations reflect the culture of the country or region where they are located, although there are instances of geocentric organizations that try to remove ethnocentric cultures from the organization (IBM, Philips, and Sony are some examples). In most instances, the local marketer, when approaching the customer, will have to be guided by both local cultural norms and the specific organizational culture involved.

Relationship Marketing

For the salesperson faced with the business-to-business marketing task, it is helpful to anticipate establishing a long-term relationship with the local buyer and the buying organization. **Relationship marketing** is the term applied to a marketing effort involving various personalized services, creation of new and additional services, and customizing a company's offering to the needs of a special buyer. Although the idea of relationship marketing is adaptable to consumer markets, it is obviously more applicable in business-to-business marketing. As an example, Citibank has tried to attract and build strong relationships with wealthy customers in many countries by offering extended banking hours, a separate lobby with attractive decor, comfortable seating, and sometimes free drinks. Needless to say, culture influences the creation of a strong relationship in myriad ways, including where to have dinner (Exhibit 5.11).

Relationship marketing takes a long-term view since without it the effort required to build a relationship is hardly worth it. The up-front costs of developing the mutual trust and confidence of a relationship are greater than the revenues from a single sale. A dependable relationship is beneficial to both parties in the long run. The buyer does not have to go through the negotiating process every time a purchase is required. The seller overcomes the barriers created against competitive entry, thus justifying the investment in learning about the organizational culture, the particular people involved, the product and service requirements, and the local culture. The relationship must create a win-win situation.

CULTURE AND CONSUMER CHOICE

In addition to being an influence on managerial behavior, culture is a strong determinant of consumer demand. For the marketer it is no longer sufficient to develop cultural sensitivity and to learn to accept individuals who act in strange ways. For marketing purposes learning about culture is useful mainly because culture is involved in understanding and predicting local buyer behavior.

Understanding Foreign Consumers

Understanding consumers in foreign cultures is often a baffling business. We see that they have common human needs through the life cycle. They grow up, fall in love, establish families, work hard, and grow old. Everybody has a life. But what kind of life, and what do people choose to make of it, and why?

Of course, many groups of people are more or less in the position of not being able to choose. A great number of people in the world live in relative poverty and showing them vast choices of brands, products, or lifestyles can be pointless or even counterproductive. They are likely to resent the inaccessible materialism they see advertised on the global communication highway.

But even among very poor people there are those who can and do, within limits, choose. The choices made will often astound an outsider. In a mud hut in central Africa, where clean water is scarce, one will find a Sony TV set. In India, a paradigm of a developing country, a poor farmer is happy to show off his new Philishave electric razor. And in China provinces, one can see Nissans and Toyotas navigating roads intended for oxcarts and Pedi cabs.

There are basically three fundamental facts about behavior that are necessary to recognize before trying to understand foreign consumers. They are

- a product's or service's core benefit,
- the goal orientation of consumer behavior everywhere,
- and the impact of social norms.

All three reflect cultural influences. In our home markets these are obvious effects and we do not usually think of them, which is why global marketers can go crucially wrong overseas. We will discuss each in turn.

EXHIBIT 5.11.
A neighborhood restaurant in Florence, Italy.
A rain delay for dinner is acceptable in Italy, but not in many other countries.

Photo by Michael T. Furick

Identify the Core Benefit

A necessary preliminary step in analyzing local consumers is to question what the product or service "means" to them. What does the product or service do for the buyer? How does it fit into the consumption and use pattern of the buyer? What are the core benefits?

This is not a question of lifestyle or preferences of the consumer but rather a question of what the product represents generically, what the core benefit is. And the core benefit often differs between local markets and cultures.

BOX: Fresh Fruit In Japan[22]

One of the long-enduring trade conflicts between Japan and other countries has been in the fresh fruit industry. Oranges from California, apples from Washington State, grapes from Chile, and bananas from the Philippines are only a few of the cases of entry being carefully examined and often stopped at the border. Japan's domestic fruit industry is small but strong politically.

The typical justification for keeping products off the Japanese markets is that they do not meet the standards expected by Japanese customers. Although this tends to hide the important reason of wanting to protect the domestic industry, for fresh fruits there is a grain of truth in this argument. This is not because Japanese consumers want quality per se—it has to do with the core benefit of fruit in Japan. Fresh fruit in Japan has always been viewed as a specialty, even luxury, product, usually bought during the gift-giving season. It had no particular role to play as a daily food supplement in salads, for snacks, and so on.

For example, fresh fruit in Japan has long been judged according to standards for apples at $5 apiece, cantaloupe at $40 a melon, and boxed grapes for $70, all turned out in beautifully wrapped *gift sets*. Not only did the customs officials deem the imported fruit below par, the consumer would not accept it. It was simply not expensive enough as a proper gift (see Exhibit 5.12).

It was not until fresh fruit took on the new core benefit of a *daily food supplement* that the imported fruit was accepted.

Some examples will clarify this. While the core benefit of an automobile may be transportation in some countries, especially large ones with a well-developed road network such as the United States, the auto is often a status symbol in less-developed countries. While disposable diapers may be bought for convenience in some countries, they are used for health reasons elsewhere. A credit card may offer more security and convenience than cash in some countries, while in others it offers a chance for parents to indulge their children. Even a simple product such as apples is not the same everywhere (see box, "Fresh Fruit in Japan").

While several benefits are intermingled in most markets, and some segments of a local market will emphasize some over the others, the identification of a different core benefit is a necessary first step in analyzing local customers.

Goal Orientation

When trying to understand foreign consumers, the good news is that there is one simple truth about buyer behavior in all markets. It is that most people are doing what they do for a reason. Consumers perceive a link between behavior and desired results. Buyers do not choose products or services for no reason, even in the most fatalistic of cultures. In other words, buyers are goal-oriented.

Thus, if one can find out what people in a local market are trying to achieve, one can start to understand their behavior. The global marketer should start by attempting to find out what motivates buyers by asking them what and why they buy, or by observing them buying certain products or choosing certain brands. The results of such

BOX: Finding the Hidden Motivators[24]

In the 1990s after Marriott, the American-based hotel chain, opened up a new luxury hotel in Jeddah, Saudi Arabia, it became an instant attraction for local luminaries and international travelers. The grandly decorated lobby with its large windows and magnificent entrance drew not only travelers and hotel guests but also local visitors. The large number of people crowded in the lobby delayed check-in and check-out operations, and long lines formed in front of the service counter. Early in the new millennium, managers of the Marriott headquarters in the United States proposed to install the new quick check-out system already in place in many of its hotels worldwide, which would allow the guests to leave quickly without waiting in line.

But when the system was proposed to local management, objections were immediately raised. The managers explained that the customers of the new Marriott wanted to spend time in the lobby, to see and be seen, and to enjoy the status it conveyed; the long lines supplied a simple but legitimate reason for doing this. It was decided that a more rapid check-out process would be a negative benefit and the proposal was scuttled.

EXHIBIT 5.12.
White peach in a Japanese gift package.
Unblemished and perfect, these peaches could easily cost as much as $8–10 each or $50 for a box of six, an acceptable lower limit for a seasonal gift.
The well-packaged and pricey fruit of Japan makes fruits a high-involvement item—you pay attention when you eat one.

Copyright © by Shutterstock/honobono.

an investigation are sometimes startling because of hidden motivators (see box, "Finding the Hidden Motivators").

Social Constraints

The third factor to remember is that the stress in the West on individual consumer choice is not necessarily the right way elsewhere. Where group pressures to comply are strong, as in many non-Western cultures, one can expect influence of social norms to override any individual evaluation. The individual consumer's attitudes, beliefs, and budget may suggest one choice, but social pressure mandates another choice. The evaluation of the available brands is modified by the social norms. The **social norms** involve two aspects: the social pressure and the individual's motivation to comply with it.

Social pressures are the normative suggestions that come from an individual's family, peer groups, social class, and other external forces. For example, an autoworker in Germany will face some pressure to buy a German car, regardless of individual preference. A successful pension fund manager in the city of London is more likely to wear an expensive Rolex than a cheap digital watch however versatile and reliable.

Motivation to comply relates to the willingness of the individual to listen to what others say and think. This is very much a matter of culture. In high context and homogeneous cultures where norms are both enforceable and enforced, the motivation to comply will usually be great. Most people will know what products, features, brands, and stores are "acceptable," and adhering to the norm will have tangible benefits.

The high value placed by Confucian cultures on the importance of social norms suggests that, in general, Eastern cultures show much more of an impact from social norms than do Western cultures. For example, in one study of Chinese and American consumers about green purchasing behavior, it was found that social norms exert stronger influences on Chinese consumers' behavioral intention than on American consumers.[25]

In another study of Korean consumers of luxury goods, conformity to social norms was a more important influence in their choices than what is commonly seen in Western countries.[26]

RELIGION

Today, religion has become a powerful cultural and political force. Many of the current ethnic and racial conflicts between nations have a religious basis. Most strikingly, the rise of international terrorism rests squarely on the rise of intolerant religious teachings. Up through 2006, the number of terrorism incidents attributable to political or nationalist-separatist or religious groups averaged around 250–300 a year each. After 2006, the number for political and nationalist groups has remained the same, while the number of incidents attributable to religious ideologies has risen three-fold, to about 1500 incidents a year in 2013.[27] In the last few years, many more fundamentalists have taken up arms in their "God's army."

Fundamentalism vs. Tolerance

This is not the place to discuss religions as such. Most major religions seem to have some fundamental documents that preach peace but also support violence. With the allegorical and metaphorical language often used, interpretations of a certain passage can vary from layperson to layperson, between academic experts, and even among the religious leaders. Religions rarely offer cut-and-dried answers. This has left the field wide open for preachers who claim to have ultimate authority for their own interpretation, convincing individuals in search of certainty to follow them.

Since the religions and their preachers tend to give conflicting messages to different groups, there is a problem in establishing a functioning social structure that can accommodate more than one dogma. One solution has been to separate worldly affairs from religious sentiment. "Render to Caesar the things that are Caesar's, and to God the things that are God's" in the words of the New Testament. Other countries have established national religions but allowed free worship under that umbrella—the solution for Henry VIII of England. In the United States with all religions deemed equal, the solution was to distinguish religious practices from other pursuits. Thus the United States' Constitution has explicitly separated religion from politics and state affairs.

In the Muslim religion, government is intrinsically religious, and legal rules and norms come directly from the Koran. In this sense, the Muslim is less tolerant of alternative worship. However, in the past, Islamic rulers have been accommodating to many non-believers. The religiously tolerant rule of the Muslims in Moorish Spain between 700–1500 has been well-documented. The Ottoman Empire (1453–1923) that began with the fall of Constantinople also allowed relatively free worship.

The rise of more fundamentalist sentiment among both Christians and Muslims, however, has recently challenged the status quo. This is a real threat not only internally to a nation, but certainly to relationships between nations. It is therefore a real threat to international business and marketing.

Major Religions

Exhibit 5.13 shows the current size and the projected growth of the major religions.

	2010 Population (Millions)	Percent of World Total 2010	Projected 2050 Population (Millions)	Percent of World Total 2050
Christians	2,168	31.4%	2,918	31.4%
Muslims	1,599	23.2%	2,761	29.7%
Unaffiliated	1,131	16.4%	1,230	13.2%
Hindus	1,032	15.0%	1,384	14.9%
Buddhists	487	7.1%	486	5.2%
Folk religions	404	5.9%	449	4.8%
Other religions	58	0.8%	61	0.7%
Jews	13	0.2%	16	0.2%
World total	6,895	100.0%	9,307	100.0%

EXHIBIT 5.13.
World population shares of major religious groups

Source: Pew Research Center.

Source: The Future of World Religions: Population Growth Projections, 2010–2050, Pew Research Center.

Among the Christians, about half (1.1 billion) are Catholic. There are also 400 million (6 percent) with traditional or "folk religions" in China, Africa, and among Native Americans and Australian Aborigines. The Vedic origin refers to the original Veda scriptures from Persia and India, the earliest literary record of Indo-Aryan civilization. "Veda" means wisdom, knowledge, or vision. Vedic scriptures are the most sacred books of India. The laws of the Vedas regulate the social, legal, domestic, and religious customs of the Hindus to the present day.[28] Buddhism has similar roots, but Buddha essentially rejected some of the Vedic pronouncements, including the caste system, finding the Brahmins too intolerant and Hinduism too constrained for enlightenment.

The three Abrahamic religions all originate with Abraham as a real historical person, typically conceived as a direct descendant of Adam. Abrahamic religions teach monotheism, that there is one God only although the name might be The Lord, Allah, or Yahweh. One important difference between the three religions is who was a true messenger from the one God. In Judaism, the Messiah has yet to come. For Christians, Jesus was the Messiah. For Muslims, the true messenger and last prophet of Allah was Muhammad.

By 2050 Muslims and Christians will represent over 60 percent of the world's population. As can be seen from Exhibit 5.13, the main factor in the growth comes from Muslims. Christians maintain their share, and other religions decline. These differences would seem quite minor were it not for the fact that both Christians and Muslims have been tasked by their spiritual leaders to convert the unbelievers to the "right" religion. This is one reason why these religions have become the two major religions in the world today. Considering the political and military might of the countries behind them, it is also not surprising if today they find themselves in an increasingly violent conflict. The late eminent scholar Samuel Huntington presciently foresaw a "Clash of Civilizations" in a 1996 book. The international terrorism threat discussed in the previous chapter derives precisely from this religious impulse, driven by some fundamentalists' beliefs about the need to fight for Islam (the "jihad").

Religion as Part of Culture

Religions in general tend to be conservative, emphasizing tradition over innovation. They tend to define the significance of individual lives as part of a greater whole. This works differently for collectivist and individualistic cultures.

In collective societies, the individual life is embedded in a clear fabric, such as a family, tribe, or social circle. In individualist societies, this fabric is weak or nonexistent—each individual life is singular and "special."

The "meaning" of one's life is less at issue in collectivist societies; people know "who they are" from birth. In strong family-oriented cultures, for example, one's family name, age order in the family, heritage from grandparents, and so on help define one's identity. In individualistic cultures, one's identity is more ephemeral, and usually tied to one's career achievements and worldly possessions. You are what you do or what you have acquired, not what you were born into.

Capitalist economies tend to kindle the latter view of the individual. American marketing assumes that products will make you happy and satisfied with your life. It might be fine as far as it goes, but for most individuals, "more stuff" cannot be all there is to life.

The differences between individualism and collectivism cultures are not hard or clear all the time, but they have become emphasized by the rise of global terrorism. We learn that many of the terrorists are in fact well-educated individuals who have grown disenchanted with the "empty" lives of Western capitalism. The terrorists tend to come from—or know of—more collectivist cultures where the identity and the meaning of one's life are clearer. They find "meaning" in the kind of violence that seems senseless to the average observer. Their lives become "significant."[29]

It is easy to dismiss these people as "failures," thinking that they have failed to accumulate enough goods or have not achieved their career goals. But this argument, although sometimes true, misses the point that products (or worldly achievement) can in general not be counted on to deliver consistent happiness and satisfaction. As all cultures (and religions) will tell you, once you reach a certain level, there will always be the question, "What is next?" Even winning the Super Bowl—or collecting all of Beyoncé's music—will not ensure a happy life, and it will not suffice to bring meaning to your life. One reason people are willing—perhaps even hope—to die for their country (or religion) is precisely that it does give them meaning, forever.

This would seem to be far away for global marketing concerns. But it is important that the marketer remembers that products are basically just that, products, and that money can't buy happiness. What free markets offer traditional countries are more products and services. For poorer countries, this is undoubtedly a good thing. Lifting people out of poverty and ill health should be a welcome gift everywhere. But if the gift carries with it a threat to the established order, culture, and religion, we should not be surprised that some will reject it. A promise of a materially better life will seem "empty" to many if it only means the erosion of one's place in the universe.

Religion-Based Segmentation

The result of the worldwide conflict has been a heightened religious preoccupation in various countries. Today, with the rise of ethnic and national pride, environmental concern, and local sensitivity, an increasing number of consumers buy products and brands—or don't buy—based on other principles than materialistic wants and needs.

This also includes religious considerations. It is no longer sufficient for an entering company to provide a better product or faster service or less expensive goods. They must now make sure that local religious sensibilities do not get ruffled—if they do, the entering company may not simply lose a sale but even be confronted with boycotts and even more violent attacks. A few examples can be used to illustrate that this is a problem not only among Islamic countries but elsewhere as well.

- Nike offended Muslims in June 1997 when the "flaming air" logo for its Nike Air sneakers looked too similar to the Arabic form of God's name, "Allah". Nike pulled more than 38,000 pairs of sneakers from the market.[30]
- In 2006 Danish firms were faced with a consumer boycott of their goods in the Arab world following a furor over cartoons of the prophet Muhammad published in a Danish newspaper. The Danish toy-maker Lego said its products had been taken off the shelves of stores in Qatar, Kuwait, and the United Arab Emirates. Iran cut all trade ties to Denmark, which exports some $280m (£160.9m) worth of goods to Iran each year.[31]
- Lowe's Home Improvement stores sponsored a U.S. television program called "All-American Muslim," which intended to introduce American society to mainstream Islamic adherents. After a conservative group known as the Florida Family Association began encouraging companies to pull their sponsorship from the program because "the Islamic agenda's clear and present danger to American liberties and traditional values," Lowe's and other firms stopped purchasing commercials. The program was canceled.[32]
- Hobby Lobby is an American arts and crafts store chain that very openly embraces Christianity. The company closes its more than 500 stories on Sundays. Its statement of purpose says: "We believe that it is by God's grace and provision that Hobby Lobby has endured. He has been faithful in the past, we trust Him for our future."[33] In 2017 the company returned about 5000 ancient artifacts that had been bought from tomb breakers in Iraqi battlefields.
- In 2008 Ford Motor Company was faced with a boycott by the conservative American Family Association because of "crude" ads. Interestingly, these ads were in European publications. Ford's U.S. dealers were buttonholed after church services by Americans telling them to pull the ads in Europe. "Have you seen these magazine ads in Norway or England? They are disgusting." Ford decided to pull the ads in Europe even though those dealers did not go to church.[34]

MULTICULTURALISM

The fragmentation of the country markets also involves what is called "multiculturalism." As the word indicates, a multicultural nation is one where the population can be divided into several cultural groups. This is of course true of a number of nations. China and Russia are good examples, as are the United States, Canada, Australia, and New Zealand, all nations established by immigrants. These countries and many like them are each home to a number of different cultural groups. What distinguishes "multiculturalism" is that the concept refers to a perspective that these groups are "separate but equal." This is in contrast to the "melting pot" notion, which is that there is a central mainstream culture, and the nation's population should gradually assimilate into that main culture.

The "melting pot" was long the model for the United States. By contrast, the multiculturalism idea was long the model for Canada, where it also was known as the "salad bowl" (since there is no real melting together of lettuce and tomato). Multiculturalism goes very well with the new emphasis on cultural identity and pride. One example of multiculturalism is the Black Panther movement of the 1960s in the United States, and also the gender equality movement and the LGBT (lesbian, gay, bisexual, and transgender) movement later on.

It is important for the international marketer to be attuned to these different movements and how they affect organizations and markets in different countries around the world.[35] Multiculturalism tends to divide markets into smaller specific segments. But the general increase in cultural and especially religious sensitivity will often go counter to one or more of these new groupings. Gender equality ideals do not usually go over well in Islamic countries, for example, where the female's role is very constrained. Among fundamentalist Christians, homosexuality and especially gay marriage is anathema, and literally so. It is easy to see that some marketing decisions can easily offend one or two of the tenets of these groups. Two examples:

- In 2012, Ellen DeGeneres, an openly gay celebrity, was picked as a spokesperson by JC Penney, a large department store. An organization named One Million Moms complained loudly: "JC Penney seems to think hiring an open homosexual spokesperson will help their business when most of their customers are traditional families." The organization asked for a boycott of the store. Although management held fast and some customers voiced support, the store has not had very strong results after that.[36]
- In 2013 American bars and restaurants announced boycotts of Russian-made spirits, liquors, and foods to protest recent anti-gay laws implemented by the Russian government. The move protests new Russian laws that ban public displays of gay affection, including men holding hands, or displaying symbols like a rainbow flag.[37]

Multiculturalism is a movement that conflicts with the idea that all of us live in the same "one world." In a multicultural world, each one of us lives in our own world. The popular 1971 Coca-Cola commercial "I'd like to buy the world a Coke" is a much better fit with the original idea that we all want the same thing.[38] Coke may be the iconic American drink, but it belongs to the "melting pot" generations of the past. Today, the U.S. has become a multicultural fragmented society.

SUMMARY

Culture involves the fundamental values that guide our lives. This is why a large part of culture relates to religion. With the recent rise of fundamentalist sentiments in the major religions, Christianity and Islam, culture with its religious roots has come to play an increasing role in international marketing. It is one of the reasons why global marketing has increasingly stressed adaptation and localization in recent years. It has become important that global brands adapt their offerings to local guidelines and cultural norms.

Culture directly affects how to do business in various countries. In particular, culture affects how negotiations should be carried out. But culture also affects consumer choice, how people behave and their preferences. These issues are much more central for most international marketing efforts, since they affect all the product, price, distribution, and promotion decisions directly. Generally speaking, global localization means that entrants need to adapt to the underlying value system of each market—or at least avoid antagonizing the citizens. But the behavior and preferences of individual consumers are usually malleable and not set in stone. With proper attention to underlying values and avoiding cultural traps, a global marketer can persuade consumers to accept a new offering and change behavior as well as preferences.

Without challenging the underlying value system, international marketers can often propose new and better ways of doing things, get a teenager to upgrade from "cool" torn jeans, change preconceived notions about what food should taste like, and even persuade a beer drinker to switch to wine. It does not always work, but it can be worth a try. So while adaptation to local market preferences might be useful in the short run, it is important to "seize the day" sometimes and propose something fresh. That can work well, provided the fundamental and underlying value system is not directly threatened.

KEY TERMS

body language
Confucianist dynamics
core benefit
cultural adaptation
cultural dilemmas
culture
diversity
high- and low-context cultures
high versus low power distance
Hofstede's cultural dimensions
individualism versus collectivism
learned behavior
managerial styles

masculine versus feminine
multicultural
nonadaptation
non-verbal communication
Rapaille's archetypes
relative income
"silent languages"
transparency
trust
type A negotiator
type B negotiator
uncertainty avoidance
universalist

DISCUSSION QUESTIONS

1. An American manager can often be heard to start out saying, "Well, the way I see it …" while a Norwegian as often will start with, "Well, as we all know …." What cultural explanation can you find for this?

2. Look for the websites of a few of the companies mentioned in this book. To what extent do they attempt to create a relationship with you? For example, do they offer screensavers with their logo for downloading, offer more information at your request, or allow you to use the site interactively? How many languages are available? Any differences for companies from different countries?

3. Discuss the extent to which electronic commerce (online purchases, Internet shopping, etc.) might be acceptable to a culture. Does this have anything to do with Hall's or Hofstede's dimensions? Give examples of cultures that would be reluctant to accept electronic commerce and others that might accept it more easily.

4. What behavioral differences would you expect to find between the managers in a large Chinese multinational and in a German MNC in the same industry? What factors might make their behavior very similar?

5. In negotiations it is often said that "silence is golden." Give an example of what this might mean. What kind of culture would you expect to favor that rule, high context or low context?

TEAM CHALLENGE PROJECTS

1. Cultures differ in terms of their aesthetic preferences and these play a major role in the design of a product and packaging. Color is a primary example with some colors such as green and blue having universal feelings of peace and gentleness associated with them. The "meaning" and feelings associated with other colors, however, can vary by culture. (In the U.S., wearing black to a funeral is customary but in other cultures wearing black to a funeral might be considered rude.) Find examples of the cultural differences associated with other colors. Explain the cultural reasons that determine this color usage.

2. Like a country, a company has a culture that provides a source of advantage and disadvantage. Team 1: Pick a company that you would like to work for upon graduation and explain its culture. Outline the type of employee who would perform well. Team 2: Pick a company that you would not like to work for upon graduation specifically because of its undesirable corporate culture. Outline the type of employee who would perform well.

3. Certain Muslim countries (Saudi Arabia, for example) do not, for religious reasons, allow women to appear in public showing their hair. Additionally women cannot be shown in advertising with their hair exposed. You are the global manager for haircare goods for a large American consumer products company and you want to enter the Saudi marketplace with your haircare items. Team 1: Develop the 4Ps for entry. Team 2: Develop the presentation that explains why you are NOT entering the Saudi market.

4. Video gaming has been slow to develop in Germany. Many Germans feel that their time is better spent on education or careers rather not sitting in front of a TV playing a video game. As a result, for many years Germany has had a strongly reading-oriented culture. In addition, German decency laws are possibly the strictest in the world and limit content video games can display. Game makers have tried to adjust, for example, by leaving out WW2 Nazi references and changing blood colors from red to green. Team 1: Create a list of marketing actions you might take to energize video-game sales in Germany. Team 2: Develop a presentation that convinces your company to abandon Germany for video-game sales.

5. Team 1: Use the Hofstede scales to explain the differences between German and American car manufacturers. Team 2: Use the Hofstede scales to explain the differences between Korean and American car manufacturers.

SELECTED REFERENCES

Brewer, Paul and Sunil Venaik, "Individualism-Collectivism in Hofstede and GLOBE," *Journal of International Business Studies*, Vol. 42, No. 3, April 2011, pp. 436–445.

Chan, Ricky Y. K. and Lorett B. Y. Lau, "Explaining Green Purchasing Behavior: A Cross-Cultural Study on American and Chinese Consumers," *Journal of International Consumer Marketing*, Volume 14, Issue 2–3, 2002, pp. 9–40.

Cuddy, Amy. "Your Body Language Shapes Who You Are," *TED Global 2012*.

Davidson, Amy, "The Attack on 'All-American Muslim'" *The New Yorker*, Dec 13, 2011.

Gannon, Martin J. and Rajnandini (Raj) K. Pillai, *Understanding Global Cultures: Metaphorical Journeys through 31 Nations, Clusters of Nations, Continents, and Diversity*. 5th ed. Thousand Oaks, CA: SAGE, 2012.

Gemperlein-Schirm, Riddley, "The Most Expensive Fruits in the World," May 24, 2014 (http://firstwefeast.com/eat/worlds-most-expensive-fruits/).

Hall, Edward T. *Beyond Culture*. Garden City, NY: Anchor, 1976.

———, "The Silent Language in Overseas Business." *Harvard Business Review*, May-June 1960, pp. 87–96.

Hall, Edward T., and Mildred Reed Hall. *Understanding Cultural Differences*. Yarmouth, ME: Intercultural Press, 1990.

Hodgson, James Day, Yoshihiro Sano and John L. Graham, *Doing Business with the New Japan: Succeeding in America's Richest International Market*. 2nd ed. Lanham, MD: Rowman & Littlefield, 2007.

Hofstede, Geert. *Culture's Consequences*. Beverly Hills, CA: Sage, 1980.

———, "The Confucius Connection: From Cultural Roots to Economic Growth." *Organizational Dynamics* 16, no. 4 (Spring 1988), pp. 5–21.

———, Hofstede, G. J. & Minkov, M. (2010). *Cultures and Organizations: Software of the Mind* (Rev. 3rd ed.). New York: McGraw-Hill.

House, R.J., P.J. Hanges, M. Javidan, P.W. Dorfman and G. Vipin. *Culture, leadership, and organization: The GLOBE study of 62 societies*. Thousand Oaks, CA: Sage, 2004.

Ito, Kenzo and John Dyck, "Fruit Policies in Japan," *USDA*, FTS 341-01, April 2010.

Karabell, Shellie, "Putin's Problem: Corruption, Not Just Sanctions," *Forbes, Leadership*, Dec, 22, 2014.

Leung, Wency. "Faith in Boycotts: Can Religious Groups Affect the Bottom Line?" *The Globe and Mail*, Feb. 27, 2012.

Lücke, Gundula, Tatiana Kostova and Kendall Roth, "Multiculturalism from a cognitive perspective: Patterns and implications," *Journal of International Business Studies,* Vol. 45, Mo. 2, Feb/Mar 2014, pp.169–190.

Nisbett, Richard E. and Takahiko Masuda, "Culture and Point of View," *Proceedings of the National Academy of Science of the United States of America,* vol. 100 no. 19, 2003, pp. 11163–11170, doi: 10.1073/pnas.1934527100.

Park, , Hye-Jung, Nancy J. Rabolt, Kyung Sook Jeon, "Purchasing Global Luxury Brands among Young Korean Consumers," *Journal of Fashion Marketing and Management: An International Journal,* Vol. 12, No. 2, (2008), pp. 244–259.

Rapaille, G. Clotaire. *7 Secrets of Marketing in a Multi-Cultural World.* Provo, UT: Executive Excellence Publishing, 2001.

——, *The Culture Code: An Ingenious Way to Understand Why People Around the World Live and Buy as They Do.* New York: Crown Business, 2007.

——, *The Global Code: How a New Culture of Universal Values is Reshaping Business and Marketing.* London: Palgrave Macmillan Trade, 2015.

Requejo, William Hernandez and John L. Graham, *Global Negotiation: The New Rules.* London: Palgrave Macmillan Trade, 2014.

Salacuse, Jeswald W. *The Global Negotiator: Making, Managing, and Mending Deals Around the World in the Twenty-First Century.* London: Palgrave Macmillan Trade, 2015.

Shaw, Alexis and Kirit Radia. "Russia's Anti-Gay Laws Incite Push for Russian Liquor, Food Boycott," *ABC News,* Aug. 5, 2013.

Shenkar, Oded, "Cultural Distance Revisited: Toward a More Rigorous Conceptualization and Measurement of Cultural Differences," *Journal of International Business Studies,* 32, no. 3 (2001), 519–535.

——, "Beyond Cultural Distance: Shifting to a Friction Lens in the Study of Cultural Differences," *Journal of International Business Studies,* 43, no. 1 (2012), pp. 12–17.

Sieczkowski, Cavan, "Ellen DeGeneres Ad: One Million Moms Angry Over JC Penney Christmas Commercial," *The Huffington Post,* 2012.

Steger, Jason, "Jo Nesbø's Hole story," *Sydney Morning Herald,* Feb 18, 2012.

Sullivan, Kevin. "For Danish Firms, Boycott in Mideast a 'Nightmare'" *Washington Post Foreign Service,* February 11, 2006.

Taylor, William. "The Logic of Global Business: An Interview with ABB's Percy Barnevik," *Harvard Business Review,* March-April 1991 Issue.

Temple, Emily, "The Best-Selling Books in 10 Countries around the World," *Flavorwire.com,* Feb. 3, 2013.

Toren, Ben, "8 Apparel Mistakes," *Fortune,* July 20, 2012.

Trompenaars, Fons and Charles Hampden-Turner, *Riding the Waves of Culture: Understanding Diversity in Global Business,* 3rd ed. New York: McGraw-Hill, 2012.

Weidenhamer, Deb. "Customer Service, Chinese Style," *The New York Times Online*/Boss blogs, Feb. 14, 2014.

White, Martha C" "Ikea's Saudi Arabian Catalog is Missing Something: Women," *NBC News, Business,* October 1, 2012.

Yuen, Laura, Mukhtar Ibrahim, Sasha Aslanian, "From MN Suburbs, They Set Out to Join ISIS," *MPRNews,* Mar 25, 2015.

ENDNOTES

1. See Steger, 2012.
2. The overview is from Temple, 2013.

3. Reported in Weidenhamer, 2014.
4. Karabell, 2014.
5. As reported by White, 2012.
6. From Nisbett and Masuda, 2003.
7. Hall, 1960.
8. See Cuddy, 2012.
9. Hofstede, 1980, still is the basic reference.
10. Hofstede, 1988.
11. In Hofstede, Hofstede, and Minkov, 2010.
12. Adapted from Hofstede, 1980, 1988, and Hofstede, Hofstede, and Minkow 2010.
13. See House et al., 2004.
14. See, for example, Brewer and Venaik, 2011.
15. See Trompenaars and Hampden-Turner, 2012.
16. From Rapaille, 2001, 2007, 2015.
17. From Gannon and Pillai, 2012.
18. See, for example, Requejo and Graham, 2014, and Salacuse, 2015.
19. Adapted from Hodgson, Sano, and Graham, 2007.
20. Adapted from Salacuse, 2015.
21. See Taylor, 1991.
22. See Ito and Dyck, 2010.
23. Gemperlein; Shirn, 2014.
24. Source: Bruce Wolff, Vice President of Distribution Sales, Marriott Hotels, Class Presentation at Georgetown University 2005.
25. Chan and Lau, 2002.
26. From Park, Rabolt, and Jeon, 2008.
27. Data from Global Terrorism Index, Vision of Humanity 2015: http://www.visionofhumanity.org.
28. Retrieved from http://hinduism.about.com/cs/vedasvedanta/a/aa120103a.htm, accessed 3/3/2015.
29. There are ongoing discussions of what actually motivates Western youth to become terrorists. This is from Yuen, Ibrahim, and Aslanian, 2015.
30. From Toren, 2012.
31. See Sullivan, 2006.
32. See Davidson, 2011.
33. The quote is from the website, http://www.hobbylobby.com/our_company/.
34. As reported by Leung, 2012.
35. See, for example, Lücke, Kostova, and Roth, 2014.
36. From Sieczkowski, 2012.
37. As reported by Shaw and Radia, 2013.
38. As of May 2015, the video was still on YouTube: https://www.youtube.com/watch?v=1VM2eLhvsSM.

ABSTRACT

In 1986 the Hyundai Excel became the most successful foreign car launch in U.S. history. Then, plagued by a reputation for producing low-quality cars, sales began to drop dramatically in the early 1990s. Uneven quality control produced automobiles with a shaky reputation among U.S. buyers.

Hyundai (B) is a continuation of the four-part Hyundai case study.

HYUNDAI (B)

"Focus groups told us that Elantra didn't look or feel like a Hyundai, and we took that as a positive sign."
Tom Ryan, Vice President-Marketing, Hyundai Motor America

Hyundai spent more than $270 million on research and development in 1990, attempting to counter the innovations of Japanese automobile producers who had been spending at a rate 10 times that of Hyundai. They invested $2.6 billion in new capacity, including a third assembly plant at Ulsan.

The Hyundai Scoupe, a sporty model priced at less than $9,000, was introduced in 1990 with the tagline, "Hyundai. Yes. Hyundai." A turbocharged Scoupe was launched in 1991, not to achieve high sales but specifically "to help improve the image of Hyundai technology."

In September 1991, Hyundai announced their Value Care program for the Elantra. The program paid for all maintenance and repairs on the car for the first two years or 24,000 miles. The program covered oil changes, filters, wipers, tires, and almost any other repair or maintenance expense. Estimated costs of the plan to Hyundai were about $500–$600 per car. By December the program was extended to the other cars in the Hyundai line—Excel, Sonata, and Scoupe. Don Hicks, owner of Shortline Hyundai in Aurora, Colorado, said, "In focus groups, customers are saying, 'Hyundai wouldn't make a promise like that if the cars weren't good.' Hyundai has to overcome a reputation for having throwaway cars. This is helping."[1]

As Tom Ryan, vice president of marketing for Hyundai Motor America, declared, "We have to overcome the perceived risk of buying a Hyundai product. Our research shows that we are better than the perception. Image is our biggest problem."[2]

---

* This case was prepared by Don Sexton, Professor of Marketing, Director, Center for International Business Education and Research, Columbia Business School. This case was sponsored by the Chazen Institute and the Columbia University Center for International Business Education and Research (CIBER).

Hyundai also increased their efforts to monitor customer satisfaction. They instituted a program of contacting each Hyundai purchaser a week after the sale and service customers a week after their appointment to ask "every question J.D. Power [a firm that evaluates products and services] would ask."[3] Dealers that received the highest customer satisfaction evaluations were rewarded.

Executive vice president and chief operating officer Rod Hayden commented:

> If we're spending $1,000 on a rebate on an automobile and another $700 to $800 [per car] to buy advertising, and [the customer] has a $100 item that goes wrong after warranty and you [get them angry], you've gained nothing and you've lost that customer. ... All we have to do is fix or have one less problem per car and we'll be in the middle of the pack on CSI [Customer Satisfaction Index].[4]

DISCUSSION QUESTIONS

1. What research did Hyundai do to identify its brand image in the United States? What else could they have done? Should they have spent more on market research? Why, why not?
2. What did Hyundai do to improve its brand image in the United States? Anything else they could have done?

REFERENCES

Bank, D. and Leyden, P. "The Once-Hot Hyundai Takes a Dive in Sales," *St. Petersburg Times,* June 10, 1990.

Breese, K. S., "Hyundai Hopes to Improve Image with Elantra Freebies," *Automotive News,* September 2, 1991.

Breese, K. S., "Hyundai Tries Free Maintenance to Repair Image," *Automotive News,* January 27, 1992.

Gadacz, O., "Hyundai Unveils Turbo Scoupe: Hopped-Up Version Hits U.S. for '93," *Automotive News,* December 16, 1991.

Kiley, D., "The Only Good Hyundai Is an Elantra," *Adweek,* October 7, 1991.

Kiley, D., "Hyundai, Maybe, Hyundai," *Adweek,* September 17, 1990.

ENDNOTES

1. Breese, K. S., "Hyundai Hopes to Improve Image with Elantra Freebies," *Automotive News,* September 2, 1991.
2. Breese, K. S., "Hyundai Hopes to Improve Image."
3. Breese, K. S., "Hyundai Hopes to Improve Image."
4. Breese, K. S., "Hyundai Hopes to Improve Image."

IN 2001, THE SENIOR MANAGEMENT TEAM OF the Mad Science Group was considering how best to go on growing revenues. It had developed a solid business model through franchising and was well-positioned in the major markets of Canada and the United States. It had also developed the Mad Science brand through other activities and partnerships. Mad Science had achieved a limited presence in a number of international markets and was now wondering whether Mexico would be a good expansion route for the company.

COMPANY BACKGROUND

The company's business involved transforming laboratory science into fun, interactive learning experiences for kids from kindergarten to sixth grade. The programs were divided into six areas of business: after-school programs, in-class workshops, birthday parties, summer and vacation camps, special events, and preschool programs. The founders of Mad Science—brothers Ariel and Ron Shlien—had a profound interest in science and this was central to their business idea. As children, the brothers conducted science experiments to amuse themselves and their friends. Later, they ran shows for kids in summer camp and at the YMCA and realized they had found a healthy business opportunity.

In 1985, Ariel and Ron established The Mad Science Group in Montreal, Quebec. They ran the company from their basement on a part-time basis over the next 10 years, including the period while they were studying commerce at McGill University. Many of the course projects undertaken at McGill focused on their fledgling company. After graduation, the brothers employed full-time people to work in the company but, because they were uncertain about the potential for

"Science can be fun"

Copyright © by Shutterstock/Poznyakov.

[1] This case was prepared by Professor Philip Rosson of Dalhousie University as a basis for class discussion rather than to illustrate either the correct or incorrect handling of an administrative situation. It was prepared using secondary sources of information and benefited from the research assistance of Rachelle Jackowski. The financial assistance of the Centre for International Business Studies, Dalhousie University, and the Atlantic Canada Opportunities Agency in preparation of the case is gratefully acknowledged.

Mad Science, took full-time positions elsewhere. After about two years, however, they were more convinced about the long-term prospects for the business and devoted themselves to it totally.

The brothers began to realize that Mad Science had wide appeal when they received phone calls from parents who had used their services in Montreal but could find nothing similar since relocating to Toronto, New York, or Florida. This was further confirmed in 1990 when Mad Science entered into an agreement to give its science shows on cruise ships catering to school kids from more than 50 countries. The kids loved the science shows and it became clear that Mad Science had an offering with nearly universal appeal (Kucharsky, 2001).

CURRENT OPERATIONS

Franchising emerged as a business model that would allow Mad Science to expand without requiring substantial investment. The company sold its first franchise in San Diego in 1995 for U.S.$23,000, followed by many others. Sales quadrupled between 1995 and 1997. Revenues grew to about $4 million in 1999, with profits totaling almost $1 million (Oliver, 2003).

In 2001, Mad Science had over 130 franchisees, located in Canada (21 franchisees), the U.S. (86), and overseas (29, in several countries). These franchisees entertained over five million children through about 150,000 interactive presentations annually. Success was viewed as resulting from the novel business idea and the dedication of the team of people who made the science shows come alive.

The Shliens' approach emphasized educating and exciting children about science and how the world works. Because company "performers" were able to spark the imagination and curiosity of children aged three to 12 years old, parents were prepared to pay $75 for an after-school program, or $150 for a private party. In response to customer requests, the services offered by Mad Science grew to include events such as preschool and in-class workshops, camps, birthday parties, and special events.

Mad Science was not just a franchise organization (or franchisor). Its business strategy emphasized brand building and it had entered into several partnership agreements with a view to further development. For example, Scholastic Press had published 12 Mad Science books with toys and workbooks through an exclusive deal. Plans were to expand this partnership through distribution to 10,000 retailers internationally. Mad Science also had a substantial presence at the Kennedy Space Center in Florida, where children learned about space through 3-D stereoscopic shows, animation, and live actors. In addition, the company had a production company (Mad Science Productions) that traveled from city to city, offering shows in large-scale theatrical venues. It was considering moving the Mad Science brand and approach into television, with all the attendant merchandising possibilities (e.g., toys, clothes, CD-ROMS, etc.) that could flow from a successful TV series (Smith, 2001).

In summary, by 2001 Mad Science had a strong franchisee network in numerous locations as well as a growing number of activities that focused on building the Mad Science brand at the household level. Senior management believed that these two elements of Mad Science's business had a reinforcing effect on one another.

FUTURE GROWTH

Not content to simply maintain business operations, the senior management team was considering a number of expansion strategies.

1. Mad Science could grow its business through signing franchisee agreements in areas of Canada and the U.S. where service gaps existed.
2. Another possibility was to expand more aggressively in international markets.
3. Mad Science could concentrate on developing its non-franchisee activities (e.g., television shows).
4. A further option was for the company to pursue some combination of strategies 1–3.

The international expansion strategy is examined below for Mexico.

Economic Indicators

One foreign market on the radar screen of the senior managers of Mad Science was Mexico. Since the North American Free-Trade Agreement (NAFTA) was signed in 1994, trade and investment flows between Canada, Mexico, and the U.S. had increased sharply and Mad Science felt that it was important to explore business opportunities. In order to analyze the attractiveness of the Mexican market, Mad Science scanned excerpts from a recent report on Mexico (Table 1). Several economic indicators were also assembled that enabled rough comparisons to be made between the company's two major markets (Canada and the U.S.) and Mexico (see Table 2). Some indicators provided clues about general market potential (e.g., GDP), whereas others were generally (e.g., population) or more specifically (e.g., cable television subscribers) related to Mad Science's business offering.

National Cultures

One of the senior managers at Mad Science felt that any economic analysis of Mexico should be supplemented with consideration of cultural factors that could impact on business development. She became aware of a large-scale study showing that four main factors explained significant differences in national cultures. The factors are shown in Table 3, along with the scores for Canada, Mexico, and the U.S. from the study.

Franchising

Mad Science managers realized that although the three countries had agreed to work to develop a free-trade area, business operated in different ways around the world. These differences might prove problematic in developing business on the ground in Mexico. One very practical question, for example, concerned franchising. Although franchising was prominent in Mexico, a recent study (Falbe and Welsh, 1998) suggested that differing views existed regarding franchise success and failure in Mexico versus Canada and the U.S. (Table 4). Given these results, Mad Science senior managers were unclear whether their normal franchise arrangements (see Table 5) would be attractive in Mexico.

MEXICO TRADE MISSION

While the Mad Science senior management team was getting to grips with these issues, it learned that a federal government trade mission was to visit Mexico in October 2001. It would be led by the Minister of International trade and organized by the Department of Foreign Affairs and International Trade. The trade mission objective was to help export-ready companies investigate the Mexican market with a view to subsequent business development. The cost of the three-day mission would be in the $4,000 per person range, which included airfare, hotel, and meal expenses, as well as a nominal charge for mission arrangements.

Table 1
The Mexican Economy in 2001

Excerpts from a report by the Economist Intelligence Unit, April 1, 2001 Editorial commentary:

Mexico's economy has performed very well in the past several years, as its trade and finance have become increasingly linked with the U.S. and Canada through the NAFTA. This integration, however, may lead the country to suffer more severely than in the past from a slowdown in the economies of its northern neighbours. Rapid growth, combined with more thorough financial regulation, has helped to stabilize a banking sector that nearly collapsed after the devaluation of the peso in late 1994 ...

Operating conditions in Mexico have improved in recent years as a result of peaceful transition to multi-party democracy, responsible economic policies, and the floatation of the peso, the local currency. Mexico has become a favoured destination for U.S. and Canadian direct and portfolio investors in particular since NAFTA entered into force in 1994, and a recent trade agreement with the European Union may produce similar inflows of capital. Tax reform, currently under debate in Congress, would further improve the economic environment ...

Multinationals and blue-chip Mexican firms rely mainly on foreign and domestic banks and international debt markets to raise capital. Local financing in Mexico has traditionally been expensive and limited to the short-term of under one year. Domestic credit remained stagnant for the seventh straight year in 2000, despite a strong economy and improved bank results. The reform of bankruptcy laws and collection procedures in May 2000 may spur banks to offer additional lending in future ...

Mexico at a Glance: EIU Country Risk Rating

Overall Rating	Overall score	Political risk	Economic policy risk	Economic structure risk	Liquidity risk
C	52	C	C	C	C

The EIU Country Risk Service provides risk assessments for 100 countries. Every country is rated by category, ranging from "A" (the lowest risk) to "E" (the highest risk), and assigning a grade for political risk, economic policy risk, economic structure risk, and liquidity risk. Overall scores can range from 0 ("A" category) to a maximum of 100 points ("E" category) for the highest-risk countries.

Adapted from Economist Intelligence Unit.

Table 2
Selected Statistics for the NAFTA Countries, 2001

Statistic	Canada	Mexico	United States
GDP (in current US$)	$705 billion	$622 billion	$10 trillion
GDP growth (annual %)	1.9%	– 0.1%	0.5%
GDP per capita growth (annual %)	0.9%	– 1.5%	– 0.6%
Household final consumption expenditure (annual % growth)	2.6%	2.5%	2.5%
Inflation in consumer prices (annual %)	2.5%	6.4%	2.8%
Population, total	31 million	99 million	285 million
Population growth (annual %)	1.0%	1.4%	1.1%
Population aged less than 14 years (%)	18.7%	33.5%	21.2%
Primary education, pupils	2.5 million	14.8 million	24.9 million
Television sets (per 1,000 people)	690.6	282.0	937.5
Cable television subscribers (per 1,000 people)	252.9	24.8	256.2

Source: Various United Nations publications.

Income Distribution for NAFTA Countries (%)

	Lowest 40%	Next 40%	Top 20%
Canada (1994)	20.4*	30.2	39.3
Mexico (1992)	11.9	32.9	55.3
United States (1994)	15.8	39.5	45.2

Note: Read as follows: In 1994, Canadians with the lowest 40 percent of incomes accounted for 20.4 percent of total income.

Sources: World Bank and Oxford University Press (1999).

Table 3
Hofstede's (1980) Cultural Factors Defined

Power distance is the degree to which less powerful persons in a culture accept inequality as a normal situation. In low power distance societies (e.g., Sweden), people tend to feel equal, and close to each other in their daily work relationships. In high power distance societies (e.g., China), people feel separated from each other.

Individualism/collectivism reflects the extent to which people in a culture are self-centred and feel little need to depend on others (e.g., U.S.) versus have a group mentality and prefer to maintain harmony (e.g., South Korea).

Uncertainty avoidance is the extent to which people feel threatened by uncertain or unknown situations. In low-uncertainty avoidance cultures (e.g., Singapore), people and institutions feel that although the future is unknown, it can be evaluated and dealt with. In contrast, in high-uncertainty avoidance cultures (e.g., Japan), uncertainty is regarded as bad and everything in society must focus on its reduction.

Masculinity/femininity reflects the degree to which "masculine" values such as assertiveness, success, money, and competition prevail in a culture (e.g., Great Britain) versus "feminine" values such as quality of life, service, and solidarity (e.g., Netherlands).

Source: Hofstede (1980).

The NAFTA Countries: Scores on Hofstede's Cultural Factors (0–100)

Cultural factor	Canada	Mexico	United States
Power distance	39 Low	81 High	40 Low
Individualism/collectivism	80 Individualist	30 Collectivist	91 Individualist
Uncertainty avoidance	48 Low	82 High	46 Low
Masculinity/femininity	52 Masculine	69 Masculine	62 Masculine

Source: Adapted from Usunier and Lee (2005).

Table 4
Franchise Success and Failure Factors

Factor	Country differences
Success: System quality (e.g., franchisor quality support, franchisor adaptation to market, operational system efficiency)	Higher impact in M vs C & U.S.
Brand name (e.g., extensive national ads, positive name recognition)	Higher impact in C & M vs U.S.
Local environment (e.g., good local market location, full-time franchisee commitment)	Higher impact in C & M vs U.S.
Communication (e.g., franchisee board representation, franchisee communication/network)	Higher impact in M vs C & U.S.
Franchise activities (e.g., franchisee sufficient capital, franchisee shows leadership, franchisee community involvement)	No differences
Failure: Franchisor failure (e.g., misrepresentation or dishonesty, market saturation, faddish product)	Higher impact in M vs C & U.S.
Franchisee failure (e.g., Unwilling to follow system, failure to pay, overstaffing)	Higher impact in M vs C & U.S.

Source: Adapted from Falbe and Welsh (1998).

Table 5
Mad Science Franchise Requirements

Characteristic	Requirement
Territory size	Must include 100–120 schools for grades kindergarten to six, within a 60–90 minute drive
Total investment (C$)	$37,300 to $79,000
Franchise fee (C$)	$10,000 to $23.500
Ongoing royalty fee	8%
Agreement duration	25 years, renewable
Qualifications	General business or industry experience with good marketing skills
Number of employees needed	3–30 people

Note: The franchise business can be run from home
About 5% of all franchisees own more than one unit
Extensive training and support is provided by The Mad Science Group

Source: Mad Science Group

(Continued)

REFERENCES

Falbe, Cecilia & Dianne Welsh (1998). NAFTA and franchising: A comparison of franchisor perceptions of characteristics associated with franchisee success and failure in Canada, Mexico, and the United States, *Journal of Business Venturing*, 13, pp. 151–171.

Hofstede, Geert (1980). *Culture's Consequences: International Differences in Work-related Values.* Beverly Hills, CA: Sage.

Kucharsky, Danny (2001). Eureka! Montrealers Ariel and Ron Shlien have discovered how to fuse kids' love of science with their own marketing savvy. *Marketing Magazine*, 106(38), p. 14.

Oliver, Lee (2003). The method of Mad Science. *Profit*, 22(3), pp. 42–49.

Smith, Devlin (2001). A teenage project becomes a full-fledged business for the two brothers who started The Mad Science Group. Retrieved October 31, 2005 from www.entrepreneur.com/article/0,4621,293790,00.html.

Usunier, Jean-Claude & Julie Ann Lee (2005). *Marketing Across Cultures.* 4th. ed., Harlow, England: Pearson Education Limited.

QUESTIONS FOR DISCUSSION

1. What are the strengths and weaknesses of the Mad Science service? What does it take to transfer the service to another country?
2. Is franchising a good option? Any other mode of entry?
3. Given the economic and cultural information in the case, is Mexico a good opportunity for Mad Science? Any threats? Overall, is Mexico an attractive market for Mad Science?
4. Does it make sense for Mad Science to participate in the trade mission to Mexico? If so, what objectives would you set for the visit to Mexico?

SINCE ITS 2005 APPEARANCE IN MEXICO'S MOTORCYCLE market, Italika had been increasing its market share to become the leading brand in this country. However, competitors had taken notice and copied this strategy, importing Chinese-made motorcycles and selling them in their stores under their own brands. In late 2011 Ricardo Salinas, Chairman of the Mexican conglomerate Grupo Salinas, was wondering how to respond to the new competition. He reflected on the actions that enabled his company to make Italika the number-one brand in Mexico in such short time. Italika had been successful targeting the low-income households, selling motorcycles with the help of installment plans facilitated by the group's bank, Banco Azteca. Could competition also copy this? What to do next?

Initially, the Salinas group had sold another motorcycle brand, Carabela, targeting a more middle-income clientele. The Carabela brand was a nationally recognized brand created by the Hessel brothers. But in 2004 its main distributor, the department store chain Elektra (also in the Salinas group) did not have enough supply of motorcycles to fulfill the demand. That year had seen strong growth, with the average number of motorcycles sold at 200,000 units, with Elektra selling 4,600, or 2.3 percent of the total. In 2005 the sales increased a further 12 percent and the import of motorcycles increased by 25 percent, while Carabela was facing problems to supply Elektra.

Salinas decided to search for a reliable supplier of motorcycles in Asia. He found the Loncin Group, a leading motorcycle manufacturer in China. The Chinese group, founded in 1996, was located in the city of Chongqing in Southwest China. It was a large motorcycle manufacturer, exporting to over 80 countries around the world. In 2005 Elektra began importing Loncin motorcycles to Mexico, and decided to drop the domestically produced Carabela brand. The new motorcycles were sold under a brand Salinas had already registered, "Italika." Selling the brand in the Elektra stores meant that Italika, like Carabela before, shared space with other consumer goods, such as furniture and electronics, providing financing for low-income consumers.

HISTORY OF GRUPO SALINAS

The Grupo Salinas conformed by *Grupo Elektra, Azteca Broadcast Television, Banco Azteca, Italika and Grupo Iusacell* started in 1906 in Monterrey City, located in the northeast part of Mexico. Benjamin Salinas-Westrup and his brother in law, Joel Rocha, started a brass beds factory. After two years of operation the company was registered as "*Benjamín Salinas y Compañia.*" Five years later, the company closed its doors temporarily because the Mexican Revolution. In the 1920s the first furniture store was established under "Salinas y Rocha" in Monterrey's downtown.

---

[1] *This case was prepared by Dr. Miguel A. Montoya, Tecnológico de Monterrey, campus Guadalajara, Mexico. It is based on secondary data.*

In 1933 a new branch of "Salinas y Rocha" was opened in Mexico City and Hugo Salinas-Rocha, son of the founder, was in charge of managing it. In 1948 "Salinas y Rocha" became a strong business and first competitor of Sears with about 20 stores in the country. In 1950 he decided to change the name of the company to *"Elektra"* in order to not be associated with a bad-quality product. Elektra made a contract with a USA manufacturer to import TV parts which were assembled by Elektra. The TVs were sold door to door and the company started to offer credits.

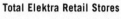

Total Elektra Retail Stores

In 1997 Grupo Elektra started its internationalization by opening branches in Latin American countries. By 2011 it had operations in Argentina, Brazil, El Salvador, Honduras, Guatemala, Panama, and Peru.

In the year of 2002, Grupo Salinas got the license to operate a bank called Banco Azteca, approved by the Ministry of Finance and Public Credit in Mexico. In 2005 Banco Azteca started with its internationalization process to other countries in Latin America. Banco Azteca was a commercial bank focused in the bottom-of-the-pyramid sector. Once the bank was launched, it began with the granting of credits that needed minimum requirements. Besides granting consumer credits, Banco Azteca offered other financial services like credit cards (Tarjeta Azteca), personal loans, car loans, and mortgages.

Banco Azteca also developed a website that allows the customers check their balance inquiry, statements, pay online for services, national and international transfers, online account opening, and check movements under the security system Token or by fingerprints. This system came to benefit the consumer because of the facilities presented in order to purchase goods; in addition it provided consumers the necessary capital to make timely payments to settle their balances by buying products in Elektra. The bank also developed cell-phone access to help check balance accounts, make transfers, and pay services.

The payments could be fixed in terms of 3, 6, or 12 months by using the webpage "*elektraonline.com*," via the authorized credit or debit cards. Since most of the people in the low-income sector did not have access to credit cards, with the support of Banco Azteca these people could obtain a credit card in just 24 hours. According to the Bank of Mexico (Banxico) the country registered an average of 24 million credit cards equivalent to the 22 percent of the Mexican population.

To open an account in Banco Azteca the process was the following: the bank executive collects the basic information of the customer (official ID, birth certification, and/or paychecks), and actually visits the customer's home to estimate his/her incomes and expenses. After the investigation, the bank established the payment capacity of the client. The transaction was completely secure. Other alternatives to pay were cash payments in Elektra's stores and banks, referred or wire transfer payment, or by using credit or debit cards.

According to Pedro Padilla, current Director of Grupo Salinas, Ricardo Salinas "wanted to improve the quality of life in people's homes giving them the items that would make their lives easier and more pleasant."

SELLING MOTORCYCLES TO LOW-INCOME HOUSEHOLDS

In 2004 Ricardo Salinas-Pliego CEO of Grupo Salinas decided to get into the transportation segment under his subsidiary Elektra. He noted that the country had several problems with the public transportation as not enough routes and an elevate transportation rates. He saw an opportunity area for developing a new system of commercialization of motorcycles in his Elektra stores, introducing the motorcycles in the same schema used for electronics and appliances, where the customer has the facility to make weekly payments according to his/her ability to pay.

The strategy of Grupo Elektra was to focus on the segments C and D$^+$ (see Exhibit) which represent the upper-middle strata of low-income classes. With that target, the group looked to offer a transportation alternative for the bulk of the population in Mexico. Available data on Segments C and D$^+$ showed the transportation sector in the third place in the table of expenses, just after food and housing.

Economic Segments in Mexico

Socioeconomic Level	Year 2000	2002	2003	2005	2006–2007	2008
A/B	19%	7%	7%	8%	8%	7%
C+		13%	13%	14%	14%	14%
ABC+	19%	20%	20%	21%	21%	21%
C	18%	17%	17%	19%	17%	18%
D+	30%	36%	34%	33%	36%	36%
D/E	33%	28%	29%	28%	25%	25%

Source: AMAI

2000	2001	2002	2003	2004	2005	2006-2007	2008
98,432,557	99,715,527	100,909,374	101,999,555	103,001,867	103,946,866	105,332,504	106,682,518

Source: CONAPO. Mid-year Mexican Population

Ricardo Salinas saw the potential of providing transportation to the Mexican population at a moderate cost, through the granting of a micro-credit system offered by the Banco Azteca.

Carabela was a traditional Mexican motorcycle marque with a reputation of good quality and low cost. As much as 70 percent of the components were produced in Mexico. Initially run by the Hessel brothers, in 1979 the company was sold to Grupo Alfa of Monterrey, one of the biggest Mexican industrial emporiums. In 1987 the company stopped motorcycle production and during the next three years it was just selling out inventory until Grupo Alfa decided to close the company in 1990.

Carabela's second phase began in 2001, when the brand was bought by Moto Road, a company formed by 70 percent of domestic capital and 30 percent foreign capital. The company imported the motorcycles from China as Complete Knock Down (CKD) kits, to lower tariffs compared to importing a fully assembled unit. It was assembled in Mexico and sold as a domestic product. Elektra stores handled the distribution. The liberal selling system generated a great acceptance by the consumers, who now had access to motorized transportation facilities, micro-credits, and cash discounts. Gradually the demand of motorcycles began to increase, causing Elektra to have problems with the supply.

The difficulties in supplying Carabela motorcycles to meet the growing demand were exacerbated by a lack of access to services and parts. This was when Ricardo Salinas decided to find a manufacturing partner in Asia. For over four months, he made several trips to China in search of new suppliers to see if any of them could solve the supply problems that Carabela was having in Mexico.

SOURCING MOTORCYCLES IN CHINA

China has a sizable motorcycle industry that supplies a large and growing market at home and abroad. By the end of 2010, more than 29 million units were sold in China, representing a growth of 19 percent compared to the previous year, according to Datamonitor. One of the biggest brands, **Haojue**, is recognized for its high quality standards and its relation with Japanese Suzuki. The company is considered one of the most important in the Guangdong province. The company behind a brand named **Lifan**, with headquarters in Chongqing, was large enough to place as the number 88 of the Forbes' 2009 Top Enterprises in China. The **Jianshe** brand is well-known for the quality of its products and its partnership with the Japanese brand Yamaha. These companies manufacture motorcycles, mopeds, ATVs, engines, and spare parts as well.

Loncin Group Company was a leader in the Chinese market and in the export area. The Group has a large production of high-quality engines. The strengths of this group include a strategic partnership with BMW where Loncin is in charge of manufacturing 800 cc engines and above, with the design provided by BMW. The company headquarters is in the city of Chongqing located in Southwest China. The company produces an average of 2 million motorcycles and 3 million engines annually.

In 2005, Grupo Salinas and Loncin signed a sole rights contract for the distribution of Loncin motorcycles in Mexico. This agreement does not allow other companies to sell motorcycles manufactured by Loncin Group in México but Grupo Elektra has the power to sell other brands of motorcycles in the country if they want. The contract can end whenever Grupo Salinas wants.

Once the trade agreement had been signed between Grupo Salinas and Loncin Group, GS decided to use the marque "Italika" for the Mexican market for the motorcycles manufactured by Loncin Group. The connotation to Italy was seen as symbolic of high quality and stylish design, and was expected to help avoid any potential negatives about a Chinese motorcycle brand.

The Loncin motorcycles in the Chinese market have their own identity. The manufacturer adds features of the Chinese culture such as dragons and Chinese symbols. Grupo Elektra requested Loncin to eliminate that ornamentation of the motorcycles because the Latin consumer is not familiar with those symbols, and that could be an entry barrier for the brand in Mexico.

THE ITALIKA IS LAUNCHED

In late 2005, Grupo Elektra started importing several models of motorcycles manufactured and assembled by Loncin Group under the name of Italika. These were stored in its distribution centers located at Tijuana, Hermosillo, La Paz, Laredo, Guadalajara, Mexico City, Lerma, Villahermosa, and Cancun. That same year, Elektra put the Italika motorcycles on their sales floors and replaced Carabela, following the same payment system used previously. A credit line was opened for the customers who could acquire goods under a weekly payments system.

Alberto Tanus, Italika's chief executive, was quoted as saying that "at the beginning there were averages of 50 units sold per month. Later on motorcycles were widely accepted by consumers, reaching average annual sales of 200,000 units between the different models available."

The Italika FT 125

Photo by case author.

The Italika introduction helped grow the total market size significantly. The company offered a low-cost product for the sector of the population neglected by other manufacturers. By 2005 their registered sales were 43,000 motorcycles. The next year its level increased to 226 percent, representing sales of 140,000 units. In 2007 the sales behavior kept increasing with a registration of 192,000 units. In 2008 Italika led with 50 percent of the Mexican market.

Due to the increasing of sales for three years, Ricardo Salinas decided to open an assembly plant in Mexico. In September of 2008, with the presence of the Mexican President Felipe Calderon, Gao Yong, Loncin Group CEO, and Grupo Salinas Chairman Ricardo Salinas, the plant Ensamblika based in Toluca Mexico was finally opened. The initial investment for this plant was 165 million pesos, 100 percent of the capital was provided by Grupo Salinas. The plant was planned to provide a production capacity of 350,000 units per year. Ensamblika offers 7,000 direct jobs and 3,000 indirect jobs. The Italika motorcycles get to Mexico from China classified as "automotive parts" with a lower 20 percent tax. Grupo Salinas is evaluating and certifying the production processes done in its plants. Since its opening in 2008 the plant Ensamblika has assembled more than 400,000 units.

The assembly plant operated under an agreement known as Complete Knock Down (CKD). Earlier the Italika motorcycles had been assembled as Semi Knocked Down (SDK the units are semi-assembled). Around 75 percent of the parts came from Loncin, and the other 25 percent from Mexican suppliers. With Mexican components the production cost could be decreased between 5–7 percent. After the depreciation of the Mexican peso (against the dollar and Yuan), at the end of 2008 and in the first months of 2009, Grupo Salinas tried to increase the percentage of the Mexican parts suppliers (brakes, chassis, whips, and other parts). Increasing local content not just lowers some costs and tariffs, but also provides a more secure supply of necessary parts components for after-sales service.

COMPETING RETAILERS IN MEXICO

In Mexico it is common to find motorcycles in department stores alongside other goods such as electronics, furniture, and clothing. The retail industry that focuses on low income customers is composed on three national chains: Elektra, Coppel, and Famsa. In recent years other retailers such as the U.S. firm Walmart and the Mexican firm Chedraui have started selling motorcycles as well.

Elektra had the competitive advantage of being the first to offer a low-cost transportation solution for lower sectors of the population. In addition, Elektra focused its efforts on strong after-sales service, with a network of workshops across the country. Italika offers rapid supply of spare parts, with a maximum of nine days since the order was placed within Mexico. Because of the wide range of models offered by Elektra, the wide distribution network, and its more than 589 service shops, Italika brand is considered the "*number one*" in Mexico.

Coppel and Famsa, numbers two and three in the ranking of position in sales after Elektra, have copied the pattern of distribution of low-cost motorcycles for the Mexican base of the pyramid sector.

Grupo Famsa has more than 40 years of operations in Mexico, offering financial services and investment products for its clients. By the end of 2010, Grupo Famsa registered 359 stores and presence in 24 states in Mexico. The company has also presence in the United States with 51 stores located in five states. To promote the company's sales, Grupo Famsa has increased the offer of personal loans and the revival of demand of some major categories of durable goods.

Coppel was founded in 1965 in Culiacan City. This department store has a national coverage, and by the end of 2010 the company had 515 traditional stores, 294 Coppel Canada Stores, and 54 Limited Variety Coppel Stores located all over the Mexican territory in more than 303 cities. Its strategy involves credit sales with lenient conditions, home delivery of products and installation of equipment with no additional charges, and two-year guarantee program in every article sold.

Even companies such as Sears and Liverpool, focused in the middle and upper classes of the country and have begun to distribute Italika substitute brands for credit accessible systems.

Liverpool, a company with wide presence in Mexco, targets the population with medium-high or high income. This corporation has 80 department stores, 57 of them are Liverpool and 23 are Fabricas de Francia, its subsidiary. **Sears Roebuck Mexico** has 50 stores located on Mexican territory. Eighty-five percent of the company's shares are property of Grupo Carso, one of the most important conglomerates of the country. Both Liverpool and Sears offer an internal credit system to people who have membership of the store. To get that membership, the customer must have a good credit record.

MOTORCYCLE MARKET SHARES

The (Mexican Automotive Industry Association, 2011) (AMIA) is a civil association in charge of the automotive sector. Its purpose is to represent the automotive companies within the industrial sector and also generates statistics of production, sales, imports, and exports of enterprises incorporated. Some of the motorcycle manufacturers affiliated to the association are Honda, Yamaha, Suzuki, Harley Davidson, BMW, and Carabela. The participation of the manufacturers in this chamber depends on its decision of they want to participate or not. Until the middle of 2011 the leader brand of the Mexican market Italika and others have not joined to the AMIA. This makes it difficult to generate reliable statistics rather than estimates.

The AMIA reports show the behavior that the Mexican motorcycle market took in 2004–2010 periods; there is a record of costumer sales of 76,018 units in 2004, in 2005 the sales increased by 12 percent. In 2006 the sales registered were 101,345 units, an increase of 19 percent in relation to 2005. 2007 also showed an increase over 2006 with a record of 106,990 units. From 2008 there was a slight decrease in sales that was increased in 2009 following the global crisis, from 104,262 to 65,927 units sold, respectively, representing a decrease of 37 percent of consumer sales in this last year. In 2010 the sector registered a small improvement with a growth of 0.4 percent over the previous year.

In 2009 Italika took 55 percent of the domestic market, in 2010 Italika took 60 percent reaffirming its leadership in the Mexican market. The remaining 40 percent is left for AMIA brands such as BMW, Harley Davidson, Yamaha, Honda, Suzuki, and Carabela and others not incorporated to AMIA (see exhibit).

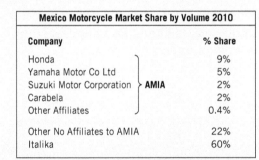

Mexico Motorcycle Market Share by Volume 2010	
Company	% Share
Honda	9%
Yamaha Motor Co Ltd	5%
Suzuki Motor Corporation AMIA	2%
Carabela	2%
Other Affiliates	0.4%
Other No Affiliates to AMIA	22%
Italika	60%

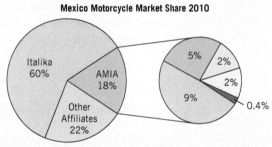

Mexico Motorcycle Market Share 2010

Calculated by Miguel A. Montoya based on data from Datamonitor.

The major brands of motorcycles have begun to wake up after the introduction of inexpensive motorcycles by Italika. Actually, the Mexican motorcycle market grew in imports 20 percent in July of 2011 in respect to the same month of the previous year, reaching an accumulated increase of 24.5 percent during the first semester of 2011. If this trend continues, the Mexican market could regain the levels reached in 2008. The companies registered at the AMIA have started to offer cheaper models in relation to those offered in the past. They have focused their efforts on products ranging from 50 to 250 cc, which are the models with highest demand in the country. Motorcycles with big powerful engines were losing share. In the report of the first half of 2011, AMIA showed a significant growth of 48 percent in sales from the previous year. As for imports on motorcycles from 50 to 250 cc, the increase has been of 22 percent in the first semester of 2011, in respect to the same period of the previous year.

DECISION

Units sold since the start of operations of Italika in 2005

Country	Elektra	Distributors	Total
Mexico	933,694	17,691	951,385
Guatemala	37,457		37,457
Honduras	19,131	721	19,852
Peru	13,225	627	13,852
Brasil	1,024		1,024
Total	1,004,531	19,039	1,023,570

Elektra's Placement Presentation 2011

Italika's success has been due to being the first-mover in the low-Income sector, offering products and services adapted to the sector's particular needs. The D⁺ and C population sectors were in fact offered an option to exchange their bicycles for low-cost motorcycles. Italika's strengths include a vast network of service workshops and a robust distribution system that offer credits for low-income people. On the other hand, Ricardo Salinas needs to face the competitors, who have already begun to focus the bottom of the pyramid as their target market. What can he do?

DISCUSSION QUESTIONS

1. What is the strategic justification for dropping Carabela and instead introducing Italika, a new brand?
2. Do you think there are first-mover advantages for Italika being the first to target the low-income market segments?
3. Would you say there are low or high entry barriers to enter the low-income segments? Justify your answer.
4. How can Italika defend its market position?
5. It is often said that "attack is the best defense." What attack strategies could Italika consider?

BIBLIOGRAPHY

Automotive News World Congress. (2009, January). Retrieved from http://www.autonews.com/assets/html/09_anwc/pdf/pres_ligocki.pdf.

Motorcycles in Mexico. (2010). *Datamonitor*, 13.

Motorcycles in Mexico. (2010). *Datamonitor*, 42.

Grupo Coppel. (2011, June). Retrieved from http://www.coppel.com/coppel/.

Grupo Elektra. (2011, June). Retrieved from http://www.grupoelektra.com.mx/.

Grupo Elektra, S.A. de C.V. (2011). *Datamonitor*, 15.

Grupo Famsa. (2011, June). Retrieved from http://www.grupofamsa.com/index_esp.php?temp=hm.

Grupo Salinas. (2011, November). Retrieved from http://www.gruposalinas.com/Default.aspx.

Italika Home Page. (2011, October). Retrieved from http://www.italika.com.mx/.

Mexican Automotive Industry Association. (2011, October). Retrieved from http://www.amia.com.mx/.

Mexican Stock Exchange. (2011, June). Retrieved from http://www.bmv.com.mx/.

Motorcycle Manufacturing in China. (2011). Datamonitor, 32.

Motorcycle Manufacturing in Mexico. (2011). Datamonitor, 32.

Reporte de autos en México. (2011). *Business Monitor International*, 72.

Ricardo Salinas Pliego's Official Blog. (2011, August). Retrieved from http://www.ricardosalinas.com.

Arnold, D., Herrero, G., & Monteiro, L. (2003). Grupo Elektra. Harvard Business School.

Echarte, L. (2010). Update Number 25. 10–11.

Lopez, H. (2008). Distribución de Niveles Socioeconómicos. 7.

Lopez, H. (2009). *Los niveles socioeconómicos y la distribución del gasto. Instituto de Investigaciones Sociales*, 40.

Lund, D. (2010). *La Base Social de la Esperanza y el Miedo en México*. Mund Group, 5.

Moreno, L. (2007). Expansión de los servicios financieros a la población de bajos ingresos de América Latina. *The McKinsey Quarterly*, 1–9.

Palacio, E. (2010, April 12). Assistant Manager of Italika. (M. Montoya, Interviewer)

Prahalad, C., & Hart, S. (2002). *The Fortune at the Bottom of the Pyramid*.

Santa, I. (2011, October 11). El peligro de abonar sólo el pago mínimo. *El Economista*.

Tanus, A., Salinas, R., Peña, E., & Yong, G. (2008, September 10). *Diversas intervenciones en la inauguración de la planta ensambladora de motocicletas Italika. Presidencia de la República, Toluca*.

THE CASE IN BRIEF

In September 2012, the European Commission launched an antidumping investigation into exports of Photovoltaic (PV) solar panels and their key components (i.e., solar cells and solar wafers) from China. Antidumping (AD) is a mechanism by which countries can seek to counteract unfair trading practices, most notably by imposing additional taxes—antidumping duties (ADDs)—on the offending exports. The system is based on the principle that selling goods below a certain value (the most widely used benchmarks are the cost of production or the price on the home market) is unfair and that retaliation is justified.

Solar panels

Copyright © by Shutterstock/Sergiy1975.

The investigation was initiated further to a complaint by an ad-hoc group of EU PV producers called Prosun. They argued that low-cost imports from China were destroying a key strategic industry for Europe and that action was needed immediately to protect EU companies from this predatory behavior (see supporting material in annex). However the EU PV industry was by no means unanimous in calling for action. EU installation companies, Chinese PV exporters and manufacturers of intermediate goods formed another group—the Alliance for Affordable Solar Energy (Afase)—to

[1] *This case was prepared by Professor Louise Curran, Université de Toulouse, Toulouse Business School, Toulouse, France.*

make the case against antidumping measures. They argued that low-cost solar was good for the EU economy and environment and that their prices were simply based on more competitive production (see supporting material in annex). Both sides commissioned studies to support their claims. They came up with very different conclusions on the potential impact of duties (see annex).

After several months of in-depth investigations, the Commission concluded in June 2013 that dumping had indeed taken place. Interim duties of 11.8 percent were imposed on the EU market for a period of two months, with the potential to rise to 47.6 percent, if a negotiated solution was not found with Chinese industry. Press reports indicated that, in a rare move, duties were imposed in spite of a majority of Member States opposing them (Curran, 2015). This fact undoubtedly weakened the Commission's negotiating position in the subsequent search for a compromise, as a majority would have been needed for final duties to be imposed.

A key concern of member states and industry in relation to the imposition of these kinds of trade defense measures was the fear of retaliation. Indeed, academic studies have found that many AD cases are instigated in retaliation, and Chinese trade officials had indicated several sectors that might be investigated for potential breaches, in case of a negative outcome to the case (Chaffin and Wiesmann, 2012). Not long after, a case was launched by China against EU Polysilicon exports in November 2012.

Furthermore, the Chinese reacted immediately to the Commission's interim decision and only a few hours later instigated an antidumping case against EU wine. China's commerce ministry said it was launching the investigation of European wine imports after complaints from domestic producers that the rapid increase in Chinese consumption of EU wine was due to illegal subsidies by home governments (Hook, Daneshkhu and Spiegel, 2013). The move promoted angry reactions in France, by far the EU's biggest exporter of wine to China and a supporter of the duties. The chairman of the French Federation of Wine and Spirits Exporters, was quoted as complaining that the wine industry had been "taken hostage" to the wider dispute (Hook et al., 2013). The solar panel case thus became strongly politicized, with a much wider production network implicated in the decisions on the case.

A few weeks after the imposition of the interim duties, the Commission announced that an agreement had been reached with the key Chinese companies in the industry securing a minimum price undertaking (CEC, 2013). This agreement established a price floor for Chinese exports, as well as a maximum volume limit. In spite of claims by the Commission that the agreement would stabilize the market, Prosun strongly opposed the agreement and launched a challenge in the European Court. Politically, the EU Member States seemed to concur that the minimum price floor was a better option than the proposed ADDs, with 20 reported by Afase to have supported the proposal (Curran, 2015). In the end, therefore, in spite of the finding that dumping had taken place, no ADDs were imposed in the EU market.

Subsequently "amicable" solutions were concluded by the EU and China in both the polysilicon and wine AD cases. The EU polysilicon industry agreed a minimum price with the Chinese administration, while the wine industry agreed to provide technical assistance to Chinese wine producers (Curran, 2015).

REFERENCES

CEC (2014) European Commission welcomes EU industry's agreement with China in the polysilicon anti-dumping and anti-subsidy cases, Brussels: Commission for the European Communities; accessed at http://europa.eu/rapid/press-release_IP-14-278_en.htm 19th March 2014.

CEC (2013). Commissioner De Gucht: "We found an amicable solution in the EU-China solar panels case that will lead to a new market equilibrium at sustainable prices." Memo. Brussels: Commission of the European Communities. Downloaded on 22th August 2013 from: http://trade.ec.europa.eu/doclib/press/index.cfm?id=955.

Chaffin, J. and Wiesman, G. (2012). EU trade officials face China dilemma, *Financial Times*. 2th September 2012. Downloaded from: http://www.ft.com/intl/cms/s/0/7873f2d2-f4e9-11e1-b120-00144feabdc0.html on 10th September 2012.

Curran, L. (2015). The impact of Trade Policy on Global Production Networks: The Solar panel case. Forthcoming in *The Review of International Political Economy*, http://dx.doi.org/10.1080/09692290.2015.1014927.

Hook, L., Daneshkhu, S and Spiegel, P. (2013). China takes aim at France with EU wine export probe Financial Times. 5th June, 2013. Downloaded from: http://www.ft.com/cms/s/0/9229031a-cdb1-11e2-8313-00144feab7de.html#ixzz2VWeEuF65 on 7th June 2013.

ANNEX: EXCERPTS FROM AFASE STATEMENTS AND PRESS RELEASE

10 Reasons for Free Trade. Afase (2013)

1. Free trade makes solar products affordable and attractive for consumers.
2. Free trade safeguards and creates jobs in the European solar sector.
3. Free trade is the backbone of a strong global solar value chain.
4. Free trade is essential for the survival of the European up and downstream industries in the solar sector.
5. Free trade drives solar companies to develop the most cost-effective and innovative products.
6. Free trade helps solar energy to become independent from subsidies in the long run.
7. Free trade helps solar energy to achieve competitiveness with traditional energy sources.
8. Free trade helps the EU and Member States to expand their solar sector and achieve their climate change targets.
9. Free trade makes solar energy affordable for developing countries, thus offering their populations climate-friendly access to energy.
10. Free trade guarantees good international trade relations and is key to economic growth worldwide.

AFASE Press release. 19th February 2013

Punitive Tariffs would cost EU up to 242,000 Jobs
"Antidumping and/or Countervailing duties at whatever level on imported Chinese solar products will lead to decreased demand for solar products immediately translating into very significant job losses and less value added along the whole European photovoltaic value chain. This is the result of a study by the independent economic institute Prognos.

A punitive tariff of 20 percent would cost 115,600 jobs in the European Union during the first year after the implementation. This would add up to 175,500 job losses until the third year. The value added lost would sum up to 4.74 billion euros in the first year and to 18.4 billion euros during three years with a tariff of 20 percent.

'The potential positive impact of duties for the EU solar producers is dwarfed by the negative impact on employment in the EU. … The jobs created by the EU solar producers represent at the very most 20 percent of the jobs lost along the PV value chain,' says Thorsten Preugschas, CEO of the German project developer Soventix, a spokesperson of AFASE."

Documents

afase_press_release_prognos_study_190213.pdf

Downloaded from: http://afase.org/en/media/punitive-tariffs-would-cost-eu-242000-jobs on 12th January 2015.

Excerpts from Prosun's statement

The Cost of EU Inaction
"If the European Union doesn't react to the predatory behaviour of Chinese solar manufacturers, there will be significant costs to our environment, economy and society:

- Thousands of people in Europe will lose their jobs—especially high-end jobs in research and manufacturing.
- All the investment that was made into developing the world's leading solar technologies will be lost to China.
- If the European PV solar manufacturing industry ceases to exist, there is no hope of rebuilding this industry in the EU ever again. This is due to the extremely high market entry barriers (high investment in research and facilities), but also the fear that any such attempt will be directly squeezed out by Chinese unfair market practices.
- If China becomes a de facto global monopoly, it will have an adverse effect on the innovation and affordability of the entire sector globally. With no competition there will be no incentives for China to develop new technologies or lower prices.
- Renewable energies are supposed to be a sustainable solution that will allow the EU to become independent from imports. However if solar PV and possibly all European manufacturers of

renewable energy products soon disappear, EU renewable energy production will become fully dependent on Chinese imports.

- If Europe doesn't react, this will send a clear message to the Chinese government that we tolerate predatory market behavior and accept losing our strategic industries to China. ProSun calls for the EU not to give up on its principles of fair competition due to Chinese political pressure or threats of retaliation.
- If EU accepts that China takes over PV solar manufacturing—a very healthy and globally competitive industry, then what is the future for other European industries?
- The EU has very high environmental standards and goals, with 2020 energy targets the region is a global model of sustainability. However if PV solar production is fully given away to China, then Europe will in fact base its high environmental standards on imports from a country that didn't sign the Kyoto protocol, has the highest CO2 emissions in the world and doesn't meet the environmental production standards."

Excerpts from the PWC report on impacts of AD Duties

"The results of the Prognos study are implausible:

- Higher job losses than total number of jobs: In the Prognos study, estimated job losses exceed in several instances the total number of existing jobs in the solar industry.
- The unexplained increase of the number of allegedly lost jobs: The first results of the Prognos study, which were presented to the public in November 2012, announced considerably fewer job losses than the results made available to the public in February 2013. By then, the number of estimated job losses was suddenly several times higher than in November 2012.
- The U.S. experience—Antidumping tariffs and job growth: The U.S. imposed tariffs on PV products in 2012. However, after the introduction of tariffs demand increased and more jobs were created. This is a useful example to illustrate that there are good reasons not to believe alarming studies which are based on vague data and questionable assumptions.

There are major flaws with regard to methodology and content:

- Central elements of the analysis like the elasticity of demand remain completely unclear.
- The Prognos study does not meet the standards for economic evidence set out by the Commission and therefore should not be taken into consideration.

It is reasonable to conclude that the beneficial effects of tariffs more than outweigh limited negative effects on demand, i.e., that the introduction of tariffs has a net positive effect on employment in Europe."

DISCUSSION QUESTIONS

1. Summarize the arguments for and against antidumping duties on Chinese solar panel imports to the EU. Which side would you be on?
2. If antidumping duties had been imposed what would the impact have been for the key actors in the PV global value chain and beyond? Summarize your thinking in a table indicating who would lose and who would gain.
3. Why do you think a minimum price floor was thought to be more acceptable than antidumping duties in this case?
4. Why do you think China instigated an antidumping investigation into EU wine? How can nations avoid retaliatory behavior?

MARTHA TILAAR GROUP IS ONE OF THE biggest beauty companies in Indonesia providing traditional, high-quality yet innovative beauty products and services. The company was founded in the early 1970s and was named after its founder, Dr. Martha Tilaar. Starting as a beauty salon in the garage of her father's house in central Jakarta, Indonesia, the Martha Tilaar Group has turned into a world-class beauty group of companies. One of its subsidiaries, PT. Cantika Puspa Pesona, offers an authentic Indonesia spa experience to answer the demand of staying young and healthy by adopting a holistic approach and using centuries-old Eastern traditions of health and beauty throughout the human lifecycle. Its spa beauty outlets have spread out in almost all of the cities of Indonesia under the brand name Martha Tilaar Salon Day Spa.

Martha Tilaar Salon Day Spa

Copyright © by Martha Tilaar Salon Day Spa. Reprinted with permission.

EXPANSION ABROAD

In 2003, Cantika Puspa Pesona started to expand its business to Malaysia, piggybacking on the well-known brand of Martha Tilaar beauty products which had been successfully distributed there since 1986. Dewi Sri Martha Tilaar Spa was opened in a five-star hotel in Kuala Lumpur with a profit-sharing partnership with the hotel owner. The name of Dewi Sri refers to the Indonesian prosperity and rice goddess and is in line with its positioning as an authentic Indonesian spa experience. Dewi

[1] *This case was prepared by Lianti Raharjo and Dahlia Darmayanti, Binus Business School, Bina Nusantara University, Indonesia.*

Lianti Raharjo and Dahlia Darmayanti, "Dewi Sri Martha Tilaar Spa Goes to Malaysia." Copyright © by Lianti Raharjo and Dahlia Darmayanti. Reprinted with permission.

Sri Martha Tilaar Spa was decorated with an Indonesian ambience and supported by six to eight well-trained and professional Indonesian spa therapists who could speak English and had been trained at the Martha Tilaar Training Center in Bali for six months to master Indonesian spa techniques.

The establisment of the Dewi Sri Martha Tilaar Spa as the overseas brand was a flagship of the Martha Tilaar brand in Malaysia. Besides the profit-sharing partnership, Cantika Puspa Pesona also granted two Dewi Sri Martha Tilaar Spa franchises to two local, personally owned companies in 2003. They were day spas located in the Plaza Hartamas shopping mall area in Kuala Lumpur and in Shah Alam, 20 km west of Kuala Lumpur.

To obtain a Dewi Sri Martha Tilaar Spa franchise, the franchisees had to pay a five-year, $40,000 (U.S.) franchise fee, to arrange working permits for the Indonesian spa therapists and to provide a place with a minimum area of 200m² to accomodate six to eight spa treatment rooms including the furniture and equipment. Meanwhile, Cantika Puspa Pesona as franchisor provided interior design, highly trained Indonesian therapists, software, and training as well as set up a point-of-sales system. All Dewi Sri Martha Tilaar Spas in Malaysia enjoyed promising demand and high revenue from the customers coming from the middle up market serving 20 to 30 clients per day with average daily revenue of RM 15,000.

CONFLICTS

Nevertheless, Cantika Puspa Pesona faced management conflict with these two franchise outlets as the owners did not fully comply with the franchise agreement, providing substandard service and substituting some of the spa elements from natural to artificial elements to cut costs.

Another issue was related to the difficulty to extend the Indonesian therapists' working permits. They required a significant amount of deposit funds at the Malaysian immigration department and a complicated process to extend the two-year working permit. In order to handle this issue, the franchisee started to employ Malaysian therapists with a ratio of 80 percent Indonesian and 20 percent local, then 50 percent Indonesian and 50 percent local, and finally 30 percent Indonesian, 70 percent local. Even though the local therapists had received intensive basic massage training from the franchisor for a month, the customers' satisfaction had decreased, with customers expecting to be treated with authentic Indonesian massage techniques and healing touch hospitality. As a result of these challenges, the franchise agreements of both outlets ended in 2008.

In the same year, the partnership of Cantika Puspa Pesona and the five-star hotel in Kuala Lumpur also ended when the hotel was bought by a new owner and installed its own spa provider. In the meantime, a brand-new five-star hotel franchised Dewi Sri Martha Tilaar spa for a period of five years in Putrajaya, a federal administrative center of Malaysia located about 25 km South of Kuala Lumpur. As the hotel had been granted a quota to hire foreign workers, it was not difficult to arrange working permits for Indonesian spa therapists. Thus, this new outlet could provide an authentic Indonesia spa experience.

INDUSTRY GROWTH

Industry specialists *Intelligent Spas* claimed a remarkable growth of the spa industry in Malaysia of almost 200 percent from 2002 to 2007. There were 151 spa facilities in Malaysia operated roughly equally between day spas (no residential accommodation) and hotel/resort spas (destination spa). After 2007, the annual growth of this industry was about 16 percent and the industry was predicted to become the fifth-largest income contributor in the Malaysian economy by 2020. The spa industry in Malaysia generated RM 20.7 million revenue in 2011 and was projected to contribute RM 6.7 million to Malaysia's annual income.

However, almost 60 percent of the spa therapist working in Malaysia were foreigners from Thailand and Indonesia. The basic reason was said to be the negative perceptions about spa therapists held by local Malaysians.

GOVERNMENT INTERFERENCE

With industry growth, the Ministry of Home Affairs decided to reduce dependency on foreign spa therapists. Starting in 2012, to protect the local industry players and to secure the employment of local talent, the Malaysian government placed a freeze on foreign therapists. The government banned the issue of new working permits for foreign therapists.

Under a temporary "6P program," the Ministry of Home Affairs allowed registered spa operators to take in illegal foreign workers as spa therapists for two years under the permit "*Pendatang Asing Tanpa Izin*" (PATI), to end by 1st January, 2017. The Ministry of Tourism endorsed the application by 66 spa operators for the intake of 257 PATI holders, with the majority coming from Thailand and Indonesia. Most of these PATI holders had been working with spa operators before and therefore had been trained.

The Malaysian Ministry of Tourism and Culture has developed a six-month training program at the Centers of Excellence Spa Training in Langkawi, Kuala Lumpur, Penang, and Petaling Jaya to encourage young Malaysians to fill the job opportunities as professional respected spa therapists. The industry aims to create more than 6,000 jobs by 2020.

As the result of Malaysian government policy, Dewi Sri Martha Tilaar Spa did not extend its franchise agreement with its Malaysian partner. The new policy did not sustain the value proposition of Dewi Sri Martha Tilaar Spa to provide an authentic Indonesia spa experience.

DISCUSSION QUESTIONS

1. What were the entry barriers for Dewi Sri Martha Tilaar Spa in Malaysia? To what extent is the expansion an example of the "cultural distance" effect?
2. What is the reason why the Malaysian government decided to regulate the industry? Is this protectionism? What is the role of industry growth in this, if any?

3. Considering the spa business is growing in Malaysia, do you think the decision to end the franchise agreement in 2013 was the right decision? If Cantika Puspa Pesona would like to continue the spa business in Malaysia, what alternatives should be considered? Justify your answer.

REFERENCES

Developing_Local_Expertise_and_Better_Regulating_the_Spa_Industry,http://etp.pemandu.gov.my/Tourism-@-Tourism_-_EPP_9a-.

Franchise Opportunities Guideline, PT. Cantika Puspa Pesona.

Growing Malaysias Spa Industry, http://malaysianbiz.my/industry/growing-malaysias-spa-industry, October 17th, 2013.

Interview with the General Manager of PT. Cantika Puspa Pesona: Ms. Palupi Candra.

Spa industry sees huge growth, http://www.ttnworldwide.com/Article/10002/Spa_industry_sees_huge_growth, June 16th, 2010.

Spa Therapist Training Programme,http://www.motac.gov.my/en/programme/courses/spa-therapist-training-programme.

The beauty of the beauty industry, http://www.themalaysiantimes.com.my/the-beauty-of-the-beauty-industry, April 14th, 2014.

SPA growth and opportunity in Malaysia 2002-2007, http://www.asiatraveltips.com/news06/1512-SpasinMalaysia.shtml, December 15th, 2006.

IN PART III WE WILL decide which country or countries to enter, and also how to enter. We will also discuss market segmentation and product positioning.

Chapter 6 deals with research necessary before deciding on country selection. It goes through the screening process by which the country opportunities can be ranked to arrive at a decision. It also suggests what published data sources may prove useful in the screening process. The chapter then presents methods for collecting market research data that can help pinpoint the best marketing opportunities in the country selected. Even though the published data sources suggest that, for example, China would be a great option, it is important to do some research on how the Chinese customers might react to the new entry. The chapter ends with a primer on basic sales forecasting tools as applied to foreign markets.

The following Chapter 7 presents the four basic modes of entry: Exporting, Licensing, Strategic Alliances, and Foreign Direct Investment (FDI). The chapter describes the modes, how they differ in marketing control, and what middlemen are needed to implement each mode. It also shows how the best or optimal mode depends on what kind of entry barriers exist for the selected country. In free and open markets, there are usually few barriers and very efficient middlemen, facilitating simple exporting and making risky foreign direct investment less necessary.

Chapter 8 covers the basic principles of market segmentation and product positioning in a global setting. It shows how global market segmentation differs from domestic-only cases and introduces a two-step approach wherein the country-level macro-segmentation precedes the within-country micro-segmentation. The chapter also covers targeting issues, discussing which of the segment(s) should be targeted, the question of diversification, and the choice between waterfall and sprinkler entry strategies. The chapter ends with a discussion of how all three strategy components—segmentation, targeting, and positioning—need to be fully integrated for maximum benefit.

In this chapter you will learn about:
1. A systematic analysis of countries to identify the most promising market to enter
2. How to conduct market research in the country selected in order to find out more about the customers
3. What kind of data is useful in each stage of the analysis and how to collect the data
4. How to do sales forecasting in the selected market

This chapter will combine the internal "self-analysis" of strengths and weaknesses of the SWOT framework, with the environmental opportunities and threats (the OT part of SWOT). Analyzing key indicators on macro variables in the economic, political, and cultural environment, the firm will be able to select the country with the best fit and highest potential. Using an actual example, the chapter will show how the country attractiveness can be systematically analyzed. Then the chapter will discuss the issues involved in local market research used to uncover the market segments, consumer preferences, and other characteristics of the country selected. This will help the company match its strengths and weaknesses to the requirements of the local market, and identify what segments to target and what appeals to use. The end of this chapter will present the basic sales forecasting techniques used to predict sales.

Country Assessment and Local Market Research

CHAPTER 6

IKEA'S PAINSTAKING COUNTRY RESEARCH

IKEA, the Swedish furniture manufacturer, has used its model of blue-and-yellow stores, ready-to-assemble furniture flat packs and very low prices to expand throughout the world and build a strong global brand name (see Exhibit 6.1).

In Europe, where IKEA has 248 stores (72 percent of its worldwide total), standardization of its business was possible. However, expansion beyond has required patience, in-depth research and detailed adaptation—and still trial and error.

IKEA's 1985 expansion into the U.S. saw Americans coming into the stores, looking at the furniture and leaving empty-handed. More research was conducted that told IKEA to modify its mix of products, prices, and locations. One small example: Americans at the time bought sets of IKEA's clear small flower vases to use as water glasses, since IKEA's European water glasses were too small for American-size drinks with ice.[2]

IKEA applied these hard-won lessons before it started its expansion in China in 1998. The company used both its own research staff and local Chinese agencies to thoroughly understand the Chinese consumer. For example, the company modified the furniture to reflect Chinese tastes and smaller Chinese apartments, located stores near railway stations since most Chinese do not have cars, and used social media instead of their usual catalogs. In spite of these successful adaptations, IKEA continues to struggle with low-cost imitations of its products, unique to the Chinese market.

Before recently taking on South Korea, IKEA spent six (6) years doing market research. The company first

used available country data to evaluate South Korea as an attractive market. The findings were then confirmed through focus groups, surveys, and in-person interviews. The data helped with big decisions such as the best location for the store, and also smaller decisions such as to stock metal chopsticks instead of wooden chopsticks. As a result, IKEA's opening of the first store outside of Seoul was deemed the smoothest and most successful of all its international openings. Currently the world's largest, it is on track to be one of IKEA's best-performing stores internationally.[3]

In its global expansion, IKEA starts with the assumption that the store, the product, and the service can be the same worldwide and then tries to make a minimum amount of changes for culture. Getting this balancing act correct between globalization versus localization is one of the key requirements for international success.

COUNTRY ATTRACTIVENESS

At a basic level, country attractiveness for a firm depends on five factors:

- Market size: larger is generally more attractive
- Market growth: fast growth opens up opportunities
- Competitive intensity: intense rivalry lowers attractiveness
- Trade barriers (including regulations): less is better
- Membership in a trade bloc: increases size and provides opportunities

Market size involves population size and income levels. Market growth relates to the speed of economic development for the country and the increase in the demand for a particular product or service over time. As an example, for a "bottom of the pyramid" strategy, the population size dominates the income level at least at the start. The "bottom of the pyramid" strategy is based on the notion that as adapted products will be accepted and bought by poor consumers, economic development will occur, and the economic growth becomes self-sustaining. Economic growth coupled with a large population will then make the country increasingly attractive in the more traditional sense.

Competitive intensity involves the competition between domestic and foreign brands and the rivalry between entering global brands. Where domestic brands are favored by consumer patriotism and loyalty, attractiveness will be lower. Many firms can get across this obstacle by acquiring a local brand. Where government policies or regulation favors domestic competitors, the hurdle will generally be harder to overcome, although joint ventures can sometimes be used.

Trade barriers include entry barriers such as tariffs and custom duties, and also transportation costs. There are also non-tariff barriers, such as a slow and cumbersome bureaucracy and various business regulations such as limits on the size of stores. There can also be various political risks, and cultural and religious obstacles to trade in the country. Because of these barriers, an otherwise attractive country may not be the best choice for entry.

Trade bloc membership can increase the attractiveness of a country significantly. For the foreign firm, two effects are particularly important:

- Membership increases the market size. The potential market is now greater than the one country.
- Membership justifies a greater effort to overcome any entry barriers and become an insider in the trading area. Once the company has established operations in one country, expansion to other member countries is facilitated.

In what follows, we will show how these basic principles impact the country selection screening process.

THE SCREENING PROCESS

To bring order to the many alternatives and wide variety of foreign opportunities it is important to follow a systematic process when selecting a country market. Actually, there are foreign endeavors that have started quite randomly and with little foresight and still panned out. Toyota, the Japanese carmaker, entered the European market after being contacted by a Danish businessman who wanted to become their first—and exclusive—foreign dealer. That businessman did very well for himself and for Toyota. In fact, it is not unusual for potential importers from a foreign country to approach large manufacturers at some trade fair and suggest collaboration. Foreign trade is a two-way affair, and not always initiated by an exporter.

But, by and large, such ad-hoc efforts will not suffice. The company intent on having sustainable presence and success in foreign markets needs to be more objective and systematic in its screening of candidate countries.

A Stepwise Process

As in most selection procedures, companies typically treat the country selection in a hierarchical stepwise manner. Broad and general factors such as political risk are applied early in the elimination process to quickly weed out more or less dangerous locations. Then more specific criteria such as regulatory and legal environments are used to further narrow down the field. Countries where government rules are restrictive tend to be difficult to do business in, raising costs and limiting the potential. By contrast, where the government is pushing for membership in a trade bloc the market potential in otherwise limited country markets will rise.

Next, economic and trade factors have to be considered. Here there is usually plenty of country-level data. The aggregated data has to be broken down and made specific to the company's products. This makes the analysis more relevant but also more intensive and costly. The level of disposable household income per capita is usually available, but estimates of the amount of money spent on the product category are not always easy to come up with. Similarly, even if trade data is available, category sales are not always easy to judge before entry, even with extensive market research.

BOX: The "Cultural Distance" Effect

There is a basic theory that explains how firms first expand abroad. Field research has shown that companies look for countries abroad where their experiences in the home market would be most useful, where the intercultural synergy would be maximized. This "reasoning by analogy" leads to selecting countries with conditions similar to the home market. Most of the expansion paths followed by firms begin in countries culturally similar to their own or to countries they already export to. The similarity involves "culture" in a broad sense, including language, religion, geographical proximity, and so on.[4] Recent research suggests that the most important factor might be language differences, partly because shipping costs are today much less of a factor compared to communications misunderstandings between headquarters and local representatives and subsidiaries.[5]

There are numerous examples of the cultural distance effect at work. The United States and Canada are each other's most important trading partners, and many small businesses in Wisconsin, for example, trade more with Canadian businesses than they trade with California or the East Coast. Japan's exporting companies generally started trade with the Southeast Asian countries before moving on to Latin America and Australia. Most European companies export first to their immediate neighbors, an old habit much encouraged by the establishment of the European Union (EU) ties.

At the next level, the consumer receptivity toward the brand has to be estimated somehow. Here social and cultural factors come into play. For example, the possibility of cultural conflicts needs to be assessed (see box, "The 'Cultural Distance' Effect").

The screening of candidate countries can be described as an elimination process, moving from a wide set of countries to a gradual narrowing of the number of countries considered, as shown in Exhibit 6.2. The exhibit shows how the process moves from general environmental variables to more specific country and market variables which usually require more in-depth market and consumer data. This is because such data is generally more expensive to collect and analyze, and it is important to quickly screen out less promising markets. On the right-hand side, the possible data sources are indicated. The last stage involves personal visits—expensive, but really necessary to confirm the soundness and feasibility of the selection made.

Next we will go through the stages in order and exemplify how the process works. The analysis will later be illustrated by an actual application at one company.

Stage 1—ID of the set of Candidate Countries

In the **country identification** stage, various statistical data are used to identify candidate regions and countries. Typically the company decides to enter a particular trade area. For example, companies opt to focus on Europe or Latin America or East Asia, and then do a more in-depth analysis within each of the regions to identify where to place their sales headquarters and which countries to enter first.

The statistical variables typically define level of development (including per-capita income) and cultural similarity of the countries. To get a sense of the total potential, population comparisons are necessary as well.

Stage 2—Preliminary Screening

After the candidate countries have been identified, the **preliminary screening** stage begins. This involves rating the identified countries on macro-level indicators such as political stability, geographic distance, and economic development. The idea is to weed out obviously problematic candidates from consideration. For example, if profit

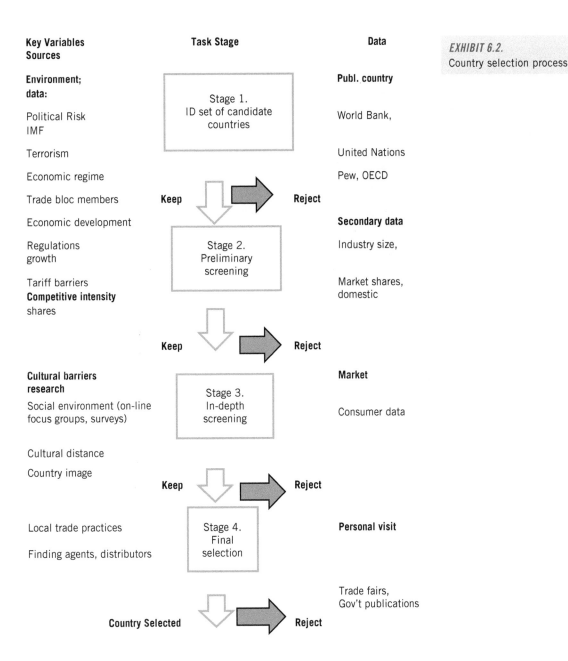

Key Variables Sources	Task Stage	Data
Environment; data:	**Stage 1.** ID set of candidate countries	**Publ. country**
Political Risk IMF		World Bank,
Terrorism		United Nations
Economic regime		Pew, OECD
Trade bloc members	**Keep** → **Reject**	
Economic development	**Stage 2.** Preliminary screening	**Secondary data**
Regulations growth		Industry size,
Tariff barriers **Competitive intensity** shares		Market shares, domestic
	Keep → **Reject**	
Cultural barriers research	**Stage 3.** In-depth screening	**Market**
Social environment (on-line focus groups, surveys)		Consumer data
Cultural distance		
Country image	**Keep** → **Reject**	
Local trade practices	**Stage 4.** Final selection	**Personal visit**
Finding agents, distributors		
	Country Selected → **Reject**	Trade fairs, Gov't publications

EXHIBIT 6.2.
Country selection process

repatriation or currency convertibility is questionable, the country may be eliminated. Also, countries with signs of political instability may be ruled out at this stage. For example, the Turkish protests against President Erdogan (see Exhibit 6.3) have probably weakened the attraction of Turkey as a market, despite a strong growth record.

At this stage, the anticipated costs of entering a market should be broadly assessed to match financial and other resource constraints. In addition to data on transportation costs and customs duty, which are comparatively easy to assemble, costs involve storage and warehousing, distribution in the country, and supporting the product in the market.

These usually have to be rough estimates, drawing on industry experts and personal experience in the country.

Stage 3—In-Depth Screening

The **in-depth screening** stage is the core of the attractiveness evaluation. Data here are specific to the industry and product markets, if possible even down to specific market segments. This stage involves assessing **market potential** and actual market size, market growth rate, strengths and weaknesses of existing and potential competition, and height of regulation and entry barriers, including tariffs and quotas. In-country micro-segmentation should also be explored, with an eye to capturing more precise target segment forecasts. Furthermore, at this stage the company resource constraints—money, managers, supply capacity, and so on—should be revisited to make sure that contemplated entries are feasible.

Several screening criteria for the in-depth stage can be useful to the prospective entrant. Generally, studies have shown that almost all entrants use information relating to market size and growth rate, level of competition, and trade barriers and regulations.

Market Size. For market size it is useful to distinguish between the current market and the potential future market. To assess the size of the current market and the target segment size, three sets of data are useful:

- Population, age-groups, no. of households (in B2B number of businesses)
- Disposable income per capita
- Per-capita spending on product category

The future potential requires an analysis of the product life cycle:

- Current stage of the PLC
- Potential saturation level
- Percent of saturation potential sold (penetration)

A crude measure of market size can be computed from local production, minus exports, plus imports. An indirect measure can be derived from the widely available GNP measure, population size, growth in GNP, and imports of relevant goods. Data for the product life cycle involves penetration data such as percentage of households in

EXHIBIT 6.3.
Demonstration in Taksim Square, Istanbul, sparked by plans to build on the Gezi Park. Regardless of the cause, political unrest is a negative when evaluating a potential market.

possession of the product or in the market versus the likely total saturation level. Data availability is discussed later in this chapter.

Market Growth. For market growth it is useful to distinguish between three growth components:

- Growth among existing customers. This could be growth in buying frequency and also growth in amounts bought.
- Growth in penetration. These are switching buyers as awareness grows and brand diffusion occurs.
- Growth rate of new buyers. With population growth and growth in disposable income, these are new incoming buyers who are old enough and have enough buying power to purchase.

Growth estimates can be obtained by getting the market size measurements for different years and computing the growth rates. When deriving the growth rate in this manner, it is important that cyclical changes in the economy are accounted for. When the business cycles turn up, even slow-growing mature markets will show strong growth.

Competitive Intensity. The level of competitive rivalry in the market can be measured by the number of competitors in the market and the relative size distribution of market shares. Distinguish the following:

- Total number of competitors
- Number of domestic and foreign competitors
- Domestic companies, market shares
- Multinational competitors, market shares

Then assess own strength in terms of competitive advantages and disadvantages to reach a range of potential levels of market share.

Many governments' Departments of Commerce track market shares for many industries in different countries in its Market Shares Report. Competition is generally toughest where a few large domestic companies dominate the market. When existing companies all have small shares, or when foreign companies have already made successful entry, the competitors will generally be less concerned about a new entrant.

Trade Barriers and Regulations. Tariffs, taxes, duties, and transportation costs can be ascertained from official government publications. One problem in analyzing tariff data is that the level of the barriers depends on the exact specification of the goods entered. The company can often decide to do some assembly in the foreign country to avoid high tariffs on finished products, for example, or it can decide to purchase a component from a local manufacturer in another country to get a better rate because of increased local content. Accordingly, the country rating on tariff barriers can only be assessed accurately after preliminary decisions have been made as to whether a final or some intermediate product will be shipped to that country. Since tariffs also vary by country of origin, it is important to research which sourcing country would be best to utilize. When a multinational has several alternative plant locations around the world, it is necessary to research all feasible locations.

The in-depth screening can be summarized using managerial judgment on the basis of the research findings. Managers can assign numerical scores to each of the most important factors for the market potential in each country. Assigning weights to these factors according to how important they are to success or failure, each candidate country can be given a comparable summary score. An example is given in Exhibit 6.4, using Under Armour, the 2014 U.S. Olympic athletic apparel maker. The exhibit shows how the possible expansion into China can be rated.

As can be seen, the market potential is high at a score of 76.5 (with 50 being "neutral"), but the country-level constraints lowers the overall attractiveness to 43.8, basically negative. The basic problems involve entry barriers

EXHIBIT 6.4.
How attractive is China to
Under Armour?[6]

Adapted from Roger Best,
Market-Based Management.
Prentice Hall, 2012.

Country: China
Product: Under Armour

Market Attractiveness Factors	Importance Weight	Rating
Score(*)		
<u>Market factors 40%</u>		
Potential demand (willingness to buy, stage of PLC)	0.25	90
Current segment size (share of population able to buy)	0.20	50
Segment growth (combine existing, new buyers)	0.35	80
Your Competitive strength (brand, country-of-origin)	0.20	80
Summed market score	**100%**	**76.5**
<u>Country factors 60%</u>		
Regulatory and Legal constraints	0.25	10
Tariffs, custom duties	0.25	20
Middleman barriers	0.15	20
Cultural barriers (religion, attitudes)	0.05	50
Infrastructure (incl. transportation, shopping malls)	0.30	30
Summed country score	**100%**	**22.0**
Total Attractiveness Score	**43.8**	

(*) The score is a judgment rating from zero (extremely poor) to 100 (extremely favorable) and 50 is a neutral rating (not good or bad).

(regulatory constraints and custom duties have very low scores), and as China opens up, these barriers will come down.

Stage 4—Final Selection

Personal Experience. The **final** selection of the country to enter cannot and should not be made until personal visits have been made to the country and **direct experience** acquired by the managers. There is no substitute for on-the-spot information and the hands-on feeling of a new market. There are lessons to be learned from the flexibility with which the hotel staff responds to unusual requests; the language capabilities of the average person in the street; the courtesy, or lack of it, in stores; the degree to which a doctor responds to a client's questions; the ease with which a telephone connection home can be made; and the speed with which currencies may be exchanged. Countless such observations may be made on the local scene. And the visits will often have serendipitous effects, creating marketing opportunities not recognized before, as happened to Microlog (see below).

CASE: MICROLOG GOES TO EUROPE[7]

To illustrate how the step-wise process works in practice, it is useful to go through an actual case in some detail. This is how Microlog went about its first expansion abroad.

Microlog Inc. is a small company located in Germantown, Maryland, just outside Washington, D.C. Its business is in telecommunications and it has managed to survive over a decade in a very competitive industry. Initially, the company marketed and serviced voice processing systems, that is, computerized electronic telephone systems that help direct incoming calls, record messages, and generally serve as an online mail and audio information service. Such integrated hardware-software systems has seen tremendous growth in the United States and elsewhere. Today the business has grown to a communications system for managing all customer interactions. From its website: "Microlog provides managed communications solutions to actively engage your customer base." Microlog was one of the pioneers that helped develop the systems. Its domestic market includes local businesses as well as the U.S. government.

Country Identification

To identify candidate countries, the marketing director and his assistant first decided to select three regions: Southeast Asia, Latin America, and Europe. All three regions showed promise, with increasing penetration of telephones and promising economic prospects. Southeast Asia showed the fastest growth, while Latin America got a boost from the North American Free Trade Agreement (NAFTA) which had significantly opened up trade between North American and South American countries. Europe was very attractive because the 28 member countries have developed as a single market through a standardized system of laws that apply in all member states.

Given their limited resources, the two managers decided to first focus on Europe, partly because of their own ease and comfort there (one manager had extensive experience in Europe, and the assistant was British). They also sensed that Europeans might be more culturally prepared for the automation than the other regions (although partially correct, acceptance in the Southeast Asian countries proved to be even quicker).

Preliminary Screening

To collect preliminary screening data on the European countries, the marketing manager and his team collected U.N. data on the size and growth of the GNP, population size, infrastructure, and level of industrial activity from the university library. Visits to the World Bank yielded information on political risk factors, ethnic diversity, and potential language and cultural problems. The preliminary screening led to a selection of 11 countries for in-depth evaluation. The set of countries included Belgium, Denmark, France, Germany, the Netherlands, Ireland, Italy, Norway, Spain, Sweden, and Switzerland.

In-Depth Screening

After the choice of the 11 countries had been decided, the team turned to the selection of in-depth screening criteria. The selected criteria involved market size, growth potential, a "loose brick" factor indicating ease of entry, competitive factors, distribution possibilities, cultural distance to the United States, technological development, likely receptivity to voice processing, and importance of the market in the EU.

Once the criteria were agreed upon, the team set about collecting data, scoring each of the 11 countries on the selected criteria.

The manager then came up with weights reflecting the importance of the various criteria for the voice-processing system's market success. The cultural and linguistic similarity with the United States and the compatibility of the phone system and its regulation were judged to be particularly important. To transact business in any other language than English would be difficult. At the same time, size of the market was seen as unimportant or even slightly negative, since it was deemed that entry into a smaller market to start with might be a more manageable task for the firm. Also, in one of these meetings the ease of expansion from the entry base into other countries emerged as an important criterion.

The weights and attractiveness scores of the countries showed that the Netherlands and Ireland were rated highest. In both cases the telecommunications market was well-developed, the industry regulations were not as severe as elsewhere, and the countries seemed to be natural entry gates for the northern European market. The Scandinavian countries, although attractive in many ways, were not sufficiently close to continental Europe to be good gateways. In addition, Sweden's Ericsson was a feared potential competitor. Germany was ruled out mainly because of its byzantine regulatory system that raised barriers and made entry costly. France's regulations were also a barrier—raised further by the dominance of Alcatel, the French telecommunications giant and a potential competitor. Because the team considered the Netherlands' location more favorable than Ireland's, it recommended the Netherlands for initial entry. As a second alternative for an entry into southern Europe, the team recommended Italy.

Final Selection

The final choice? The Netherlands. A first trip to the European CeBIT fair in Hanover, Germany (the world's largest and most international computer expo held every year in Hanover) yielded several contacts. The manager met with executives at Philips, the big electronics manufacturer. Philips was interesting not simply as a prospective customer, but as a partner in the European market. With the kind of strong European connection provided by Philips, Microlog would be able to quickly establish credibility and create a base for future European expansion. Of course, this also meant that Microlog did not establish its own brand name in the end market of Europe—but with its small size, the company still considered it a very successful deal.

DATA SOURCES

Despite the important role of personal visits to the top candidate countries, most of the data used in the screening of countries come from **secondary data**, not **primary data**. Secondary data is information that has been collected for a purpose other than your current research project but has some relevance and utility for your research. Primary data is information that is collected specifically for the purpose of your research project. An advantage of primary data is that it is tailored to your research questions and needs.

Country identification. In the country identification stage, the analysis usually has to make do with general information.

- A good place to start is with the United Nations annual compilation of world economic and social data, which will give a broad picture of the various countries.
- This can be followed by data from Department of Commerce and other government offices and data from international organizations such as the EU Commission, World Bank, and the International Monetary Fund (IMF).

Preliminary screening. In the preliminary screening phase, more in-depth data becomes desirable.

- The *U.S. Department of Commerce* and its counterparts in other countries publish data at the industry level, even some market share data for various countries and products. Where trade conflicts have occurred, more data tend to be available.

- The *Euromonitor International* is another source that offers data on attitudes and opinions in addition to socioeconomic data not only on European countries. It also offers in-depth analyses on consumers for specific product categories.
- A good data source for the preliminary screening phase is the *Business International Market Report (BI),* published by the Economist Intelligence Unit. The report gives weighted indicators of market size, growth, and market intensity for 200 countries. The market intensity measure is intended to capture the dynamics of the marketplace by double-weighting the private consumption expenditures, the car ownership figures, and the proportion of urban population.

The *World Values Survey* (WVS) is a global survey of values and beliefs, covering some 57 countries and 85,000 respondents. Done as repeated surveys, the WVS allows the identification of trends over time. The most recent sixth wave covered years 2010–2014. The WVS measures attitudes toward democracy, tolerance of foreigners and ethnic minorities, the role of religion, the impact of globalization, and attitudes toward the environment.

The *Eurobarometer* survey series is a cross-national longitudinal study designed to compare and gauge trends within member states of the European Union. The surveys investigate a wide range of topics such as agriculture, consumer behavior, elderly people, immigration, poverty, regional identity, working conditions, and youth attitudes from a European perspective.

The *European Social Survey* (ESS) is a social scientific endeavor to map the attitudes, beliefs, and behavior patterns in Europe covering 30 countries. It is a more recent data source started in 2002 and held every two years.

In-depth screening. In the in-depth screening stage, when data on specific markets are needed, the data availability varies by industry. The *Euromonitor* and *BI* reports are still very useful here. There are also other sources:

- Trade associations are usually the place to start, followed by government agencies. The U.S. Department of commerce and its counterparts in other countries do assist industry-level research. In highly visible industries such as automobiles, computers, and consumer electronics, good data are usually available from the trade press.
- There are also **syndicated data,** industry-wide data for sale from commercial sources and available to all competitors. Frost and Sullivan in New York, for example, provide worldwide studies of market growth and potential for specific industries. Various independent firms, from advertising agencies to international research firms to electronic news media, have emerged to gather and sell information on specific industries across the globe.

In most markets the local marketer is faced with competition from both domestic competitors and other foreign competitors. Who the competitors are and how intense the competitive rivalry is are important factors to assess.

- This type of information is usually available from middlemen, trade magazines, and even newspaper articles.

Final selection. The final selection stage requires no new secondary information in principle, but it is here that the subjective judgments and experiences during the visits to the prospective country play a bigger role.

- Trade fairs are a good place to find and interview industry experts in the foreign country. Managers can substitute subjective "guesstimates" for missing data and correct other data that seem out of line.

LOCAL MARKET RESEARCH

Once the country selection process is over, there is a need for further market research to better understand the local customer and prepare the introductory campaign. Now there is a need to match the company strengths and weaknesses with the specifics of the local market. What FSAs and CSAs will be particularly useful and should be stressed in the new market? This requires more in-depth market research data.

The typical marketing research process to collect **primary data** is shown in Exhibit 6.5.[8] Except for the last stage, data analysis, all the stages can be affected by a foreign environment. The main components will be discussed in what follows.

Qualitative Research

Although there are many forms of qualitative research, the well-known *focus groups* have become standard for initial **exploratory research** in many markets. It helps determine the best research design, data collection method, and selection of respondents.

What are focus groups? A **focus group** is a small number of people (usually between 4 and 15, but typically 8) brought together with a moderator to participate in a guided discussion about a particular product or topic before launch or to provide ongoing feedback. The aim of a focus group is to generate a discussion instead of collecting individual responses to formal questions and focus groups thus provide qualitative data on preferences and beliefs.

Pros and Cons. In foreign markets, focus groups have the advantages of being relatively inexpensive, completed quickly, and can reach local pockets of the total market. Online focus groups in particular can be completed in a couple of weeks. The cost is minimal, although any data analysis can be time-consuming and costly. The evidence from focus groups is often clear from the direct responses of the participants, and little further analysis may be necessary.

Unfortunately, focus groups can constitute a sample that may be **unrepresentative** of the potential customer segment. They are not similar to the client's customer base. This happens either because the focus group is too small to properly represent a market, or because the screening criteria are incorrect.

In general, the small nonrandom sample sizes of focus groups make assumptions about representativeness tenuous at best. Furthermore, respondents get paid, the amount varying by participants' perceived opportunity cost. The payment tends to inhibit the expression of negative feelings.

Correcting the drawbacks. These and related problems can be overcome with careful planning of the focus groups. Representativeness in terms of geographical areas is usually dealt with by selecting certain cities that are leading markets for the products. In the United States, New York and Los Angeles are often viewed as trendsetters—in Germany, it is Berlin and Munich. Few UK studies can avoid London, and the same is true for studies in France (Paris), Italy (Milano), Spain (Madrid), and Scandinavia (Stockholm).

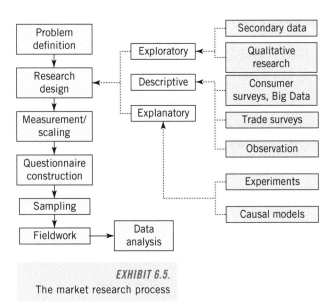

EXHIBIT 6.5.
The market research process

The moderators chosen should be professionals who can identify with the subjects and make them feel at ease. The amount paid should be sufficient to make a difference and thus be an incentive, but not so large as to invite praise. Local users in mature markets are often ideal key informers for the adaptation of a global product.

Consumer Surveys

Surveys of relatively large (n = 2000 and above) random samples drawn from a sampling frame of representative product users constitute the core of **descriptive market research**. Whether administered online, by phone, or in person, such surveys are used for a variety of marketing purposes, including segmentation and positioning, concept testing, and customer satisfaction and competitive product evaluation.

The emergence of cloud-based services for doing surveys internationally has really changed the survey landscape, although the basics remain the same. We will deal with the many issues concerning international questionnaire construction and sampling first, then get back to discussing how the new online survey companies can help the global marketer.

Questionnaire Construction. There are many cultural aspects affecting the application of the kind of direct questioning involved in the typical consumer survey. In high-context cultures the idea that one can understand consumers from their responses to a formal survey can be questioned. Answering truthfully to a stranger is not necessarily proper in some nations, especially those in which an authoritarian regime has made people wary of questions. Open-ended questions are often left blank by respondents in hierarchical cultures who are not used to explaining their reasoning or are afraid of being too transparent.[9]

In questionnaire construction for cross-cultural consumer research there are three major issues:

- Pretesting and back translation
- Mode of administration
- Equivalence of scales

1. <u>Pretesting and back translation</u>. The questionnaire employed in the typical consumer survey needs to be carefully *tested before its deployment*, especially if it is simply a translation from a standardized version in another country. Translated questions are often very prone to misunderstandings, even when literally correct, because of differences in context. Also, a word in one language may have no equivalent in another language, or could have a completely different "meaning" or effect in the translated language (see box, "Translations may vary").

BOX: Translations may vary

Even mundane and simple language can create problems and misunderstandings. For example, British English is not the same as American English.

<u>"British" versus "American" English:</u>[10]
- Boot: Trunk
- Chips: French fries
- Nappy: Diaper
- Chemist: Pharmacist
- Fairy Cake: Cupcake

Spanish is another language where there are differences between the home land and previous colonies:

"Blanket" in Spanish[11]
- Spain: manta
- Argentina: acolchado
- Chile, Dominican Republic, Peru: frazada
- Columbia, Ecuador, Venezuuela: cobija
- Cuba: colcha
- Costa Rica, Mexico: sabana

Rule: Always double-check with a native speaker!

EXHIBIT 6.6.
Market researcher intercepting a shopping center customer. In on-the-spot interviews, the interviewer has to be pleasant but the questions have to be short and to the point, so as not to waste anybody's time.

Copyright © by Bigstock/andres.

The global market researcher should first translate the original questionnaire into the foreign language and then have someone else "***back translate***" the questionnaire into the original language. Back translation is the process of translating a document that has already been translated into a foreign language back to the original language—preferably by an independent translator. When differences appear, they have to be resolved through discussions, pretests with target respondents, and repeated back translations.[12] It is common for this process to yield a questionnaire of different length than the original, since different languages require different levels of polite indirectness.

2. Mode of administration. Today, much of the research in developed markets is done online. In many countries this will exclude many potential respondents. Phone interviews are also possible and fairly cost effective, but again many respondents will not be reached. This leaves personal interviews, common in the new emerging markets where interviewers are available and can be trained. Personal interviews are not always very cost-effective, but intercepts at shopping malls are usually feasible (see Exhibit 6.6).

It is important to recognize that face-to-face interviews are prone to bias because of **demand characteristics**, that is, respondents who try to answer in a way that satisfies the interviewer (or the respondent's own ego). Such demand pressure is handled differently in different cultures. Western people are known either to try to please ("yea-sayers") or go against ("nay-sayers") according to their attitude toward the assumed sponsor. Respondents everywhere may try to answer more or less conscientiously, often opting for the least inconvenient multiple-choice alternative. Or they may lie. For example, respondents may be eager to show off a socially desirable image (see box, "Telling It Like It Is").

3. Equivalence of scales. **Equivalence** issues involve questions about the comparability of the concepts across cultures. For example, does the Western conception of "love" mean the same thing in all cultures? Probably not in those countries where marriages are still arranged. There are several kinds of equivalence issues that arise in cross-national marketing research.[14]

BOX: Telling it Like it is[13]

Sometimes qualitative research is useful simply as a check on the validity and reliability of self-reported data from consumers. One example comes from a doctoral researcher at the University of California, Berkeley, whose thesis dealt with consumption behavior in his home country in the Middle East.

The researcher followed the family on the weekly Saturday shopping trip to the local open-air market. The goal was to document spending patterns for various household products by urban families. Walking by the various stalls offering all kinds of produce, clothing, and electronic products, the observer dutifully recorded the family's bargaining for a better deal and the actual prices paid. Returning home, he discussed the trip with the husband and double-checked the figures. The husband corrected him, doubling the price for the shirt bought, and lowering the price for the red wine. "But I saw how much you paid," protested the researcher. "You don't understand," responded the husband. "I can't wear such a cheap shirt, and I can't spend that much on wine."

Survey responses sometimes do not match reality.

A typical example of equivalence problems occurs in lifestyle segmentation research. For example, "independence" in the United States is described as "self-orientation and resourceful," while in Japan the concept involves "life orientation and attitudes toward social change."[15]

Another example is **scale points and cutoffs.** This is a difficult issue for two reasons. First, the type of scale can influence the answer. For example, a scale of 1 through 5 or -2 through +2 can produce different answers even though both have five points (some respondents don't like negative numbers). Secondly, the groupings of choices (i.e., the cutoffs) can alter the answers. For example, what should be the cutoffs for "high" or "low" income levels for households? Using the same cutoffs in different countries might mean that high incomes in one country might be barely above the poverty level elsewhere.

In **attitude scaling,** the way of measuring an individual's intensity of feeling vis-à-vis some product or company, it is common to use numerical scales. But the use of numbers as indicators of emotions or value ("he's a 10") may be easy to grasp for Westerners used to quantification, but can be confusing to others. On an even more basic level, the cognitive and emotional concepts measured might not be equivalent across cultures. For example, "assertive" is a notorious English language concept for which there are few counterparts in any language. In yet other instances the foreign language has a much more nuanced set of emotions—the word "disagree," which is commonly used in attitude scales, can be expressed in at least five different ways in Japanese.

It is important to remember that *double-barreled questions* always give ambiguous results. A double-barreled question is a single question that asks about more than one issue, but only allows for one answer. Double-barreled questions result in confusion and inaccuracies in the answer because there is no indication which issue in the double-barreled question the respondent is thinking of. An example:

Question: Religion plays an important role and I go to church regularly (check one)
☐ YES
☐ NO

- 75 percent in the UK answered YES yet only 10 percent attend church regularly (in England, religion is important but not church attendance).

- Only 30 percent of Italians answered YES yet 55 percent attend church regularly (to Italians, attending church does not mean religion is important).

In addition to the problem with double-barreled questions, different people and different cultures have different *response patterns to a survey*. This can ruin comparability across countries. An example:

- Italians tend to circle toward either ends of a scale.
- Germans tend to circle toward the middle of a scale.[16]

Sampling. The lack of comprehensive and reliable **sampling frames** from which to sample respondents has long been holding back survey research in many countries. Sampling frames are simply the list of all those within a population who can be sampled, and may include individuals, households, or institutions. Telephone directories are not very useful when few households have telephones. Postal addresses won't work well when people are mobile, when one address covers many individuals in extended families, and when postal service is unreliable. Today, of course, online surveys are increasingly feasible, fast, inexpensive, and also representative, as Internet penetration and online access has increased exponentially.

BOX: Getting to Know the European Consumer[17]

Despite all the talk about an integrated European Union, the European consumers are hardly homogeneous and continue to baffle marketers. According to Tom Broeders, an independent marketing consultant in Belgium, "Europe is a collection of different cultures related to language and habits." Especially in the contentious EU climate of 2015, it is not clear "how consumers balance the 'new' realities within the EU and their influence on consumption behavior" as one article puts it.[18]

Language differences make the creation of pan-European survey questionnaires difficult and expensive. These problems have diminished as the European nations provide more data for cross-national comparison and market researchers test pan-European strategies. Also, scale cutoffs on income and related measures have been simplified by the introduction of the euro in many countries, allowing more direct comparisons across countries.

One result has been the joint European development of a standardized questionnaire that is administered annually and collects comparable data on a number of socio-demographic, political, and economic indicators. Called the *Eurobarometer*, it was originally written in French and English, translated by native speakers into the various languages across the EU market, then back translated into French and English to check for subtle variations in meaning. Standard and Special Eurobarometer surveys are conducted in two waves per year, consisting of approximately 1000 face-to-face interviews in each of the 28 EU member states. For example, a special survey of attitudes toward privacy was conducted via 28,000 personal interviews, demonstrating Europeans' overwhelming desire for control of their personal information and 63 percent indicated their distrust of online business.[19]

Even if consumer surveys are afflicted by a number of problems and potential distortions in many foreign markets, they can be very useful. Many of the difficulties can be overcome by careful design of the questionnaire, back translation, and painstaking pretesting. One example is the *Eurobarometer,* an annual survey of attitudes and opinions in the European Union (see box, "Getting to Know the European Consumer").

Online surveys. With the recent growth of cloud-based survey services, the use of survey research has been greatly expanded. Companies such as SurveyMonkey, InstantSurvey, Qualtrics, and Amazon's Mechanical Turk offer a number of easy to use and inexpensive research services that allows both large and small companies to do research internationally at very low cost and with fast results.

These companies offer several services:

- Design of the questionnaires. The firms offer a wide variety of alternative question formulations, in different languages, and already pretested in different countries. Not all languages are necessarily available, but the companies are moving quickly expanding their reach.
- Sampling. The typical model for these companies is to maintain access to a large panel of volunteer respondents who sign up to complete surveys for payment. The fee is usually low and paid per completed (and accepted) questionnaire. The respondents' profile data (age, gender, etc.) allows the pre-qualification of the respondents, making sure they are in the target population. The panel is often managed by an independent company such as Cashbackresearch.com and Quickrewards.net. For international research, these panels are organized in the respective countries.
- Data collection. The actual administration of the survey is done by the survey firms once the questionnaire and sample have been decided on in collaboration with the marketing client. The survey is uploaded, and the panel is flagged that the survey is up, and the survey closes when the required number of respondents has been reached. Time is usually short, days or even hours.
- Data tabulation. The service firms provide basic tabulation of the responses, often on a real-time basis so that the client can follow how the responses stack up. More advanced analytics is often also available, but these analytics—such as a market segmentation analysis or price sensitivity assessment—will incur extra charges.
- Low price. The basic price is determined on the basis of number of respondents and length of questionnaire— some services offer a "free sample" by allowing a few questions and, say, 50 responses for free. Since the surveys draw on pre-tested questions and questionnaires that can be assembled by the client working online, the service is low-cost and the software is usually very flexible.

There are still questions that a client needs to answer before using these services, especially internationally.

One is whether the panel participants really constitute a representative sample. The companies go to great length to recruit a broad selection in each country, but still the necessary PC or tablet (or soon the smartphone) is simply not available to all people.

There is also a question of whether the submitted profile truthfully describes the respondent. It is difficult for companies to double-check and inquire about what is in fact private information, but the best firms try hard to weed out cheaters. One way is to check each respondent over several surveys and try to spot any inconsistencies, and the data collection companies preserve the right to reject a completed survey they suspect is fraudulent.

But given the convenience and the ease, speed and low-cost of collecting valuable data on new markets, it seems clear that these cloud-based online survey providers will become increasingly important for global marketers in all countries. The volume is great already. For example, SurveyMonkey is said to receive three million survey responses every day, with an average of 29 million questions answered, in 55 languages. The resulting reports, which is available free or as paid versions, can be paid in 28 different currencies.[20]

Big Data

The data generated by consumers' use of the Internet in social media, online purchases, and other activities on the Internet is huge. It is increasingly known as **"Big Data."**[21] In many countries there are virtually limitless data available on individual behaviors. Your credit card payments are routinely collected, as are your search patterns online, the transactions on Amazon.com and elsewhere, your subscriptions, your uploaded photos and social media activity, and so on. Although privacy concerns and legal restrictions prohibit the use of your actual identity, your home and work address can be matched to zip codes and thus to the kind of classification that shows what kind of household you are likely to live in.

If only the company could find a way to harness all this information—provided freely—and somehow put it to good use in tracking their brands in the marketplace, in conjunction with the large data banks already compiled, they could really target the individual consumer with the right product. This was the birth of the Big Data concept.

The use of Big Data for the analysis of consumer data is rapidly increasing. The basic problem is not to find something about a particular segment—this can be done readily. For example, you can get the comments about your brand from of someone active on Twitter, and also the comments from others (this is now a standard way of tracking brand image). Of course, in a foreign market, you need to hire native speakers to interpret the comments. The problem has more to do with the kind of data and the magnitudes involved. How do you summarize all the comments? How do you make sure that you are not just adding comments from one individual but from relevant target members? How do you match the verbal comments to transactional data on purchases?

Today, companies access huge databases tracking individual consumers across the many "touch-points" that the electronic and digital technologies have spawned even in foreign markets (although differing privacy rules and censorship limits the use in countries like Germany and China). The new type of data collection involves "scraping" the Internet to gather information from Twitter, Facebook, and other social media vehicles. It is a collection, typically verbal, of the "buzz" out there. It is collected in real time, and continuously updated. Even though the social media platforms do not release individual data for privacy reasons, they increasingly offer aggregated summaries of what was being said and by what groups of people.

The basic analysis usually involves using a search engine to find specified key words—a brand, a country, a product, a current topic—and an assessment of whether the sentiment expressed is positive or negative. The first marketing report is usually a quick indicator of whether a brand was quoted positively or negatively, and in what context. As summary measures, the analysis simply adds up the relative number of positive versus negative comments, screening out multiple posts from each individual.

These are new developments that are only starting to play themselves out. But the impact on marketing practice is already underway. One effect has been the need for a completely different style of data analysis. While traditional market research has employed statistical methods and sampling probabilities, with Big Data the only real need is for trying to summarize and average what the market is saying. The technology of how to analyze verbal expressions is not yet very advanced, but things are likely to gradually change, and quite quickly at that.

Trade Surveys

The quickest, least expensive, and most commonly used method for learning about customers in a market is to do a **trade survey**. This typically involves interviewing people at trade fairs, in the distribution channels, and at trade associations. These intermediaries can often explain the basic segments in the market, who the buyers are, the type of buying processes used, and the sources of buyer information. These people provide a good starting point for further data gathering and analysis.

In the United States, the use of middlemen for information about consumers is usually limited to the sales and scanner records of retailers and wholesalers. For example, a wholesaler may only know that a product is selling well in retail distribution and not why it is selling well. More attention is usually given to middlemen in the business-to-business sectors, if only because there are a limited number of ways to use formal research methods on business customers. In many other countries the middlemen are a much more important—and perhaps the only—source of information.

Interviewing middlemen is, it should be remembered, only one aspect of getting data on the trade. Store visits to observe customers and talk to them directly, inspecting store layouts and atmospherics, and collecting sales and turnover data are other activities that yield market information.

Observational Research

Research involving **direct observation** of customers buying and using existing products can be very beneficial. Existing products give important clues to customer preferences, especially in mature markets.

By analyzing bestselling products—and those that don't do so well—the global marketer can start to identify which features of a product are valued by the market and which are not. Although these points are in a sense obvious, Western marketers have been slow in exploiting this potential. The Asian companies have been much faster. The Japanese successes in Western markets have not been based on thorough market research in the traditional sense. Instead, they have learned about customers and design preferences by analyzing the products that are successful in Western markets.

For example, the way drivers enter their cars has a direct bearing on design. The Japanese small cars were built originally for men, who can easily put one leg in and then sit down in the driver's seat pulling the other leg after. But in the West, the small Japanese cars became popular with women, whose skirts prohibited such an entry. Thus, the Japanese had to make the door larger, to allow the woman driver to first sit down, and then pull both legs in. This redesign came about when Toyota engineers traveled to Los Angeles and watched people get in and out of their cars. Similar research lies behind the lowered threshold of the trunk (to make it easier to slide baggage in and out), the coffee cup holders in cars, and the height of the fastback door.

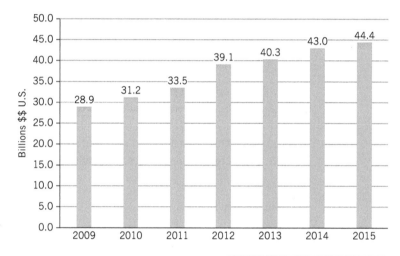

[22]**EXHIBIT 6.7.**
Global revenue of market research companies
Consistently topping the chart are the five largest research companies in the world: Nielsen (USA), Kantar (UK), IMS Health (USA), Ipsos (France), and GfK (Germany). Together these represent 37% of the total revenue for 2015.

Source: American Marketing Association: The 2016 AMA Gold Report Top 25 Global Market Research Firms

Explanatory Research

Explanatory marketing research involves determining the cause of what is happening, the "why" that explains the behavior of consumers. This research involves experimental methods advanced causal modeling. It is used to fine-tune choices such as color of the product, choosing between two ad campaigns, and similar options. Much of this research follows from focus group findings, and provides a more rigorous assessment of the underlying reasons for consumer opinions.

The problem in this research is that the samples involved tend to be very small and possibly unrepresentative. In emerging markets this kind of research is rarely worth the cost. The decisions to be made are too basic to need that much fine-tuning, and the action alternatives facing the global marketer are often rather crude. Observing actual usage is often a better approach. But in mature markets where consumers pay attention to fine nuances—such as design features of a product—this research is very common and actually necessary for companies. Understanding that consumers were not adverse to larger cell phones gave Samsung a (brief) head start over iPhone.

Fieldwork

Fieldwork is the actual collecting of data and can include interviewing via house to house surveys, telephone interviewing, street intercepts or shopping center intercepts, mystery customer or mystery shopper roles, and structured observation. Throughout the research process, and in particular when it comes to the fieldwork, usually the firm will work with a market research firm, sometimes a full-service advertising agency because of the large number of hours needed to collect data and the familiarity with the culture needed for success. In fact, there are over 7000 market research companies worldwide helping with the data collection and analysis process and generating increasing revenues (see Exhibit 6.7).

Market research is a growing field internationally, as companies try to understand the often baffling customers in the global marketplace.

FORECASTING COUNTRY SALES

Before finally committing to a new market entry strategy, it is necessary to forecast the likely unit sales and market share that can be captured. Without the forecast, it is not possible to assess properly the likelihood of a successful entry.

The forecasting of total market sales and market share involves technical skills, many of which are valid in any market. But there are additional factors that need to be considered in foreign markets.

A Basic Equation

There are two basic components that companies use to estimate in order to generate a forecast. They are sales in the industry or market in total, and the share that the firm can expect to capture. The unit sales can then be forecasted using the basic equation

- Unit Sales = Market sales × Market share

The division between market sales and market share serves to identify and separate what factors need to be considered.

To develop an estimate of *market sales*, environmental determinants such as economic growth, disposable incomes, social and political developments, as well as dynamics of the product life cycle need to be considered. The *market share* prediction, on the other hand, relates directly to factors such as competitive situation and marketing effort. What affects the market size is one thing, what affects the share we get in the market is another. Although in international marketing this represents an oversimplification because of various trade obstacles (tariff and nontariff barriers), such factors can be incorporated and accounted for as we will show.

Market Forecast in Early PLC Stages

The forecasting of market sales is different depending on what product life cycle (PLC) stage the market country is in. In the early stages of the product life cycle the market size is not easily gauged (since it is not yet established). Three types of forecasting techniques can be used in the early stages.

- "Build-up" method from industry experts and distribution channels
- "Forecasting by analogy," doing a comparison with a lead country
- "Judgmental" methods

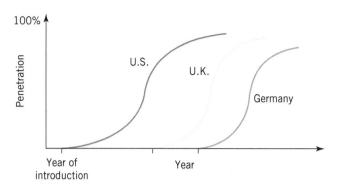

*The **Build-Up Method**.* The "build-up" connotation comes from the fact that the market sales are estimated on the basis of separate estimates from industry experts and knowledgeable channel members about certain segments of the market. These single estimates of various parts of the market are aggregated or "built up" into an evaluation of total market size.

Given that these estimates are subjective, it is important that the marketer gather additional information from whatever other sources are available so as to develop a sense of the reliability of the subjective estimates.

The information from the build-up method should always be compared to managerial experiences of the product in other countries—provided of course there are other countries further along the product life cycle process. In these cases forecasting by analogy has become quite popular.

Forecasting by Analogy. The basic premise underlying **forecasting by analogy** is that the sales in one "lagging" country will show similarities to sales in another "leading" country where the product is already marketed. Such similarities have been used to forecast the rate of acceptance of a new product in many different countries, especially those belonging to a common regional grouping. A typical example is television.[23] Its introduction in the United States exhibited a growth curve replicated with minor modifications in a number of other countries (the so-called "demonstration effect"). Exhibit 6.8 shows the basic logic.

The similarities between the U.S., UK, and (then West) Germany penetration curves are striking. Only the starting point is shifted by several years as Europe recovered from World War II.

To account for the difference in size between countries, the sales figures are usually weighted by a measure such as GNP or population size. For example, forecasted sales might be computed from an expression such as the following:

$$S_b(2020) = [S_a(2016)/\text{GNP}_a(2016)] \times \text{GNP}_b(2020)$$

where S stands for unit sales, the subscript a stands for the leading country, b stands for the lagging country, and there is a lag of four years (2020–2016). In words, the ratio of sales to

GNP in the lead country in 2016 gives the unit sales per dollar GNP. By multiplying this factor into the lagging country's GNP in 2020, a sales forecast is arrived at.

Clearly, the validity of this formula requires a careful assessment of the comparability between the two countries.[24] The United States and Canada might show a similar pattern of penetration, but they may not be useful comparisons for emerging countries where income inequality prevents a rapid penetration in the middle- and lower-income segments.

Judgmental Forecasts. Judgmental forecasting is used in cases during completely new and unique market conditions. Judgmental forecasting techniques generally attempt to introduce a certain amount of rigor and reliability into otherwise quite arbitrary guesses. The most widely used technique is the Delphi technique.

The **Delphi method** consists of a series of "rounds" of numerical forecasts from a pre-selected number of experts. These experts may or may not know the identity of the other members of the panel. They are asked to provide individual estimates, independently of their colleagues. The estimates are tallied, the average forecast is computed, and summary statistics (but not individual estimates) are returned to the experts. Another round of estimates is collected, tallied up, and the summary is again distributed. As these rounds continue, the feedback provided will tend to bring the estimates into line. The anonymity provided serves to ensure that everybody "has a voice" as the process gradually converges towards a consensus forecast.

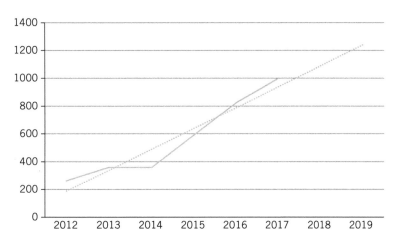

EXHIBIT 6.9.
Extrapolating end of year stock price for Amazon.com (AMZN). Actual stock price and linear trend line with two year forecast. This trend line indicates that the stock was slightly overpriced in 2017 relative to the historical trends.

Source: Amazon stock prices.

Market Forecast in Late PLC Stages

When the product in the market country has reached a more mature stage in the product life cycle, forecasting using past data becomes possible.

Time Series Extrapolation. **Extrapolation** refers to the method by which a time series of (sales) data observed over some periods in the past is extended into the future. The primary requirements for statistical forecasting of foreign sales are (1) that data are available, (2) that past events are relevant for the future, and (3) that statistics will be a better judge of what happened than more informal or anecdotal accounts. Although in domestic forecasting the reliance on statistical analysis often seems great (because the requisite data are indeed available), in international marketing all three requirements typically pose problems. For example, recent dramatic political and economic changes in Asia, Eastern Europe, and Latin America suggest that historical time series may be a poor guide for the future.

Exhibit 6.9 shows the idea behind extrapolation. A fitted regression line is extended along the trend line into subsequent years.

The smooth trend line is the regression line that reduces the variation, provides some direction, and helps one to make a forecast.

Extrapolation represents a very naive form of forecasting in that the only information employed is the numbers of the sales series in past periods. The focus of the forecaster's job is on projecting the shape of the past data into the future. The basic mathematical function is a simple regression:

$$\text{Market Sales} = f(\text{time}),$$

where "time" might be scored simply in terms of years. For shorter forecasts, a linear function might well be sufficient, but for longer periods a curvilinear function will usually be more applicable. There are many excellent texts on this topic, and since the international context adds little to these treatments, they will not be covered here.

Regression-Based Forecasts. Where good data are available across countries, extrapolation and forecasting by analogy can be improved by the use of multiple regression forecasts. The approach starts by looking at the size of the potential market for this product, and then predicts the willingness and ability to buy the product. [25]

The size component deals with how many people are potential customers. A useful approach is sometimes to segment the total number into homogeneous subsets: how many households with children, how many with incomes over a certain level, how many in the big cities versus the rural areas, and so on for a product such as a video camera. This type of evaluation can usually be done using the "chain ratio rule," in which the initial figure of size is broken down by the percentages falling into the separate segments: For example, the size M of one segment may be calculated as

$$M = \text{Number of households} \times \text{Proportion with children} \times$$
$$\text{Proportion with income over \$40,000 a year.}$$

The *willingness to buy* is determined by the need for the product among consumers, their existing attitudes toward family fun, the fit between product use and lifestyles, and other similar considerations. The data for such a regression can come from other countries where the product has already been introduced. For example, using data for the Chinese in the more developed Asian "tiger" countries—South Korea, Singapore, Hong Kong—could be useful for predicting willingness for mainland China.

The *ability to buy* relates to consumers' available funds to spend for the product. Variables here are income, household expenditures on related products, and other similar economic factors. Again existing data from related countries can be useful.

Combining the willingness and ability to buy, one can develop an estimate of the amount of probable *sales per customer* (units or money) in the target segment:

$$\text{Sales per customer} = f(\text{Willingness to buy} \times \text{Ability to Buy}),$$

with the relevant right-hand side variables behind willingness and ability the ones identified above, with data from the Asian tiger countries.

The *market sales* forecast combines customers' willingness and ability to buy with the potential market. Using the market size multiplied by the average sales per customer, a simple version of the model is:

$$S = M \times r$$

where r is the average sales per customer (in units or money). It should be made clear that this data-based forecast is possible only when data are available for the market country on the variables underlying willingness and ability to pay. They are needed to enter on the right-hand side to generate predictions for a China forecast.

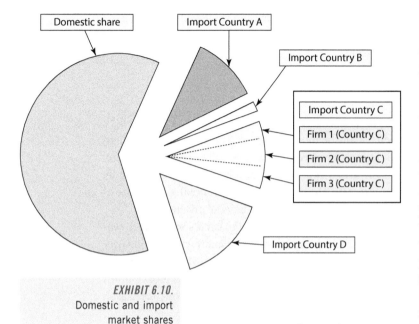

Domestic share

Import Country A

Import Country B

Import Country C

Firm 1 (Country C)

Firm 2 (Country C)

Firm 3 (Country C)

Import Country D

EXHIBIT 6.10.
Domestic and import
market shares

Forecasting Market Share

After forecasting market sales it becomes necessary to predict **market share**, the portion of total market sales the particular company can obtain. This entails a forecast of market share.

Market share forecasts are usually done best by breaking up the problem into its separate components. First, the likely competitors must be identified, including domestic firms and multinational companies operating in the country. Second, country-specific advantages of the domestic companies over foreign competition should be well-understood. Third, the company's strengths against the other firms have to be objectively assessed, particularly against other foreign firms operating in the country.

Identifying Competitors. Drawing on informal in-house knowledge and on selected contacts in the market country, a list of competitors is compiled. It is important that potential entrants be included. When a competitor is already well-established in other markets, entry into a new market can be undertaken quite quickly. A good example is the burgeoning auto market in China that has been rapidly covered by major automakers.

Domestic Competitors. The fact that tariff and nontariff barriers make entry difficult by raising foreign firms' prices and giving advantages to domestic producers must be considered very carefully. For forecasting purposes, the critical figure is the proportion of the market available to foreign competitors ("country share").

Apart from political considerations, the forecaster needs to evaluate the strength of a possible "pro-domestic" attitude on the part of buyers. There is sometimes covert or overt pressure on buyers to stay loyal to their domestic companies, the "Buy American" movement being one example.

In the end, the forecaster should be able to come up with a reasonable estimate of the market share "available" to imports (import share versus domestic share). This step serves well in accounting for factors affecting market performance that are not encountered in the home market.

Foreign Competitors. How well will the company fare against other foreign competitors in the local market? Here more objective data are sometimes available, since these firms might have been encountered in other world markets. Market share estimates can't be assumed equal to those in other markets, but a fair evaluation can be made.

If appropriate, this last step can be broken down into evaluating foreign competitors first and then firms from the company's home country. A typical example would be automobiles in the EU. Semiofficial quotas help Italian and French authorities keep domestic auto firms' market shares up to protect employment. Once the "desired" domestic share has been ascertained from industry experts, the foreign automakers can focus on the remaining available market share. This approach yields a quick approximate forecast in established markets such as automobiles in the United States, for example. Exhibit 6.10 shows the partitioning of the market "pie."

Final Forecast

To summarize, once the market share forecast is made, it can be combined with market sales using the basic equation

$$\text{Unit Sales} = \text{Market sales} \times \text{Market share.}$$

These unit sales can then be converted into a revenue forecast by multiplying in the price:

$$\text{Forecasted revenues} = \text{Unit sales} \times \text{Received Unit Price.}$$

Note that "received" price will usually be the export price to the intermediary overseas, not the market price in the new market.

SUMMARY

This chapter has shown how to use market research to select the best country to enter. The solution lies in matching the internal "self-analysis" of strengths-and-weaknesses of the SWOT framework with the environmental data on threats and opportunities, the OT part of SWOT. The chapter showed how the analysis should move from the broader country indicators useful for the preliminary assessment to more specific and in-depth indicators of the likely success in the candidate countries. The chapter showed how an "attractiveness index" for each candidate country can be derived using a weighted sum of the factors important for the success of the entering firm. The final country selection should only be done after personal visits to the most promising countries.

The chapter also showed the different data sources useful at different stages of the screening process. The chapter went further into the question of collecting new data specifically on the chosen country market, including the possible use of Big Data from social media. Primary data is necessary in order to project product acceptability and to design the introductory campaigns. The intended marketing campaign, including the likely pricing policy, is necessary to help set the stage for the forecasting of sales and projected profitability.

The last section of the chapter discussed techniques of forecasting. It emphasized the usefulness of separating the total market sales forecast from the prediction of market share. The determinants of the market size are basic economic and demographic variables such as per-capita income, population size, and so on, while market share has to do with competition against domestic and foreign firms. The forecasted sales can then be projected from a simple equation, multiplying market size by market share.

KEY TERMS

attitude scaling

back translation

build-up method

causal marketing research

country identification

Delphi method

demand characteristics

descriptive market research

direct observation

exploratory research

extrapolation
final selection
focus groups
forecasting by analogy
in-depth screening
market potential
market share forecasts
personal experience
preliminary screening
primary data

questionnaire
sales forecast
sampling equivalence
sampling frames
scale equivalence
secondary data
surveys
trade surveys
unrepresentative sample

DISCUSSION QUESTIONS

1. What factors would you consider when helping an already global manufacturer of household vacuum cleaners choose between Mexico, India, and China as the next country to enter?
2. Access the available online services to create a database that would help a company decide how attractive a country market is. Product category and country are your choices.
3. New high-tech products—such as the Apple iPod—are often said to generate their own demand. What does this imply about the possibility of forecasting sales when such a product is first introduced? How could one forecast sales for it when later entering a market such as Russia?
4. How would you go about doing consumer research to find if a product has different core benefits for different local markets abroad? Motivate and explain your research design.
5. How would you go about finding out whether consumers in a country are against global brands or not? Whether they are anti-American brands only? Whether they are more in favor of domestic brands than before?

TEAM CHALLENGE PROJECTS

1. Developing a market research program requires progressing through five steps: a) define the problem; b) analyze the situation; c) collect data; d) interpret the data; and e) develop a conclusion. As a marketing manager, you are uncertain which of your product lines to introduce first into the Chinese market. You will hire a market research firm to help with this question. Team 1: What instructions will you give the market research firm about what to do? Team 2: What instructions will you give the market research firm about what NOT to do?
2. Use the country screening process to decide which country represents the best opportunity for expanding vacuum cleaner sales. Team 1: Start with a minimum of 10 countries as potential targets and narrow your results to one country. Outline the criteria you used and explain the weighting of each. Team 2: Identify 10 countries that would be bad choices for expansion of the vacuum cleaner business. Outline the criteria you used and explain the weighting of each.
3. Identify three countries with rapidly improving levels of economic development that are NOT good candidates, i.e., not attractive for international expansion. Explain your reasoning. Team 1: Use countries from the African region. Team 2: Use countries from the Asian region.

4. Pick a product you like and use forecasting techniques from the chapter to develop an estimate of the market potential in one country. Team 1: Pick a product and use a country in Asia. Team 2: Pick a product and use a country in Latin America.

5. Interview a manager from an internationally operating company and determine the criteria they use to assess a country's attractiveness. How does this compare to the information presented so far in the chapters?

6. A U.S. manufacturer of eye glasses wishes to expand internationally and is interested in Japan and South Korea as its first countries for expansion. Team 1: Prepare an analysis that argues the Japanese market is the best country to enter first. Team 2: Prepare an analysis that argues South Korea is the best country to enter first.

SELECTED REFERENCES

Adams, Jonathan; Shubber Ali; Leila Byczkowski; Kathryn Cancro; and Susan Nolen. "Microlog Corporation: European Market Evaluation." Class project, School of Business, Georgetown University, May 12, 1993.

Armstrong, J. Scott. "An Application of Econometric Models to International Marketing." *Journal of Marketing Research* VII (May 1970), pp. 190–98.

Baumgartner, Hans and Bernd Weijters, "Response Biases in Cross-Cultural Measurement," in Ng, Sharon and Angela Y. Lee, *Handbook of Culture and Consumer Behavior*, New York: Oxford University Press, 2015, pp. 150–167.

Best, Roger. *Market-Based Management*, 6th ed. Upper Saddle River: Prentice Hall, 2012.

Dani, Marco, "Assembling the fractured European consumer," *LEQS* Paper No. 29/2011, January 2011.

Douglas, Susan, and Samuel R. Craig. *International Marketing Research*, 3rd ed. New York: Wiley, 2009.

European Commission, *Data protection, Eurobarometer Special Report*, June 24, 2015.

Goodwin, Paul, Seik Meeran and Karima Dyussekeneva, "The challenges of pre-launch forecasting of adoption time series for new durable products," *International Journal of Forecasting*, Volume 30, Issue 4, October-December 2014, pp. 1082–1097.

Hardy, Quentin, "How SurveyMonkey Is Coping After the Death of Dave Goldberg," *The New York Times*, June 22, 2015, B1.

Harzing, Anne-Wil and Markus Pudelko, "Do we need to distance ourselves from the distance concept? Why home and host country context might matter more than (cultural) distance." *Management International Review*, 2015 (In press).

"IKEA at a Glance," *Forbes*, Most Valuable Brands List, 2014.

Johanson J, and Vahlne, J. "Internationalization process of firm-model of knowledge development and increasing foreign market commitments," *Journal of International Business Studies*, 8(1): pp. 23–32, 1977.

Kowitt, Beth, "How IKEA took over the world," *Fortune Magazine*, 2015.

Lindberg, Bertil. "International Comparison of Growth in Demand for a New Durable Consumer Product." *Journal of Marketing Research,* August 1982, pp. 364–71.

Lisa Bertagnoli, "Continental Spendthrifts," Marketing News, October 22, 2001, pp. 1,15.

Makridakis, Spyros G. and Steven C. Wheelwright, *Forecasting Methods and Applications,* 3rd edition, WSE Publications, 2008.

Marr, Bernard. *Big Data: Using SMART Big Data, Analytics and Metrics To Make Better Decisions and Improve Performance*. New York: Wiley, 2015.

Penz, Elfriede and Barbara Stöttinger, "Consuming 'European': capturing homogeneity and heterogeneity in consumer culture of five European countries," *European Journal of International Management*, Volume 9, Issue 3, 2015, DOI: 10.1504/EJIM.2015.069162.

Statista.com 2015: Data from www.Statista.com website: http://www.statista.com/statistics/242477/global-revenue-of-market-research-companies/.

Steenkamp, Jan-Benedict E.M., and Frankel Ter Hofstede. "International Market Segmentation: Issues and Perspectives." *International Journal of Research in Marketing* 19 (September 2002), pp. 185–213.

Tung, Rosalie, L., Julian Birkinshaw and Mary Yoko Brannen, editors, "Special Issue: Qualitative Research in International Business," *Journal of International Business Studies,* Vol. 42, No. 5, June/July 2011.

Williams, Jim, "Constant Questions or Constant Meanings? Assessing Intercultural Motivations in Alcoholic Drinks." *Marketing and Research Today*, 19 (August 1991): pp. 169–177.

ENDNOTES

1. See "IKEA at a glance," 2014.
2. From Kowitt, 2015.
3. As reported by Kowitt, 2015.
4. The seminal work here is by Johanson and Vahlne, 1977, but the theory has been validated and refined several times since then, including Harzing and Pudelko, 2015.
5. See, for example, Harzing and Pudelko, 2015.
6. The example is adapted from Best, 2012.
7. Sources for the Microlog illustration include class reports such as: Adams et al., 1993, interviews and corporate reports as well as websites: http://mlog.com/; Used with permission from the Microlog Corporation.
8. Drawing on Douglas and Craig, 2009.
9. For more on cultural biases in questionnaire responses, see Baumgartner and Weijters, 2015.
10. The web is rich with examples. See http://www.english-zone.com/vocab/ae-be.html.
11. For more see http://www.speakinglatino.com/the-matrix-spanish-words-comparisons.
12. The proper procedure is discussed at length in Douglas and Craig, 2009.
13. Tung, Birkinshaw, and Brannen (2011) offers several examples of anthropological, ethnographic, and case studies applicable to international marketing issues.
14. Steenkamp and Ter Hofstede, 2002, provide an in-depth survey of equivalence issues.
15. See Baumgartner and Weijters, 2015.
16. These examples come from Williams, 1991.
17. Sources: Bertagnoli, 2001; Dani, 2011; Penz and Stöttinger, 2015.
18. Penz and Stöttinger, 2015.
19. European Commission, 2015.
20. See Hardy, 2015.
21. See Marr, 2015.
22. Source: Statista.com, 2015.
23. Lindberg, 1982; Goodwin, Meeran, and Dyussekeneva (2014) show some of the weaknesses of forecasting by analogy.
24. See Goodwin, Meeran, and Dyussekeneva, 2014.
25. See Armstrong, 1985; Makridakis and Wheelwright, 2008.

" Across the river and into the trees "

In this chapter you will learn about:

1. The four basic modes on entry: Export, Licensing, Strategic Alliance, and Foreign Direct Investment (FDI)
2. The many new tasks involved in direct exporting, but also how a number of independent middlemen can assist the company
3. How the "internationalization process" reflects companies' increasing skills and capability in doing business abroad
4. How the types and height of entry barriers influence the choice of entry mode

Modes of Entry

CHAPTER 7

STARBUCKS' MODE OF ENTRY

Starbucks operated only in the U.S. until 1996 when the company started its international expansion by creating Starbucks Coffee International (SCI) to co-ordinate the international expansion. The company's international expansion was based on two strategies: To provide licenses in countries to reduce market risk. Or, preferably, to create a joint venture with a branded local company in the target host country.

Starbucks' first foreign move was a joint venture in Japan in 1996 as Japan had the second-largest economy in the world at the time and the third-largest coffee-consuming population after the U.S. and Germany. Starbucks formed a 50/50 joint venture with Sazaby,

Inc., an operator of upscale retail and restaurant chains and formed Starbucks Coffee Japan.[1] Starbucks handled decisions relating to brand, product-line advertising, and corporate communications, while decisions regarding real-estate operational issues and human resources were handled by Sazaby.[2] Starbucks is very focused on local HR issues as it sees coffee quality, uniformity of customer service experience, and the training and positive attitude of its baristas as a key part of its company success. Despite strong local competition, the Japanese venture was success-ful from the start and profitable more than two years ahead of plan.

Starbucks continued to use these licensing and joint-venture models in the early years as its preferred mode of entry as it expanded internationally (see Exhibit 7.1).

EXHIBIT 7.1.

Starbucks' early market entries

Source: Trefis Team, 2014.

Source: Anna Jonsson and Nicolai J. Foss, "International Expansion through Flexible Replication: Learning from the Internationalization Experience of IKEA," Journal of International Business Studies, vol. 42, no. 9.

Country	Year	Type of Entry	Partner
Japan	1996	JV	Sazaby Inc.
Malaysia	1998	License	Berajaya Group Ltd
New Zealand	1998	License	Restaurant Brands
Taiwan	1998	JV	President Coffee Company
Kuwait	1999	License	Alshaya
Philippines	2000	License	Rustan's Coffee Corp
Austria	2001	License	Bon Appetit Group
Germany	2002	JV	Karstadt Qualle AG
Greece	2002	JV	Marinopoulos Brothers
Puerto Rico	2002	JV	Puerto Rico Coffee Partners LLC
Spain	2002	JV	Grupo Vips

EXHIBIT 7.2.
A Starbucks coffee shop in China. This shop, currently the largest in all of China, is near the popular tourist destination of Gulangyu in the city of Xiamen, China.

Copyright © by Bigstock/elemery.

Once a company learns how to manage a certain mode of entry, it often becomes the preferred choice for later entries.[3]

China

Starbucks first entered the Chinese market in 1999 using a licensing approach because of its concern about the government and its uncertainty about trying to penetrate a country with a tea-drinking tradition going back centuries. With good early success, Starbucks switched to a joint-venture model in the early 2000s. Since China has many different local cultures, Starbucks uses three joint ventures in China. In the north, Starbucks entered a joint venture with Beijing Mei Da coffee company (see Exhibit 7.2), in the east, Starbucks partnered with the Taiwan-based Uni-President, and in the south, Starbucks worked with Hong Kong-based Maxim's Caterers.

Global brand does not necessarily mean "global products," and Starbucks has highly localized menus of beverages and foods, the *East meets West* blends, for example that are tailored to Chinese consumers in each region.[4] In addition, Starbucks formed a distribution licensing agreement in 2015 with Chinese leading food and beverage producer Tingyi Holding Corp. to manufacture and distribute Starbucks ready-to-drink (RTD) coffee products throughout mainland China. Starbucks will be responsible for providing coffee expertise, brand development, and future product innovation, and Tingyi will manufacture and sell.[5]

India

Starbucks announced in 2012 a joint venture with Tata Global Beverages to enter the Indian market. Indian regulations require that any foreign entity must own a maximum of 51 percent in an Indian venture and must source at least 30 percent of its inputs from local Indian companies. Starbucks' joint venture with Tata Global will actually source 100 percent of its coffee and tea products from within India through a subsidiary named Tata Coffee Ltd. Sourcing completely locally is a first for any of Starbucks' international locations.[6]

What's next?

Starbucks has been operating in the international markets for over 20 years now and is feeling confident about its ability to understand and localize to international markets. As of 2016 it had 25,085 retail stores worldwide, with nearly 65 percent of these stores in 75 foreign countries (Exhibit 7.3). These foreign stores generated about 35 percent of Starbucks' $21.3 billion total revenue in 2016. Starbucks' opened 2,042 net new stores globally in fiscal 2016, including the first Starbucks stores in Cambodia, Kazakhstan, Andorra, South Africa, Slovakia, and Trinidad and Tobago. Starbucks used their strategy of opening via licenses in these seven countries likely to better understand the country risk before making a large investment.

The international confidence is beginning to produce a change in Starbucks' strategy back toward its origin of owning its own stores through Foreign Direct Investment/Wholly Owned Subsidiaries. In September 2014, Starbucks bought out its Japanese joint-venture partner and now owns all its Japanese stores directly, closing a circle from its first-ever joint-venture international expansion. Starbucks entered the UK via acquisition and continues to own all 784 stores there. Starbucks also previously bought out its partners in Austria and Switzerland and owns these stores. It is likely that FDI will become a more common strategy for Starbucks as its brand becomes established in international markets and Starbucks' confidence and success internationally grows.

Country	Company owned stores	Licensed or JV	Total
USA	7880	5292	13172
China	1272	1110	2382
Canada	1035	364	1399
Japan	1140	0	1140
S. Korea	0	952	952
U.K.	366	532	898
Mexico	0	563	563
Taiwan	0	392	392
Turkey	0	314	314
Philippines	0	293	293
Thailand	273	0	273
Indonesia	0	260	260
Malaysia	0	226	226
Germany	0	161	161

Source: https://www.statista.com/statistics/306915/countries-with-the-largest-number-of-starbucks-stores-worldwide/

EXHIBIT 7.3.
Starbucks largest countries by store count. Starbucks continues to use a variety of entry modes to balance the business opportunity with country regulations and risk.

FOUR BASIC OPTIONS

After selecting the country to enter (the "host" country), the question becomes which tactic is most suitable for entering the chosen country from the "home" country. This is a question of **mode of entry**.

Exporting
- Indirect exporting via piggybacking, consortia, export management companies, trading companies
- Direct exporting, using market country agent or distributor
- Direct exporting, using own sales subsidiary
- Direct sales, including mail order and e-commerce

Licensing
- Technical licensing
- Contract manufacture
- Original equipment manufacturing (OEM)
- Management contracts
- Turnkey contracts
- Franchising

Strategic alliance
- Distribution alliance
- Manufacturing alliance
- R&D alliance
- Joint venture

Wholly owned manufacturing subsidiary
- Assembly
- Full-fledged manufacturing
- Research and development
- Acquisition

EXHIBIT 7.4.
Entry modes for foreign markets[7]

Adapted from Root (1994) and Brouthers (2013).

It is common to distinguish between four principal modes of entry into a foreign market: exporting, licensing, strategic alliance, and wholly owned manufacturing subsidiary. The four modes break down into several different activities. A typical breakdown is given in Exhibit 7.4.

THE EXPORTING OPTION

For the newcomer to the international scene, exporting is often the first international business experience. Exporting involves shipping the product to a customer in a foreign country market with the help of various middlemen. In "direct" exporting the firm arranges for the shipment. In "indirect" exporting, the firm outsources the exporting work to a trading company in the home country. Direct exporting has the advantage over indirect exporting in the control of operations it affords the producer. Going through an intermediary trading company, the firm may not even know in which country the product is ultimately sold.

Indirect Exporting

The simplest way to manage the firm's export business is to employ outside specialists. An **Export management company (EMC)** is an independent agent working for the firm in overseas markets, going to fairs, contacting distributors, organizing service, and so on. They serve basically as an external "export department" for the firm, an example of value chain deconstruction.

Alternatively, the firm may hire a trading company, which becomes the "export department" for the producer. Many smaller Asian companies use trading companies in Singapore, Hong Kong, and Seoul to handle exporting. This helps the companies sell abroad even with limited resources and little knowledge of the foreign markets. Alibaba, the new Chinese online marketplace, functions as a facilitating middleman for a large number of small and medium-sized Chinese producers, providing communications and sales leads but not transportation and warehousing as most trading companies do.

This type of "indirect" exporting has the advantage that payment is ensured and the firm avoids the overhead costs and administrative burden involved in managing their own export affairs. On the other hand, there is the disadvantage that the skills and know-how developed through experiences abroad are accumulated outside the firm, not in it.

Direct Exporting

With direct exporting, the firm is able to more directly influence the marketing effort in the foreign market. The firm also learns how to operate abroad. It is not until the firm decides to hire its own staff in the home office that a more strategic involvement in foreign markets becomes feasible. For the direct exporter, the principal choice is between establishing a sales subsidiary and employing independent middlemen.

The principal middlemen used in direct exporting are shown in Exhibit 7.5.

Choosing the independent alternative, two independent middlemen will be particularly important. One is an **agent,** to manage sales and administration, and is paid through fees and commissions. The other is a local **distributor** who houses inventory, supplies the product to the trade, and adds a markup to the cost. The agent or the distributor often serves as the "importer," although the importer can also be a legally separate firm (express shippers such as FedEx and UPS do sometimes serve as the importer, guiding shipments through the customs). A **sales subsidiary** is a legal corporation established by the exporter in the foreign market. This corporation, staffed by the company's own hires, expatriates, and locals, assumes the dual roles of agent and distributor.

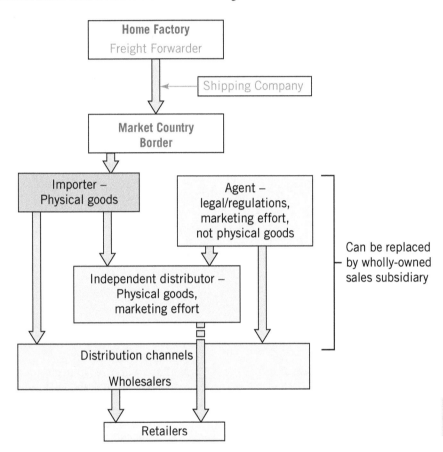

EXHIBIT 7.5.
Middlemen in direct exporting.

The choice between a sales subsidiary and independent middlemen depends on the degree to which control of the marketing effort in the country is desired and on the resources the firm can muster. To strike the optimal balance, the firm must consider the volume of operations (current and anticipated), the firm's willingness to take risks, and the availability of suitable local distributors. Investing in a wholly owned **sales subsidiary** is a bigger commitment and requires more resources than the use of independent middlemen. But where the market is potentially large, the firm would generally be better off with more central control of the marketing effort.

We will next discuss the tasks involved in exporting, and how the independent middlemen that can help these tasks. Then we will get back to the sales subsidiary issue.

The Exporting Tasks[8]

There are several separate functions to be taken care of in direct exporting. The major tasks are listed in Exhibit 7.6.

The exhibit and the discussion to follow cover only the major tasks. Some of these, such as those relating to legal issues, are only marginally related to marketing, while others, such as after-sales support, directly relate to marketing and customer acceptance. Many of the functions can be handled by independent specialists who can be found through *Department*

EXHIBIT 7.6.
Exporting tasks

Product shipment
1. Transportation to the border
2. Clearing through customs
3. Warehousing

Export pricing
1. Price quotes
2. Trade credit
3. Price escalation
4. Dumping

Local distribution
1. Finding distributors
2. Screening distributors
3. Personal visit
4. Negotiating a contract

Getting paid
1. Checking creditworthiness
2. Getting paid in local currency
3. Hedging against currency losses
4. Converting funds to home currency
5. Repatriating the funds

Legal issues
1. Export license
2. Hiring an agent
3. Transfer of title/ownership
4. Insurance

After-sales support
1. Service
2. Parts and supplies
3. Training of locals
4. Creating a sales subsidiary

EXHIBIT 7.7.
Principal documents used in exporting[9]

Adapted from International Trade Administration, "A Basic Guide to Exporting: The Official Government Resource for Small and Medium-Sized Business." (2012).

Foreign customer
1. Pro forma invoice
2. Acceptance of purchase order
3. Ocean (airway) bill of lading
4. Certificate (or policy) of insurance
5. Packing list

Exporting manufacturer
1. Purchase order
2. Letter of credit or draft (trade) acceptance

Freight forwarder
1. Shipper's letter of instructions
2. Domestic (inland) bill of lading
3. Packing list
4. Commercial invoice
5. Letter of credit (original copy)

U.S. government
1. Export declaration
2. Export license (strategic goods and shipments to designated unfriendly nations)

Foreign governments
1. Certificate of origin
2. Customs invoice
3. Consular invoice

Exporter's bank
1. Exporter's draft
2. Commercial invoice
3. Consular invoice
4. Insurance certificate
5. Ocean (airway) bill of lading

of Commerce contacts, at industry fairs and conventions, through the local telephone directories, or by contacting the consulate. Associated with these tasks are many different documents needed for exporting. Exhibit 7.7 gives a list of the principal documents. They will also be discussed below.

Product Shipment

Transportation. The shipment of the product to the border of the country is usually handled by an independent freight forwarder in combination with a shipping agency. In the typical case, freight forwarders who might specialize in certain types of products or countries pick up the product at the factory, transport it to the embarkation point, and load it onto the transnational carrier. Federal Express, UPS, and DHL serve as freight forwarders in the case of express mail, and they usually own their own transportation fleets (although some shipments, such as air transport to Africa, might go by a regular airline).

Clearing through Customs. Unloaded at the national border, the product will go from the ship or airline to a customs-free depot before being processed through customs. This depot can be a large free-trade zone, such as the one outside of Canton in China or in Gibraltar at the bottom of the European continent. From this free-trade area the product can be shipped to another country, never having crossed the border. In the typical case, the free-trade zones allow workers to further add value to the product. For example, along the Mexican border with the United States, the so-called maquiladoras are small factories located in the free-trade zones, and Mexican workers can be used to work on the products with no cross-border shipment of products. Thus, they can be shipped anywhere in the United States after the Mexican labor value added, without having to cross custom lines.

The customs officials will process the goods for entry once a claimant appears. This is usually the buyer, but can also be an independent importer or customs facilitator who specializes in custom clearance. By presenting shipping documents—called a **bill of lading**—the buyer or his agent can get access to the goods after paying the assessed duty. The tariff rate is decided on by the local customs official on the spot. In some countries, this is where there is often a temptation for bribes, the buyer "inducing" the customs official to assign a lower tariff classification.

Warehousing. After entering the country, the goods will often require storage, and there are usually facilities in the destination port for rent. The price is often quite high—as is the daily storage rental for goods waiting to be processed in the free-trade zone. Companies try to save money by getting the goods through customs quickly and warehoused at a less expensive location.

Export Pricing

Price Quotes. Export pricing quotes are considerably more complex than domestic quotes. The more common pricing terms of shipment have been standardized by the International Chamber of Commerce and codified as Incoterms (see Exhibit 7.8).

The firm selling abroad would generally be in a stronger competitive position by quoting prices CIF (cost-insurance-freight, that is, by accepting the responsibility for product cost, insurance, and freight, and factoring these items into the quote) rather than FOB (free on board). An FOB quote means that the buyer has to arrange shipping to his country. Quoting CIF still leaves the buyer with the responsibility for checking and adding tariff charges and other duties, and if, in addition, the buyer has to arrange transportation from the seller's country, the transactions costs can be very high.

EXHIBIT 7.8.
Terms of shipment[10]

Adapted from International Trade Administration, "A Basic Guide to Exporting: The Official Government Resource for Small and Medium-Sized Business." (2012).

Ex-works (EXW)
at the point of origin

Free Alongside Ship (FAS)
at a named port of export

Free on Board (FOB)
at a named port of export

Cost and Freight (CFR)
to a named overseas port

Cost, Insurance and Freight (CIF)
to a named overseas port

Delivery Duty Paid (DDP)
to an overseas buyer's premises

Trade Credit. Trade credit is an arrangement to buy goods and/or services on account without making immediate cash or check payments and is usually referred to as "open account." Trade credit is a helpful tool for growing a business because there is less pressure on cash flow and thus is helpful in reducing and managing the capital requirements of a business. Open-account trade credit is short-term (usually 30 to 90 days) deferred payment terms offered by a seller to a buyer to encourage sales.

The importance of the level of price quoted depends very much on what credit arrangements can be made. A high price can often be counterbalanced by advantageous **trade credit** terms, especially where the seller takes the responsibility for arranging the trade credit.

In many cases the competitive advantages critically depend on the credit question. Selling to the consumers at the bottom of the economic pyramid usually requires special credit arrangements (for example, offering credit for one washing machine to a whole village). At the upper end of the pyramid, Airbus sales are generally made at relatively high prices per plane but are accompanied by advantageous loans extended by the governments involved in the consortium (France, Germany, United Kingdom, and Spain). This is one reason the Boeing aircraft company is at risk with the temporary suspension of funding for the U.S. Export-Import Bank, possibly to be lifted in the 2017 budget.

Price Escalation. There are several added costs incurred when selling overseas. Shipping costs are only part of the problem—added are applicable tariffs and customs duty, insurance, and value-added taxes. Also, the fact that several middlemen (importer to take the goods through customs, freight forwarder to handle the shipping documents, dock workers) are involved in the channel adds to the costs and cuts into the profit margin unless prices are raised. The resulting increase in price overseas is commonly called **price escalation.**

The escalation of price means not only that price will be higher than intended; it also makes it more difficult to anticipate what exactly the final price in the market will be. The methods used to cope with the problems are several. Companies attempt to redesign the product so as to fit it into a lower tariff category, sometimes by shifting the final stages in the assembly process abroad. For example, truck tariffs for completed assemblies are usually higher than for semi-finished cars, and the industry has responded by creating a "knockdown" (KD) assembly stage, putting a flatbed on the chassis and "knocking it down" into place.

Dumping. Even though pricing on the basis of costs alone is not recommended in theory (demand must be taken into account, for example), cost-based pricing has one strong justification: It is the pricing procedure easiest to defend against dumping charges.

Dumping is defined as selling goods below cost. There are sometimes good management reasons for doing that. A typical case is an entry into a large competitive market by selling at very low prices; another case is when a company has overproduced and wants to sell the product in a market where it has no brand franchise to protect. **Reverse dumping** refers to the less common practice of selling products at home at prices below cost. This would be done in extreme cases where the share at home needs to be protected while monopolistic market positions abroad can be used to generate surplus funds ("cash cows" in foreign markets). Regardless, dumping is typically illegal and should be avoided if at all possible.

Local Distribution

Finding a Distributor. The next step is to get the product into the distribution channels. The most common approach is not to try to create new channels, but to use existing ones. This means identifying one or more independent distributors who can take on storage and transportation to wholesalers and retailers. An **independent distributor** takes ownership of the goods, paying the producing firm, and often will handle the importing and customs process, in addition to storage and distribution in the country. Generally, the firm appoints one exclusive distributor for the whole country. However, in large nations such as the United States overseas-based companies often have two or

three independent distributors in various parts of the country (East Coast, Midwest, and West Coast, for example).

Identifying potential distributors can be often done with the assistance of governmental agencies. Many countries maintain trade facilitation agencies to assist in the search for local distributors. The U.S. Department of Commerce, for example, will assist in identifying the names and addresses of many potential distributors in various countries and industries. But more commonly, potential distributors will be found at international trade fairs.

Trade fairs (trade shows, exhibitions or "expos") are regular events at which a large number of competing manufacturers present their products to distributors, wholesalers, retailers, and end users. International trade fairs attract potential customers and distributors from all over the world and provide widespread interactions and exposure. Trade fairs are a popular means of sales promotion because a manufacturer is able to meet face-to-face with a large number of potential partners, vendors, and clients at a low cost (see Exhibit 7.9).

These fairs are held in places such as Frankfurt, Hong Kong, Dubai, and Las Vegas. The export manager participating in a fair should try to identify beforehand potential distributors who might come to the fair and arrange meetings ahead of time.

Screening Distributors. Once a few select candidates have been identified, they must be screened on key performance criteria. The criteria include:

- Experience
- Whether they are handling competing products

- Reputation in the trade
- Financial strength
- Services offered and marketing support
- Government relations

Which of these criteria are judged important and which not depends on the situation and the significance the company attaches to the criteria. For example, consumer nondurables typically require little after-sales service. The financial strength of the distributor is less important if the firm can support the company in the start-up period. Distributor strength can even be a drawback when the initial arrangements are seen as temporary, to be superseded by a more permanent, FDI position if the market is as large as expected. A strong distributor is more likely in a position to demand some significant compensation to give up a lucrative contract.

Personal Visits. Once some promising leads have been developed, a personal visit to the country is necessary. On the trip managers should do three things:

- Talk to the ultimate users of the equipment to find out from which distributors they prefer to buy and why. Two or three names will be likely to keep popping up.
- Visit these two or three distributors and see which ones you would be able to sign up.
- Before making the final choice, look for the distributor who has the strongest individual to champion your line. Experience has shown that the successful distributor is the one who has one person in the organization willing to take the new line to heart and treat it as his or her own baby.

Negotiating a Contract. The contract has to be very specific with regard to the rights and obligations of the manufacturer and the distributor, the length of the contract, and conditions for its renegotiation. A detailed checklist is given in Exhibit 7.10.

The conditions under which competitive product lines might be added, and the degree of exclusivity that the distributor is granted, figure prominently among the rights and obligations. Although local regulations and the letter of the law naturally must be followed, the usual situation is one in which the actual formulation of these contracts hinges directly on the size and strength of the two parties.

One example of how a partnership for distribution works is that between Coke and the high-end Italian espresso producer Illy Caffe. The two have signed a global joint venture focused on premium Ready to Drink (RTD) coffee. Coca-Cola has long attempted to introduce coffee in their vending machines, and their Georgia coffee developed in Japan is one example. By tying up with Illy Caffe, the RTD coffee will presumably be very high-quality espresso. It also helps Illy Caffe keep Starbucks at bay.

For purists, of course, the whole notion behind the tie-up is heresy. One wonders what it will do to Illy Caffe's brand image.[12]

Territory–products
- Territory covered
- Advertising
- Minimum purchases
- Trademarks and copyrights

Operations report
- Distributor resale prices
- List prices
- Inventory
- Product warranty
- Reporting requirements

Effective date and duration
- Rights and obligations upon termination
- Competitive adoption
- Guiding law

EXHIBIT 7.10.
Master foreign distributorship agreement checklist[11]

Adapted from Folson, et al., International Business Transactions in a Nutshell. West Academic Publishing, 2012.

Payment

Creditworthiness. In most countries, checking on the credit-worthiness of the buyer can usually be done through banking connections. Regardless, many exporters avoid relying on credit, not shipping goods until an intermediate bank, preferably in the seller's country, guarantees payment. With the diffusion of credit cards and other intermediate processors like PayPal, payments have been considerably eased. The original process for buyer-seller international payments is via banks and a letter of credit.

Letter of Credit. Payment in advance is traditionally done via some form of **letter of credit (L/C).** The links involved between the buyer, seller, and their banks are shown in Exhibit 7.11.

The L/C is arranged for by the buyer. First, the buyer approaches the local bank, opening a credit line, and this bank will contact its corresponding bank in the selling firm's country. This latter bank will inform the seller that a letter of credit has been issued, which assures the seller that payment will be made. Once the seller ships the goods, the bill of lading can be presented to the bank, which will contact the overseas bank in the buyer's country and will pay the seller. This transaction usually takes place before the goods have reached the buyer's country. Once they arrive, the buyer can claim the goods at customs against the bill of lading sent by the bank.

A letter of credit solves two main problems of international transactions: (1) the seller wants to make certain that funds are available before shipping a product and (2) the buyer wants to know that once the product is received, there is still a possibility of getting the money back (in case of a defective or otherwise unacceptable product). The popular PayPal payment system is a simplified version of letters of credit. By asking the customer to pay via PayPal, money is deposited into the seller's PayPal account. The seller knows funds are there. To assure the buyer, PayPal does not release the money to the seller until the transaction is completed. In international transactions it is not uncommon for the delay to last as long as 21 days.

Converting Funds. As international financial markets and banking institutions become further integrated, conversion to home currency and payment is likely to become less of a problem. The diffusion of internationally accepted credit cards has greatly reduced payment risks, since funds can be obtained before shipping an order.

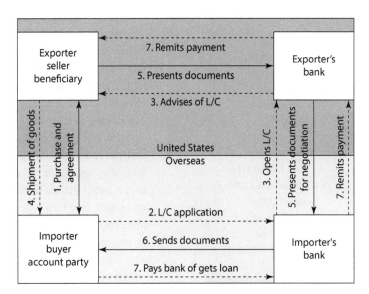

EXHIBIT 7.11.
How a Letter of Credit (L/C) works

Legal Issues

Export License. An export license grants permission to conduct a certain type of export transaction and a license is issued by the appropriate licensing agency after a careful review of the facts surrounding the given export transaction. A relatively small percentage of all U.S. export transactions require licenses from the U.S. government but it is up to the exporter to determine whether the product requires a license, to research the end use of the product in the country of delivery and to obtain a license before shipment.

EXHIBIT 7.12.
Master foreign agency appointment checklist[13]

Adapted from Folson, et al., International Business Transactions in a Nutshell. West Academic Publishing, 2012.

Transferring Title. The **title** of ownership of the exported goods generally follows the bill of lading. Whoever holds the bill of lading has access to the goods. The business risk—and thus exposure to normal loss, such as lack of sales in the marketplace—shifts with the title. The local distributor who borrows money to pay for the goods will be exposed to risk at the point when the bill of lading is accepted by the seller's bank—or, sometimes, as the seller's bank delivers the bill of lading to the buyer's bank.

Insurance. In exporting, the recommended procedure is for the seller to quote a **cost-insurance-freight** (CIF) price, in which case the seller will arrange for insurance. This simplifies the whole exporting process but also makes the seller responsible if damage to the goods occurs during transit. Alternatively, the seller can quote an FOB price (free on board), in which case the buyer is saddled with the need to arrange for shipment and insurance. Good marketing thinking suggests that the company should quote its prices at the higher CIF price and help with insurance claims. This provides better service, although at a cost.

Hiring an Agent. The seller must pay attention to legal matters in the market country. Product liability and warranty issues can become a problem; after-sales service responsibility questions may come up; conflicts with distributors about contracted quotas and sales efforts may arise; and so on. Since most countries do not allow foreigners to work on legal questions, a company representative, an agent, is needed.

The agent will be the legal representative of the firm (the principal) in the local market, usually working for a retainer fee and a contract that provides hourly compensation on special cases. Exhibit 7.12 offers a checklist of things to consider when hiring an agent.

Where their responsibilities involve some sales activities—such as, for example, visiting distribution outlets to monitor in-store support—agents can also be remunerated via a commission percentage of revenues. Many agents work for more than one principal, but not for competing firms. Agents can be found through the same sources as distributors.

After-Sales Support

Service, Parts Supply, Training. In order to support the local marketing effort, the firm needs to establish after-sales service, stock spare parts and supplies, and train local staff. These tasks are often managed by the distributor, aided by the agent. The contract specifying the responsibilities of the distributor (see Exhibit 7.10) should make clear what marketing role the distributor should play, and the agent is expected to enforce the contract.

Sales Subsidiary

As the firm's sales in a country grow larger, control of the local marketing effort becomes a very important issue. At that point the company often decides to establish a sales subsidiary, staffed with locals and a few top managers from headquarters. For marketing effectiveness, the control of the sales effort will then be in the hands of the company itself.

A *sales subsidiary* is a commercial operation fundamentally different from a wholly owned manufacturing subsidiary.

A sales subsidiary manages distribution and marketing of the product in the local market. Such a sales subsidiary will run the local marketing effort, conducting market research; dealing with local advertising agencies; monitoring distributors' performance; providing information on competitors, market demand, and growth; and generally managing the local marketing mix—sometimes going against top management's recommendations and shared wisdom. BMW USA is a sales subsidiary of BMW located in New Jersey, responsible for U.S. marketing and sales of BMW vehicles. The company that produces the BMW X-series and SUVs in South Carolina is BMW U.S. Manufacturing Company, a wholly owned manufacturing subsidiary.

LICENSING

Licensing refers to offering a firm's know-how or other intangible asset to a foreign company for a fee, royalty, and/or other type of payment.

Pros and Cons

The *advantages* over exporting are three:

1. The avoidance of tariffs and other levies that might be assessed against an imported product.
2. For the new exporter, it also has the advantages that the need for market research and knowledge is reduced.
3. In addition, as opposed to the use of a distributor, it is often possible to induce the licensee to support the product strongly in the market. This is because in licensing, the firm in the host country gets specific know-how from the licensing firm and thus is able to develop some skills on its own; it does not just resell the product as the distributor does.

The main *disadvantage* of licensing is that it transfers technology. Because the licensee gets access to certain firm-specific knowledge and know-how, it will share in the competitive advantage of the licensor—and can then potentially use this knowledge in further applications other than the ones specifically stated in the licensing contract.

To avoid the dissipation of firm-specific advantages, the licensing firm needs to handle contract negotiations with considerable skill. It is important, for example, to limit the geographical area within which the licensee might sell the product so as not to engender competition with the firm's own sales in other countries (see box, "How (not) to do it").

> **BOX: How (not) to do it.**[14]
>
> A neophyte American firm decided to avoid managerial and research expense to explore foreign markets and to simply license the manufacturing and sales of their product to a UK firm. The English firm was granted the right to sublicense the process know-how to other parts of the world. After a few years the foreign markets for the company's product increased greatly in potential, but the U.S. company gained only a small share of the increase in revenues. It had already "sold" those markets to the English company and could only watch as that company's sales took off.

Technology package
- Definition/description of the licensed industrial property (patents, trademarks, know-how)
- Know-how to be supplied and its methods of transfer
- Supply of raw materials, equipment, and intermediate goods

Use conditions
- Territorial rights for manufacture and sale
- Responsibility for defense/infringement action on patents and trademarks
- Exclusion of competitive products

Compensation
- Running royalties
- Minimum royalties
- Technical assistance fee

Other provisions
- Duration and renewal of contract
- Cancellation/termination provisions
- Procedures for the settlement of disputes

EXHIBIT 7.13.
Elements of a licensing contract[15]

Adapted from Folson, et al., International Business Transactions in a Nutshell. West Academic Publishing, 2012.

A problem in licensing is that the firm does not adapt to the local market, but expects to simply earn a royalty on an existing product or service. When KFC first entered China via Hong Kong, they quickly opened and closed 11 non-adapted restaurants. Appointing local management, KFC then changed the menu and also the restaurant interiors, stressing the red color associated in China with good fortune. They introduced new dishes such as "congee," a kind of Chinese breakfast porridge, and also played up the advantage of chicken over beef for the average Chinese palate. Today, KFC is twice as large as McDonald's in China, whereas the reverse is true elsewhere in the world.

It is also important to make sure what the conditions for terminating the contract are, what the time limit is, and how the specific know-how is to be used. Contracts identify the level and kind of marketing support the licensee is supposed to generate and the appropriate steps to be taken should this support not be forthcoming. The licensor, for his part, pledges his supply of the requisite transfer of knowledge, including managerial and technical support, patents with or without trademark, or brand-name transfer. Exhibit 7.13 shows the main elements of a typical licensing contract.

The basic payment for the license is in the form a royalty paid to the trademark owner. The royalty level and payment structure vary with different forms of licensing. Typically **royalties** are computed as a percent of revenues, often 5 percent of gross revenues, sometimes less, sometimes more (the Disney World Corporation receives 7 percent from its Japanese licensee).

Franchising

A special variant of licensing is franchising, in which local investors provide resources, including capital and manpower, in order to gain the use of a well-known brand name. Franchising has become particularly popular in services because it allows foreign expansion with limited financial resources. An example is Subway's expansion into Eastern Europe where the menu is largely the same as in the U.S. home country (see Exhibit 7.14).

The four main components of successful franchising are:

1. The basic "product" sold by the franchisor is standardized with a well-recognized brand name, nurtured carefully through global advertising and promotion, including sponsorship of various events.
2. The franchisor provides a wide range of market support services to the franchisee, in particular local advertising to sustain the brand name, of which the franchisee usually will pay a portion.
3. Additional services provided to the franchisee are assistance with analyzing best location, training manuals for employees, help with product lines and production scheduling, and accounting manuals.

4. In return, the local franchisee raises the necessary capital to establish the business, staffs and manages the franchise, paying an initial fee and a royalty percentage on total sales to the franchisor.

In franchising, *product lines* and *customer service are standardized*, two important features from a marketing perspective. Although cultural differences might require adaptation—in Europe, McDonald's serves beer, and in Asia, rice is added to the menu—the franchising concept works precisely because of standardization of product and service.

If the franchisor does not perform acceptably, the company will terminate the contract. When the McDonald's restaurant on Champs Elysees in Paris gave mediocre service in unclean premises, the McDonald's corporation stepped in and took over. Such close supervision of the various aspects of far-flung operations requires well-developed global management systems and labor-intensive monitoring. Because of the managerial skills required, international franchising has become successful largely among those businesses having long experience with franchising at home before venturing out globally.

Original Equipment Manufacturing (OEM)

In **original equipment manufacturing (OEM),** a company enters a foreign market by selling its unbranded product or component to another company in the market country. This company then markets the final product under its own *brand name.* For the supplier firm, there is little or no expense in marketing its product overseas, and the buyer gets a product ready to use and to market. The supplier has to give up its own effort to market the product overseas, but often tries to change its strategy later if the overseas market for its product is strong.

Some examples will illustrate the principles. Canon provides the cartridges for Hewlett-Packard's very successful laser printers in an OEM arrangement. After several years of successful market development, Canon now also markets its own copiers with success.

The large Korean consumer goods manufacturers such as Samsung and LG initially opted for the OEM entry mode in the U.S. market. By selling unbranded color television sets and microwaves to resellers such as Sears, Amana, and Emerson, they gained distribution and avoided the need to spend money on establishing a brand in the market. Later, however, they established their own now-strong brand names. Opting for a direct approach, the Korean automaker Hyundai decided to establish its own dealer and service network in the United States. To gain instant credibility, the company offered an unheard of warranty period of 10 years on its cars. The pros and cons of the two approaches were

EXHIBIT 7.14.
A Subway restaurant in Poznan, Poland.
Subway's spokesperson Jared Fogle, popular in the United States as "the Subway guy," has also been used internationally as a "brand ambassador." But in 2015 he was suspended after allegations of impropriety surfaced.

Copyright © 2014 by Shutterstock/Authentic Creations.

hotly debated among observers, but with the rise of brand importance in many markets, the OEM approach has today been discredited.

STRATEGIC ALLIANCES

An international **strategic alliance (SA)** is typically a collaborative arrangement between firms, sometimes competitors, across borders. The joint venture (JV) is an *equity-based* SA, with new capital invested. New forms of alliances involve *non-equity-based* collaboration (partnerships, agreements to share, contractual participation in projects).

Non-Equity SAs

Non-equity strategic alliances between competitors have become so common that they have acquired a new term, **co-opetition.**[16] The economic gains from non-equity alliances are usually quite tangible. Five common ones are:

1. *Access to technology.* A company accesses technology it otherwise would not get.
2. *Rapid market entry.* Markets are reached without a long build-up of relationships in channels.
3. *Less investment need.* Efficient manufacturing is made possible without investment in a new plant, and so on.
4. *Less need for control.* Even though patents can be policed across borders, the speed with which technology ages makes leakage less of a problem.
5. *Need to be in many markets.* Having a presence in leading markets is often necessary to observe customers, monitor competitors, and to disturb competitors' sources of cash.

Since their marketing implications differ considerably, we will distinguish between three types of non-equity alliances: distribution, manufacturing, and research and development (R&D).

Distribution Alliances. An early and still common form of SA is the *shared distribution* network. Examples include the licensing of Molson's of Canada to brew and sell Kirin beer in North America, and the tie-up between SAS, KLM, Austrian Air, and Swiss Air to share routes in European air corridors. More recently, the STAR alliance involving United Airlines, Lufthansa, Air Canada, SAS, and other airlines (now 28 airlines) has been created to provide global route access and seamless booking through code-sharing agreements.

Manufacturing Alliances. Another form of strategic alliance is **shared manufacturing**. Shared manufacturing means that one company manufactures products for several competing brands. For example, when IBM decided not to manufacture its own PCs, Panasonic produced IBM-branded PCs in a plant with excess capacity. Shared manufacturing is more common in outsourcing situations. A Chinese factory, for example, will often produce for several different apparel brands and Taiwanese factories manufacture computer parts for several computer makers.

R&D Alliances. SAs in R&D are different from those in distribution and manufacturing. In addition to providing favorable economics, speed of access, and managerial resources, *R&D alliances* are intended to solve critical survival questions for the firm.

In many markets the products must embody the new technology even to be considered by buyers. A cell phone without camera is unheard of today. A smartphone without a touchscreen is unsaleable. It is this relentless emphasis on the most recent technology in new products that has raised the ante of global participation in so many industries and has led to the need for SAs in R&D—and the protracted patent lawsuits between Apple and Samsung.[17]

Equity SAs: Joint Ventures

Even though **joint ventures (JVs)** have undeniable strengths from a marketing viewpoint, many corporations have been reluctant to enter into JV agreements unless forced to by government regulations or pressure. The JV involves direct investment, and many firms would rather invest in a wholly owned subsidiary or simply do some form of licensing to overcome entry barriers (if tariffs and entry barriers are low, most would even rather do exporting). The more an investment in specific foreign assets is needed (for example, training of local employees) the more likely the entering firm will opt for a wholly owned subsidiary.[18]

The JV involves the transfer of capital, manpower, and usually some technology from the foreign partner to an existing local firm, whose main contribution tends to be expertise and understanding of the local market.

The Chinese have been very active with joint ventures, using them to bring in foreign technology. One example is in the development of high-speed railroad service. China's vast geographical expanse favors air transportation, but high-speed rail has become increasingly popular since it allows more stopovers. One example of a joint venture is that between Siemens of Germany and Beijing Automotive Industry Holding Co., Ltd. (BAIC), creating the high-speed train CRH3. The CRH3 is a version of the Siemens Velaro high-speed train, with an operating speed of 220 mph. It is mostly built locally with German engineering help (see Exhibit 7.15).

Russia is another country with vast geographical expanse that calls for high-speed rail service. As in China, Russia has developed these infrastructure improvements with the help of joint ventures necessarily involving government business. One example is the Allegro high-speed train connecting Helsinki with St. Petersburg. The trains, with a maximum operating speed of 220 kph (approx. 136 mph), are owned by Karelian Trains, a joint venture between the VR Group (Finnish Railways) and Russian Railways.

Trust is obviously important in JVs. Research shows not surprisingly that trust is higher when both partners come from similar cultures and when both hold each respective culture in high esteem.[20] It is also common to specify procedures to be followed for dissolution of the partnership. The contract guiding the formation of a JV has often been likened to a marriage contract, and for good reason.

EXHIBIT 7.15.
The CRH3 in the south railway station in Beijing, China. Introduced first for the Shanghai to Nanjing and the Shanghai to Hangzhou routes in 2010, the CRH380 model has the current world record of 486.1 kmph (302 mph) among fast trains.[19]

Copyright © 2013 by Bigstock/ Markus Mainka.

MANUFACTURING SUBSIDIARIES

Foreign direct investment (FDI) is undertaken by the international firm for several reasons. The aims could be to acquire raw materials, to operate at lower manufacturing costs, to avoid tariff barriers and satisfy local content requirements, and/or to penetrate local markets. The last rationale is of prime interest in the marketing context.

Pros and Cons

Manufacturing FDI has several advantages in market penetration.

1. *No price escalation.* First, local production means price escalation caused by transport costs, customs duties fees, local turnover taxes, and so on can be nullified or drastically reduced.
2. *Availability of goods.* Product delivery can usually be guaranteed to resellers, minimizing potential channel conflicts over allocation decisions and eliminating delays for ultimate buyers.
3. *Local adaptation.* The most striking marketing advantage of local production is usually the projection of an ability and willingness of the company to adapt products and services to the local customer requirements. Examples include U.S. automakers' production of cars for European markets and French ski manufacturer Rossignol's location of plants in the United States and Canada. In both cases there was a desire to be closer to major markets and to be able to anticipate and quickly adapt to major changes.

There are three distinct disadvantages to FDI in manufacturing.

1. *Risk exposure.* The major disadvantage is the risk exposure that comes with a resource commitment on the scale usually required. Even joint ventures are not free from this commitment and risk since most agreements stipulate heavy costs for one partner's withdrawal.
2. *Lower quality.* Location of production in the market country may lead to lower quality. In many cases initial reluctance to do manufacturing abroad has been the risk of lowered quality. Today, however, with the global spread of manufacturing skills, the risk of lower quality is reduced, and companies can count on local suppliers to provide quality and service.
3. *Losing a COO cachet.* There is a potential problem in overseas manufacturing when country-of-origin effects are strong, that is, for products whose quality consumers tend to judge by the "made in" label. In luxury brands, for example, going abroad is not usually the preferred option. Research shows there can be a significant effect on product and brand evaluation from a shift in manufacturing location.

Still, some companies decide the pros outweigh the cons (see box, "A BMW Made in America?")

BOX: A BMW Made in America?[21]

The BMW Z3 roadster was a slick, sporty automobile, a product of German precision engineering and craftsmanship. It was the "ultimate driving machine," James Bond's vehicle of choice in the movie *GoldenEye.* Where was the BMW Z3 made? The last place you'd think of would probably be Spartanburg, South Carolina. A German icon mass-produced in the heart of the United States? Yes. The Spartanburg facility is the first full BMW manufacturing plant to be located outside Germany.

The BMW Spartanburg plant was launched in March 1994. The company invested roughly $1.4 billion in the facility, employing more than 3500 workers ("associates"). Today the plant produces the SUV models X3, X4, X5, and X6 cars for both the domestic and the international markets.[22] The Spartanburg plant is in fact the only BMW plant that makes the sport utility vehicle. Although the BMW brand is uniquely German, the SUV concept is purely of American origin.

Why would BMW consider the United States as a manufacturing facility location? You would think the main reason is ready access to the large market. But with tariff barriers low or nonexistent, and with transportation and logistics increasingly efficient, market access is not the major factor. Instead, the main reason for the move to North America was for better supplier relations.

BMW found that U.S.-based suppliers were nimbler and more flexible than their European counterparts. European suppliers, used to comfortable relationships with the abundant European automakers, were less open to new part requirements, just-in-time systems, and supply-chain improvements. The company was able improve its supply chain by using American suppliers.

The number of BMW customers in the United States has tripled over the last 10 years. And BMW reached a new global sales record in 2016, delivering 2,003,359 vehicles to customers around the world where 18% of these vehicles were sold in the U.S. with another 25% sold in China.

Given the possible buyer backlash, the solution adopted by many companies is to shift lower-skill operations overseas, keeping more advanced operations at home. Although companies are sometimes criticized for this strategy, it is often justified not only because it protects product quality and established brand equity, but also because it is a natural step in the gradual upgrading of labor skills in low-wage countries. Finally, companies with global brands strive very hard to ensure that quality standards are met, and research suggests that a strong brand image can override any negative country-of-origin effects.

Acquisitions

Rather than establish the wholly owned subsidiary from scratch, sometimes called a **greenfield investment**, the multinational company can consider the **acquisition** of an existing company. An acquisition is a corporate action in which a company buys most, if not all, of the target company's ownership stakes in order to assume control of the target firm. The advantage lies in the speed of penetration: an existing company will already have a product line to be exploited, the distribution network and dealers need not be developed from scratch, and the company can simply get on with marketing its new product(s) in conjunction with the existing line. German Siemen's purchase of compatriot Nixdorf (now Wincor Nixdorf AG, an independent company) to improve penetration in the European minicomputer market is a case in point. Another example is the purchase of American Borden by Swiss Nestlé in order to expand in the U.S. dairy food market and Unilever's acquisition of Ben and Jerry's ice cream.

The disadvantages of acquisition are many, however. In a narrow sense, the existing product line and the new products to be introduced might not be compatible, and prunings and adjustments that have to be made require reeducating the sales force and distribution channels. In general, it is not so easy to find a company to acquire that fits the purposes of entry very well. In many countries the acquisition of a domestic company by a foreign firm is not looked upon favorably by the government, employees, and other groups. From a marketing viewpoint the particular advantage of acquisition lies in the market acceptance of the company's products, gaining sales as a spillover from goodwill toward the acquired company's lines. But this benefit can be gained from a joint venture, and many of the political drawbacks of acquisitions are eliminated with a joint venture.

THE INTERNATIONALIZATION PROCESS

When the sequence of entries into several countries is examined for any one firm, a typical pattern can often be identified. Initially, countries that are similar are entered—the cultural distance effect—often including those similar countries that are also geographically close.[23] Thus, for example, the early markets for German autos included France, Benelux, and the Scandinavian countries. As more know-how and skill in international affairs are accumulated—a "learning curve" phenomenon—management becomes less tied to the similarities requirement and more "off-beat" market countries are explored. Thus, at some stage, an excursion into a country far away culturally takes place. The accumulated skills and experiences are then leveraged in further expansion into an increasingly varied group of markets.

As several researchers have found, this gradual expansion sequence is reflected in the mode of entry chosen.[24] Although companies differ, the general pattern is for gradually increased commitment to foreign markets. Several **internationalization stages** can be identified:

Stage 1: Indirect exporting, licensing
Stage 2: Direct exporter, via independent distributor
Stage 3: Establishing foreign sales subsidiary
Stage 4: Local assembly
Stage 5: Foreign production

Several variations of these internationalization stages have been proposed. For example, the early use of licensing has been questioned by proponents of the *internalization* school, which places more importance on preservation of the FSAs. In licensing there is a risk that the firm could lose its proprietary assets through dissipation of its technology or knowledge resulting in an erosion of its competitive advantage.

For example, in 1977 when a newly elected Indian government demanded that Coca-Cola share its secret formula with an Indian licensee, Coca-Cola opted to exit the country. Another more recent trend, as strategic alliances have become common, is that companies utilize joint ventures and alliances at almost any stage in the process. In fact, the traditional notion that firms will go global gradually and stage-wise has been challenged. Some firms, especially in the high-tech industries, have a global outlook from the beginning.

FOREIGN ENTRY BARRIERS

Before selecting the appropriate mode of entry, it is important to examine the barriers to entry in more detail. The height and nature of the market entry barriers directly influence the optimal entry mode for a company. Entry barriers increase the cost of entry and constrain the options available, and where they are high, the company might have only one choice of entry mode or else have to stay out.

Entry Barriers Defined

The concept of entry barriers connotes any obstacle making it more difficult for a firm to enter a product market. Thus, entry barriers also exist in the home market, as when limited shelf space prohibits a company from acquiring sufficient retail coverage to enter a local market. Overseas it can mean that customs procedures are so lengthy that they prohibit an importer's fresh produce from getting to the stores before spoiling. It is common to distinguish between **artificial barriers**, imposed on foreign products, and **natural barriers** that affect any competitor. Artificial barriers are imposed by the authorities to keep imports out, such as tariffs, quotas, and special taxes. Natural barriers are competitive barriers that arise naturally when companies compete. Brand loyalty, home-country preferences, and need for adaptation to local preferences are typical natural barriers.

The main entry barriers are the following.

1. *Tariff* barriers are "artificial" obstacles to entry into the country. High tariffs assessed as a percent of the value of imports means customs duties will be high and price escalation is likely. For the WTO in Geneva, lowering tariffs around the globe is a primary objective.

2. *Nontariff* artificial barriers can also be important. For example, slow customs procedures, special product tests for imports, and bureaucratic inertia in processing import licenses will make entry difficult.

3. Government *regulations* of business, domestic as well as foreign, constitute another set of market barriers. Some regulations are directly intended to protect domestic business against foreign competitors.

4. *Access* to manufacturing technology and processes, component suppliers, and distribution channels can be restricted by territorial restrictions, competitive collusion, or close ties between transacting partners (see box, "Sky-High Entry Barriers").

5. *Transportation* costs constitute a "natural" barrier. Although gradually less important because of dramatic improvements in technology, high transportation costs can prevent entry. When the market potential is high, firms will invest in manufacturing to be close to the market. Proximity of supplies and service also matter when transportation costs are high.

6. There are also "natural" entry barriers that arise because of *competitive rivalry*. Many of the typical marketing efforts—creation of brand loyalty, differentiation between products, high levels of promotional spending—are factors that, when successful, lead to barriers or defenses against competitive attack.

BOX: Sky-High Entry Barriers[25]

So-called "open skies" bilateral agreements between countries, intended to provide easy access for all comers to an international airport, have proven almost impossible to negotiate because of conflicting national interests.

One artificial airport barrier is a government's refusal to assign parking slots at an international airport to a foreign airline—or having their flights dock farthest away from check-in and baggage facilities. Furthermore, each country's national airline usually has first pick of the slots available and a strong voice in the approval (or rather disapproval) of new competitors entering. The national airline also has first pick of routes and times of flight, optimizing profitability and passenger convenience. And when airport facilities are upgraded, the main beneficiaries tend to be national airlines. For example, if more passport controllers and baggage handlers are added, they are likely to show up at the times when the national airline's flights arrive. The Middle East carriers Emirates (out of Dubai, in 2014 the world largest airline in terms of seats times distance flown), Etihad (out of Abu Dhabi), and Qatar Airlines also gain by strong financial support from their governments.[26]

As a result, seasoned travelers interested in convenience and service—and for whom price is no object—choose airlines based on national destination. Into Paris, fly Air France, with the best facilities at Charles De Gaulle Airport. Heading for London? Fly British Airways, "the world's favorite airline," which controls most slots at Heathrow. Frankfurt is virtually synonymous with Lufthansa, Hong Kong is Cathay Pacific, and Singapore is, yes, Singapore Air. Flying out of Tokyo, you can use All Nippon Air, but you can't use the air terminal check-in service, which is reserved for national flag carrier JAL (Japan Airline) travelers.

Another example of how these barriers limit competition is the covert agreement among airlines not to compete on certain routes. For example, in 2015, when oil prices fell by almost 50 percent, air fares in the U.S. stayed high. The four major airlines—Delta, United, Southwest, and American—basically agreed not to price compete on some major routes.[27]

Today, with the rising conflict between Russia and the West, the entry barriers into Russia might well become quite real and tangible (see Exhibit 7.16).

The economic costs of entry barriers can be considerable. The inefficiency created by barriers translates into higher prices for consumers. Where "personal contacts" are important for entry, **gatekeepers** who can arrange access can be costly. Where regulations require government approval, individuals with good contacts in the

bureaucracy are needed. The cost of doing business is very high in some countries because of entry barriers.

Firms try to deal with the main obstacles to entry in several ways. We will look more closely at the major barriers.

Tariff and Nontariff Barriers

It is common to lower or even waive a tariff when the imported product or component has a certain level of "**local content**" or when imports involve production for re-export. The foreign entrant has an incentive, therefore, to add parts and labor from the local market. When such parts are not available, it is not uncommon for the entrant to help establish a supplier of the parts in the country so as to obtain the lower tariff rate. This is an example of how tariff barriers can lead to foreign investment in plants.

Government Regulations

Governments can play a major role in raising entry barriers. Today, with rising conflict between Russia and the West, the entry barriers into Russia are very real and tangible (see Exhibit 7.16). Government regulations may be so severe and limiting that the company can do little without a native partner. A good example is China in the early years of its opening.

A joint venture was typically required by China as it opened up its market. The native partner had the task of carrying out negotiations with government authorities and local regulators. When Toys "R" Us established its operations in Japan, it appointed Mr. Den Fujita, the general manager of McDonald's Japan, as its representative. The most pressing problem, getting building codes and retail regulations changed, required a strong local presence. Once established in Japan, the firm has become an insider with claims on the same local protection as domestic firms.

Distribution Access

It can be difficult to get members of the distribution channels to carry the firm's product. In many countries, including the United States, new brands need to pay a "slotting" fee— a "tip" or bribe—to get the trade interested. This adds costs and the negotiations slow the entry down. When Belgian beer brewer InBev bought the Canadian Labatt brewer the stated reason was to get access to its North American distribution (when Budweiser was later acquired and InBev became AB InBev in 2008, Labatt had to be sold off for antitrust reasons).[28]

Lack of access to distribution channels usually means that the firm has to consider a JV, or non-equity strategic alliance, or even sell the product unbranded in an OEM (original equipment manufacturing) arrangement with a firm already established. Since 2012 Coca-Cola has partnered with Illy Caffe, the Italian espresso maker, to bring chilled ready-to-drink coffee, Illy Issimo, to convenience stores.

Effect on Entry Mode

In the end, barriers to entering a foreign market make entry-mode decisions more complex than just the arithmetic of a simple geographical expansion.

Each mode of foreign entry involves quite different operating skills. Overseeing a number of licensees in various countries is one thing, running a network of wholly owned subsidiaries quite another. Direct exporting involves learning about overseas transportation, international trade credit, tariff barriers, and so on, quite an investment for the beginner. The growth of various forms of cross-border strategic alliances in the recent past has been accompanied by the emergence of a cadre of international contract lawyers and managers skilled in international negotiations. The start-up costs of learning to manage any one of these modes of entry are considerable, and it is not surprising that companies tend to leverage their particular skills by staying with the same approach.

Consequently, even though the firm's value chain may be broken up to get under a certain country's barriers or in accordance with government regulations, its expansion path will be likely to follow the same mode of entry everywhere. Xerox and 3M are good at running international joint ventures; IBM and Ford like wholly owned subsidiaries; Subway and McDonald's prefer franchising. Staying with the "tried-and-true" leverages the company's expertise properly, minimizes the obstacles to entering, and maximizes the chances of success. When these companies have used another mode of entry, chances are they were forced to do so by government regulation or some other market access barrier.

SUMMARY

Once the country selection has been made, the mode of entry has to be considered carefully. In fact, it would be a good idea to pay attention to entry barriers before getting too deeply into the country selection. But understanding the entry modes available requires more than marketing know-how, and it is often not until the mode of entry is contemplated that more careful assessment of entry barriers is possible. As the chapter has emphasized, the height and character of entry barriers determine what the optimal entry mode should be.

This chapter focused on a detailed description of the four major modes of entry: exporting, licensing (including franchising), strategic alliance, and wholly owned manufacturing subsidiaries. Where trade barriers are low, exporting is often the preferred option, with independent middlemen providing importing and distribution assistance. The chapter stressed the importance of establishing more control over the local marketing effort. After entry, when market penetration becomes a priority, a sales subsidiary is commonly established, allowing the firm to take more control over the local effort. It should be stressed that this is common even without a manufacturing subsidiary in the country—marketing control can be gained even when the entry mode is exporting.

The internationalization process involves a sequential expansion into increasingly different markets, as the company learns to do international marketing in widely different countries. With the ease and low cost of expansion using the Internet, today more and more companies, especially in high-tech industries, target the global market from the beginning.

The chapter discussed the non-exporting modes of entry emphasizing their possibly increased risk of dissipation of key knowledge assets. Offering local licensees or alliance partners some of the technology involved in R&D and production will always carry some risk of dissipation through copying. At the same time it is important not to be too timid about reaching out to partners abroad—many companies have learned a lot from their partnerships, and the exchange is not a one-way street. In today's super-connected world, good ideas and highly skilled individuals can be found in any country.

KEY TERMS

acquisition
agent
artifical barriers
bill of lading
CIF
co-opetition
direct exporting
dissipation of FSAs
distribution access
distribution alliance
entry barriers
exporting
export license
export management company (EMC)
FDI in wholly owned manufacturing
FOB
foreign direct investment (FDI)
foreign sales subsidiary
franchising
gatekeeper
government regulations
greenfield investment
independent distributor
indirect exporting

insurance
internationalization stages
joint ventures (JVs)
letter of credit (L/C)
licensing
local content
manufacturing alliance
modes of entry
natural barriers
nontariff barriers
original equipment manufacturing (OEM)
price escalation
R&D alliance
royalties
sales subsidiary
shared manufacturing
straight licensing
strategic alliances (SAs)
tariff barriers
title
trade credit
trade fairs
trading companies
wholly owned manufacturing subsidiary

DISCUSSION QUESTIONS

1. Because it is located in the Southern Hemisphere, Chile's strong fruit-growing industry has the advantage in northern markets of counterseasonal harvesting (an example of a CSA). What is involved in arranging for the exporting of the fruit crops to a market such as the European Union? What trade barriers might Chilean fruit growers face with this entry mode? How would you try to control the marketing effort in Europe?

2. For an industry or product of your choice, use Internet websites, library sources, Department of Commerce publications, and trade publications to find out when and where the major international trade fairs and conventions are held. Estimate how much participation would cost for a company (registration fees, booth charges, travel, food and lodging, preparation of pamphlets, etc.).

3. What might be the natural entry barriers against foreign cars, if any, in the United States? In Germany? In Japan? Any natural barriers against foreign foods for the same countries?

4. While Disney World entered the Japanese market by licensing its name to a Japanese company, EuroDisney (now Disneyland Paris) outside Paris was established as a joint venture with European backing but with Disney holding majority control. To what would you attribute the difference in entry mode? Given the lack of early success in Europe, do you think another entry mode would have been better? Why or why not?

5. How can control over local marketing be managed in exporting? In franchising? How can Starbucks, the specialty coffee retailer, maintain marketing control over its franchise operations in Japan?

TEAM CHALLENGE PROJECTS

1. Ikea is a Sweden-based retailer that designs and sells ready-to-assemble furniture as well as appliances and home accessories. Ikea is usually listed as the world's largest retailer of furniture products, operating over 370 stores in 47 countries as of May 2017. Ikea has over 40 stores in the U.S. and has used a number of different entry modes in that market: licensing/franchising, FDI—building their own stores, and acquisition and rebranding of other stores. Team 1: Develop arguments for Ikea's further expansion in the U.S. using licensing/franchising. Team 2: Develop arguments for Ikea's further expansion in the U.S. using FDI and acquisitions.

2. Team 1: Research U.S. government websites (and others) to determine what mode of entry strategy has been used by American companies most frequently to enter markets in Africa. Explain why. Team 2: Research U.S. government websites (and others) to determine what mode of entry strategy has been used by American companies most frequently to enter markets in Latin America. Explain why.

SELECTED REFERENCES

Banalieva, Elitsa R. and Charles Dhanaraj, "Home-region orientation in international expansion strategies," *Journal of International Business Studies*, Vol. 44, No. 2, Feb/Mar 2013, pp. 89–116.

Brouthers, Keith D., "Institutional, cultural and transactions cost infleunces on entry mode choice and performance," *Journal of International Business Studies*, Vol. 44, No. 1, Jan. 2013a, pp. 1–13.

_____, "A Retrospective on: Institutional, cultural and transaction cost infleunces on entry mode choice and performance," *Journal of International Business Studies*, Vol. 44, No. 1, Jan. 2013b, pp. 14–22.

Cavusgil, S. Tamer. "On the Internationalization Process of Firms." *European Research* 8, no. 6 (1980), pp. 273–81.

Chowdhry, Amit, "Apple And Samsung Drop Patent Disputes Against Each Other Outside Of The U.S." *Forbes, Tech*, Aug. 06, 2014.

De Kluyver, Cornelis A. *Fundamentals of Global Strategy*. Business Expert Press, 2010.

Elfes, Holger and Keith Campbell, "AB InBev Sells Labatt USA to KPS," *Bloomberg News*, February 23, 2009.

El Gazzar, Shereen, "Gulf airlines have double advantage, says Swiss airline chief," *The National/Business* (Arab Emirates), June 2, 2014.

Ertug, Gokhan, Ilya R.P. Cuypers, Niels G. Noorderhaven and Ben M. Bensaou, "Trust between international joint venture partners: Effects of home countries," *Journal of International Business Studies*, Vol. 44, No. 3, April 2013, pp. 263–282."Export Licenses," *Export.Gov*, April 27, 2011

Folsom, Ralph, Michael Gordon, John Spanogle and Michael Van Alstine, *International Business Transactions in a Nutshell Paperback*, 9th ed. St Paul, MN: West Academic Publishing, 2012.

"Former U.S. Transportation Officials Say American Airlines/British Air Lays Pact Would Harm Competition, Lead to Higher Fares," *PR Newswire*, Dec. 19, 2001.

Goodger, Ben, "Brand Licensing in Emerging Markets – Top 10 Mistakes," *Ipstrategy.com*, October 2, 2012.

Hennart, Jean-Francois, "Down with MNE-centric theories: Market Entry and Expansion as Bundling of MNE and Local Assets," in Buckley, Peter J. and Pervez N. Gauri, ed's, *International Business Strategy: Theory and Practice*, New York: Routledge, 2015, pp. 383–409.

Jonsson, Anna and Nicolai J. Foss, "International expansion through flexible replication: Learning from the internationalization experience of IKEA, *Journal of International Business Studies*, Vol. 42, No. 9, Dec. 2011, pp.1079–1102.

Mace, M.L. "The President and International Operations," *Harvard Business Review*, November–December 1966, p. 76.

Maekelburger, Birger, Christian Schwens and Ruediger Kabst, "Asset specificity and foreign market entry mode choice of small and medium-sized enterprises: The moderating influence of knowledge safeguards and institutional safeguards," *Journal of International Business Studies*, Vol. 43, No. 5, June/July 2012, pp. 458–476.

Root, Franklin R. *Entry Strategies for International Markets,* Revised and Expanded. San Francisco: Jossey-Bass Inc. Publishers, 1994.

Ross Sorkin, Andrew, "As Oil Prices Fall, Airfares Still Stay High," *The New York Times*, B1, March 24, 2015.

Singh, Puneet Pal, "Can Sony succeed where Sony-Ericsson partnership failed?" *BBC News, Singapore*, Oct. 13, 2011.

Spence, Ewan, "Sony's Smartphone Surrender as it Abandons Android and Xperia," *Forbes, Tech*, Feb. 18, 2015.

Starbucks Newsroom, "Starbucks Opens Spectacular Flagship Store in Mumbai," Oct. 19, 2012.

Starbucks Newsroom, "Starbucks Signs Agreement with Tingyi," Mar. 18, 2015. http://news.starbucks.com/news/starbucks-signs-agreement-with-tingyi-holding-corp.

Trefis Team, "Starbucks' Full Ownership of Japan Unit to Boost International Revenue Growth." *Forbes*, 2014.

Wang, Helen H., "Five Things Starbucks Did To Get China Right." *Forbes*, Aug. 10, 2012.

ENDNOTES

1. See Trefis Team, 2014.
2. From de Kluyer, 2010.
3. Jonsson and Foss, 2011, show how the preferred entry mode at IKEA (basically own stores) has been repeated flexibly over the years.
4. From Wang, 2012.
5. Starbucks Newsroom, 2015.
6. Indian data is from Starbucks Newsroom, 2012.
7. Adapted from F.R. Root, 1994, and Brouthers, 2013b.
8. The information on terms of trade, contracts, etc. can be culled from online sites, usually government sponsored such as http://export.gov/exportbasics/eg_main_017485.asp. A good general reference book is "A Basic Guide to Exporting: The Official Government Resource for Small and Medium-Sized Business," published by International Trade Administration, 2012 (available on Amazon.com, also on Kindle).
9. From "A Basic Guide to Exporting: The Official Government Resource for Small and Medium-Sized Business," published by International Trade Administration, 2012.
10. From "A Basic Guide to Exporting: The Official Government Resource for Small and Medium-Sized Business," published by International Trade Administration, 2012.
11. Folsom et al., 2012, is a good source for the legal issues involved in the agreement.
12. The new Illy Issimo's slogan is "The Pleasure Of Illy On The Go."
13. See Folsom et al., 2012.
14. Source: Adapted from Mace, 1966; Goodger, 2012.
15. Folsom et al., 2012 is a good reference source. It is advisable to get lawyers involved in these contracts.
16. See, for example, Ybarra and Turk, 2011.
17. The largest lawsuit was finally dropped in 2014; see Chowdhry, 2014.
18. The choice between JV and 100 percent ownership is treated at length in academic research. See, for example, Brouthers, 2013a, Hennart, 2015, and Maekelburger, Schwens, and Kabst, 2012.
19. http://www.railway-technology.com/projects/crh380a-high-speed-china/.
20. See Ertug et al., 2013.

21. Source: http://www.bmwgroup.com.
22. From the factory website: https://www.bmwusfactory.com.
23. See, for example, Banalieva and Dhanaraj, 2013.
24. See Cavusgil, 1980; Jonsson and Foss, 2011; Banalieva and Dhanaraj, 2013.
25. Sources: "Former U.S. … " 2001; Ross-Sorkin, 2015.
26. See El Gazzar, 2014.
27. See Ross-Sorkin, 2015.
28. See Elfes and Campbell, 2009.

In this chapter you will learn about:

1. How to identify macro-segments, groups of countries that are sufficiently similar that a pan-regional strategy might be beneficial
2. How to follow up the macro-segmentation with micro-segmentation, where the target market(s) within the macro-group can be identified
3. How to position your product so as to fit with the local market's preferences and provide competitive advantages
4. How new features of a product can disrupt the existing market and allow a company to break into a mature market against established competitors

Market Segmentation and Product Positioning

CHAPTER 8

OPENING VIGNETTE

BUICK CONQUERS CHINA – AGAIN

Since the 1930s GM has used a marketing strategy for its five car divisions of a *ladder of success*, creating five separate brands and five price ranges for five different types of consumers. An entry-level buyer would start out at the bottom with the "basic transportation" from Chevrolet, then rising through Pontiac, Oldsmobile, Buick, and ultimately to Cadillac as both the customer's age and income rose.[1] This strategy existed for over 75 years (until GM's bankruptcy in 2008) and positioned Buick as an affordable luxury car near the top of the ladder but with an average buyer's age in the U.S. of 72 in 2000 and 66 in 2010.

When GM began its expansion into China, it saw a country with an expanding middle class and rapidly rising incomes, exactly the conditions that produce a fast growing "affordable luxury" car segment. More importantly, GM's usual competitors of Lexus, BMW, and Mercedes did not have many offering in that segment in China. GM positioned Buick as an affordable luxury car for 30- and 40-year-olds and began designing and manufacturing cars in China specifically for that market segment (see Exhibit 8.1).

The promotion in China has been hip and trendy. What helped was also that one old Buick from the early years in the century had been acquired by Chou En-lai, long the second-in-command to Mao Zedong. Having played a leading role in the Communist revolution, Chou was an unabashed automotive fan and his Buick, pre-owned by the last emperor of China, became the pride of his collection.

In a market that remembered fondly the proud Buick history, GM created a new identity. "It's stylish, fashionable and dynamic. I was attracted at first glance."[2] Buick's segment of 30- and 40-year-old,

Country	2013	2016	percent of worldwide total
China	809,918	1,100,503	76.8%
U.S.	205,509	229,631	16.0%
Canada	14,310	19,053	1.3%
Mexico	2,319	4,068	0.3%
Total Worldwide	1,032,056	1,432,679	

Source: http://gmauthority.com/blog/gm/buick/ buick-sales-numbers/

EXHIBIT 8.2.
Sales of Buicks worldwide by largest country (number of vehicles). It is becoming increasingly difficult to think of Buick as an American brand.

mostly businesspeople, who want upscale transportation differed greatly from the Tesla segment that we saw in an earlier chapter. Tesla's segment is the superrich buying their third or fourth car as a statement (i.e., toy).

The results have been impressive with GM selling 1.1 million Buicks in China in 2016. In addition, the new hip Buick styling cues are beginning to affect car design in the U.S. and Canada and sales have increased here as well (see Exhibit 8.2).

But the average age of Buick buyers in the U.S. is still 57 in 2014, an improvement but a long way to go, demonstrating that market positions for products, once firmly established, are difficult to change.[3]

The basic management question in market segmentation is to find homogeneous groups of customers with high demand potential for the firm's products or services. This used to mean that one key criterion for a viable market segment was **ability to buy**, that is, whether the segment members had enough money to pay for the product.

What is new, however, is that global marketers today understand and accept that the bottom of the pyramid (the four billion poorest people who live at the bottom of the economic pyramid) also demand attention, and can become attractive consumers.[4] This means the able to buy condition has been broadly expanded from earlier practices. Such new customers, of course, are relative newcomers in the marketplace, and often have only weakly developed preferences. They have simply not seen products and services yet that they can use. While the product usage conditions of a middle-class consumer can be quite similar across countries, poor people tend to have very unique needs. Take shampoos. Apart from formulation for different hair characteristics, the poor may also need smaller packages, one-time usage options, soap that strains the water, and less lather in communal baths. So segmentation involves more than just asking for preferences—what they want—but what they need. Segmentation in such cases needs to start with understanding the customers' usage situation, and adapt the product so it fits to the actual use.

The first section demonstrates the basic principles of global market segmentation. It also shows how global market segmentation differs from domestic-only cases. This leads to a two-step approach wherein the country-level macro-segmentation precedes the within-country micro-segmentation. The chapter continues with the clustering techniques for grouping similar markets and the procedures to identify segments across counties.

The chapter then turns to targeting issues, identifying which of the segment(s) should be targeted. Here the chapter also covers the question of diversification, selecting different countries in a portfolio of markets. In addition, the speed of expansion is considered, contrasting waterfall and sprinkler strategies. Then positioning methods are discussed.

The case in which global coordination involves a standardized product with a global brand helps to illustrate the methods. The chapter ends with a discussion of how all three strategy components—segmentation, targeting, and positioning—need to be fully integrated for maximum benefit.

GLOBAL SEGMENTATION BASICS

Segment Requirements

Differing segments exist, of course, in all country markets. People's lifestyles, usage levels, demographics, and attitudes vary among any population. But to be useful for marketing purposes, targeted segments need to possess the following characteristics. They have to be:

1. *Identifiable* (What distinguishes the segment members?)
2. *Measurable* (How many people belong to each segment?)
3. *Reachable* (How to distribute to and communicate with each segment?)

Each of these requirements can be more difficult to satisfy abroad than at home, especially in emerging and less developed markets. Nevertheless, it is important that these requirements be kept in mind when assessing a segment's revenue potential and costs. A company marketing to a minority cultural or religious group—such as Muslims in France—will usually have a relatively easy segmentation task because the members tend to congregate and live close to each other. A company marketing a product to a minor political movement such as libertarians in Canada might find it harder since libertarians tend not to congregate.

Segmentation Criteria

How to best segment a country market is a recurring problem in global marketing. A number of options exist, especially toward the later stages of the PLC when consumer preferences tend to get more diverse. The most common criteria for segmentation are the following:

Economics
The most basic global segmentation criterion is still economic development. Even for low-priced consumer necessities such as detergents, soap, and toothpaste, level of GDP per capita matters. The reason is that it is necessary to adapt marketing mixes where package sizes have to be downsized, distribution channels are different, and some communications media are unavailable.

Demographics
Demographics refer to the age and family structure in different countries. Demographics also play an important role in determining global segments, especially in terms of size. The fact is that for many consumer products, age and family size are strong determinants of consumption levels. As in the case of economics, published data are usually available and quite reliable. But they rarely determine the choice between competing brands. Demographics, like economics, help determine consumption levels, but they do not always satisfy the requirement that a good segmentation should also influence choice between competing brands.

Values

One general culture-related criterion popular in global segmentation is **value-based segmentation**, for example segmenting consumers according to how much they value social justice versus individual responsibility. Because individual values are so basic, the derived segments are often found to be similar across countries. What differs is the percentage of a population that falls into each of the segments.

Greenpeace, the international activist organization against corporate environmental degradation, is one organization that uses value-based segmentation. In its campaigns Greenpeace segments people into three broad profiles: settlers, prospectors, and pioneers.[5]

- Settlers: people concerned about safety and security, belonging and roots
- Prospectors: people who care about esteem of others and self, who are dreamers and followers
- Pioneers: people who think in terms of self-actualization, are concerned ethicals and individualists

Two examples of how Greenpeace uses this segmentation come from Brazil and the UK[6]

- To prevent offshore oil drilling in Brazil, Greenpeace identified the local community as fitting the "settler" profile. It then created messages that resonated with the values of family and personal safety.
- In the United Kingdom a website called *Global Cool* was set up to communicate with "prospectors" about climate change. The website is focused on eco-fashion and celebrities acting on climate change.

Value-based segments have the advantage of being stable over time. They are also applicable for a wide variety of products, but because they represent very fundamental characteristics of individuals they often need to be coupled with more product-specific criteria in order to be effective.

Ethnicity

One cultural factor that has become increasingly important as globalization progresses is ethnicity. As people move away from their home country in search of better work and living conditions elsewhere, they start forming enclaves of their home culture in the new country. Gradually, as more immigrants arrive and as economic progress continues, these ethnic groups become large and prosperous enough to justify targeting as separate segments. In the United States, for example, a number of firms target the Hispanic population. The same opportunity is of course open also for companies from the old home country, which is why you can find food products from many countries in any large urban supermarket in the developed world. As the ethnic groups grow, their influence spreads to the rest of society, and we all learn to like Mexican flautas, Korean kimchi, Moroccan couscous, and Indian pan. Gradually, the influence diffuses further and affects not only what we eat but what we see and hear (see box, "Global Entertainment: Bollywood and Telenovelas").

BOX: Global Entertainment: Bollywood and Telenovelas[7]

It was once safe to assume that every moviegoer and TV watcher around the world sought entertainment from Hollywood films and American must-see TV. Emerging markets and Third World markets caught a glimpse of a "better life" via the window of multi-million dollar Hollywood movies and American prime-time TV. This is changing. America is taking a backseat when it comes to the film and TV industry.

Enter Bollywood. Every year, the Indian film industry turns out 800 to 1000 films. These films reach an audience of such staggering size no one seems to be sure how big it is, with estimates ranging from 12 million *per day* to the 23 million per day suggested by the *Encyclopedia of Indian Cinema*. And that doesn't count the global communities of nonresident Indians, estimated at upward of 3.6 billion souls.

Bollywood outside of India first manifested itself in the United Kingdom, where the largest ethnic minority is Indian. Films such as *Bend it Like Beckham, Monsoon Wedding,* and *Moulin Rouge* embrace Bollywood influences. Indian music is becoming more mainstream through hip-hop samples and pop song remixes. *Bombay Dreams,* a musical about the Indian movie industry imported from London and revised for American audiences, has brought Bollywood to Broadway. The millions of South Asians who live in America retain a very vibrant link with their motherland through Bollywood. They keep their culture alive watching Bollywood movies.

Bollywood is giving viewers an alternative to the typical Hollywood movie laden with computer-generated explosions and car chases. Compared to Hollywood, Bollywood features less violence and more dance—but also sex (see Exhibit 8.3).

Jumping from Indian movies to Mexican television, there is a surging popularity in the telenovela all over the world, targeting Spanish-speaking ethnic populations.

The telenovela or television novel (the usual but inapt translation is soap opera) offers audiences love, drama, and hope through plots that unite the right couples, where good triumphs over evil, people can be redeemed, and impossible love is given fruition. The programs are exported via Miami or Mexico to the various Spanish-language markets in various countries. In heavily Hispanic cities such as Los Angeles, the telenovela sometimes gets higher prime-time ratings than any English-language network. They are also dubbed into other languages and sent to networks in Singapore, Thailand, Canada, the Philippines, Brazil, and the Czech Republic. Just as the Bollywood movies, the telenovelas threaten the assumed global dominance of American entertainment. In the Czech Republic, for example, English-language soap operas have only achieved market shares of a few percent while telenovelas may garner 50 percent of viewers.

During the 1990s, the global audience was watching U.S.-produced *Friends* and *Baywatch* on TV, and Julia Roberts and Tom Cruise in the movies. In the mid-2000s it was shows like *House MD* and *The Simpsons.* Now the global audience, while still watching American-produced shows, is also watching *Lo Que La Vida Me Robó* (*What Life Stole From Me*), *Mi Corazón Es Tuyo* (*My Heart Is Yours*) and remakes of *La Mentira* (*Twisted Lies*) and *La Madrastra* (*The Stepmother*) on TV, and Indian stars Aishwarya Rai Bachchan, Abhisheck Bachchan, and newcomers Arjun Rampal and Deepika Padukone in the theaters.

EXHIBIT 8.3.
The musical *Bollywood Love Story* performed at Theatre Victoria in Barcelona, Spain. Bollywood uses a successful mixture of genres (comedy followed by music followed by dance followed by romance followed by drama) that's called the masala style.

Copyright © 2009 by Shutterstock/ Christian Bertrand.

Peer Groups

Despite being globally connected through digital technology, individuals still care about their immediate **peer groups,** including friends, classmates, and colleagues. Well-known companies such as Benetton, Nike, Levi's, and British Airways have promoted their universality only to find that customers still want to be recognized for what kind of groups they belong to, and want their brands to reflect that.

Thus, global segments are still often defined in terms of group belonging: Benetton's target is generation X, Nike's runners are rebels, Levi's target is the American "wannabes" in foreign countries, and British Airways targets Anglo-Saxon businesspeople around the world. These segments are no longer bound by country borders, but they have a strong group identity nevertheless. Furthermore, global peer groups influence choice between competing substitutes more than actual consumption levels.

Lifestyle

As economic development takes place, and buying behavior involves more than simple necessities, consumers start developing their own lifestyle. They choose products and brands on the basis of what they want, not simply on what they need. Consumers become more sophisticated and fickle, and markets move toward the maturity stage. Their AIOs (activities, interests, and opinions), not economics or demographics, determine what they choose.

Lifestyle segments tend to be similar to value-based segmentation, although more geared to consumption patterns. For the China market, a lifestyle segmentation study employed a massive representative data set of over 70,000 individuals. The study adapted a standard AIO questionnaire by adding some basic personality items to account for typical lifestyles of Chinese consumers, such as dependent or independent, impulsive or intellectualism.[8] After massive data analysis, the result was a surprisingly limited number of four lifestyle segments (the relative size of the segments in percent):

1. Fashion-oriented consumers (15.7 percent)

- Like to keep up with latest fashion. They prefer fashionable to practical. They like to try new brands and new products. They are impulsive, affective, and sociable. For example, they like karaoke, drinking and chatting with friends, seeing films, eating at KFC or McDonald's, and longing for a romantic and comfortable life. They lack independence and are prone to be affected by other people's opinions.

2. Tradition-oriented consumers (29.4 percent)

- Conservative, they don't like change and fashion. They emphasize job security rather than high income. They are family-oriented, enjoying the family, and believe that family is more important than their career. Watching TV at home is their main leisure pastime. They are price-conscious. They prefer to buy domestic brands due to lower price compared to foreign brands. They don't pay much attention to advertisements.

3. Achievement-oriented consumers (23.4 percent)

- Place a lot of value on their personal achievement, hoping to get to the very top in their career. They are self-confident and are generally rational, decisive, and independent. They want to be seen as individuals. They like fashion and but they are not as enthusiastic for entertainment as are fashion-oriented consumers. They pay attention to social problems such as environment protection. They prefer high-quality products and famous brands.

4. Moderate-oriented consumers (31.5 percent)

- Deeply impacted by Chinese traditional culture with moderate attitudes toward different activities and issues. They normally express neither very positive nor very negative attitudes. They represent the largest of the lifestyle segments of Chinese consumers.

Benefits

A more product-specific criterion useful in global segmentation is one that focuses on the benefits sought. In this **benefit segmentation**, different people may look for different benefits, but global segments can be identified that are looking for roughly the same benefits. Anita Roddick's Body shop (now part of L'Oreal) seems to have identified a global segment that looks for green products in personal care, with benefits both in terms of functional quality and environmental care. Benefit segmentation requires good understanding of the local markets, solid marketing research, and of course a product that scores high on the specific benefits sought.

TWO-STAGE GLOBAL SEGMENTATION

Global segmentation typically combines these alternative and complementary criteria by a **two-stage segmentation** procedure, the first stage being macro-segmentation and the second stage being micro-segmentation.[9] In the **macro-segmentation** stage, countries are grouped using more general criteria, to identify clusters of countries that are similar in socioeconomic and cultural characteristics.

In the second **micro-segmentation** stage, market research is used to collect data on the potential customers in each of the countries belonging to a selected cluster. These data are then used to define cross-country segments to target.

We will first look at the macro-segmentation clustering process in more detail, then micro-segmentation, and then discuss how the two-stage procedure has been implemented in one actual case.

Macro-Segmentation

In the first macro-segmentation stage countries are grouped on the basis of common characteristics deemed to be important for marketing purposes. With more than 200 independent country markets to consider, many companies often start with the existing trade blocs or geographical regions when clustering countries. The EU, NAFTA, or ASEAN, or geographical regions such as Southeast Asia, Oceania, and the Middle East, are often already treated as relatively autonomous organizational units. The necessary data tends to be readily available for such regions, facilitating the segmentation.

The variables typically used in macro-segmentation include socio-demographic data on population size and character, disposable income levels, educational background, and primary language(s), religion and cultural identity, as well as indicators of level of development, infrastructure, rate of growth in GNP, and political affiliation. Exhibit 8.4 shows the indicators used to indicate level of economic development, cultural affinity and socio-demographics.

To identify regional groupings (macro-segments) of countries, it is possible to use computerized techniques such as **cluster analysis**.[10] Clustering maps show a picture of which countries are similar and which are far apart. To incorporate more than two criteria at a time, it is common to do an initial factor analysis before clustering the

EXHIBIT 8.4.
Macro-segmentation clustering criteria

- *Economic*: GNP per capita, Exports as a percent of GNP, Air travel by passengers, Energy use per capita, TV sets owned per household.
- *Cultural*: Religious orientation, Importance of the family, Respect for authority, Ethnocentrism, Score on Hofstede's dimensions (especially individualism vs collectivism), Primary language.
- *Socio-demographic*: Population size, Percent below 30 years of age, Number of children per household, Level of Urbanization, Literacy rate.

countries. The factor analysis helps combine all the criteria into a manageable few dimensions, although at the price of making interpretation of the dimensions less clear. The interested reader is referred to the many available statistical texts.

A publication by Budeva and Mullen illustrates how a macro-segmentation is performed.[11] The authors used criteria data on two broad dimensions, economic and cultural factors.

To represent *culture*, the study used two factors identified the World Values Survey at the University of Michigan.[12] They were *Traditional versus Secular-Rational Orientation* and *Survival versus Self-Expression* factors. Manifestations of traditional values are a strong sense of national pride and more respect for authority, while the *Secular-Rational Orientation* emphasizes opposite values. The *Survival versus Self-Expression* dimension consists of items tapping trust, tolerance, and quality of life. People at the *Survival* end of the scale tend to describe themselves as not very happy and are very careful about trusting people. *Self-expressive* people, on the other hand, show mutual trust and tolerance and feel more secure.

Exhibit 8.5 shows the clustering based on the two cultural factors.

EXHIBIT 8.5.
Six macro-economic clusters[13]

Source: Desislava G. Budeva and Michael R. Mullen, "International Market Segmentation: Economics, National Culture and Time," European Journal of Marketing, vol. 48, no. 7/8.

Cluster 1	Cluster 2	Cluster 3	Cluster 4	Cluster 5	Cluster 6
Argentina	France	Bulgaria	Belgium	Austria	U.S.A.
Brazil	Germany	Czech Rep.	Ireland	Canada	
Chile	Italy	Hungary		Finland	
India	Japan	Russia		Iceland	
Mexico	Spain	Slovakia		Netherlands	
Poland		Slovenia		Norway	
Portugal				Sweden	
S. Africa					
Turkey					

The cultural groupings turn out to be similar to the East-West and North-South categories typically employed in economic policy analyses.[14] The exhibit shows some very typical and consistent patterns. The United States, alone in Cluster 6, is often an outlier, a special case because of its high income, cultural diversity, and size. The EU countries in Cluster 2 are joined by Japan, basically a mature, slow growth, advanced cluster. Cluster 3 is Eastern Europe, including Russia. Cluster 5 is the usual Scandinavian and egalitarian grouping. Clusters 1 and 4 are less clear. Cluster 1 consists of several Latin American countries joined by a few others, and probably reflects the medium-level economies in these countries. Cluster 4 is small, with two countries that are not quite at the top rung in the European community.

Other variables have been used for macro-segmentation to get closer to ultimate consumer choices. Cannon and Yaprak proposed a framework that blends consumers' culture-based value orientations with product/service characteristics.[15] In their framework cultural values condition consumers' symbolic and functional needs for various product characteristics that drive product and brand choice. For example, you buy cowboy boots for their functional and, to a greater degree, symbolic benefits, allowing you to satisfy culture-based needs. This bridges the gap between the macro-segmentation using broad cultural and economic variables and the micro-segmentation that relates to brand-specific choices.

Micro-Segmentation

The micro-segmentation stage resembles what is typically done in any domestic market segmentation analysis.

- For each country in a chosen Cluster, the data collected involve variables related to product usage patterns, benefits desired, price sensitivity, media usage, and shopping behavior.
- Data are also collected on individual socio-demographics, income, and other background variables.
- The statistical analysis involves factoring out dimensions along which customers in a country market differ from each other and from customers in other countries in the Cluster.
- Then, the research assesses the size and sales potential for each group or segment of similar consumers.
- Finally, the data are analyzed to find the best ways to reach and communicate to each of the segments.

For example, in micro-segmentation a typical segment that can be found in the beer market of most countries is the **heavy-user segment** (defined as, say, those who consume more than two beers a day). For obvious reasons, this segment is often an attractive target segment for a beer brewer. However, the proportion of beer drinkers who belong to that segment can vary (a higher percentage in Germany and the United States, for example; much smaller in Italy and France). This affects the need to coordinate strategies across countries. Also, the way to reach the heavy users of beers might seem the same in principle—sponsorship of sports events, for example—but which sports are popular varies across countries. Thus it might not be useful to coordinate the marketing communication mix either.

A Case Illustration

To see how the two-stage procedure works in practice, a case study of a pan-European segmentation scheme for a consumer packaged goods (CPG) company is instructive.[16] The company had initially used an un-segmented strategy in Europe, and had been disappointed by the performance of some its brands. Although successful in one or two countries, several new products were less successful when introduced in other European countries. The company had become aware that not all the receptive target segments were of equal size in each country, and decided to do an in-depth analysis of pan-European segmentation.

Stage 1. The company first clustered the EU countries using economic data on market size and demographics coupled with some product- and company-specific data (e.g., presence of the company in a country market). This stage resulted in two macro-segments, the largest five countries (Germany, United Kingdom, France, Italy, and Spain) and the other countries. Since the five largest countries accounted for 80 percent of the population, the company decided to focus on that cluster.

Stage 2. In the second stage, market research was conducted in the five countries to identify similarities and differences. Because the managerial problem involved new product acceptance rates, it was decided to focus the survey questions around the concept of innovativeness. Following past research in the diffusion of innovation literature, the basic hypothesis was that each country would show some pioneers and early adopters, the kind of people important for the success of a new product in the early stage of the product life cycle. By identifying these innovator segments and measuring their size in the different countries, the company could then decide whether a coordinated introductory campaign would be likely to succeed in all five countries.

Stage 3. A key question facing the managers was where to make the cutoff for the innovative segments. There is no hard and fast rule that says that someone is an innovator if he or she scores higher than, say, a 5 on a 7-point innovation scale. But from past research it has been determined that the pioneers and early adopters constitute approximately 16 percent of any population. So, the researchers pooled the data for all five countries, and found the scale score above which 16 percent of the total number of respondents from all five countries was classified as innovators. They then identified from which countries these innovative respondents came, and could then determine whether all countries had an equal portion of innovators.

Stage 4. What did the company find? It found that the innovativeness among consumers differed considerably between the five countries. Some countries had significantly more innovators than others. This meant that if innovators were targeted everywhere, the strategy would do well in some countries but not in others.

Although disappointed, management uncovered the reason for lackluster sales of new products in some of the countries. Many of their initial new product introductions took place in one country (the United Kingdom) with a large proportion of innovators. When the product rollout then continued across Europe with a similar product formulation and marketing mix, the later countries did not respond as anticipated, simply because they had fewer innovators in the marketplace. A standardized pan-European strategy could not work. By using an adapted segmentation strategy the company estimated it was able to increase the effectiveness of its new product introductions by 50 percent on average.

TARGETING SEGMENTS

Which segment or segments the company decides to target depends on several factors. The likely revenues have to be projected as well as the costs of getting those revenues. Let's begin with the revenue side.

Projecting Revenues

Two main factors affect projected revenues.

- *Segment size.* The size component involves both number of consumers in the segment, and their spending level. From these data it is possible to compute a sales potential for each candidate target segment. Remember that spending level involves both amounts bought and frequency of repurchase.
- *Market share.* To estimate revenues the firm needs also to develop a forecast of the market share the firm is likely to gain in the segment. This means that targeting decisions need to be based on the firm's competitive advantages and disadvantages in the segment. The firm should have a clear grasp on its own strengths and weaknesses, and it becomes important to match those against the competitors in a segment. Picking a target segment involves choosing which consumers to appeal to, but at the same time the firm actually picks its competitors. Targeting a segment means choosing customers and choosing competitors.

At this stage it is important to recognize that the target consumers might see other benefits in the product than marketers or consumers in the original country. For example, the original advertising for Red Bull in Asia emphasized the product's ability to keep people awake, alert, and safe. Introduced in Europe, Red Bull's target market shifted dramatically. From blue-collar workers, the targeting first shifted to athletes, and then to the party crowd and bar-hoppers.

Forecasting market share involves assessing the strength of the competitors in the segment. The firm first has to determine which domestic and global competitors operate in the market and which segments they target. This is usually easy to find out.

The next step is assessing how strong these competitors are. When the competitors are global brands, this is also usually easy. The firm very often can gauge the competitors' performance in other markets. It is usually more difficult to judge how strong domestic competitors are.

A domestic company that can count on local brand loyalty can be a much more formidable competitor than an analysis by numbers only might suggest. Thus, for example, the very fragmented German beer market, with most citizens favoring their own town beer, would seem a very easy conquest for a large global brewer such as Heineken. But the fact is that the locals are very loyal. For example, the citizens of Cologne still favor "Kölsch," a fresh draft beer served in small juice-size glasses to be finished in minutes before it turns bad.

To gauge how difficult it will be to take market share from them, the financial strength of the competitors is one important factor. This can usually be judged from annual reports, trade press, and news reports. Also important is the degree to which the competitors are committed to defend the segment. Microsoft's search engine Bing has faced an uphill battle against Google as the incumbent leader. Google is defending its turf vigorously, as also Yahoo has learnt.

Cost Analysis

Finally, the targeting decision needs to be based not only on forecasted revenues but also on costs of achieving those revenues. This brings back into focus the question of standardized versus adapted marketing strategies. Even with today's localization mindset, managers need to consider the costs of complete adaptation versus the savings from standardization.

It will be tempting for many companies to target segments for which the needed adaptations are minimal. From this perspective the former neglect of the poor bottom of the pyramid is understandable. The costs of localization were seen to outweigh the benefits, especially since the low prices made for very slim margins.

Where to strike the balance between complete standardization and local adaptation of the marketing is perhaps the major problem in global marketing. Today, as manufacturing technology has made mass customization feasible, global companies often can tweak their products without increasing costs much. Still, it is also true that many global companies have trouble striking the right balance between global coordination and complete adaptation.

A good illustration of the problem is Dell's initial entry into China.[17] In the mainland China market, the office segment involves sales to many government-owned businesses, for which high-level contacts and personal relationships are important. Chinese customers still value the **guanxi**, or "mutual good feeling and trust" between old friends. Face-to-face contacts are not easily replaced by e-mail and Internet connections, the communication media employed in the Dell direct sales model. Direct sales also assumes a certain technical sophistication on the part of the buyer, rarely the case among government bureaucrats.

Going against local sensitivities, Dell took a chance that its low price would be a competitive and followed the same standardized sales model used by Dell elsewhere. Despite predictions, the company was successful by hiring and training Chinese sales engineers who could handhold and lead the less technical sophisticates in the government agencies. The sales engineers were also instructed to gain access to Chinese purchasing managers of technology hardware who were willing and able to accept less personal interaction—and a better price. (Unfortunately, as so often happens in global competition, soon Lenovo responded by copying Dell's model, and Dell's performance slipped.)

EXPANSION STRATEGIES

As we have seen, the clustering approach to macro-segmentation leads generally to the identification of markets with similar macro-economic characteristics. However, in developing a targeting strategy, some companies make a conscious effort to be a player in different markets and different regions. This has become increasingly important since political risk remains high and financial turmoil spreads quickly through tightly integrated global markets.

Diversification vs. Focus

A **diversification strategy** aims to balance market countries so that the international portfolio of countries and regions provides diversification protection against the risk of large losses.

Examples of diversification strategies are common. Volvo, the Swedish-Chinese carmaker, limited its U.S. market involvement to 25 percent of total output for many years. In personal interviews with top management, Toyota executives reported feeling uneasy when their exports take more than 50 percent of their home market demand. The recent tendency is for global exporters to limit their unit shares going to the U.S. market. The fear of too great a reliance on the U.S. market is palpable, especially at times when the United States seems to be vacillating in its adherence to free trade.

However, even though there may be strong diversification benefits from entering several markets or regions, a case can be made for focusing on a few similar markets in the same cluster. A **focus strategy** allocates the marketing resources to one or two key markets in a region so as to achieve high brand penetration. These markets can be given more attention and market positions fortified. Since the other countries within the region are relatively similar, spillover effects can be shared more easily. Product lines can be the same. Good advertising copy is more likely to play well in a similar country.

How should a company strike a balance between diversifying and possibly overextending itself versus being too dependent on a few single markets? High-growth markets require more marketing support for a brand, and a focused strategy tends to be desirable. On the other hand, instability and competitive rivalry in the market increase the benefits of diversification. When decisions have to be adapted to the local market, there is greater need for focus.

Empirical research has shown that generally diversified strategies tend to lead to greater sales abroad, while concentrated or focused strategies tend to result in somewhat higher profitability.[18] One prime determinant of profitability is whether the firm can identify and track costs, something that is easier in focused strategies. In firms aiming for diversification, sales objectives and market orientation tend to be more important than costs, leading to greater sales.

Expansion Paths

The rate of expansion into different markets typically follows one of two alternative paths. Under the **waterfall strategy**, the firm gradually moves into overseas markets, while in the **sprinkler strategy** the company tries to enter several country markets simultaneously or within a limited period of time.

Waterfall Strategy

Traditionally, the waterfall strategy (see Exhibit 8.6) was the preferred choice.

After success in the home market, the company gradually moves out to culturally close country markets, then to other mature and high-growth markets, and finally to less developed country markets. This is the pattern followed by many well-known companies including Panasonic, BMW, and General Electric.

The advantage of the waterfall strategy is that the expansion can take place in an orderly manner, and the same managers can be used for different countries, which helps to capitalize on skills developed. For the same reasons it is also a relatively less demanding strategy in terms of resource requirements. This is why it is still the most common approach also for relatively young global companies such as China's Haier and Alibaba, Spain's Zara, and America's Under Armour. Even for "born global" companies which tend to view the world as one market from the start, the sequential waterfall strategy seems preferable.[19] But in fast-moving markets the waterfall strategy may be too slow.

Sprinkler Strategy

Compared with the waterfall, the sprinkler strategy (see Exhibit 8.7) has the opposite strengths and disadvantages.

Sprinkler is a much quicker way to market penetration across the globe, it generates first-mover advantages, and it preempts competitive countermoves by sheer speed. The sprinkler strategy is a response to increasing competitive rivalry and the need for speed when competitors imitate quickly. The drawback is the amount of managerial, financial, and other resources required and the risk potential of major commitments without proper country knowledge or research.

Examples of the sprinkler approach are becoming more frequent as the competitive climate heats up and as global communications such as the Internet make access to country markets easier. The typical cases involve new product launches by companies with established global presence such as Samsung (the Galaxy cellphone models), Microsoft (the Xbox game player versions), Gillette (the Fusion, for example), and L'Oréal's Revitalift series.

But the sprinkler strategy is also used by expanding companies to establish a global presence. For example, catalog-based retailers such as Lands' End, Eddie Bauer, and L.L.Bean have entered a large number of foreign countries within a limited time period. Telecommunications companies have also followed the sprinkler strategy, although partly by necessity: not many country markets were open to foreign competitors before deregulation and privatization. The fact is that with the great advances in global communications in the last decade, the sprinkler approach has become much less resource-demanding, and companies can reach almost anywhere on the globe to sell their wares.

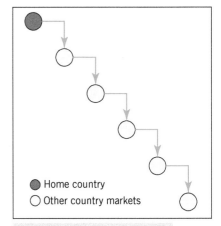

EXHIBIT 8.6.
Waterfall expansion

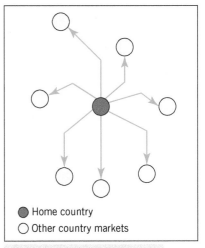

EXHIBIT 8.7.
Sprinkler expansion

GLOBAL PRODUCT POSITIONING

After the segment(s) to target has been decided, the firm will need to develop a positioning strategy.

Product positioning refers to the activities undertaken by the marketer to adapt and communicate the features and the benefits of the product and the image of the brand to the actual and potential customer.[20] This is where the core of "global localization" lies. As mentioned throughout this text, the early efforts at globalization involved standardization—bringing everybody the identical product. Today, this is not acceptable. The product or service that is offered by the company in the local marketplace has to be adapted at least to a degree. It has to be "positioned" as close as possible to what the consumer wants, his or her "ideal point." The firm has to identify what attributes and benefits the customers look for, and make sure the product or service measures up on these features against competition.

In some ways, global product positioning is no different from positioning in the home market.

The Product Space

To predict what happens when a new (possibly global) brand is introduced in a local market, the product space maps that are commonly used in product positioning will be useful.

To describe a brand's position relative to other products on specific characteristics, marketers typically use **perceptual maps,** also known as **product space** or **positioning maps.** We will show some of these maps below—one good example is Steve Jobs' positioning map used at the introduction of the iPhone (see box).

To be accurate, the product space requires data from market research in the specific country market targeted. The map is constructed from four sets of consumer data.

Salient attributes. First is the data on which attributes are "salient," that is what a customer looks for in a product. For example, in considering automobiles, individuals may look for handling, gas economy, comfort, reliability, and so forth.

Evoked set. A second set of data involves identifying which brands are considered by the buyer, that is what the evoked set is. These are the brands (car makes, for example) which compete for the buyer's purchase.

Attribute ratings. The third set of data shows how the individual rates the brands in the evoked set on the salient attributes. How does the BMW rate in terms of handling, for example, and how does the handling of the Audi rate?

Preferences. Finally, the fourth set of data involves how the brands rank in terms of overall preference. That is, respondents rank the brands in the evoked set in terms of desirability—a preference measure—usually without considering the prices.

The data are typically collected with survey questionnaires, using standard attitude and rating scales ranging from 1 to 7. Each brand's scores on the salient attributes becomes the brand's profile or "position." Using statistical techniques to collapse the attributes, the product space maps are usually shown as two-dimensional graphs (see below).

Positioning and Consumer Choice

The distances in the diagram between the brands reflect the degree to which they compete for the same consumers. The traditional idea of product positioning was that new entries simply were added somewhere in the consumer's existing perceptual maps. This is still the basic rationale behind the use of these maps. Identify the

BOX: The iPhone Disruption

When Steve Jobs of Apple introduced the iPhone in 2007, he used a very simple illustration to show the superiority of the new product. He showed a two-dimensional positioning map, a "Business school 101 graph" as he called it, with two axes, "Smart" and "Easy to Use."[21] The iPhone was positioned far away from competitors, demonstrating how unique it was (see Exhibit 8.8).

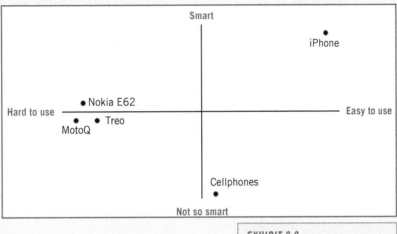

EXHIBIT 8.8.
Steve Jobs' iPhone positioning

Adapted from Apple, Inc. (2013).

This graph expresses the degree to which the iPhone disrupted and re-invented the cell-phone market. The professional segment was interested in smarter phones, while younger users were more concerned with style and extra features. The iPhone showed how you could have both a smarter phone and ease of use. A positioning graph today would look quite different, with the Android system and me-too products from Samsung and other makers crowding the iPhone space.

These two-dimensional maps are based on customers' ratings of competing brands on the various attributes that are important, and show the position of each brand on the map. The product space can also indicate the preferences of the customers, as well as what kind of combination or bundle of attributes they prefer (more power, better mileage, etc.).

existing competitive positions and consumers' ideal points, and then target an empty space in the market where no competitor is positioned but where a potential target segment of customers is located.

Judging from Exhibit 8.9, one can deduce that the success of microbreweries is probably due to shifting consumer preferences, toward the upper northeast corner of the market map. Local microbrewery beers tend to be heavier and quite special.

As we will see below, when new strong brands enter a market such as this, the existing positioning map is usually disrupted. This is why the static positioning maps are only useful as a snapshot of a market at one particular time. In today's competitive markets, markets are continually contested, making it necessary to track new products and shifting consumers—and construct new positioning maps.

A typical example of a positioning map for beer is given in Exhibit 8.9.

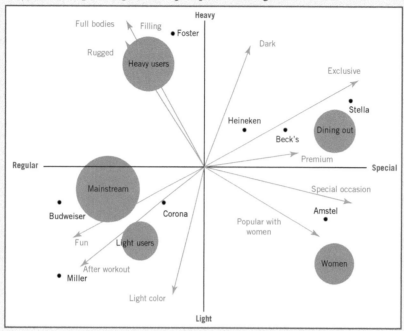

EXHIBIT 8.9.
Beer positioning graph with ideal points and segment sizes

The axes of the diagram are described in terms of the various attributes that people consider important. The location of the various brands on the axes—their "position" in product space—is derived from people's ratings of the beers on the various attributes. The map also shows the preferences of different market segments through **ideal points** (the circles). The size of the circles reflects the size of the market segment. The location of the circles—which is drawn from people's expressed preferences—shows what kind of attributes would appeal to the segments. For example, the relatively small segment for women would like a light beer for a special occasion. Of the rated beers, they would probably prefer an Amstel.

It is important to note that positions can be different in different countries. Compared to the U.S. graph in Exhibit 8.9, for example, Heineken is not very exclusive in Holland, but the brand scores well with women in the rest of Europe.

Global Positioning: Same or Different?

As with segmentation and targeting, a key question in global positioning is the degree to which the position should be identical in all countries. Many global brands attempt as much similarity as possible to reinforce their image, not always succeeding. Coca-Cola is fun, refreshing, and young everywhere. Its "Always" slogan is omnipresent. Sony is innovative and higher-priced everywhere, even at home in Japan. But McDonald's has had to change its American fast-food image to a more localized destination position in several European countries by adapting menus, changing decor, and providing more comfortable chairs. And even if the same segment is targeted everywhere, it does not follow that the positioning need be the same. A classic example is Levi's jeans, targeting young people all over the globe, but positioned as fun and practical at home in the United States while overseas it is positioned on status as the original jeans.

Two major considerations play a role in the chosen positioning strategy: the degree to which the market is global, and the stage of the product life cycle (the PLC).

Global Markets. In a **global market**, the product attributes and benefits customers look for are similar. Technology markets tend to have these characteristics. In B2B technology markets in particular, the important attributes and customer preferences are often similar across markets (as we saw in the Dell in China case above). But also in consumer technology markets the similarities are often strong. In cell phones, for example, most consumers seem to look for the same attributes, even though the constant stream of new features changes what those features are, seemingly overnight. In these kinds of global markets, uniform positioning is feasible and desirable. **Uniform positioning** means that products, brand names, marketing communications, and distribution channels are similar across countries to provide demand spillovers and cost efficiencies.

In more **multi-domestic** markets, where preferences vary by country, such as food and clothing, consumers in different countries will be looking at products with different eyes. They will prefer more salt to more sugar, less to more butter, practicality and durability more than fashion, and so on. As we saw in the segmentation section, there could still be segments that are similar across countries, but their sizes vary. Uniform positioning in these kinds of multi-domestic markets is less beneficial, as we saw in the McDonald's and Levi's examples above.

Stage of the PLC. A second major factor in global positioning decisions is the stage of the PLC. Typically, different country markets are at different stages of the PLC, and this makes a uniform positioning less attractive.

As a rule, product positioning is particularly important in the mature stages of the PLC. In some sense positioning is not possible at too early a stage, because in the introductory stage customers have not yet learned enough about the product to understand the attributes and form preferences. This is why the first mover has a chance to educate potential customers and create an advantage as the original innovator. In global marketing this is a common case, with an entrant from a leading market—which has matured, and where sales growth is slowing down—expanding abroad to capture new markets.

In the later stages of the PLC, customers tend to understand product features well; they have established preferences and even loyalties to existing brands. Positioning becomes much more important, because the firm needs to communicate exactly what its brand's particular strengths are relative to competition. Because of the spillover benefits and cost savings of uniform positioning, where all countries in a selected cluster have markets at the maturity stage of the PLC, the firm needs to consider a uniform global positioning strategy. Of course, where usage conditions differ significantly, the fact that the markets are mature everywhere does not necessarily mean that consumers should be approached similarly (see box, "Positioning an Old Gas-Guzzler: The Chevy Suburban").

Disrupting the Product Space

What global localization means today is something akin to product space disruption. Global marketers today introduce new features, and new product or services that change the existing local markets—in positioning language, they change the existing product space. The disruption can be due to incremental innovations or truly new innovations.

Extending the product space. The elongation of the dimensions defining the product space occurs when the new entrant offers more of the salient features. This is more of an incremental advance, like adding more pixels to a

BOX: Positioning An Old Gas-Guzzler: The Chevy Suburban[22]

The Chevy Suburban was one of Chevrolet's pickup truck offerings already back in 1936, and it is still one of the more popular brands of SUVs (Sport Utility Vehicles) in America. The 2015 Suburban features some of the most advanced technology and a 355-horsepower 5.3-liter engine that's the latest in GM's legendary line of V8s. Although only getting 18 miles per gallon highway, GM's Surburban and related products (Yukon, Tahoe, and Escalade) command over 60 percent of the full-size SUV market. G.M.'s largest SUVs also reach profits of up to $10,000 a vehicle, while its smaller cars make about $1,500 to $2,000.[23]

The Suburban does stand out from its competing brands—but mainly because of its lack of aggressiveness and with no special image (see Exhibit 8.10). How come it has been so successful?

Research uncovered an answer. Among dozens of SUV models from other automakers, the Chevy Suburban rated above all other brands (except Jeep) in terms of levels of engagement. **Engagement** referred to the amount of mental meaning (stories, associations, imagery, ideas) the Chevy Suburban name evoked, and how personally engaged consumers were in the brand name. The long history and tradition of the Suburban had implanted the brand into the consciousness from the time when the now-adult Americans had been small children. This traditional theme was emphasized explicitly in the positioning statement and the promotional campaign, helping to differentiate the car from the newcomers.

But such an American traditional image—not to mention its gas-guzzling—is hard to market overseas. Consequently, while the sales of the Suburban have stayed high in America, its sales elsewhere are negligible—in terms of units sold, that is. But for special purposes, the Suburban has become a favorite. In the Middle East, for example, the journalists covering the Iraq war and then the ISIS onslaught tracked across the desert terrain, followed military vehicles, and avoided IEDs and grenade attacks in Suburbans. In Latin America, the SUV is favored by VIPs, dignitaries, celebrities, or other important officials because of a customized feature: armored and bulletproof Suburbans. This customized Suburban is also a favored vehicle of the U.S. Central Intelligence Agency for their covert operations in foreign countries.

Mass market here becomes a niche market there.

camera. This happens frequently, since the global products often incorporate the newest technology.

A good illustration of extending the product space is the introduction of the Honda Accord in the U.S. auto market in 1982. Exhibit 8.11 shows a positioning map with the Accord and several competing models included.

As can be seen, the Accord offered a unique mix of characteristics, being much more economical than even the Japanese competitors. As the overall rating vector shows, the BMW was the preferred choice—but the price was much higher for that car. The American makes were not competitive in this market segment without large rebates.

New features. The new entrant is likely to offer novel features as well. This means that new salient dimensions are added. Products that do not offer the new features (digital audio, antilock brakes, and low cholesterol) will be left out of the consumers' **evoked sets,** meaning that consumers will not even consider the brands as one of their possible choices. Older brands, often local-only, are now mis-positioned. They might not even register in the appropriate evoked set any longer. The main players are global. See, for example, what is happening when Starbucks moves into a new neighborhood or a new market and the local cafes that don't offer the same selection or quality have to add to their menu or close.

The phone-with-camera is a good illustration. Introduced by Samsung in 2000, the first phone camera that allowed users to send the photos came from Sharp later in the year. The technology rapidly developed, adding auto-focus, flash, and added megapixels for higher resolution. By 2004, two-thirds of phone shipments came with cameras.[25] In a few short years, cell phones without cameras had become museum pieces.

Changing Preferences. Finally, the entry of a global brand might well change customer preferences in addition to perceptions. Traditionally, consumers' tastes and preferences were formed by brands and products they could see, touch, and buy. With global communications, things have changed. Global media and sponsorships of events ensure that many people will be exposed to a brand name even before they have seen the real product.

The fact is that a brand name can cross trade barriers much more easily than a product or service can. This means that a pent-up demand for a branded product in a protected market can easily be created by global communication of the brand name.

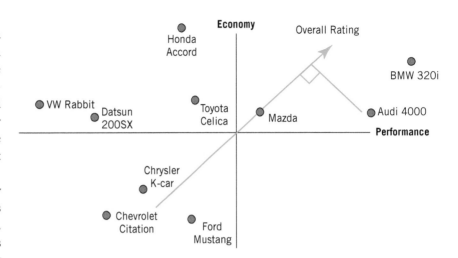

EXHIBIT 8.11.
Honda extends the product space.[24]

Adapted from Johny K. Johansson and Hans B. Thorelli, "International Product Positioning," Journal of International Business Studies, vol. XVI, no. 3.

GLOBAL STP STRATEGIES

What kind of segmentation, targeting, and positioning (STP) strategies do global marketers employ and under what conditions? There are of course a number of alternative strategies depending on the level of similarity across segments targeted and the degree to which the positioning is uniform.

Two marketing professors, Salah Hassan and Stephen Craft, have developed a general segmentation and positioning framework by distinguishing four generic situations:

similar segments and similar positioning; similar segments but different positioning; different segments but similar positioning; and different segments and different positioning.[26] The cross-classification in Exhibit 8.12 identifies the four alternatives and gives illustrative examples.

In the exhibit two alternative market segmentation cases (similar and different) are crossed against two positioning appeals (similar, different). A similar segment refers to a segment that is basically universal, the same across country markets—teenagers, say, or young professionals. A different segment is one that is unique in each country (for example, college students in country A, and families with children in country B). For the product-positioning dimension, similar indicates a positioning that is uniform across countries, while different indicates that the positioning theme is adapted across countries.

Cell 1: Similar segment, similar positioning. This is a true global strategy. Exemplifying this cell, Nike's global brand appeals to young boys and aspiring athletes, whether they play on the streets of Buenos Aires, Philadelphia, Seoul, or Helsinki. The high-performance positioning is underscored by the use of well-known athletes.

Cell 2: Similar segment, different positioning. Here the positioning is adapted. As mentioned in several places in this book, Levi's jeans are a status symbol in many countries, while the American home market takes a more prosaic view of the denims. Similarly, Pampers, P&G's globally very successful baby diaper brand, has a positioning message in Asia that focuses on happy babies rather than on the inconvenienced mothers in the West.

Cell 3: Different segments, similar positioning. Here segments differ but the positioning appeals stay the same. Across the world IKEA offers largely the same selections and offers the same furniture as self-assembled kits, immediately available. But whereas the target segments everywhere include families with children, in the United States there is much greater stress on singles while in Europe newly married are a prime target. In the case of mobile phones, this "must-have" product for young professionals in most places was in Scandinavia first used by delivery men.

Cell 4: Different segments, different positioning. This is a localized, non-global strategy. That target segment and positioning appeal can differ even though the product is standardized is easily seen in the case of Volvo cars, a car for the rugged individual in Europe. Volvo users in the U.S. market, families with small children, have traditionally been appealed to in terms of safety and upscale income. Another case in this cell is the Chevy Suburban, the big Chevy car already discussed in the box above on "Positioning a Gas-Guzzler."

Hassan and Craft found that a few key factors influence company choice. For the cell 1 strategy (similar segment, similar positioning) to be preferable, the countries should be similar in terms of macroeconomics (GDP per capita, economic growth rate). The consumers should be similar in terms of attitudes and product usage, and the local cultures and lifestyles should be similar.

	Local Micro-Segment	
	Similar	Different
Similar	Nike	IKEA / Mobile Phones
Different	Volvo / Pampers	Levi's / Chevy Suburban

Positioning (row axis)

EXHIBIT 8.12.
Global S-T-P strategies.
Source: Hassan and Craft, 2005.

For the cell 2 strategy (similar segment, different positioning) to be optimal, the consumers should be similar in terms of attitudes, product usage, and local culture, but the macroeconomic factors and socio-demographics differ, making an adapted positioning strategy necessary. The cell 3 strategy (different segments, similar positioning) is advantageous when product usage, attitudes, and demographics are similar, but local cultural and economic factors make it difficult to target the same segment everywhere. Finally, the cell 4 strategy (different segment, different positioning) is the best option when brand loyalty in the marketplace is high, regardless of other conditions. This is natural since this is the true localization option.

SUMMARY

The first task for the marketer intent on coordinating global marketing strategy is to find a way to group countries into more homogeneous subsets. Global segmentation involves such macro-segmentation, followed by more precise targeting of consumers, micro-segmentation.

In the first macro-segmentation stage, trade blocs or regional similarities or statistical procedures are used to form clusters of similar countries on broad economic and social indicators. In a second stage, micro-segmentation analysis is used to identify which segments are similar across the countries in a given cluster.

To select segments for targeting, the analysis has to be extended to competitive intensity and the firm's competitive advantages and disadvantages in a segment. This evaluation should result in a prediction of the market share that the company can be expected to capture in a given segment with a standardized or a locally adapted strategy. Then revenues and costs can be forecasted for the target segments and the projected strategy. It is important to assess the costs of any adaptation, and balance it against increased consumer acceptance. Especially when selling to the bottom of the pyramid, paying attention the consumers' usage situation is mandatory so the product offered is sure to fill a need.

The expansion into foreign markets also needs to consider adding different kinds of markets into the "portfolio," diversifying in order to protect against political or economic turmoil in any one market. Firms also choose between a speedy "sprinkler" strategy, entering many countries at once to preserve first-mover advantages, or a more gradual "waterfall" strategy in order to solidify gains before moving on.

Global product positioning involves predicting how local markets abroad might react to the introduction of a standardized product with a global brand. Several scenarios are possible, including the shifting of the product space with the introduction of new features. The global marketer has to evaluate the risk that the standardization might lead the brand to be mis-positioned, and to assess the degree to which the cachet of a global brand can counter the lack of ideal fit. If not, price may have to be reduced—or, more likely, the product has to be adapted to local preferences. This is often necessary in today's markets, as localization is becoming the new imperative.

Universal segments can often be approached with relatively uniform positioning. But the relationship is not that simple. Even universally similar segments (such as teenagers) might need some adaptation of product or positioning. In other cases, globally coordinated strategies, standardized products, and even uniform strategies can be employed even where the segments approached are different.

KEY TERMS

benefit segmentation	focus strategy
cluster analysis	heavy-user segment
demographics	ideal points
diversification strategy	lifestyle segmentation
evoked set	macro-segmentation

micro-segmentation	salient attributes
mis-positioned	segmentation criteria
multi-domestic market	sprinkler strategy
peer groups	two-stage segmentation
perceptual maps	uniform positioning
product positioning	value-based segmentation
product space	waterfall strategy

DISCUSSION QUESTIONS

1. What are the differences and similarities between the positioning of the iPhone and that of Apple's computers (like the iMac)? What market segment(s) does iPhone seem to target? The iMac?

2. Why is a high-tech product more likely to appeal to the same segment everywhere, compared with a frequently purchased packaged good? Any examples?

3. Would services be more or less likely to have universal segments than products? Is the success of global fast-food restaurants (a service category) an exception or typical of services?

4. What are the advantages of "similar segments, similar positioning" in a product such as digital cameras? In cell phones? In leisure clothing? In athletic shoes? Any disadvantages?

5. When discussing product positioning, the chapter used examples of Japanese cars entering Western markets. Using this framework, how would you analyze the reception given to the Japanese luxury marques (Acura, Infiniti, Lexus)? What did change in people's perceptions—and what did not?

TEAM CHALLENGE PROJECTS

1. The chapter discusses both micro- and macro-segmentation. Many organizations collect country-level data that could be important for marketing purposes. One such organization is The World Bank which collects World Development Indicators (WDI; http://wdi.worldbank.org/tables) that provide a comprehensive macro-view of a country. Team 1: Identify 10 WDIs that could be important in segmenting for the sale of personal computer products (PCs, tablets, etc.). Explain each choice. Team 2: Identify 10 WDIs that would NOT be important in segmenting for the sale of personal computer products (PCs, tablets, etc.). Explain your choice.

2. Starbuck's coffee has expanded internationally but is struggling with how to segment the worldwide coffee market. Team 1: What segmentation criteria should be used if the target was to enter the countries that drink the most coffee? Develop the 4Ps. Team 2: What segmentation criteria should be used if the target was to enter the countries that drink the least coffee? Develop the 4Ps.

Coffee Consumption Per Person			
	Cups Per Day		Cups Per Day
Netherlands	2.41	Russia	0.55
Finland	1.84	Brazil	0.48
Sweden	1.35	South Africa	0.12
Denmark	1.23		
Germany	1.23	Egypt	0.02
Slovakia	1.20	India	0.02
Serbia	1.18	Uzbekistan	0.009
Czech Republic	1.17	Pakistan	0.008
Poland	1.15	Kenya	0.007
Norway	1.12	Azerbaijan	0.006
Slovenia	1.07	China	0.003
Canada	1.00	Nigeria	0.002

Source: The Atlantic (2014).

3. In many developing countries, a large portion of the population is young (i.e., under the age of 25). The young in China comprise 14.7 percent of the population or about 200 million people and in Brazil 16.5 percent or about 35 million people. If you can interest this young demographic in your brand now, they may become lifetime consumers of your products. Do all young populations worldwide have the same characteristics? Team 1: What segments would you use to describe the typical 15-year-old in China? Team 2: What segments would you use to describe the typical 15-year-old in Brazil?

SELECTED REFERENCES

Bjornstad, Eric. "How Alfred Sloan and GM changed American history," *Bellperformance.com*, 2013.

Budeva, Desislava G. and Michael R. Mullen, "International market segmentation: Economics, national culture and time," *European Journal of Marketing*, Vol. 48, No. 7/8, 2014, pp. 1209–1238.

Cannon, H.M. and Yaprak, A., "A dynamic framework for understanding cross-national segmentation," *International Marketing Review*, Vol. 28 No. 3, 2011, pp. 229–243.

Carpenter, Susan, "Hollywood, Meet Bollywood," *Los Angeles Times*, April 15, 2003, p. 37.

Cato, Jeremy, "Suburban is solid, stalwart and, surprisingly, nimble: Quadrasteer turns the new Suburban into a very nimble machine," *The Standard (Ontario)*, May 8, 2003, p. D1.

Churchill, Gilbert A., Jr. and Dawn Iacobucci, *Marketing Research: Methodological Foundations,* 10th ed. Mason: South Western Cengage, 2010.

DePaula, Matthew. "Buick Draws Younger Buyers With Regal Sedan, Which Improves For 2014," *Forbes*, 2014.

Einhorn, Bruce, Christina Larson, and Aaron Ricadela, "In China, Dell Clings Tightly to the Waning PC," *Bloomberg Business*, Nov 7, 2013.

Greenspan, Alan, "Europe's crisis is all about the north-south split," *Financial Times*, Oct. 6, 2011.

Hashai, Niron, "Sequencing the expansion of geographic scope and foreign operations by 'born global' firms," *Journal of International Business Studies*, Vol. 42, No. 8, Oct/Nov 2011, pp. 995–1015.

Hassan, Salah S., and Stephen H. Craft. "Linking Global Market Segmentation Decisions with Strategic Positioning Options." *Journal of Consumer Marketing* 22 (Fall/Winter 2005).

Indiantelevision team, "Top 10 Bollywood actors to look out for in 2015," *Indian Television.com,* Dec. 27, 2014.

Inglehart, Ronald, Miguel Basanez. and Alejandro, Moreno. *Human Values and Beliefs: A Cross-Cultural Sourcebook.* Ann Arbor, MI: The University of Michigan Press, 1998.

Jeffries, Stuart, "The rise of the camera-phone," *The Guardian,* Jan. 7, 2010.

Jensen, Camille, "Values Segmentation Drives Successful Campaigns, says Greenpeace," Dec. 1, 2012.

Johansson, Johny K. and Hans B. Thorelli. "International Product Positioning." *Journal of International Business Studies* XVI, no. 3 (Fall 1985), pp. 57–76.

Keegan, Warren. "Multinational Product Planning: Strategic Alternatives." *Journal of Marketing* 33 (January 1969), pp. 58–62.

Kessler, Aron, "Sales of Big S.U.V.s Pulling the Weight at General Motors," *The New York Times,* July 24, 2014.

Kotler, Philip and Kevin L. Keller. *Marketing Management,* 14th ed. Upper Saddle River, NJ: Prentice-Hall, 2015.

Ma, Forest, "Lifestyle Segmentation of the Chinese Consumer," *Sinomonitor International, China,* March 2004.

Ng, Pauline and P. Lovelock. *Dell: Selling Directly, Globally.* Centre for Asian Business Cases, The University of Hong Kong, HKU 069, Jan. 1, 2000.

Nijssen, Edwin J. and Susan P. Douglas, "Consumer World-Mindedness and Attitudes Toward Product Positioning in Advertising: An Examination of Global Versus Foreign Versus Local Positioning," *Journal of International Marketing:* September 2011, Vol. 19, No. 3, 2011, pp. 113–133.

Pallotta, Frank, "Super Bowl XLIX posts the largest audience in TV history," *CNNMoney,* Feb. 2, 2015.

Phelan, Mark, "2015 Chevrolet Suburban has massive appeal," *Detroit Free Press,* November 9, 2014.

Philipson, Alice, "World Cup 2014: BBC pulls in four times as many viewers as ITV," *The Telegraph,* Jul. 14, 2014.

Piercy, Nigel. "Export Strategy: Concentration on Key Markets vs. Market Spreading." *Journal of International Marketing* 1, no. 1 (1982), pp. 56–67.

Prahalad, C.K. (2010), The Fortune at the Bottom of the Pyramid: Eradicating Poverty Through Profits, 5th anniversary ed. Wharton School Publishing, Upper Saddle River, NJ.

Rose, Chris, What Makes People Tick: The Three Hidden Worlds of Settlers, Prospectors and Pioneers. Leicester, UK: Matador, 2011.

Schlefer, Jonathan, "Global Must-See TV: Telenovelas," *The Boston Globe,* January 4, 2004, p. 12.

Steenkamp, Jan-Benedict E.M., and Frankel Ter Hofstede. "International Market Segmentation: Issues and Perspectives." *International Journal of Research in Marketing* 19 (September 2002), pp. 185–213.

Tinoco, Armando, "Telenovelas 2015 Preview: 'El Señor De Los Cielos 3,' Remakes Of 'La Mentira,' 'La Madrastra' Coming To Univision, Telemundo And MundoFOX," *Latin Times,* Dec. 31, 2014, www.latintimes.com.

Turan, Kenneth, "By Way of Bombay; a UCLA film series is proof: Bollywood has arrived with a flourish," *Los Angeles Times,* April 15, 2004, p. 36.

Vansickle, Abbie. "Not just your grandma's car, Buicks shine in Chinese luxury market," *The Seattle Globalist,* 2014.

Wadhwa, Vivek, "My Entertaining Education in Movieland," *BusinessWeek Online,* August 11, 2004.

Wind, Jerry and Susan Douglas. "International Market Segmentation." *European Journal of Marketing* 6, no. 1 (1972).

Zandpour, Fred, and Katrin R. Harich. "Think and Feel Country Clusters: A New Approach to International Advertising Standardization." *International Journal of Advertising,* Vol. 15, No. 4, 1996, pp. 325–44.

ENDNOTES

1. See Bjornstad, 2013.
2. From Vansickle, 2014.
3. See dePaula, 2014.
4. As proposed by Prahalad, 2010.
5. From Rose, 2011.
6. See Jensen, 2012.
7. Sources: Turan, 2004; Carpenter, 2003; Wadhwa, 2004; Schlefer, 2004; Indiantelevison Team, 2014; Tinoco, 2014.
8. See Ma, 2004.
9. The two-stage process, now standard, was first proposed by Wind and Douglas, 1972.
10. See, for example, Churchill and Iacobucci, 2010.
11. See Budeva and Mullen, 2014.
12. See Inglehart, Basanez, and Moreno, 1998.
13. From Budeva and Mullen, 2014.
14. See Greenspan, 2011.
15. See Cannon and Yaprak, 2011.
16. From Steenkamp and ter Hofstede, 2002.
17. From Ng and Lovelock, 2000; Einhorn, Larson, and Ricadela, 2013.
18. See, e.g., Piercy, 1982.
19. See Hashai, 2011.
20. See Kotler and Keller, 2015.
21. The presentation at Apple's MacWorld event is available on YouTube: https://www.youtube.com/watch?v=9hUIxyE2Ns8.
22. From Cato, 2003; Phelan, 2014.
23. See Kessler, 2014.
24. Adapted from Johansson and Thorelli, 1985.
25. From Jeffries, 2010.
26. From Hassan and Craft, 2005.

ABSTRACT

FACED WITH FLAT-LINING SALES IN 2006, HYUNDAI conducted an extensive study to better understand some consumers' aversion to the brand. What strategy would help Hyundai to overcome its image as a value (i.e., "cheap") product?

Hyundai (C) is a continuation of the four-part Hyundai case study.

HYUNDAI (C)

"We have no brand." Steve Wilhite, Chief Operating Officer, Hyundai Motor America[1]

In 2006 Hyundai Kia Automotive Group was the sixth-largest automobile company in the world, larger than Nissan and Honda.

In 1987 Hyundai exported 263,000 cars to the United States, but sales had dwindled to fewer than 100,000 cars in 1999 due to ongoing quality problems. Helped by the 2000 introduction of a 10-year/100,000-mile warranty on Hyundai engines and transmissions and a five-year/60,000 mile warranty for bumper-to-bumper coverage, plus a five-year/unlimited-mile warranty for 24-hour roadside assistance, Hyundai's product reputation increased. In 2006 J.D. Power and Associates ranked Hyundai No. 3 on their overall product quality list, just behind Porsche and Lexus.

Partly as a result of the improvement in the perceptions of their brand, from 2001 through 2005 Hyundai sales in the U.S. increased an average of 14 percent per year, reaching 455,012 units in 2005. However it appeared that Hyundai still needed to improve their brand perception. In 2006 U.S. sales were only 455,520—a growth rate of only 0.1 percent over 2005.

Despite making progress on their brand, Steve Wilhite, chief operating officer of Hyundai Motor America, was not satisfied. He believed that many U.S. buyers still saw Hyundai as a small South Korean company making small, inexpensive cars. Said Wilhite, "We're seen as a 'value' car company."[2] (In the U.S. automobile industry, "value" is another word for "cheap.") Wilhite further commented, "It is not that we don't know who we are. The problem is that not many people outside of the company know who we are. We haven't done a good job of telling our story."[3]

Survey results confirmed Wilhite's observations. Despite high ratings from J.D. Power and Associates, more than twice as many new-car buyers were willing to consider Toyota or Honda rather than Hyundai.

---

[1] This case was prepared by Don Sexton, Professor of Marketing, Director, Center for International Business Education and Research, Columbia Business School. This case was sponsored by the Chazen Institute and the Columbia University Center for International Business Education and Research (CIBER).

	Hyundai	Toyota	Honda
J.D. Power Initial Quality Study—2006	3	4	6
New-car buyers who in 2006 considered:	23%	65%	50%

In another study two hundred people were shown the Hyundai Veracruz. Without Hyundai identification, 71 percent said they would purchase the car; with Hyundai identification, only 52 percent said they would buy it. By contrast, in the same study Toyota identification on a car *increased* consumer intent-to-purchase by 20 percentage points.

Wilhite and John Krafcik, vice president for product development and product planning at Hyundai Motor America, were trying to craft a strategy to stimulate sales growth in the U.S. Any strategy had to take into consideration Hyundai's 755 dealers in the United States, who had long sold "value" to budget-minded customers, many of whom had low credit ratings.

DISCUSSION QUESTIONS

1. How did Hyundai increase its U.S. sales to 455,520 automobiles in 2006?
2. What were the branding challenges facing Hyundai in 2006?
3. What might Hyundai do to change potential customers' perceptions of the Hyundai brand?

ENDNOTES

1. David Kiley, "Hyundai Still Gets No Respect," *Business Week*, May 21, 2007.
2. Warren Brown, "Hyundai's Mission Possible: Beat the Luxury Brands," *The Washington Post*, April 1, 2007.
3. Brown, "Hyundai's Mission."

COMPANY OPERATIONS 2015

By early 2015, Mad Science Group had franchise operations in 20 countries outside Canada. It employed 30 people in its offices in Montreal, Quebec. As a privately held company it did not publish financial accounts. The company employed two business models—one for North America and another for international markets—as shown in Table 1. (For more information on the Mad Science Group, please see Mad Science case (A)).

Mad Science Group emphasized its strength as a global consumer brand that had close connections to its customers. Its reach was extensive:

- 20 countries outside Canada
- 160 locations worldwide
- 127 locations in North America
- Access to over 25,000 schools, 350,000 teachers and school administrators, and 6.5 million children

The company was proud of its collaborations with various corporate partners. It worked with others to offer targeted educational and social awareness programs such as "Be tobacco-free," "Build your bones," and "What do you know about H_{20}?"

The partners included:

- GlaxoSmithKline
- Kennedy Space Centre
- L'Oréal
- McDonald's of Europe
- NASA
- Oral-B
- Scholastic
- Time Entertainment
- Toys "R" Us

The company had grown its franchise operations over the past few years in international markets. In Canada and the U.S., its principal focus was on improving current franchisee distribution and performance. Some franchises were terminated and new ones established as the company sought the best market coverage.

[1] *This case was prepared by Professor Philip Rosson of Dalhousie University as a basis for class discussion rather than to illustrate either the correct or incorrect handling of an administrative situation. It was prepared using secondary sources of information. The data are drawn from the Mad Science Group website,* Entrepreneur *magazine, and a Government of Canada website.*
Copyright © 2015 by Philip Rosson, Dalhousie University.

Philip Rosson, "Mad Science: From Canada to the World (Part B)." Copyright © 2015 by Philip Rosson. Reprinted with permission.

Year	U.S.	Canada	International	Total
2011	114	22	29	155
2012	103	23	33	159
2013	100	23	35	158
2014	99	23	38	160

Mad Science Group had gained the following recent rankings as a franchisor.

- Franchise 500: ranked #483 (2013), #452 (2012)
- Low-cost franchise: ranked #93 (2013), #100 (2012)

INTERNATIONAL DEVELOPMENT

Table 2 shows the development of international markets by Mad Science Group over the years. Some current markets were fully covered for the time being but, in others, there were opportunities for additional franchises. The company was also exploring new markets around the world.

TABLE 1. **Mad Science Group Business Models**

	North America Model	International Model
Territory	Large metropolitan area	Countries, states, provinces
Office	Home or office based	Office or center based
Territory	Protected with 100 elementary schools (K to grade 6)	Protected with over 500,000 in population
Investment	$71,8000–$87,300	$80,000–$300,000 depending on territory size
Franchise fee	$23,500	–Negotiable
Equipment package	$25,000	–Negotiable
Employees required	3–30	
Franchise royalty	8%	
Franchise duration	10 years, renewable	
Training:		
At location with Account Manager	5 days	8–10 days
At Mad Science Group in Montreal	Yes	No
Support:		
Assigned Account Manager	Yes	
Access to company extranet	Yes	
Training videos and instructional materials	Yes	
Annual conference in Montreal	Yes	

TABLE 2. Mad Science Group International Market Development

Country	First Franchise	Number of Franchises/Locations	Franchise Opportunities
Canada	1993	23	Yes
USA	1995	95	Yes
UK & Ireland	2005	10	?
Bahrain	2007	1	No
Brazil	2008	1	Yes
China	2013	2	Yes
India	2010	4	Yes
Kuwait	1998	1	No
Mexico	2001	Numerous	No
Netherlands	2004	6	Yes
Nigeria	2007	1	No
Oman	2005	1	No
Peru	1999	1	No
Philippines	2002	1	No
Qatar	2012	1	No
Saudi Arabia	2001	1	Yes
Singapore	2011	1	No
Spain	2009	2	Yes
Thailand	1999	1	No
Turkey	2006	1	Yes
United Arab Emirates	2005	1	No

DISCUSSION QUESTIONS

1. How would you characterize the international expansion path of Mad Science—incremental, sprinkler, or something else?
2. In what ways does cultural distance play a role in the expansion path? Does cultural distance also affect acceptance of the Mad Science services?
3. Given your answers to 2, what country or countries would you suggest Mad Science next explores for expansion? Explain the rationale (pros and cons) for your recommendation. What changes, if any, would you propose for the franchising terms?

REFERENCES

"Mad Science Group Inc." Retrieved February 1, 2015 from www.madscience.org.

"About Mad Science Group Inc." Retrieved February 1, 2015 from www.entrepreneur.com/franchises/madsciencegroupinc/282546-0.html.

"The Mad Science Group." Retrieved February 1, 2015 from www.ic.gc.ca/app/ccc/srch/nvgt.do?lang=eng&prtl=1&sbPrtl=&estblmntNo=123456198616&profile=cmpltPrfl&profileId=1921&app=sold.

FREZITE, A MEDIUM-SIZED PORTUGUESE ENGINEERING COMPANY, HAD an early start in international expansion. Just a few years after its foundation in 1978 it started doing business with nearby countries, including Spain and France. The experience acquired during these years led the company to face a new and more difficult challenge: the launch of an operation in Brazil, a distant continent from its headquarters close by Porto. Although a daunting challenge, entry into Brazil would allow the company to compete in one of the largest markets in the world.

HOME COUNTRY BACKGROUND

Portugal shares with Spain the Iberian Peninsula in the southwest corner of the European continent. The peninsula's southernmost tip, the rock Gibraltar, is in British hands. Portugal occupies about one-fifth of the peninsula, along its western edge. Its population is roughly 11 million whereas Spain has about 48 million people (see Exhibit 1). There are about 5 million Portuguese living outside of Portugal, and a large number of descendants from the Portuguese colonial rule in Asia, South America, and Africa.

Exhibit 1. A statistical comparison of Portugal and Spain.

	Portugal	Spain
Area	92,090 sq km (slightly smaller than Indiana)	505,370 sq km (slightly the same as Texas)
Population	10,813,834 (July 2014 est.)	47,737,941 (July 2014 est.)
GDP per capita	$22,900 (2013 est.)	$30,100 (2013 est.)
Main exports	$61 billion (2013 est.): agricultural products, food products, wine, oil products, chemical products, plastics and rubber, hides, leather, wood and cork, wood pulp and paper	$458 billion (2013 est.): machinery, motor vehicles; foodstuffs, pharmaceuticals, medicines, other consumer goods
Main exports destination	Spain 22.7%, Germany 12.4%, France 11.9%, Angola 6.5%, UK 5.3%, Netherlands 4.2% (2012)	France 16.8%, Germany 10.8%, Italy 7.7%, Portugal 7.1%, UK 6.5% (2012)
People that speak the language	250 million (PT is the official language of 9 countries): 202 million located in Brazil	470 million (SP is the official language in 20 countries)

---

[1] *This case was prepared by Susana Costa e Silva(Católica Porto Business School) and Tássia Hanna Frade(Pontifícia Universidade Católica de São Paulo). The case study was developed to be used as a basis for discussion in classroom and illustrates a typical internationalization situation. The case was developed in cooperation with Frezite.* ©2014, Catolica Porto Business School. None or part of this case study can be copied, saved, transmitted or reproduced, in any form, without the authorization of the copyright holder.

Susana Costa e Silva and Tássia Hanna Frade, "Portugal's Frezite Goes to Brazil." Copyright © 2014 by Catolica Porto Business School. Reprinted with permission.

Colonial History

Portugal and Spain have a similar colonial history. Portugal was the first European country to initiate an overseas expansion, creating a seaborne empire starting in 1415. In 1488 Portuguese explorer Bartolomeu Dias discovered the Cape of Good Hope, the southernmost point on the African continent. Spain explored westward, and in 1492 Christopher Columbus discovered and claimed America for the Spanish king (after having been denied support from the Portuguese king). The Portuguese explorer Vasco da Gama found the path to India for Portugal in 1498, sailing around the Cape of Good Hope and into the Indian Ocean. To this day, several of the countries along the path have Portuguese as the main language, including Mozambique in Africa and Goa, Daman, and Diu in India. The Portuguese reached as far as Japan in 1543, opening new trade routes. Portuguese Jesuits attempted to convert the Japanese to Christianity, until 1638, when the imperial rulers in Japan locked the country to the westerns (the *sakoku*).

In 1500, the Portuguese arrived in Brazil. From the 16th to the early 19th centuries, Brazil was a colony of Portugal. Brazil became independent in 1822, when the regent, Dom Pedro I, who had been appointed by his father, King João VI, declared his independence from Portugal. The current Brazilian republic was constituted after a coup d'état against Pedro II, the son of Dom Pedro I.

Company Background

Frezite was founded in 1978 to supply a Portuguese market with engineering cutting tools that the country lacked (Exhibit 2 shows the product line). Since the founding of the business, management had always looked for growth opportunities in product and market development. The company strove to introduce innovative solutions and to improve their products and services. Frezite prospered at a time when Portugal benefited from fast economic growth. The company gained more and more share in the domestic market and developed expertise in production and customer service.

Exhibit 2. The product line of Frezite.

Inspired by the international economic news on the television, Frezite's president, Mr. Manuel Fernandes, realized that foreign market development could also be important for company growth. He undertook to systematically analyze which country markets would present higher chances of success for the company already in the 1980s. His enthusiasm while facing these international expansion challenges and opportunities was crucial for Frezite's success in the markets it entered.

Frezite started to participate in International Trade Fairs, including the major one in Hannover (Germany). Germany was a leading manufacturer of cutting tools, and had several strong manufacturers. Being close to customers and competitors in German and European markets, the company took its first learning steps into international expansion. The early expansion was close to its national borders, where technical and cultural knowledge allowed an easier of transition across borders.

The Internationalization Process

In the early stage of internationalization, entering into foreign markets and operating in different countries will usually give rise to uncertainty, complexity, and risk. Companies face new and strong competitors, different cultural habits than they are used to, and there is also financial, material, and personnel risk going across borders for the first time. Over time, however, when the entry barriers in new foreign markets can be overcome, international expansion produces benefits that contribute to company growth. Developing new skills, the company becomes an experienced international player.

This situation was not different for Frezite. However, this challenge had also encouraged Mr. Fernandes to look for market opportunities beyond Portugal. In fact, the company had successful met competition in the European market before its entry into the Brazilian market. Its main competitors came from Germany, a country with a very positive country-of-origin image in the tools sector. Even nowadays, in a global market, German companies Leitz and Leuco remain strong competitors in the business of wood-cutting tools.

Initially looking at the European countries in close proximity, Frezite's first real step toward the company's international expansion was the 1988 creation of Frezite Galicia in Spain. Besides establishing an office in Spain, in this period Frezite also saw an increase in its exports to several other European countries.

Some companies find the best moment to pursue opportunities overseas in crisis situations at home. More commonly, companies identify these opportunities in times of favorable economic conditions, when they are able to spend time and effort to spot new opportunities as they appear. Frezite is of the second type, its management having considered international expansion very early. This made it natural for Frezite to gradually move to strengthen its future relations with Brazil, a country with large potential and with a shared Portuguese language and colonial history.

Host Country Brazil

In the mid-1990s Brazil had a population of about 160 million inhabitants, a figure that represented a large domestic market to be supplied by various industries. Brazil was undergoing a major period of profound economic changes that led to the implementation of the so-called "Real Plan." Established in 1994, the plan involved a change of the currency (from the cruzeiro to the real) in order to stop hyperinflation. It restored vitality to the economy and established a pro-business environment which led to prosperity for business in the years that followed. In addition, the program established by the government also aimed to promote greater trade openness in the country. The measures included exchange-rate stability and the reduction of tariff and nontariff restrictions on imports, encouraging competition and improving the local industry.

Brazil left behind the country that had experienced a "lost decade" in the 1980s, choosing to become a country for the future and showing the world a sign of commitment made with modernity and sustainable growth. During this same period, other Latin American countries did not have the benefit of economic renewal as healthy as the one Brazil was experiencing, representing more hostile environments for business. This, for example, was the case of foreign-exchange crisis experienced by Mexico in 1994.

Mr. Fernandes saw a great business opportunity and the strong potential that Frezite products had in the Brazilian market. Brazil had important furniture makers in the south and southeast regions. Currently, the furniture industry has about 17,500 companies in the country, having manufactured 492,200 pieces in 2012. According to a report of Movergs (Association of Furniture Industries of the State of Rio Grande do Sul), São Paulo had the largest number of companies in the sector, while Rio Grande do Sul had the largest hubs of producers/exporters. In the 1990s there were few suppliers in the sector of cutting equipment. The most technologically advanced equipment of the furniture industry was imported mainly from Germany and Italy. The vast untapped potential of this sector and its growth potential prompted Frezite to enter.

Exporting to Brazil

The first entry into the Brazilian market was via exports through independent distributors. But Frezite reassessed the potential of the market and decided in 1990 it was worth to put a more definitive stake in the country. A sales office was established in São Paulo in order to facilitate and enhance trade relations with Brazilian customers.

As the company began its selling operations in Brazil, seeking partners and bringing their products from Portugal to customers and dealers in Brazil, it quickly gained significant market share. Still, despite the success of operations in the country, Frezite soon realized a huge problem related to exports received in Brazil: customs issues. Nowadays, Brazil still presents uncertainty for companies exporting to the country, and in the 1990s this problem was even more dramatic. In fact, initially as well as today, customs clearance in Brazil can be quite complicated and time-consuming, even for companies like Frezite with minimal language barriers. There are also costs associated with clearance of goods and delivery time to customers. Brazil is also quite protectionist in some sectors. This is the case for manufactured products, which are taxed by two different types of tax to enter the country. Besides the ordinary import tax, the industrialized product also has its own separate tax (IPI), thus turning imported products much more expensive than domestically produced products. This fact undermined the competitiveness of Frezite's exports, reaching the Brazilian market with prices far less competitive than those produced domestically.

Given this reality and the problems brought to Frezite's business in Brazil, the company decided to change the organization of its activities in the country. After establishing a sales office and gaining a good part of this market through strong commercial work, brand awareness, and customer relationship, Frezite decided to start a manufacturing plant in southern Brazil to meet demand, and eliminate the problems with delivery deadlines and customs.

FDI in Brazil

Apart from the issue of improved customer relationships, the constant problems the customs created for imported products led Frezite to make an important decision: to engage in foreign direct investment (FDI) and start production in Brazil.

The company had started its exports to Brazil basing its sales office in São Paulo. This location for the office was chosen by the strong economic growth of São Paulo and proximity to most established companies in the country. Despite the great economic potential of São Paulo, when considering FDI, Frezite realized they should be closer to its major customers, who were in the southern region.

The southern region of Brazil had a large furniture center in São Bento do Sul (SC), a town of some 74,000 people, many of German origins, situated 100 km (60 miles) south of Curitiba. This is where Frezite located its manufacturing plant (see Exhibit 3).

Exhibit 3.

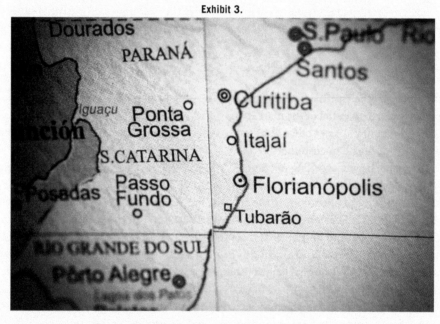

Copyright © by Shutterstock/Victor Maschek.

According to the Association of Furniture Industries of Rio Grande do Sul, the state's furniture exports represented about 30 percent of the Brazil's total furniture exports in recent years, thus proving the productive capacity of the region. The association also shows that between 2008 and 2012 the Rio Grande do Sul represented 19 percent of the country's revenue in the sector, growing 52.2 percent in the period.

The production unit of Frezite installed in the south became responsible for 95 percent of its units sold to the local market, complemented by a small portion of imports. Since 2000, the Brazilian furniture sector grew 55 percent in terms of exports, which amply justified Frezite's investment in domestic production to improve the supply to these industries and avoid the cost inherent to imports. The cost reduction related to the import tax made Frezite's products more price competitive, and also reduced the uncertainties related to timely delivery and customer service.

Cultural Adaptation

Brazil presents a large domestic market and potential for many industries. But it is necessary to have a good understanding of the Brazilian customer and operation of businesses in the country to be successful. Frezite, unlike many of its fellow Portuguese companies, gave great importance to these issues to overcome barriers overseas.

In general, going to a foreign country to establish a production unit demands a lot of attention to local conditions. This was still true in the case of Frezite. The linguistic proximity, while facilitating communication, could not always be relied on transfer to another Lusophone (Portuguese-speaking) country like Brazil. The executives had to understand the market and show cultural sensitivity, factors that were critical to the operation's success.

The company's executives had to go to the country prepared to face a new reality and cultural challenges. Although speaking the same language, there were many different expressions that created misunderstandings. Mr. Fernandes was surprised to encounter situations in which different linguistic expressions caused reactions different from the expected. For example, he realized that often the meanings of words are exchanged, and a "little problem" in Brazil may actually be a "big problem" to his company. To Frezite managers Brazilians seemed to be overoptimistic. For instance, when Brazilians said "Deixa comigo!" (Leave it to me!), the Portuguese understood that the issue was going to be taken care of. However, they soon realized that expression did not literally have that meaning in Brazil. Learning about small details like these was of course important to Frezite's executives not only how to act in the foreign country. It was essential to have a better understanding of how to interpret local expressions of the performance and market feedback from the Brazilian subsidiary.

According to another Frezite executive—Tiago Fernandes—the full product line offered by the group was initially also introduced and sold in Brazil. But the Brazilian market often required adjustments, said the manager. Against expectations, the firm had to develop a different line of adapted products for Brazil. So changes in the marketing mix of Frezite were made, as the products sold in Brazil had to be adapted from those sold in the rest of the world.

In Brazil, the preference was for products typically less expensive and "ready to use" for the user. For example, in Portugal the user of a cutting tool can be requested to turn a screw in order to replace the blade on the saw. By contrast, in Brazil users want more user-friendly solutions—something ready to use. Similarly, whereas in Germany, for instance, customers would be willing to pay extra for a superior-quality blade, in Brazil customers value price more. So, cheaper and more user-friendly products had to be developed.

Besides adapting the products, executives realized early that Frezite also needed to adapt to the way of doing business with Brazilian people. The adaptation had to be made not only in the relationships with customers and suppliers, but in the behavior of the Portuguese expatriate executives dealing with the local employees. There was a different atmosphere in meetings, much more informal when compared to Europeans. The much more relaxed way of Brazilian people was also reflected in the business environment, often demanding more selling dedication and patience in getting responses.

The Company Currently

Despite strong competition, Frezite has managed to position itself strongly in international markets and to be among the leaders in many countries:

The internationalization of Frezite has led the group name to every corner of the globe, with presence in over 50 countries. The company's receives 70 percent of its sales from outside of Portugal, through exports and subsidiaries in Brazil, Spain, United Kingdom, France, Czech Republic, Slovakia, and Germany, as well as sales offices in Romania and Poland installed in 2011. The company's next step is said to involve further penetration in Latin America, with a factory in Mexico, and also entry into Africa, with the creation of a subsidiary in South Africa.

In addition, the company has created another products division, the FMT-FREZITE Metal Tooling, which offered cutting tools for metal, thus extending their product line, entering a new market and also improving their presence in the global market. With an investment of approximately two million Euros, FTM was created in Trofa, Portugal, manufacturing high-tech metal-cutting tools.

FTM has also expanded into Brazil. In 2011, the company's revenues in Brazil had reached around five million Euros, justifying the investment in the new facility to further expand business in the country. The installation of this new division has brought diversification in terms of product offers and market coverage, raised Frezite's brand presence and the chances for success of the company in the coming years.

Frezite has a well-established position in Brazil. According to Tiago Fernandes, despite the lack of data for measuring the "market share" of the companies in the sector, Frezite brand is the second-most recognized in engineering tools for cutting wood in Brazil. In terms of communication, promotion of the company's products is made through nationwide network of dealers, offering the products and after-sales service to customers and helping to promote the brand and its quality.

Going Forward

The experience gained through the years in Brazil should help Frezite to develop its operations in Mexico and South Africa, as both countries exhibit similar culture-related difficulties in the way of doing business, plus their own tariffs issues and imports problems. Success in Brazil was gained through a great effort to understand the local market and develop sensitivity to important commercial issues. These are key factors to be taken into account in further international expansion, particularly in countries with cultures distinct from the Portuguese.

DISCUSSION QUESTIONS

1. How would you characterize the strengths and weaknesses of Frezite in the European market? In the Brazilian market? Is there a country-of-origin factor involved, and if so, is it positive or negative?
2. What were the factors that led Frezite to shift from exporting to FDI? What alternative modes of entry could Frezite have considered? Was FDI the best choice?
3. Identify the key factors in the success of Frezite in Brazil.
4. What has Frezite learnt in Brazil? To what extent is the experience in Brazil helpful in other international entries?
5. Frezite is considering entry into other Latin American markets. What are the pros and cons of this strategy? Any alternatives?

BIBLIOGRAPHY REFERENCES

Azevedo, A. F. Z & Portugal, M. S. (1997) "Abertura Comercial Brasileira e Instabilidade da Demanda de Importações" *Scientific Research UFRGS*.

Gorini, A. P. F. (1998). "Panorama do setor moveleiro no brasil, com ênfase na competitividade externa a partir do desenvolvimento da cadeia industrial de produtos sólidos de madeira" *BNDES Publication*.

Johanson, J. & Vahlne, J. E. (1977), "The internationalization process of the firm—a model of knowledge development and increasing foreign market commitment," *Journal of International Business Studies*, Vol. 8 No. 1, pp. 23–32.

Johanson, J. & Wiedersheim-Paul, F. (1975), "The Internationalization of the Firm—Four Swedish Cases," *Journal of Management Studies*, Vol. 12 No. 3, pp. 305–322.

E-mobile—*Furniture Industry magazine*. Article about Frezite in March 2011, p. 78.

INTERNET

Association of Furniture Industries of Rio Grande do Sul, http://www.movergs.com.br, on 10/04/2014.

Aicep Portugal http://www.portugalglobal.pt/PT/PortugalNews/Paginas/NewDetail.aspx?newId= %7B816B86C4-712C-4EAF-94FB-47286C504808%7D, on 20/05/2013.

ON A SUNNY DAY IN MARCH 2015, Ahmed Badr, the vice president of ITWorx, was sitting in his office recalling a lecture he attended in his MBA class, back in 2010. The lecture was on "How to enter a new market" which caused his thoughts to drift away. He started thinking of his own global software services company, ITWorx, which he and his other two partners, Wael Amin and Youssri Helmy, established in 1994. Then the idea hit him, isn't it the time to expand and enter a new market? The steady pace of development of ITWorx made the thought even more desirable and attractive, especially that they started with one customer, "Corel Corporation," in Canada, and reached out to be one of the fastest-growing market leader companies. Although his expansion plans were put on hold due to the political unrest that took place in Egypt between 2011 and 2014, Badr believed that the economy now was starting to move again and it was time to reconsider his plans.

Headquartered in Cairo, the company offered portals, business intelligence, enterprise application integration, and application development outsourcing services to Global 2000 companies.

Cairo, Egypt—the old and the new worlds meet

Copyright © 2010 by Bigstock/Baloncici.

---

[1] *This case was prepared by (Dr) Marina Apaydin and Hend Mostafa based on materials from Ahmed Badr, Maha Gaber, Doaa Hazem, Nevine Ghonema and Mohamed Mohsen, at the American University in Cairo.*

ITWorx already covered a wide range of customers including governments, financial services firms, educational institutions, and telecommunication operators and media companies in North America, Europe, and the Middle East. ITWorx was able to customize software applications to satisfy customers' needs.

All of this made Ahmed Badr see growing opportunities in different new market that the company could penetrate especially after having offices in KSA, USA, and UAE. After their successful expansion in the Middle East, he thought that it was time for the next step of expansion but this time to Africa, to diversify and to take advantage of being the market leader, which would enable the company to have first-mover advantage as many countries in Africa are still entering the phase of technological advances.

ITWorx's current financial position helped trigger the idea of expansion, especially after being privately held in 2008, with financial backing from the Euro Mena Fund, Venture Capital Bank, and Proparco and fortunate to have industry-leading customers United Technologies, Vodafone, and Mellon Bank. The lecturer interrupted his thoughts by asking "how should we choose this new market?" This question trigged a serious of questions in Badr's mind: What countries in Africa should we choose? What method of expansion was most suitable?

POLITICAL OVERVIEW

During former president Gamal Abdel Nasser's tenure, Egypt's economy was highly centralized, which changed later during the 1970s by former president Sadat to an open-door policy. Between 2004 and 2008, former president Mubarak pursued economic reforms to attract foreign investment and increase GDP. However, the economic growth in recent years was not reflected on living conditions. Accordingly on 25th of Jan. 2011, the Egyptian revolution took place where citizens demanded political and economic reforms. On the 11th of Feb. 2011, Mubarak resigned and the Egyptian military assumed leadership. By June 2012, Mohamed Morsi was elected as president; however, massive anti-government demonstrations took place against his government and the Egyptian Armed Forces intervened, removed Morsi, and replaced him with an interim president, Adly Mansour, in July 2013. During June 2014, presidential elections took place, and Abdel Fattah al Sisi became the president.

ECONOMY

After the Egyptian revolution took place in January 2011, the Egyptian economy was deeply affected. The sectors that were affected most in the economy were tourism, manufacturing, and construction. Moreover, the political instability decreased economic growth, increased unemployment, and reduced government's revenues. In 2011, the GDP growth rate dropped to 1.8 percent and the GDP per capita was $6,600. There was a minor increase in the GDP growth rate in 2012, reaching 2.2 percent however it dropped again in 2013 to 1.8 percent. In 2012 the public debt reached 88 percent of the GDP and it increased to 92.2 percent of GDP in 2013. Moreover the external debt accounted for $38.69 billion in 2012 and increased to $48.76 billion in 2013. The government spending has also increased to address the dissatisfied public, and accordingly Egypt had been using its foreign-exchange reserves and was now depending on foreign assistance especially from the gulf countries.[1]

SOCIAL

Population

Over the last 30 years, the Egyptian population has almost doubled from 44 million in 1980 to over 84 million persons today, making Egypt one of the most populous Arab countries. According to central Intelligence Agency, the annual population growth rate is almost 2 percent.

Religion

Islam was the main religion of Egypt; nearly 90 percent of the population were Muslims. The majority of the Muslim Egyptians were Sunni. The Mufti and Sheikh Al Azhar University were the two religious leaders in Egypt and they were elected by the government. Family traditions and structures were influenced by the Islamic concepts.

Nevertheless, the Coptic community was an important group in the Egyptian society despite the fact that it accounted for only 10 percent of the population. Muslims and Copts lived together peacefully as there was no discrimination.

Language

Arabic was the official language of Egypt. The Colloquial Egyptian Arabic known as Amayia, had been spread throughout of the Arab countries which revealed the impact of the Egyptian's strong cultural influence. Amayia adopted terms from other language such as French, English, Persian, and Turkish over the last 100 years.

Education

Almost 71.4 percent of Egyptians over the age of 15 were literate but there was a wide gap in literacy between males (83 percent) and females (59.4 percent) due to the Egyptian rural customs which restricted the education of females. One big challenge that resulted from the poor educational system was matching the laborers' skills with the skills needed by employers.

EGYPT'S ICT

Back in 1980, the elite Egyptian had only a transistor radio as source of communication, however, nowadays due to the globalization influence in spreading the improvement of technology, more than half of the Egyptian population has cell phone while the telephone main-line users are 10.313 million. Furthermore, the number of Internet users reached 11.414 million.

The information and communications technology (ICT) had become one of main drivers of the economy. In the first quarter of 2010, the IT sector had witnessed a growth of 11.3 percent, contributing to a substantial increase of 5.8 percent in the total GDP.

Egypt had become one of the world growing outsourcing destinations due to reforms which included local employment subsidies, lower corporate taxes, deductions for training costs, the increased availability of attractive business properties like Smart Village, and flexible income-tax regulations. Furthermore, the government was encouraging the expansion in ICT Sector by investing in infrastructure and by supporting SME IT start-ups. The underutilization of the extensive Egyptian workforces who had computer and linguistic skills represented competitive advantages for multinational companies.

Although the IT market in Egypt was expected to grow, the political unrest since 2011 highly impacted the IT market. The revolution that took place in 2011 followed by many political instability forced many retail outlets and distributors to suspend their operations. Moreover, the spending on consumer electronics dropped causing temporary closure of country's bank and the drop off in consumer confidence. The mobile operators had a large drop in revenues and a number of multinational vendors suspended local sales and marketing activities. However sales were expected to recover, but the uncertainty about the future direction of economic policies limited business investment. These uncertainties in the Egyptian market hindered the country to develop its IT market and become a hub between Middle East and Africa.

Despite the period of uncertainty that Egypt witnessed, the IT market was expected to improve in the coming years. The large population of Egypt and the strong government support for the IT industry was expected to boost the IT market in Egypt. The emergence of a more affluent middle class in Egypt, urbanization, and the growing acceptance of modern retail concepts would allow the consumer electronics market to grow steadily over the next five years. The growing Internet usage during the political uncertainty in Egypt, the large growth of DSL, mobile broadband, and the economic recovery in 2015 would also contribute to the growth of the IT market in Egypt.[2]

The government initiatives such as "PC for Every Home" would also support growth in the industry. The computer hardware sales increased from $956 million in 2011 to $1.0 billion in 2012. The computer penetration was forecasted to rise by 20 percent in 2016.[3]

Software Sector

The software industry in Egypt remains in its early stage of development, consisting of four market segments. The first was software tools which were computer programs used to create, maintain, or support other programs and applications. The second market segment was packaged applications which were a bundle of two or more computer programs that were used together to address a specific business need. The third segment was the customization of existing applications to align with customers' needs. Finally was arabization software that allowed existing applications to be used for inputting Arabic text. ITWorx was currently active in two segments: packed applications and customization of existing applications.

According to the BMI Egypt report 2010, the overall spending on software remains low: "being projected at U.S.$187M in 2010. The estimated 14 percent share of the total Egyptian IT spending accounted for by software reflects the relative immaturity of Egypt's IT market." However, the domestic software market was expected to grow at a CAGR of around 11 percent over the forecast period until end-2014.

Software piracy was the main obstacle that was hindering the development of software industry. According to Business Software Association, illegal software usage was 59 percent.[4]

ITWorx[5]

ITWorx was one of the leading software professional services company in Egypt. With its headquarters in Cairo, the company offered different IT services to more than 2000 companies in North America, Europe, and the Middle East. ITWorx had a list of clients among leading Fortune 500 repeat customers such as United Technologies, Microsoft, Vodafone, and Mellon Bank. Moreover, ITWorx partnered with top players in the IT market such as Magic Quadrant technology vendors—Microsoft, Vignette, IBM, Oracle, MicroStrategy, Informatica, Ounce Labs, and Intel.

ITWorx developed a successful project methodology through expertise and using best practices to ensure the delivery of products on time, on budget, and to customers' needs. The company's mission was "improving people's lives through technology." Its vision however was to work, live, and learn better. ITWorx encourages different values such as passion, integrity, accountability, quality, and innovation and productivity.

ITWorx developed products to four different industries: government, education, Teleco, and enterprise. For the government, ITWorx developed innovative software products that would facilitate their business processes. These products enhanced citizen's experience by managing e-permits, e-license issuing, and e-services. For the education sector, ITWorx was considered a market leader in educational software solutions. The company developed unique e-learning platforms that employ the latest technologies and cutting-edge education techniques, tools, and applications. The company was able to customize software solutions for more than 1400 schools.

ITWorx also developed telecom application that transforms businesses process and organization to an online core. Finally, in the enterprise sector, ITWorx delivered enterprise solutions to consolidate data, visually represent data, analyze data, and build analytical models to enrich decision-making.

In 2003, ITWorx started to reposition itself from being a generic custom software services provider to highlight its expertise in specific industries such as software for telecommunication operators. ITWorx had been rapidly growing thus opening new markets and learning new technologies was essential to keep this position and to achieve customer satisfaction. The company's revenues had been growing at phenomenal rates above 40 percent with revenues from the Middle East growing at almost 100 percent in 2008. The yearly turnover reached 10 percent a year and ITWorx was considering further expansion in new markets.

Reverse Growth

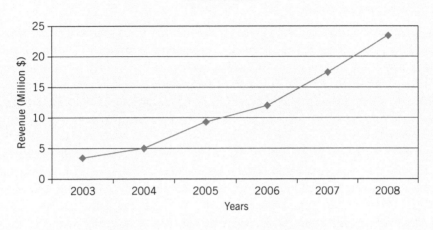

Source: ITWorks

Through gaining experience and delivering high-quality products, ITWorx was able to build a strong brand name in the Egyptian and international market. The company had three centers of distribution in Egypt and a fourth one in China; these centers were the basis of outsourcing to all of their regional and global offices.[6] In 2014, the company had around 700 employees.

COMPETITION

ITWorx had different local and international competitors. In the local market the main competitors were two small companies, Link development and OMS. These companies also competed with ITWorx in the Middle East market as they share the same language and cultural advantage. Link development was a subsidiary of OTVentures that was founded in 1996 and employed 300 employees. The company operated through offices in Egypt (Headquarters), UAE, KSA, Qatar, Italy, and Canada. The second local competitor was OMS, an information and communication technology services provider that was founded in 2000. The company has three branches in the Middle East; UAE, Saudi Arabia, and Lebanon, and has 19 partners in the Middle East.

In the international market, however, the main competitors were Wipro and Infosys. These two large companies were Indian and they competed with ITWorx in the U.S. and the Canadian markets.

Wipro was a global information technology, consulting, and outsourcing company. It employed around 156,866 employees and operated in 175 cities across six continents. Infosys, another competitor, was also a global leader in consulting, technology, and outsourcing solutions. The company had clients in 50 countries and employed 165,000 employees.

Cultural and Language Barriers

Being an Egyptian company impacted ITWorx in different ways. International clients were usually suspicious about Egypt's ability to develop quality IT solutions. Accordingly ITWorx had to open offices in each market it decided to go to. "Although it was a huge burden on us, we had to open offices and hire sales people to convince the clients to try our products," indicated Badr. In the U.S., for example, ITWorx used to approach its clients as a U.S. company that off-shores its development center in Egypt. This approach was also followed by other IT companies such as large Indian companies.

The language however was not a barrier for ITWorx in international markets. As indicated by Badr, Egypt had a large population of well-educated engineers who spoke different languages, mainly English. Moreover, ITWorx provided training to its engineers to improve their language skills and allowed them to travel to their clients to better understand their needs. Unlike Indian and Chinese competitors, ITWorx could communicate easily with its clients and deliver the software services required. However, language represented a barrier in non-English-speaking countries. "That is why we never considered working in Germany or France," added Badr, "as it would be very difficult to communicate."

The culture, however, could sometimes represent a barrier to ITWorx when dealing with international clients. Communicating with customers in Canada and U.S. would not be possible unless they were open to off-shoring. According to Badr, international clients should have an "appetite for off-shoring" in order for the communication to succeed. Otherwise it would be very hard to understand customers' needs and deliver software that satisfy these needs.

In the Middle East market, however, ITWorx had an advantage for being an Egyptian company. Sharing common language, religion, and culture allowed ITWorx to communicate easily with its clients, understand their needs, and deliver software solutions that suit these needs. ITWorx had an edge over its Indian competitors, not only because of the language barrier, but also due to the time zones. ITWorx could respond immediately to its customers and get their feedback often as they share the same time zone. Unlike Indian companies who had large time gap that hindered the communication and fast response for customers in the Middle East. Moreover, customers in the Middle East preferred ITWorx because it was a certified company that delivered products with international standards.

ITWorx Competitive Advantage

ITWorx was able to establish itself in the Egyptian and international market. The company had different competitive advantages that allowed it to attract customers and compete with large international companies. The first edge of the company was off-shoring its operations. Most international companies found it very difficult and expensive to build their own software systems and accordingly used companies such as ITWorx to develop these systems for them. However, the cost of engineers in the U.S., Canada, and even the Middle East was very high. Accordingly, ITWorx used off-shoring in Egypt to develop software solutions for its clients. The company hired highly skilled Egyptian engineers who were less costly, compared to other countries, and developed high-quality software solutions at low costs.

Another competitive edge that ITWorx possessed was its large expertise in intranet, enterprise portals, and business intelligence. ITWorx's experience was developed through its strategic partnerships with global technology leaders such as Microsoft, IBM, Vignette, etc. Through engaging in different projects, whether in the private or public sector, ITWorx's team became very skilled and experienced. Moreover, ITWorx provided continuous training for its team to improve their efficiency and skills.

ITWorx was also able to differentiate itself from competitors, mainly Indians, through the high quality of its products. The company was certified and developed products with international standards. In addition, ITWorx had received different awards such as the Microsoft Worldwide Customer Experience Award in 2004. Later in 2007, ITWorx received the Adobe's "Site of the Day" award, for Vodafone Egypt 3G website, that recognized websites based on their strong visual designs, superior functionalities, and innovative use of adobe products. In 2014, the Ooredoo group intranet that was developed in partnership with ITWorx was among the world's 10 best intranets in 2014.[7]

Opportunities in Egypt's IT Market

The IT market in Egypt had different opportunities especially ITWorx's goal to make Egypt a regional center for outsourcing, especially with the strong government support for the industry in general, and exporting the production to other countries. Another important opportunity was that the IT industry had been expanding to be essential part of other industries. It used to be only related to educational and governmental institutes but now IT investments in the oil and gas, telecom and banking sectors had been growing significantly. Thus ITWorx should begin to deal with oil and gas sector. This was besides the growing potential in domestic market with computer penetration above 2 percent for a population of 80 million.

CHALLENGES IN THE EXTERNAL ENVIRONMENT

Between 2011 and 2013, ITWorx went through a very difficult period. Due to the political instability in Egypt, many international clients started to refrain from doing business with ITWorx. When the revolution started in 25 Jan. 2011, the political authority decided to cut the Internet throughout Egypt on 28 Jan., in an effort to minimize communication and control the situation. Although the government failed to control the demonstrations, the Internet cut off remained for a week. "The

Internet cut had huge impact on the company," indicated Badr, "we were unable to communicate with our customers nor deliver our products on time." Although the Internet came back a week later, many customers were worried that the Egyptian authority could do it again and accordingly refrained from demanding ITWorx's products. To overcome this problem, ITWorx developed a recovery system through satellites to act as a back-up in case the Internet went off again.

Another problem that ITWorx faced during this period was the closure of Cairo airport during the revolution. This hindered ITWorx's team to travel to its clients. Although the airport was open few days later, customers were still worried that it would happen again and that their businesses get affected. As a result of the political instability that Egypt was going through, demand decreased tremendously and revenues accordingly decreased. Most clients were continuing the existing projects with ITWorx but none wanted to start any new products. The situation in Egypt was very unclear and customers wanted to monitor how would this affect ITWorx before deciding to continue with new projects. All this had huge impact on the expected growth of ITWorx.

The Middle East market however was not affected severely like the international market. In 2015 the situation got better and international customers started to gain confidence in Egypt and ITWorx.

PLANNING COMPANY STRATEGY

After passing the tough situation between 2011 and 2014, Egypt's political environment started to stabilize and the economy started moving slowly. At this stage, ITWorx started to reconsider its expansion plans that had been put on hold for a few years.

Ahmed Badr focused on entering a new market where they could gain first-mover advantage. Africa as one of the least developed markets with the least competition was his choice. The company would be market seeking not resource seeking as there was no technological resources or labor with advanced technological education in these markets that could be an opportunity for the company. However, the opportunity was in the market itself with huge population and potential growth.

The company could enter the market through exporting with opening sales representative's offices thus eliminating the threat normally associated with exporting which included losing control over distribution and lack of knowledge of the market. Trained representatives would go to government institutions, educational institutions, and multinational companies to present the products. The products would be customized based on the customer's need.

Opening small offices in Nigeria and South Africa might be the first step. The industry attractiveness in both countries was strong. There is a threat of new entrants but still the current competition status wasn't strong which made the buyer bargaining power relatively low. Since software could be considered a service, and then there was no supplier needed as production would remain in the same places. Outsourcing wouldn't be considered for now for unstable political factors and lack of needed resources such as skilled labor.

The target market would be the same globally including: educational institutions, governmental institutions and multinational or big companies. Segmentation strategy would be used as the company also offered customized products. The strategy would be of a service company focusing on a personal visit to the target market and making it easy to try the services provided by the company. An important step was to be able to develop general awareness about the industry in the developing countries through awareness campaigns. Maintenance of after-sales services and continuous relations with the customers was essential.

Nigeria

Nigeria was one of the highest importers of software products in the Sub-Saharan African continent as all its operating systems, system software, network software, and development tools were 100 percent imported. There was an over-dependency on foreign software due to the nonexistence of software quality assurance, poor investment in software development, poor product standards, and absence of proper documentation.

The financial sector was the principal consumer of foreign software, as it relied 100 percent on foreign software to drive its operations.

The fact that the majority of Nigerian software companies did not offer customized software as they only provided existing off-the-shelf software signified the presence of a market gap in the specialized application development markets. This represented a golden opportunity for software developers especially to ITWorx as it was one of their core activities. However, Nigerian businesses usually did not invest their money in buying customized software due to either their ignorance of the benefits of the software or their preference in buying the foreign software as it was regarded as better quality as opposed to the local specialized software which was known for its dreadful quality and poor function.

The Nigerian government had established the Nigerian Software Development Initiative (NSDI) jointly with Nigerian software practitioners in recognition of the importance of software.

According to the Oracle of the Nigerian IT industry, ISPON had initiated strategies to establish a National Policy and **tactics for Software Development,** "ISPON indicated that the Nigerian software market potential was currently worth about $5.2 billion U.S. dollars and could grow to more than $15 billion annually, provided that an exclusive, independent, and professionally constituted framework was established to harness its immense potential."

South Africa

The ICT industry in South Africa was booming, it currently contributed to about 7 percent of the country's gross domestic product. South Africa had about 3000 IT companies, mainly in Gauteng, Western Cape, and Kwazulu provinces.[8] In 2009, the spending on software was estimated at ZAR 11,732 million of which 50 percent came from imported packaged software, and its growth was estimated at 7.2 percent a year until the end of 2013.[9] The growth was supported by the low and stable exchange rate that makes the local products price competitive and a capable labor market. Local companies usually were usually associated with foreign companies; South African developers had a good reputation especially concerning the financial services sector.

The country's economy was continuously developing and the ICT industry was currently booming as it contributed to about 7 percent of South Africa's gross domestic product. The country also ranked 72nd freest in the 2010 economic freedom index; which was higher than the world average. Since ITWorx was trying to expand their client base, the fact that South Africa had more than 3000 IT companies and ranks 22nd worldwide in IT spend in 2001 reaffirms it as a good choice. As a service provider, Human resources were especially significant for ITWorx. South Africa's widespread poverty and weak educational system might very well deny the company access to qualified labor and thus hinder business success. Moreover, South Africa still had considerable political risk due to high corruption perception, non-transparent regulations, rigid labor laws, and crime. And what most of all, as a software company they could stand to lose a lot in terms of potential sales because end-use piracy is not criminalized in South Africa yet. ITWorx also needed to consider the international and local competitors in South Africa before making its final decision.

After the full analysis of the situation, Ahmed Badr was sure that the expansion to the African market especially Nigeria and South Africa was the right decision. However, still unresolved issues and questions were still in his mind. How to know much more about the customs and habits of the population there and how to effectively reach them? What was the possibility of failure and how would it be handled? How could the company benefit and create spillover effect to the other near African countries? What and when potential competitors would enter the market and how this would affect the position of the company, its revenues and the market in general?

DISCUSSION QUESTIONS

1. What firm-specific and country-specific advantages does ITWorx have in the Middle East? Do they transfer also to Nigeria and South Africa?
2. Are there first-mover advantages in these markets? Can they work in Nigeria? In South Africa?
3. What should be the entry strategy of ITWorx in Nigeria? In South Africa? Does the company need a local partner?
4. What segment should be targeted in these countries? Which segments are most likely to have high entry barriers, and which ones would have strong competition?
5. What should ITWorx do—enter one (which one), enter both, or none at all, focus on the Middle East?

EXHIBITS

DEMOGRAPHIC INDICATORS[10]

Demographic Factors	Nigeria	South Africa
Population (millions)	177	48
Population growth rate (%)	2.47	−0.48
Urban population (%)	49.6	62
Rate of Urbanization (%)	3.75	1.21
Literacy Rate (%)	61.3	93

ECONOMIC INDICATORS[11]

Economic Factors	Nigeria	South Africa
GDP ($) (billions)	478.5	595.7
GDP ($) (billions)	502	353.9
GDP (%)	6.2	2
GDP – per capita ($)	2,800	11,500
Labor force (millions)	51.53	18.54
Unemployment rate	23.9	24.9
Investment (% of GDP) (gross fixed)	9.8	22
Public debt (% of GDP)	19.3	45.4
Debt – external ($)(billions)	15.73	139
Inflation rate (%)	8.7	5.8

ENDNOTES

1. "Egypt," The World Fact book, Retrieved 20 March 2015 from https://www.cia.gov/library/publications/the-world-factbook/geos/eg.html.
2. "Egypt Broadband Market," Research and Markets. Retrieved from http://www.researchandmarkets.com/reports/2103389/egypt_broadband_market_insights_statistics#pos-4.
3. "Egypt Information Technology Report Q2 2012," Research and Markets. Retrieved from http://www.researchandmarkets.com/reports/2134527/egypt_information_technology_report_q2_2012#pos-1.
4. Ibid.
5. ITWorx, 2015, Retrieved 20 March 2015 from http://www.ITWorx.com/Company/Profile/.
6. "Corporate profile," ITWorx, 2010, retrieved 12 Nov 2010 from http://www.ITWorx.com/Company/Profile/.

7. ITWorx. Retrieved on 20 March 2015 from http://www.ITWorx.com/PressRoom/PressReleases/Pages/2014.aspx.

8. "Business opportunities within the IT and telecommunication industry," Ministry of Foreign Affair of Denmark, 2010, Retrieved 27 Nov 2010 from http://www.um.dk/NR/rdonlyres/920458AC-6BC6-4E3E-9D69-A0E7B0665DC7/0/SouthAfricawww.pdf.

9. "Aid to recovery: the economic impact of it, software, and the Microsoft ecosystem on the economy," Microsoft, Retrieved 29 Oct 2010 from http://blogs.microsoft.nl/blogs/ruud_de_jonge/archive/2009/10/07/aid-to-recovery-the-economic-impact-of-it-software-and-the-microsoft-ecosystem-on-the-economy.aspx.

10. The Demographic Indicators are in year 2014.

11. The Economic Indicators are in year 2013.

Source: CIA – The World Factbook, Retrieved 24 Feb 2015 from www.cia.gov.

IN 2004, TEKNOSA, A LEADING CONSUMER ELECTRONICS and home appliances retailer in Turkey was facing a major strategic turning point. How should Teknosa respond to the increased competition among retailers in the new shopping malls that were springing up all over Turkey? Teknosa had also lost some key personnel, including the founding General Manager and Head of Retail SBU at Sabanci, Mr. Demir Sabanci, who had been rumored to start his own retail chain after resignation. Would the company be resilient enough to bounce back?

Teknosa had established a strong track record over the previous three years, had grown fast, helped create a strong consumer electronics retail market, and become the market leader. It was now feeling the need to move into a new growth stage and face the threat of upcoming foreign competitors. So what should be done and how? Was a change of strategy needed and if so in what direction? These were some of the key questions that the new leadership of Teknosa had to find answers to.

TURKISH RETAIL MARKET TRANSFORMATION

In Turkey, retailing was predominantly run by traditional, unorganized channels in the 1990s. In fact, this was the result of a closed economic structure in the country until 1983 when a switch was made to liberal economic system. The first modern shopping mall in Turkey opened its doors in 1988 in Istanbul and the industry had to wait for more than a decade to pick up its growth curve. The first retail-related industry association was formed in 1994 which later became the Turkish Shopping Centers and Retailers Association.

Retail chains at that time were very limited and stores were located on high streets of major cities. The majority of both food and nonfood retailers were mom-and-pop stores. At the end of 1994, there were 10 shopping malls in Turkey and this number went up to 50 by the end of 2000. Consumer electronics retailing was done through individual stores that ran the spot markets for foreign brands and through the exclusive dealer networks of the major Turkish brown and white goods manufacturers such as Arçelik, Vestel, and Profilo. From 2000 onward, however, a structural transformation of the retail industry started which significantly speeded up with the entrance of international retail real-estate developers of foreign origin into the Turkish market.

---

[1] This is the first part of an abbreviated version of a case prepared by Dr. Cüneyt Evirgen with the assistance of Yüksel Kaplancık both at Sabanci University, Istanbul, Turkey. Dr. Evirgen was also a Member of the Board at Teknosa starting in 2005. The author would also like to thank Teknosa top management and Jones Lang LaSalle, Turkey for their support during data collection for the case. The case is intended as a basis for class discussion and not to serve as an endorsement, source of primary data or as an illustration for good or bad practice. Not to be reproduced or quoted without permission.

THE SABANCI GROUP AND RETAILING

Teknosa was one of the companies of the Sabanci Group, the second-largest Turkish conglomerate, whose businesses were mostly in banking and industrial manufacturing (business-to-business) areas. "Sabanci" was the surname of the founder of the Group which was a very well-known and highly respected and trusted name in Turkey. Names of all Sabanci Group companies ended with "SA" and the letters S and A placed in circles was the mark of this in company logos. Hence, "SA" at the end of Teknosa pointed out that Teknosa was also a Sabanci Group company and everybody in Turkey could easily recognize this.

Teknosa logo

Source: Teknosa.

The involvement of the Sabanci Group in brown goods (consumer electronics) and white goods (home appliances) retailing went back to 1996. The Group had its first retail experience when a joint venture was formed with Carrefour to form CarrefourSA in Turkey in 1996. However, executive management of the company was controlled by the French partner and Sabanci was only represented on the company Board. Thus, this joint venture had not given Sabanci Group a chance to be directly involved in retail operations, but rather being an influencer and decision-maker as an investor. There were probably other venues of retail that could be promising.

Up until that time, the experience of the Group with Japanese companies had been very promising. Successful 50/50 joint ventures formed with Toyota, Bridgestone, and Mitsubishi had been profitably growing. Looking for an area of new investment and growth, assessment was made that Japanese brands of white goods were underrepresented in Turkey. A distributorship agreement was signed with Sharp Inc. to market their products in Turkey. Sharp washing machines were not included in the agreement since they were top-loading types and Hoover brand front-loading washing machines were also added to the product portfolio. Additionally, distributorship agreement was made with the French Thomson brand for TV and audio equipment.

Hence, Sabanci Group became the wholesale distributor for Sharp, Hoover, and Thomson in Turkey. The retail structure was initially based on nonexclusive dealers, but, after a while, the decision was made to enter the retail side of the business. The first company-owned store was opened at the end of 1998 in Izmir under the name Direct Shop. Izmir was a smaller market than Istanbul where the majority of trade took place, yet being the third-largest city in Turkey it also represented a good test market. The results of the first month following the opening were rather promising. With 70 SKUs, $250,000 revenue was generated. The total revenue of the wholesale business at that time was $20 million.

March 2000 marked the establishment of the new company, Teknosa, where Demir Sabanci (third-generation family member) was both the founding General Manager and President of the

Board and Mr. Mehmet Nane was the Vice-President. The first six months of operation passed dealing with IT software issues since the existing ERP (Enterprise Resource Planning) system was not suitable for a retail business. Gradually the company grew to 12 stores and the brand name was changed from Direct Shop to Klik. However, it turned out that the name "Klik" was already registered by a different company. Eventually, the store name was changed to Teknosa and the first invoice was written in October 2000.

2000–2002: Currency Shock

The early months of Teknosa's operations were not auspicious. A very significant political crisis that broke out in February 2001 in Turkey was followed by a 50 percent devaluation of the Turkish Lira against the U.S. dollar. Teknosa was hit by a $20 million currency loss when the annual revenues were at the same level. Ten of the total number of 24 stores of Teknosa were shut down, the company contracted, and a new game plan was needed.

The 2002 budget aimed at an ambitious revitalization of the business. However, shareholders (i.e., Sabanci family members) seriously challenged the draft budget and asked for downsizing of the number of stores as well as staff size. The revised budget targeted 15 stores in total with a total staff size of 330. Shareholders approved the revised budget and agreed to invest $25 million of equity into the company.

One major decision made was to hedge the currency risk. Instead of directly importing the products, they were purchased from local distributors of the brands or local manufacturers. The first manufacturers that offered their products to Teknosa were Arçelik and Vestel, the two leading Turkish brown and white goods companies. This was accomplished even though the manufacturers had their own exclusive mono-brand dealer networks in the country. Teknosa became the first multi-brand retail store chain of brown goods (consumer electronics) and white goods (home appliances) in Turkey.

In 2001, franchise agreement was signed with Radio Shack (a U.S. consumer electronics retailer, now closed down) and three stores were opened under the Radio Shack name. A lot of things regarding running a consumer electronics retail business was learned out of this experience. However, later on it became clear that the product range of Radio Shack (mostly electronics parts and accessories) was not appropriate for Turkey at that time and eventually, Radio Shack stores were all converted into Teknosa stores.

2002–2004: Teknosa Grows Capabilities

In 2001, governance structure in the Sabanci Group was changed and strategic business units (SBUs) were formed. A Food and Retail SBU was formed under which the packaged consumer goods and retail businesses were placed. Later on, in 2002, this SBU was split into two separate SBUs as Food SBU and Retail SBU where Mr. Demir Sabanci became the Head of Retail SBU.

The revitalization road map for Teknosa in 2002 included several critical initiatives and operational investments. One of these was a contract for Sabanci University to run a retail business analysis of Teknosa. The company aimed to become a world-class retailer and set up a modern retail sales performance system in the stores. Sabanci University worked with leading foreign retail consultants such as Retail Performance Specialists (UK) who was also the European representative for Friedman International, a well-known retail consultancy firm. Thus, a bridge was formed for transfer of world-class retail sales know-how to Teknosa. This was a visionary decision that radically changed the retail sales management at Teknosa.

Results of the initial situation analysis clearly indicated improvement areas for Teknosa such as human resource practices, IT infrastructure, store sales management, regional area management, and managerial processes. Hence, in 2003 significant operational investments were made to implement a world-class sales performance management system and retail ERP & IT system. Key retail sales performance indicators such as conversion rate, number of invoices written, sales, and items per invoice became key performance measures that were measured, tracked, and targeted as standard practice.

The system was integrated across all levels of the retail sales force, starting from the individual sales consultant at each store and moving up to store managers, area managers, and sales director. The Sales Director was able to see the real-time full sales performance dashboard for Teknosa retail stores at his fingertips sitting in his office. Store sale scorecards that used to be prepared manually using MS Excel spreadsheets were now produced electronically once a sale was run at the cash register. Real-time tracking of sales at store level enabled area and store managers to make effective and fast decisions and catch up with the pace of retail. Moreover, ongoing, uninterrupted training programs were executed for all new and existing sales staff at all levels.

An organizational change was also implemented in late 2004 where managerial positions reporting directly to the General Manager were redefined. Sales, marketing communication, and category management functions were separated and a director was assigned for each.

Overall, the period 2002–2004 represented a fast-track expansion period for Teknosa. By the end of 2004, Teknosa had 56 stores (all company-owned) around Turkey. The stores were on average 250 square meters in size and were mostly located in shopping malls with some being on high streets.

A typical Teknosa store

All through this period, in essence, Teknosa created the multi-brand consumer electronics retail chain industry in Turkey and became the market leader through its growth. During this period, Teknosa also launched alternative sales channel initiatives including setting up a call center for sales by telephone and an e-sales store (www.teknosa.com) for sales over the Internet. Both of these initiatives were pioneering initiatives in consumer electronics retailing in Turkey. Teknosa also led the usage of periodic monthly sales promotion inserts or flyers distributed with national newspapers and at the stores.

The strategy of Teknosa was based on a service oriented modern retail concept and differentiation was the key. The core concept was based on the customer experience within the store and the objective was to be the store of choice for the targeted consumer electronics consumer. The differentiation involved a wide variety of leading brands, flexible methods of payments offered, convenient store locations, professionalism of the sales staff, modern merchandising and displays within the stores, and extensive after-sales services.

Increased Competition

The growth of the consumer electronics retail business led by Teknosa soon began to attract a lot of attention, both locally and internationally. Some local consumer electronics retail chains that had been around for 10–20 years with stagnant growth got spurred by the growth triggered by Teknosa and turned to growth strategies as well. Among these were Bimeks, Gold Bilgisayar and Vatan Bilgisayar. Moreover, foreign consumer electronics retail chains such as MediaMarkt (part of Metro Group, Germany), ElectroWorld (part of the Dixons Group, UK), Darty (part of the Kesa Group, France), and Best Buy (U.S.) began investigating the Turkish market and signaling their intentions to enter.

Turkey, with its total population close to 70 million, 45 percent of which was under 40 years old, growing per-capita income and relatively low levels of consumer electronics product penetration was representing huge growth opportunities. This attractiveness was further amplified by the fact that the U.S. and Western European markets were reaching saturation levels.

One of the imminent reflections of foreign retailers' entry plans was that Teknosa became a source of staff recruitment by these companies. Since history of modern retailing was very short in Turkey, and even shorter in consumer electronics retailing, there was a significant lack of experienced local talent at all levels of the retail business. By that time, Teknosa was the home of experienced and well-trained talent in consumer electronics retail in Turkey.

Another critical issue was that Teknosa began to come across these other consumer electronics retailers for rental space in new shopping mall development projects that were underway. Now, for real-estate developers there were alternative renters in the consumer electronics category and very strong and aggressive competition for limited supply began to build up.

Furthermore, in late 2004, the founding General Manager and Head of Retail SBU at Sabanci, Mr. Demir Sabanci, resigned and left the Sabanci Group following some other Sabanci family members to build his own business. Mr. Mehmet Nane left the Retail SBU and became the General Secretary of Sabanci Holding while his Board membership at Teknosa continued. There were rumors in the business circles that Mr. Demir Sabanci was going to re-enter consumer electronics retailing business with a foreign partner.

The company had established a strong track record over the previous three years, grown fast, created the consumer electronics retail market, and became the market leader and was now feeling the pressures of moving into a new growth stage and threat of upcoming foreign competitors. So what should be done and how? Is a change of strategy needed and if so in what direction? These were some of the key questions that the new leadership of Teknosa had to find answers to.

DISCUSSION QUESTIONS

1. Describe how the local Sabanci group learned to do retailing. What factors seemed to have been key in this learning process? What role does the 1983 market opening seem to have played? What slowed the group down? Would a less family-oriented group have been quicker or slower?

2. What factors make the Turkish market in the case an attractive electronics market? What are the negative factors?

3. If you were asked by Best Buy or another foreign white and brown goods retailer to make a recommendation for entry (or not), how would you respond? If entry, what mode of entry would you recommend?

4. Given the information in the case and what you know from the textbook about Turkey and emerging markets in general, how would you describe the typical customer of Teknosa? Are there several segments? Do you think there is any loyalty among consumers toward shopping in a Sabanci store?

5. What should Teknosa do to prepare its defense against the foreign competition?

GLOBAL LOCALIZATION STRATEGIES

GLOBALIZED MARKETING

Localization has limits. For companies that expand globally and start marketing in several local markets, there is usually a need to standardize the product and develop a strategy that is uniform across countries. There are many reasons for this. On the cost side, unnecessary duplication (meaningless differences in product designs, separate advertising campaigns, different brand names) is wasteful. On the demand side, global communications make for positive spillovers from keeping the same brand name. Some compromise between standardization with a uniform global strategy on one hand and complete localization on the other is unavoidable. This is the goal of global localization.

GLOBAL LOCALIZATION

Global localization is the concept that global strategies should still leave a lot of room for local adaptation. The economies of scale made possible by global strategies—including standardized products and multi-country advertising campaigns—are important factors in helping marketers offer products and services at affordable prices around the globe. But companies have also learnt "mass customization," offering options and modular systems to help local adaptation. Global strategy no longer means complete uniformity.

Part Four deals with the global localization of marketing management, that is, how a firm coordinates and integrates its local marketing efforts globally while still preserving local adaptability. Its six chapters follow roughly the standard marketing division of "the 4Ps," but cover also digital global marketing

- Chapter 9 focuses on *global products and brands*, discussing the management of standardized product lines and global brand management.
- Chapter 10 discusses the increasing importance of *global services* and how the management of global services differs from the management of products.
- Chapter 11 covers *global pricing*, and shows how companies deal with transfer prices, price coordination across borders, and the problem of fluctuating exchange rates.

- Chapter 12 covers *global distribution and e-commerce*, and includes a discussion of the massive changes in global logistics technology.
- Chapter 13 deals with *global advertising and promotion*. It covers global ad campaigns and agencies, online advertising and sales promotions, and global personal selling.

- Chapter 14 deals with the new *digital global marketing* model, what the new tools can do, the "pure play" companies that only have digital presence, and how consumers in different countries react to digital media.

In this chapter you will learn about:

1. How firms strike a balance between standardization and adaptation of their products
2. How global products are developed and why so few new products can be global from the start
3. The increased importance of brands in all markets, and why local brands can also be strong against the large global brands
4. How it takes both a strong state-of-the-art product and a strong brand to have a sustained success in any market

Global Products and Brands

CHAPTER 9

UNDER ARMOUR GOES INTERNATIONAL

Under Armour is a U.S. manufacturer and retailer of specialty athletic clothing, exercise clothing, and footwear primarily for men. The company success is based primarily on its innovative athletic apparel, using new materials that were moisture-wicking and provided unmatched athletic flexibility and dryness. Apparel was a category where the two main competitors, Nike and Adidas, had had limited success and to some extent the UA products complement the focus on shoes by both Nike and Adidas.

The innovative apparel was quickly accepted by a number of teams in American football, and UA received unprecedented access to athletes. The popularity of football in America helped UA build awareness, excitement, and allegiance for its brand. Beyond American football, in 2015 the company-sponsored Jordan Spieth became the youngest golf player to win both the Masters and the U.S. Open in the same year.

About 85 percent of the company's revenue comes from the U.S. market so far and the company has achieved spectacular growth over the past few years (see Exhibit 9.1).

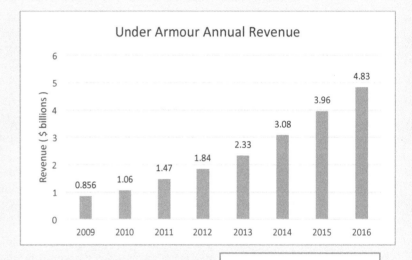

Under Armour Annual Revenue

Revenue ($ billions)

Year	Revenue
2009	0.856
2010	1.06
2011	1.47
2012	1.84
2013	2.33
2014	3.08
2015	3.96
2016	4.83

EXHIBIT 9.1.
Under Armour has grown rapidly. International revenues represented 15 percent of total revenues in 2016, up from 11 percent in 2015.[2]

Source: http://investor.underarmour.com/income.cfm.

Under Armour's primarily U.S.-only revenue stream is in sharp contrast to Nike and Adidas. Nike generates about 59 percent of its sales outside its home region, while Adidas, based in Germany, gets about 60 percent of its sales outside its home market of Europe.[1]

To continue this growth, UA has begun an expansion strategy that focuses in three directions: expanding its women's clothing business, expanding internationally, and expanding further into footwear (after a start in 2006), putting the company in direct competition with the two world leaders.

International Expansion

International expansion beyond its current 6 percent of revenue is important for Under Armour's long-term success since more than half of global spending on athletic clothing and equipment happens outside North America.[3] Recognizing the opportunity, Under Armour started its efforts to expand internationally in 2012 by hiring an executive with Latin American experience to head its international efforts.

The company began by outfitting several teams at the 2014 Winter Olympics in Sochi and signing an eight-year deal with the U.S. speed skating team through the 2022 Olympics (although some athletes complained about air-resisting outfits, the sponsorship continues).[4] At the 2020 Games in Tokyo, the U.S. gymnastics teams will be outfitted in Under Armour gear.

In Latin America, Under Armour has targeted Mexico, Chile, and especially Brazil, which hosted the 2014 World Cup and the 2016 Summer Olympics. Under Armour is selling its products to consumers in 70 stores in Brazil and other store locations in Mexico, and Chile. Under Armour is also the sole sponsor of Brazil's most famous soccer club team Santos, Pelé's team. The Sao Paulo club has won six national titles and 12 international titles, including three club world championships. The company also sponsors the Tottenham Hotspur FC of the English Premier League, Colo-Colo of the Chilean Primera Division, and Cruz Azul and Toluca of Mexico's Liga MX.[5]

In China, Under Armour sells its products directly to consumers through its 13 Under Armour stores with a plan to open 50 stores total. In Shanghai the company is piloting a retail theater store concept that combines both product sales and storytelling with the life stories of famous athletes on video. In Australia, Rebel Sport is the largest sports equipment and clothing chain and is now the exclusive distributor of Under Armour products.[6] The company logo (see Exhibit 9.2) is becoming recognized around the world.

In total Under Armour has expanded into nine countries so far. Under Armour has also partnered with international shipping solution BorderFree to make their products "shippable" from the U.S. website into 85 countries with payment in the local currency.[7]

The Women's Market

Under Armour also hired a woman executive from Tokyo to head its new women's clothing business. Expanding its product line into women's products is seen as necessary for international success. Currently women's apparel sales account for 30 percent of Under Armour's business and UA has an ever-growing line of women's studio fashion wear designed to be worn in training, on the field and in public.[8] As an example, Under Armour has signed a multiyear sponsorship deal with Misty Copeland, a soloist at New York's American Ballet Theatre, in an attempt to dial down its macho men-only image. Under Armour president Plank said, "We think the reality is that this shift is more permanent than some may expect. Women in essence see life as a workout."[9] Putting this idea into action, Under Armour has opened a test store in hometown Baltimore that has ditched the company's prevailing locker-room vibe for natural light, cheery colors, and 10 times as many mannequins. The outreach to women is part of efforts to broaden out beyond performance apparel.

Future Expansion

Under Armour thinks expansion into the footwear business can help it to further expand internationally. Footwear is a standardized global business with products identical around the world (pull up the tongue of any athletic shoe and one can find sizes for a dozen various countries). U.S.-designed footwear should work everywhere. Athletic clothing, on the other hand, because of the "fashion" content, operates with both aspects of global and localization. Particularly with the expansion into women's clothing, it is likely that Under Armour will have to adapt or localize its clothing designs by region or possibly even by country to fit into the local acceptable "fashion." Clothing design is Under Armour's core business and they understand how to do this in the U.S., but internationally this would be a business model with a much higher cost structure.

Under Armour recognizes that success internationally must be a long-term commitment and forecasts its international revenue to grow modestly from 6 percent to 12 percent by 2016. This is more than a doubling of international sales but still a small number when compared to Nike and Adidas, implying a potentially untapped international opportunity.[10]

One of the first questions in global product management is, "Can this product be standardized globally?" While a customized offering is closest to the marketing ideal, there are cost savings in large scale that make global standardization preferable. There are also demand spillover effects from a uniform approach—in brand-name recognition, trade support, prestige, and word of mouth. This chapter discusses the management of global products and brands, including standardization, new product development, and the building of strong global brands.

A **local product** or brand is one sold only in one country. But global is not always completely "global." Marketers generally make a distinction between global and regional products and brands. **Regional products** are those sold in a group of countries, but not everywhere. **Global products** are available in all countries, usually standardized with some uniform features in all countries. In particular, brand names are often the same across countries. Global brand examples include Gillette razor blades, Colgate toothpaste, Sony television sets, and Benetton sweaters. By contrast, regional products and brands are unique to a particular trading region, often a trading bloc or one of the regions discussed in the Factbook. Examples include P&G's Ariel and Vizir in Europe, Brazilian Natura's cosmetics in its Pan-American market, and Korea's ginseng tea makers covering the East Asian market.

This chapter first discusses the pros and cons of standardization and how managers balance the demand for local adaptation against the benefits of uniformity. A possible distinction between localization and adaptation is clarified. The following section covers global new product development and the diffusion of new products across countries.

EXHIBIT 9.2.
British tennis star player Andy Murray at the French Open in 2015.
Murray is completely outfitted by Under Armour—from shoes and socks to shorts, shirt, and wristbands—although the racquet is a Head.
The gray-and-black color combination is typical for Under Armour's gear, but for the Wimbledon tennis tournament, where a stricter dress code is imposed, UA and Murray developed a completely new all-white outfit.

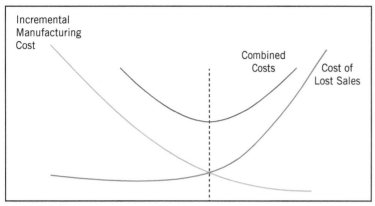

Incremental Manufacturing Cost

Combined Costs

Cost of Lost Sales

Fully Adapted

Fully Standardized

Then a section on global product lines leads into a discussion of the important role that global brands play today. The way companies build and manage a global brand is discussed in depth. The final section deals with the competition between global brands and today's rising local brands.

THE PROS AND CONS OF STANDARDIZATION

For most companies some product standardization is unavoidable. Cost savings from longer product series often outweigh the disadvantages of not being perfectly adapted to customers' precise requirements. At the same time, the customer satisfaction advantages of a high level of adaptation are well understood by most companies. The point at which the combined costs are at a minimum (see Exhibit 9.3) is the optimal level of standardization.

Finding this point in practice is often a delicate balancing act. The actual costs involved relate to predicted gains and losses, not always easy to estimate before entry into a local market. In *bottom of the pyramid* markets especially, a long-term perspective is needed since it is often difficult to predict the speed of channel penetration and customer acceptance.

To evaluate the potential benefits of a standardized product or service strategy, it is useful to first summarize and review the basic advantages and drawbacks of standardized offerings.

The Advantages of Standardization

There can be several positive effects of standardization:[11]

Cost Reduction

Cost reductions gained by *scale* economies constitute one major benefit from product standardization. Because of the longer production series, i.e., producing more units with the same product specifications, there are considerable savings to be gained in manufacturing as well as purchasing. Product development costs can be spread over a larger number of units, thus lowering the average unit cost. Unnecessary duplication of effort, with minor variations in color or design of a product, can be avoided. Centralizing the purchase of media spots for advertising generates quantity rebates and other savings. When one global brand name is used in several countries, there are savings in media advertising and sales efforts.

Furthermore, performing the same marketing activities with other products or services, known as scope economies, produces other cost savings. The use of a globally standardized advertising campaign makes it possible to exploit good creative ideas to their fullest potential. So, for example, Under Armour's goodwill can be extended from apparel to sports gear. Advanced technology and new features can be used across a whole product line. New carbon material can be used for all tennis rackets, not just the upper end of the market.

Improved Quality

The standardized product or service is likely to offer improved quality in terms of components, parts, and functioning. Since additional resources can be focused on the product development effort and the design, the standardized product or service is likely to be more thoroughly tested. Investment in state-of-the-art production processes is justified. This leads to higher quality in terms of durability and reliability. The customized product may have more status and extra quality features—an expensive luxury car, for example, may have more expensive wood on the dashboard—but in terms of functionality, a standardized product is more likely to be both up-to-date and function well.

Global Customers

There is also a special advantage to standardization because of global customers who demand uniform quality and services wherever they happen to be and buy. In consumer goods, global communications and the growth of international travel and tourism have helped spawn global markets for products as diverse as chocolate, watches, and apparel. In business-to-business markets, as firms grow more global and their purchasing function is centralized on a global basis, standardization of requirement specifications becomes necessary.

Cross-country Segments

Furthermore, standardization has the advantage that it fits with the emergence of cross-country customer segments. As we have seen, the customer segments in one market can often be similar to those in other markets. In technology-based product categories—computers, cameras, televisions—there are customer segments in various countries that all want similar products, and as these segments grow, the potential benefits of standardization grow as well.

Enhanced Customer Preference

Early in globalization, it was assumed that standardization enhances customer preferences. The argument was that "everyone wants the same thing."[12] For consumers in emerging markets especially, getting the same product and brand as they see in advanced markets (the so-called "demonstration" effect) seemed obvious to observers. Some of this still is true. Seeing attractive ads for the same camera at home and in a foreign country reinforces a customer's purchase decision. Rolex, capitalizing on the recognition value of Roger Federer, the tennis player, features him endorsing Rolex watches in airport advertisements around the world.

But today, these are not automatic consumer responses, even in emerging markets. For luxury brands, yes, most consumers want and expect standardized products. But for non-luxury brands—the majority of products by far—consumers today prefer products adapted to their wants and needs. Whether it is a global or domestic product, an increasing number of consumers around the world feel empowered to demand what fits them.

The Drawbacks of Standardization

There are clear negatives to standardization:[13]

Off-Target

A big drawback of standardized products or services is that by focusing on the cost savings, the products are likely to miss the exact target in any one country. Since "One size fits all" is not usually the best strategy, standardized products are potentially mis-positioned relative to buyer preferences. Where needs and wants across countries are homogeneous, this is a lesser threat, but even within countries there is heterogeneity in tastes and preferences. The problem is more obvious in markets where customers in different countries have widely different tastes or needs. Offering only jumbo-sized packages of bathroom tissue makes no sense where storage capacity in the homes is limited. As we have seen throughout this text, for the "new" global marketer usage conditions are one important consideration in adaptation, in addition to wants, tastes, and preferences.

Lack of Uniqueness

There is also a drawback in the lack of uniqueness of standardized products. If customization or exclusivity is one of the purchase considerations, a standardized offering is by definition in a weak position. As markets grow more affluent, uniqueness is likely to become increasingly salient. By contrast, in a period of recession, the luxury of being "special" might be forgone by the consumer.

Strong domestic competition.

Standardization can also fail simply because local competitors are capable and manage to mount a strong defense. At an early stage of globalization domestic loyalties were thought to offer local companies protection. They did, for a while, as domestic brands tried to kindle patriotic loyalties. But over time, patriots also demand competitive products. Many local competitors could not respond and failed. But many others offered improved products and became worthy competitors.[14] Working closely with local channel members, many local competitors have been able to hold off standardized global brands. For example, Pepsico's *Lays* potato chips could not compete with the local Egyptian brand *Chipsy*. Finally, Pepsico bought the local brand and kept both brands.[15] As we have seen throughout this text, strong local competition is one reason why global companies increasingly localize and adapt their offering.

LOCALIZATION VS ADAPTATION

So far in this text we have used localization and adaptation interchangeably. In considering product standardization, however, it is useful to make a distinction between the two concepts.[16]

Localization is often used by companies to refer to changes required for a product or service to function in a new country. Localization is closely related to the usage conditions. For example, when a fax machine is fitted with a new type of telephone jack for a foreign country, it is localized. Automobiles are typically standardized products whose localization involves **homologation**, certification that the car meets regulatory standards and specifications, such as safety and technical requirements.

By contrast, **adaptation** is when changes are made to match customer tastes or preferences. When a tablet comes with a smaller size for the Asian market, it is adapted. Optional equipment helps a car maker target different segments.

Generally speaking, localization helps local customers use the product, while adaptation gives customers a positive reason for choosing it. Localization is a positive for all potential customers in the market, while adaptation aims to target some special segment or segments. Disneyland Paris was originally called Euro-Disney, but was renamed to be more attractive to the French (Exhibit 9.4).

The problem with such adaptation is increased costs. Manufacturing costs go up since scale economies are forgone, sales costs rise as re-training, and promotional costs go up as consumer ads need to be re-designed.

In the past, the costs made standardization the preferred option, but the increasing maturity of foreign markets make consumers more demanding and more likely to reject products that are not adapted. Using focus groups and test markets, managers do product research to determine whether the cost of adaptation is balanced by the projected increased revenues (Exhibit 9.3). Companies like Procter & Gamble with long experience judge the acceptability of an adaptation by the percentage of respondents that would prefer the adapted version. Depending on the price, to get the go-ahead an adaptation would need to muster a significant majority of the respondents.

The distinction between localization and adaptation is useful in analyzing the pros and cons of product standardization. An adaptation can be used in advertising appeals, for example, but localization is usually taken for granted. Even a globally standardized product needs to be localized.

HOW TO LOCALIZE/ADAPT?

In practice, 100 percent standardization is rare. Usually some features of a product need to be localized. For example, packaging should show information in the native language. Some global firms solve this problem by providing information in three or four languages on the same package. Personal care products in Europe typically come in packages with up to four languages (English, French, German, and Spanish, for example), making it possible to produce longer manufacturing runs of the same product and gain scale economies. Likewise, Russian products sold to the ex-Soviet Union countries come in eight languages, including Armenian.

Companies actually have a number of tools to customize products even while retaining some of the economies of scale in standardization. This is now called **mass customization**.[18] Today's manufacturing processes are often assemblies of modular and standardized components and parts, akin to building an IKEA bookcase. Coupled with the use of flexible computer-aided design and manufacturing systems (CAD-CAM), it is often possible to make incremental design changes which help localization and adaptation. Mass customization can take several forms:

- *Product platform.* Since adapting the product to each particular market or segment is not cost-efficient for technology products, companies try to identify basic product attributes that can be standardized. A common strategy is to work from a basic product platform, such as the base frame of an automobile (the chassis). The designers then try to develop alternative packaging options (the body) that can be adapted to each local market.
- *Modular design.* Another approach is to design products in modular fashion, with different components that can be assembled into different versions. Camera producers and smartphone producers tend to use this approach. Different features can then easily be combined into unique and adapted offerings for different countries and segments. Most automobile producers provide different body styles and engine sizes in different parts of the world to accommodate different road conditions and fuel-efficiency requirements.

- *Adaptable products.* A literal application of adaptation, some products come with multiple systems, options, and expansions that can be used in different parts of the world to customize products. Consumer electronics firms tend to favor this approach, with adaptation relating to electric supply, plugs, and added capabilities such as extra memory boards and external disk drives.

GLOBAL PRODUCT LINES

Product lines in even the most global company are rarely identical across countries. Procter & Gamble has not introduced its detergents *Ariel* and *Vizir* in the United States (although its *Tide* brand in the U.S. incorporates similar technology; and in the Middle East *Tide* is a low-tier detergent with *Ariel* the top P&G brand). Coca-Cola sells its *Georgia* iced coffee and *Aquarius* isotonic drink in Japan but not at home. Honda's City automobile is sold in Asia and the Middle East but not in North America.

There are actually several reasons why product lines differ. Many are simply historical accidents, while others represent true adaptation.[19] Product lines differ between countries because of:

- *History.* The different local products were well-established before standardization and coordination were feasible and the benefits recognized. Several of P&G's brands in soaps and detergents fall into this category.
- *M&A.* If the product lines are formed through mergers and acquisitions, complete integration is usually difficult. Although the company has tried to sell off unrelated businesses, after acquiring Findus, Nestlé found itself in the canning business in Europe.
- *Plant capacity.* Global product lines need large production capacity, often through plant locations in several countries. A firm will take some time to develop that capacity, especially since forecasting demand is not without uncertainty. Because of strong demand in the North American target market, Toyota initially did not have enough capacity to sell its Lexus model in Japan.
- *Channel requirements.* Differences in channel structure can make it difficult to support the same product lines. Coca-Cola's isotonic drink Aquarius is a "me-too" version of a popular Japanese drink, Pocari Sweat. By introducing Aquarius in addition to Georgia, the iced coffee, Coca-Cola made sure that its vending machines could be stocked with the variety demanded by the Japanese consumer.
- *Adaptation.* But the most basic reason for differences in product lines is local adaptation. For many businesses the simplest adaptation can be to add versions to the product line. This is the standard approach in fast food, for example. Menus for companies such as McDonald's, KFC, and Wendy's are not identical across the globe, but feature additional choices plus several of the standard core offerings—a falafel burger in Egypt, rice and chicken in Hong Kong, veggie burgers in India, and so on. PC makers offer smaller keyboards in Asia, you find more colorful smartphones in Japan, and the largest supermarkets in the United States typically offer a wide variety of food products for its diverse citizens while the large supermarkets in China might offer deeper assortments (which is why Walmart's superstore in Shanghai features live turtles as part of its soup section).

Going further, larger companies often end up developing new products and brands for the particular market. Procter & Gamble and Unilever are two companies that have done this, P&G for China especially, Unilever for a long time in India. In other cases the adaptation simply consists of buying up a local producer and either keeping the local brand (the typical strategy in the beer industry—as with Baltika in Eastern Europe, now owned by Danish Carlsberg) or co-branding with the global brand (the typical pattern in appliances, such as Olympic in Egypt bought by Electrolux).

As with all product line management, well-managed global lines also need to offer a certain rate of new product introductions (see box, "Montblanc's Product Line Extensions"). To be successful in globally competitive markets, a significant percentage of sales and profits should come from new products.

BOX: Montblanc's Product Line Extensions[20]

When is a pen not a pen? When it is an "art form." This is how Switzerland's Compagnie Financière Richemont positions its Montblanc pens. The fancy writing instruments boast individually numbered gold nibs and are topped with a white mark representing a bird's-eye view of snow-capped Mont Blanc, a mountain in the Alps. A single fountain pen will set you back $235 to $13,500 (for one made of platinum). Its most iconic product is the Montblanc Meisterstück which allegedly is at the desk of the most important decision-makers in the world. The myth of the Meisterstück is as the Power Pen (signifying your power when signing important documents).

Apparently, the pen's style and quality have succeeded in making it more than just a status symbol. The upscale readers of *Robb Report,* a monthly magazine that rates products associated with an affluent lifestyle, voted Montblanc the best writing instrument in the world.

For Richemont subsidiary Montblanc North America, this reputation presents an opportunity to extend the product line. The company has opened stand-alone boutiques offering jewelry and leather accessories such as wallets, briefcases, organizers, and garment bags.

To support the brand extension, the company designed marketing communications reinforcing Montblanc's image of fine quality. This promotional effort included magazine advertisements that link the Montblanc pen with the "art of writing." Newspaper ads announce the opening of the boutiques and the introduction of new products. Cultural events at the boutiques included displays of rare manuscripts, letters, and autographs. Together, such efforts were intended to convey, in the words of the ad agency's creative director, "an image that Montblanc isn't only a writing-instrument company but a European luxury brand. We hope that the Montblanc brand will stand not just for a pen, but for a certain lifestyle." In line with this extension strategy, the company now offers fragrances and eyewear under the Montblanc name.

DEVELOPING NEW GLOBAL PRODUCTS

In the past, most globally standardized products did not start out as global products. They were products that turned out to be successful in the home market and were then gradually introduced in markets abroad, following a kind of waterfall strategy, one country at a time. A good example is the Ford Fiesta from Europe, Ford's first attempt at a global car. Other examples include P&G's Pampers diapers, Coca-Cola's overseas expansion, and Marlboro cigarettes.

Today, as in the case of the Ford Focus, new products are developed with an eye toward the global market. This is particularly true for many companies characterized as "born global," whose products often involve computer software, peripherals, and other high-technology products.

Born Globals[21]

Based on research among newly formed high technology start-ups, the term *born global* was first coined by a McKinsey report.[22] **Born global** firms are firms that from the outset view the world as one market. They are typically small technology-based businesses, and their FSAs lie in new innovations and technological breakthroughs which are naturally standardized products. The threat of competitive imitation and alternative technologies mean that rapid internationalization is necessary to capture the first-mover advantages in world markets.

Born global firms may start as exporters, selling to customers identified and reached through alliances and network relationships. Their FSAs involve technical eminence, with substantial added value and differentiated designs. Because of limited organizational and managerial resources, the born global firms tend to rely on e-mail, the Internet, and electronic data interchange (EDI) to reach their customers in different countries. The advanced communications allow the company low-cost exchange with partners and customers. In addition, substantial market data availability on the Internet, previously unavailable to smaller firms, facilitates their overseas penetration. [23]

The typical characteristics of a born global firm are several.[24]

- Born global firms tend to market value-added offerings—innovative differentiations at the cutting edge of technology—rather than completely new products.
- The change-agent is a strong leader, often founder, who drives the internationalization.
- The risk of going international is discounted because the leader perceives an internationalization premium.
- The product or service market is global.
- The born global builds an effective network that allows both low-cost reach and energized collaborators.
- The home country market is typically small relative to the global market.

Some observers argue that advances in global communication have made traditional internationalization patterns simply history. Still, even born global firms tend to employ a waterfall expansion strategy, to prevent overtaxing their limited resources.[25] There are reasons to suspect that in the future many small companies will see the world as their market from the beginning, using the Internet to research foreign markets, identifying distributors and potential partners on the World Wide Web, and rapidly creating alliances and relationships through e-mail, Facebook, and LinkedIn.

Starting with the global market in mind is natural for new products from companies whose home market is small and the great opportunities really lie abroad. Taiwan's Acer laptops are designed with the global market in mind. So are Switzerland's Swatch. But today also more and more products are designed for global appeal with the requirements of customers in multiple countries considered in the development. The list includes not only hardware products such as automobiles, home appliances, consumer electronics, and phones, but also movies, music, and apparel. Design decisions about these products are no longer made with one local market in mind but with eyes firmly focused on the global marketplace.

Product Development Stages

How are global products and services developed? Almost all new products, whether aimed for the home or global market, are developed along a well-known new product development path. The process can be divided into five sequential stages: idea generation, preliminary screening, concept research, sales forecast, and test marketing (see Exhibit 9.5). Most new product texts will discuss these stages in detail.[26] Here we will focus on the way the global perspective changes what companies do.

1. Idea Generation.
"Ideas are cheap?" Yes and no. In some ways ideas come easily. There are several sources for new global product or service ideas.

The most common source of new product ideas, especially for global products, is new technology. As we have seen, in technology-based products the market is usually inherently global, since the technological solution can often be applied everywhere. Satellite guiding systems for automobiles are a typical new product where technology has made it feasible to beam orientation maps to the driver's monitor. Smartphones, tablets, and personal computers are all technology-driven products sharing globalizing characteristics.

But not all new ideas are winners. Four-channel stereo (quadraphonic sound), a "sure" winner, failed. Ski-sailing, adapting wind-surfing to snow, failed. Soccer is still in the embryonic stage in the United States. And so on. A common assumption is that it takes 64 new product ideas to generate one successful new product (Exhibit 9.5 shows the fast drop-off at the idea stage). The figures vary but an 80 percent failure rate is a commonly accepted number[27] (see Exhibit 9.5).

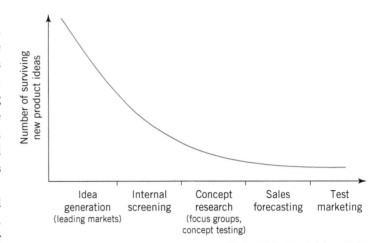

EXHIBIT 9.5.
New product development stages

To reduce the chances of failure, most R&D undertaken for new products in multinational companies is still focused not so much on completely new products as on modifications and upgrading of existing products. In a personal interview, a Sony executive estimated that even an innovative company like Sony spends over 80 percent of its new product activity focused on improving and upgrading existing products.

2. Internal Screening

Once a promising idea has been identified, companies tend to assign the responsibility for new product development to *cross-functional and cross-country teams.*

At this stage the factors requiring localization of a global product are usually uncovered. For example, the size of parking spaces, the narrowness of streets, and the gasoline prices affect what size car is acceptable. Voltage levels, fire regulations, and circuit overloads affect what changes may be necessary in electrical products. Language, operating systems, and functions used affect what PC software applications may or may not be acceptable. When it comes to removing obstacles to convenient and proper local use, the local members of the development team will be particularly useful.

3. Concept Research

The next step is to collect data on the acceptability of the concept in the various markets. These data can come from standard marketing research tools, including focus groups and surveys, and from trade-off analysis of alternative design features.

Combining focus groups with more formal survey questions is also possible. Available cloud-based research services such as Survey Monkey, Qualtrics, and Amazon's Mechanical Turk can quickly and inexpensively get customer reactions to proposed designs. Comparing responses across countries makes it possible to determine which features can be similar and where there may be need for adaptation.

Concept testing is notoriously difficult. One reason is that consumers tend to be wary of complete new ideas. For dramatically new products, firms often have to take a risk, betting that the product will succeed even though consumers are doubtful. One example is the iPad, a great success that introduced a whole new category of products. According to Jobs, no market research was done for the iPad because, he said, "It's not the consumers' job to know what they want."[28] Jobs seems to have had an unusual knack in deciphering consumer behavior around the world (see Exhibit 9.6).

An alternative (and complementary) approach short-cuts the concept research process and speeds it up. It is called **target research**. By analyzing the leading brands and their attributes, firms are able to understand what appeals to consumers. Targeting one of the brands, that brand's customers can be questioned directly for possible improvements. By reverse engineering the brand and producing a new version incorporating the existing leader's strengths minus the weaknesses—a so-called me-too-plus product—Asian companies have been able to capture large market shares abroad. Examples include Toyota's Lexus, Camry, and Corolla, Samsung's cell phones, and Hyundai's Sonata. Catching on, the Chinese company BYD has created a "me-too" version of a Toyota Corolla and is selling a similar car under the BYD F3 marque.[29]

4. Sales Forecast

After the market research is done a more precise forecast can be produced.

In mature markets unit sales can conveniently be broken up into two multiplicative components, product category sales and market share.

Emerging and developing markets are likely to exhibit the typical product life cycle characteristics of an introductory period followed by a growth period. In these cases, sales forecasting is best focused on leading users and markets in analogous countries (for more technical detail, see the chapter on Local Market Research).

5. Test Marketing

Once the sales forecast looks promising, the new product is usually test marketed. Many companies find it useful to simply let customers use the product and offer feedback. It is done routinely by consumer goods companies going into emerging and developing markets, as it helps them understand the localization requirements. For example, when German electric irons were first introduced in Asia, their cords were too short. In Europe there are usually several electric outlets in the wall, while in Asia at that time electric outlets connected to the one bulb in the ceiling.

EXHIBIT 9.6.
Two ophthalmologists checking test results. Steve Jobs might have been able to imagine all kinds of uses for the iPad before it was introduced, but it is hard to believe that he could have foreseen the way the tablets have revolutionized the way doctors are able to access all patient data on the spot as they make their rounds.

Copyright © by Shutterstock/Lorena Fernandez.

GLOBAL BRANDING

Brands are legally protected trademarks that identify the product maker or service provider. A brand assigns responsibility for product (or service) performance to a particular manufacturer or distributor. The name, together with its logo, has to be registered in each country where the products are sold. If not, the trademark cannot be protected from copying and infringements.[30]

Brands matter a lot for consumer perceptions even those who deny their importance. For example, you see a great car on the street. How do you rate it without knowing the make? Many cannot decide until they know. Research shows it is the same for drinks if you cannot see the bottle. Loyal Coke drinkers served Coca-Cola from a Pepsi can "hate the taste."

With open markets and intense competitive rivalry, most consumers also come to assume that any product will work fine. This means the only major difference is the brand. In emerging markets this is also increasingly the case. According to most observers, Asian markets in particular tend to be brand-conscious, but brands matter everywhere today. It also means that strong brands can demand a price premium.

We will start by discussing the pros and cons of global brands for consumers and companies. We then will show how brand valuation is done, which helps show why "going global" is such an attractive brand proposition. The management of a brand portfolio and the way brand names are changed following acquisitions is discussed. We end with the defense of local brands and how they often start their own global expansion.

PROS AND CONS OF GLOBAL BRANDS

As usual, for companies the pros of global brands involve scale economies and lower costs. But there is also some evidence that global brands are more attractive to consumers.

Consumers and Global Brands

For many consumers around the world, the lure of global brands is hard to deny. Especially in emerging markets, the sense of being part of the greater world after years of poverty and isolation is clearly exhilarating. Later on, as economic growth advances consumer aspirations, appeals like "exclusivity" may become more attractive than "belonging." But in the meanwhile, even luxury brands now expand into countries like China to satisfy a wide and growing clientele. And for companies in emerging markets the dream of establishing their own global brand is evident among companies from Turkey to India to Brazil.

According to research, consumers tend to judge global brands differently from local brands.[31]

Three kinds of favorable reactions stand out:

- *Quality.* The most common perception is an assumption of quality, global brands seen as providing higher quality than local brands. If the brand is well-known around the world, the product quality cannot be bad.
- *Aspirational.* Second, global brands tend to be brands that consumers aspire to. Especially in emerging countries, a global brand is one that people have been waiting for, for example.
- *Cosmopolitan.* Third, even in advanced countries, global brands naturally elicit a sense of belonging to the larger cosmopolitan world, a sense of global identity.

Strikingly, the research shows that these perceptions are quite similar among consumers in a diverse set of countries, including Brazil, China, Egypt, France, Japan, and the United States (although the importance of global identity is weaker in the United States than in the other countries).

There are consumer negatives to global brands as well. In the past the negatives tended to be less than the positives, but recently the tide shows signs of changing.

- *Local loyalties.* Local brands tend to have greater allegiance than global brands, at least in advanced markets. Gradually, the same phenomenon is appearing also in emerging markets, for example in China and Russia, as the economy grows and local brands offer high quality products.
- *Anti-globalization.* Another problem for global brands has been that they are the natural targets for anti-globalization actions. For example, Naomi Klein's "No Logo" primer for activists that effectiveness of any anti-globalization demonstration requires a prominent global target.[32] If a smaller brand is attacked, the public's sympathy will easily be swayed in favor of the underdog. But anti-globalization is today a broader political sentiment, less of a concern among consumers.
- *Awareness.* The high brand awareness for a global product can have its drawbacks. Consumers demand more in terms of CSR and sustainability. Any negative incident will hurt more. Intel, the PC chipmaker, used a "piggybacking" approach to promote its name by inducing hardware manufacturers to indicate "Intel inside" on advertising materials. Consumer awareness, though, helped exacerbate the negative public relations damage when the company had problems with its Pentium chip.

Companies and Global Brands

There are several cost and revenue issues for companies using global brands. The three major *positive* factors are:

- *Scale economies.* A main reason favoring a global brand is the chance to capture **economies of scale**, which provides lower costs per unit as fixed costs are spread out over more units of output. The standardization of logo, packaging, and production lowers manufacturing costs. As for promotional expenses, the cost for producing a global TV commercial can easily run into more than U.S. $1 million, much higher than a local campaign. Celebrity spokespersons with global reach are expensive but can be used everywhere, lowering unit costs—Beyoncé was allegedly paid $50 million for a long-term contract with Pepsi.[33] When used for campaigns all over the world, the production costs can be spread over a much larger volume, making global TV commercials very cost-effective. The same goes for the volume discounts in global media and global distribution.
- *Global customers.* A second way that benefits are gained is through global customers. In business-to-business markets, where the consumers might be large multinational firms, global customers are common. But this is also the case in consumer goods markets. As people travel internationally for business or pleasure, airport shops become important distribution outlets for product categories such as cosmetics, cameras, and fashion goods. These global customers are naturally more attracted to global brands with wide reach that they can find in many places.
- *Demand spillover.* **Demand spillover** occurs when sales in one country market generates demand in another country and is a third factor favoring the global brand. Media coverage spills over into new country markets, and the brand name becomes well-known and easily recognized. What people in one country buy is what other people want; they know about it through news reports, television coverage, and magazines. To capitalize on spillovers the brand name needs to be the same everywhere, so a global brand has a clear advantage

over local brands. A global brand name also makes a difference on the Internet, since research shows that well-known brands attract more hits.

The two main *negative* factors for global brand management are the following:

- *Local motivation.* Global branding necessarily imposes constraints on the brand management at the local level. This easily leads to a lack of motivation at the local level. Most companies allow local managers to manage some local brands in addition to the global brand.
- *Brand mis-fit.* The brand could be a **mis-fit**, because the name, slogan, or mantra may not fit the local market. Changing a name is serious business—more on this below. The slogan and mantra can usually be simplified making an acceptable version easier. Coca-Cola's "Always" is one solution.

GLOBAL BRAND VALUE

A company's global brands are major assets, worth billions to their firms. Exhibit 9.7 shows what one study found to be the world's most valuable brands in the most recent ranking. The amount of imputed dollar values are remarkably high—below we will discuss in some detail how the values are figured.

Other surveys tally roughly the same set of brands, although the ranking varies by country, region and over time. In the ranking a decade earlier, neither Apple nor Google or Samsung scored very highly. But as can be seen, all of the brands belong to companies that market globally standardized products. Global brands are worth a lot, partly because of their customers' allegiance and partly by sheer size of reach across countries.

How does one know how much a brand is worth? The answer in principle requires an assessment of how much the company would make without the brand. This is akin to asking how much a generic brand would make—for example, how much could L'Oréal charge if it just offered an unmarked face cream? The answer can be derived in two steps. First, for the product category, how important is the brand relative to other factors? Second, how strong is the brand relative to other brands? Thus, for, say, cosmetics, how important is the brand itself in the choice of cosmetics? Then, how strong is, say, L'Oréal, relative to competition? Those two factors together are assumed to explain how much the brand is worth.[34]

Brand Equity and Brand Value

For global marketers it is useful to distinguish between brand equity and brand value. **Brand equity** is the level of allegiance that customers have for the brand. A brand with high equity will generally have a deep relationship with its customers, with favorable attitudes and high brand loyalty. The many dedicated Coca-Cola drinkers and loyal Apple fans mean that both brands have high brand equity. The many books on branding tend to focus on how managers can build brand equity, moving customers from brand awareness and familiarity to liking and preference and ultimately to "bonding" and even "love" of a brand.

The equity for a given brand will typically vary across markets. The allegiance to a brand will usually be stronger in its home market than abroad. Lenovo, the Chinese PC maker, is strong in China, less so in the United States and Europe. Acer, the Taiwanese PC brand, is stronger in Europe than in the United States. Even inside countries there are differences. The Corona beer brand has higher equity in the American South and West than in the Northeast.

EXHIBIT 9.7.

The world's most valuable brands (2016). Becoming a valuable brand for customers is not simply a matter of annual revenue or advertising dollars spent.

Rank	Name	Brand Value	Annual Revenue	Advertising	Industry
1.	Apple	$170 B	$214.2 B	$1.8 B	Technology
2.	Google	$101.8 B	$80.5 B	$3.9 B	Technology
3.	Microsoft	$87 B	$85.3 B	$1.6 B	Technology
4.	Facebook	$73.5 B	$25.6 B	$310 M	Technology
5.	Coca-Cola	$56.4 B	$23 B	$4 B	Beverages
6.	Amazon	$54.1 B	$133 B	$5 B	Technology
7.	Disney	$43.9 B	$30.7 B	$2.9 B	Leisure
8.	Toyota	$41.1 B	$168.8 B	$4.3 B	Automotive
9.	McDonald's	$40.3 B	$85 B	$646 M	Restaurants
10.	Samsung	$38.2 B	$166.7 B	$3.7 B	Technology

Source: Interbrand.

For a brand manager aiming to raise brand equity, one major decision is whether it is better to focus on building increased loyalty in an already strong market segment or to reach out to improve equity in another market. Going international is one way to raise a brand's visibility and gain more customers.

By contrast, brand value is the dollar worth of a brand (as in Exhibit 9.7). **Brand value** has more to do with how many customers are reached by the brand. The more customers a brand attracts, the higher the value. In general terms, brand value can be viewed as a product of the level of allegiance (i.e., brand equity) to the brand from its customers, multiplied by the number of customers.

The increased brand value is one reason why entering foreign markets is so attractive to companies. Expanding the reach of the brand across markets is a good way to leverage the equity and increase the value of a strong brand.

But it is not clear that the new customers will have the same level of affinity to the brand, so a large brand cannot necessarily count on high loyalty. Also, paying more attention to foreign expansion can make current loyal customers lose faith. When Lenovo tried to expand overseas, its Chinese competitors Founder, Hasee, and Haier took the chance to improve product and prices for the Chinese home market, forcing Lenovo to retreat back to home. Most companies try to strike a balance between nursing customers at home with high loyalty and reaching out to leverage the strength of a brand overseas.

Brand Value and M&A

The development of the brand value formula was spurred by the need to assess company value in acquisitions, mergers, and takeovers. For example, in 2008 the Indian Tata Group paid $2.3 billion for Jaguar and Land Rover, a price tag that analysts claimed was too high. But by March 2012 Jaguar Land Rover posted a 27 percent jump in retail sales and became the primary driver of growth and profit for Tata Motors (see case IV.8 "Tata buys Jaguar Land Rover" in this text).

In 2010, Google offered to purchase Groupon for $6 billion but was rebuffed. Since then Groupon has begun to struggle with competitors such as Living Social. In 2016 Alibaba bought part of Groupon and in 2017 Groupon finished the acquisition of Living Social, its largest competitor. Still, Groupon's market value dropped to about $2.25 billion in early 2017.[35]

Extending the Brand

A **brand extension** involves applying the same brand in new product categories. This is a common strategy to leverage a strong brand. The Montblanc example earlier in this chapter is a good illustration. But it can be a risky strategy that sometimes fails when the new product category is too different. Coca-Cola's efforts in jeans and other apparel have not been very successful, and neither was Nike's excursion into leisure shoes.

Expansion into new markets is often the simpler and safer alternative, especially when media spillovers have created a latent demand for the brand. Leveraging the brand by introducing the products in new markets under the same name becomes the natural solution to growing brand value.

Of course, when a brand goes international, it does not always manage to maintain the same level of allegiance. A new market may need some time before customers have broken their loyalty with existing local brands and developed a new bond. In the meantime, the brand equity is lower than at home. Also, when a brand ventures abroad, management attention and advertising spending is diverted and some customers at home may feel ignored, resulting in lower equity at home.

However, focusing on just a few customers at home can be too limiting. These customers may not buy very much and not very frequently. This is why even a company like Harley Davidson, with perhaps the most loyal customers of any business, is expanding into new segments (women, young adults between 18 and 34, African Americans, and Hispanics) and international markets.[36]

The trade-off between geographical reach and the depth of brand equity is shown in Exhibit 9.8.

Domestic brands often possess high brand loyalty among its customers, but the few customers might not be sufficient to sustain the business. On the other hand, expansion around the globe can help sell a lot of product but at discount prices, unless the brand is strong. The optimal middle ground combines geographical expansion with protection of existing loyal customer allegiance, a balancing act that strong global brands successfully navigate.

THE INTERNATIONAL BRAND PORTFOLIO

Many multinational companies have more local brands than global brands. Especially among packaged goods companies with a history of growth through mergers and acquisitions, companies are likely to have a few global brands and several local brands. The combination of their global brands and local brands is called a **brand portfolio**.

The brands in the portfolio are typically divided into a **brand hierarchy** with the largest international brands at the top and smaller local brands and sub-brands below.[37] This is the typical branding scheme of companies such as Nestlé and Sara Lee. SAB-Miller, the beer giant from South Africa, follows a similar model. Four of its brands have been designated "Global" brands: Grolsch, Peroni, Pilsner Urquell, and Miller Genuine Draft. A second level is designated "Flagship" brands with 21 brands. The flagship brands include local favorites such as Blue Moon (U.S.), Castle Lager (South Africa), Haywards 5000 (India), Snow (China), Aguila (Colombia), and Gambrinus (Czech Republic). The support brands are the local brands, extending the product line in one or two countries. SAB-Miller was taken over by Anheuser-Busch InBev in 2016 and had to jettison the Miller Genuine Draft and Coors brands.

The portfolio can also be managed by giving each brand a strategic role, with several brands worldwide. One such case is shown Exhibit 9.9, which depicts the brand portfolio of L'Oréal, the French cosmetics multinational.

The different strategic roles of the brands are clearest in the primary Consumer Products division. While L'Oréal Paris represents the basic French identity and upscale positioning of L'Oréal, the company's strategic brands are targeted to more specific consumer segments. Garnier is such a strategic brand, offering value-based skin and hair products, with active natural ingredients. Garnier Fructis shampoo and Garnier Nutritionist for

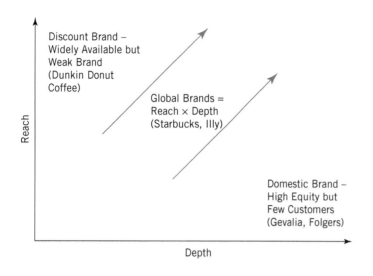

- Discount Brand – Widely Available but Weak Brand (Dunkin Donut Coffee)
- Global Brands = Reach × Depth (Starbucks, Illy)
- Domestic Brand – High Equity but Few Customers (Gevalia, Folgers)

Reach

Depth

skin care are the main sub-brands. Maybelline is another strategic brand, with cosmetics products targeting a younger segment. SoftSheen-Carson is a world leader in hair care products for people of African descent.[38]

For most companies only a few brands are truly global and available practically everywhere under the same name. The financial and monetary resources required for global brand management are too great. A study by ACNielsen found that among consumer packaged goods, there were only 43 truly global brands.[39] And consumer panel data from Young & Rubicam show that local brands account for somewhere around 75 percent of the top brands in most markets.[40]

GLOBAL BRAND NAMES

You may have heard already of some of the classic failures of foreign brand names. When McDonalds' began opening outlets in France, it translated its "Big Mac" hamburger as "Gros Mec." In French slang, it means "Big Pimp." The name is now "Le Big Mac." The Chevy Nova translates in Spanish to "No-go" and the name was dropped in some markets.

Checking the Name

To evaluate the potential of globalizing a strong brand name, it is useful to systematically go through a checklist of factors.

1. Does the brand name make sense outside of the source country? What does it mean? What associations are generated? Often a simple translation of the brand name will not be sufficient (see box, "What's in a Name? Plenty!").

L'Oreal Luxe (sold in department stores, cosmetics stores, own boutiques)	Lancome, Biotherm, Kiehl's, YSL Beauté, Diesel, Giorgio Armani et.al.
Consumer Products (sold in retail stores)	L'Oreal Paris, Garnier, Maybelline, Softsheen Carson, Createurs de Beaute.com, Essie
Professional Products (sold in salons)	L'Oreal Professionnel, Redken, Shu Uemura et al.
Active Cosmetics (sold in healthcare and drugstores)	Vichy, The Body Shop et.al.

2. If the name suggests a country association, is the effect positive? Haier from China, a leading company in home appliances, is not unaware of the fact that its name sounds vaguely German. In fact, it is intentional. "Haier" comes from the last two syllables of the Chinese pronunciation of Liebherr (in China "Li-bo-hai-er"). The German company Liebherr was the first European partner to Qingdao Refrigerator, Haier's original Chinese name.

3. Is the name available legally in the country? Philips, the Dutch electronics giant, has been hampered continuously in the North American market because the Phillips oil company was the first to register its similar brand name there. The Dutch company uses Norelco instead in North America.

BOX: What's In A Name? Plenty![41]

Even though global brand managers would like to use the same brand name everywhere, there are numerous examples where this has failed because of difficulty of pronunciation, unfortunate associations, or ambiguous meaning—or simply because the name had already been taken. Mr. Clean is Mr. Propre in France, Toyo Kogyo became Mazda in the West (and then changed to the same name in Japan), and Philips became Norelco in the United States. But when the brand is introduced in a country such as China where the written characters are entirely different, the problems escalate dramatically.

A language such as English has a phonographic writing system, where the alphabet and the words represent the sound of the spoken language. By contrast, the Chinese writing system is logographic, with words and concepts represented by icons, or *kanji* characters, which were originally derived as pictures of the things described. There is no necessary link between the sound of the word and the *kanji* used to write it. To some extent the Chinese *kanji* ideographs are in fact also well-known to Koreans and Japanese, with the same meaning but with often completely different pronunciations.

This means that a Western brand introduced into China might be "translated" in two different ways. The translation can be by sound or by meaning. To get the sound right, the chosen *kanji* might well be meaningless or worse. Coca-Cola's first effort has become famous: the characters chosen as correct-sounding said in fact, "Bite the wax tadpole," whatever that means. Shifting to a more meaningful set of characters, the Coca-Cola brand emerged as, "Tastes good and makes you happy," a much preferred suggestion. On the other hand, the pronunciation is slightly off, with a suggestive Hawaiian flavor, "Ko-kou-ko-le."

The Electrolux brand of home appliances is used in China, but the company has also introduced new names for products designed specifically for China. An award-winning refrigerator OuYu (欧宇, roughly "Western style" or "Western space") targets the middleclass, while another more sophisticated model is simply named "Willow" with no translation, more foreign and cosmopolitan.

Since brands become symbols of people's lifestyles, it is important to match the name to what the consumers aspire to.

Changeover Tactics

When a global brand name is preferable and acceptable, some local brands may have to be changed. Companies use two alternative strategies to change names.

Fade-in/Fade-out. The **fade-in/fade-out** option usually consists of a period with dual branding, where the new brand name is featured together with the old name. It is common to support the brand with public announcements and advertising, showing both names together. After some time, usually some months, the old name may get a smaller font, with the new name featured more prominently. Finally, the old name disappears.

When China's Lenovo bought IBM's PC business in 2004, they also acquired the ThinkPad sub-brand. For a period of four years, the company was allowed to also keep the IBM name. The advertising for the "new" ThinkPad featured both the Lenovo and the IBM name for a while, but even before the four-year "grace period" was up, Lenovo dropped the IBM name.[42] Lenovo, using its own name, is now the leader in worldwide PC market share at 19.4 percent in 2015 and over 26 percent in Asia Pacific.[43] In this case, Lenovo correctly recognized the fading relevance of the IBM name in PC sales.

Summary axing. In **summary axing** the old brand is simply replaced on the market by the new brand. After the Berlin Wall fell in 1989, Mars, the family-owned confectionery multinational headquartered in the U.S., decided to take Snickers into Eastern Europe. While Snickers had been their leading brand in the Americas and Asia, Europe had kept the old name Marathon for basically the same candy bar.

Once Eastern Europe opened up, the company saw the need to use the one name for global advertising— Snickers had long been associated with team sports events. Since the purchase of a candy bar usually does not involve a very long consideration phase, the company decided that simply changing the brand would be sufficient. Bolstered by a strong advertising and event promotional push, the 1990 brand changeover was quite successful, and Snickers is now a leading confectionery brand worldwide. However, in 2008 Mars reintroduced Marathon in Britain, riding a nostalgic "retro" wave.[44] Global marketers cannot stand still.

STRENGTH OF LOCAL BRANDS

As the experiences of many travelers attest, in open markets many local brands survive and prosper next to global brands. In audio products, shoes, apparel, and other consumer goods, local brands coexist with well-known world brands. In business-to-business markets local vendors do well with custom software and supplies. Local beers are successful throughout North America and Europe, even though in some cases their market is directly targeted by global competitors (see box, "This Bud Is Not for You!").

The typical reason for the success of local products is the familiarity and loyalty involved. They are also better at local customization. In industrial goods markets, personal attention, fast delivery, and prompt after-sales service are all factors tending to favor local products.

In consumer goods, global companies often buy up local competitors and leave their local names intact. Some even develop global products but use local brand names to avoid any negative sentiment against foreign brands. Thus, while global brands may capture a large segment of the market, local names are used for a standardized product (see Exhibit 9.10).

Today, with local brands growing stronger, the most significant story for the future of local brands is perhaps that of Coca-Cola's fate in India (see box, "ThumsUp strikes back").

BOX: This Bud is Not For You![45]

Even before being acquired by InBev 2008 to become AB InBev, St. Louis-based beer maker Anheuser-Busch had long tried to market its leading Budweiser brand globally. But the rights to the Budweiser name in Europe belong to a much smaller beer-maker, Budejovicky Budvar, the Czech brewer of Budweiser. The word Budejovicky is the equivalent of Budweiser, or German for "from Budweis" in the Czech language. The Czech company has the leading market share at home and has a growing export business to other European countries as well.

After the fall of communism in 1989, when the Czechs started to privatize industry and sell off government-owned businesses, Anheuser-Busch figured it had another chance and decided to try again to buy the little beer-maker and the trademark.

But the Czech managers and workers in the still state-owned company were not about to be bought up by the American giant. They did not want any part of a company that they suspected would only pull the plug on their operation, siphon the profits away, and try to take their beer off the market. And they did not like the idea of replacing their own great beer with the lightweight watery-tasting beer of the American namesake.

To soften up the folks, Anheuser-Busch opened up a $1 million cultural center in Ceske Budejovice, the town where the brewer is located, inaugurated baseball and basketball teams, opened a marble-floored cafe, and offered scholarships and English lessons. But to no avail. In 2001 the fight was joined in the courts and prolonged litigation followed.

By 2014, in much of Europe Budejovicky Budvar still has the rights to the name Budweiser, forcing Anheuser-Busch InBev to use the name Bud.[46] The reverse is true in much of the rest of the world. In the United States and Canada the Czech beer is sold as Czechvar. Trademark disputes need to be resolved country-by-country. As a result there have been hundreds of legal cases in the last decade. The companies don't want to give up their rights in any country that may be the next big market.

Even cases that appear resolved may reopen again. A court decision in the United Kingdom in 2013 resolved that both companies had the rights to the name on the grounds that consumers can tell the difference. To consumers this seems a reasonable compromise, and the brands can coexist. But the companies themselves do not agree. In 2013 Budvar tried to gain control of the Bud name, but was rebuffed by the European Union court.[47]

AB InBev has not yet tried to buy Budejovicky Budvar, but odds are that it will one day. As to that, said Frantisek Nedorost, a 52-year-old electrician: "I absolutely disagree with the Americans buying part of our company. I like Americans, their culture, their films. But I know American beer doesn't reach the quality of Czech beer. It's much poorer, much weaker."

Local Brands Go Global

As the leading local brands gain confidence and resources, they also start exploring options abroad, starting with neighboring countries. Local brands can suffer from their lack of scale economies but in the large BRIC economies, for instance, the "local" population is large enough to provide scale economies. This is why Haier's small refrigerators from China can now be found in many countries around the world. India's Tata is doing well with the Jaguar marquee, and in China Lenovo's 2004 takeover of IBMs ThinkPad at a price of $1.75 billion seems to have been a good bet. Beko appliances are already in more than 100 countries outside of its Turkey home under its own name. Natura, the cosmetics maker from Brazil, is now making a push for foreign markets as well. If you have not heard of Huawei phones from China or Bisleri water from India or Efes beer from Turkey, chances are you soon will.

Global branding is no longer for the well-established multinationals in advanced countries, not even in the luxury category. Toyota's Lexus luxury marque shows what can be done against old stereotypes. And the Indian tractor maker Mahindra is making significant inroads in the North-American market, defying country-of-origin and farmer stereotyping.

SUMMARY

This chapter has discussed the emergence of standardized global products. It emphasized the distinction between localization to a country's infrastructure and adaptation to customer preferences. Localization is always necessary, but adaptation to customer preferences is more a matter of managerial judgment. The key is whether a product feature is important, and preferences vary across countries. If both conditions are fulfilled, there is no avoiding adaptation.

The chapter also examined the new product development process as it applies to global products. It showed how global products are today developed with an eye toward standardization across markets.

BOX: ThumsUp Strikes Back[49]

Family-owned ThumsUp was a leading soft-drink brand in India when market barriers came down in 1990. Pepsi Cola entered quickly, and Pepsi and ThumsUp fought for leadership. In 1993 Coca-Cola entered and managed to buy ThumsUp for a relatively low amount of $60 million. ThumsUp had fought Pepsi to a standstill and the two shared the lead in a large and growing cola market.

Coke's strategic intent was to gradually eliminate ThumsUp and replace the brand with Coca-Cola. But despite reduced marketing expenditures, ThumsUp still claimed considerable loyalty among consumers, especially young men who were attracted to its macho image. In the end Coca-Cola was forced to reinstate marketing expenditures for ThumsUp and has repositioned its own brand further toward the very young market segments. Coca-Cola's ThumsUp brand is now the cola leader in the Indian market with a 15 percent share of the soft-drink market (42 percent share of the cola market) and is targeted at the older "young and restless."[50]

The Coca-Cola website says "ThumsUp is known for its strong, fizzy taste and its confident, mature and uniquely masculine attitude. This brand clearly seeks to separate the men from the boys." Coca-Cola Classic is also sold and the ingredients listed are nearly identical with the exception that ThumsUp lists sugar as its sweetener while Coke uses high-fructose corn syrup. [51]

Coca-Cola Classic's market share is 8.7 percent and India is one of the few markets where Coke Classic lags behind Pepsi in sales. The company wants to get new consumers to sample the Coke Classic brand in rural areas and in 2015 started "Happiness on the Go" vans, which will serve the Classic brand at Rs 5 (8 cents U.S.) per serving price point.

The chapter also dealt with the management of the firm's brand portfolio, including the building and management of local and global brands. The global marketing successes almost always involve global branding, with superior reach leveraging brand equity and brand value. Managing the global brand portfolio is a demanding task because a balance has to be struck between a few powerful global brands and many local brands that help the localization to local markets.

Today such localization is mandatory as the attractiveness of competitive domestic brands is increasing in many markets. Many domestic brands have responded competitively to the incoming foreign brands, and in the process become potentially global brands in their own right. The dynamics of open markets and free competition have led many countries to economic growth and also the entrepreneurial development of their own global companies.

KEY TERMS

adaptation	global products
born global	imitative
brand	innovative
brand equity	localization
brand extensions	local brands
brand mis-fit	local products
brand hierarchy	mass customization
brand portfolio	modular design
brand value	regional products
concept testing	economies of scale
global brand management	scope economies
global brand	target research
adoption rate	test marketing
new product diffusion	

DISCUSSION QUESTIONS

1. Analyze the extent to which a particular multinational (such as Benetton, Procter & Gamble, or Nokia) offers the same product line in different countries by comparing the company web site entries for different countries.
2. Today many start-up companies are "born globals." What are the factors that help a startup to go global from the beginning? What factors make it difficult?
3. Why do you think brands are so important today? Are you or your peers influenced by brand names? For which products? Why, why not?
4. Give an example of a local brand or product that you are aware of. Check first to make sure that it has in fact not gone abroad (yet). Then explain why (or why not) this product or brand should stay local.
5. Analyze the reasons why some local products (such as local beers) might have an enhanced potential when standardized global brands enter the market.

TEAM CHALLENGE PROJECTS

1. While 99 percent of homes in the U.S. and Europe have a refrigerator and 90% in China, only 29% of homes in India have one. Appliances have different significances in different cultures. For example, in China the refrigerator is located in the living room rather than the kitchen. When some rural Indian villagers get their first refrigerator, they hold a religious ceremony dabbing vermillion on the appliance to ward off evil spirits. Team 1: Redesign the typical American refrigerator to be more attractive to Indian consumers to increase market share. Team 2: Develop the argument that the Indian market is not a good country choice for the sale of refrigerators no matter how the product is redesigned.

2. Recently, BRICS companies have been aggressively moving into premium-product markets. For example, both Jaguar and Land Rover are now owned by Indian companies, and Chinese companies have purchased luxury British yacht maker Sunseeker (the James Bond boat) and the French winery Rolland Mallet. While premium luxury watches with names such as Rolex, Piaget, Cartier, and Grubel Forsey have a Swiss or Italian or French brand name and country of origin, Chinese companies are examining this market for expansion but wish to build their own brand. Team 1: Develop the 4Ps necessary to build a Chinese brand for a line of premium watches. Team 2: Argue that a premium watch "Made in China" is a non-starter with no chance of success. Explain your reasoning.

3. Visit the website of Interbrand (http://www.bestglobalbrands.com) to view the 100 most valuable brands in the world for 2016. The top 10 are shown in the chart to the right:

Rank 2016	Company	Country	Brand Value $B
#1	Apple	USA	$170 B
#2	Google	USA	$101.8 B
#3	Microsoft	USA	$87 B
#4	Facebook	USA	$73.5 B
#5	Coca-Cola	USA	$56.4 B
#6	Amazon	USA	$54.1 B
#7	Disney	USA	$43.9 B
#8	Toyota	Japan	$41.1 B
#9	McDonald's	USA	$40.3 B
#10	Samsung	S. Korea	$38.2 B

Source: Best Brands (2014).

Team 1 and Team 2: Roll the clock forward to the year 2026. Develop the list of the top 20 brands that you expect in that year. How many brands will be from the BRICS countries? Explain why.

SELECTED REFERENCES

ACNielsen. *Reaching the Billion-Dollar Mark: A Review of Today's Global Brands.* Chicago: ACNielsen Inc., 2001.

Adams, Ariel, "Montblanc: On How To Be A Luxury Brand For Many," *Forbes*, March 14, 2013.

Berger, Peter L. and Samuel P. Huntington, *Many Globalizations.* New York: Oxford University Press, 2003.

Bodoni, Stephanie, "AB InBev Wins Court Fight Over Bud EU Trademark for Beer," *Bloomberg News*, Jan. 22, 2013.

Buzzell, Robert D. "Can You Standardize Multinational Marketing?" *Harvard Business Review*, November-December 1968, pp. 102–13.

Casserly, Meghan, "Beyoncé's $50 million Pepsi Deal Takes a Cue from Jay Z," *Forbes*, Dec 12, 2012.

Cavusgil, S. Tamer and Gary Knight, "The born global firm: An entrepreneurial and capabilities perspective on early and rapid internationalization," *Journal of International Business Studies*, Vol. 46, No. 1, Jan 2015, pp. 3–16.

Chabowski, Brian R., Saeed Samiee and G. Tomas M. Hult, "A bibliometric analysis of the global branding literature and a research agenda," *Journal of International Business Studies*, Vol. 44, No. Aug 2013, pp. 622–634.

Chailan, Claude, "Brand portfolios and competitive advantage: an empirical study," *Journal of Product & Brand Management*, Vol. 17, No. 4, 2008, pp. 254–264.

Clark, Julie. "The outlook for the global sports market to 2013," *Pricewaterhouse Coopers'*, 2010.

Cooper, Robert G. *Winning at New Products*, 4th ed., New York, NY: Basic Books, 2011.

Cunningham, Benjamin, "Where a Budweiser Isn't Allowed to Be a Budweiser," *Time Magazine*, Jan. 27, 2014.

Dekimpe, Marnik G.; Philip M. Parker; and Miklos Sarvary. "Global Diffusion of Technological Innovations: A Coupled-Hazard Approach." *Journal of Marketing Research* 37, February 2000, pp. 47–59.

"Disneyland Paris condensed: fun facts and figures of the 2013 Annual Review," *DLP Today*, February 15, 2014.

Douglas, Susan P.; C. Samuel Craig; and Edwin J. Nijssen. "Integrating Branding Strategy across Markets: Building International Brand Architecture." *Journal of International Marketing* 9, no. 2 (2001), pp. 97–114.

El-Shenawi, Eman, "Egypt United? Well, at least the Ramadan advertisers think so," *Al Arabiya*, July 31, 2013.

Gillette, Felix, Diane Brady and Caroline Winter, "The Rise and Fall of BlackBerry: An Oral History," *Bloomberg Business*, December 05, 2013.

Hashai, Niron, "Sequencing the expansion of geographic scope and foreign operations by 'born global' firms," *Journal of International Business Studies*, Vol. 42, No. 8, Oct/Nov 2011, pp. 995–1015.

Holt, Douglas B, John A. Quelch, and Earl L. Taylor (2004), "How Global Brands Compete," *Harvard Business Review*, 82 (9), 68–81.

Hughes, Sam, "Thums Up for Indian Cola," *Serious Eats*, July 23, 2013.

"Japan tablet market sales—iPad Apple," *IDC Japan*, November 2014.

Johansson, Johny K. and Kurt A. Carlson, *Contemporary Brand Management*, Thousand Oaks, CA: Sage, 2015.

Jones, Chuck, "Apple's iPhone Continues To Lose Market Share Month To Month," *Forbes*, May 7, 2015.

Kell, John. "Under Armour Arrives on Global Stage," *The Wall Street Journal*, 2013.

Klein, Naomi. *No Logo*. London: Flamingo, 2000.

Knight, G. A., & Cavusgil, S. T. (2004). Innovation, organizational capabilities, and the born-global firm. *Journal of International Business Studies*, 35:124–141.

_____ & _____ (2005). A taxonomy of born global firms. *Management International Review*, 45: 15–35.

Kudina, Alina, George S. Yip and Harry Barkema, "Born Global," *Business Strategy Review*, London Business School, 2010.

Kurien, Ashok & Elsie Nanji, "Thums Up, the most successful campaign we created," *The Economic Times of India*, August 19, 2009.

"Lenovo Surges after Profit Beats Estimates on Smartphones," *Bloomberg Business*, February 2, 2015.

Levitt, Ted, 1983, "The Globalization of Markets," *Harvard Business Review*, May-June 1983, pp. 92–102.

Lindemann, Jan, "Brand Valuation." Chapter 2 (pp.27–45) in Clifton, Rita and John Simmons, *Brands and Branding*. New York: Bloomberg Press, 2004.

Linton, Ian, "What Is the Failure Rate of New Items Launched in the Grocery Industry?" *Houston Chronicle*, 2009.

Lohr, Steve, "Without Its Master of Design, Apple Will Face Many Challenges," *The New York Times*, Business, 2011, B1, August 11.

Macalister, Terry, "Bentley and Jaguar Land Rover enjoy global sales success," *The Guardian*, April 10, 2013.

McKinsey and Co., *Emerging Exporters: Australia's High Value-Added Manufacturing Exporters*. Melbourne: Australian Manufacturing Council, 1993.

Meehan, Sarah. "How Under Armour plans to grow its women's line into a $1B business," *Baltimore Business Journal*, 2013.

Mirabella, Lorraine, "Under Armour will sponsor Brazil's most decorated soccer club," *The Baltimore Sun*, 2015.

Myerberg, Paul, "Under Armour defends suits as U.S. speedskaters go cold," *USA Today*, February 17, 2014.

Ning, W.E., "Spy Shots: facelifted BYD F3 is testing in China," *Carnewschina.com*, Feb 27, 2015.

Perlez, Jane. "This Bud's Not for You, Anheuser." *New York Times*, June 30, 1995, pp. D1, D4.

Primack, Dan, "Let's stop laughing at Groupon," *Fortune*, Jan 26, 2015.

Quelch, John and Carin-Isabel Knoop, *Lenovo: Building a Global Brand*, Harvard Business School case no. 9-507-014, 2006.

Salvador, Fabrizio, Pablo Martin de Holan and Frank Piller, "Cracking the Code of Mass Customization," *MIT Sloan Management Review*, Vol. 50, No. 3, Spring 2009, pp. 71–80.

Schuiling, Isabelle and Jean-Noël Kapferer, "Executive Insights: Real Differences between Local and International Brands: Strategic Implications for International Marketers," *Journal of International Marketing*, 12 (4), 2004, 97–112.

Sharma, Samidha, "Coke eyes rural push to topple Pepsi in 1 year," *The Economic Times*, February 4, 2014.

Statler, Matt, and Johan Roos. "A Place to Play: Redefining Strategy Research." *Imagination Lab Working Paper* 2001–8, December 11, 2001.

Steenkamp, Jan-Benedict E.M., Rajeev Batra, and Dana L. Alden, "How Perceived Brand Globalness Creates Brand Value," *Journal of International Business Studies*, 34 (1), 2003, 53–65.

Stock, Kyle, "Under Armour Goes en Pointe in Its Bid for Women," *Bloomberg Business Press*, 2014.

Stremersch, Stefan and Gerard J. Tellis. "Understanding and managing international growth of new products," *International Journal of Research in Marketing*, Vol. 21, Issue 4, December 2004, pp. 421–48.

Sui, Sui and Matthias Baum, "Internationalization strategy, firm resources, and the survival of SMEs in the export market," *Journal of International Business Studies*, Vol. 45, No. 7, Sep 2014, pp. 821–841.

Townsend, Matt. "Under Armour Finds Feminine Side to Go Beyond $2 Billion," *Bloomberg Business Press*, 2015.

Under Armour website, "Region Selection," 2015. https://www.underarmour.com/en-us/change-region.

Yi, Jeannie J. and Shawn X. Ye, *The Haier Way*. Dumont, NJ: Homa & Sekey Books, 2003.

Yip, George S and G. Tomas M. Hult. *Total Global Strategy II*. Upper Saddle River, NJ: Prentice Hall, 2011.

Zhang, Shi and Bernd H. Schmitt. "Creating Local Brands in Multilingual International Markets," *Journal of Marketing Research* XXXVIII (August 2001), pp. 313–25.

ENDNOTES

1. See Kell, 2013.
2. Source: Under Armour financial statements.
3. From Clark, 2010.
4. See Myerberg, 2014.
5. Mirabella, 2015.
6. See Under Armour website, "Region Selection."
7. From its website: www.underarmour.com.
8. See Meehan, 2013.
9. From Stock, 2014.
10. According to Townsend, 2015.
11. Buzzell, 1968, was the first to clearly articulate the cost benefits of standardization, then elaborated by Yip and Hult, 2011.
12. The claim first made by Ted Levitt in his seminal 1983 article "The Globalization of Markets" (in the *Harvard Business Review*, May-June 1983).
13. See, for example, Yip and Hult, 2011.
14. See Berger and Huntington, 2003.
15. From El-Shenawi, 2013.
16. See Stremersch and Tellis, 2004.
17. See "Disneyland Paris condensed: fun facts and figures of the 2013 Annual Review," February 15, 2014.

18. See Salvador, de Holan and Piller, 2009.

19. See Chabowski, Samiee, and Hult, 2013.

20. Sources: Adams, 2013; www.worldlux.com.

21. Sources: Knight and Cavusgil, 2004 and 2005; Kudina, Yip, and Barkema, 2010, Sui and Baum, 2014.

22. See McKinsey, 2003.

23. See Kudina, Yip, and Barkema, 2010.

24. From Cavusgil and Knight, 2015.

25. See Hashai, 2011.

26. See, for example, Cooper, 2011.

27. See Linton, 2013.

28. From Lohr, 2011.

29. See Ning, 2015.

30. From Johansson and Carlson, 2015.

31. See, for example, Steenkamp, Batra, and Alden, 2003; Holt, Quelch, and Taylor, 2004.

32. See Klein, 2000.

33. See Casserly, 2012.

34. Lindemann, 2004, gives a good explanation of Interbrand's calculations.

35. See Primack, 2015.

36. According to its website, http://ar.harley-davidson.com/stories-Global.php.

37. See Douglas, Craig, and Nijssen, 2001.

38. Chailan, 2008, describes the strategic roles of the L'Oreal brands in depth.

39. See "ACNielsen ..." 2001.

40. See Schuiling and Kapferer, 2004.

41. Sources: Zhang and Schmitt, 2001; "Art, innovation and function inspires fridge range in China," *Electrolux Consumer Insight*, Nov. 11, 2011.

42. From Quelch and Knoop, 2006; from Yi and Ye, 2003

43. See "Lenovo Surges After Profit Beats Estimates on Smartphones," 2015.

44. "Farewell Snickers, now Marathon bars make a comeback," Daily Mail, May 12, 2008.

45. Sources: Perlez, 1995; Koenig; 1995; Bodoni, 2013; Cunningham, 2014.

46. See Bodoni, 2013.

47. See Cunningham, 2014.

48. Source: Unilever Company.

49. From Kurien and Nanji, 2009; Johansson and Carlson, 2015.

50. See Sharma, 2014.

51. See Hughes, 2013.

In this chapter you will learn about:

1. The wide variety among the businesses that are classified as services and how their importance has grown in international business
2. The reasons service exports and imports are so difficult to track and quantify
3. What determines the quality of a service and how companies go about transferring their services abroad
4. Why franchising has been so successful as the mode of entry for services

Global Services

CHAPTER 10

OPENING VIGNETTE

MEDICAL CARE AS AN INTERNATIONAL SERVICE BUSINESS

Since 2003, Massachusetts General Hospital has been sending its digitized X-ray and MRI files to India to be read by radiologists there. The Indian radiologist reviews the digitized file, prepares the report, and offers suggestions on treatment. More and more hospitals have begun outsourcing the reading of X-ray and other scans to teleradiology companies based in India and other countries and the market for these diagnostics services in India alone is over $1.8 billion.[1] There are three major reasons for this rapid growth. The first is lower costs: a board-certified radiologist in India earns about $60,000 annually versus the U.S. radiologist who earns $350,000 and there is a U.S. shortage. Secondly, there is an abundance of skilled IT and business process professionals in India who can set up and monitor the technology needed for the entire process. Thirdly, the time differences means that off-hours in the U.S. are business hours in India.[2]

Beyond just reading X-rays internationally, patients began in earnest in 1999 taking tours outside their home country to actually receive medical treatment (what has come to be known as "medical tourism"). This occurred when the U.S.-based Joint Commission, which accredits hospitals in the U.S., also began to accredit hospitals internationally. According to Patients Beyond Borders, "An international hospital must meet the same set of rigorous standards set forth in the U.S. by the Joint Commission. … More than 600 hospitals and clinical departments around the world have now been awarded U.S. Joint Commission accreditation and that number is growing by about 20 percent per year."[3] For example, as of 2017 there were 13 accredited hospitals in India, 18 in Thailand, and 24 in Turkey. Established agencies that accredit outpatient clinics, such as The Accreditation Association of Ambulatory

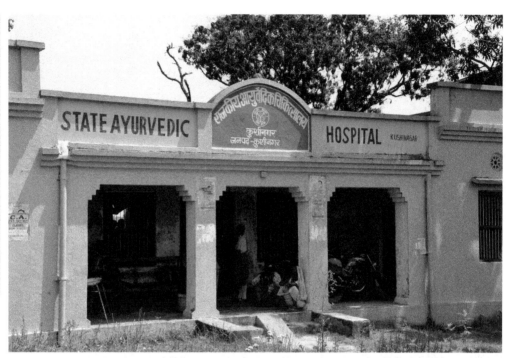

EXHIBIT 10.1.
State ayurvedic hospital in Kushinagar, India. Accreditation ensures adherence to international medical standards and solves the intangibility and heterogeneity problem typical with international services by ensuring a consistently high level of quality. This hospital is not accredited, although the traditional Indian ayurvedic medicine is getting increasingly popular as the yoga movement makes further inroads in the West.

Copyright © by 123RF/svglass.

EXHIBIT 10.2.
Where to travel for medical care[4]

Source: Healthy Travel Media.

	Medical Tourism Number of Patients (000)	Typical Percentage Cost Savings from U.S. Prices
Mexico	1000	40%–65%
India	250	65%–90%
Thailand	1000	50%–75%
Brazil	180	20%–30%
Singapore	500	25%–40%
Malaysia	650	65%–80%

Health Care (AAAHC) and The American Association for Accreditation of Ambulatory Surgery Facilities (AAASF), have launched international initiatives as well. This makes for internationally consistent high-quality care (see Exhibit 10.1).

It is estimated that about 14 million patients (1.6 million Americans) traveled internationally in 2016 to receive medical care. Developing countries have been aggressive in attempting to provide these services since an estimated $50 billion annually is being spent (see Exhibit 10.2).

There are five factors that could limit the appeal of services internationally: 1) restrictions and regulations, 2) logistics, 3) delivering quality customer service, 4) managing cultural differences, and 5) staffing and Personnel. With medical tourism, delivering quality customer service and managing the cultural issues are probably the most important and these developing countries have done well so far.

Global services have received increasing attention as the importance of services in virtually all economies has grown considerably over the last decade. Both the share of GNP attributable to service, and the employment share in the service sectors have increased significantly even in basically manufacturing countries such as China and South Korea. This in turn has meant that the international trade and foreign direct investment in services have grown, as firms turn to foreign markets for growth and new communications technology makes global service delivery possible. This chapter deals with the global marketing of services in different service industries.

The service industries comprise a wide variety of businesses, including hotels and other lodging places; establishments providing personal, business, repair, and amusement services; health, legal, engineering, and other professional services; educational institutions; finance, insurance, and real estate; wholesale and retail trade; and general government, transportation, communication, and public utilities.[5] Exhibit 10.3 gives a list of the many diverse businesses officially classified as service industries.

Although some of these services are not very significant globally, only few have no international involvement. Services are in fact traded internationally at an increasing rate. The international trade in services actually accounts for a significant share of foreign trade, especially in advanced countries, but also in a country such as India—see Exhibit 10.4. One task of this chapter is to explain how such trade is done.

- Accounting
- Advertising
- Banking
- Broadcasting
- Computer services
- Consulting
- Data processing
- Design & engineering
- Distribution
- Education
- Entertainment
- Healthcare
- Insurance
- Investment banking
- Leasing
- Legal Services
- Lodging
- Media
- Reservation systems
- Restaurants
- Tourism
- Telecommunications
- Transportation
- Utilies

EXHIBIT 10.3.
The diverse service industries

SERVICES IN INTERNATIONAL TRADE

When international trade is discussed the focus is typically on trade in physical goods. Services tend to confound such discussions. When one has in mind automobiles, wheat, or shoes, questions of tariff rates, transportation charges, and customs inspection come naturally. But how do these things apply when it comes to professional consulting services? Airline tickets? Sports and entertainment events? Are these exports, and if they are, how do countries record them?

It is possible, but not simple. Take a rock band such as the Rolling Stones, for example. Their World Tour in 2015 will take them to Argentina and Peru.[6] They are likely to make a fair amount of money there, for themselves and for the organizers. What is this, a service export? The answer is, yes, it is a service export from the UK to Argentina and Peru.

This also means the income (the band revenues minus the costs) will be taxed as UK income. The income is typically "self-reported," that is the band has to declare how much they made. But it might not be so clear what costs are and what the net income is. The band members probably "don't remember" everything. If the tax is high in the UK, the Rolling Stones may shift their "home base" out of England. In fact, in the early 1970s, the band

EXHIBIT 10.4.
When thinking about international trade it is important to include the large trade in services.

Source: https://data.oecd.org/trade/trade-in-goods.htm#indicator-chart.

	Services Exported 2016	Services Imported 2016	Goods Exported 2016
	Billion $$	Billion $$	Billions $$
Australia	52.9	56.1	192.5
Germany	332.2	201.3	1321.4
France	236.5	235.5	506.9
USA	752.4	504.7	1455.7
Brazil	33.3	63.7	184.4
Russia	50.6	74.4	281.8
India	161.8	96.1	268.6
China	208.4	452.6	1989.5
South Africa	14.3	14.9	75.1

Source : Organization for Economic Co-operation and Development Trade Statistics 2016 https://data.oecd.org/trade/trade-in-goods.htm#indicator-chart. International trade in services represents a significant share of overall foreign trade, especially in advanced countries.

moved its base to France to avoid taxes, and sheltered their earnings in a holding company in the Netherlands. So the UK "exports" disappeared.[7]

The band's performance also will be an import to Argentina and Peru. The import will be paid for by the ticket price, which thus will include a portion for tax, including possibly a sales tax (which is why the announced ticket price is usually lower than what you actually pay for the ticket). If it is considered a luxury, the tax will usually be higher. The organizers will pay the regular income tax on their net take. The import amount is the total import plus sales tax on the ticket.

If you find this complicated, you are not alone. Actually, given the prominence of the Rolling Stones and their many world tours, this is a relatively easy and well-rehearsed case. What happens when lawyers, doctors, and other professionals travel abroad? When tourists travel? When a patient gets medical care abroad? How the nations cope with the various implications for taxes and tariffs is not always clear.

Those who created the General Agreement on Tariffs and Trade (GATT), a precursor of today's World Trade Organization (WTO), labored several years trying to fashion an agreement on services that mirrored those already in place for trade in goods. In 1993 about 88 of the then 117 nations pledged to liberalize trade in a wide range of services. However, air transport, labor movement, financial services, and the telecommunications sectors demanded special provisions.

Separate financial services and telecommunications agreements were negotiated in 1997. Further liberalization of trade in services was then placed on the agenda for the 2000 WTO Seattle meeting, but that meeting failed because of the anti-globalization demonstrations. The service progress at the Doha, Qatar, 2001 meeting was mainly confined to intellectual property rights and patent protection. Prodded by the United States, which stands to gain an estimated $860 billion of increased exports of services, about 50 trading partners have agreed to start negotiations again in Geneva. By mid-2014 the Trade in Services Agreement (TISA) was seen on their website as "the most promising opportunity in two decades to improve and expand trade in services."[8]

Government restrictions still constitute a major barrier to international trade in services. For example, in a service such as financial data-processing privacy concerns can be paramount (although this has not prevented credit cards going multinational on a grand scale—see box, "Visa and MasterCard Want to Be Everywhere").[9]

BOX: Visa and MasterCard Want to be Everywhere[10]

While credit cards are alternatively reviled and adored, they have become an integral part of the payment system all over the world. Visa spent lavishly for years on sponsorship and advertising to achieve market dominance. So has rival MasterCard, starting with the soccer World Cup sponsorship in 1998, 2002, and 2006. But Visa struck back, snatched the sponsorship away from MasterCard starting in 2010, and is for the time being king of the credit card business.

Although Visa and MasterCard both bill themselves as associations, they are foremost franchisers and protectors of their respective brand marks. Visa's share of fees from charge cards with its logo results in more than $1 billion in annual revenue. In return, Visa spends about one-third of this amount on advertising and sponsorship to promote its brand and encourage greater use of its members' cards. Visa also pays the slotting fees required to be listed as the first (default) card on e-commerce checkout sites such as Amazon.com.

This level of investment has been rewarded with industry leadership and success in differentiating its brand in a basic commodity business. In order to stay ahead, Visa has been using new technology. The 2014 World Cup in Brazil was a good place to show off. In Brazil, Visa utilizes contact-less transactions, where a credit card is not swiped to make a transaction, but merely held close to the point-of-sale terminal. Furthermore, in Brazil 93 percent of the local volume is going through chip-and-pin transactions.[11] In fact, Visa credit card transactions in Brazil are as advanced as in Europe, and more advanced than the United States.

Of course, as with soccer champions, there is no guarantee of a repeat. Only time will tell whether Visa can continue as the champion.

Services as a valuable part of a country's economy can be examined as percent of GDP (internal) and services as percent of exports (external). Looking internally, services constitute a higher percentage of GDP in advanced countries than in emerging countries. In Exhibit 10.5, for example, the percentages range from 79.2 percent for the France to 51.6 percent for China.

This chapter will discuss how these services exports are accomplished and how global services are marketed. The chapter starts by showing the differences and similarities between goods and services. The next section shows how managers analyze service globalization potential and how the mode of entry differs between the different types of services covered.

The following section shows the cultural influences on quality perceptions and suggests how localization of the service can be accomplished. The chapter ends with a brief discussion of two special global services, fast-food franchising and professional services.

SERVICES VS. PRODUCTS: A COMPARISON

There are several differences but also similarities between services and physical products. We will start with the differences.

Characteristics of Services

Although there is great variety among the industries in Exhibit 10.3, they tend to share four characteristics that make them different from physical goods and that affect their mode of entry. Services are characterized by:[12]

1. **Intangibility.** You cannot easily touch a service. This means that the tactile evaluation possible with physical products is not really possible. More, the touching is actually not very important. You can actually touch an ATM cash machine, but that is not a major aspect—more important is how easy and convenient it is to get the cash.

   One effect of intangibility is that service quality becomes quite subjective. Subjectivity is no problem in individualistic cultures, but in collectivist cultures subjectivity is easily swayed by group thinking. Most consumers will also judge service quality by augmenting factors such as the physical surroundings. A restaurant with a fireplace will easily be judged to have warm and friendly service. Individualistic low-context cultures tend to have consumers less influenced by their surroundings.

2. **Heterogeneity.** The service is not exactly the same each time. Last time you might have had a different waiter, for example, and this time you feel disappointed. In traditional societies with low economic growth, few things change abruptly. Consumers will not take easily to new entries and new services, and will need more time to adjust. Of course, younger consumers will more readily accept innovations, new services, and will also be less prone to judge variations in services.

   Service companies going abroad go to great length to maintain their service standards abroad, and in franchising local employees are usually trained quite thoroughly in the proper approach. Disneyland Paris workers (or actors, as they are called) were educated in the Disney approach before going on stage in the park. But what has worked at home is not always what will work in another

	Services as % of GDP
Australia	73.1
Germany	68.9
France	79.2
USA	78
Brazil	73.3
Russia	62.8
India	53.8
China	51.6
South Africa	68.6

Source: The World Bank national accounts data, and OECD National Accounts data files.http://data.worldbank.org/indicator/NV.SRV.TETC.ZS

EXHIBIT 10.5.
Services as a percentage of GDP

Source: http://data.worldbank.org/indicator/NV.SRV.TETC.ZS.

EXHIBIT 10.6.
Call center in India.
To facilitate communications
employees are typically
assigned easily understood
names such as "Peter" and
"Mary."

Copyright © by Bigstock/
Nosnibor137.

culture. Disneyland Paris employees are not quite as cheerful and friendly as the original bouncy Californians, but slightly more distant and reserved, as befits Parisians and the colder climate. Personal service is notoriously heterogeneous.

Personal service is also expensive since it involves labor time. This is one reason the company call centers tend to be located in countries like India, which has well-educated English-speakers but relatively low wages (see Exhibit 10.6).

The call center is often chosen to be on the opposite side of the globe from the company's main operations, facilitating 24/7 service availability.

3. *Inseparability.* Services are produced when they are consumed. With physical products, what you see is what you get. But in services, the product is the experience of consuming it. In Starbucks, for example, you might get great coffee, but what you are served is the totality of the experience in ordering, picking up, and drinking it. Many marketers have suggested that Starbucks sells an experience, and this is true of many service companies (some companies have adopted the same approach to products; BMW sells a driving experience, for example).

Inseparability means that controlling the quality of a service is not very easy. Every sales occasion is in fact a test of the product. Companies go to great lengths to ensure each occasion is as successful as intended, but it is unfortunately easy enough for a waiter to spill some soup on your table cloth and the engagement dinner is a mess. The uncertainty of the actual service delivery has been coined *the moment of truth*, something we will discuss more about later. Here it is sufficient to note that one reason American-style fast food has been globally successful is that the service delivery has been routinized to the extent possible. This prevents mishaps. The service is minimized, in a way, precisely to avoid human error.

4. *Perishability.* You cannot store a service. This follows from the inseparability. If you could store a service (as you can a physical product), the consumer could just call on it whenever. The ATM machine is in fact a kind stored service, in that the bills are stored there, but the service is not produced until you to activate it. This is true of most service businesses.

A service business model is basically a contingency setup, waiting for a consumer to activate it. Then it must be ready to deliver the service. This means that a service business is directly dependent on a country's infrastructure. ATM machines depend on a functioning banking system. A restaurant is dependent on food supplies and good transportation. So is a hospital, which is even more dependent on functioning electric systems, medical supplies, doctors, and so on. These need to be on the alert, ready to offer their services. A physical product, by contrast, can simply be produced and shipped, even with no buyer yet.

The upshot of these four characteristics is that services tend to come much later to international expansion than physical products. There is simply more need in the local market for the business setup, for finding partners, for training employees, for adapting the service, and so on, than for products. We will cover more of this later in the chapter.

Not all the service industries shown in Exhibit 10.3 possess the four characteristics to the same degree. For example, a restaurant exemplifies 2, 3, and 4 well, and even 1, although in a sense you can touch the food, the table, the hot plate, and so on.

Services can sometimes be viewed as products (just like products can sometimes be viewed as a service—a car offers transportation, for example). Most offerings fall somewhere on a scale between pure services at one end and pure products at the other end providing customers with some portion of both. As examples, having your lawn cut falls toward the pure services end, a restaurant meal is somewhere in the middle as a combination of service expectations and product/food expectations, but buying a bottle of juice is toward the product end (see Exhibit 10.7).

We will discuss the similarities between services and products next.

EXHIBIT 10.7.
Most offerings exist somewhere on a scale between pure services at one end and pure products at the other end, having characteristics of both.

Source: https://openclipart.org/detail/216933/dancing-lesson.

Source: https://openclipart.org/detail/27369/apple-spritzer-bottle.

A Product Equivalence

From a marketing viewpoint there are actually many similarities between physical goods and services. For example, one standard marketing definition of a product is as a bundle of benefit-generating attributes. There is nothing inherently physical about this bundle. The same definition can be applied to an intangible service such as an insurance package. In fact, the similarities can be so strong that for some purposes there is no difference. In many ways the product is simply the packaging of a problem-solving service. For example, a book replaces the telling of a story, a car offers transportation, a cash machine replaces a teller, and so on.

Similar to product marketers, service marketers distinguish between three levels of the service offering: the core service, the basic service package, and the augmented service. Exhibit 10.8 demonstrates the relationships between these three concepts.

The **core service** is what the buyer is really buying. For instance, the person getting a tune-up for her car is really buying trouble-free operation and transportation. The individual checking into the Hilton in Manila is really buying a night's comfort and reliable service.

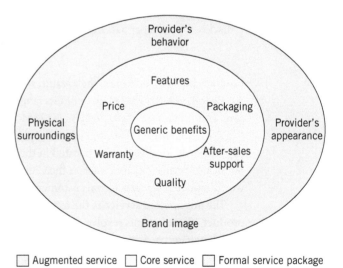

☐ Augmented service ☐ Core service ☐ Formal service package

EXHIBIT 10.8.
The service as a "Product" has multiple levels defining it.

The first task. The first job of the global services marketer is to make sure that these core service benefits can be delivered in the foreign markets. While this task establishes a necessary condition for expansion, it is not sufficient by itself for success.

The **basic service package** refers to the specified services offered the customer, which include service features, the price, the packaging, and the guarantees offered. The basic service package of a bank involves the various

---

BOX: When Less is More[13]

Commercial airlines constitute an industry where the differences between the core service, the basic service package, and the augmented service are very clear. The core service is rapid transportation between two or more points. The basic service package is what is included in the ticket price—first class, business class, or coach, free meals, free drinks, baggage checks at the hotel, free limo service, and so on. The augmented service is in the personal touch, the attention from a stewardess, the willing accommodation of special seating requests, and so forth.

Since different segments of the traveler market desire different combinations of the complete service package, there is room for service differentiation. An interesting case is EasyJet, a no-frills airline operating out of Luton, England. By focusing on the core service, minimizing the basic service package, and eliminating the augmented service altogether, EasyJet is able to provide low-cost travel within the European Union. Its tickets are between one-half to one-third of the regularly scheduled airlines' prices.

At the other end you can find Emirates airline based in Dubai. As with everything else, the UAE businesses do not scrimp. The Emirates has ordered 140 of the new Airbus 380 behemoth airplane. The A380 has caught the imagination of travelers. Its two full-length decks total 6,000 square feet, 50 percent more than the original jumbo jet, the Boeing 747. Its wingspan barely fits inside a football field. Its first-class cabin features hotel-size suites, complete with bed and showers, and a business-class bar at the tail of the upper level with big chairs and couches.[14]

Successful? You bet. Emirates airline is adding the popular plane on long-haul routes such as Dubai to Johannesburg. Airbus is not quite so happy since few airlines have plans for the big-hub concept behind a 500-plus-passenger airplane. EasyJet flies over five million passengers annually, has an 80 percent utilization factor, high in a very competitive industry, and makes roughly $2 profit on each passenger. The airline has not disclosed profits per passenger, but its calculations certainly involve a different price per ticket.

---

products the bank offers and their features, including free checking, high-interest certificates of deposit, and so on. An airline provides a set of more or less tangible in-flight services such as food, drink, duty-free sales, special baby care, and movies (see box, "When Less Is More").

The second task. The second job of the global services marketer is to develop a basic service package that can be appropriately localized and replicated in the various markets around the world. Offering innovative and hard-to-duplicate service packages, such as the Club Med all-inclusive vacations in its own villages in different parts of the world, can help develop a loyal customer base and a sustained competitive advantage.

The **augmented service** is the totality of benefits that the individual receives or experiences when buying the product. These benefits revolve around the service delivery, the way the provider is dressed, the tone of voice and body language used, the confidence and credence imparted, and so on. These benefits also involve the brand image and status of the service provider, as well as the physical surroundings of the service.

The third task. The third job of the global services marketer is to create a customer-oriented augmented service package.

Although they do play a role for physical products as well, these augmenting features can make a big difference in relatively standardized services. They can become the FSAs (firm-specific advantages). For example, the salon's furniture, the music played, and the other customers there are all factors contributing to whether the hair styling itself will seem acceptable or not.[15] These augmenting benefits are often so inextricably linked to most services that without them the service can't be replicated properly elsewhere. Without such duplication, exporting to other countries is less likely to succeed. One key factor in global services marketing is not whether the core benefit is desired or whether the basic service package can be replicated but whether the total **service delivery system**—the linked activities, hardware and software, which make the service delivery work—can be successfully transplanted abroad. If not, quality and customer satisfaction are jeopardized (see box, "Service Standardization").

Service Standardization: Impersonal Personal Service?

Just as with products, the standardization of services typically starts with a certain "core" service. Most fast-food restaurants, following McDonald's, focus on the basic principles of friendliness ("smile!"), cleanliness of the premises, and quick service. But given the cultural diversity in the world, the human element can become an obstacle to **service standardization.** That is, attempting to make the service delivery uniform in every market can be difficult, given that people from different cultures behave differently.

Thus, the consensus among many service marketers is that one can globally standardize the **backroom operations** of the service—quality control in fast-food restaurants, computerized bookings within a hotel chain, inventory control for retailers—but not necessarily the customer interactions, the **frontline operations**—those facing and interacting with consumers.[16] The frontline personnel in even the most global service companies are usually natives, whose command of language and customs enables them to deliver the service appropriately—or, as some fast-food companies seem to aim for, standardize the personal service to make it impersonal.

SERVICE GLOBALIZATION POTENTIAL

Even if more and more services are going global, not all services have the same **globalization potential**, that is, the appropriate preconditions for globalization. The basic drivers of service expansion are the same as those for products market drivers, competitive drivers, cost drivers, government drivers, and technology drivers. These drivers define whether a particular service industry is ready for globalization. As we discussed earlier in this chapter, the government factors in terms of regulations and other restrictions often constitute the main obstacles to global expansion.

Assuming that these drivers are relatively favorable and the obstacles not too high, the feasibility of globalizing a particular service business depends on some factors that are unique to services as compared to products.

Stage of the Life Cycle

As with a product cycle, development of a business service over time follows a cycle from birth through growth and maturity to decline. In the typical marketing illustration, the product life cycle (PLC) follows an S-curve, with the growth period corresponding to where the "S" has its steepest ascent. This is when a new product is often introduced in foreign markets to capture first-mover advantages. However, for services, it is in the maturity stage that the potential for global expansion of the service concept is the highest.

In the early and growth stage of the cycle, the production process employed by the service company is often still under development. The concept is still being created. In maturity, the software and hardware ingredients in the service have been fully developed, and the standardization of key components and features takes place. It is this standardization—whether it be in advertising, medical care, fast-food restaurants, accounting, or hotels—that is the basis for global expansion of the service. FSAs in services are often in innovative standardization—from Subway's insistence on fresh bread, meat, and produce, to Hilton Hotels' training in how to greet guests, to Boston Consulting Group's growth-share matrix, a durable and successful consulting "product."

Infrastructure Barriers

The global applicability of a service depends on whether appropriate infrastructure is available in the foreign market. The availability of advanced telecommunications, a well-developed logistics infrastructure, and skilled local labor are typical requirements for many service businesses. So are usually more basic infrastructure features such as uninterrupted electricity, paved roads, reasonable housing and personal safety.

Government regulations are often a problem. In brokerage firms, for example, a very sophisticated service concept that works well under a certain type of regulatory and economic environment might lose all relevance when the financial regulations and/or the institutional members change character. The buying and selling of call and put options or other derivatives, for example, is not feasible where there is no futures market.

Idiosyncratic Home Markets

An often-overlooked inhibitor of services exporting is that many service systems exist as ingenious solutions to very special problems faced in the home country. Even with great success at home, their globalization potential can be limited because conditions elsewhere are different. The typical supermarket in the United States has developed partly as a response to the growing availability of automobiles and parking lot space in many suburban areas of the nation. They may not work well where these conditions are missing.

Regulatory constraints in the local environment determine the specific shape of the service organizations found in many countries. The retail regulations in Germany at the local level can still regulate opening hours, in-store promotions, and magnitude of discounts, making it difficult for large American style retailers to succeed. German retailers may find it difficult to expand to more open markets.

What is needed for services globalization is (1) a distillation of exactly what the key features of the service concept are, clearer in late PLC stages, (2) a reasonable similarity to the home country situation in terms of infrastructure, and (3) hope that the home country's service regulations and other factors are not too idiosyncratic but a similar service model can fit also in the foreign environment. Because of intangibility and perishability, services cannot usually be simply handled by an independent overseas partner the same way products can. To maintain service quality, investment is necessary in hiring and managing local people, training and training courses, modifying your service to "fit" into the local culture and possibly bringing expatriates into the country.

Then, as always, what is required is the localization of the key features to another environment while still maintaining the FSAs of the firm. And to overcome cultural obstacles, adaptation of the service will often be required, just as with products.

FOREIGN ENTRY OF SERVICES

Next we explore how the service characteristics influence mode of entry abroad. First we need to be clear on how foreign trade in services occurs.

Entry Modes in Services

To understand service exporting, *tourism exports* provide a good illustration. For example, as Japanese tourists descend upon Rome, their spending is done in local currency, bought by exchanging yen for euros. This means that hotel bills in Rome, food in the restaurants, payment for taxis, entrance tickets to the Coliseum, and similar expenditures are payments for services exported to Japan.

A Subway franchising expansion provides an illustration of a *licensing* mode of entry. As a potential Subway franchisee in, say, Mexico applies for a franchise, s/he will have to demonstrate appropriate business skills and access to sufficient financial resources and is likely to be interviewed by a Subway manager. Then, given support in how to establish and manage the business, including finding an appropriate location, the franchisee will be able to order and sell the typical Subway foods. From the revenues Subway will then be paid a certain percentage as a royalty payment and can transfer those funds to the U.S. (or leave the funds for further local expansion).

In consulting services, *foreign direct investment* is sometimes necessary. For consulting to local companies, it is typically necessary to have a local place of business to facilitate communication between the firm and its clients. Thus, consulting companies such as Accenture and McKinsey have branch offices in several large cities around the world, with local staff and some headquarters managers. This is an example of FDI in services, where the locals pay taxes to the host countries, but a share of the consulting fees is re-invested or transferred back to headquarters.

Entry and Exit Barriers

As with products, the mode of entry choice in services is affected by entry barriers and by the strategic objectives of the firm. Entry barriers in services are generally greater than for products. The reason is the uncertainty of control that comes with the intangibility of services, which induces governments to regulate services and causes firms to have problems with quality controls.

Studies have identified the most common barriers to service expansion abroad:[17]

1. *Host-country restrictions and regulations.* Often the biggest hurdle, local regulations tend to protect local service providers. Wal-Mart's problems in Germany had partly to do with limits on store size and opening hours.
2. *Logistics.* On-time supplies can also be a problem, because infrastructures differ. Getting the fresh supplies to a new Subway restaurant is a challenge in many countries.
3. *Delivering quality customer service.* Basic education is important for personal service providers, so customer requests can be easily understood and fulfilled. "Being polite" is not the same everywhere. Chinese service can seem crude and unpolished to many foreign visitors.[18]
4. *Cultural differences.* Cultural factors can make it difficult to move a personal service into a foreign setting. The local consumers want a different approach. Wal-Mart's greeters were only an unexpected annoyance to Germans.
5. *Staffing and Personnel.* Finding the right kind of frontline people can be a challenge. Attitudes toward work differ, for example. Disneyland Paris initially had to allow their cast members to smoke, for example. When a culture considers "serving someone" a low-level role, as in the Middle East, people cannot offer quality service.

If you compare this list to the previous listing of the factors that affect the feasibility of global expansion (section of "Globalization Potential" above), you can see that in many cases the barriers make international expansion infeasible. For example, it might simply be impossible for a famous French restaurant to go international and keep its cachet.

BOX: Starbucks' Japanese Roast[19]

Starbucks' distinctive green and circular logo can be found on busy street corners, in shopping malls, as well as at airports and train stations in an increasing number of countries around the world. One early entry was Japan.

Since Japan is the world's third-largest coffee consumer after the United States and Germany, Starbucks viewed the island nation as a huge challenge and opportunity for the firm. Entering Japan in October 1995, Starbucks entered into an equity-based joint venture with Tokyo's Sazaby, Inc. This joint venture, amounting to a small 25 million yen ($2.33 million) in capitalization, helped Starbucks open its first 12 stores in Japan by the end of 1997. A humble beginning but Starbucks was concerned that the Japanese were not used to Italian-style coffees. Starbucks executives' concern was that the Japanese consumers would not embrace the Starbucks concept.

The positioning in Japan for Starbucks was in the middle between two contrasting coffee bars. One was the traditional coffee houses (*kissaten*) where couples and friends are likely to spend time away from their small apartments in a slow and leisurely environment. The other end of this spectrum was exemplified by Doutor Coffee Company, started in 1980. Doutor was Japan's leading coffee-bar chain with over 466 shops in and around Tokyo. Its focus was on speed of service and quick turnover of customers. The average customer stayed in a Doutor coffee shop only about 10 minutes (and many for even less time), about one-third the stay in a typical *kissaten*. In terms the services vs product scale (Exhibit 10.6), the traditional coffee houses were at the services end offering an "experience." Doutor was at the products end, focused on the coffee.

EXHIBIT 10.9.
There is just enough tweaking of the basic concept to make the shops avoid a legal challenge from Starbucks for copyright infringement.

J.K. Johansson

Starbucks tried to position between these two extremes and placed its usual emphasis on the coffee but also wanted to have an enjoyable store experience, but with less stress on the social aspects. It also targeted single people.

Starbucks' format proved successful and helped the coffee market in Japan to five years of uninterrupted growth. The only problem was that much of that growth accrued to competitive look-alikes. In true Japanese fashion, the Japanese competitors quickly imitated the Starbucks formula, and created their own me-too versions of the Starbucks coffeehouses. The imitations were, also as usual, sometimes as good as the original. If you enter a Doutor's me-too coffee house in Tokyo, named "Excelsior Caffe," you'll find the typical Starbucks menu of coffees posted behind the counter, the various brews are offered in the well-known paper and plastic cups, the coffee-making procedure and serving is the same, the atmosphere with comfortable seating and Internet access is indistinguishable from a Starbucks, and the store front looks pretty much like a Starbucks, complete with logo and coloring (see Exhibit 10.9).

Today, Starbucks is still holding on to a lead in this competitive coffee market, has over $1 billion dollars in revenue in Japan and as of 2014, it had 1034 stores in Japan. Surprising most observers, its decision to stick to its no-smoking policy turned out to be a smart non-localization move as Japan's anti-smoking campaign kicked into gear. (When Starbucks first entered Japan in 1996 over 50 percent of Japanese men smoked, the highest rate in the world.[20]) In 2014 the company decided to buy the remaining 60.5 percent share of Starbucks Japan in a deal valued at about $913.5 million.[21] From humble beginnings, Starbuck's executives clearly think they know this market now.

LOCAL MARKETING OF GLOBAL SERVICES

When marketing the service in the local market the similarities with products can be used to advantage. There are several such similarities where product marketing and service marketing become indistinguishable. A few examples will help illustrate the point.

The competitive advantage of an entering service business needs to be profiled strongly, just as with products. Country-of-origin is one factor that can help or hinder positioning. When Hard Rock Cafe opens a restaurant abroad, its American popular music heritage is played to the hilt. By contrast, Starbucks, the unlikely American coffee store chain, enters foreign markets downplaying its roots, serving lattes and cappuccinos brewed with coffees from Africa, Asia, and Latin America (see box on the following page, "Starbucks' Japanese Roast").

Because of the intangibility of services and their other differences from products, branding becomes even more important for services. Services are experience goods, hard to evaluate before experiencing them. While a product can be inspected and tested before purchase, the service is produced only when consumed, so to test it you need to buy it first.

Restaurant guide authors, movie critics, and concert reviewers all have consumed the service before reporting on it. A well-known brand therefore becomes a way of getting past the first hurdle of customer acceptance and induces the buyer to try the service. A 7-Eleven or a Citibank sign offers less risk and more comfort to non-locals than does a domestic-only brand.

BOX: *Lord of the Rings* in New Marketing Era[22]

Once upon a time the conventional wisdom held that Hollywood movies were introduced in the United States and Canada to assess their box office potential, with the winners being introduced some months later in a variety of markets around the world. This waterfall strategy has lately turned into a sprinkler strategy, a simultaneous launch in several countries. Part of the reason is the need to preempt the distribution of pirated copies that would typically start to appear within a week after a movie's release from moviegoers with video cameras. Another reason is the increased ability to use the Internet to build up the prelaunch anticipation of the movie and speed up demand penetration.

Marketing executives rationalized that since J. R. R. Tolkien's trilogy *Lord of the Rings* had such global publishing appeal, the film version would have a simultaneous December 19, 2001, global release date in 16 countries: Austria, Belgium, Canada, Denmark, France, Germany, Greece, Iceland, Malta, Norway, South Africa, Switzerland, Sweden, United States, United Kingdom, and Venezuela. Subsequent releases were scheduled over the next few months in an additional 45 countries around the world.

Demand had been building for months prior to the movie's release on the official Internet site (www.lordoftherings.net) and a plethora of unofficial websites started by fans around the world. International clubs quickly became established in Denmark, Finland, France, Germany, Norway, Spain, and Sweden, each in the host country's language and linked to a fan club home page.

The Fellowship of the Ring was only the first installment. The trilogy was filmed in New Zealand in a single production run spanning 274 days, but to avoid consumer overload the three films were released a year apart. *The Two Towers* was released in December 2002 and the final film, *The Return of the King*, in December 2003.[23] In each case the same pattern has been followed, with simultaneous release around the world.

The results have been spectacular. *The Fellowship of the Ring* has earned more than $871.5 million since its 2001 release, while *The Two Towers* has earned $926.0 million since its 2002 release. *The Return of the King* has made $1,119.9 million (eighth on the all-time list), taking the trilogy to a $2.9 billion total by 2013. The next three movies in this series focused on *The Hobbit* (*An Unexpected Journey* 2012, *The Desolation of Smaug* 2013 and *The Battle of the Five Armies* 2014) and earned an additional $2.9 billion bringing the total for all the films of "Middle Earth" to $5.88 billion.

And these are only direct ticket sales. Movie revenues move down a long food chain. It starts with the U.S. and international box office receipts, followed by DVD and video sales and rentals, continuing with pay-per-view, cable, network, and ultimately to local television. Licensing for toys and clothing is also in the mix. "Once you have a successful movie, it drives revenue down the line," says Mark May, senior analyst with Kaufman Brothers. "For example, *Lord of the Rings* has driven a 150 percent increase in DVD sales" for Time Warner.

Hollywood has quickly learned that the real success for movies is now written in the international markets not just the North American markets (Exhibit 10.10).[24]

Services also need to be advertised and promoted just as products do. In some services—law, medical, and other professional services, for example—restrictions on promotions make it necessary to generate word-of-mouth advice by using existing customers and established contacts for referrals. In other cases services can be easily promoted without advertising. Movie stars routinely appear on TV shows and in person when films open, artists show up for autographs and photo signings, and rock bands go on tour to promote their latest music release. And nowadays, of course, the Internet makes it possible to go virtually global from the beginning (see box, "*Lord of the Rings*").

LOCAL SERVICE QUALITY

Distribution is the one area where services and products really do differ. The reason is the inseparability: a service is fundamentally produced and consumed at the same time. Thus the service delivery is identical to the service production, and the distribution cannot be separated out.

The Local Servicescape

The production and distribution of service generally occurs in what has become called a servicescape. The **servicescape** is defined as the environment in which the service is assembled and in which the seller and customer interact, combined with tangible commodities that facilitate performance or communication of the service.[25] The actual servicescape becomes an important factor in customer perceptions of the level of service provided, including perceptions of value for money. For example, Starbucks chain aims to provide a cozy environment, with music, free wi-fi and comfortable seating (an "experience") helping it to charge high prices.

Franchise	No. of Movies	USA Box Office (billions$)	Worldwide Box Office (billions$)	International Revenue (% of total worldwide)
Marvel Cinematic Universe	22	$4.77	$12.07	60.5%
Harry Potter	11	$2.63	$8.53	69.2%
Star Wars	12	$3.73	$7.60	50.9%
James Bond	25	$2.11	$7.08	70.2%
Peter Jackson's Lord of the Rings	6	$1.85	$5.89	68.6%
Fast and the Furious	10	$1.51	$5.14	70.6%
X-Men	11	$2.04	$5.02	59.4%
Batman	16	$2.23	$4.57	51.2%
Pirates of the Caribbean	5	$1.45	$4.45	67.4%
Transformers	6	$1.45	$4.28	66.1%

Source: The Numbers: Movie Franchises. http://www.the-numbers.com/movies/franchises/sort/World

EXHIBIT 10.10.
Highest-grossing movie franchises (2016)[26] To be a high grossing movie franchise, the movies must consistently appeal to international audiences.

Source: http://www.the-numbers.com/movies/franchises/sort/World

To cover the various aspects of what constitutes a servicescape, in service marketing it is now common to add three more "Ps" to the customary 4Ps: people, physical evidence, and process. For the international expansion, these factors pose additional entry barriers. Two factors stand out:

1. *Transfer of the servicescape.* It is not so easy reproduce the same servicescape abroad. The training of the people, establishing the same physical setting, and introducing the same service-flow process. Even if the company can define precisely what constitutes a good replication (usually in the later stages of the PLC at home as we have seen), in a new culture the same servicescape may not achieve the same effect. Jazz music and soft chairs might need to be replaced by a samba beat and light rattan chairs in Brazil's Starbucks, for example.

   It is also the case that the transfer of a service may necessitate significant consumer education and rethinking of tradition. For example, while self-service might have a promising market in some countries, more traditional cultures will find the practice a sign of low status. In the Middle East, for example, service is often outsourced because the work is viewed as less worthy. Thus, in Dubai, taxi drivers are typically from Pakistan and waiters are often from the Philippines. (Of course, outsourcing of this kind can be found elsewhere, but the usual rationale is cost).

2. *Imitation by competitors.* Entry barriers in consumer services are notoriously low. It does not take much to open a small boutique, a small restaurant or a coffee shop. As the record shows, there are numerous local imitators of the successful fast-food chains, coffee shops and small stores—even cupcake outlets.

The servicescape is difficult to replicate because of the many intangibles, but a well-known brand facilitates the transfer significantly. A strong brand affects the subjective assessments involved in judging services driectly. This is one reason why international franchising based on a strong brand has been so successful.

The servicescape sets the stage for the encounters between the consumer and the producer of the service. These encounters have come to be known as *critical incidents* or *moments of truth*. The encounters (face-to-face, on the phone, online, etc.) help determine the consumer's evaluation of the service quality and customer satisfaction. Such assessments are highly subjective and depend critically on cultural expectations.

Service Quality is Subjective

Service quality cannot be assessed the same as product quality. For product quality, objective tests can be carried out, the performance can be judged by using the product, and the looks and design can be rated more or less objectively. There are subjective factors—like color and styling, say—but tangibility makes product quality a more objective measure (as in *Consumer Reports*).

Service quality involves the subjective assessments by the customer on five major dimensions:[27]

- *Reliability*. Ability to perform the promised service dependably and accurately
- *Assurance*. Knowledge and courtesy of employees and their ability to inspire trust and confidence
- *Tangibles*. Physical facilities, equipment, and appearance of personnel
- *Empathy*. Caring, individualized attention the firm provides its customers
- *Responsiveness*. Willingness to help customers and provide prompt service

Although all of these aspects reflect some degree of objectivity—and the service firms do a considerable amount of training of personnel to assure they deliver on these aspects—in the end it is the consumers' perceptions that matter. As some research has found, these perceptions can be affected by the level of customer involvement in the service production process. Getting the consumers to do parts of the job themselves can make them perceive higher value, something well-recognized in online marketing.[28] Consumers are not always right—but in services even more than in products, what they think is, in a way, the true measure of the service. This is the basic rationale behind analyzing the critical incidents when service is delivered and service satisfaction is registered or not.

A **critical incident** or **moment of truth** is defined as the period of time during which a consumer directly interacts with a service. Once the pros and the cons in the critical incident are identified, the service encounter can be appropriately designed both in terms of a person's behavior and in terms of the physical surrounding or servicescape.

A Cultural Gap Model

The customer satisfaction of a service during a critical incident or moment of truth is typically measured in terms of the gap between the customer's expectations of the service and the perceived actual performance, or **gap model**.[29] If the latter is at or above the expected level, the customer is satisfied. If it's above the expected level, the customer is positively surprised. If the perceived performance is below this level, the customer is dissatisfied and rates the quality low. Thus, according to this gap model, service quality in the end becomes a matter of whether the customer is satisfied or not.

There are four different levels of perceptions at work:[30]

- The *desired* service is the highest or ideal quality.
- The *adequate* service forms the lower limit below which the service quality is unacceptable.
- The *expected* service lies somewhere between the desired and the adequate service.
- The *actual* service level as experienced and perceived by the customer.

The relationships between these service levels are depicted in Exhibit 10.11.

As long as the perceived service performance lies between the desired and the adequate service levels there is no gap and the customer is satisfied. If the performance drops below the adequate level, there is a gap and dissatisfaction. Between the desired and the adequate service levels is the **zone of tolerance**, where the customer will be more or less satisfied. If the performance is above that expected the customer is positively surprised.

In intercultural service encounters the expectations are influenced by the home country culture. The expectations on the part of the customers are formed partly by their cultural background and past experiences. For example, what we like—our taste—is largely determined by culture and past experiences in the product or service category. This means that the service firm entering a foreign market is not necessarily met with the same expectations as a domestic firm. In the gap model, the standard against which services are judged abroad can be very different from at home.

This means that what is perceived as high-quality service will often differ between countries. By comparing two culturally different places (say, New York City and Tokyo), great differences in approach—and service—can easily be seen. The direct, explicit, and "professional" approach of a New York department store clerk is far away from the Japanese clerk's softness and courteous demeanor. A person raised in a particular service environment might be surprised by what passes for high-quality service in another.

Still, the global service marketer entering a new country can succeed without completely adopting the local behavior. Keeping the cultural factors well in mind and localizing by hiring skillful natives as employees, the global entrant can educate local customers about the potential quality of the new service.

As we saw earlier in this chapter, when Starbucks coffee shops in Tokyo decided to keep the "no smoking" policy just before the Japanese government launched its anti-smoking campaign.

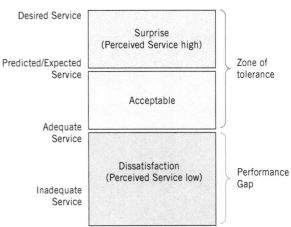

EXHIBIT 10.11.
Customer satisfaction: the gap and the zone of tolerance

CLOSE-UP: FAST-FOOD FRANCHISING

The franchising of fast-food restaurants has witnessed an unprecedented growth in the last three decades. The brand names McDonald's, Dunkin' Donuts, Wendy's, and others

EXHIBIT 10.12.
KFC restaurant on Xa Dan Street, Hanoi, Vietnam. The standardization of colors and design of premises in fast-food franchising is responsible in large part for the similarities in the suburban landscape of different countries, sometimes complained about as being "too American."

are well-known the world over. How and why have these exports proved so viable? The answer is franchising.

Many multinational service firms are increasingly turning to franchising as a way to enter foreign markets while still retaining some control over their brand image. It reduces the financial exposure of directly investing in a market and simplifies the problem of managing a foreign venture. Franchising also appeals to local entrepreneurs who can adopt of a business model that has succeeded in other markets. These franchisees typically pay an up-front fee to purchase a license and annual royalties based on sales volume. In return, they receive management assistance setting up their business and running the franchise operation.

A wide variety of firms have utilized franchising to penetrate new markets by leveraging on their brand name and the local market knowledge of their franchise owners. U.S. fast-food firms have fueled the growth of franchising over the last decade, driven by such brand names as McDonald's, KFC (see Exhibit 10.12), Taco Bell, Pizza Hut, Burger King, and Wendy's. All of these firms were able to successfully identify the core features of their service systems and their product specific advantages in order to determine how to export their winning concepts.

BOX: The McDonald's Way[31]

With more than 35,000 restaurants in over 119 countries, McDonald's is in all likelihood the world's largest and best-known food service retailer. The chain serves an estimated 68 million meals every day. Despite already possessing possibly the most developed global franchise system anywhere, McDonald's is still driven to expand. It aims to serve 1 percent of the world's population. This vision is focused on three worldwide strategies: be the best employer for its people in each community around the world; deliver operational excellence to its customers in each of its restaurants; and achieve enduring profitable growth by expanding the brand through innovation and technology.

Currently, about 70 percent of McDonald's worldwide restaurant businesses are owned and operated by independent businessmen and women. A new franchise investment runs around $1–2 million depending on the size of the facility, inventory, decor, landscaping, and other factors. An initial fee of $45,000 must be paid to McDonald's and the company charges a royalty rate of about 12.5 percent.[32] Additional support is available for prospective franchisees throughout the countries in which McDonald's operates.

In certain countries such as Russia, McDonald's has ownership interests in restaurants. When McDonald's opened its first Moscow outlet in 1990, its 700-seat restaurant served 30,000 meals in one day, still a record for an initial store opening. McDonald's now serves more than 1 million Russians every day, which is particularly notable considering that its food prices are comparable worldwide while Russian incomes are only a fraction of those in developed countries.

From the initial Pushkin Square restaurant, which received its ingredients almost totally from abroad, McDonald's now purchases almost 100 percent of its ingredients from independent Russian suppliers. The Moscow-McDonald's invested in a $45 million warehouse McComplex in order to supply its restaurants with the quality ingredients necessary to meet their global standards. Although most supply functions have now been outsourced, today this centralized distribution facility still supplies McDonald's 330 restaurants throughout Russia as well as those in 17 other countries, including Austria, Belorussia, Czech Republic, Germany, Hungary, Moldova, and Ukraine. In 2012, the company agreed to allow a Russian firm, Rosinter, to be its first franchisee as it pushes for further penetration. Under a deal running until 2023, Rosinter has rights to open and operate McDonald's outlets at Moscow's three international airports of Sheremetyevo, Domodedovo, and Vnukovo, as well as in all terminals of Pulkovo airport in St. Petersburg. So far it has opened two of these.[33]

Even with McDonald's new flexibility toward local preferences, it is hardly surprising that some non-Americans—as well as some Americans—consider McDonald's a threat to cultural traditionalists. It is also an attractive target for anti-American sentiments, as we saw in the opening vignette to Chapter 1.

While the franchise's core features are legally protected by the licensing agreement, franchisers are typically granted some latitude in adapting the marketing mix to the local environment. For instance, McDonald's sells black courant rather than apple pies in central Europe because of local tastes and preferences.

Standardization in franchise operations is essential to ensuring a high degree of brand consistency. For instance, McDonald's successful system consists of not only the cooking method and serving procedure but also the training of the workers, their attire and attitude, and the management and bookkeeping system. Franchisees are required to attend *Hamburger University* in order to learn how to manage the business and train their staff. These franchisees must also adhere to established McDonald's standards in terms of the quality of the ingredients and the preparation and sale of the product (see box, "The McDonald's Way").[34]

Franchisor Assistance. Franchisors provide a host of preplanning tools to help prospective local investors. These include analyses of key factors in choice of location (traffic patterns, competition and synergy from similar outlets, offices versus private residences), checklists of positive and negative attraction factors in the market area (population mix, income levels, age, and family size), and building advice (size, layout, and construction materials).

These tools have to be localized to the conditions in the foreign markets. "Traffic pattern" in one country may refer to cars, in others to motorcycles, in still others to bicycles or pedestrians. "Population mix" is a nonfactor in homogeneous countries such as Norway but important and based on religion in countries such as Malaysia. "Building advice" in the desert sands of Kuwait is far different from that in North Dakota—not to speak of the building permits that of course differ across countries as well as between municipalities.

Franchisee advantages. Franchising enables a franchisee to start a business with limited capital and to benefit from the business experience of the franchiser. So an investment in a globally advertised franchise literally assures the franchisee of customers from the outset. In the event business problems develop, the franchisee can obtain guidance and advice from the franchiser at little or no cost. Thus, franchised outlets are generally more successful than independently owned businesses. Oftentimes the franchisee even receives materials to use in promotional campaigns and benefits from a franchiser's global image advertising and strong brand equity.

Franchisee drawbacks. Franchise agreements also have certain drawbacks. For instance, a franchiser's ability to dictate the many facets of business operation could prove overly intrusive. Franchisees would usually know more about the local market conditions but may be unable to adapt due to contractual obligations. In addition to a one-time franchise fee and continuing royalty payments, many franchisees also borrow for a larger investment than is comfortable. They have to work long hours in order to pay back the investment. Lastly, their entrepreneurial spirit might suffer because franchisees give up a large measure of control when entering into a franchise agreement.

Government regulation can preclude franchising in some countries. When McDonald's of Canada investigated opening a restaurant in Moscow, the Soviet government did not allow any individual ownership and also prohibited foreign majority ownership of any business. Therefore, Moscow-McDonald's operates to this day as a joint venture between McDonald's Canada and the Moscow city government.

SUMMARY

Foreign trade in services has grown much faster than trade in manufactured goods during the last decade although according to the World Bank it is still less than a third of trade in goods for the United States. In particular, advanced economies tend to show a great deal of services export. The liberalization of trade in services has not been smooth and the WTO still has several issues to negotiate. Still, the basic trend is for services to increase even further as a share of international trade.

A global service is generally a more intricate and fragile export than a physical good. The intangibility and other characteristics that make services different from physical goods also make it difficult for the marketer to re-create the service and control the quality level abroad. In terms of marketing, however, many of the standard concepts and tools from product marketing are still applicable. The one major difference comes with distribution, where the inseparability of consumption and production of services makes the service delivery the moment of truth for quality and customer satisfaction. The necessary reliance on the customer's subjective judgment means that cultural factors play a very prominent role in determining quality and satisfaction levels.

Global service expansion is driven by the same factors that drive globalization of products. Services also have a life cycle, just like the PLC. But services tend to go global later in the service life cycle, because the crystallization of what exactly the service experience consist of needs to be carefully defined first, which usually happens later in the life cycle. Other issues that arise when going global involve determining how the same service delivery system can be reproduced abroad, whether the necessary localization to the new markets can be made without jeopardizing the firm-specific advantages, and how the necessary local personnel can be properly trained. Judging from the successes, many companies are up to the challenge.

KEY TERMS

adequate service
augmented service
backroom operations
basic service package
core service
critical incident
desired service
expected service
franchising
frontline operations
gap model
globalization potential
heterogeneity

inseparability
intangibility
moment of truth
perceived service
perishability
professional services
service delivery system
servicescape
service quality
service satisfaction
service standardization
zone of tolerance

DISCUSSION QUESTIONS

1. In what ways are services different from products? How do these differences affect mode of entry?
2. Give some examples of how the inseparability of consumption and production of services makes for moments of truth in banking. How does a cash machine solve the problem of heterogeneity? Is there a moment of truth with a cash machine?
3. Discuss how culture influences one's perception of what would be considered good service in a restaurant. Do the same for a store visit. (Use cultures with which you have some personal experience.)
4. Check out the websites of some service companies (for example hotels, brokerage firms, auto dealers), and analyze how they try to translate their offering to the new medium. Are services more or less adaptable to online shopping than products?
5. Why are most personal services not easily globalized? Give some examples that show how a service has to be standardized before going global—and how standardized personal service is almost always impersonal.

Country	Services as % of GDP
Australia	73.1
Germany	68.9
France	79.2
USA	78
Brazil	73.3
Russia	62.8
India	53.8
China	51.6
South Africa	68.6

(*Source*: http://data.worldbank.org/indicator/NV.SRV.TETC.ZS.)

TEAM CHALLENGE PROJECTS

1. As countries progress along the PLC (Product Life Cycle) from emerging to developing to mature, their economies tend to progress from farming to manufacturing to services. Services eventually come to dominate the economies of mature developed countries.

   GDP is an internal measure and does not imply exports. (For example, while the U.S. economy has a high percentage of GDP as services, the U.S. exports over $2T but actually 70 percent is merchandise and 30 percent is service.) Team 1: Pick an emerging/developing country in Africa and develop a plan that enables that country to generate more GDP from services. Team 2: Pick an emerging/developing country in Latin America and develop a plan that enables that country to generate more GDP from services.

2. Team 1: Develop the 4Ps for Citibank to expand its credit card business and financial services in China. Team 2: Develop the 4Ps for Citibank to expand its credit card business and financial services in Brazil.

3. Team 1: Pick a country in Latin America and a service that is used widely in that country. Define "service quality" for that service. What criteria are important to the customer? How would you as a business ensure that this quality is consistent?

   Team 2: Pick a country in Asia and a service that is used widely in that country. Define "service quality" for that service. What criteria are important to the customer? How would you as a business ensure that this quality is consistent?

4. Team 1: What are the reasons that the U.S. should adopt the metric system as the country's system of weights and measures?

   Team 2: What are the reasons that the U.S. should not adopt the metric system as the country's system of weights and measures?

SELECTED REFERENCES

Baertlein, Lisa, "Starbucks buying full control of Japan unit for $914 million," *Reuters*, September 24, 2014.

Bitner, Mary Jo. "Servicescapes: The Impact of Physical Surroundings on Customers and Employees." *Journal of Marketing*, April 1992, pp. 57–71.

Chalabi, Mona & John Burn-Murdoch, "McDonald's 34,492 restaurants: where are they?" *The Guardian*, Wednesday 17 July 2013.

"Deloitte is biggest global firm," *Economa*, January 28, 2015.

Ducker, Michael, "New Free Trade Talks On Services Key to U.S. Job Growth," *Forbes Opinion*, Jan 18, 2013.

Ekeledo, Ikechi and K. Sivakumar, "International market entry mode strategies of manufacturing firms and service firms: A resource-based perspective," *International Marketing Review*, 2004, Vol. 21 Iss: 1, pp. 68–101.

Grönroos, Christian. *Service Management and Marketing*, 3rd ed. Chichester, UK: Wiley, 2007.

Higgins, Kevin T., "Marketing Visa Everywhere It Wants to Be," *Marketing Management,* November-December 2001, p. 14.

Jensen, J. Bradford, *Global Trade in Services: Fear, Facts, and Offshoring*. Peterson Institute for International Economics, 2011.

Jessop, Alicia. "Visa Relies Heavily Upon Technology as An Official World Cup Sponsor," *Forbes*, June 13, 2014.

Lubin, Gus and Mamta Badkar, "15 Facts About McDonald's That Will Blow Your Mind," *Business Insider*, Nov. 25, 2011.

Mastropolo, Frank, "How the Rolling Stones, Rod Stewart and David Bowie Ran from the Taxman," *Ultimateclassicrock.com*, April 15, 2014.

"McDonald's franchisee in Russia not to reconsider plans for expansion," *Tass Russian News Agency*, 2014.

Mouawad, Jad, "Giant Airbus A380 finds sales not so big," *Seattle Times,* August 18, 2014.

Nielsen, Rachel, "Q&A: For McDonald's Khasbulatov, It's All About People," *The Moscow Times*, Oct. 19, 2012.

"Patients Beyond Borders," *Medical Tourism Statistics & Facts*, 2014.

Peeters, Carine, Catherine Dehon and Patricia Garcia-Prieto, "The attention stimulus of cultural differences in global services sourcing," *Journal of International Business Studies*, Vol. 46, No. 2, Feb/March 2015, pp. 241–251.

Pollack, Andrew, "Who's Reading your X-Ray?" *New York Times*, 2003.

PR Newswire, "New Line Cinema's *Return of the King* Reigns Worldwide with $312 Million in First Seven Days," December 24, 2003.

Punch, Linda, "How Exposed?" *Credit Card Management,* November 2001, pp. 26–32.

Reardon, James; M. Krishna Erramilli; and Derrick Dsouza. "International Expansion of Service Firms: Problems and Strategies," *Journal of Professional Services Marketing* 15, no. 1 (1996), pp. 31–46.

Rheubottom, Robert, "Rolling Stones reported as performing fall 2015 tour dates in Brazil," *AXS*, January 4, 2015.

RNCOS Business Consultancy, *Indian Diagnostic Services Market Outlook*, 2013.

Samiee, Saeed. "The Internationalization of Services: Trends, Obstacles and Issues." *In Hult*, 1999, pp. 319–28.

Schilling, Melissa and Suresh Kotha, "Starbucks Corporation: Going Global." *University of Washington, School of Business Case*, 1997.

"Smoking in Japan," Facts and Figures, 2014.

"Starbucks celebrates 30 years of success," *DJC Orgeon*, September 7, 2001.

"Starbucks on track to open 1,000th store in Japan," *Japan Today*, May 13, 2013.

Stauss, Bernd, and Paul Mang. "'Culture Shocks' in Inter-Cultural Service Encounters," *In Hult*, 1999, pp. 329–46.

"Lord of the Rings: The Two Towers Extended Edition commentary," *New Line Cinema*, 2003.

"Top 100 Movie Franchises by Revenue," *IMDB, Universal Box Office*, Dec 10. 2013.

Weidenhamer, Deb, "Customer Service, Chinese Style: You're the Boss," *The New York Times*, Feb. 14, 2014.

Westbrook, Bruce, "DVD Release: *The Return of the King*," *The Houston Chronicle*, May 24, 2004, p. 1.

"Worldwide Box Office Grosses," Box Office Mojo, 2014.

Zeithaml, Valarie A., Mary-Jo Bitner, D.D.Gremler," *Services Marketing*, 6th ed., McGraw-Hill, 2012.

Zhang, Xiao, Weiguo Zhong and Shige Makino, "Customer Involvement and service firm internationalization performance: An integrative framework," *Journal of International Business Studies,* Vol. 46, No. 3, April 2015, pp. 355–380.

ENDNOTES

1. See RNCOS, 2013.
2. See Pollack, 2003.
3. See Patients Beyond Borders, 2014.
4. From Patients Beyond Borders, 2014.
5. See Samiee, 1999.
6. From Rheubottom, 2015.
7. See Mastropolo, 2014.
8. See Jensen, 2011, and www. servicescoalition.org.
9. See Ducker, 2013.
10. Sources: Higgins, 2001; Punch, 2001; Jessop, 2014.
11. See Jessop, 2014.
12. From Zeithaml, Bitner, and Gremler, 2012.
13. Sources: Grönroos, 2007; Mouawad, 2014.
14. See Mouawad, 2014.
15. See Zeithaml, et al., 2012. The original article is Bitner, 1992.
16. From Grönroos, 2007.
17. From Reardon, Erramilli, and Dsouza, 1996; Ekeledo and Sivakumar, 2004.
18. See Weidenhamer, 2014.
19. Sources: Schilling and Kotha, 1997; "Starbucks Celebrates …, 2001; "Starbucks on track …" 2013.
20. See "Smoking in Japan," 2014.
21. See Baertlein, 2014.
22. Sources: Westbrook, 2004; PR Newswire, 2003; "Top 100 Movie …," 2013.
23. See "*Lord of the Rings* …," 2003.
24. See "Top 100 movie franchises …," 2013.
25. See "Worldwide Box Offices Grosses," 2014.
26. From Bitner, 1992.
27. From Zeithaml, et al., 2013.
28. See, for example, Zhang, Zhong, and Makino, 2015.
29. See Zeithaml et al., 2012.
30. From Stauss and Mang, 1999.
31. See Lubin and Badkar, 2011
32. Sources: Nielsen, 2012; Lubin and Badkar, 2011; Chalabi and Burn-Murdoch, 2013; http://www.aboutmcdonalds.com.
33. See McDonald's corporate website "Franchise Details."
34. See "McDonald's franchisee in Russia not to reconsider plans for expansion," 2015.

In this chapter you will learn about:

1. The many added factors that have to be considered in setting prices when going abroad
2. How transfer pricing of goods shipped between a company's foreign subsidiaries affect local prices and profitability and local taxes paid, and how companies need to stay clear of legal complications
3. The role of countertrade in international business
4. The need to use pricing tolls such as price corridors to limit and help avoid gray trade

Global Pricing

CHAPTER 11

APPLE'S PRICING APPROACH

Apple's strategy for pricing of the iPhone revolves around four main ideas

1. Focus on the high end
2. Offer a small number of products
3. Profits are more important than market share
4. Create a shortage that makes people want new Apple products

A key to this strategy's success is that Apple's phone products must be unique and technologically ahead of its competitors, essentially providing a lot of value for the price.

Apple uses a retail pricing strategy called "minimum advertised price" or "price maintenance." Normally as products move from manufacturer to end user, they pass through a network of distribution and each is free to set their own price levels using "cost plus a markup"

approach. For example, if a phone has a manufacturer suggested price (MSRP) of $500, the retailer may buy this phone for $250. That gap between cost and suggested price leaves the retailer a lot of room to set their own margins and prices and produces a significant range of market prices for the same product (this is the shopping experience that we all love).

Apple however offers only a tiny discount between cost and suggested selling price thus forcing prices into the small range that we see in the market today. To interest retailers in carrying its products, Apple then offers large monetary incentives if retailers will advertise its products at or above a minimum price (securing the profit margin for most Apple retailers).[1]

The lack of competition has positioned Apple prices far above its rivals but with significant market share worldwide based on its technologically advanced designs (see Exhibit 11.1).

EXHIBIT 11.1.	Samsung	31.0 %
Smartphone worldwide market shares[2] Apple and Samsung are losing market share as Chinese brands continued to increase their sales. While Chinese brands sell most phones in their home market, they are also starting to do well in emerging markets.	Apple	25.4 %
	Huawei	7.4 %
	Xiaomi	6.3%
	Oppo	5.5 %
	Vivo (Chinese)	4.0%
	LG	3.4%
	Sony	2.8%
	Motorola	2.7%
	Others	11.5 %
	Total	100 %

Source: https://newzoo.com/ insights/trend-reports/ global-mobile-market-report-light-2017.

So why, then, if Apple carefully manages the price levels of its phones, do Apple prices (see Exhibit 11.2) vary so significantly from market to market?

Using a "cost plus" pricing approach some of the variation has to do with higher and varying costs to do business internationally country by country, and some related to costs from potential changes to exchange rates. Using a "perceived value" pricing approach Apple, along with many other companies, has the opportunity to charge higher prices overseas aided, in Apple's case, by the local customer's perception of its advanced technology (i.e., value) and also by point 4 above, the possibility of shortages.

Apple's strategy however is being put to the test as 90 percent of cell-phone users in Brazil have the less expensive Android phones and 75 percent of the cell-phone users in Argentina and Mexico use Androids, raising the questions as to whether Apple's strategy of dominating the most profitable, high end of each market can work long term internationally.[4]

EXHIBIT 11.2.	Apple iPhone S7 Prices (May 2017) (US$$)	
iPhone prices around the globe[3]	United States	$ 815
	Japan	$ 815
	Hong Kong	$ 821
	Malaysia	$ 846
	Canada	$ 855
	....	....
	Poland	$ 1,005
	Greece	$ 1,028
	Russia	$ 1,086
	Brazil	$ 1,115
	Turkey	$ 1,200

High import tariffs are one reason for wide price discrepancies.

Source: https://www.businessinsider. com.au/ ranked-what-an-iphone-7-costs-in-33-countries-2017-5#KeFO8XJSrcGjllff.99.

Pricing globally is more complicated than pricing in the home market. In the domestic market, deciding on price levels, promotional rebates to middlemen, and consumer deals requires careful analysis; but once the decisions are made, the implementation is straightforward.

The opposite generally holds true for markets abroad. The level of price is often a minor headache compared with the problems of currency fluctuations and devaluations, price escalation through tariffs, difficult-to-assess credit risks, FOB versus CIF quotations, dumping charges, transfer prices, and price controls—all common issues in global pricing. In global marketing the actual height of the product price is sometimes less important than currencies quoted, methods of payment, and credit extended.

It is perhaps fair to say that it is in pricing that the existing know-how from domestic marketing is least valuable for global operations. Market segmentation and product positioning principles can be extended abroad. Advertising and sales campaigns can be standardized for foreign markets. But the practical and institutional know-how required for global pricing decisions is of a wholly different order of magnitude.

A GLOBAL PRICING FRAMEWORK

Global pricing involves a number of thorny issues. Exhibit 11.3 provides a framework for our discussion.

It is useful to distinguish at the outset between pricing considerations facing the company as an exporter and the pricing problems specific to global coordination and integration.

- *Export pricing.* The export pricing concerns are several:
    - Currency **exchange** rates vary, sometimes dramatically (as in the Russian ruble's 30 percent decline against the dollar 2014 to 2015). An exporter that offers credit terms in a local currency (such as the ruble) would suffer a big drop in earnings. Many exporters demand payment in a strong currency such as euro or U.S. dollar—which unfortunately can make their products uncompetitive in markets with a volatile currency.
    - Another question is whether the additional costs of tariff (and nontariff) barriers should be passed on to the customer through higher prices, also lowering competitiveness.
    - As for positioning strategy, a high **skimming price** and an "import" status image necessitate niche targeting but also slow down market penetration and leave windows of opportunity for the competition. A skimming price strategy assumes that a marketer can charge a price significantly above the competition and focus on obtaining high profits per unit rather than high sales. On the other hand, choosing a low **penetration price**, the firm runs a risk of inviting competition, and also being accused of dumping, that is, selling its products below cost. A penetration price strategy attempts to obtain significant sales and market share by offering a very low price compared to competition even if profits are low.
- *Multinational pricing.* For the multinational company with subsidiaries abroad, there are additional problems of pricing strategy.
    - The first strategic task is that of deciding in which currency to price and what hedging tactics to employ against a currency shift.
    - Next is the task of determining **transfer prices**—the prices charged country subsidiaries for products, components, and supplies—that are equitable in terms of performance evaluation between country units and still optimal from the overall network perspective, including a desirable profit repatriation pattern. Foreign tax authorities have grown increasingly impatient with pricing schemes that rob a country of "fair" tax returns and, consequently, subject transfer prices to great scrutiny.

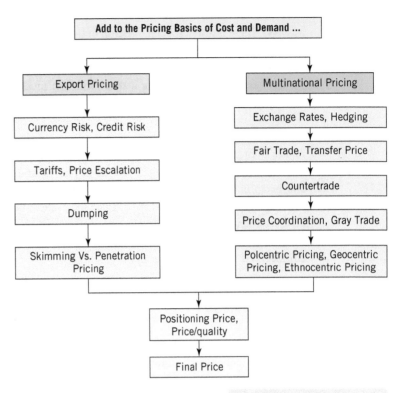

EXHIBIT 11.3.
A global pricing framework

- There is also a special question of how to price when fair trade products are acquired and used as inputs to production or in final products.
- Then there is the problem of coordinating pricing across countries, to satisfy multinational customers, without imposing a straitjacket on local subsidiaries and illegally fixing prices for independent distributors.

The manager might also have to face **countertrade** which is the term for a transaction where the customer makes all or part of the payment in goods instead of hard currency (essentially a form of bartering).

The chapter will start with the basics of pricing and then move to the financial issues of currency exchange and hedging. The chapter will then turn to transfer pricing, countertrade, and systems pricing. The roles of the price–quality relationship and the product life cycle in positioning strategy are discussed next. This is followed by an assessment of the feasibility of global or regional price coordination with particular emphasis on firms' "gray trade" experiences. The last section of the chapter deals with the relative merits of polycentric, geocentric, and ethnocentric pricing strategies in the global firm.

PRICING BASICS

The basic principles of global pricing derive from the traditional pricing approaches in home markets. These revolve around production costs, competitive factors, and demand considerations. Going abroad with a fairly standardized product or service, the price can then be adjusted depending on the conditions in any one local market.

Cost-Plus Pricing

The standard pricing procedure for exporting consists of a **cost-plus pricing** formula. Cost-plus pricing is a simple pricing strategy in which a company determines the cost of their product and then adds a percentage on top of that cost to determine the selling price to the customer. The firm presumably arrives at prices in foreign markets by adding up the various costs involved in producing the product at home (cost-based pricing) and then adding a markup ("plus") to this figure for shipping and border crossing costs. This is the "price escalation" that seems logical as a first step. The cost components include manufacturing costs, administrative costs, allocated R&D expenditures, selling costs, plus the transport charges, insurance, tariffs and various customs duties, and requisite fees to importers and agents.

Often simplified products will be cheaper to produce, and if so, even if the scale returns are not achieved, a lower price for the poorer markets may still yield a positive profit margin because direct costs are low. Even with lower gross margins, the huge market at the bottom of the pyramid will still be profitable enough because of the large volume sold to satisfy the large multinationals and their investors. This is the logic behind the bottom of the pyramid argument.[5]

The sole reliance on a cost-based pricing system is acceptable only in rare circumstances. It is frequently resorted to in the firm starting its exporting, since the know-how and the financial resources are not yet sufficient for market-oriented pricing. In most cases, however, it becomes absolutely necessary that competition and demand be factored into the decision process.

Experience Curve Pricing

The use of a cost-based price has become more common after the discovery of the **experience curve** effect. While scale economies relate directly to the size of a plant (a larger plant will have lower unit costs up to a "minimum efficient scale"), the **experience curve** shows how unit costs go down *over time* as successively more units of a product are produced (see Exhibit 11.4).

Through the "learning by doing" that comes from experience, the company's employees develop skills and capabilities that translate into lower costs. Thus, a firm entering a new foreign market will gain in capabilities from accumulated production and market experience.

The learning behind the experience curve will also help the company develop scope economies. **Scope economies** are efficiencies that emerge as a company and its employees learn to operate in related products and markets. Scope economies can be significant at the bottom of the pyramid, when companies learn how to diversify into new products and services once the situation of the poor is better understood. In a way, scope economies give rise to CSR and related activities. Once the companies realize the need for further education and healthcare among the poor, it becomes natural to invest in better social structures. When Procter & Gamble starts a school in India ("Program Shiksha"), they are not simply doing CSR and filling a need—they are also ensuring a better local labor supply for a growing economy, including their own company and suppliers.[6]

Experience curve pricing has been adopted primarily by companies entering an existing market in the maturity stage. Many firms from emerging countries operate with this strategy in advanced markets, since it allows them to maintain a penetration price level in foreign markets.

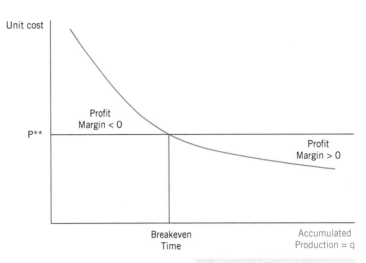

EXHIBIT 11.4.
The experience curve

Perceived Value Pricing

The competitive analysis in pricing might be as simple as finding out what global and domestic competitors in the particular country market charge for their products. These prices tend to set the **reservation prices** in the local market, that is, the limit beyond which the firm's product will not be bought. The analysis can go further and attempt to isolate the differential advantages that the firm's product might have over these existing offerings, using so-called perceived value pricing.[7]

Perceived value pricing consists of dividing price into a "commodity" part and a "premium price differential" part. The commodity portion of price relates to underlying demand factors, while the premium differential focuses specifically on the competitive factors.

The **premium price differential** refers to the degree to which the firm might be granted a higher price by the market because of the particular strengths of its product. The company needs to research how important various product attributes are to customers, and assess how competition is perceived on the salient attributes. Caterpillar uses this approach to price its products in relation to its competitors, including Japanese Komatsu and China's Joy Global (see Exhibit 11.5).

Example: Caterpillar vs main competitor.

$ 20,000	Is the Competitor's Price
$ 3,000	Is the Premium For Superior Durability
$ 2,000	Is the Premium For Superior Reliability
$ 2,000	Is the Premium For Superior Service
$ 1,000	Is the Premium For Longer Warranty
$28,000	Is the *Total Value*
$ 4,000	Offered Discount
$24,000	*Final Price*

EXHIBIT 11.5.
Perceived value pricing

EXHIBIT 11.6.
Balinese villagers participating in the traditional religious Hindu procession before Balinese New Year in Ubud, Bali. Pricing in B-O-P markets means thinking outside of the box: Perhaps sharing the use of a new product makes price affordable? If credit is necessary, how can it be extended safely? Is some kind of countertrade possible—for example, could we help sell the crop from a village?

The final price is higher than competition, but the premium price still includes a $4,000 "discount."

In domestic markets the research to identify the specific strengths and weaknesses is typically done via comprehensive and in-depth marketing research. In foreign markets informal data from existing customers, distributors, and country experts can usually offer a preliminary guide.

Demand Pricing

Naturally, demand also needs to be considered when setting prices; and most firms do, however implicitly, pay attention to what the various local markets "will bear."

The **price elasticity** associated with the demand curve in economic theory identifies how many customers are willing to buy how much of the product at various price levels. The price elasticity is the economics term usually called **price sensitivity** by marketers.

It is easy to assume that emerging markets are more sensitive to price level than more advanced markets—after all, the poor are more financially constrained. But this is too simplistic. Even in advanced markets there are segments of people who have less money.

In a recent large-scale study, the authors found that price sensitivity is at least as high in advanced countries as in emerging countries.[8] Because the better infrastructure enables more effective distribution, availability of competing brands is greater in advanced countries. Since competing brands are typically close substitutes, this leads to greater price sensitivity. The researchers concluded that distribution is the most important factor in emerging markets, with price most important in advanced markets.

In addition to making the products available through distribution, pricing clearly becomes an important issue for bottom-of-the-pyramid markets. How much can people pay? In such cases, the pricing analysis needs to first carefully evaluate what exactly a price would consist of—an individual outlay, or can several consumers share? (See Exhibit 11.6.)

The point here is that the analysis starts with an acceptable price. Then the question is: Can the company produce a functional product at that price? That is, can we adapt our product, however it is done, to yield a production cost that still gives the company some kind of positive return margin? This is not so farfetched as it might seem. This kind of pricing approach has come to be called **target pricing**.

Target pricing is typically used by new companies from emerging markets, trying to break into advanced markets. For example, cell-phone manufacturers other than Apple tend to follow this approach. The issue is how much of a price discount is necessary to incite consumers to consider our brand, given that the functional quality is comparable? In some sense their situation is the opposite of a price premium case, with the differential being a price discount rather than premium.

SKIMMING VS. PENETRATION PRICING

When entering a new foreign market, the company is usually faced with the choice between a high skimming price and a lower penetration price. The choice has implications for the revenues and the long run profitability of the entry (see Exhibit 11.7).

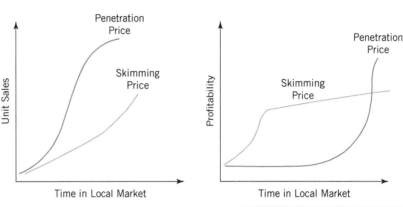

EXHIBIT 11.7.
Skimming vs. penetration pricing

It is generally agreed that in the introductory stage of the product life cycle (PLC) customers are relatively insensitive to price levels. The innovators and pioneers who venture to try the new product are not very much concerned with price but act out of a desire to experience new things. Thus, the firm entering a market in the early growth stage could possibly maintain a relatively high so-called *skimming* price, charging what the market will bear. Apple's pricing policy (see Opening Vignette) is intended to skim the market, for example.

However, today a **demonstration effect** often serves to speed up the introductory phase of many products. A demonstration effect describes the fact that customers in the new market already know about the product from other markets. Potential customers are prepared for the eventual arrival of the new product by exposure via television and related global media so the introductory phase of the market is shortened and the market jumps to the growth stage.

Consequently, the best entry pricing approach in many markets will be a relatively low-priced so-called *penetration* strategy. This is also the one followed in recent years by most companies, including those as diverse as Microsoft with its office products, Mercedes' new model autos and Samsung's smartphones. The competitive rivalry is potentially intense, the buyers in the global village already know much about the product, and the producers use the experience curve argument to justify very low prices based on marginal costs.

FINANCIAL ISSUES

Pricing basics are only the start of global price determination. As we saw in Exhibit 11.3, there are a number of international finance issues related to pricing.

BOX: Argentine Woes Pegged to the Peso[10]

In early 2015, Argentina was faced with the possibility of a default. Its bond-holders around the world cannot get paid the annual interest charges and the redemption costs. Funds were available and even deposited in banks in New York City, but a legal challenge by a handful (7 percent) of bond-holders stopped any payouts. The problem was, they demanded full payment of the original debt, while 93 percent of bond-holders were willing to accept 30 cents on the dollar, a major loss for these bond holders but something (i.e., 30 percent of your investment) is better than nothing.

This debacle had a decade-long history. In 2002 Eduardo Duhalde, Argentina's fifth president in two weeks, was faced with whether or not to devalue the country's peso and avert the nation's largest financial crisis in history.

For a decade, Argentina had kept the peso pegged one-to-one to the U.S. dollar as a means of providing monetary stability in the face of hyperinflation in the late 1980s. While most Argentines earn pesos, an estimated 80 percent of debts, from home mortgages to corporate loans, were denominated in dollars. So a break of the currency peg was likely to result in widespread bankruptcies.

The peg meant that peso was overvalued, making Argentine exports uncompetitive on world markets—and resulting in four years of recession. The dollar's strength resulted in Argentine exports being more expensive than competitive offerings in many cases. Argentine businesses were scrambling to remain solvent.

The decision? The peso's peg to the dollar was abandoned in January 2002, and the peso was floated in February. The medicine worked. The exchange rate plunged and inflation picked up rapidly, but by mid-2002 the economy had stabilized, albeit at a lower level. Led by record exports, the economy began to recover with output up 8 percent in 2003, unemployment falling, and inflation reduced to under 4 percent at year-end. Despite the success, Mr. Duhalde was not re-elected. On May 25, 2003, Nestor Kirchner was declared the winner of a runoff presidential election by default after Carlos Saul Menem withdrew his candidacy. The new president, proud of his leftwing political past, fought hard with the IMF for forgiveness of Argentina's outstanding foreign debt of about $100 billion.

On his death in 2007 he was succeeded by his wife, Cristina, who continued the fight. As of 2014, Argentina had succeeded in shaping a so-called "haircut" on the outstanding foreign debt, i.e., the agreement to pay 30 cents on the dollar previously mentioned. This was accepted by most bond-holders, but some hedge-fund leaders (the seven percent) saw an opportunity and having acquired an amount of Argentine bonds at cut-rate prices, they demanded full payment, 100 cents on the dollar and sued in U.S. court. The case was finally resolved in 2016 with holdout bondholders getting close to 100 cents on the dollar

Exchange Rates[9]

Fluctuating exchange rates will routinely create problems with revenues and prices in a foreign market and can powerfully affect the performance of local subsidiaries. A particularly potent threat is the chance of government devaluation, as happened in China recently and has long been a problem in Argentina (see box, "Argentine Woes Pegged to the Peso").

The currency shifts that are most crucial are the cases where the currency specified in a contract suddenly loses its value. This can happen when a country encounters steep inflation or when an unexpected shock happens. Foreign companies paid in the local currency suddenly receive significantly less funds than before. When the Brexit vote surprisingly made for Britain's exit from the EU, the pound sterling lost around 15 percent of its value overnight against the dollar. American companies paid in pounds could receive significantly fewer dollars than before. On the other hand, American tourists suddenly found London to be much cheaper than expected. The impact of depreciating and appreciating currency on prices can be seen in the example in Exhibit 11.8.

		if the home company needs this amount of home currency per product	..... then the sales price in the foreign country must be this:
Normal	1 home currency = 1 foreign currency	<u>100</u>	<u>100</u>
Home currency depreciates (i.e., is worth less so more is needed to buy foreign currency)	1.2 home = 1 foreign	<u>100</u>	<u>83.3</u>
Home currency appreciates (i.e., is worth more so less is needed to buy foreign currency)	.8 home = 1 foreign	<u>100</u>	<u>120</u>

EXHIBIT 11.8
Currency fluctuations can alter prices in the international markets. Management must constantly be monitoring exchange rates to ensure competitive international prices.

The Big Mac Index

To understand exchange rate fluctuations and their impact on market prices, the McDonald's Big Mac prices around the world has long been a favorite illustration among economists. The so-called "Big Mac index" was spearheaded by *The Economist* who did it first in 1986 as a lighthearted guide and has been doing it every year since then (see Exhibit 11.9). In most local markets, McDonald's positions its products as affordable for a broad-based family segment. In addition, the Big Mac is pretty much the same across countries, although the local prices vary widely. These differences, when translated into dollar terms, can show the strength and weakness of the local currency.

The Big Mac index is based on the notion that the local price of a Big Mac relative to the price of a Big Mac in the United States, its home market, will show whether the local currency is over- or undervalued relative to the U.S. dollar. To translate the local price of a Big Mac into U.S. dollars, the official exchange rate is used. Since the U.S. dollar is often the default choice as a globally accepted currency, the over- or undervaluation vis-à-vis the U.S. dollar becomes important for global trade and investment decisions.

Country	Currency	Big Mac Price (2017)	Currency Status Raw Index	Currency Status Adjusted Index
Switzerland	Swiss Franc	$6.74	overvalue 27.2%	overvalue 5.6%
Norway	Kroner	$5.91	overvalue 11.6%	undervalue 3.5%
Sweden	S Krona	$5.82	overvalue 9.8%	overvalue 15.4%
USA	Dollar	$5.30	baseline	baseline
Brazil	Real	$5.10	undervalue 3.7%	overvalue 56.9%
Israel	Shekel	$4.77	undervalue 9.9%	overvalue 6.2%
Canada	C Dollar	$4.66	undervalue 12.2%	undervalue 1.1%
China	Yuan	$2.92	undervalue 45.0%	overvalue 9.6%
India	Rupee	$2.76	undervalue 48.0%	undervalue 6.5%
Russia	Rouble	$2.28	undervalue 57.0%	undervalue 30.3%
South Africa	Rand	$2.26	undervalue 57.3%	undervalue 27.6%

EXHIBIT 11.9.
The Big Mac index The "raw" index is based on official exchange rates, the "adjusted" corrects for local cost-of-living expenses.

Source: *The Economist* (http://www.economist.com/content/big-mac-index.

In Exhibit 11.9 we can see that in 2017 Big Mac prices ranged from $2.26 in South Africa to $6.74 in Switzerland (that still uses its own strong Swiss franc and has not adopted the Euro). For a Swiss visiting the United States will be like going to a discount store, while an American visiting Switzerland might well skip some meals.

The Big Mac index is centered at the U.S. price, where the index = 0. The index is obtained by subtracting the U.S. price from the local price in U.S. dollars (at official exchange rates), dividing the result by the U.S. price and multiplying by 100. For example, the average price of a Big Mac in America in July 2017 was $5.30; in China it was only $2.92 at market exchange rates. So the "raw" Big Mac index based on official exchange rates says that the yuan was undervalued by 45% at that time (1-2.92/5.30 = .45). Since 2.92 can actually buy a Big Mac, it is more money than it would seem, actually more like $5.30, which is why the yuan seems undervalued. The adjusted Big Mac index uses the Purchasing Power Index to adjust this figure. Even though 2.92 might seem undervalued, the PPP adjusts for the fact that other products in China are less expensive as well. So, although 2.92 can buy a Big Mac, when compared to other products in the China market, the 2.92 Big Mac is actually pretty expensive. It shows that the yuan is overvalued, meaning that 5.30 in the U.S. is less money than $2.92 in China. The 9.6% overvalue suggests that the 2.92 is more like $5.80 (5.30 x 1.096) in the U.S.

Hedging

In the big picture, the effect of exchange rate fluctuations on the market prices of the products sold is limited not only by what managers can do but also by what they can't do. Prices can't be changed overnight, even if exchange rates do. To avoid the risk of wide fluctuations in short-term profits, the global company will often turn to hedging.

Hedging involves the purchase of insurance against losses because of currency fluctuations. Such insurance usually takes the form of buying or selling "forward contracts" or engaging in "currency swaps" with the help of financial intermediaries (banks and brokerage houses).

Hedging allows a company to protect itself, but comes as sometimes steep price. The insurance premium is not low, but sometimes worth it. Here is how Bloomberg reports two contrasting cases:

> "Wal-Mart Stores Inc. took a $680 million hit to sales last quarter because of the stronger dollar, show-ing the risks that companies face when they don't hedge against swings in the U.S. currency. Wal-Mart, operates stores worldwide in local currencies but reports results in U.S. dollars and does not use hedg-ing. … Some companies have been successful in blunting the effect of currency fluctuations. Yahoo! Inc. recorded $165 million in gains in the second quarter from steps the web portal took to guard against swings in the Japanese yen, bringing its total benefit from such currency hedges to $438 million."[11]

A **forward contract** refers to the sale or purchase of a specified amount of a foreign currency at a fixed exchange rate for delivery or settlement on an agreed date in the future or, under an options contract, between agreed upon dates in the future. A **swap** may be defined as the exchange of one currency for another for a fixed period of time. At the expiration of the swap each party returns the currency initially received. While the forward contract represents a simple insurance policy against downside risk—the firm buys today so as not to lose by a deteriorating currency in the foreign market—the cost of the contract reduces the gain from a favorable change in rates.

Hedging has become a major financial activity of the international division in many MNCs. From a market-ing viewpoint, the most desirable arrangement would be for the seller to assume responsibility for currency fluctuations and quote prices in the local currency. This is not done very often by Western companies, however. Their prices, especially in commodities and industrial markets, tend to be quoted in the "hard" currencies, in particular the U.S. dollar. A company such as Boeing, for example, quotes prices in U.S. dollars only and lets its customers worry about the exchange-rate fluctuations and the conversion from the local currency.

Government Interventions

There are various types of government intervention that affect pricing. Chief among these are the antitrust laws, in particular as they relate to **price fixing** and **discrimination**. Price fixing is an agreement (written, verbal, or inferred from conduct) among competitors that raises, lowers, or stabilizes prices rather than allowing prices to be determined naturally through free-market forces. Price fixing is illegal in the U.S. but not always in other countries. Price discrimination is the practice of charging a different price to different customers for the same good or service. Not all price discrimination is illegal. For example, different customers may pay different prices based on larger or smaller quantity purchased.

The firm's legal counsel is the person most likely to be involved in these matters. In terms of price fixing it is important to point out that in certain countries price cartels are common. A price **cartel** is an agreement between competing producers to set a common price—oil prices are basically set by a cartel, for example. But cartels are often opposed by governments when the benefits accrue to foreign entrants (see box, "Chinese antitrust").

BOX: Chinese Antitrust[12]

In 2014, China's antitrust agency stepped up enforcement against price fixing among multinationals in China. It fined 12 Japanese auto parts and bearings suppliers approximately $200 million, a new record for Chinese enforcement. The 12 suppliers cited in the ruling were accused of fixing prices for parts and components used in the manufacture of more than 20 car models, assembled by the Chinese joint ventures of Toyota, Honda, Nissan, Suzuki, and Ford.

Observers interpreted the action as targeting Japan, perhaps as a result of territorial disputes over three islands on the China coast, and also over disagreement over the two countries' conflicting versions of their World War II experiences.

In a related effort, the Chinese regulator is also trying to determine whether foreign automakers are colluding with dealers to compel customers to buy expensive replacement parts from the automakers' own factories. They are supposed to allow customers to choose replacement parts from independent parts manufacturers. Perhaps to forestall further actions, Tata Motors (Jaguar and Land Rover), Mercedes-Benz, and BMW are among seven foreign automakers that have announced price cuts on replacement parts in China.

China is becoming more like us? Not yet. Any rulings can in theory be appealed by companies to the courts. But the Chinese government tightly controls the judiciary, so lawyers and companies have generally concluded that this is fruitless.

When it comes to price discrimination, there are very few laws around the world that prohibit discrimination, as the American Robinson-Patman law does. However, many laws do question discounts not tied to specific functions performed: The issue of bribery surfaces easily. The firm needs to get some legal advice on what is acceptable and what is not in the particular country. In the Middle East, for example, it is customary to give large functional rebates to the middlemen handling the product as distributors. It is usually necessary to offer such rebates for any newcomer who wants to enter the market.

FAIR TRADE AND PRICING

Fair trade is a movement whose goal is to help producers in developing countries to get a fair price for their products so as to reduce poverty, provide for the ethical treatment of workers and farmers, and promote environmentally sustainable practices. This fair price is not determined by market conditions but through an agreement between buyer and seller of what is "fair." Although the products involved are basically produce, the movement has relevance beyond produce. It sensitizes consumers to the sourcing of raw materials and to the treatment of workers in outsourced contract manufacturing.

Fair trade is based on the notion that the producers in poor countries should be ensured a minimum level of price for their products without regard to what the actual world price is for their commodity. The Fair Trade International's website lists the fair trade minimum price levels for a wide range of produce, from apples and bananas to rice, sugar, and zucchini, broken down by country of origin.[13] Actual prices can be higher, depending on market prices. The exact wording is:

"When the market price is higher than the Fair Trade Minimum Price, producers should receive the current market price or the price negotiated at contract signing."

There is also a price premium allowed for upgraded products. "Organic" farming of coffee can raise the minimum by around 15 percent, for example, for coffee that is of higher quality.[14] In return for the endorsement that comes with the Fair Trade label, Fair Trade International insists that producers adhere to high environmental standards. The produce does not have to be "organic," but is guaranteed to be free of GMOs (genetically modified organisms). The use of pesticides and fertilizers is also limited. Sustainability is demanded. For example, the producers must:

- Protect water resources and natural vegetation areas
- Demonstrate erosion control
- Show proper management of waste, water, and energy

These kinds of requirement are now affecting many multinational manufacturers who rely on outsourcing in low-wage countries. As we have seen throughout the text, such MNCs are also increasingly focused on sustainability and CSR.

Fair trade is not "free trade." Standard economic theory would suggest that guaranteed price levels to producers will raise consumer prices. However, the Fair Trade International organization argues that prices are not necessarily higher. But in many cases Fair Trade products are in fact more expensive. One reason is that there are incentives for producers to upgrade their produce—many begin "organic" farming, for example. Consequently their products will fetch higher prices than "conventional" produce. But the higher prices can be discounted (see Exhibit 11.10).

The same effect has been recognized by multinational companies, allowing their investments in sustainability and CSR to be reflected in slightly higher prices, a premium based on increased consumer "goodwill."

TRANSFER PRICING[15]

A considerable amount of international trade is accounted for by shipments between headquarters and subsidiaries. For example, the share of exports that is intra-firm (that is, going to the same firm in another country) is regularly around one-third or more across

EXHIBIT 11.10.
Fair Trade products can be organic—and discounted too. Because many consumers are willing to pay more for fair trade and organic produce, the Fair Trade label has attractive in-store appeal.

J.K. Johansson

countries.[16] The question of how companies price these internal shipments naturally arises. This is the problem of "transfer" prices.

What is a Transfer Price?

The **transfer price** is the price charged for the products shipped between units of the same organization when the shipment crosses national borders (see Exhibit 11.11A). The transfer price is the base on which the correct duties and taxes can be paid. The price escalation in turn affects the final consumer price (see Exhibit 11.11B).

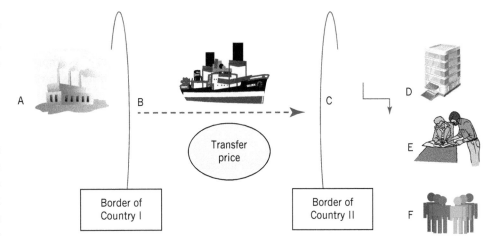

A = manufacturing price
B = cost at the shipping dock
C = cost at the dock in country
D = cost at the local subsidiary after customs
E = cost to the local distributor
F = cost to the consumer

EXHIBIT 11.11A
Effect of transfer price on final consumer price

Ex. 11.11a: Source: http://www. pdclipart.org/displayimage. php?album=search&cat=0&pos=0.

Ex. 11.11b: Source: http://www. pdclipart.org/displayimage. php?album=search&cat=0&pos=62.

Ex. 11.11c: Source: https:// openclipart.org/detail/216806/ office-building.

Ex. 11.11d: Source: https:// openclipart.org/detail/6970/ reference-desk.

Ex. 11.11e: Source: https:// openclipart.org/detail/138967/ people.

		Example One	Example Two	Example Three
A	Manufacturing price		$100	$100	$100
B	Price at dock (The Transfer price)		$100	$150	$200
	Shipping and insurance (20% fees)	$20		$30	$40
C	Cost at dock		$120	$180	$240
	25% import tariff	$30		$45	$60
D	Landed cost to importer		$150	$225	$300
	Importer profit added (25%)	$38		$56	$75
E	Price to local distributor		$188	$281	$375
	Distributor profit (50%)	$94		$141	$188
F	**Price to local customer**		**$281**	**$422**	**$563**

Taxes paid in international country			
Import tariff	$30	$45	$60
30% income tax on importer profits	$9	$14	$18
30% income tax on distributor profits	$28	$42	$56
Total local tax paid	$67	$101	$134

EXHIBIT 11.11B
Price escalation to consumers and taxes paid

Since the transfer price directly affects costs at the foreign subsidiary, it has a direct influence on the subsidiary's financial performance. Because of this transfer prices have become a mechanism for the multinational company to shift profits from one country to another. If the headquarters of a company sets a high price on the shipment to a subsidiary in a foreign country, this subsidiary might have trouble showing a profit; and if the transfer price is set low, the subsidiary will be more profitable.

Transfer of Taxes

Transfer pricing becomes a key influence on a corporation's worldwide tax burden. In particular, as the levels of corporate income tax and tariffs vary considerably across different countries, transfer prices may be set in part to help minimize a firm's worldwide tax bill.

Reportedly, the use of transfer prices for tax-shifting purposes is not as widespread as it once was because the governments have caught on to abuses.[17] Profit repatriation has come under the close scrutiny of many governments whose tax revenues have diminished because of it (see box, "How to Transfer Income?").

BOX: How to Transfer Income? Carefully[18]

Because of the tax and dumping implications of transfer prices and governments' insistence on transparent accounting rules, public accounting firms have developed detailed guidelines for the transfer pricing process in large multinationals. These guidelines stress the need to document carefully how the decision was made and justify each step taken.

If convicted of cheating, the penalty can be severe. The case of Roche in Australia is an illustrative example. Roche is a Swiss-based pharmaceutical company with global operations. The case at issue was the transfer prices charged to its Australian subsidiaries between the years 1993-2003. In 2006 the Australian government audited the transfer prices to the Australian subsidiary for Roche products acquired from the company's operations in Switzerland and Singapore and decided that those prices were excessive. This assessment increased the subsidiary profits by 126 million Australian dollars (1 Australian dollar at this time was worth about .80 of U.S. dollars).

Going to court, Roche challenged the assessments with the help of economists who calculated the transfer as being market-based and arm's-length. The government retained its own economists who demonstrated that the prices were in fact not arm's-length but significantly higher than market prices. The case was resolved in 2009 on appeal, with the final verdict a compromise, the assessment lowered but still $45 million.

As another example, in 2006, the U.S. Internal Revenue Service successfully resolved a transfer pricing dispute with Glaxo SmithKline Holdings which represents the largest tax dispute in the history of the Internal Revenue Service. Under the settlement agreement, GSK will pay the Internal Revenue Service approximately $3.4 billion for transfer pricing which failed to maintain "arm's-length transactions."[19]

Amazon is currently battling the U.S. IRS related to transfer prices with their EU operations. The IRS has proposed slapping the company with $1.5 billion in back-taxes for their EU operations from 2005 to 2012. Due to differing national tax policies and inter-country money transferring rules, especially in Europe, the IRS claims that Amazon re-arranged their foreign business structures and their transfer pricing to enjoy extraordinary tax benefits.[20] Amazon and IRS accountants and lawyers are currently working on this issue.

In transfer pricing, as in many other matters, economists, accountants, and tax collectors can disagree.

Transfer Pricing in Practice

In practice, the two main approaches to transfer pricing are market-based transfer pricing and cost-based transfer pricing.[21]

Market-based transfer prices. Judging from their public statements, several companies have taken the logical step of introducing an option for subsidiaries to buy on the open market, should price and quality there be more favorable. For example, many of Ford Motor Company's subsidiaries around the world now have this option. This is also called the **arm's-length price**.

Cost-based transfer prices. To assist in determining a cost-based transfer price, a functional analysis can be useful. A **functional analysis** is the process of decomposing the transactional price in order to determine a justifiable price.[22] The purpose is to review and evaluate the functions performed, assets utilized, and risks assumed by the subsidiary in question.

Where the market position is strategically important for the global position of the MNC, headquarters might well transfer more funds to the subsidiary by simply charging low prices for some key product components or parts. The approach is equivalent to government subsidies, but in this case it is carried out within a corporation. An example is the entry of many South Korean companies into the U.S. market. The American offices are usually staffed by people paid directly from South Korea which keeps its costs low. In this way, transfer prices can be used to support a subsidiary's competitive position in an important market.

COUNTERTRADE

Countertrade is the term for transactions in which all or part of the payment is made in kind rather than cash. The practice has been known as "barter trade" throughout recorded history, and often involves a great deal of negotiations, patient persuasion and "haggling." The practice has a long tradition in the Orient, especially the countries around the Silk Road between Xian in China and the cities in Eastern Mediterranean, including Tyre in Lebanon and Istanbul (then Constantinople) in Turkey (Exhibit 11.12).

The primary moving force behind countertrade has been a shortage of hard currencies available to developing countries, in particular those lacking a strong export sector to generate foreign earnings. In addition, the failure of the globally integrated financial markets to support the stability of domestic currencies has made countertrade again appear as a viable alternative payment.

It is useful to distinguish between five kinds of countertrade:[23]

- barter,
- compensation deals,
- counter-purchase,
- product buy-back, and
- offset.

Barter

Barter is the oldest form of countertrade. It is the direct exchange of goods between two trading partners. For barter to make economic sense, the seller must be able to dispose of the goods received in payment. To assist companies that engage in barter trading and cannot count on such arrangements, several barter houses have been

established, primarily in Europe, where many of the exchanges are negotiated.

A famous barter transaction involving consumer goods was Pepsi-Cola's entry into the Soviet Union (see box, "Bartering Russian Vodka for Pepsi Cola").

BOX: Bartering Russian Vodka for Pepsi Cola[24]

One of the classic countertrade cases was Pepsi-Cola's entry into the Soviet Union back in 1972. At that time the Soviets did not have access to much hard currency since the Cold War was severely limiting trade outside the Soviet bloc and the oil that today accounts for much of Russia's foreign exchange was considered a strategic good and not exported.

The American president at that time, Richard Nixon, had been an attorney at Pepsi-Cola and had maintained a close relationship with Donald Kendall, Pepsi's CEO. Kendall convinced Nixon that a trade relationship between Soviet Russia and the United States would help ease tensions, and what better symbol of this relationship than selling Pepsi-Cola to the Russians? For the opportunity to become the first Western consumer product sold in the Soviet Union, Pepsi would be willing to consider any countertrade offer.

Pepsi-Cola's relationship with the Soviet Union actually dated back to 1959 when then Soviet leader Nikita Khrushchev was photographed sipping Pepsi-Cola at an American national exhibition in Moscow. But it was on a visit to Soviet Russia in 1971 that President Nixon proposed to his Soviet counterpart President Leonid Brezhnev that Pepsi-Cola be allowed to build a bottling plant and sell its cola in the Russian market. The proposal was accepted and as a quid pro quo the Russians offered Pepsi the exclusive American distribution rights for the number one Russian drink, Stolichnaya vodka.

Exchanging cola for vodka was an offer that PepsiCo executives could not refuse. A $2 billion landmark countertrade agreement was reached in 1972 to exchange Pepsi-Cola concentrate for the rights to sell Stolichnaya vodka in the United States. Pepsi-Cola's first Soviet bottling plant opened in 1974 and soon 22 plants were turning out the concentrate. Fortunately for Pepsi, Stolichnaya became the best-selling imported vodka in the United States for the first 10 years of the agreement and is still near the top of the vodka market.

At the time Pepsi managers had few alternatives for entering a closed market that lacked a fully convertible hard currency. Soviet officials were unwilling to part

EXHIBIT 11.12.
Inside the Grand Bazaar in Istanbul.
The Grand Bazaar is one of the largest and oldest covered markets in the world, with 61 covered streets and over 3,000 shops.
The tradition of negotiating prices over a cup of tea or coffee is still alive in many emerging countries.

with any foreign exchange reserves, so a barter arrangement appealed to both sides. The difficulty, as in any other barter agreement, was being able to independently assess the value of the goods or services involved. Compounding this assessment was Pepsi's inability over the agreement's first 15 years to utilize any modern marketing techniques in the Russian market, since television advertisements, radio commercials, and supermarket promotions with entertainment celebrities or top athletes were all unavailable to the soft drink giant.

However, once the Berlin Wall fell in 1989 and the Russian market opened up, the Pepsi head start proved a handicap. Rather than gaining first-mover advantages, the brand seemed old and tainted by the old regime. Although Coca-Cola took some time to develop its Russian distribution network, it seemed only a matter of time before Pepsi would be overtaken. By 1994 Pepsi still had 60 percent of the Russian market compared to Coke's 38 percent. However, an estimated $500 investment in Russia vaulted Coke to a 51 percent share in 1996 versus Pepsi's 44 percent, and Coke has been leading ever since. As of 2013, Coca-Cola had double the market share of Pepsi (36 percent vs. 18 percent, respectively) in the carbonated soft drink category in Russia.

Pepsi had some consolation in that its entry into a traditional Russian category Kvass, a local fermented drink, is successful. Its "Russian Gift" brand is in the number three spot, ahead of Coca-Cola.

The World Trade Organization estimates that 15 percent of the $5.62 trillion in international trade is conducted on a non-cash basis. Commercial arrangements involving bartering across countries involve as many as 450,000 businesses with 10 percent annual growth.[25] Hundreds of companies and websites now exist to help with international barter transactions including The International Barter Alliance, a trade group.

There is a darker side to counter trade. As an example, in December 2016, Paris-based International Council on Museums (Icom) issued a list and report on ancient manuscripts and historic religious items looted by extremists in the west African country of Mali. The fear is that these antiquities will be sold via barter in non-cash transactions to avoid alerting the world banking community and police.

Compensation Deals

Compensation deals are a type of countertrade that involves the exports of goods in one direction but the payment back is usually split into at least two parts. The first part of the payment is in cash by the importer in the usual manner and for the rest of the payment the original exporter makes an obligation to purchase some of the buyer's goods. Essentially the payment is made in both cash and goods. In one case GM sold locomotives to former Yugoslavia for $12 million and was paid in cash plus Yugoslavian machine tools valued at approximately $4 million. The introduction of the cash portion is to make the deal more attractive to the seller, and most companies faced with the possibility of a countertrade agreement will in fact insist that at least some portion of the bill be settled in cash. As in the case of barter, the goods portion of the payment has to be sold in a third market, and the additional transaction costs should logically be added to the original amount invoiced.

Counter-Purchases

Counter-purchases represent the most typical version of the countertrade. Here two contracts are usually negotiated: one to sell the product (the initial agreement) at an agreed-upon cash price, and a second to buy goods from the purchaser at an amount equal to the bill in the initial agreement. This type of contract simply represents one way for the buyer to reuse valuable foreign currency and force exports and is usually introduced relatively late in the exchange negotiations. In practice the seller gets its money and then has a limited period of time (usually 6 to 12 months) before its purchases from the country must be completed. In some of these cases the second contract is sold (at a steep discount) to a third party (a barter house, for example), but this is not always easy. For a classic example, McDonnell Douglas, the American aircraft manufacturer now merged with Boeing, once had to buy and then resell ham from China in order to sell a few of its aircraft there.

Product Buy-Backs

In **product buy-backs** both the seller and buyer agree to accept payment in goods rather than cash and these usually come in two types. In one type of product buy-back agreement the seller accepts a certain amount of the output as full or partial payment for the goods sold. Alternatively, the seller can agree to buy back some of the output at a later date. Levi Strauss is accepting Hungarian-made jeans (bearing its brand name) in partial payment for setting up a jeans factory outside Budapest. Another Western company has established a tractor plant in Poland and agreed to buy back a certain number of Polish-built tractors as part of the deal.

Offset Deals

In **offset deals**, the seller contracts to invest in local production or procurement to partially offset the sale price. In aircraft, for example, it is not uncommon for a national airline buying airplanes to demand that the manufacturer procure certain components, parts, or supplies in the buyer's country, or invest in some assembly operation there. This helps justify the purchase price paid to the manufacturer from cash-strapped nations.

Business Evaluation

For the seller evaluating a countertrade proposal, the following points are important to consider:

1. Is this the only way the order can be secured?
2. Can the received goods be sold?
3. How can we maximize the cash portion?
4. Does the invoiced price incorporate extra transaction costs?
5. Are there any import barriers to the received goods (so that we will have trouble disposing of the goods at home, say)?
6. Could there be currency exchange problems if we try to repatriate the earnings from sales in a third country?

If these issues receive a positive evaluation, countertrade might be a useful alternative. When the opposite happens, the firm might be better off curbing its appetite for foreign sales.

PRICE AND POSITIONING

Before settling on a final price, the targeted positioning needs to be considered. Positioning as a premium brand, for example, necessarily involves a premium price, typically meaning a higher than average competitive price. For bottom-of-the-pyramid products, where low prices are necessary, a premium brand cannot be used. For most multinationals, there are several brands and models and versions in their product lines, and it is important for positioning purposes, that they reflect different price points. Price will not be the only positioning tool even in poor markets, but it will be the clearest and most important one.

Customers will often attribute high quality to a product with high price. They assume that it costs more to produce a high-quality product, and thus its price will be higher. This is commonly known as the **price–quality relationship.**

Although much research confirms this bias, research has also shown that this price–quality relationship varies in strength by products category. It is strong, for example, for many durable products, but weaker for daily consumables and supermarket items.[26]

The price–quality relationship is also weakened in markets protected by trade barriers and taxes. In such markets imported products will usually show an artificially high price (because of the price escalation due to tariffs and nontariff barriers and entry taxes), and thus a high price signals an imported product, not necessarily a high-quality product.

Because of price escalation from high tariffs and taxes, some imports will make no inroads against established domestic brands. An example is the situation in an emerging market such as China where taxes and nontariff barriers have made markets "dualistic," with a domestic and an import segment. The majority of the market falls to the domestic producers, between whom competition is intense, while the imports garner a small fringe segment of the market, whose primary buying appeal is not "quality" but "status." But with prices of luxury brands in China at 50 percent or more above prices elsewhere, it is hardly surprising that many Chinese travel abroad to go shopping.[27]

PRICING TO LIMIT GRAY TRADE

When a company manufactures in several nations and sells its products in many countries, the same product might appear on the market in different countries at widely different prices. Regardless of the company's price policy, fluctuations in exchange rates tend to produce temporary misalignment in prices between countries. Entrepreneurial spirits in a country can exploit such so-called "arbitrage" opportunities by purchasing the product abroad, shipping it to the market, selling it at a discount, and still clearing a profit.

These imports are sometimes called **parallel imports**, also called **gray trade.** Unauthorized middlemen import the genuine (not counterfeit) products and brands from countries whose prices are lower because of exchange rates. Today, such parallel importers operate quite openly on the web, from a variety of countries, including New Zealand and Singapore. Parallel trade is not illegal—but, of course, as with most things on the Internet, you can never be sure that the brands are authentic. Some are, some aren't.

The problem of gray trade is particularly acute in trade areas where barriers have recently been dismantled and exchange rates fluctuate. China is one example, where despite its WTO membership import tariffs and taxes still make imports much more expensive. This creates big **arbitrage** opportunities meaning that the price within China is significantly higher than the price for the same product outside of China. This price difference is exploited by **consumer tourism**, with people traveling to different countries for the sole purpose of shopping. In China, such shopping trips are sometimes organized for group buying or *tuángòu*, meaning that the overseas traveler buys the branded items for a group of consumers at home, often local neighbors.[28]

Controlling gray trade involves more than trying to set prices that eliminate price differentials between countries, an impossible task in a world of floating exchange rates. Nevertheless, some pricing actions can be taken to help reduce the gray trade problem.

Four approaches to coordinating prices under the threat of gray trade can be identified.[29] They are not mutually exclusive, since a company can pursue them in combination:

Economic Controls

The company can influence price setting in local markets by changing the prices at which the product is shipped to importers or by outright rationing of the product. This usually is most feasible in the case of transfer prices to wholly owned subsidiaries.

Centralization

The company can attempt to set limits for local prices. These usually involve so-called **price corridors**, a range between maximum and minimum prices within which all local prices in a trading area must fall. The corridor should consider market data for the individual countries, price elasticity in the countries, currency exchange rates, costs in countries and arbitrage costs between them, plus data on competition and distribution.

Formalization

Headquarters can standardize the process of planning and implementing pricing decisions in order to direct the pricing at the local level.

Informal Coordination

The company can institute various informal coordination mechanisms, including explicit articulation of corporate values and culture, human resource exchanges, and frequent visits to share experiences in other markets.

The choice between these approaches is affected by many factors, but two have been identified as particularly important: level of marketing standardization and strength of local resources. Exhibit 11.13 helps identify how these factors affect choice of method.

EXHIBIT 11.13.
Pricing strategies to limit gray trade

Adapted from Gert Assmus and Carsten Wiese, "How to Address the Gray Market Threat Using Price Coordination," MIT Sloan Management Review, vol. 36, no. 3.

Level of Marketing Standardization		
	High	Low
Strength of Local Resources High	Economic controls	Informal Coordination
Low	Centralization	Formalization

The different situations can be assessed from the exhibit:

1. When *marketing standardization is high*, target segments and the elements of the marketing mix are known well enough for headquarters to help set local prices.
   a. If local resources are on a high level, *economic controls* tend to be preferable, since raising and lowering transfer prices or rationing will send clear signals to local representatives without imposing final prices.
   b. But if local resources are weak, *centralization* of the pricing decisions may be necessary, creating limits beyond which prices may not deviate.

2. In the *low standardization case*, when marketing is multi-domestic in orientation with locally adapted mix elements, headquarters' role will be less directive. Local managers are likely to be better informed about local conditions than headquarters.

   a. When local representatives are less resourceful, *formalization* of procedures can be helpful in ensuring that the appropriate factors are taken into account when local prices are set.

   b. With strong local resources, *informal coordination* is likely to be preferred, preserving local autonomy—but still using a stick if the carrot is not enough (see box, "Informal Coordination").

BOX: Informal Coordination: The Carrot And The Stick[30]

One company in high-tech medical equipment was faced with a sticky problem. In some countries, doctors needed extensive service support to operate the equipment, while in other countries hospitals had more trained staff. The transfer prices to these latter countries were set higher since sales costs for the subsidiaries were lower. But hospital purchasing managers in these countries were able to lower procurement costs by ordering equipment directly from subsidiaries in countries with lower transfer costs.

To solve the problem, headquarters first organized discussion groups with subsidiary managers to find an acceptable solution. After several meetings, the following strategy was adopted.

- First, the three most important markets were defined as lead countries. The main pricing authority was given to the local managers in the lead countries, who were to set prices so that gray trade would not be lucrative.
- Second, the country managers were trained and rotated between countries to better understand local competition and profit responsibility.
- Third, the reward system was changed by basing part of the local manager's annual bonuses on the success of the whole group. Managers who were uncooperative and hindered progress were laid off.

After one year, the problems were solved. Prices were coordinated, and profitability increased by more than 10 percent.

In the end, it is useful to remember that in isolated instances, not all effects of gray trade might be negative. It is also possible to gain some advantages because gray trade tends to enlarge the market for a product through lower prices.

GLOBAL PRICING POLICIES

Apart from the coordination of prices on specific products and services, global firms usually adopt one of three alternative pricing policies that cut across all their product lines. These pricing policies can be classified as polycentric, geocentric, and ethnocentric.

Polycentric Pricing

Polycentric organizations are those firms that leave a wide margin of discretion to local management. In these firms, prices are set at their appropriate levels in each local market separately, without constraints from headquarters. This is called **polycentric pricing.** Naturally, prices might vary considerably between countries in polycentric pricing creating risk of gray trade. On the other hand, there is the undeniable advantage of really being able to adjust prices to the particular conditions facing the product in any one country.

Polycentric pricing is particularly useful when price sensitivity differs between markets and when the problem of gray trade is minimal. This can be the case in global service marketing (see box, "Pricing in Global Services").

BOX: Pricing in Global Services[31]

Global service companies rarely face the problem of gray trade. The reason is that services are typically characterized by intangibility, perishability, and inseparability of production and consumption. This means polycentric pricing with different prices in different countries is more feasible for services than for physical products.

This does not mean, however, that prices cannot be usefully coordinated across countries. In an interesting article discussing global pricing by a provider of system support services for business customers in telecommunications, healthcare, and finance, Bolton and Myers show how global or regional prices can be coordinated. The key is whether the price elasticity differ by segment or by country.

Rather than allowing each country subsidiary to set local prices, the company decided to explore the possibility of setting coordinated prices by segment. It identified the different price elasticity in different user segments (telecommunication firms versus hospitals, for example) and found that the different service levels required meant that price elasticity differed as well. But across countries in any region (such as Asia) there were similarities of price elasticity that made it possible to use regionally coordinated pricing strategies for several of these segments.

In this kind of case, the centralized pricing strategies might be preferable to locally set prices not only for control purposes. The local subsidiary is likely to set a uniform price within the country to facilitate its control. This means the different price elasticity in the different segments are not adapted to, and the local price is likely to be suboptimal. By setting prices centrally, the local prices become more optimal.

Geocentric Pricing

The most common **geocentric pricing** scheme revolves around the use of a global or regional standard plus a markup that is variable across countries. The comparison price is derived for the home country or some other lead country for the world or a regional trading bloc. This base price is computed from a cost-plus formula. The markup is then adjusted for the particular situation the product faces in each country. When demand is strong and competition is weak (a "cash cow" situation), the added-on markup will be high; if competition is strong, the markup will come down.

One big headache in geocentric pricing is the question of **product line pricing**. Product line pricing refers to the standard practice of separating different models in a product line by charging different prices for different models. In automobiles, for example, the Mercedes C, E, and S classes are separated by price points. According to its U.S. website, in 2015, the C-class started at $38,400, the E at $52,650, and the S-class at $94,400, meaning that the E-class was 37 percent more expensive than the C, and the S was 79 percent more expensive than the E. But in Germany, with the C-class starting at €31,683 ($35,168 at the exchange rate in mid-2015, not much different from the U.S. price), the E-class at €41,412 ($45,967) was only 31 percent more expensive than the C (and meaning the E is relatively less expensive in Germany than in the U.S.), and the S-class at €1,753 ($90,745) was a whole 97 percent more expensive than the E, almost twice as high.[32] The difference reflects market conditions (and exchange rates—the euro had declined against the dollar during the first six months of 2015).

The example shows how the optimal markup changes depending on the competitive situation. Mercedes has more competition at the middle-to-lower end in Germany, and less at the very top. The opposite is the case in the United States market.

Ethnocentric Pricing

In **ethnocentric pricing** the same price is charged to all customers regardless of nationality. It provides a standard worldwide price, usually derived on the basis of a full-cost formula to ensure that general overhead, selling expenses, and R&D expenditures will be covered. This type of pricing approach is most useful when the company is producing a relatively standardized product with uniform usage patterns across many countries.

This is the typical pricing scheme for large-ticket items in industrial goods. Examples include aircraft and mainframe computers. IBM maintains this type of pricing policy, partly for the reasons stated above. Boeing, the aircraft company, is pricing its commercial aircraft in this fashion, only making adjustments because of special customization requirements and quantity discounts—as well as Airbus competition. Ethnocentric pricing is also a natural pricing procedure when the company is small and the international sales are few and far between. This is the kind of pricing scheme most acceptable to global customers since homogeneity of prices worldwide makes planning easier and concentrated purchases from central headquarters possible.

Managerial Trade-Offs

The ethnocentric approach to pricing in global companies has the great advantage of simplicity and allows headquarters to coordinate prices at the subsidiaries. But its drawbacks, primarily in terms of non-adaptation to the individual local markets, usually make it not useful to the multinational facing multi-domestic markets and different competitive situations in each country.

The polycentric approach is the one favored by most local managers of subsidiaries since it increases their control and allows complete attention to competing in the local market. But it leaves the company open to the arbitrage possibilities of gray trade. Many different product categories such as cameras, watches, jeans, and compact disks suffer from parallel imports. Gray trade creates a headache for multinationals trying to manage their regular distribution channels and motivate authorized resellers to support and service their products.

Geocentric pricing, especially as regionalized by trading blocs, emerges as a well-balanced compromise between global coordination and local adaptation. The variable markup, or the use of price corridors, allows the subsidiaries to adapt to the specific conditions within their particular regional markets. And the distance between different regions discourages gray traders at least to a degree.

SUMMARY

This chapter has dealt with the many complex pricing issues facing the global marketer, showing how differences between countries constrain purely strategic considerations in global pricing. This chapter placed the global pricing question in the context of pricing in economic theory and in marketing theory and practice, and then focused on issues and problems related to transfer prices and the global coordination of prices.

Many factors combine to determine what the actual price of a product will be when it finally appears on the market abroad. This final price might be quite different from the intended positioning: In global marketing it is not always easy to control what the final price will be because of regulatory limitations, exchange-rate fluctuations, the number of independent middlemen and facilitating agents, and the need to motivate managers in local subsidiaries. Transfer prices to local subsidiaries have various functions over and above that of stimulating local sales, in particular a role in performance evaluations of the subsidiaries. Another complicating factor is the need to evaluate countertrade options and, in business-to-business settings especially, the possibility of bundling software and hardware together in larger systems.

As one ingredient of the product positioning mix, global pricing still has to take into account how customers in different countries evaluate high and low prices, as well as the stage of the PLC in the particular market. At the same time, the pressure from multinational customers to be quoted the same price anywhere in the world, along with the specter of gray trade, means that global coordination of prices is a necessary task of the global marketer. The chapter discussed the pricing aspect of the gray trade problem with special reference to the EU market, along with various schemes that companies use to counter gray trade. In the last section of the chapter we described the relative merits of polycentric, geocentric, and ethnocentric pricing strategies in the global firm.

KEY TERMS

arbitrage	hedging
arm's-length prices	offset deals
barter	parallel imports
cartel	penetration price
compensation deals	perceived-value pricing
consumer tourism	polycentric pricing
cost-plus pricing	premium price differential
counter-purchases	price controls
countertrade	price corridors
demonstration effect	price discrimination
devaluation	price elasticity
ethnocentric pricing	price–quality relationship
exchange-rate fluctuations	product buy-backs
experience curve pricing	product line pricing
fair trade	reservation price
fair trade minimum price	skimming price
forward contract	swap
functional analysis	systems selling
geocentric pricing	transfer pricing
gray trade	turnkey sales

DISCUSSION QUESTIONS

1. With the coming of the global marketplace on the Internet, will all prices be the same all over the globe? Why or why not? What are the ways in which the prices in local markets can still be different?
2. Would you be willing to pay more for a Fair Trade product? For an organic product? Why (not)? In what kind of countries would find consumers willing to pay higher prices for Fair Trade products? In what countries would you expect only few such consumers to exist? Explain your reasons.
3. As a marketing manager for a non-European business, what obstacles would you face in attempting to coordinate prices between European countries? Why would you attempt it?
4. From a marketing viewpoint, what are the advantages and disadvantages of allowing local units to set their own prices?
5. What are the problems in implementing a coordinated pricing system to control gray trade?

TEAM CHALLENGE PROJECTS

1. Team 1: Pick one country from each of the five regions and find the retail price for an Apple iPhone in that country. Explain drivers for this foreign market pricing for each country. Team 2: Pick one country from each of the five regions and find the retail price for a bottle of Listerine Mouthwash in that country. Explain drivers for this foreign market pricing for each country.

2. Pharmaceutical drug makers such as GlaxoSmithKline and Merck sell AIDS drugs at very different prices around the world from expensive in the U.S./Canada and other Western countries to much less expensive in developing regions such as Africa. Team 1: Develop the reasons that this pricing makes sense and should be continued. Team 2: The U.S. government currently limits a person's ability to import drugs into the U.S. due to safety and distribution concerns. Argue that U.S. consumers and doctors should be able to import drugs from anywhere in the world to greatly reduce healthcare costs.

3. Team 1: Argue that the Internet and e-commerce are making prices around the world available to consumers so prices will tend to converge (i.e., high price transparency so prices become nearly the same) in every country. Show an example. Team 2: Argue that although the Internet and e-commerce are making prices around the world available to consumers, prices will still tend to be specific to a particular country and the Internet does not have the power to force prices the same worldwide. Show an example.

SELECTED REFERENCES

Assmus, Gert, and Carsten Wiese. "How to Address the Gray Market Threat Using Price Coordination." *Sloan Management Review* 36, no. 3 (1995), pp. 31–42.

Bahadir, S. Cem, Sundar G. Bharadway and Rajendra K. Srivastava, "Marketing mix and brand sales in gloal markets: Examining the contingent role of country-market characteristics," *Journal of International Business Studies*, Vol. 46, No. 5, June/July 2015, pp. 596–619.

Bernard, A. B., Jensen J. B., & Schott, P. K., "Importers, exporters and multinationals: A portrait of firms in the U.S. that trade goods." *Report from the U.S. Census Bureau and NBER*, May 8, 2007.

Best, Roger J., *Market-Based Management*, 6th ed. Upper Saddle River: Prentice Hall, 2012.

Bolton Ruth N. and Matthew B. Myers, "Price-Based Global Market Segmentation for Services," *Journal of Marketing*, Vol. 67, no. 3 (July 2003), pp. 108–28.

Bradsher, Keith, "China Fines Japanese Auto Parts and Bearings Makers in Price Rigging," *The New York Times*, August 21, 2014, p. B5.

Cain, Alexandra, "Australia Tightens Transfer Pricing Regulations: 'Arms-Length' Principle Applied," *InTheBlack. com, Tools Of The Trade*, Dec. 11, 2013.

Chan, Vinicy, Kevin Buckland and Lauren S Murphy, *Bloomberg Business*, August 19, 2013.

"China's addiction to luxury goods," *The Economist explains*, Apr 29th 2014.

Cho, Young-Sam and Chua Kong Ho, "China Levies Record Antitrust Fine on Japanese Firms," *Bloomberg News*, August 20, 2014.

"Cola Wars In Russia (Part 1)," *Trefis.com*, Dec.19, 2013.

"Does Fair Trade Coffee Cost More To The Consumer?" *Equal Exchange Fairly Traded*, 2015.

Dovi, Emily, "Apple Price Policies: How the Brand Maintains Popularity and Profit Margins," *Dealnews.com*, 2013.

Edwards, Jim, "Apple's iPhone 6 Faces a Big Pricing Problem Around the World", *Business Insider*, 2014.

Faiola, Anthony, "Devaluation Imminent in Argentina," *Washington Post*, January 3, 2002, p. A12.

Hollie, Pameal, "Pepsico Renews Deal with Russians," *New York Times*, May 22, 1985, p. D5.

International Data Corporation, "In a Near Tie, Apple Closes the Gap on Samsung in the Fourth Quarter as Worldwide Smartphone Shipments Top 1.3 Billion for 2014," *IDC Press Release,* January 2015.

"IRS Accepts Settlement Offer in Largest Transfer Pricing Dispute," *IRS Bulletin IR-2006-142*, Sept. 11, 2006.

Kapadia, Kaushal. "Arm's-Length Principle and Transfer Pricing Methodologies," *I.T. Review,* October 2001, pp. 36–40.

Kouremetis, Dena, "Bartering for Survival – 'Have I Got A Deal for You'" *Forbes*, October 22, 2012.

Lelyveld, Michael, "Innovation Is the Key to Keep Vodka Flowing to U.S. Shores," *Journal of Commerce*, July 29, 1993, p. 2C.

Li, Hao, Ping Zhao, Yan Wang and Gao Wang, "A Qualitative Research of *Tuangou*: Modes, Characteristics and Roles of the New E-Business Model," *International Symposium on Information Engineering and Electronic Commerce,* IEEE Computer Society, 750–53, 2009.

Livingstone, John Leslie, and Theodore Grossman, eds. *The Portable MBA in Finance and Accounting,* 4th ed. New York: John Wiley and Sons, Inc., 2009.

Matthews, Nick, KPMG, Melbourne, personal interview, 2006.

O'Brien, Thomas J. *Applied International Finance: Managing Foreign Exchange Risk and International Capital Budgeting.* New York: Business Expert Press, November 30, 2013.

Parks, Michael, "For Pepsi, Road to Moscow Was a Trip Back in Time," *Washington Post*, July 6, 1988, p. A1.

Prahalad, C.K. *The Fortune at the Bottom of the Pyramid.* Revised and Updated 5th Anniversary Edition. Wharton School Publishing, 2009.

Rosenheck, Dan, "Argentina's Rational Default, *The New Yorker*, Aug. 7, 2014.

Seyoum, Belay, *Export-Import Theory, Practices, and Procedures*, 3rd ed. London: Routledge, 2013.

Shulman, James S., *Transfer pricing in the multinational firm.* Scholar's Choice, February 15, 2015.

Temple-West, Patrick, "Amazon fights $234 million tax liability in Tax Court," *Reuters*, January 15, 2013.

Toumi, Mondher, Cécile Rémuzat, Anne-Lise Vataire, Duccio Urbinati,, "External reference pricing of medicinal products: simulation-based considerations for cross-country coordination," *Final Report*, European Union, 2014.

Zask, Ezra, *All About Hedge Funds*, 2nd Edition. New York: McGraw-Hill, February 14, 2013.

Zeithaml, Valarie A., "Consumer Perceptions of Price, Quality, and Value: A Means-End Model and Synthesis of Evidence," *Journal of Marketing*, Vol. 52, No. 3 (July 1988), pp. 2–22.

ENDNOTES

1. See Dovi, 2013.
2. Source: International Data Corporation, 2015.
3. Reported on the website of www.thetechstorm.com.
4. See Edwards, 2014.
5. See Prahalad, 2009.
6. The program is extensively documented on the P&G website: (http://www.pg.com/en_IN/sustainability/social_responsibility/social-responsibility-programs-in-india.shtml).
7. See, for example, Best, 2012, pp. 243–44.
8. See Bahadir, Bharadwaj, and Srivastava, 2015.
9. A good primer on exchange rates is O'Brien, 2013.

10. Sources: Faiola, 2002; Rosenheck, 2014.

11. Source: Chan, Buckland, and Murphy, 2013.

12. Bradsher, 2014; Cho and Ho, 2014.

13. See www.fairtrade.net.

14. See "Does Fair Trade Coffee Cost More ..." 2015.

15. A good primer on transfer pricing is Shulman, 2015.

16. See Bernard, Jensen, and Schott, 2007.

17. From Matthews, 2006.

18. Sources: http://law.ato.gov.au; Cain, 2013.

19. See "IRS Accepts Settlement Offer ..." 2006.

20. See Temple-West, 2013.

21. See Livingstone and Grossman, 2009.

22. See Shulman, 2015.

23. Seyoum, 2013, ch. 12, offers a good discussion of countertrade options.

24. Sources: Hollie, 1985; Lelyveld, 1993; Parks, 1988; "Cola Wars In Russia," 2013.

25. For an overview, see Zeithaml, 1988.

26. See "China's addiction to luxury goods," 2014.

27. See Li, Zhao, Wang, and Wang, 2009.

28. From Assmus and Wiese, 1995.

29. Sources: Assmus and Wiese, 1995; Toumi, et al., 2014.

30. Source: Bolton and Myers, 2003.

31. These numbers come from two websites, http://www.mbusa.com/mercedes/index for the U.S. figures, and http://www.mercedesbenz.de/content/germany/mpc/mpc_germany_website/de/home_mpc/passenge rcars.html for the German prices.

In this chapter you will learn about:

1. The globalization of wholesale and retail trade
2. How advances in logistics have made transportation a much smaller trade barrier than in the past
3. How price differences and inexpensive logistics have together made for an increase in gray trade
4. How e-commerce has become the fastest-growing distribution channel internationally

Global Distribution and E-Commerce

CHAPTER 12

ALIBABA ACHIEVES UNPRECEDENTED GROWTH

Alibaba Group Holding Limited (NYSE: BABA) is a Chinese e-commerce company started in 1999 that provides consumer-to-consumer, business-to-consumer, and business-to-business sales services via web portals. It also provides electronic payment services, a shopping search engine, and data-centric cloud computing services. Alibaba has become the world's largest e-commerce company in terms of gross merchandise volume or GMV selling over a staggering $550 billion worth of merchandise annually, including $7 billion in just two hours in 2016 during Alibaba's "Singles Day" sale.[1]

Alibaba's number of sales transactions are larger than Amazon and eBay.com combined.[2] Alibaba's consumer-to-consumer portal Taobao, similar to eBay.

com, features nearly a billion products and is one of the 20 most-visited websites globally.[3] The Group's websites account for over 60 percent of the parcels delivered in China and 80 percent of the nation's online sales.[4] Alipay, an online payment escrow service similar to PayPal, accounts for roughly half of all online payment transactions within China.[5] Alibaba generated 2016 revenue of $23.0 billion and its Initial Public Offering (IPO) in 2014 was the world's largest, raising over $25 billion. Its headquarters are in Hangzhou, just south of Shanghai, a city that combines ancient traditions with modern architecture (see Exhibit 12.1).

Several forces worked in Alibaba's favor to produce this growth. The first is China's rapid acceptance of Internet and technology in the last 10 years.

Hangzhou Civic Centre Building, a famous symbol of the new China.   **Traditional ship on the Xihu (West lake), Hangzhou, China**

EXHIBIT 12.1.

Hangzhou, China, Alibaba's "home town," is a city with historical and cultural ties to both ancient and new China. Its mix of old and new buildings, placid lakes, and traditional entertainment make the city a favorite tourist destination. With a population of approximately 2.5 million, it is a relatively "small" city in China (see also the Apple store in Exhibit 12.14).

Copyright © 2015 by Shutterstock/Zhao Jian Kang.gui Copyright © by Shutterstock/Gui Jun Peng.

The second is that online shopping, which represented 13.5 percent of total China consumption in 2016, is projected to continue its rapid growth as more Chinese consumers shop online and e-commerce spending per consumer increases (see Exhibit 12.2).[6]

Third, the company has achieved first mover advantage in all three markets of C2C, B2B, and B2C plus online payment systems. Alibaba's brand is firmly planted in the minds of Chinese consumers.

China's sheer population size has helped Alibaba to reach dominance comparable only to Amazon. As Alibaba is poised to go global, a confrontation between the Goliaths looms large.

EXHIBIT 12.2.

Largest Internet countries 2017[7]

Source: http://www.internetworld-stats.com/top20.htm.

	Country	Population, 2017 Est. (millions)	Internet Users 2017 (millions)	Internet Penetration	Growth multiplier between 2000–2017
1	China	1,388.2	731.4	52.7%	32 times
2	India	1,342.5	462.1	34.4%	91 times
3	United States	326.5	286.9	87.9%	2 times
4	Brazil	211.2	139.1	65.9%	27 times
5	Indonesia	263.5	132.7	50.4%	65 times
6	Japan	126.0	118.5	94.0%	1.5 times
7	Russia	143.4	104.6	72.9%	32 times
8	Nigeria	191.8	93.6	48.8%	47 times
9	Germany	80.6	71.7	89.0%	2 times
10	Mexico	130.2	69.9	53.7%	25 times
	TOP 20 Countries	5,038.7	2,738.9	54.4%	9 times
	Rest of the World	2,480.3	993.0	40.0%	10 times

Source: Internet World Stats: Usage and Population Statistics; Top 20 Countries with the highest number of internet users. http://www.internetworldstats.com/top20.htm

DISTRIBUTION OVERVIEW

This chapter will deal with the distribution issues facing the global marketer. There are three major tasks:

- *Traditional channels.* The first task is to establish the traditional links of intermediaries between the company and its customers—and also the links to suppliers abroad if needed. The marketer will have to find wholesalers and retailers in the foreign markets, but also importers, distributors, and agents. One problem is usually that the channel intermediaries successful at home might not be available abroad—or might not offer the same functions or be very effective. This chapter will detail some of these differences.
- *Logistics.* Distribution also has to find ways of shipping products to the foreign markets. Fortunately, global logistics have improved greatly over the years, and transportation speed and efficiency have increased while costs have decreased. This has also helped create a problem of gray trade, for manufacturers as well as local distributors. The chapter will discuss more of these developments as well.
- *E-commerce.* In the new global marketing environment, there is also something else to consider: The Internet and online channels. The global marketer has to find a way to integrate the online channel into the distribution mix and decide what the role of e-commerce should be.

The Internet Effect

The arrival of the Internet has had a dramatic impact on global marketing in both marketing communications and distribution. It has created a whole new way of doing global marketing.

1. *Communication.* Initially, the Internet was seen as a revolutionary—and disruptive—innovation for fast and inexpensive global communications. Communication via e-mail was cheap and fast, databases could be attached and sent overseas, photographs could be shared, text messaging was facilitated cost-free, and Skype connections eliminated long distance and international phone calling charges. The vaunted fax machines, just invented a few years earlier, were now obsolete, but scanners still had some use to digitalize files. Internet-based digital gaming now threatens to eliminate the need for separate game players. Soon the rise of the Internet enabled the blogs, chat-rooms, and interactive sites like Facebook that have now morphed into the world of social media.

2. *Distribution.* Very soon, e-commerce showed that communication was only one side of the coin. The Internet was turned into a new sales and distribution channel. Products and services could be digitalized, and shown on the web for prospective buyers to inspect designs, read reviews, and compare prices. With a credit card, buyers could order and pay for products, leaving shipment in the hands of independent express shipping services. Spearheaded by Amazon in books, e-commerce soon became the preferred mode of shopping for airline tickets, computer software, toys, and consumer electronics. Today, e-commerce has grown to include groceries, fast-moving consumer goods, apparel and shoes, and many more categories.

   Defining the difference. For companies, web-based marketing is both a promotional tool and a new sales and distribution channel. The distinction is not always very clear, but one separation is clear: As a sales tool, e-commerce necessarily ends with "Place your order." As a promotional tool, the ending command is "Send for more information."

A small difference in a sense, but it is important. Many companies from a large number of countries will have presence on the web, but they will not have a "store" on the web. Especially in global marketing, the Internet has made for a widely available and inexpensive global communication tool—and thus a promotional tool—but to get to e-commerce, there has to be a *Cart* and a *Checkout* and a *Payment* and a *Place your order*. The main obstacles are usually how to pay and how to ship across borders—both critical issues in e-commerce, but not issues in communications.

In the present chapter we will deal with the e-commerce aspect, with an emphasis on *distribution and sales*. But since the traditional channels of distribution are still the dominant ones, we will start there.

Distribution Advantage

It is important to remember at the outset that distribution can be part of a company's competitive advantage. This has special relevance for global marketers, since distribution advantages are often difficult to transfer to new countries.

If distribution is a key success factor in a product category, global expansion can be difficult and expensive. A successful distribution system at home might be hard to reproduce abroad. This makes global coordination and control more difficult. Even Coca-Cola has had trouble replicating some of its bottling and distribution systems abroad, although the company expanded after World War II when many countries were rebuilding. Today, in mature markets, the situation is decidedly different. The favored locations in retailing might already be occupied by strong domestic players.

Starbucks has trouble using its saturation strategy where the number of store locations is limited by regulations as in many European countries. Toys "R" Us needed rezoning in many countries to make room for its large warehouse-style stores. In this chapter we will see that retailers often go global by acquiring domestic chains simply to get access to distribution points. But they often find that introducing a new way to do retailing into an existing foreign business is not always easy. Wal-Mart's purchase of Asda in Britain proved successful, but its venture into Germany via Wertkauf and Interspar was less so.

Logistics is the part of distribution that involves transportation and tracking of shipments. The increased distance between manufacturing and point-of-sale that goes with global marketing makes the logistics also more important than at home. Even when distribution is not a major success factor in the home market, slow and costly logistics might be a major disadvantage abroad. For example, problems with lack of supplies, delivery delays, lost shipments, and access to spare parts can be magnified when shipping is across borders.

Fortunately, as this chapter will show, with the vastly enhanced global communications capability (not least through the Internet) and much-improved technology, logistical problems are usually manageable. The global success of companies such as H&M and Zara owes much to their ability to manage logistics across many borders successfully. We have not yet reached "the death of distance" as some Internet writers claimed early on. Physical products still need to be shipped, and the greater the distance the greater the chance that something may go wrong. But the logistical disadvantage of being far from the market and the ultimate buyer—a traditional "trade barrier"—has been reduced considerably in recent years. That does not mean, of course, that being close to the customer is not important—the global marketer still has to learn the desires and preferences of the local customer.

WHOLESALING

A wholesaler is a person or firm that buys large quantity of goods from various producers or vendors, warehouses them, and resells to retailers or industrial users. Their main functions involve making contact, negotiating, buying, selling, and warehousing; but they might also be involved in shipping, financing, and packaging as well as other middleman functions. Wholesaling is a major component of a country's infrastructure, and its structure offers important clues as to the country's stage of development.

Exhibit 12.3 lists the number enterprises, the number of firms per 1000 people, the number of employees, and the sales revenues of wholesalers in selected countries. The exhibits also show the average number of employees per enterprise to give a sense of the size of the firm, and also sales per enterprise, to give a sense of the likely profitability. Comparable data are not always available, but the numbers generally do not change very quickly (one exception will likely be China due to its rapid growth of retail markets).

Country	Firms	Number of Firms Per Capita (no. Per 1000 People)	Employees		Revenues (Euro)	
	(in 000)	(estimated)	(in 000)	Per firm	Total	Per Firm
Belgium	42.1	3.96	229.3	5.1	192.3	4.57
Denmark	16.5	3.02	173.4	10.5	112.2	6.8
Germany	96.1	1.13	1283.8	13.4	775.8	8.07
France	182.4	3.03	1,084.90	6	637.5	3.5
Ireland	7.9	1.79	87.7	11.1	62.8	7.95
Italy	406.1	7.01	1115	2.8	454.4	1.12
Netherlands	59.9	3.5	479.2	8	305.6	5.1
Poland	122	3.2	706.5	5.8	130.2	1.07
Portugal	81.8	7.75	293	3.6	66.9	0.82
UK	109.7	1.84	1189.2	10.8	815.2	7.43
U.S.A.	435	1.11	6227	14.3	4862.7	11.18
Japan	334.8	2.61	3526	10.5	2563.9	7.66
China	60.9	0.04	2,495.90	41	998.1	16.4

*Average exchange rate used is 1 euro = 1.34 US$, 10.58 Chinese yuan, and 161.29 Japanese yen.

EXHIBIT 12.3.
Size and number of wholesalers in selected countries*[8]

Sources: U.S. Census, Ministry of Economy (Japan), National Bureau of Statistics (China) and Eurostat Regional Yearbook (2014).

There are several striking facts in Exhibit 12.3. The first is the large number of people employed in wholesaling. As consumers we do not usually notice wholesalers, but behind the retail stores we shop in there are almost always a large number of wholesalers who help supply the products to the store shelves. The second is that the estimated number of wholesalers per 1000 people varies widely from 1.11 in the U.S. to over 7 in Portugal and Italy possibly giving an indication of the efficiency and complexity of a country's market. The third is the varying number of employees per wholesalers from an average employee headcount of 2.8 in Italy (probably tending toward family-run business) to larger firms in other countries. Lastly, China's consumer markets are still in the early stages of developing without an apparently adequate wholesale industry (thus driving the growth of e-commerce).

As the exhibit shows, the total revenues reflect (as they should) the economic size of the country. In wholesaling, there can be many levels, with companies selling to each other, especially in countries with complex distribution systems. This will tend to raise the total revenues recorded and cloud the actual picture.

In countries with lower economic activity, distribution tends to be carried out by smaller enterprises. Notice the contrasts between Portugal and Italy on one hand, and Germany and the UK on the other. Over time as growth occurs, wholesale enterprises tend to consolidate, and what once was a large number of individual firms becomes dominated more by large units.

Functions of Wholesalers

Wholesalers can provide a number of functions for the retailer and also for the manufacturer. The most crucial services for global marketing include the following:

- *Take title*. Wholesalers buy in large quantities on their own account.
- *Physical distribution*. Wholesalers ship to customers in smaller quantities.
- *Warehousing*. Wholesalers provide inventory management usually in two main areas. First they often offer quick and frequent pickup and deliveries, as needed, which allows both the producers of the goods and wholesale customers to avoid the risks associated with holding large inventories. Secondly, they consolidate shipments from multiple vendors into a single truckload. The retailer receives one delivery from the wholesaler with the goods from many manufacturers rather than the multiple deliveries needed if the goods were purchased separately.
- *Market planning*. Wholesalers support retailers by market planning and promotion assistance and keep producers up to date on market conditions.
- *Credit*. Wholesalers often provide financial assistance and extend credit as needed.

Not all wholesalers offer this range of services. It is important to find out exactly what services are offered when entering into a contract with a wholesaler in a new country.

- *Full-service*. In general, the so-called **full-service wholesalers** offer all of the functions mentioned above. In addition physical distribution many times includes management of the importation process for the product. But because of their size and tie-ins with existing brands and chains, they might not be willing, or the best ones, to distribute the firm's product.

The full-service concept should be carefully assessed for each country entered. Full-service might mean take title (and thus ownership) to American sellers, but it might not prohibit a Middle Eastern wholesaler from returning a product that does not sell well, expecting a full refund. Full service might not include service backup in European countries, but in India retailers expect to be able to return defective products to the wholesaler rather than the manufacturer.

- *Limited line*. Limited-line wholesalers provide some of the functions of the typical full-service wholesalers but as a business strategy chose to limit their services and scope. This limitation usually is in the range of the products offered, but could be also in other areas such as the credit terms available, marketing support available, etc. A wholesaler that handled air-conditioning parts for only two manufacturers would be an example of a limited-line wholesaler. Limited-line wholesalers have a number of different names including rack jobbers, brokers, drop shippers, and others.

Wholesaler Consolidation

The size distribution of wholesalers in many countries approximates the well-known *80–20 rule*: 80 percent of the transactions are handled by 20 percent of the firms. In Malaysia, for example, fewer than a dozen European merchant houses handle over half the import trade, while hundreds of small local trading companies handle the remaining volume. The giant Israeli wholesaler Hamashbir Hamerkazi handles a variety of products and has full or partial ownership of a dozen major industrial firms, representing approximately one-fifth of Israeli wholesaling trade.[9]

The trend toward vertical integration and larger enterprises reflect the technological developments that have made large-scale economies and technical coordination feasible. It is an example of technological diffusion across the globe. The emergence of freezing equipment, automatic (and computerized) materials handling, models of optimal inventory control and large-quantity reordering, and reliable and fast communications (telecommunications and transportation) has made the growth of the large individual wholesaler possible and economically desirable. As the infrastructure in various countries has improved with economic development, the introduction of these technical innovations has become feasible.

As entrepreneurial distributors adopt the new technology, they leave others behind; if the wholesalers don't do it, there are always eager retailers and manufacturers who will. In many countries the wholesalers have, in fact, been too slow to innovate and have been pushed aside by aggressive retailers integrating upstream and manufacturers eager to simplify their distribution channels downstream. The functions carried out by the wholesalers still remain necessary for the movement of the product from producer to consumer: It is just that wholesalers are not always the most efficient at it, especially with new direct importers providing stiff competition.

RETAILING

Retailers are those middlemen who sell directly to the ultimate consumer. They fulfill similar functions as other middlemen, including ordering, creating assortments, presenting the merchandise, storing and packaging, and perhaps also shipping and financing. The variety in retailing across countries is, if anything, greater than in wholesaling. In some countries such as Italy and Algiers, retailing is composed largely of small specialty houses carrying a narrow line of products. By contrast, in the northern European countries there are many stores with a broad assortment of products. According to its website, the large British chain of department stores, Marks & Spencer, maintains 454 retail stores around the world (in addition to its 979 UK stores) and attracts thousands of customers per day.[10] The bazaars of the Middle East, on the other hand, contain as many shops as customers on some days.

Exhibit 12.4 shows the number and size of retail outlets in different countries.

Country	Firms	Number of Firms Per Capita (no. Per 1000 People)	Employees		Revenues	
	(in 000)	(estimated)	(in 000)	Per firm	(Euro bill*)	Per firm
Belgium	78.4	7.37	318	4.1	83.438	1.06
Denmark	21.6	3.95	223.4	10.3	40.413	1.87
Germany	325.1	3.33	3333.3	10.3	474.357	1.46
France	422.1	7.07	1904.9	4.5	419.219	0.99
Ireland	21.8	4.95	211.3	9.7	33.264	1.53
Italy	644.9	12.12	1893.2	2.9	312.599	0.48
Netherlands	93.4	4.84	810.4	8.7	100.368	1.07
Poland	330.9	8.68	1291.6	3.9	96.669	0.29
Portugal	157.7	14.92	459	2.9	47.211	0.3
UK	187.3	3.33	3043.9	16.3	385.883	2.06
U.S.A.	1128.1	2.11	15515	13.8	2923	2.59
Japan	1137.9	8.88	7579	6.7	835.2	0.73
China	549	0.41	8369	15.2	433.5	0.79

*Average exchange rate used is 1 euro = 1.34 US$, 10.58 Chinese yuan, and 161.29 Japanese yen.

The data show clearly the smaller size of firms in Portugal and also Italy, where the small neighborhood stores still dominate the channels. This produces a high number of stores per 1000 population. The U.S. is at the other end with a low number of stores per 1000 people, implying larger stores and maybe lower costs but probably lower service. Germany and the UK both have large chains that raise the average number of employees in both wholesale and retail units. France is quite different, with many smaller enterprises, not unlike Japan in retailing. Relative to the population, Japan has a very large number of people employed in retailing.

Among Western companies, the United States has a relatively large number of people employed in retailing (relative to the population) with each store quite large (the United Kingdom is the closest country in this regard). Most European countries have fewer people in retailing relative to the population and have smaller stores, with the exception of the United Kingdom, where consolidation has gone further than in the U.S. Japan has more stores than the United States with quite low revenues per store, the classic Mom and Pop pattern.

Distribution in China

The atypical China data demands further discussion. The wholesaler data in Exhibit 12.3 show relatively few but large enterprises with more employees and higher sales per enterprise. The retail data in Exhibit 12.4 are more in line with the rest of the world, but the number of enterprises is still surprisingly low for such a large country.

Part of the explanation is in the statistics—the official numbers in Exhibit 12.4 are probably too low, omitting unofficial smaller units. The Chinese market remains highly fragmented, with small, independent retailers throughout the countryside serving a population who buy food and clothing at, or slightly above, subsistence level. As seen in Exhibit 12.5, while individual incomes are projected to continue growing, the overall income per capita is still relatively low implying a continuation of the uncounted but numerous small-store retail environment.

However, in the cities, malls, and department stores are becoming the preferred shopping venues for many consumers. An increasing number of tier 2 cities, particularly Tianjin, Shenyang, and Chengdu, now have sizeable Western-style shopping centers but there is still an overwhelming number of small retail operations. Overall, local domestic operators still dominate the market, making up an estimated 75 percent of the total stock of retail outlets.[13]

The official data reflect the general trend of increased privatization of China's economy. But overall the government still controls a large share of distribution, directly and often indirectly, and the individual units are very large.

An example of a state-owned company is the Bailian Group, a large enterprise in Shanghai which is one of the top retail enterprises in China. Founded on April 24, 2003, Bailian (Group) Co., Ltd. is a consolidated company among Shanghai Yibai (Group) Co. Ltd., Hualian (Group) Co., Ltd., Shanghai Friendship (Group) Co., Ltd., and Shanghai Materials (Group) Corporation.[14] The main business covers department stores, shopping malls, outlet, large stores, supermarket, convenience stores, specialty retail formats, operating non-ferrous metals, ferrous metals, automotive, chemical light, electrical, timber, fuel, etc. involving e-commerce, logistics, consumer services, electronic information, and other fields. In 2015 they have over 7000 retail stores and consolidated revenue of over $19 billion.[15]

But also private enterprises in China tend to grow large. Suning Commerce Group Co., Ltd., another top retailer, is a private company that operates a home appliance retail chain in China. The company offers consumer appliance, computer, and communication products. Its products include TVs, refrigerators, washing machines, digital products, small household electronics, and air conditioners.[16]

Overall, it is clear that for distribution in China, big size really is an unusually prevalent factor. The wholesalers and retailers are big diversified firms, whether government-owned or private.

China per Capita Income, U.S. $

EXHIBIT 12.5.
Fast growth in Chinese consumers income have led to a buying boom of consumer products. The Chinese government claims that over 70% of the population have now been lifted out of poverty.[12]

Source: http://www.marketresearch.com/Business-Monitor-International-v304/China-Retail-Q3-9142683/

Global Retailing

Retailing is dynamic. As economic growth takes place and global trade expands, new alternatives emerge. Even the least developed countries experience dramatic changes in distribution channels as innovations such as self-service, discounting, vending machines, mail-order houses, and fast-food outlets are diffused globally. Today, convenience stores such as 7-Eleven and its emulators, fast-food restaurants such as McDonald's and its similar offshoots, and catalog merchandisers such as L.L.Bean and Eddie Bauer can be found in a number of countries around the globe.

Exhibit 12.6 shows the world's 15 largest retailers in terms of sales.

Rank 2017	Company	Country	Retail Revenue (billions$$) (2016)	Number of Countries
1	Wal-Mart Stores, Inc	US	482.1	30
2	Costco Wholesale Corporation	US	116.2	10
3	The Kroger Co.	US	109.8	1
4	Schwarz Unternehmenstreuhand KG	Germany	94.4	26
5	Walgreens Boots Alliance, Inc.	US	89.6	10
6	Home Depot, Inc.	US	88.5	4
7	Carrefour S.A.	France	84.9	35
8	Aldi Einkauf GmbH & Co. oHG	Germany	82.1	17
9	Tesco PLC	UK	81	10
10	Amazon.com, Inc.	US	79.2	14
11	Target Corporation	US	73.7	1
12	CVS Health Corporation	US	72	3
13	Metro Ag	Germany	68	31
14	Aeon Co., Ltd	Japan	63.6	12
15	Lowe's Companies, Inc.	US	59	4

Source: http://ceoworld.biz/2017/01/24/giants-retail-worlds-25-largest-retailers-revenue-2017/

As the exhibit shows, Wal-Mart is by far the largest retailer, followed by other Supercenter stores (stores that sell everything from groceries and produce to apparel and electronics), Warehouse Clubs (with membership discounts) and basic discount stores. As products have become standardized and global brands get established, consumers around the world expect to find the global brands available everywhere, a demand that these global giants have capitalized on. But even these giant stores are coming to realize that they have to localize their operations. This is why Wal-Mart sells live turtles in its Shanghai store.

Remarkably, although several large retailers have tried international expansion, for every one that has succeeded, there are two or three that failed. Home Depot and Wal-Mart are successful in Latin America, but Home Depot failed in China and Wal-Mart failed in Germany. France's Carrefour introduced the hypermarket concept to the east coast of the United States with little success. Belgium's Delhaize, a successful top-of-the-line supermarket at home, has had trouble in the United States, and plans for a merger with Ahold, its Dutch competitor, was announced in 2015 combining Food Lion and Giant supermarkets in the U.S.[18]

In retailing, a company's firm-specific advantages, whether in merchandising, supply chain, or service, do not seem to translate well into foreign markets. This seems to hold for department stores in particular. The large marquee stores dominating in their home markets—Bloomingdales and Saks Fifth Avenue in the U.S., Harrods and Selfridges in London, Printemps and Galeries Lafayette in Paris, Mitsukoshi and Takashimaya in Tokyo—have little presence outside of their home country. They have made some efforts—Takashimaya and Mitsukoshi have stores catering to Japanese tourists overseas, for example—but have not been successful attracting foreign customers. Britain's Marks & Spencer, with scattered successes overseas, failed in North America and closed its flagship Paris store in 2000, and its compatriot Tesco pulled out of China in 2013.[19]

But there are successes also in global retailing. The rise of global chains in fast-fashion retailing in particular is a remarkable development. "**Fast-fashion retailing**," or **fast fashion** for short, is a manufacturing model characterized by quick response to changes in demand. The term originated with the corporation behind Japanese Uniqlo, a company that is actually named Fast Retailing. Exponents of fast fashion include Uniqlo, Zara, and H&M, all with global ambitions, presence in major markets, and still expanding into new countries.

In fast fashion, speed is naturally important. These firms go to great lengths not just to predict coming fashion trends, but to help create them, and to track closely in real time what colors, designs, and styles seem to catch on (and which do not), and then respond quickly. Zara is a good example of what fast fashion involves (see box, "Zara, Fast-Fashion Retailer").

BOX: Zara, Fast-Fashion Retailer

Zara, the Spanish apparel chain (owned by Inditex, SA), began in 1963 as a supplier of women's lingerie in La Coruna, a city on the northwestern tip of Spain. The first Zara store did not open until 1975. The company now has over 2000 stores in 44 countries, typically in the larger cities (see Exhibit 12.7), and generated revenues of $14.3 billion in 2014.[20]

Over the years Zara gradually learned to synchronize design, production, distribution, and sales with increasing precision and speed. Fashion—what catches on and what does not—is notoriously difficult to predict. Zara managers realized that a solution would be to simply track closely the new designs from the fashion houses in Europe, America, and Japan, and China, combine this information with consumer feedback from the market, and then quickly create new styles for the mass market. With a flexible and fast production system, the factories could then produce and distribute the new designs quickly and the stores would have new designs early. Over time, Zara learned to cut this design-to-production-to-store cycle down to weeks rather than the months that most competitors needed.

Zara produces about 10,000 different styles annually, and store managers choose from that range twice a week. They receive information via handheld PCs, where they can see images of the product and then key in the orders for each style, including quantities, sizes, and colors. Orders have to be placed at pre-designated times: stores in Spain and southern Europe on Wednesdays before

EXHIBIT 12.7.
The "Kaunas Zara," the Zara store in Kaunas, Lithuania. The arrival of a Zara store becomes a sign that the country's consumers are now participants in the global market.

Copyright © 2014 by Shutterstock/ Vytautas Kielaitis.

3:00 in the afternoon and Saturdays before 6:00 in the evening, in the rest of the world on Tuesdays by 3:00 in the afternoon and Fridays by 6:00 in the evening. Orders must be on time. If, for example, a store in Belgium misses the Wednesday deadline, then it would have to wait until Saturday for a shipment.

This system has a drawback: distribution problems are magnified. In 2014, the stores in Venezuela had trouble getting inventory replenished because the country's weak currency (the bolivar) and price controls reduced inbound transportation. Zara took the unprecedented step of limiting the number of items customers could buy to five per month.[21]

Zara is another illustration of the power of fast and flexible production systems. Its business model is based on the just-in-time methods of the automotive industry pioneered by Toyota. With figures showing year-on-year growth of 25 percent in sales despite slowing consumer markets, Zara is beginning to look like an unstoppable global fashion force.

But despite the success of fast retailing, the globalization of retail firms still lags that of companies in other industries. For some comparisons, in 2013 foreign revenues accounted for 29.8 percent at Wal-Mart, 64.8 percent at P&G, 50.4 percent at Dell, and 58.9 percent at Coca-Cola.[22]

GLOBAL LOGISTICS

Global logistics can be defined as the transportation and storage activities necessary to transfer the physical product from manufacturing plants and warehouses in different countries to the various market countries. Global logistics is a subset of global distribution, which also involves the management of the channels within a country. It is a useful distinction for the global marketer, since the management of channels within a country requires a lot of interactions with local subsidiaries, distributors, and agents. By contrast, the distribution between countries is usually a matter for headquarters and the shipping partners alone.

Supply Chain Logistics

Managing the global supply chain involves coordinating and rationalizing the global logistics function of the firm operating in many markets. It is not a simple task. The number of independent suppliers is one factor that complicates matters. A typical automobile assembly might today contain 80 percent of parts from independent suppliers located in different countries. In addition, the company might have located manufacturing facilities in various countries, each specializing in only part of the complete product line, so that a particular local market needs to be supplied from a number of countries.

The Nissan trucks sold in France might come from the company's United States plant in Tennessee, the Micras from its Sunderland plant in England, while the Maximas are imported from Japan by its European subsidiary located in Amsterdam. Furthermore, Nissan's engine plant in the United Kingdom might be supplying engines to its American and Spanish plants. From a marketing perspective this might seem quite irrelevant, but it means that parts for after-sales service and repairs have to be ordered from factories in several different countries. Global logistics in the heavily globalized automobile industry might be particularly complicated, but similar problems afflict most companies that attempt to implement a global strategy. Fortunately the arrival of the Internet and e-commerce has helped supply chain management considerably (see box, "E-Procurement Energizes Supply Chain Managers").

BOX: E-Procurement Energizes Supply-Chain Managers

The first businesses to develop e-commerce were B2B businesses who used the Internet to purchase standardized parts and components, otherwise known as **e-procurement**. Many U.S. and European firms soon reported impressive savings from eliminating wholesalers and other middlemen, instead conducting their procurement over the Internet: 20–30 percent on the cost of indirect goods and 0.5–2 percent on the cost of direct materials.

Lower prices were the most immediate benefit from instituting an online supply chain management program but new levels of collaboration and the speed of delivery soon eclipsed even those gains. Just-in-time inventory management was enhanced considerably by e-procurement. All along the value chain, from product development through production, distribution, and managing customer relationships, e-commerce tools allowed collaboration on many levels with suppliers, distributors, and customers.

General Motors integrated its supply chain to link maintenance scheduling and needs with component suppliers. General Electric conducted direct purchasing online by linking 1500 corporate buyers and 16,000 suppliers. Hewlett-Packard cut its procurement costs by 17 percent and its automated purchase orders jumped from 20 percent to 70 percent of all orders. Wal-Mart uses its mammoth purchasing power to shape suppliers' behavior which also drives down costs. The evolution of Wal-Mart's supply chain includes three elements: distribution practices, operating its own fleet of trucks, and implementing technology. Benefits from its supply chain efficiency result in time savings, more cost-effective inventory management, and improved product forecasting.[23] These practices have now been applied in other companies to great effect (see Exhibit 12.8).

1. Apple
2. McDonald's
3. Amazon
4. Unilever
5. P&G
6. Samsung Electronics
7. Cisco Systems
8. Intel
9. Colgate-Palmolive
10. The Coca-Cola Company

EXHIBIT 12.8.
Top-ranked firms in supply chain management[24]

Source: http://www.gartner.com/newsroom/id/2747417.

Logistics and supply chain management are no longer optional if a company wants to compete with the best companies in Exhibit 12.8, who move and manage massive amounts of inventory accurately and at low cost. Right from the start, e-commerce translated into immediate B2B savings and improved corporate procurement performance. As we will see below, these e-commerce savings soon also extended into the B2C businesses.

Technological Advances

Technology has spawned a number of new global logistical options available for the global marketer. Global transportation is an area where considerable cost savings are often possible. Four of the main sources of savings are the following:

- *Consolidating shipments* in larger units rather than shipping smaller units
- *Eliminating duplication* in cross-border procedures by using common shipping documents and customs declaration
- Investments in *specialized equipment* (cranes, freezer containers) at transfer points
- *Inventory management*, creating savings through just-in-time practices and adding customer value by reducing delivery times

Freight forwarders, ship lines, air express outfits, and airlines now offer more reliable and faster services than before and also offer services not available before, such as tracking of shipments and overnight delivery. In fact, the recent growth of outsourcing manufacturing and other business functions to low-wage countries is made possible largely through this new technology.

Air Express

Technical innovations in computerized inventory systems and numerically controlled machines for goods handling, including robotics, coupled with the speed and reliability of the jet aircraft, made possible the growth of air express systems exemplified by American-based FedEx, UPS, DHL (now German-owned), and TNT (Dutch-owned).

Typically, the logistics involve shipment systems offering local pickups, the transportation of packages in the evening to a single transshipment point, sorting according to addresses during the night, and then shipping out to their destination by the early morning for local delivery. The competition can be fierce (see box, "DHL Gets Back to Roots").

BOX: DHL Gets Back to Roots

DHL is a global shipping giant now owned by the German Post Office, with more than 170,000 employees worldwide. It is comparatively unknown in the United States, which is striking since it was founded in 1969 by three young Berkeley students (Adrian *D*alsey, Larry *H*illblom, and Robert *L*ynn—hence *DHL*). It started as an express carrier between San Francisco and Honolulu. From the beginning DHL focused only on international shipping, leaving the U.S. domestic market to its competitors: Federal Express, United Parcel Service, and Airborne. But as these companies expanded abroad and moved into international shipping, DHL found its traditional international markets under attack and thought it necessary to strike back. DHL decided it needed to have a presence in the U.S. domestic market and be both an international and domestic package delivery service.

The first step was to acquire Airborne, the smallest of the three American express carriers which it did in 2004. DHL then spent the next years implementing an aggressive integrated marketing plan to establish brand awareness in the United States, and go head-to-head with FedEx and UPS. DHL tried an ambitious advertising campaign, Olympic team sponsorships, customer service initiatives, and special pricing.

Alas, it was not to be. After years of large losses, DHL announced it would return to its roots and be once again only an international shipping company. Competition inside the U.S. market was simply too tough—the two big companies, FedEx and UPS controlled the market and aggressively defended their turf. DHL is still using a hub in Cincinnati for its international shipments that was originally intended for domestic shipping. Its profitability is much improved and has returned to its normal range. One of the 10 points that Google includes in its mission statement is to "be best at doing one thing really, really well."[25] DHL may have learned this lesson with their return to the business that made them successful initially: international shipping.

As one might have expected, the duopoly of FedEx and UPS has been good for business but not for customers. According to reports, annual price increases have been in the range of 5 percent-7 percent for the period 2007–2017, a period when inflation ranged less than 2%. The Federal Trade Commission is considering an investigation.[26]

Today, shipping computer software, cameras, many consumer electronic products, and even apparel overseas often starts with a call to the local express mail office for a pickup. Instead of taking one to two weeks or much more in the case of ocean shipping, the merchandise can arrive in a couple of days. The goods are cleared through customs faster by using the express carrier's dedicated access ports at the point of transshipment, usually away from crowded entry ports for general merchandise. The computerized system makes it possible to track the packages, monitor the progress, and resolve obstacles or trouble. The increasing demand for package shipments from the e-commerce economy has been very good for the shipping business.

Ocean Carriers

The development of fast and efficient air transportation has opened up new international distribution channels, in particular for items high in value per unit weight. For shipments of bulky and low-value-per-unit products—such as automobiles, produce, dry goods, beer, and soft drinks—ocean-going vessels are still the most economical carrier alternative overseas. A few of these products—autos, oil, grain—are transported in specially designed ships owned by the producers. But mostly the shipping is done by independent ship lines through containers, ship-to-truck, or rail. Even here global requirements have made for changes.

Sharing resources and providing integrated one-stop services to the shipper makes great scale economies possible. Accordingly, there have been a number of **global carrier alliances** in the shipping industry. For example, American President Lines (APL), Orient Overseas Container Line from Hong Kong, and Mitsui O.S.K. Lines from Japan have joined in a global alliance consortium. APL and Matson Navigation Co., another American ship line, have shared vessels in a U.S.–Hawaii–Asia service since 1996. In another alliance, Sea-Land Service in Seattle and Maersk Line of Denmark have started a world partnership. Again, terrorism has affected this traffic, as the true story in the *Captain Phillips* 2013 film vividly showed.

The advantages of these alliances are similar to those in the airline industry. Sharing routes, vessels, and port facilities, better utilization of fixed assets is made possible, cargo destinations are expanded, and economies in documentation and customs clearing can be realized. The larger scale makes investment in specialized assets economically justified, reducing transfer costs further and offering lower prices to users. These specialized assets include

- Large-capacity lifting cranes
- Up-to-date storage facilities
- Ever larger and faster ships.

The upgrades put pressure on competitors and particularly on ports. Shipping terminals and their surrounding areas face mounting pressures from the global economy to accommodate large freight flows which are increasingly containerized. **Containers** are standard units of ocean shipping that have been designed for simplicity and functionality. The container is filled at the factory, mounted onboard a ship, taken to and off-loaded at its final port, loaded onto a train or truck and delivered to its final destination. There is thus the setting of a "mega logistics" framework that must insure a continuous circulation and tracking of freight containers worldwide. Ports respond by rapidly expanding to accommodate huge ships, speed up container loading and unloading to reduce the "dwell time" (the time that unloaded containers wait on the dock for further transportation via truck or rail) expansion of rail and truck facilities and expansion of technology investments to track everything. These are being referred to as **mega-ports**.

Overland Transportation

The increasing volume of international trade has put the system under pressure not only in ports but also inland. The connection is clear. For example, containers with tobacco products from Richmond, Virginia, destined for Eastern Europe are unloaded in Bremerhaven, loaded onto trucks, and sped overland to Eastern Europe on the

Overloaded small truck on the Beijing expressway, China   Motorcycle overloaded with straw baskets, Phnom Penh, Cambodia.

German Autobahn—creating traffic problems, safety hazards, and long lines at border-crossings (eased for those Eastern European countries now in the EU).

One solution to this problem has been the **roll-on-roll-off (RORO)** system, in which a loaded container is simply rolled onto a railcar and shipped by rail for part of the way, avoiding congested freeways. Even quicker is the new *RoadRailer* system, in which a rail wheel carriage can be attached to the bottom of the trailer carrying the container on the road. Then the container can go directly on the rail and be hooked up to a train without the need for a railcar.

In Europe, the typical overland transportation involves trucking, and the changeover to rail requires a special truck/rail terminal with a capability of lifting the container off the trailer and then placing it on a railcar. The special equipment required and the time lost in the transfer mean that European roads are likely to be clogged by trucks for some time to come. In developing countries trucks and roads are lifelines that also can be quite clogged at times (see Exhibit 12.9).

Warehousing

The competitive need on the part of global companies to be "close to the customer" and provide fast and efficient service has placed increased demand not only on transportation but also on warehousing and inventory management. While increased speed on the part of independent carriers has made it possible to fill orders faster and cut response time for parts requests, increased competition has escalated customers' demands for service.

Thus, companies try increasingly to locate warehouses close to customers. But if the company does not want to invest in its own distribution center, some of the middlemen in global logistics provide inventory services. For example, FedEx, DHL, and also smaller outfits offer warehouse space for rent at their transshipment points. Companies rent the space to store products in high demand. A company such as Eddie Bauer can stock some of the more popular catalog items in Memphis at the FedEx central location and ship directly from there, lowering the shipment time significantly.

GRAY TRADE

Gray trade (parallel trade or parallel importation by unauthorized distributors) goes against global companies' need for control. Three main factors motivate independent entrepreneurs to engage in gray trade:

1. *Wide price discrepancies.* There are substantial price differences between national markets, for example, because of currency fluctuations.
2. *Limited availability.* There is limited availability of certain models or versions in one market. Demand outstrips supply and is likely to push local prices even higher relative to other markets.
3. *Inexpensive logistics.* Transportation and importation can be accomplished with relative ease. The increased availability of global modes of transportation and the added services offered by carriers and freight forwarders have meant that the logistics problems are usually few. Gray traders can use the independent middlemen as well as any manufacturer.

Exhibit 12.10 shows some of the ways in which gray traders infiltrate the global distribution of Seiko watches. The Japanese company exports watches to the importer, often a sales subsidiary, in the various countries. From there the watches are shipped to the distributors and on to retailers. These are the authorized channels where the company offers merchandising support and sales training and, in turn, demands service support.

As can be seen in the exhibit, the gray trade arises from several sources. Some of the distributors in price-competitive markets, such as Hong Kong, will divert part of their shipment to more lucrative markets. They may sell directly to unauthorized (or even authorized) European or American distributors or retailers, getting higher prices that more than offset any transportation charges. Alternatively, Japanese distributors and retailers backed by a strong yen can go abroad to get watches from overseas distributors or retailers for sale at home. And for new models in great demand, a Hong Kong distributor may send people to Tokyo to buy at retail, sometimes in duty-free shops, and bring back watches that fetch premium prices.

Gray trade is extensive for global brands in certain product categories. Although exact figures are hard to come by, since identification of gray goods is uncertain and the volume varies annually by exchange rate changes, the following are some estimates from U.S. industry sources:

-   10 percent of PC sales
-   20 percent of Sharp electronics
-   22 percent of Mercedes cars

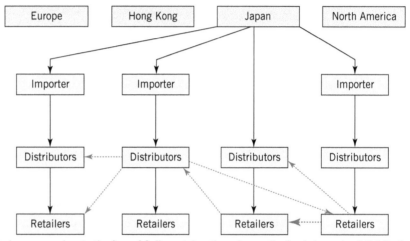

Broken arrows denote the flow of Seiko watches through unauthorized channels of distribution. Solid arrows denote the flow of Seiko watches through authorized channels of distribution.

EXHIBIT 12.10.
Seiko's channels of distribution

Total volume was estimated at $40 billion by KPMG in IT-related technology products alone, causing loss of about $5 billion for producers.[27] In cameras, a notorious gray trade product category since value per unit is high and brands are well-recognized, the average manufacturer might have recently lost sales of about $7.4 million annually and the volume is increasing. The Indian government estimates that gray trade cost their manufacturing sector over $16 billion in 2014 and is growing at 44 percent annually.[28] Seven manufacturing sectors seem to be the most impacted—auto components, alcoholic beverages, computer hardware, personal goods, packaged foods, mobile phones, and tobacco. (Of these, alcoholic beverages and phones are the largest gray markets in India.)

Effects of Gray Trade

The damage from gray imports falls into four categories. Gray trade threatens to:

- Erode brand equity
- Strain relationships with authorized channel members
- Lead to legal liabilities
- Complicate global marketing strategies

Brand equity can easily be eroded. For example, products with date marks, such as film and batteries, may be resold in gray markets with dates changed or obliterated, and the unwary buyer will find photos ruined and batteries dead. The strain with channel members arises from the fact that they will face intra-brand competition, the identical brand sold at lower prices elsewhere, and they will be asked to do service and repairs for gray imports.

The legal liabilities problem usually involves warranties that can't be honored and performance criteria that can't be fulfilled. These problems are especially acute for pharmaceutical products because of the potential injuries involved. Taking medication that has expired or whose dosages are meant for adults can severely harm children.

Gray trade affects global marketing management in a number of ways. Forecasted sales in a market may not be realized when there is a sudden influx of gray goods. Roll-out campaign plans for new product introductions might have to be changed if gray traders introduce the product prematurely, as happens frequently in film videos and popular music.

Channel Actions against Gray Trade

What can global marketers do in the distribution channels about gray trade? There are a number of actions available to help reduce the volume of gray trade and limit the damage done.

Supply Interference

Most companies engage in some interchange and relationship building with their distributors in various countries, asking them to help stop gray trade at the source by screening orders carefully and being careful how they dispose of surplus inventory. Software makers, in an effort to stop dealers from ordering large quantities of popular programs at volume discounts and then selling the excess to gray traders, have been known to announce their determination to terminate any distributor that supplies the product to unauthorized dealers. These practices have to be done with care, since putting pressure on suppliers can easily turn into an illegal restriction of trade.

Dealer Interference

A more drastic measure is to search for gray imports at the gray traders' outlets in the importing country and then ask the dealers—or help them—to get rid of their inventory. Companies sometimes attempt to simply destroy gray merchandise in the stores. This kind of "search and destroy" action requires a substantiated legal justification, such as an illegal change in the valid dates or improper packaging, and is more common for counterfeit goods.

Demand Interference

Some firms use advertising and other promotional means to educate potential customers about the drawbacks of gray goods and the limitations on warranties, returns, and service. Companies such as Rolex, Seiko, Mercedes, Microsoft, and IBM have engaged in these practices. There are two problems with this solution. One is the legal problem of threatening to limit service to products sold through authorized dealers only, not an acceptable practice in most countries. Second, firms are reluctant to call attention to the gray trade phenomenon and create hesitation on the part of potential buyers of the brand.

Strategic Attack

A more constructive solution is to go on the attack and create stronger reasons for customers to patronize authorized dealers. Caterpillar, the heavy machinery company, helped authorized dealers develop customized warranties the individual buyer could tailor to his or her own special needs.

Manufacturers also support their dealers by regionalizing their offerings, differentiating model features and numbers between trade areas to make it possible to spot gray imports and restrict servicing liability. Most Japanese camera makers use different model numbers and introduce slight differences in features between their Asian, North American, and European markets. By stressing features and model numbers in the advertising, their global advertising copy can remain uniform with the same brand name (Canon, Nikon), helping to support a global brand. Even legal action can be considered when brand equity is threatened, as a new legal ruling takes effect (see box, "Why Gray Markets May Turn Black").

BOX: Why Gray Markets May Turn Black

In a landmark 2001 case that lingered several years in the courts, Levi Strauss, the maker of Levi's jeans, tried to prevent England's Tesco from selling Levi's jeans imported from the United States, Mexico, or Canada at discount prices in the EU market.[29] Tesco had sourced the product from low-priced North American suppliers and stores, and then resold them at home for prices up to 30 percent below regular prices for Levi's in Europe. In its suit, Levi's argued that their global distribution system has been developed to safeguard the quality of their products and that products destined for different continents may be significantly different. The company claimed the right to control distribution.

The European Court of Justice ruled that Tesco could not sell Levi's jeans imported from outside the European Economic Area. The judges ruled that a retailer must be able to prove that its goods were obtained from legitimate sources within the EU or could be prevented from selling them. Thus, this ruling now places the onus on a vendor to prove that cheap designer goods were not obtained on the gray market but through legitimate wholesalers approved by the manufacturer.

Activists argued that the ruling smacks of being anti-consumer, since it will lead to higher prices for branded goods. Trademark holders, like Levi Strauss, hailed the decision as the dawn of a new era. In the past, gray goods were not illegal as such. That is, even if a shipment of a branded product was intended for a particular market, once a distributor had paid for the shipment, the right of ultimate disposal of the product was its alone. Of course, a reseller who consistently undercut other retailers would be cajoled into proper behavior or else could have trouble getting its orders filled, but in the law very little could ultimately be done.

The Levi's-Tesco ruling changed all that and even more than a decade later the ruling still stands. In August, 2017 the UK Supreme Court decided that two managers in an LLC company importing via gray trade could be held criminally liable for the gray trade. Understanding the importance of global branding, the judges have established a precedence of importance for global marketers. In specific cases where the brand strategy is well-justified, gray markets may be as illegal as black markets are.

Since the Levi's-Tesco case, many countries have been developing a legal framework for addressing gray trade. Because of the large impact that gray trade has on India's market (which we have previously discussed), the Indian government and courts have been particularly active in this area. A number of high-profile cases have been decided in favor of the manufacturer, including *Cisco Technologies v Shrikanth*, 2006, *Samsung Electronics Co Ltd v Mr G Choudhary*, 2006, *General Electric Company v Altamas Khan*, 2010, and *Kapil Wadhva v Samsung Electronics*, 2013.[30]

A country's decision on whether to allow grey trade is thus ultimately a choice between quality control and price control. The countries that are attempting to address this issue argue that trademark owners can take legal action against traders dealing in goods if those sales will compromise the goodwill, reputation, or quality of the trademark.

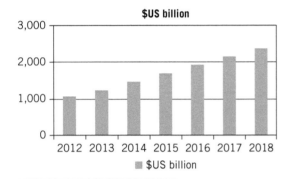

EXHIBIT 12.11.
Global B2C e-commerce sales[31]

Source: http://www.statista.com/statistics/261245/b2c-e-commerce-sales-worldwide/

EXHIBIT 12.12.
E-commerce shares across major regions

Source: http://www.emarketer.com/Article/Global-B2C-Ecommerce-Sales-Hit-15-Trillion-This-Year-Driven-by-Growth-Emerging-Markets/1010575.

THE E-COMMERCE CHANNEL

Today global distribution also includes e-commerce. **E-commerce** can be defined as buying and selling of goods/services online. Using the Internet, e-commerce is naturally global, and increasingly so as Internet penetration deepens across the globe. Using their own websites or portal sites such as Amazon.com and Alibaba.com, large and small companies in both B2B and B2C have found in e-commerce a widely available and inexpensive distribution channel.

E-Commerce's Global Growth

E-commerce to consumers (B2C) has been growing fast and is expected to continue growing in the foreseeable future (see Exhibit 12.11).

The growth has been particularly strong in Asia-Pacific, spearheaded by China's emergence.[32] Exhibit 12.12 shows that Asia-Pacific has already surpassed North America in total B2C e-commerce.[33]

B2C E-Commerce Sales by Region (billion $$)						
	2012	2013	2014	2015	2016	2017
Asia Pacific	301.2	383.9	525.2	681.2	855.7	1052.9
North America	379.8	431	482.6	538.3	597.9	660.4
Western Europe	277.5	312	347.4	382.7	414.2	445
Central & Southern Europe	41.5	49.5	58	64.4	68.9	73.1
Latin America	37.6	48.1	57.7	64.9	70.6	74.6
Middle East & Africa	20.3	27	33.8	39.6	45.5	51.4
Worldwide	1058.2	1251.4	1504.6	1771	2052.7	2357.4

The growth is not uniform across all countries, but the trend is quite clear: e-commerce is a growing distribution channel in most countries.

However, e-commerce still represents only about a small fraction of total retail sales. Exhibit 12.13 shows the steady growth of the percentage e-commerce relative to total retail, but e-commerce might not even reach 10 percent before 2018.

There are differences across countries. In 2015, China's share is about 10 percent, for example, and the U.S. is expected to rise to 10 percent by 2017.[35] Still, traditional retail is much larger than B2C e-commerce.

The B2C e-commerce tends to be a greater factor in emerging markets generally.[36] There are various reasons for this, not the least the underdeveloped state of the retail infrastructure and the burgeoning middle classes in many emerging markets. Also, hefty markups in stores and high taxes on many products make online purchasing attractive. In China, for example, e-commerce makes buying overseas possible even without traveling. Many Chinese use **online shopping agents,** independent operators who aggregate requests from individuals, buy the requested foreign goods at a discount, and then deliver to the buyers.[37] Foreign websites, including Amazon, now offer direct delivery to China for certain products, and local e-commerce giants such as Alibaba run cross-border services.

Although the majority of e-commerce spending in the U.S. still occurs on PCs, mobile's share is growing significantly faster. International Data Corporation's Mobile Phone Tracker also estimates that more than $50 billion will be spent on merchandise globally using smartphones in 2014.[38] In emerging markets where cell-phone penetration is much greater than landlines or PC penetration, smartphones (and tablets where affordable) become particularly attractive as alternative buying platforms.

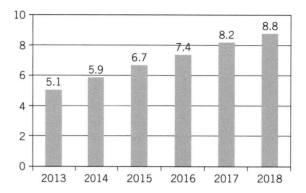

EXHIBIT 12.13.
Global B2C e-commerce % of total retail.[34] While still a small part of total retail sales, B2C e-commerce is a greater factor in emerging markets generally.

Source: http://www.statista.com/statistics/261245/b2c-e-commerce-sales-worldwide/

E-Commerce Models

It is useful to distinguish between four kinds of e-commerce models.

- *Pure-play web stores.* No brick-and-mortar establishment. Amazon was one of the first pure-play businesses, with the original book store simply established online without any physical brick-and-mortar store (although Amazon opened some stores in 2017). Another example is Zappos.com for shoes, and Spreadshirt.com in T-shirts.
- *Company websites.* As online purchasing technology became simplified and standardized, producers started establishing their own checkouts on their websites. Examples include Dell, Apple, and Intel. This direct sales model is now common in B2B technology products, in the process challenging established wholesalers as well as retailers.
- *Store website.* Playing defense, brick-and-mortar stores established a website channel alternative from which customers could buy. Examples include the Barnes & Noble bookstore, Brooks Brothers' suits, and Marks & Spencer apparel. Newspapers and other print media similarly started to offer alternative subscription-based access online. For catalog retailers, the e-commerce channel is a natural—see, for example, L.L.Bean's online global catalog below.

- *Portal channel.* The seller uses an online portal to attract customers via links, paying for the storefront with a fee to the portal owner. Buyers complete the purchase either through the portal or in-house. The portal could be a search portal (e.g., Google) or an established online store (e.g., Amazon or Alibaba).

The portal channel has become the dominant model for many small and medium-sized businesses (SMB). The portals serve to attract customers, and by linking its offering to key search words, a business can attract customers that have an interest in the product. Using Google, the business has to create its own checkout process. With Amazon the business can even outsource the fulfillment to Amazon, including the warehousing of company products. Alibaba is similar, but will usually not keep inventory for the business.

For their part, the portals charge a fee, how much depending on the amount of services rendered. Amazon offers extended services, including not only links and advertising, but also warehousing, user reviews, payment mechanism, and order fulfillment, all useful services for smaller businesses. China's Alibaba is similar, but without inventory, but with ability to handle payments in different currencies (see box, "Two giants square off?").

BOX: Two Giants Square Off?[39]

Most Americans are very familiar with Amazon.com, as some consumers elsewhere might also be (Amazon has 10 separate country sites, including Germany, Japan, and China). But in China the biggest e-commerce site is Alibaba.com which was discussed in the opening vignette. Alibaba was established in 1999 in China by Jack Ma, a young entrepreneur inspired by Amazon's rapid rise. After exponential growth, Alibaba is now expanding overseas including the United States and Russia, and in 2014 the company completed an initial public offering (IPO) of shares on the New York Stock Exchange.

This seems to set the stage for a clash of titans. But there are significant differences between two companies. It seems safer to predict that rather than directly confronting each other, the two giants will cause collateral damage among smaller players in various online niches.

Amazon is basically a B2C business. After its 1994 bookstore beginning it quickly moved into a wide variety of product categories—records and CDs initially, then consumer electronics and cameras, computer hardware and software and further into shopping goods like apparel and shoes and even consumer packaged goods. Amazon is a competitor with existing retail stores in virtually all product categories.

By contrast, Alibaba.com started out as a B2B portal, providing an online trading platform for Chinese manufacturers. Through Alibaba, the firms were able to connect with buyers and trading partners in China and were also able to find overseas buyers. Alibaba's main mission is still helping the Chinese producers to trade nationally and especially internationally. Since foreign-exchange issues were important, Alibaba assisted with currency exchange and transfer or funds.

In 2003 a subsidiary Taobao was established as a consumer-to-consumer (C2C) business, essentially a competitor to eBay, the auction site. Using Alibaba's experience with arranging transactions, the Taobao initiative also led to the creation in the same year of an online payment system, Alipay.com.[40] Taobao is Alibaba's biggest shopping site. It's home to seven million merchants selling everything from tiger-striped leather jackets to origami decorations and allows consumers to buy goods directly from small businesses.[41]

Amazon's 2014 revenues of $88.9 billion dwarf Alibaba's $12.3 billion.[42] But Alibaba does not take ownership of inventory, or stock it in large distribution centers, and then fulfill the orders as Amazon does. Instead Alibaba has an e-commerce platform and a "community" to connect buyers and sellers, and simply charges a fee. Fund transactions on Alibaba's online sites exceeded $250 billion in 2014, more than twice Amazon's. And Alibaba was very profitable, Amazon barely so because of its large overhead costs.

So, none of Alibaba's activities would seem to compete with Amazon's. However, in 2008 Alibaba established a new unit, Tmall.com. Its purpose is to sell branded products, many foreign, to the newly affluent Chinese consumer, a B2C business which does in fact look similar to the Amazon business. Tmall, connects larger brand retailers to consumers selling verified brands like Nike, Apple, and P&G. This is an effort to eliminate the fake goods that appear frequently on Alibaba's main Taobao website. It has become a very popular site for China's consumers. Given the rapid rise of e-commerce in China, one would expect Tmall to be a fierce competitor to Amazon. And even though Amazon is in China (as a joint venture "Joyo.com" since 2004), and has operated their own branded website "Amazon.cn," it is difficult to predict how successful they will be against Alibaba.[43] It is estimated that Amazon lost over $600 million in China in 2014 and has less than a 1.5 percent market share. Some analysts say that it is time for Amazon to abandon China but Amazon's chief financial officer said in 2015 that, in China, Amazon is "investing a lot and trying to grow the business."[44]

For one thing, when it comes to currency-exchange issues, Alibaba is ahead. Even through Visa and Mastercard are in principle globally available, not many Chinese consumers possess these cards. This gives Alipay an edge. Alipay supports transactions in 12 foreign currencies and its transactions fees are much lower than the credit card fees. In addition to the vast number of Chinese businesses using it, Alipay has currently more than 300 foreign merchants who use it for direct sales to consumers in China.

If Amazon cannot break through in China, it may find itself needing to defend itself on its home U.S. turf.

Digital Modes of Entry

In e-commerce mode of entry becomes a question of how to arrange for order fulfillment.

To see what is involved, it is useful to examine an experienced international online business (see box, "L.L.Bean's global catalog").

BOX: L.L.Bean's Global Catalog

L.L.Bean is a well-established catalog retailer in Maine, USA, that has long placed its catalog online, with particular success in Canada and in Japan. It is instructive to see how the company manages the online interaction with international customers.[45]

- Customers are told upfront that all transactions are in U.S. dollars.
- For orders to destinations outside the U.S., Canada, and Japan, the site notes that duties and taxes are not calculated or collected by L.L.Bean and customers are notified simply that they will be responsible when the goods are delivered.
- Shipping to Japan is treated slightly differently—Japan is one of L.L.Bean's largest markets and its customs procedures are particularly demanding. The wording is more polite, but essentially the same, L.L.Bean does not take responsibility for the calculation and collection of duties and taxes.
- Orders sent as gifts are subject to the same warning that the recipient will responsible for taxes and duties.
- A chart shows the times and costs involved, offering standard airmail, higher rates for international express, and estimated delivery times.
- The shipping rates increase with the value of the order, not so common in e-commerce but partly a reflection of anticipated volume and weight. Such a policy also discourages the team buying or club buying which is common in Asia, and, importantly, discourages gray trade.

With companies like L.L.Bean, the buyers from some countries will have difficulty to get orders placed because of convertibility might be questionable and custom duties are not always easy to establish. This is why portals like Alibaba has decided to get into the currency exchange business and help customers with border issues. Thus, Alibaba, like PayPal, can establish the creditworthiness of individual customers, and allow the transaction to be completed even without the standard credit cards. Alibaba can also provide guidance for importers to China with regard to tariffs and duties.

Retailing Impact

The biggest threat from e-commerce against "brick-and-mortar" retailing has been the portal stores, especially Amazon who has been a real pioneer in e-commerce. Two factors in particular have had major impact. One, Amazon learned very early how to make the shopping experience online an acceptable alternative to in-store shopping. Two, Amazon invited other businesses to use its platform, and substantially assisted other businesses by allowing their use of Amazon's own trusted and simple fulfillment routines. By first attracting customers, Amazon then leveraged them to attract other businesses to use Amazon as their portal, attracting even more customers in a virtuous spiral.

The e-commerce model has gradually come to dominate in many product categories around the globe.

E-commerce is taking on grocery stores with deliveries, luxury brands are bought and sold on eBay, some fake, consumer electronics and cameras are routinely bought on the Internet, as physical stores have closed shop. One hesitates to claim any business to be off limits—not only jewelry stores and clothing stores but even automobile dealerships are struggling to pay the steep rents at prime physical locations when more merchandise can be moved inexpensively online. And with well-known brands the risks of buying online are reduced. Although counterfeits do proliferate, strong and well-known brands go to great length to protect their brand names. In the process they help to increase buyer trust in their online offerings, inadvertently drawing customers from their established retailers.

Retailers Fight Back

The brick-and-mortar stores have tried to fight back. As so often, attack seems to be the best defense.

The first line of defense has been "If you can't fight them, join them." Stores open their own online sales channel. The stores also try to stay ahead of the curve by introducing their own online "apps" tied to their store credit cards, points system, and loyalty rewards.

The second line of defense has been to invite shoppers to use the Internet in the stores. Free wi-fi is a simple but now common service to allow access to the Internet in-store. Stores also provide tablets with intra-chain connections, so that assortments throughout its warehouse and other stores can be accessed, allowing stores to offer the wider assortments online stores do. Trial shipments with free returns and "personal shopper" benefits for a wider clientele are also introduced.

The third and surprisingly successful line of defense has been to make the actual store visit a special experience, to make the store a place for entertainment, aesthetics and excitement. A new type of retail strategy, emphasizing global retail flagship stores has emerged.[46] As in so many other instances, Steve Jobs and Apple helped initiate this effort, by opening stores with extraordinary and innovative architectural touches in major cities around the world. One recent example is the Apple store in Hangzhou which opened in 2015 (see Exhibit 12.14).

Other companies from Adidas and Nike to H&M and Zara have also adopted the flagship concept. New flagship stores include one for Japan's Uniqlo (casual wear) in Berlin and one for Italian apparel maker Benetton in Moscow. In the Benetton store the clothes are displayed on movable metal tubes, and rather than displaying products according to category, the format showcases them by themes and colors, and features total looks across clothing, footwear, and accessories. Such a complete look is presumably less easy to achieve by an individual online consumer, giving the store an edge over e-commerce competitors.

In many ways the best surviving stores today—which include the luxury brands' boutiques in particular—are much more enjoyable and pleasing to customers than ever before. At the same time, the failing stores are the ones that focus on costs, cutting staff, merchandise, targeting a shrinking loyal base, and going through a slow and painful death spiral.

Omni-Channel Strategies

Online purchasing options added to the existing traditional channels of distribution represent an **omni-channel** strategy. "Omni-channel" is a multichannel approach to sales that seeks to provide the customer with a seamless shopping experience whether the customer is shopping online from a desktop or mobile device, by telephone, or in a brick-and-mortar store. Since the channels may compete for the same customers, conflicts are often unavoidable and need to be managed. A version of this is "dual channel" distribution where two channels are being used, say a direct sales force and a chain of retail stores.

Multiple channels are actually not so new and have long been common among companies going abroad. Part of the reason is that the channels used in an early entry stage might not be the best as market penetration in a country increases. Many luxury brands, for example, enter first via some established high-end retailers, but after the market shows potential, they will establish their own boutiques. Naturally, the negotiations with the initial stores can be sensitive, and quite often the luxury brand ends up offering slightly different models and designs (and prices) in their own boutiques, typically offering the very top end. Armani, for example, develops slightly different styles of suits for upscale department store such as Saks 5th Avenue, where the customers tend to be more conservative, and presents the more avant-garde and daring styles in his own boutiques (plus has introduced Armani Exchange for a younger crowd).

EXHIBIT 12.14.
Apple store in Hangzhou at night. The leaf of the huge Apple logo was turned green on Earth Day, an annual event. This store is Apple's largest store in China. The Apple aesthetic of simple transparent lines has helped make its stores destination points around the world.

Copyright © 2015 by Shutterstock/August_0802.

Duty-free shopping at airports have long been—and still is—an alternative channel for higher-end brands. When the European Union abolished border controls between member countries and created a single currency, duty-free shopping was no longer a viable option for travelers within EU. Many sellers of cosmetics and liquor expected that retail sales would decline at the countries' international terminals.

But sales quickly rebounded as marketers discovered that the duty-free stores can be used effectively for product sampling and demonstrations and sales at regular prices. A busy airport such as Heathrow outside of London turns out to be an excellent location to reach travelers that are heavy shoppers, buying gifts for friends and relatives, stocking up on items that are scarce abroad, or simply killing time. So even though marketers can no longer promise duty-free savings, an opportunity to deal one-to-one with a large number of consumers with time on their hands and money in their pockets is one that many firms continue to exploit.[47]

Although some manufacturers do try to control their channels completely with a strong in-store sales effort—Swatch and Rolex are two that do—for many manufacturers the job is too big. They concentrate on trying to keep the abuses and damages at acceptable levels. Through model changes, pricing and advertising support, and interpersonal appeals—they try to minimize inter-channel conflict so that synergy can develop between the parallel channels through which the product moves.

E-commerce is intrinsically global. If it is sold here, it can be sold there. The global marketer today necessarily has to consider e-commerce as one great opportunity to sell to new foreign markets—or a threat to one's established business in an existing market anywhere. But as the e-commerce channel is explored, it will also have to be integrated with the traditional channels—except for pure-play businesses, the global marketer has to manage multiple channels.

SUMMARY

In this chapter various aspects of the international distribution strategy have been discussed: first some of the differences in wholesaling and retailing in various countries and the emergence of global retailing; then the independent organizations that facilitate global logistics between countries, emphasizing how competition and technology have pressured them to increase speed, reliability, and service; next problems with parallel distribution, especially gray trade.

The chapter then dealt with e-commerce, the new channel which is rapidly increasing in importance especially in emerging countries. The chapter discussed some of the advantages and disadvantages of e-commerce relative to traditional channels, and showed how threatening e-commerce through portals has become for traditional channels. More will be covered in a later chapter on online marketing and social media. The chapter ended with a discussion of how multiple channels into a country have become a fact of life for the global marketer and how conflicts may be resolved.

In the end, the degree to which channel policy in different countries should be made consistent through a global strategy hinges on the degree to which FSAs are explicitly lodged in distribution channels and the degree to which the channel members' activities can be coordinated and controlled. If channels are very important because of FSAs, the company has to evaluate the alternatives very carefully and decide whether the available channels provide sufficient support. If they do not, the firm might have to establish its own distribution network, focus on e-commerce alone, or else forgo entry.

KEY TERMS

air express

channel captains

dual distribution

duty-free shopping

e-procurement

fast fashion

full-service wholesalers

global carrier alliances

gray trade

limited-line wholesalers

mega-ports

omni-channel

parallel distribution

point-of-purchase (p-o-p) technology

roll-on-roll-off (RORO)

supply chain management

vertical integration

DISCUSSION QUESTIONS

1. Compare and contrast the food retailing systems in two countries you are familiar with. Why have the differences occurred? Is a convergence underway?

2. Why is coordination of global logistics so complex? What technological innovations have made coordination easier?

3. Discuss how the phenomenon of gray trade affects the ability of the global marketer to control distribution. How can the difficulties be overcome? How will the emergence of the Internet spawn more gray trade, or will it?

4. Use the websites of FedEx, DHL, and UPS to analyze how the service is marketed. What are the competitive advantages of each? How do the firms attempt to keep air freight distribution from becoming a commodity?

5. Using library and Internet resources, investigate one of the successful cases of an introduction of a new approach to channels in foreign countries (Avon, 7-Eleven, Toys "R" Us, or L.L.Bean, for example). What customer factors were important determinants of the success? What did competition do? What are some lessons for other companies?

TEAM CHALLENGE PROJECTS

1. The Dubai Mall, United Arab Emirates, is the largest mall in the world by square footage (over 1200 stores), The SM Megamall in the Philippines is the largest mall by visitors (i.e., nearly 292 million people per year with over 1000 stores), and West Edmonton Mall, Canada, is the largest mall in North America (over 800 stores). Team 1: Visit the website of these malls in Dubai and Philippines. What are the malls doing differently and the same? Team 2: Visit the website of the malls in Canada and Philippines. What should the Canadian mall do differently to increase the number of visitors as the Philippines mall has done?

2. Team 1: Develop a list of U.S. companies that should expand its international e-commerce business. What rationale did you use? Team 2: Develop a list of companies that should not expand their international e-commerce business and explain. What rationale did you use?

3. An auto parts manufacturer in South Carolina wants to export an order of 1000 transmissions. Team 1: Develop in detail the logistical steps that must be completed for this order to arrive safely and on time into a Russian city. Team 2: Develop in detail the logistics steps that must be completed for this order to arrive safely and on time into a German city.

SELECTED REFERENCES

"Alibaba: The world's greatest bazaar," *The Economist*, March 23, 2013.

"Amazon Leads Web Site Retailers." *iMedia Connection*, August 24, 2014.

Attwood, Karen, "British retailers going global," *The Independent*, Nov. 7, 2007.

"B2C e-commerce sales worldwide from 2012 to 2018 (in billion U.S. dollars)," *Statista*, 2014.

"Bailian Group Introduction," *Bailian Group*, 2015.

Bajpai, Prableen. "What is Alibaba?" *Investopedia*, Nov. 13, 2014.

Baker, Lianna B., Jessica Toonkel, Ryan Vlastelica. "Alibaba surges 38 percent on massive demand in market debut," *Reuters*, Sept. 19, 2014.

Banker, Steve, "Amazon vs. Alibaba: Omni-channel Competitor and Collaborator," *Forbes*, July 1, 2014.

Cendrowski, Scott, "Humbled Amazon turns to rival Alibaba for help in China," *Fortune*, March 6, 2015.

"China Retail Report, 2015," *BMI Research*, Q2, 2015.

Dickie, Mure. "Amazon Buys into Growing Chinese Online Retail Market." *Financial Times (London),* August 20, 2004, p. 20.

"Duty Free Philippines," *Duty Free Philippines Corporation,* 2014.

"E-commerce in China: Driving a new consumer culture," *KPMG,* January 2014.

"E-Commerce in China: The Alibaba Phenomenon," *The Economist,* March 23, 2013.

Farfan, Barbara, "Global Flagship Retail Stores—Worldwide Retail Destination Stores," *About Money* 2014.

Fung Group, "Retail Market in China," *Fung Business Intelligence Center,* September 2013.

"Gartner Announces Rankings of Its 2014 Supply Chain Top 25," *Gartner Newsroom,* May 22, 2015.

"Global B2C Ecommerce Sales to Hit $1.5 Trillion This Year Driven by Growth in Emerging Markets," *Retail & E-Commerce,* February 3, 2014.

"Global Power of Retailing," *Deloitte,* 2015.

Hao Li, Hao, Ping Zhao, Yan Wang and Gao Wang, "A Qualitative Research of *Tuangou*: Modes, Characteristics and Roles of the New E-Business Model," *2009 International Symposium on Information Engineering and Electronic Commerce,* IEEE Computer Society, 750–53.

"How Global is the S&P 500?" *S&P Dow Jones Indices,* McGraw Hill Financial, March 2015.

"Internal Help / Duties and Taxes," *L.L.Bean,* 2015.

"Internet Users by Country 2014," *Internet Live Statistics,* 2015.

"Key Facts" *Marks and Spencer,* 2015.

KPMG, "Effective Channel Management Is Critical in Combating the Gray Market and Increasing Technology Companies' Bottom Line," *KPMG Gray Market Study* Update 2008.

Lambert, Bruce. "In Philippines, Duty-Free with a Difference (or Two)," *New York Times,* June 24, 1995, p. 34.

"Manufacturing sector losses increased 44 percent due to illicit trade: Study" *Economic Times,* April 8, 2015.

Riley, Charles, "Alibaba is not the Amazon of China," *CNN Money,* September 16, 2014.

"Shanghai Bailian Group Co Ltd Income Statement," *Reuters,* March 31, 2015.

Smith, Cooper. "How Alibaba Became the World's Largest E-Commerce Company," *Business Insider,* May 14, 2014.

Smith, Craig, "Leader-Parallel Importers Punish Brands for Distribution," *Marketing,* July 19, 2001.

Solomon, Mark "Five years on, DHL's U.S. exit continues to cause pain—for parcel shippers," *Transportation,* Nov. 25, 2013.

Strom, Stephanie and Chad Bray, "Global Grocers' Merger Plan Points Up Challenges in U.S.," *The New York Times,* Business, June 25, 2015, B1, B4.

"Suning Commerce Group Co –A," *Bloomberg Business,* June 10, 2015.

"Ten things we know to be true", *Google Corporate website,* 2015.

"Tesco on the retreat as overseas expansion turns in rotten returns," *The Guardian,* Aug 11, 2013.

"Walmart: Keys to Successful Supply Chain Management," *University Alliance,* 2015.

W.S. Kane and Company, "Parallel import issues under Indian trademark law," *Lexology,* March 20, 2015.

"Worldwide Quarterly Mobile Phone Tracker," *IDC Corporate,* 2015.

Worstall, Tim, "Inditex's Zara and the Power of Comparative Advantage," *Forbes,* 2015.

"Zara rations its stores in Venezuela, allows only five items per customer a month," *Fox News Latino,* November 17, 2014.

ENDNOTES

1. See Smith, 2014.
2. See Alibaba 2014 SEC filings.
3. See "E-Commerce in China: The Alibaba Phenomenon," 2013.

4. See Baker, 2014.

5. See "Alibaba: The world's greatest bazaar," 2013.

6. See Bajpai, 2014.

7. Exhibit data from World Bank statistics and Internet Live Statistics. See "Internet Usage by Country 2014," 2015.

8. Data from U.S. Census, Ministry of Economy See Japan, National Bureau of Statistics-China and Eurostat Regional Yearbook, 2014.

9. See *Encyclopaedia Judaica*. © 2008 The Gale Group.

10. See "Key Facts," 2015.

11. Data compiled from Eurostat Yearbook 2014, U.S. Census, Ministry of Economy See Japan, China Business Review.

12. See "China Retail Report," 2015.

13. See "China Retail Report," 2015.

14. See "Bailian Group Introduction," 2015.

15. See "Shanghai Bailian Group Co Ltd Income Statement," 2015.

16. See "Suning Commerce Group Co –A," 2015.

17. See "Global Powers of Retailing," 2015.

18. See Strom and Bray, 2015.

19. See Attwood, 2007; "Tesco ..." 2013.

20. See Worstall, 2015.

21. See "Zara rations its stores in Venezuela ..." 2014.

22. See "How Global is the S&P 500?" 2015.

23. See "Walmart: Keys to Successful Supply Chain Management," 2015.

24. See "Gartner Announces Rankings of Its 2014 Supply Chain Top 25," 2014.

25. See "Ten things we know to be true," 2015.

26. See Soloman, 2013.

27. See KPMG, 2008.

28. See "Manufacturing sector losses increased 44 per cent due to illicit trade: Study."

29. See Smith, 2001.

30. See W.S. Kane and Company, 2015.

31. See "B2C e-commerce sales worldwide from 2012 to 2018 ..." 2014.

32. See Fung, 2013.

33. See "Global B2C Ecommerce Sales to Hit $1.5 Trillion This Year Driven by Growth in Emerging Markets," 2014.

34. See "Internet Users by Country 2014," 2015.

35. See "E-commerce in China: Driving a new consumer culture," 2014.

36. See "Global B2C Ecommerce Sales to Hit $1.5 Trillion This Year Driven by Growth in Emerging Markets," 2014.

37. See Hao, Zhao, Wang, and Wang, 2009.

38. See "Worldwide Quarterly Mobile Phone Tracker," 2015.

39. See Banker, Toonkel, and Vlastelica, 2014.

40. See Alibaba Corporate website: History and Milestones.

41. See Riley, 2014.

42. See "Amazon leads website Retailers," 2014.

43. See Dickie, 2004.

44. See Cendrowski, 2015.

45. See "Internal Help / Duties and Taxes," 2015.

46. See Farfan, 2014.

47. See Lambert, 1995.

"One voice, many languages"

In this chapter you will learn about:

1. How advertising spending differs across countries in line with economic growth and the openness of markets
2. How global advertising is possible, especially using pattern standardization
3. How online advertising is done and its effectiveness measured
4. How sponsorship and events play huge roles in global brand promotions

Global Advertising and Promotion

CHAPTER 13

RED BULL, A SUCCESSFUL BORN GLOBAL FIRM

Red Bull was founded in the mid-1980s by Dietrich Mateschitz, and the company sold its first can of energy drink on April 1, 1987, in Austria, its home market. According to the product's homepage, "This was not only the launch of a completely new product, in fact it was the birth of a totally new product category."[1]

Mateschitz's attitude toward globalization was summed up when he said that from the beginning "there is only one market, that is the world. ... from zero on we have gone for global brand philosophy, global pricing, global media plans."[2] In less than 30 years, Red Bull has grown to employ over 10,000 people in 171 countries with a total of 6,026 billion cans of Red Bull sold worldwide in 2016."[3] The main reasons for such positive figures include outstanding sales in the Red Bull markets such as Chile (+28%), Scandinavia (+13%), Poland (+13%), the Netherlands (+12%) and South Africa (+10%), combined with efficient cost management and ongoing brand investment.[3]

Red Bull's success has attracted a number of competitors with suggestive names like Amp, Full Throttle Monster, and RockStar. Red Bull recognized from the start that energy drinks do not sell because of taste, they sell primarily on image and Red Bull's promotional efforts to build and maintain the brand have always been outsized. Some years the company spends 30 percent of its sales on advertising and promotion.[4] The strategy ranges "from guerrilla tactics to publicity stunts to big-name sponsorships and national advertising campaigns."[5] "Keeping the brand in the public eye" has become the mantra embodied by its preposterous but eye-catching can-carrying mini-cars which are often driven by college students around campuses offering free samples (see Exhibit 13.1).

In line with its slogan "Red Bull gives you wings," the company has allied its brand and financial resources to adventure sports such as Formula One racing. In 2012 Red Bull sponsored the highest ever free-fall parachute jump from the edge of space at 39 kilometers above the Earth. It also created new high-involvement events such as the Flugtag (Flight Day or Flying Day). Red Bull Flugtag events have contestants attempt to fly home-made, human-powered flying machines off a 30-feet-high cliff into the sea. Hundreds of these have been held worldwide, with the largest attracting over 200,000 people in Cape Town South Africa in 2012. The Flugtags in Nashville, TN and Long Beach, Ca. regularly attract over 100,000 people. Most of the attendees at these events are in the core energy drink market's demographic of 18- to 35-year-old males. On Twitter there are nearly 300,000 followers of Red Bull activities and Red Bull has over 21 million consumers "like" them on Facebook.

There is a balancing act between global brands and local brands, but Red Bull shows that if properly managed, "all marketing is potentially global marketing."

GLOBAL ADVERTISING EXPENDITURES

The global advertiser faces a challenging task. The communication has to be appropriate for each local market, while at the same time there is a need to coordinate campaigns and control expenditures across the globe. Because of the varying media availability in different countries and differing effectiveness of global media, including digital media, the feasible channels for advertising will differ. Furthermore, the variations across country markets in customer behavior make for variable receptivity to advertising and message construction. This chapter deals with these managerial issues and shows how advertising and other promotional tools can be managed to strike the right balance between cost-efficient global campaigns and more adapted local campaigns.

Global advertising can be defined as advertising more or less uniform across many countries, often, but not necessarily, in media vehicles with global reach. In many cases complete uniformity is unobtainable because of linguistic and regulatory differences between nations or differences in cultural values or media availability, but as with products, with some changes advertising can still gain scale economies.

	2014	2017	Growth %
U.S.	176.2	197.2	11.9
Japan	45	48.4	7.6
China	45.41	58	27.7
Germany	24.6	25.8	4.9
UK	22.6	26.8	18.6
Brazil	15.7	19.1	21.7
France	13.1	13	-0.8
Australia	12.3	13	5.7
South Korea	11.4	12.7	11.4
Canada	11.1	11.8	6.3

Advertising Spending

The data in Exhibit 13.2 shows the advertising expenditures in the 10 largest markets.

As the affluence of countries grows, new products/services appear, and customers need more information. Advertising becomes more important and advertising expenditures as a percentage of GDP increase. In fact, advertising expenditures increase and decrease to reflect economic growth closely:

- When economic growth is fast, advertising spending tends to grow even faster.
- When economic growth falters, advertising spending decreases at a faster rate.

There is a role for advertising to play in all economies, socialist as well as capitalist. At the same time, there is little doubt that the role of advertising in advanced capitalist countries is considerably greater than in many other places. The advertising per capita figures in Exhibit 13.3 illustrate this.

Data highlights:

- Advertising intensity varies a great deal between countries. Advertising is simply not a very common form of communication in some countries and may not be an effective promotional tool there.
- Digital advertising is lower than more traditional advertising, taking about 24 percent of ad spending in the United States, for example. But digital is growing fast and accounts for as much as a third of all spending in some countries.
- Generally the higher the GDP, the more is spent on advertising in per-capita terms. The more developed the country, the more money is allocated to advertising. Norway's high spending is especially reflective of their high per-capita income, partly based on the oil finds in the North Sea.
- Total amount of advertising spending per person and in total is very high in the United States. This is partly a result of three factors: the population size, the cultural diversity that makes social norms and interpersonal communication (word-of-mouth) relatively less reliable, and the U.S. economy which is dependent on consumer spending. This has now been recognized by many foreign companies, which find that they have to spend much more on advertising in the United States than expected.[8]

	2012	2014	2016	2018	Growth Rate
U.S.	525	564	617	670	4%
Norway	538	538	550	566	1%
Australia	493	504	515	525	1%
Canada	374	397	416	434	2%
Sweden	397	393	398	403	0%
Denmark	389	385	393	399	0%
UK	331	366	393	414	3%
Germany	325	337	346	354	1%
Japan	370	318	332	341	−1%
Netherlands	316	318	320	321	0%
Finland	345	313	321	334	0%
France	236	232	234	238	0%
South Korea	188	198	207	215	2%
Italy	193	186	192	200	1%
Spain	144	132	136	140	0%
Brazil	83	100	121	141	8%
Argentina	97	87	96	101	1%
Russia	59	76	93	108	9%
Indonesia	30	43	58	74	14%
Mexico	36	41	46	52	5%
China	31	37	42	48	6%
India	4	5	5	6	6%

EXHIBIT 13.3.
Advertising spending per person (U.S. $$ based on 2014 exchange rates)[7] Mature markets in developed countries require high advertising expenditures to differentiate your product, making them expensive markets to enter.

Source: http://www.emarketer.com/Article/Global-Ad-Spending-Growth-Double-This-Year/1010997.

Different cultures, target segments, and regions have different receptivity to advertising and this has affected spending (Exhibit 13.4).[9]

This affects the desirability of having a job in advertising as well. In parts of Asia and the Middle East, advertising agencies have difficulty hiring the best people. But things are changing. Free-market advertising crowds out traditional norms and inefficient ways of communicating. But even as more and more countries are taking to voice mail, Twitter, and texting, differences persist.

	Percent
Americas	41.30%
Asia Pacific	29.70%
Europe	25.70%
Middle East	2.30%
Rest of World	1.00%

EXHIBIT 13.4.
Global advertising spending by region

Source: "MarketLine Industry Profile: Global Advertising," Marketline (2015).

Category	Percent
Food Beverage Personal Healthcare	25.6%
Retailers	12.8%
Media Telecommunications	10.0%
Automotive	8.7%
Financial Services	6.5%
Other	36.3%

EXHIBIT 13.5.
Global advertising by industry[10]

Source: "MarketLine Industry Profile: Global Advertising," Marketline (2015).

EXHIBIT 13.6.
Largest Global Advertisers by Expenditures ($ mil.)[11]
The United States is home to 46 of the world's top 100 advertisers, but the rest are spread across the globe. The top 100 advertisers represent about 47.8% of total spending.

The amount of money spent on advertising differs a great deal between *product categories* (Exhibit 13.5).

Companies in cosmetics and personal care products tend to show the highest advertising-to-sales expenditures, sometimes as high as 30 percent. Consumer packaged goods in general are big spenders, as are automobile companies, although advertising-to-sales ratios are in the 5–10 percent range. [...]

The rankings in the exhibit are based on worldwide advertising spending. The leaders Procter & Gamble and Unilever are fierce competitors in a wide range of household products. They are both in most major markets (70 and 190 countries, respectively, in 2017), and while P&G is strong in the United States, Unilever tends to have a more even global spread, and is very active in Europe. Nestlé, the Swiss food company, another large advertiser, is similar to Unilever in its global reach.

The high advertising expenditures reflect the fact that many companies have a large number of brands. Unilever owns about 400 brands, including *Axe/Lynx, Dove, Omo, Becel/Flora, Heartbrand ice creams, Hellmann's, Knorr, Lipton, Lux, Magnum, Rama, Rexona, Sunsilk, Surf,* and *Ben & Jerry's* ice cream. Nestlé owns over a thousand brands, including *KitKat, Nescafé, Milo, Nestea, Nesquik, Maggi, Herta, Purina, and Perrier.* P&G owns 23 brands with over $1 billion in sales, including *Pampers, Bounty, Tide, Pantene, and Head and Shoulders.* In 2014 P&G adopted a strategy of focusing on its top 70-80 global brands and exiting the unrelated food business. The company sold off about 100 of its smaller local brands and also larger brands such as Pringles crisps and Folgers coffee.[12] As of 2017, a slimmer P&G had 10 product categories with about 65 brands.

These advertisers reach most of the major markets and more. For one thing, the media spillover from satellite TV and other communications is likely to help spread the message to most peoples of the world. The ads may be broadcast from less than 50 percent of the countries, but they are likely to diffuse into the remotest corners of the globe.

Rank	Company	Headquarters	2015 total worldwide advertising spending (billions$$)
1	Procter & Gamble Co.	U.S.	$10.4 billion
2	Unilever	Netherlands/U.K.	$8.9 billion
3	L'Oréal	France	$8.2 billion
4	Volkswagen	Germany	$6.6 billion
5	Comcast Corp.	U.S.	$5.9 billion
	World's Largest Advertisers: Top 5		$40.1 billion
	World's Largest Advertisers: Top 100		$240.5 billion

Source: http://adage.com/article/advertising/world-s-largest-advertisers/306983/

Media Spending

The advertising media have shifted considerably in the last decade. Television advertising is still important, but the new digital media have eroded some of the print media positions. Exhibit 13.7 shows the global advertising by media in 2008, 2013, and 2018 (forecasted), and also the compounded annual growth rate (CAGR).

MEDIA	2008	2013	CAGR	2018	CAGR
Digital advertising	56,619	123,041	15.6%	248,661	15.1%
TV advertising	153,350	181,117	3.4%	250,011	6.7%
Audio (incl. Radio)	32,401	30,950	-.09	35,607	2.8%
Magazines	32,951	25,703	-4.8%	25,729	0.0%
Newspapers	106,600	81,056	-5.3%	78,857	-.05%
Video games	1,262	2,805	17.3%	6.330	17.7%

EXHIBIT 13.7.
Global advertising by media ($U.S. mil.) and compound annual growth rate (CAGR) (percent) 2008–13 and 2013–18[13]

Source: "Global Media Report 2014 Global Industry Overview," McKinsey & Company (2014).

As can be seen in the Exhibit, there has been very strong growth in digital advertising over the last few years. **Digital advertising** refers to promotional messages to consumers and other customers using Internet technologies for delivery. Digital advertising includes promotional advertisements and messages delivered through e-mail, social media websites, and online advertising on search engines, banner ads on mobile, or websites.

By 2018 digital advertising is projected to equal TV advertising. Television is still holding on (some TV advertising will in fact be online) but newspapers and magazines are seeing declines. Video games are a new medium for advertising which is also expected to grow strongly in the future. By 2018, online and mobile games will make up 86 percent of the consumer video games market.

Across regions, the overall increase in global advertising hides weaknesses in some regions and obscures strong gains elsewhere. In Western Europe and Middle East/Africa there was little or no growth between 2008 and 2013, while Central and Eastern Europe grew by 3.6 percent. (Middle East/Africa is projected to grow advertising by 7.6 percent from 2013 until 2018, however). Asia-Pacific rose 6.4 percent fueled mainly by China. Latin America increased spending at 10.5 percent, strong but also reflecting a small starting base. North American spending increased only 0.6 percent annually from 2008 to 2013. Predictions are that the majority of new growth in global advertising in the years up to 2018 will come from Latin America, Asia-Pacific, and Central and Eastern Europe.[14]

Mobile media amount to about 51 percent of digital in 2016, and rapidly rising. Mobile media refer to cell phones, especially smartphones, tablets, and other electronic media that individuals can access "on-the-go." Global mobile advertising rose 83.9 percent and will increase by 34.5 percent compounded annually over the next five years.

The figures in Exhibit 13.7 do not show the emergence of truly global media vehicles. Traditional global media are still alive:

- In *television,* for example, Cable News Network International (CNNI) reaches into many of the globe's remote corners. The British Sky Channel can be seen in most of the EU countries. British BBC is present in many foreign countries, but Al Jazeera has pulled back from developing a global network.
- In *magazines* such as U.S.-based *Time, Cosmopolitan,* and *National Geographic,* overseas editions in the English language have editorial content adapted to the local country. For major markets they also have more completely localized editions and offer, for example, Japanese-language editions.
- In *newspapers, The Financial Times* and *The Wall Street Journal* still have global reach; *The Wall Street Journal* has Asian and European editions.

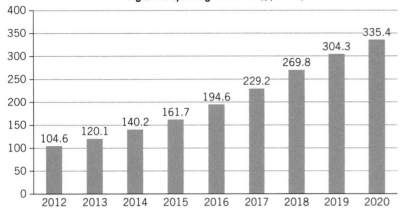

Digital Ad Spending Worldwide ($$billion)

Source: Statista.com. https://www.statista.com/statistics/237974/

online-advertising-spending-worldwide/

EXHIBIT 13.8.
Digital advertising is on pace to represent more than one third of all advertising spending by 2020.[15]

DIGITAL ADVERTISING

In the beginning, digital advertising simply meant **web advertisements**. Internet or web ads are those boxed "inserts" on the screen that pop up as you arrive at a website, still very common. They are interactive in the sense that you can point to them with the mouse and click to get more information about the product or service advertised. By clicking on the ad, you are linked electronically to the company home page. The effectiveness of the ads is typically measured via the CTR, or click through rate.

There are several kinds of web ads, including *Banner* ads, "*Tickers*" that move across the screen, *Pop-up ads*, and so-called *Roadblocks*, the full-screen ads that users must pass through to get to the other screens they wish to view. But the web advertising is today only a small part of digital advertising, which has grown rapidly in recent years (see Exhibit 13.8).

The major alternatives in digital advertising are the following:

- **Search advertising**. Search engines such as Google make advertising space available for products and services associated with the search "keywords." Offering companies the option of tying their ads to relevant keywords (its "AdWords") allowed ads to appear when consumers searched—which is why you see those sidebars and those top of the menu listings that crop up when you search. By charging for these ad listings—more for the top of the line, less for the sidebar, and also allowing advertisers to come ahead in line—search engines "monetized" their free search. Of Google's $66.0 billion in revenues in 2014, $77.7 billion came from advertising (86 percent).[16]
- **E-mail advertising**. E-mail has become another advertising channel. For the average consumer, e-mail ads account for more than 50 percent of incoming messages. Your address is gathered usually with your consent at store visits, purchases, and, most certainly, on online website visits. It is a very inexpensive advertising venue for companies, although promotions need to be coordinated with in-store activity so customers can redeem coupons and deals. Also, e-mail ads are not always an obvious choice even though inexpensive—the offers may be screened out as "spam," and can also irritate consumers, leading to anti-brand animosity. Furthermore, these e-mails can be relegated to a "Promotions" bin in Google's e-mail service, lessening their impact further.

Several additional media are now also available for digital advertising.

- *Blogs*. Advertising on popular blogs (Huffington Post, for example) has become the main way for a few full-time bloggers to make a living.
- *SMS*. Short Message Service or "texting" is an appendix to e-mail and phone advertising. Well-adapted to mobile advertising.
- *YouTube*. Now owned by Google, YouTube has become an increasingly popular medium as broadband access diffuses and even mobile videos can be watched.

	2012	2013	2014	2015	2016	2017	2018
North America	11%	21%	33%	43%	53%	60%	67%
Western Europe	6%	12%	21%	30%	39%	48%	57%
Asia-Pacific	9%	12%	18%	23%	28%	33%	36%
Latin America	2%	4%	6%	9%	13%	18%	24%
Central & Eastern Europe	2%	4%	6%	9%	12%	15%	18%
Middle East & Africa	2%	4%	5%	6%	7%	9%	11%

EXHIBIT 13.9.
Mobile ad spending as percent of total digital ad spending[17]

Source: http://www.emarketer.com/Article/Global-Ad-Spending-Growth-Double-This-Year/1010997.

- *Social media.* Even though Twitter and Facebook have only recently opened up for advertising, social media are becoming increasingly used for digital advertising.
- *Classified listings.* There is Craigslist and Yellow Pages, for example.

Mobile Advertising. Mobile advertising is less of a new digital medium than simply a new transmission method. It is poised to become the next "new thing" around the world as tablets and especially smartphones proliferate (see Exhibit 13.9).

Mobile ads include new interactive and personalized ad media that companies have been experimenting with for some time. Appearing when you search for addresses on a smartphone was only the beginning. The cameras that recognize you on arrival to a store or on the street are likely to become more prevalent and possibly annoying, as advertisers try to kindle personal attention and build relationships. Already in 2007 a Mini Cooper billboard in San Francisco was using a signal emitted from approaching cars to flash personalized messages to the driver.

In Western countries the smartphone is complementary to the PC and tablets, but in many emerging countries, smartphones are the only Internet access tool. India is expected to have about 651 million smartphone users by end of 2019.[18] Some Indian consumers will still access the Internet via a PC at home or at work or in cyber-cafes, but the majority will likely use their phones.

GLOBALIZED ADVERTISING

The most obvious part of global advertising is uniformity of visuals and message. There are three levels of uniformity to a global advertising strategy.

Identical Ads

The ads can be identical ads, usually with localization only in terms of language voice-over changes and simple copy translations. Worldwide advertising featuring the Marlboro cowboy is one example (see Exhibit 13.10).

The Marlboro cowboy ads ran in the United States from 1954 to 1999 when all cigarette advertising was banned. They continued running in the EU till the mid 2000s and are still running in Japan and China where smoking is still widespread especially among the male population.

Exxon gasoline's slogan "Put a tiger in the tank" is another iconic example. This campaign has long been used in Europe, Australia, and the Far East and Exxon's

EXHIBIT 13.10.
The macho "Marlboro Man," with a cigarette dangling from his lips, on a building in Berlin, Germany. The European directive against cigarette advertising does not include advertising in cinemas and on billboard. The iconic cowboy has been used so long that for many people the image is imprinted on their minds, and supposedly no brand logo is needed. Marlboro is the largest selling brand of cigarettes in the world because in part of the effectiveness of the global "Marlboro Man" image.

Tiger even appeared on the cover of *Time* magazine. "Esso's tiger" is still used around the world (see Exhibit 13.11).

In some cases the identical ads or commercials can be used without any translation at all. Levi's, the jeans manufacturer, sometimes uses cartoons with rock music and unintelligible, vaguely Esperanto-sounding vocals in one commercial where the Levi's-wearing hero rescues a beautiful woman from a burning building, an easily comprehended message. In other cases the commercials simply carry subtitles. IBM shows Italian-speaking nuns discussing the pros and cons of Internet surfing with subtitles translating the conversation: global ad, with a local touch.

Esso gas pump in Toronto, Canada   **Esso petrol station in Bangkok, Thailand.**

EXHIBIT 13.11.
Early globalization:
Esso's Tiger. Esso is the
international trade name for
ExxonMobil and its related
companies. The name is a
phonetic version of the initials
of the pre-1911 Standard Oil.
The use of the name in the
United States has been
blocked by the regional
Standard Oil companies.

Copyright © 2015 by Shutterstock/
rmnoa357.

Copyright © 2015 by Shutterstock/
MrNovel.

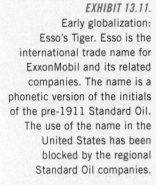

Prototype Advertising

In prototype advertising the voice-over and the visuals are changed to avoid language and cultural problems; the ad may also be reshot with local spokespeople but using the same visualization. Apple's early iPad ads fall into the prototype category, with strict adherence to a certain formula (see Exhibit 13.12).

As another prototype example, Drakkar Noir, a man's fragrance, in a print ad from the Middle East shows a woman's hand caressing a man's hand holding the product; in France the same hand grasps the man's wrist, showing a more assertive woman. Cultural adaptation.

Pattern Standardization

A less structured approach to global advertising involves **pattern standardization,** in which the positioning theme is unified and some alternative creative concepts supporting the positioning are spelled out, but the actual execution of the ads differs between markets. L'Oreal's ads with female celebrities in different countries follow a facial shot with a product visual and some copy. The ads have the same basic message and "feeling" although the words and product selections are different.

Despite such pitfalls, pattern standardization has become the most common approach to global advertising. For global brand building, it allows creative flexibility at the local level but still makes for some consistency in the brand image. For example, MasterCard's "Priceless" campaigns represent an example of pattern standardization, with executions localized around the world including Hong Kong and India.[19] Nike's repeated use of different soccer stars in advertising the World Cups is another example of pattern standardization.[20]

UK, iPad Air

Russia, iPad with financial app

Ukraine, iPad2 with FIFA football game

EXHIBIT 13.12.
Apple iPad ads from three different countries. The finger touch and hands are prominent repeated features to explain how to use the iPad and how easy it is. Later on the prototype changes to a pattern standardization approach, when users are shown in various settings (as in the medical example in Chapter 9, Exhibit 9.6).

Core Benefit Pitfalls

Global advertising works best when the core benefit of the product is similar across markets. It is sometimes easy to assume that foreign people see the same advantages in products as we do. In-depth market research is often necessary to identify potential pitfalls.

An example that shows the how different core benefits can ruin pattern standardization in advertising comes from Procter & Gamble. P&G often creates its own storyboard behind its commercials, and a favorite approach has long been the "problem-solving" story. The typical commercial starts with a consumer "problem," then brings in some individual with "expertise" who suggests the use of a P&G brand to "solve the problem," shows how the product works, and ends with the customer smiling and happy, "problem solved." A 30-second commercials can easily show the sequence, with some quick cuts and voice-overs. A simple example is the typical Head & Shoulders ad first showing the dandruff on someone's shoulder, a friend recommending H&S, a shower and hair wash, and then the happy individual on a date. This pattern standardization has been repeated for P&G's detergents, soaps, diapers, and so on.

In Asia, the problem-solving approach has met with some resistance. One early example involved the introduction of Pampers, P&G's disposable diapers, into Japan. Following its formula, P&G ran commercials showing how a crying baby was pacified, and how a distraught mother was comforted by the use of disposable diapers. Sales were lackluster for several years before P&G realized the cause. In Japan, babies are not "problems" and if they cry (which is rare, hard for P&G to imagine), the mother is at fault. The commercials were actually insulting to the Japanese mothers. P&G then shifted to focus on the babies alone, with the mothers not shown, with the commercials demonstrating how disposable diapers made babies happy (see Exhibit 13.13).

In the West: Helping to solve the mother's problem with the crying baby.

In Asia: Helping to make your baby happy and beautiful.

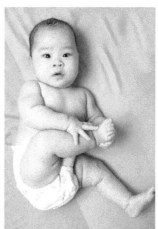

Procter & Gamble has learned from its experience. In China, for example, the Head & Shoulders shampoo is positioned not as a dandruff fighter, but as a shampoo that makes women's hair shimmering, silky, and soft. The "core benefit" is different. H&S is now one of the leading brands in China.

GLOBAL ADVERTISING PROS AND CONS

As we have seen, global advertising is not always the correct strategy. By far the most advertising spending in the world is for ads adapted to the local marketplace. Even for the largest global companies, a typical allocation of global advertising budgets is one-third for global campaigns, two-thirds for local campaigns. The global portion might involve product placement in major movie (ex. Samsung's Galaxy in the *Matrix* trilogy), and TV advertising for global on major international channels such as CNN International, and then follow-up promotional efforts at the local level. The local portion involves local broadcast media, targeted social media campaigns, and channel merchandising. Global sponsorship of a major event such as the World Cup (ex. Visa) or the Olympics (ex. Lenovo) needs to be supported by on-site promotions, local advertising, and local channel support, leveraging the global sponsorship. Local adaptation is necessary even for global campaigns.

The most immediate benefit of global advertising usually involves the cost advantages of unified campaigns.

Cost Advantages

From a cost viewpoint a globally uniform campaign is usually advantageous. The creative ideas once developed can be used globally; the illustrations and messages can be developed once and for all or employed with only minor modifications. Media availability forces some changes, since a broadcast approach might not be directly translatable into print, but generally costs can be held down below those generated by original work for the local market.

Globalized campaigns can also be the basis for savings in media buying. Several media provide global services, especially print, through their international editions. Because media ownership is becoming multinational there are sources of scale returns available to a globalized campaign not easily tapped by local buyers.

Global Markets

In general, global advertising will be most useful when the market itself is global. Air travel is a case in point. International airlines offer a typically standardized "product"—or service—and compete for passengers in a global marketplace. The various international airlines attempt to differentiate themselves by superior preflight, in-flight, and post-flight service. Global advertising has become an important competitive weapon and a prime source of differentiation.[21]

Global Brands

It might be assumed that global brands need global advertising. This is often true. The campaigns for Swatch watches, Club Med, Benetton, and Reebok are very similar across continents. But there is often a need to do some local adaptation of global campaigns. Sometimes a brand's global campaign has misfired and the company has retreated to a more multi-domestic adaptation. Parker Pen, a globally recognized American brand name, shifted to global advertising using identical ads worldwide in the mid-1980s only to return to multi-domestic advertising (and renewed success) after sales slumped badly.[22] The cause of failure was the lack of cooperation on the part of the company's country subsidiaries, whose previously successful campaigns were discontinued.

The *disadvantages* of global advertising are basically the lack of "fit" in local markets. The "misfit" reasons can be several:

- *Image.* The image communicated cannot be identical across countries. Levi's jeans is one example. Another is the premium Buick image in China in contrast to the old image in the United States. Still another is Mercedes' mainstream image at home in Germany versus luxury in India.
- *Symbols.* The symbols used do not carry the same meaning across countries. Colors can play a role, for example. Orange is a spiritual color in the East, but not good in Ireland where it stands for Protestants—the French telecom company Orange had to tone down its logo. Coke's red color signifies happiness in China, excitement in the United States.
- *Features.* The product features desired are not the same. The fuel-saving lighter cars favored by Asian car companies do not always appeal to Western buyers who kick the tires and slam the doors to test stability and durability. Levi's worn day-to-day need more durability than when jeans are style items.
- *Usage.* The usage conditions are not similar across markets. Iron-free shirts might be practical in Southern Europe with its dry summers, but in the Caribbean's humidity you need cotton shirts. Car suspensions need to be reinforced in countries where potholes are common, compromising the riding comfort.

When one or more of these conditions hold—as in the case of Levi's jeans—even standardized products may need adapted multi-domestic advertising. If the conditions are not right, global advertising will fail. If none of these conditions hold, as in the case of the airlines, say, global advertising is a natural.

GLOBALIZATION EXAMPLES

The best illustration of global advertising is probably Coca-Cola's campaigns. For its main cola brand, Coca-Cola typically hires a global agency. McCann-Erickson had the account on and off for many years, but as of 2014 it is divided among several agencies. Traditionally the agency developed prototypes of advertising messages and layouts in the United States with input from its local agencies abroad. The local offices were allowed to make changes so as to accommodate language differences and possible differences in regulations, but they are generally expected to follow the main script for the campaign. Today, the basic theme can come from anywhere in the global network.

Over the years, Coca-Cola has developed several memorable slogans. Experts have singled out three as most successful:

- "Things Go Better With Coke" (1963-69): created by McCann-Erickson.
- "It's the Real Thing" (1969-1976): Another by McCann-Erickson, who also introduced the popular "I'd like to buy the world a Coke" song by The New Seekers who incorporated the slogan into the song. One early commercial in 1971 called "Hilltop" was also one of the first truly global commercials, with young people gathered on a hill outside Rome singing together.[23]
- "Always Coca-Cola" (1993-2006): by Creative Artists Agency; this was when the animated Polar Bears campaign started, a globally successful campaign that targeted the Winter Olympics 1994 but proved of universal appeal.

In 2009, Coca-Cola and the Wieden & Kennedy agency introduced the "Open Happiness" campaign and this campaign was rolled out to 200 markets globally (this campaign theme is still ongoing). The campaign involves vignettes of real people in surprising and fun situations, using a wide variety of media, print ads, television commercials, and online search advertising. The global commercials tend to be short clips with a mix of activities and people, laughing and happy.

The campaign also features specific local adaptations with longer commercials, filming odd events created by Coca-Cola. In one, migrant workers from South Asia in Dubai are able to use Coca-Cola cap tops as coins for telephone calls back home. In another, Indian and Pakistani citizens can meet each other virtually through the webcam hookups in two Coke-like vending machines placed in two cities on the border.[24] This 2013 commercial inspired an American commercial from Google just a few months later.[25] After six years of "Open Happiness," the brand has asked 10 advertising agencies to pitch ideas for Coke's next global campaign. A rep said Coke is looking for new messaging now to ensure it continues to have global appeal, engages and entertains consumers, and drives business growth. It's unclear how long the selection process will take, or when the brand might unveil a new marketing effort.[26] In 2017 it seemed that finally a new campaign theme had been found. "Taste the Feeling" is poised to become the new global slogan.

More serious campaigns are also common. One example is from Philips, the Dutch multinational (see box, "Philips turns to B2B").

A number of companies are practitioners of global advertising. They include the L'Oreal company (cosmetics), the Ralph Lauren Polo and Chaps brands (men's clothing and accessories), Johnnie Walker, a leading global Scotch whisky brand, most high-fashion companies such as Louis Vuitton, Chanel, and Dior, and home electronics

BOX: Philips Turns to B2B.[27]

The large Philips corporation has traditionally been more of a multinational than a truly global company, with significant autonomy for its country subsidiaries and less a centralized globally directed organization. Its product line includes medical instruments, infrastructure projects, and computer chips, but also Norelco electric shavers, light bulbs, consumer electronics, and coffee makers.

To establish the Philips name as an umbrella brand for this product line, the company first developed a new campaign in 2004 with a tag-line "Sense and Simplicity." The new tag-line represented a common thread among all these disparate products. The global campaign involved a series of print and TV commercials around the "Sense and Simplicity" theme.

The campaign kicked off strongly by Philips as the "official technology supplier" to the 2004 blockbuster movie *Ocean's Twelve* filmed in Europe, starring George Clooney, Brad Pitt, Matt Damon, Catherine Zeta-Jones, and Julia Roberts. It wanted to create some "buzz" around the brand.

But by 2014, the company was changing tack. Finding the efforts to establish a strong consumer brand too challenging in the face of strong Asian competition (Japan, Korea, China), Philips decided it was time for a re-brand. It wants Philips to be seen as a business-to-business (B2B) brand, in many ways a more authentic identity since two-thirds of its overall business is in enterprise and government work (see Exhibit 13.14).

The new B2B campaign involves posting digital documentaries that showcase how its innovations are helping businesses and people around the world. The documentaries showcase how other industries, particularly in infrastructure and healthcare, are utilizing Philips products to benefit people every day. From making streets safer for children at night through street lighting, making bedtime easier for a little girl in London, to showing how a loving husband and wife can live together and receive high-quality healthcare at home, the stories show how Philips' innovation is improving people's lives around the world.

The campaign slogan is "Innovation and You," and is featured on major business magazines' websites, coupled with targeted TV spots and print advertising.[28] To appeal to local businesses around the world, the documentaries are filmed in various parts of the world by the Ogilvy agency and will be posted on the "Innovation and You" Philips website. So far, the online effort seems to have paid off better than *Ocean's Twelve*.

The Norelco electric shaver, developed by Philips.

The portable heart defibrillator introduced by Philips.

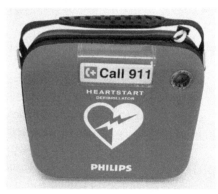

EXHIBIT 13.14.
Two of the top products from the Philips Company in the Netherlands. The company is a leading B2B company but also strong in consumer products. One problem has been that its leading electric shaver is marketed under the Norelco brand name in the United States because the Philips name cannot be used there.

Copyright © by Shutterstock/Natan86.

Copyright © by Bigstock/Leonard Zhukovsky.

companies such as Samsung and Sony. There are others from which one might expect globalized campaigns but that do not use them. Canon cameras employ different campaign material in Japan, Europe, and the United States, as do the Japanese automobile companies. The European car manufacturers develop special campaigns for their North American markets even though many of the selling propositions remain the same.

Agency Group	Worldwide Revenue 2016 (Billions$)
WPP Group	17.1
Omnicom	15.4
Publicis Groupe	10.3
Interpublic	7.8
Dentsu	7.1
Havas	2.5
Hakuhodo DY	2.3
MDC Partners	1.4
Cheil	0.87
Bluefocus	0.82

Source: Global Agency Family Tree 2017, http://www.rthree.com/en/insight/detail/190JVCO.html

EXHIBIT 13.15.
World's largest agency networks 2016 (by Worldwide Revenue)[29]

Source: http://www.rthree.com/en/insight/detail/190JVCO.html.

THE GLOBAL ADVERTISING AGENCY

The drive toward global advertising has been supported by **global advertising agencies**, those with worldwide networks of subsidiaries or affiliates.

Agency Globalization

The world's largest agencies are listed in Exhibit 13.15.

The large agencies listed in the exhibit comprise industry groupings, called "super-agencies" by some. The four largest of these are the Omnicom Group and the Interpublic Group of Companies of New York, the WPP Group of London, and Publicis in Paris. These larger groupings represent a consolidation of the industry to capture scale returns—especially in media buying—and also eliminate duplication and maybe eliminate competition. The Omnicom Group for example had a 2014 total revenue of $14.58 billion but consists of 62 individual advertising and public relations companies ranging in size from $17 million in annual revenue up to $1.49 billion.

The new super-agencies take advantage of the scale returns in media buying. But trying to keep the creative component small and inspiring, the original agencies are left intact. The agency names tend also to remain because of the brand equity vested in the name. The media buying component, on the other hand, shares in the discounts offered to the large super-agencies.

With consolidation into larger agency groupings many competing agencies have actually ended up in the same super-agency. This has become an ongoing problem, since two agencies in the same grouping can be working for competing clients. For example, at one point PepsiCo switched $350 million of its ad business from an agency acquired by Interpublic to an Omnicom shop because Interpublic also represents Pepsi's archrival, Coca-Cola. A short while later, Coca-Cola shifted work on its Sprite brand from Interpublic to a WPP-owned agency, saying it didn't want to rely on a single advertising conglomerate.

Message Creation

One main function of the advertising agency is to craft the global ad message. Here the local branches of the ad agencies play a major role, since translations are often involved. Small nuances in words sometimes matter a lot. An American manufacturer in the auto industry advertised its batteries as "highly rated." In Venezuela the translation made it "highly overrated." The advertising of a global shirt brand in Mexico also had trouble with the Spanish language. Instead of declaring, "When I used this shirt I felt good," the character in the advertisement asserted "Until I used this shirt I felt good."

Sexual connotations under the surface of day-to-day language create pitfalls. Chrysler tried to use its American slogan "Dart Is Power" in Latin-American markets only to find that the message implied that drivers of the car lacked sexual vigor. An airline advertising its "rendezvous lounges" on its flights did not realize that to many Europeans a rendezvous carries the distinct connotation of meeting a lover for an illicit affair. Otis Elevators promoted parts of its line in Russia as "completion equipment," which in Russian became "tools for orgasms."

Spanish Word for Tires	Countries Using Each Word
Cauchos	Venezuela
Cubiertas	Argentina
Gomas	Puerto Rico
Llantas	Mexico, Peru, Guatemala, Colombia
Neumaticos	Chile

Sometimes there is no easy way out. Goodyear found there were four different ways to say "tires" in Latin America, and a fifth way to say it in Puerto Rico. In some of these countries one of the expressions occurs less frequently, while in other countries expressions other than the main one either will not be understood or may convey an entirely different meaning.

It's obviously important to pick the right word for each local market.

But there are also examples of successful advertising messages used in many different countries with only a modicum of modification. A classic example was Nokia's legendary tag-line, "Connecting people," now discontinued. Unilever's Lux soap was long advertised around the world as "the soap used by 9 stars out of 10"; Sony positions itself as "the innovator" in most country markets; and Audi's "Vorsprung durch technik" (roughly translated as "Advantage through technique"), emphasizing its German roots, can be seen in Asia, Europe, North America, and Latin America.

Media Selection

Traditional media selection is another area where the agency and its local representatives are in charge. The reason is primarily expertise. Local knowledge of the availability of media alternatives is absolutely necessary so that the optimal media, given the constraints, are chosen. It might be possible to direct an advertising campaign from overseas insofar as budgeting, message creation, and general direction go, but the media choices must be negotiated and made locally.

The effectiveness of different media has always been a big question mark. The most common measure has been the **cost-per-thousand (CPM**, or cost-per-mille) criterion, suggesting that the vehicle with the lowest CPM is the more efficient choice.

The CPM calculation divides the cost of one ad or commercial spot with the audience (in thousands) reading the newspaper or watching the program. For example, a full-page ad in *The New York Times* costs $70,000. With a daily circulation about 2.5 million in 2014, the CPM is 28.0. A Super Bowl 30-second ad that reaches an estimated 112 million viewers (2014) and costs $4 million, has a CPM of 35.7. Both are high numbers, meaning these are expensive media. A digital ad can be much less costly for a given audience and tend to have a much lower CPM.

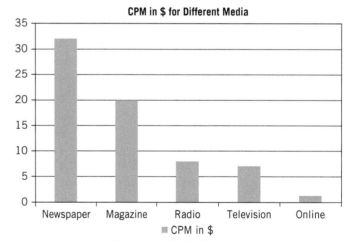

EXHIBIT 13.16.
Cost-per-thousand (CPM) of advertising media (U.S. 2014)[30]

Source: Richard Marshall, "'Triple Advantage' for Responsible Supply Chains, Says WEF Report," HHGlobal, 2015.

Which medium is least expensive depends on a number of things, but generally digital is ranked as the least expensive. One example is the media cost graph for the U.S. in 2014 which shows that the Super Bowl costs are not representative of TV ads in general (see Exhibit 13.16):

There is, unfortunately, no guarantee that the people in the audience actually see the ad. This has always been a problem for all media. For digital advertising, however, audience and exposure can be approximately measured. The number of visitors to a website is recorded, and the **click-through rate (CTR)** to an ad can be measured. That is, given the exposures to an ad with a link, what proportion of consumers actually clicked on it? The CTR can also be used to design advertising. Google's AdWords program is helping advertisers design online search ads that generate higher CTR scores, for example.

GLOBAL SALES PROMOTION

Sales promotion involves a variety of activities, ranging from point-of-purchase displays and trade promotions to Sunday newspaper coupons and the sponsorship of symphony orchestras and athletic events such as the Olympics, soccer's World Cup, and major tennis tournaments.

In-Store and Trade Promotions

In-store or **point-of-purchase (p-o-p) promotions** (also referred to as POS, point-of-sale) involves promotional activities inside the store; **trade promotions** are targeted at channel intermediaries ("the trade"). Both are important in the U.S. market and are becoming more important in many other markets as well.

Typically, in-store sales promotion is a much more localized activity than advertising. Promotions are not always welcomed by the trade or the consumers. Several factors play a role in this.

- *Regulations.* Sales promotion is often more rigidly regulated than advertising. Cents-off coupons, free samples, and two-for-one offers can be prohibited in some countries where regulation is aimed at ensuring orderly markets and steady margins for local retailers. The many coupons available on digital channels in some countries will not be allowed in certain countries. Similarly, premiums, gifts, and competitions are sometimes allowed but with major restrictions. Outright prohibition is unusual, but most countries impose limits on what can be done. These restrictions vary between countries. In France, for example, a gift can't be worth more than 4 percent of the retail value of the product. In Germany, requiring proof of purchase for participation in a competition is illegal.
- *Cooperation from the Trade.* The aim of sales promotion is to "move product," and retailers and upstream wholesalers need to be induced to cooperate and increase the product flow. This is usually done through trade discounts, cooperative advertising, and sales support. If the trade is not compensated, middlemen may not cooperate. For example, ACNielsen tried to introduce cents-off coupons in Chile, but the nation's supermarket union opposed the project and asked its members not to accept them.
- *Attitudes toward Coupons.* The retailers need to handle promotions such as coupons professionally and not embarrass the coupon-using consumer, often difficult in countries with a history of producers dominating the customers.
- *Limited Capability.* Since distribution infrastructure is often different between countries, some promotions may simply not be feasible. Procter & Gamble tried to introduce its Cheer detergent in Japan using the

type of trade promotion employed in the United States, including coupons, cents off, and trade discounts. The stores in Japan, however, were too small to handle the necessary volume and quickly ran out of stock.[31] Consumers were disappointed, retailers were frustrated, and the introductory campaign was a failure.

- *Presold Customers.* In-store promotions work best when the is consumer expected to make choices in the store. In some cases the choice is already made before entering the store: preselling a product through advertising or newspaper coupons, for example, often means that no in-store choice is necessary. Brand loyalty has the same effect. When channels are dominated by manufacturers (as is common in many emerging markets), stores may feature only one brand and the store choice dictates which brand will be bought.

Trade promotions have their own problems. When General Electric broke into the air-conditioning market in Japan, the company offered overseas trips to outstanding dealers and a free color TV set to purchasers of high-end models. The successful campaign drew complaints from the trade association, and new rules to limit promotions were approved by the Japanese Fair Trade Commission. A limit was set on the size of the premium that could be offered, and no overseas trips were allowed as dealer incentives for any home appliances.[32]

Japan has long been a difficult market because of regulation. In 2013 the *Wall Street Journal* reported that after promising to open over-the-counter drugs to online sales, the government decided to renege on its promise because of opposition by the trade. Instead, prescription drugs recently converted to over-the-counter status would be blocked from online sales for up to three years, pending a safety assessment.[33] As another example, to protect its wildly uncompetitive and inefficient farmers, Japan has erected one of the world's highest tariffs: the 2015 duty on imported polished rice is 777 percent, essentially preventing importation and promotion of rice.[34] The TPP accord abolished by President Trump would have changed that.

Digital "Middlemen"

A vast number of new digital-based businesses have cropped up as promotional middlemen to support the linkage between consumers, products, and the stores. Just as with traditional middlemen, these **digital middlemen** create and foster valuable exchanges between consumers and producers. Some are simple applications ("apps") for the tablets and smartphones, some are bots or crawlers that search the web for lowest price, others are free-standing enterprises that offer completely new products and services that consumers never knew they needed before the Internet.

Many of these new applications begin as local services, and many stay that way. The "Embark NYC" for updates on the New York City's subway system's breakdowns is a local app. A bot such as *www.thecouponsbot.com* scours manufacturers' and stores' advertising to find coupons for products you want. You can download and redeem the coupon in a store near you. Shopkick.com is a new enterprise that offers the consumer "points" for visiting stores and buying certain products. Here is how its website introduces its new service on shopkick.com/tour:

"Shopkick is the shopping app that helps you discover all the best products at stores near you. It shows you popular products and rewards waiting for you at stores like Target, Macy's, Best Buy, Old Navy, American Eagle, JCPenney, Sports Authority and Crate & Barrel. And it rewards you with kicks (points) just for walking in the door. Get even more kicks when you scan items and make purchases. Redeem your points for gift cards at your favorite stores. Now you can do even more of what you love—shop."

Even though these examples are basically local, the technology is available globally. It is not surprising, therefore, to find out that in many countries local application with different names have cropped up. When that happens, the originators tend to start looking at international expansion, to also share in the new consumer demand opening up. A good example is Groupon.com (see box, "Groupon goes global").

BOX: Groupon Goes Global

Groupon stands for group coupon. The business was started in 2008 in Chicago, offering consumers online access to discount gift certificates as "deal-of-the-day" for local area businesses—restaurants, art and entertainment events, and travel. It soon expanded into other major metropolitan areas in the United States.[35]

The company offers basically a deal a day to consumers who have signed up in that location. If enough consumers buy the deal, it is on—else it is scrapped (to limit the exposure to retailers). The retailer and Groupon divide the daily total equally.

Groupon's business model can be easily copied and with a low barrier to entry has led to increased competition in the daily deals space. Within a couple of years the Groupon business model had been copied in about 50 foreign countries. Deciding to respond to competition, the company raised money from local investors overseas and bought up local competitors.[36] Within a short span of time, the company expanded as follows:

- Europe—Groupon purchased CityDeal, a large European clone based in Berlin. The acquisition added 600 employees to Groupon's payroll of 300 before the deal. CityDeal was active in 80 markets in 16 countries, including the United Kingdom, Germany, and France. In 2013, the company announced the acquisition of travel app Blink, which primarily deals in same day hotel bookings in Europe. With Blink's 2000 hotel partners in eight European countries, the company intends to bolster its Groupon Getaways business.
- Russia—Groupon acquired a majority stake in Darberry.ru, a similar site based in Moscow. With the investment, Darberry was renamed Groupon Russia. The site served seven cities in Russia, and 180,000 subscribers.
- Japan—Groupon put up $10 million to buy a majority stake in Qpod, a Tokyo-based start-up. The site has been re-branded Groupon Japan.
- Latin-America—Groupon entered Latin America by buying one of its imitators in Chile, a site called ClanDescuento. Groupon quickly became the most-visited coupon site in Latin America with 4.8 million visitors, the largest audience in Brazil (2.5 million visitors reaching 6 percent of online users), the highest reach in Argentina (922,000 visitors reaching 7.1 percent) and Chile (481,000 visitors reaching 6.6 percent).[37]
- India—Groupon entered India by buying a popular site SoSasta.com, first rebranding it to Crazeal.com. The SoSasta name, which derives from the Sanskrit word Sasta for "cheap," did not find favor with users in the south of India where Sanskrit is not particularly popular. It is now Groupon.co.in.[38]
- China—Currently there were over 100 clones of Groupon in China, including an exact replica of the original site with address groupon.cn. Gaopeng is the name of the Groupon joint venture partner, but Groupon has only a minor stake in the firm, while Hong Kong based Tencent owns the majority. After years of trying in China, Groupon decided in 2014 to exit the Chinese market.

In addition, in 2014, Groupon exited Romania, after three losing years. The Internet penetration in Romania was apparently not sufficiently up to acceptable technical standards yet.

Groupon continues to evolve from a daily-deal provider to a more traditional e-commerce merchant that sells physical goods. Groupon Inc. wants shoppers to think of Groupon as an online retailer and marketplace, and not just a supplier of discount vouchers. It remains to be seen if this expansion strategy can work long term. Even support from Alibaba has not stopped the decline in capitalization, from $6 billion in 2010 to some $2.2 Billion in 2017.

From a consumer behavior perspective what is striking here is how quickly these promotional services diffuse globally. Apparently many of the market-driving innovations of the Internet are readily applicable and acceptable in many markets around the world. Globally, buyer behavior seems to be increasingly similar.

Sponsorships

With the advent of global media the possibilities for global **sponsorships** are opening up. Sponsoring a World Cup match by plastering the brand name on the bleachers and piggybacking on the television broadcasts has helped companies such as Mars (Snickers), Samsung, and Emirates establish a strong identity in the global marketplace. More direct spending involves sponsoring tennis tournaments (Volvo, Virginia Slims), Formula One race cars (Coca-Cola, Marlboro), single-man treks to the South Pole (NordicTrack), and athletic team wear (Nike, Under Armour). Red Bull is one company that has gone all out to sponsor a Formula One race car. The energy drinks giant has spent more than $1.2 billion on its flagship Formula One auto racing team over the past decade (see Exhibit 13.17).[39]

EXHIBIT 13.17.
Sebastian Vettel in the Red Bull F1 on the track at Jerez de la Frontera, Spain. Red Bull has spent over $1.2 billion on Formula One racing, a passion of Red Bull founder Dietrich Mateschitz. F1 racing is pretty exclusive and does not necessarily reach the typical Red Bull target of young people, but the "extreme sport" angle is one that the Red Bull image aspires to.

The Olympic sponsorship, which started seriously in Los Angeles in 1984, and reached new heights (or depths, for some purists) in Beijing 2008, then London 2012, and the Winter Games in Sochi in 2014, has now spilled over into promotional sponsorship of Russian hockey players (Visa) and Italian basketball teams (Sony). It is somewhat unsettling to see newspaper pictures of the national soccer team of Brazil and find it sponsored by Nike. Nike still stands behind Neymar and Brazil, even though Adidas, the World Cup sponsor, scored a win in 2014 when the German team trounced Brazil 7-1. Adidas reportedly pays $70 million every four years for the sponsorship rights to the World Cup until 2030.[40]

The global reach of sporting events, which has created possibilities for products to become associated with globally recognized sports figures, has made the sports figures rich in addition to famous. Maria Sharapova, the tennis player, is a spokesperson for Samsung, Tag Heuer, Evian, Porsche—and, again, Nike—and has also put her name on a line of products.[41] These, however, need to be marketed well and can't stretch too far: former tennis great Bjorn Borg's adventure in personal hygiene products and leisurewear was not successful, for example.

The use of well-known athletes has its downside. Athletes don't last forever. Tiger Woods was dropped by Gillette, Accenture, AT&T, Tag Heuer, Electronic Art, and Gatorade—but not by Nike. His Nike sponsorship remains one of the biggest in sports with the $28.8 billion-in-sales sportswear giant building a $789 million golf division on the back of Woods.[42] After a few lackluster performances since 2014–15, Tiger Woods' position seems quite precarious, however. Sharapova was banned for drug abuse in 2016–17, but has recently come back.

Companies also help arrange events and contests at which their brands can be promoted. For example, aiming for global expansion, Glacéau vitamin water, a subsidiary of Coca-Cola, did a 2014 World Cup promotion called "Shoot to Win." The digital promotion encouraged fans of photography to capture an "everyday colorful moment" on their camera for a chance to win one of several World Cup-themed prizes. Running until mid-May before the start of the competition in June, the campaign offered football fans the chance to win the ultimate prize of a trip for two to Rio and watch a quarter-final match.[43]

Global media can also be useful as vehicles for local campaigns. In an interesting twist, local Airbnb hosts in Rio de Janeiro used the 2016 Olympics platform to attract traffic from abroad. Airbnb became an official "alternative accommodations" sponsor of the Olympics. The opportunity arose when local owners realized that Rio had just half the 40,000 beds required for the games, creating an obvious demand gap.

Paying a sponsoring fee, Airbnb was listed in the Olympics' ticketing website, with a link to a page where customers were able to rent private homes and apartments in Rio. Another link on the official Olympic website also served to connect the Airbnb service to people traveling to Rio for the Olympics. One small advantage: since Airbnb starts with an A, the name was listed first among the suppliers for the Olympics.

Airbnb then extended its global #StayWithMe campaign which invites Airbnb hosts to post photos or short videos on social media to showcase their countries. The Olympics version created Rio-specific videos and content starring the local hosts and sports fans at the game venues.

The Swiss watchmaker Swatch relies extensively on sponsorship of special events. The company has a policy of spending a major share of its promotional budget on special-events promotion. The company organizes "launch parties" in various countries, when a new collection of Swatches is introduced. The company has positioned its watches as fashion products, and its product policy is to keep the Swatch designs fresh by introducing new styles twice a year, in the spring and in the fall.[44]

Cross-Promotion

The **cross-promotion** of related products from successful events and stars represents one of many promotional tactics. A cross-promotion is a marketing program that targets buyers of a product with an offer to purchase a related product. There is a big global business in selling products associated with Elvis Presley, James Dean, various successful films (*Hunchback of Notre Dame*, *Titanic*), and TV shows (*Star Trek*, *The Simpsons*). The technique has been perfected by Disney, starting with the Mickey and Minnie Mouse cartoons, theme parks, and films, with t-shirts, bags, wallets, and various trinkets emblazoned with the beloved characters' face and logo. Today it is possible to buy dolls and Elsa's dress featured in Disney's film *Frozen*, provided you can find them on the shelf—the success of the film has led to stock outs around the world.[45]

Today many non-luxury brands use cross-promotions—you can buy Caterpillar (or "Cat") caps, clothes, and boots online, for example. American colleges have long used a promotion strategy with their sweatshirts and athletic gear. Surprisingly, not many universities abroad have yet adopted that idea. It might be only a matter of time.

Publicity

Publicity, the publishing of news about the company and its products, is an increasingly important part of global companies' promotion function.

"Good News ..."

Publicity is more credible than paid advertising, and since a global expansion effort is inherently more newsworthy than expansion at home, global companies often get featured in news media. The press coverage can even be orchestrated by the firm as could be seen in Apple's launch of the iPhone 6 and the iWatch. The event was covered by news media in Asia and Europe and elsewhere, supported by promotional film made available by Apple.

In general, high-technology products, potentially important for security reasons or for national competitiveness, also enhance engagement and potential reader interest. Managing publicity—including coordination with the public relations function—is important when foreign direct investments or trade barriers become news, as they often do. The wide press coverage of Alibaba's entry into the West via its 2014 share offering on the New York Stock Exchange clearly helped establish the brand outside China.

Publicity has the obvious advantage that there is no need to pay for airtime or press coverage. But it is not always without cost. Publicity requires some management and can be labor-intensive. Media contacts need to be created, nurtured, and maintained. Press coverage of the opening of a plant or warehouse in a new market involves travel, food, and sometimes lodging for journalists. The preparation of **press releases**, copy written for immediate news publication, requires skill, especially when the information is about a technical breakthrough. Making top managers available for personal interviews takes their time and diverts their attention. Still, the payoff in goodwill and free advertising can be considerable and the investment well worth it.

"... and Bad News"

Even "negative" publicity can have its rewards since it serves to keep the brand name in the public eye. The Chinese antitrust fines against foreign automakers in 2014 and 2016 are newsworthy issues that are important for the countries and the brands involved.[46] For China the effect may be negative, but the brands are kept in the public eye.

Benetton, the Italian apparel maker, is another example. Through its famous (or infamous depending on one's views) realistic TV commercials and large full-page magazine ads of a man dying from AIDS, a priest kissing a nun, an automobile ablaze after a car bomb, and a boatload of refugees without copy but with the brand logo displayed after the commercial or below the picture, Benetton has garnered plenty of publicity, mainly negative. The ads seem to be in bad taste, and Benetton has been accused of exploiting human suffering to sell its products. In Germany, irate store owners refused to stock Benetton products unless the advertisements were withdrawn, claiming that the ads kept customers away.[47] But the company argues that it is doing a positive thing—and to help prove it, it opened a new store in war-torn Sarajevo. It also developed a new campaign theme of "UnHate."[48]

Product Placement

The last few years have seen an increase in the use of product placement for promotional purposes. **Product placement** refers to the use of branded products in films and television. One of the first early famous example was done by Steven Spielberg in the movie *ET: The Extraterrestrial*, where an alien creature was seen eating "Reese's Pieces," a peanut-flavored candy; sales of the product subsequently increased by 70 percent. More recently Mercedes Benz has 14 models of its cars in the movie *A Good Day to Die Hard*, and the hero in the American TV show *House of Cards* is obsessed with playing Sony's PlayStation 3 (and only that product).

The master at product placement however appears to be Apple as Apple products appeared in nine of the 35 films that ranked #1 and topped the U.S. box office in 2014. Apple's brand cameos that year ranged from the passing mention in *The Lego Movie* to an outstanding Apple Store scene in *Captain America: Winter Soldier*.[49] Product placement involves contracting with producers about using the branded product as a natural prop in the film or TV program. In many cases the product is offered free, and no guarantees about its use are made by the producers. Partly because of this, the impact can be negative as well as positive. A Mercedes car used as a prop in one film was set on fire, not a particularly successful product placement. Still, in 2016 Mercedes-Benz took the top spot for the Brandcameo Product Placement Awards.

Apple's logo on their laptops, easily recognized, shows nicely when a popular movie actor opens up the computer, a feature clearly intended if not originated by Steve Jobs. Under Armour, the new sweatshirt manufacturer from the U.S. seems to have taken some lessons from Apple's playbook. In 1999, just three years after the brand's founding, the well-known actor Jamie Foxx appeared in an Under Armour jockstrap in the film *Any Given Sunday*. Under Armour outfitted the Gotham Rogues football team in *The Dark Knight Rises*. The brand has also partnered with the blockbuster *Captain America: Winter Soldier* as part of a larger deal with Marvel Comics. Under Armour even garnered a 2013 "Lifetime Award" from one branding blog, Interbrand's "Brandchannel."[50]

Cause Marketing

When companies get engaged in promotion social causes by sponsoring social-issue advertising, special events, or agreeing to produce adapted products such as pink shoes for the drive against breast cancer, they are doing cause marketing. One example is marketing to gay customers. After decades of ignoring gay consumers, automakers are now courting them in advertisements and through sponsoring gay events, awards, and causes. For example, Japanese automaker Subaru, which was a founding sponsor of the Rainbow card, has an affinity card program that has raised more than $1 million for gay causes. Subaru led the way in opening up gay consumers as a potential market when it hired former tennis star Martina Navratilova, perhaps the world's best-known lesbian athlete at the time, to star in television spots.

The fact is that gay consumers and gay publications have demographics that are very appealing to advertisers. For instance, *Out* and *The Advocate* have an average reader that is a 39-year-old white-collar professional man with a college degree and a "household" income of $95,000.

These kinds of numbers prompted Daimler-Chrysler, Ford, and General Motors to sponsor the annual show of the Lambda Car Club, a group of 2000 gay collectors. In 2014 a Chevrolet ad made its LGBT-friendly message clear: against a montage of different families including both heterosexual and single and same-sex parents, a voice-over intones, "While what it means to be family hasn't changed, what a family looks like has." The acronym LGBT (for lesbian, gay, bisexual, and transgender) is no longer unknown among at least American advertisers.

But for global marketers, it will difficult to standardize that advertising commercial. North America and Northern Europe might be two areas where it could play well, but for the rest of the world—in fact for the vast majority of the world's population—it will not be suitable. In due time, perhaps, things will change, but probably not very soon.

Global Public Relations

Similar to publicity, **global public relations** is a form of indirect promotion of products and services that focuses on creating goodwill toward the corporation as a whole. The corporate communications staff at headquarters and its counterpart in the various host countries serve as promoters of the corporation to various stakeholders interested in the company's foreign expansion. These stakeholders can include a wide variety of groups:

- Employees
- Customers
- Distributors, Suppliers
- Stockholders, Financial community
- Media, Activist groups, General public
- Government

These groups all can lay some legitimate claim on a company to conduct itself ethically and to operate with a certain level of transparency in accordance with the free-market system. However, for the many countries in which a global company is likely to do business, ethical standards and customary business secrecy can vary considerably. This easily creates conflicts between host country stakeholders' claims and headquarters' policy guidelines. One job of the public relations staff is to make sure that such potential conflicts do not erupt and, when they do, to carry out "damage control."

Conflicts typically arise when a firm enters a new country by acquiring a local company or by investing in manufacturing. When American companies such as Ford, GM, IBM, Xerox, Honeywell, and General Electric became big investors in Europe in the 1950s and 60s, Europeans became alarmed by the "American challenge." As Japanese companies like Nissan (trucks), Mitsubishi (real estate), Matsushita (electronics), and Honda (automobiles) established presence in the United States by large investments, many Americans voiced misgivings. When Arab investors acquired port facilities on the coast of the United States, and when Chinese investors tried to acquire American firms, lawmakers complained.

Even though the economic justifications of these and other FDI entries are usually sound, and the host countries also benefit, the companies' PR departments have to work hard to establish the "good local citizen" image among stakeholders. This involves compiling statistics about the number of natives employed, the local content of the products, and the tax contribution made to the local municipality—and publicizing this information.

Effective **damage control**, actions taken to limit the spillover into a negative public opinion, requires both public relations and timing. The German automaker Audi stood firm in defending its Audi 5000 model design against repeated accusations of malfunctioning. Several accidents had happened because drivers mistakenly (as the courts found) stepped on the gas pedal instead of the brakes. The Audi engineers won their court case, consumer damage was contained with attractive new models, and Audi market share has kept rising.[51]

Another example of how confrontation can be a problem was what happened to Nestlé with its baby formula in Africa (see box, "Nestlé's baby (mis)steps").

BOX: Nestlé's Baby (Mis)Steps.

The large Swiss multinational Nestlé is a major global company in the food industry. Its Nestlé instant tea, Nescafé coffee, Libby's juices, and Carnation milk products are household names all over the world.

The company got its baptism by fire in global PR in the latter half of the 1970s. Having developed a superior infant formula that could effectively supplant a breast-feeding mother, the company saw great potential among malnourished third-world children particularly those in Africa. Distributing the formula through clinics and wet-nurses, the company was able to tap into the market effectively. There was only one problem. Some mothers, partly to offset the relatively high cost of the formula, took to diluting it with water. As a consequence, many babies on formula did not get the requisite nourishment, and in a few cases, the water used for the dilution was infected and there were some deaths.[52]

Activist groups in Europe and North America soon learned about the situation. As initial appeals to the company in Vevey, Switzerland, were rebuffed, the groups started a massive international campaign against Nestlé and its products.

Through press conferences and media releases as well as in direct meetings with activist leaders, Nestlé argued that withdrawing a beneficial product would do more harm than good. The company undertook scientific research projects designed to establish the superiority of the product against weak mothers' milk and projected the expected death rates should the product be withdrawn.

In the end, the activists were fought off and the company prevailed, succeeding in maintaining its product in the third-world markets and reducing the damage to its brands. But the process is still ongoing, with the activists still calling a boycott.[53] The argument is that breast milk has many natural benefits lacking in formula, the bond between baby and mother can be strengthened during breastfeeding, and breastfeeding can also delay the return of fertility, which can help women in developing countries to space their births. Essentially the sale of formula in developing countries is simple profiteering. A number of leading international NGOs, including Save the Children, Oxfam, CARE International, Plan International, and World Vision, continue to describe Nestlé's marketing of infant formula in developing countries as unethical and urge boycotting its products.[54] As of 2015, The United Nations is discussing the role of companies and rich nations in determining the food types and nutrition needs of poor nations.

The lesson? Ethical conduct and corporate standing that might seem spotless and self-evident at home need to be explained, justified, and defended actively in other places. And in all cases, flexibility and respect for local norms are a must. However, in a recent video on YouTube, the Head of the Nestlé group Peter Brabeck might have put Nestlé's foot in the mouth again. He argues against natural and organic foods. Taking on the NGOs, he argues that to view the right to water as a basic right is an "extreme" viewpoint. He favors privatization of the water supply, perhaps not surprising since Nestlé's portfolio has a number of water brands, including Perrier, Poland Spring, S. Pellegrino, and Vittel.[55] Social media are abuzz.

Corporate Social Responsibility

Throughout this text we have stressed the increasing importance of corporate social responsibility and the triple bottom line. Although such efforts should be more genuine and of more fundamental value to the community than simply PR, they need to be coordinated with PR efforts. Good corporate citizenship means that a company may sponsor a drive for aid to a disaster-stricken area, print and distribute informational booklets about illnesses such as AIDS, or fund activist environmental groups or local symphony orchestras. Such good deeds should not go unrecognized.

One example is the Procter & Gamble "Hope Schools" project in China. Thanks to the project, a program in partnership with the China Youth Development Foundation, children now have better access to education in poverty-stricken rural areas of China. P&G China has founded over 200 P&G Hope Schools throughout rural China. P&G Hope Schools have benefited over 100,000 children across China in the last 12 years, and over 5000 P&G China employees have actively supported its program activities.[56]

Generally, such efforts are not easily measured in terms of financial bottom-line payoffs, but companies find them worthwhile for the goodwill and positive image created (the triple bottom line again). But in some cases such PR efforts can go against the business interests of the company. For example, big multinational Unilever found itself sponsoring anti-globalization groups after its purchase of Ben and Jerry's ice creams, a firm with a long-standing commitment to anti-GMO issues and local foods. This poses a difficult ethical quandary for the company—but the uneasy relationship seems to have survived so far.

INTEGRATED MARKETING COMMUNICATIONS

Any one customer, whether home or abroad, receives information about a brand from a number of sources. It is naturally important that the message coming through be consistent. This is the task of integrated marketing communications, or IMC for short.

The integrated marketing communications concept stresses the need to combine the various communication disciplines—for example, media advertising, digital media, sales promotion, web advertising, and public relations—to ensure clarity, consistency, and maximum communications impact. It argues for a broad perspective that takes into account all sources of brand or company contacts that a customer has with a product or service. Instead of seeing Facebook advertising, media advertising and in-store promotion as separate major promotional vehicles, IMC says that all tools need to be managed jointly to achieve maximum impact.

The IMC concept may be difficult to implement globally since it enlarges the number of communication functions that need to be coordinated. It also runs up against the problem that different rules and regulations govern the use of promotional tools in different countries. Nevertheless, the IMC concept is valuable globally since it forces the company to define the brand identities and communication platforms more clearly. It may not be possible to use the same promotional tools in different countries, but the message put across can be uniform and consistent.

A good example of an integrated global campaign is Pepsi-Cola's campaign in the soccer World Cup in Rio in 2014, a natural event for an integrated global campaign.

Pepsi was not the official sponsor of the Cup—Coca-Cola was—so the campaign's primary aim was to blunt Coke's advantage globally. The Pepsi campaign was what experts call a "guerilla" effort.

The global theme of Pepsi's campaign was "Now is what you make it," playing off of Pepsi's 2012 slogan "Live for now." The campaign was simultaneously launched in 100 countries as the World Cup got under way. It included 30- and 60-second television spots, as well as a two-minute interactive video that allowed consumers to unlock an additional four minutes of content. The spots featured Stony, a YouTube celebrity intended to draw in the younger soccer audience. Commercials were also shot with soccer stars, including Leo Messi of Barcelona and Argentina and Sergei Ramos of Real Madrid and Spain. For the American spots, an American player, Clint Dempsey, was used, the idea being that soccer was not yet very big in the United States.

The television campaign was largely shot on location in Brazil. In addition to commercials, the campaign involved drawings and photographs of soccer stars which exhibited at stadiums and bars where fans would be found. The campaign took on the character of a film opening, with special exhibits and sponsored stars appearing at the matches. There were a series of announcements and launches which served to generate excitement and involvement with the brand.

Of course, Coca-Cola tried to match the effort by Pepsi-Cola. As the official sponsor, Coke had the advantage of being featured on banners and logos inside and around stadiums to a much greater extent than Pepsi. Coca-Cola's television effort emphasized "marketing through storytelling." The company shot a number of commercials around the theme "One World, One Game." The spots told uplifting stories of soccer fans from around the world who have overcome major hurdles in inspiring situations. The individuals told their emotional stories and how the love of soccer had helped them through hardships.

In terms of sales results, the Pepsi–Coke matchup seems to have resulted in a draw. Or if you want, their game went into extra time, still going. In business, there is no penalty shoot-out and no golden goal.

IMC forces advertising and promotional specialists to "think outside the box," that is, to take a broader view of their communication means and goals. This can be particularly useful when entering new markets where communication media are different. Intel, the chipmaker from Silicon Valley, placed television and billboard ads throughout China to establish brand awareness for its microprocessors. The company also distributed nearly 1 million bike reflectors—which glow in the dark with the words "Intel Inside"—in China's biggest cities. Taiwan-based Yonex Corporation pays $2 million annually to be the exclusive equipment sponsor for Indonesia's powerful national badminton team. Nike sponsors four teams in China's new professional soccer league, including one owned by the People's Liberation Army. Citibank captured 40 percent of Thailand's credit card market relying on a sales force of 600 part-timers who are paid a fee for each applicant approved.[57]

SUMMARY

Despite the pitfalls of standardized and translated messages, global ads have become an important alternative to adapted multi-domestic advertising. The technological advances in global communications, the growth of digital media, and the strength of global advertising agencies have combined to make global advertising possible. And the positive spillovers from unified messages and the increasing homogeneity of many markets have made global advertising desirable.

As the affluence of countries grows, new products and services appear and customers need more information. Advertising becomes more important and advertising expenditures as a percentage of the GDP increase. For the global marketer, faced with increasing spending needs in all markets, a coordinated effort with synchronized campaigns, pattern standardization, and unified message across trade regions is usually more effective and cost-efficient than multi-domestic campaigns.

Although much of the execution of sales promotion strategies needs to be localized because of varying regulations in different countries, the growth of global communications, digital media, and global events in sports and other areas has made global promotion feasible. Sponsorship and creation of global events, and a global public relations perspective, including global publicity, are promotional tools for the company's global marketing effort. The increasing feasibility of digital promotions with the help of digital facilitators and e-commerce helps even smaller companies capitalize on global opportunities.

The various promotional tools discussed in this chapter play an important role in developing and sustaining the equity in global brand names. This is accomplished by globally integrated marketing communications, with all promotions based on a unified brand identity and global copy platforms, but with room for local implementation taking into account local promotion regulations and availability of promotional tools.

KEY TERMS

cause marketing
click-through rate
closing tactics
conversion rates
cost-per-thousand (CPM)
cross-promotion
damage control
digital advertising
direct response
global advertising
global advertising agencies
global advertising budget
global public relations
gross exposures
handling objections
hierarchy of effects
in-store promotion
integrated marketing communications

local advertising
media selection
message translation
mobile media
multi-domestic advertising
on-site promotions
pattern standardization
point-of-purchase (p-o-p) promotions
press releases
product placement
prototype advertising
publicity
salesman as a person
salesmanship
sponsorship
trade promotions
viral diffusion
web advertisements

DISCUSSION QUESTIONS

1. Using library sources and the Internet, find three examples of global advertising. What characteristics make these campaigns global? Do they use "pattern standardization"?

2. Using the same sources, can you find examples of global advertising for which the markets are not global but "multi-domestic"? Are websites more or less important for multi-domestic brands than for global brands?

3. Discuss what an advertiser may do to avoid conflicts with country managers when a global advertising campaign is contemplated.

4. Analyze how some companies' websites serve as both a source of information and an engagement promotional site. What do the companies—such as M&M—do in order to create an interactive, highly involved encounter? Do they try to induce "action"?

5. Drawing on the cultural discussion in Chapter 5 and your own cultural background, compare the salesmanship skills needed to sell an automobile in Germany, in the United States, and in Japan (or some other countries of your own choice). What skills would be most advantageous? Which ones could land you in trouble?

TEAM CHALLENGE PROJECTS

1. Cola Turka is attempting to overtake Coca-Cola as the leading brand of Cola in Turkey. The company is using a set of TV and Internet ads staring the American actor Chevy Chase to establish its brand: https://www.youtube.com/watch?v=6W_26ArnZHw; https://www.youtube.com/watch?v=oi_LKnQmqLc.

    The Cola Turka product has now grown to capture over 13 percent of the Turkish market and continues to expand.

    Team 1: Discuss the strategy that Cola Turka is using and develop the 4Ps to continue to attack Coca-Cola. Team 2: What should Coca-Cola do to maintain its dominant position and hold back the growth of Cola Turka?

2. As of 1996, U.S. law requires that any cloth "substantially altered" (woven, for example) in another nation must identify that country on its all-important label. This means that $300 Hermes ties must have a "made in China" label instead of a "made in France" label. Similarly $500 Italian scarves from Ferragamo and Versace must have the "made in Italy" label removed and replaced by "made in China." Manufacturers have tended to ignore this law claiming that their product's country of origin is not really China for various reasons. (The French once claimed they were making silk in France, an impossibility due to climate.) The U.S. is beginning to enforce the law. Team 1: Develop an advertising campaign that reduces a customer's nervousness about spending so much money on fashion products with a "made in China" label. Team 2: Develop an ad campaign for the U.S. government informing customers of the law and asking them to look for the "made in label" before making a purchase.

3. In business-to-business marketing, trade shows (or trade fairs) have historically been an important avenue for reaching potential customers. More than 2,000 trade shows are held annually worldwide (even 70 held in Africa). The Hanover Industry Fair (Germany) is the largest with 6000 booths and 600,000 visitors. Team 1: Argue that trade shows will be an important part of B2B promotions for the foreseeable future. Team 2: Argue that trade shows, like the yellow pages, are a relic from the past and in the Internet age, there are much more effective ways to spend advertising/promotion budgets which is why American firms spend less than 5 percent of ad budgets on trade shows.

SELECTED REFERENCES

"2014 Marketing Fact Pack," *Ad Age Research Report*, December 29, 2013.
"Advertising expenditure at the world's largest ad markets," *Statista*, 2015.

"Advertising Revenue of Google," *Statista*, 2015.

"Agency Family Trees 2014; World's 20 Largest Agency Networks," *Advertising Age*, 2014.

"Announcing the 2015 Brandcameo Product Placement Awards," *Brand Channel*, February 20, 2015.

Arthur, Charles. "Smartphone Explosion in 2014 Will See Ownership in India Pass U.S.," *The Guardian,* Jan. 13, 2014.

"Average Ad Spending Per Capita: US Tops List," *Marketing Charts*, March 4, 2015.

Badenhausen, Kurt, "Maria Sharapova Tops List of the World's Highest Paid Female Athletes," *Forbes*, August 15, 2013.

———, "Tiger Woods Inks Huge Sponsorship Deal Ahead Of Return to Golf," *Forbes*, December 2, 2014.

"British Airways 1983," *Online video clip, Youtube*, May 25, 2007.

"Coca-Cola Small World Machines—Bringing India and Pakistan Together," *Online video clip, Youtube*, May 19, 2013.

Crawshaw, Steve, "Benetton Sued Over Shock Ads," *The Independent,* Jan. 22, 1995.

Davies, Robin, "The Uncomfortable Truth About Online Ad Measurement and Viewability," *The Guardian,* Sept. 20, 2013.

Dolan, Kerry A. "The Soda with Buzz," *Forbes,* March, 28, 2005.

Fineberg, Seth, "Philips Continues B2B Rebranding Push with Digital Stories," *Ad Age Reports*, Marc h 19, 2014.

"Global—Advertising," *Marketline,* 2015.

"Global Ad Spending Growth to Double This Year," *eMarketer*, July 9, 2014.

"Global Media Report 2014 Global Industry Overview," *McKinsey & Company*, 2014.

"Google Indian Commercial, Connecting India and Pakistan," *Online video clip, Youtube*, Nov. 14, 2013.

Greyser, Stephen A. *Siemens: Corporate Advertising.* Harvard Business School, case 593–022, 1996.

"Groupon's Expansion Strategy," *INC.,* 2014.

"Groupon Leads Latin America as Most-Visited Coupon Site in Region," *Comscore*, June 1, 2011.

Horsnell, Chris, "Glaceau Kick Off World Cup Promo," *Drink-Brands*, March 24, 2014.

"India to have 651 million smartphones, 18.7 million tablets by 2019," *The Economic Times*, February 3, 2015.

Joel, Mitch, "Online Advertisers Still Don't Have it Figured Out," *Huffington Post*, August 21, 2102.

Johansson, Johny K. and Ikujiro Nonaka, *Relentless: The Japanese Way of Marketing.* New York: Harper Business, 1995.

Klor, Achim, "B2B Case Study: Philips Aligns Marketing and Innovation," *Business 2 Community*, April 12, 2014.

"LAOS: NGOs flay Nestlé's infant formula strategy," IRIN, June 23, 2011.

"Largest global advertisers in 2013, by ad spending (in billion U.S. dollars)," *Statista*, 2014.

Lippman, Joanne. "Marketers Turn Sour on Global Sales Pitch Harvard Guru Makes," *The Wall Street Journal*, May 12, 1988, p. 1.

"MarketLine Industry Profile: Global Advertising," *Marketline*, March, 2015.

Marshall, Richard. "'Triple Advantage' For Responsible Supply Chains, Says WEF Report," *HHGlobal*, April 14, 2015.

Martina, Michael, "EU Lobby Piles In on Foreign Criticism of China's Antitrust Enforcement," *Reuters*, Sept. 9, 2014.

MasterCard, "MasterCard Priceless Surprises," *Online video clip, Youtube*, May 10, 2014.

Monllos, Kristina, "Coca-Cola is Looking for Its Next Big Global Campaign," *Ad Week*, March 23, 2015.

Müller, Hans, Helmuth Leihs, and Lee Dahringer. *International Marketing: A Global Perspective.* Thomson Learning, 2006.

"Nestle: The Bottled Milk Scandal That Won't Go Away (1970's-Present, Still Unresolved)," *Business Ethics Cases*, April 1, 2014.

"Nestle CEO: Water Is Not a Human Right, Should Be Privatized," *Online video clip, Youtube*, Apr. 25, 2013.

Nike Football. "Nike Football: Winner Stays," *Online video clip, Youtube*, Apr. 25, 2014.

"P&G and Hope Schools: A Long-Term Commitment to Education Success," *P&G Chemicals*, 2015.

"P&G Walks Away From Foods, Sells Pringles for $2.35 Billion," *Trefis*, April 6th, 2011.

Primack, Dan, "Let's stop laughing at Groupon," *Fortune*, Jan. 26, 2015.

Ribeiro, John, "Groupon Rebrands, Repositions in India," *PC World*, Oct. 3, 2011.

"Rice farming in Japan," *The Economist*, November 30, 2013.

Rom, Fiona, "The Man Who Built a Brand That Changed the World," *Emerging Stars: How to Make It in Emerging Markets*, 2015.

Sauer, Abe, "The Envelope, Please: The 2014 Brancameo Product Placement Awards," *Broadchannel*, Feb. 27, 2014.

Sekiguchi, Toko "Japan Limits Scope of Online Pharmaceutical Sales," *The Wall Street Journal*, November 6, 2013.

Shirk, Martha. "Simple Formula No Answer for Hungry Children," *St. Louis Post-Dispatch*, September 23, 1991, p. 18.

Soergel, Andrew, "Adidas and Nike Face Off at World Cup," *U.S. News*, June 28, 2014.

Strohl, Daniel, "Class of '86 – Audi 5000CS," *Hemmings Daily*, Aug. 5, 2011.

Sylt, Christian, "Revealed: Red Bull's $1.2 billion Bet on Formula One," *Forbes*, April 3, 2014.

Terpstra, Vern, and Ravi Sarathy. *International Marketing*, 6th ed. Fort Worth, TX: Dryden, 1994.

"The Company Behind the Can," *Redbull*, 2015.

"The Front Tells the Time," *Swatch*, 2015.

"The 'Hilltop' Ad: The Story of a Commercial," *Coca-Cola Television Advertising Home Page*, no date.

"The History of Groupon," *Groupon Works*, 2014.

"Tiger Woods Is Back on Top of the World's Highest Paid Athletes," *Forbes*, June 5, 2013.

Unhate Foundation. www.Benetton.com, 2015.

Warner, Fara, and Karen Hsu. "Intel Gets a Free Ride in China by Sticking Its Name on Bicycles," *Wall Street Journal*, August 7, 1996, p. B5.

Wood, Zoe. "Frozen: Parental Panic as Unexpected Disney Hit Leads to Merchandise Sellout," *The Guardian*, May 17, 2014.

ENDNOTES

1. See "The Company Behind The Can," 2015.
2. See Muller, 2006.
3. See "The Company Behind The Can," 2015.
4. See Dolan, 2005.
5. See Rom, 2015.
6. See "Advertising expenditure at the world's largest ad markets," 2015.
7. See "Average Ad Spending Per Capita: US Tops List," 2015 and "Global Ad Spending Growth to Double This Year," July 9, 2014.
8. See Greyser, 1993.
9. See "MarketLine Industry Profile: Global Advertising," 2015.

10. See "MarketLine Industry Profile: Global Advertising," 2015.
11. See "Largest global advertisers in 2013, by ad spending (in billion U.S. dollars)," 2014, and "2014 Marketing Fact Pack," 2013.
12. See "P&G Walks Away From Foods," 2011.
13. See "Global Media Report 2014 Global Industry Overview," 2014.
14. See "Global Media Report 2014 Global Industry Overview," 2014.
15. See "Global Ad Spending Growth to Double This Year," 2014.
16. See Google Corporate website: Income Statement Information, and "Advertising Revenue of Google," 2015.
17. See "Global Ad Spending Growth to Double This Year," 2014.
18. See "India to have 651 million smartphones, 18.7 million tablets by 2019," 2015; Arthur, 2014.
19. See Mastercard, 2014.
20. See Nike Football, 2014.
21. See "British Airways," 2007.
22. See Lippman, 1988.
23. See "The 'Hilltop' Ad," no date.
24. See "Coca-Cola Small World Machines – Bringing India and Pakistan Together," 2013.
25. See "Google Indian Commercial," 2013.
26. See Monllos, 2015.
27. See Fineberg, 2014.
28. Klor, 2014.
29. See "Agency Family Trees 2014," 2014.
30. See Marshall, 2015.
31. From Johansson and Nonaka, 1995.
32. See Terpstra and Sarathy, 1994.
33. See Sekiguchi, 2013.
34. See "Rice farming in Japan," November 30, 2013.
35. See "The History of Groupon," 2014.
36. See "Groupon's Expansion Strategy," 2014.
37. See "Groupon Leads Latin America," 2011.
38. See Ribeiro, 2011.
39. See Sylt, 2014.
40. See Soergel, 2014. Adidas actually uses lower case adidas for its brand name, but here we are following grammatical convention.
41. See Badenhausen, 2013.
42. See "Tiger Woods is back ..." 2013.
43. See Horsnell, 2014.
44. See "The Front Tells the Time," 2015.
45. See Wood, 2014.
46. See Martina, 2014.
47. See Crawshaw, 1995.
48. See Unhate Foundation, 2015.
49. See "Announcing the 2015 Brandcameo Product Placement Awards," 2015.
50. See Sauer, 2014.
51. See Strohl, 2011.

52. See Shirk, 1991.
53. See "Nestle: The Bottled Milk Scandal That Won't Go Away" (1970s-Present, Still Unresolved), 2014.
54. See "LAOS: NGOs flay Nestlé's infant formula strategy," 2011.
55. See "Nestle CEO: Water is not …," 2013.
56. See "P&G," 2015.
57. See Warner and Hsu, 1996.

In this chapter you learn about:

1. How the deep Internet penetration has removed most obstacles around the world for digital marketing, but fraud and government interference are still problems
2. The rise of social media around the world and what it means for how consumers behave
3. What it takes to be a marketer when the point is to be found by the consumer, not the other way around
4. How the new digital marketing tools can be managed by established companies through outsourcing and new organizational units

Digital Global Marketing

CHAPTER 14

UBER DISRUPTS AN INDUSTRY WORLDWIDE

Uber, the taxi service launched in the U.S. in 2009, allows passengers to arrange for a car pickup using an "app" on their smartphone. It is a good example of how the digital revolution can disrupt existing businesses.

The Uber app will signal Uber drivers in the vicinity of the passenger's whereabouts and the closest car will pick up. Rather than flagging down a random taxi on the street, or walking to the nearest taxi stand, or calling a central taxi dispatcher, Uber simply shows the passenger the closest driver using the GPS. Riders can track the location of their dispatched drivers using GPS, and pay directly on their phones. They can also rate the drivers, and drivers, in turn, can rate unruly passengers. If either party gets a low enough rating, the system closes them out. The Uber drivers simply use their private cars, and are accepted into the network after a basic screening.

There's nothing especially novel, or proprietary, about the system Uber has built. This is by now standard uses of off-the-shelf mobile technology. This could have already been implemented by existing taxi services. But the highly regulated taxi and limousine companies in every city Uber has entered have instead gone out of their way to block Uber.

Uber can't operate in Miami, for example, where existing laws protect taxicabs from competition even from other licensed services. Limousines are prohibited from picking up passengers less than an hour after receiving a reservation, for example, and the minimum fare by law is $80. The number of limousine licenses has long been limited to 550. In fact, Uber has met opposition in virtually all cities it has entered, also internationally. However, after adjustments to the service in line with court injunctions, Uber now operates with

full services in New York and London. One effect in New York has been that the the the value of a taxi permit (a "medallion") has lost more than 50% of its value to the holder. Most medallions are selling for less than half of the $1.3 million price recorded in 2013 and 2014. A medallion sold for $241,000 in April 2017, representing a new low-water mark for NY City medallions. NYC banks that made loans on medallion values are having to write down these loans.

Germany, especially is proving to be a particularly hard nut to crack. Their well-organized unions and local bureaucracy have long had a tradition of limiting competition. In beer, local brewers were long protected by the *Reinheitsgebot*, a law requiring no preservation ingredients in beer, limiting imported beers. Stores were long required to close on weekends and often at lunchtime. These restrictions have gradually been lifted, but the process has been slow. German taxi drivers are also protected, with a good income and nice cars (see Exhibit 14.1).

In 2014, a Frankfurt state court banned Uber's low-cost UberPop product from operating in the country until a hearing on whether it unfairly competes with local taxis. The court found that Uber posed unfair competition to the local taxi industry. It said Uber did not have the necessary licenses and insurance for its drivers and noted that the company could be selective in providing rides, while taxi drivers are required to accept anyone needing a ride.[1]

The usual Uber service offering standard cars driven by freelance drivers was permanently suspended in Germany in 2015. Uber responded in Germany with the *Uber Black* service which provides professional drivers in luxury sedans. Germany's highest court ruled in May 2017 that Uber's Black service had also violated the country's competition laws, but referred the case to the European Court of Justice before taking action. Since a European Court case typically takes about a year, Uber will find out its fate in Germany in 2018.[2]

GOING DIGITAL

Digital business is growing fast everywhere on the globe. Online shopping is not only putting book and record stores out of business, but is challenging many other established retailers, including department stores, drugstores, and even supermarkets. The e-commerce sector added 355,000 jobs from 2007 to 2016 while the brick and mortar general retail sector lost 51,000 jobs. Consumers buy shoes and apparel on their PCs, use tablets and smartphones to find restaurants, buy tickets, and stream their music. Customer reviews trump companies' product information and promotional messages, and social media connections offer immediate peer advice and word-of-mouth (WOM) on intended purchases. The emergence of digital commerce enabled by the Internet is changing the marketing landscape in many ways. For many businesses, going digital has become as imperative as going global used to be.

At the start, though, we have to be realistic. In the big picture, the actual numbers for digital business are still not yet very high. B2C e-commerce accounts for less than 10 percent of total retail sales across the globe. The e-commerce share of total U.S. retail sales in the first quarter of 2017 was 8.5 percent totaling $431 billion in 2017 (see Exhibit 14.2).[3] Even in the leading e-commerce country of China with $1.2 billion in sales, e-commerce represents only 12.6 percent of retail sales for physical goods.[4]

The growth of digital business is especially strong however in most of the emerging markets in Asia, with China setting the pace.

Country	2014	2015	2016	2017	2018	2019
China*	$472.91	$672.01	$911.25	$1,208.31	$1,568.39	$1,973.04
US	$298.26	$340.61	$384.89	$431.84	$481.94	$534.95
UK	$86.81	$99.39	$110.32	$121.36	$132.28	$143.19
Japan	$78.55	$89.55	$100.30	$111.33	$122.46	$134.10
Germany	$55.21	$61.84	$68.95	$76.47	$82.58	$87.54
France	$38.34	$42.60	$46.10	$49.68	$53.23	$56.69
South Korea	$35.01	$38.86	$42.75	$46.59	$50.55	$54.14
Canada	$22.98	$26.83	$30.82	$35.08	$39.80	$44.98
Brazil	$16.87	$19.49	$22.12	$24.66	$27.13	$29.65
Australia	$17.40	$19.02	$20.66	$22.31	$23.94	$25.61
Russia	$15.37	$18.86	$22.51	$26.42	$30.39	$34.86
Spain	$13.95	$15.89	$17.93	$19.96	$21.73	$23.33
India	$6.10	$14.00	$24.61	$39.45	$55.26	$68.47
Italy	$11.27	$13.41	$14.74	$15.98	$17.15	$18.24
Norway	$8.52	$9.61	$10.58	$11.54	$12.44	$13.27
Netherlands	$8.08	$9.41	$10.33	$11.22	$12.13	$13.04
Sweden	$8.25	$9.39	$10.36	$11.38	$12.32	$13.23
Denmark	$7.82	$8.48	$9.15	$9.83	$10.46	$11.03
Finland	$6.45	$6.86	$7.24	$7.56	$7.84	$8.09
Mexico	$4.38	$5.70	$7.24	$9.04	$11.03	$13.27
Argentina	$3.55	$4.96	$6.85	$8.84	$10.60	$12.38
Indonesia	$1.94	$3.22	$5.29	$8.21	$10.92	$13.16

EXHIBIT 14.2.
B2C E-commerce Sales Growth Rate by Country

Source: http://www.emarketer.com/public_media/docs/eMarketer_eTail-West2016_Worldwide_ECommerce_Report.pdf.

Source: Emarketer.com Worldwide Retail E-Commerce Sales, Dec 2015. http://www.emarketer.com/public_media/docs/eMarketer_eTailWest2016_Worldwide_ECommerce_Report.pdf

China has the most Internet users in the world with over 731 million users in 2017 (more than double the U.S.'s 290 million users). Even so, Internet business in 2016 will only account for about 6.9 percent of GDP in China, slightly higher than the U.S.[5] However, the digital business share of GDP in China is expected to rise into double digits in the next few years.[6] Chinese consumers in small and midsize cities spend as much as 27 percent of their disposable income on online purchases. It is less, but still high in the big cities, with 18 percent for those living in metropolises such as Beijing and Shanghai.[7] But foreign Internet-based businesses still find the going difficult in China (see box, "China's Great Firewall").

BOX: China's Great Firewall.[8]

Throughout this textbook, we have stressed the global reach of the Internet. But especially in China there is a problem with that alleged reach. In reality, Internet does not reach all corners of the world.

Already in Chapter 4, we discussed the censorship that the Chinese government routinely exercises on Internet content, and its willingness to block access and sites. By mid-2015, this censorship had become increasingly more constraining, with major Internet companies denied access. The list includes Google, Twitter, Facebook, Instagram, YouTube, Reuters, *The New York Times*, Wikipedia, and several thousand other companies whose websites are blocked by the Chinese government.[9] *The New York Times'* English and Chinese-language websites have been blocked since an October 2012 article about the wealthy family of prime minister Wen Jiabao.[10] In 2017, the last of Facebook's major products that still worked in China was disrupted by the government as Beijing broadly tightened its controls over the internet.

The product, WhatsApp, a messaging app used across the globe, was partly blocked by Chinese filters, leaving many unable to send videos and photos and some also unable to send text-based messages. Beijing's track record with other American social networking services does not bode well for American companies. Besides Facebook and Instagram, Twitter, Google and Gmail are all blocked in the country. A Beijing official says the Chinese have no need for these blocked websites.[11] Behind what is now known as the Great Firewall, alternative competing Chinese Internet business flourishes. Alibaba, Tencent, and Baidu are doing well, keeping the millions of Chinese customers satisfied and pocketing monopolistic profits.

As we have also stressed in this textbook, most scale and scope economies can be captured with a sufficiently large market. Given China's enormous population base, it is clear that the Chinese companies can reach sufficient scale without venturing abroad. The Chinese government is also eager to develop its domestic technological base, and seems to be succeeding very well. In 2017, Apple opened its first data center in China. The company said the move was made to comply with the law that calls for companies to store their data in China. What one would hope for, as a global marketer, is that President Xi Jinping's desire to be a global force will also compel him to open up the China market to foreign Internet companies as China has done in other industries. Otherwise a company such as Alibaba will probably find mounting obstacles in its global expansion.

Lack of modern retail stores in rural areas makes online shopping more attractive. With the fast growth, it is quite possible that digital marketing will one day become the dominant form of marketing, especially in emerging countries. Increasing Internet access is a positive driver everywhere, and in emerging countries mobile access compensates for weak established infrastructure.

This chapter will clarify how digital commerce has impacted global marketing. Of course, digital marketing know-how is still evolving in domestic markets and the international dimension of digital business is even more recent. But it is gradually coming into focus and it is possible to discern some emerging patterns.

B2B AND B2C DIFFERENCES

In this chapter, we will be mostly concerned with digital B2C businesses. For B2B businesses, digital is mainly an augmentation to a traditional business model, serving to add channels of communication and distribution. This means that the new marketing capabilities are not particularly disruptive in B2B, where digital marketing was quickly adopted. By contrast, they are almost revolutionary in B2C.

In business-to-business (B2B) the new marketing channels can usually be incorporated into the existing operations. The increased reach of communications, the speed of digital transmissions, and the lower costs involved are all factors making digital natural to B2B operations. With business customers, connecting via digital links is actually not very new. Companies are always in search of more efficient supplier links and lower costs distribution channels. Digital intra-firm networks have long been in place. Adding new digital capability involves little or no disruption and customer resistance is usually low. Upgrading information systems used for communication, transactions, and service is often routine business (although in mergers, for example, there can be huge problems in aligning different systems).This is why B2B businesses have quickly adopted online digital transaction models.

In B2C, business to consumers, the consumer's situation is very different. Consumers are not typically looking for more efficiency or new products. In fact, most evidence shows that consumers are by and large resistant to change. And in digital B2C, consumers surely have to change a lot as we have already seen in our daily lives:

- Consumers have to decide between options where new technical words, concepts, and tools crop up every day.
- Consumers have to learn—and purchase—new modes of Internet access on products that need to be continuously updated—from desktops to laptops to tablets.
- Consumers have to accept rapid and dramatic changes to routine behaviors in order to accommodate new technologies—from buying records to CDs to streaming music, replacing books with e-readers.

Consumers everywhere have to continuously decide if it's time for a new PC, a new cell phone, a tablet, faster Internet access, change of passwords again, worry about viruses, and much more. Being online is a different way of life. In a business setting, these kinds of decisions are typically made by the ever-expanding technology group, with experts that assist company executives who cannot be at the cutting edge of technology. Not so for most consumers. Of course, in time many of these new capabilities make life easier for all—paying by credit card is more convenient and faster and less prone to error than paying cash—but this takes time and effort to develop, and is not always easy to foresee at the beginning. Consumers resist change for good reason.

As we saw in the data above, consumers in Asia seem to accept online shopping faster than elsewhere. There are two underlying reasons.

- One is the fact that these countries (with the exception of Japan) have a much greater percentage of young people than more mature countries in the West. As of 2016, 30.3% of China's population was under 24 years old, in Brazil it was 39.2%, in Germany only 23.1% were under 24 years old. Digital, being new and often requiring a change in behavior, tends to do better in countries with a younger population.
- The second reason is the lack of well-established routines. In advanced countries, well established distribution channels have largely resisted the new digital world, since it threatens their established business models. In emerging countries, with less developed retail infrastructure, the new digital way has been met with less resistance. It is opening up opportunities that did not exist before.

In what follows, we will first discuss the many obstacles that potentially stand in the way of digital global marketing in B2C. Then we will present a discussion of the social media landscape, the various networking sites, and the global rise of mobile Internet access. The following section presents what is known so far about online consumer behavior in different countries. A marketing research section is followed by a section discussing the marketing strategy implications of digital commerce. The last section shifts to the organizational capabilities needed for global expansion and how outsourcing can help.

OBSTACLES TO DIGITAL GLOBAL MARKETING

To gauge the potential of digital global marketing, a few basic questions about possible obstacles need first to be answered:

- *Internet penetration.* Do people in different countries have access to the Internet?
- *Language.* What can be done about the language barrier?
- *Payment.* Are there inexpensive and secure payment systems?
- *Fraud.* How common is credit card theft?
- *Counterfeits.* Are the products and brands genuine?
- *Political and regulatory threats.* Will local authorities intervene?

In what follows, we will discuss these potential obstacles in order. We will first show that Internet penetration has risen exponentially. We will also show that language questions are easily solved, and that new payment methods are being put in place. Fraud is still an issue and counterfeits will be an ongoing problem that needs to be addressed by the online outlets.

Internet's Global Penetration

As could be expected given the rise of e-commerce, the percent of population with Internet access has risen dramatically around the world. The 2016 numbers for selected countries are given in Exhibit 14.3.

As you can see from the exhibit, the penetration rate has been very fast, and the reach of the Internet is really quite impressive. In total, over 3.7 billion people around the world had access to the Internet in 2017, about half the world's population.[12] There are very few countries where people do not have Internet access. A few results should be highlighted:

- For the very poor countries access is still not widely available.
- The Internet can be blocked (see North Korea).
- Northern African countries, former Eastern European countries, and Latin American countries have penetration around 40 percent, helping to explain citizen uprisings if nothing else.
- Most advanced countries have reached saturation levels with no more increase—the Internet is a mass medium in many countries.

The rates for India have been rising spectacularly in the last few years. Note also the strong results for Russia, underscoring the social (and political) potential the role of the Internet. China is very strong, despite the censorship and control by the government.[13]

	Countries	Internet Users (2016) (million$$)	Penetration as percent of population	One Year Growth Rate
1	China	721.4	52.2%	2.2%
2	India	462.1	34.8%	30.5%
3	U.S.	286.9	88.5%	1.1%
4	Brazil	139.1	66.4%	5.1%
11	France	55.9	86.4%	1.4%
12	Indonesia	53.2	20.4%	6.5%
13	Viet Nam	49.1	52.0%	3.3%
14	Turkey	46.2	58.0%	5.1%
15	Philippines	44.5	43.5%	4.4%
99	Afghanistan	2.28	6.8%	4.7%
109	Mozambique	1.83	6.4%	5.0%
120	Myanmar	1.35	2.5%	6.1%
127	Malawi	1.16	6.5%	6.7%
130	Madagascar	1.07	4.3%	7.3%
136	Benin	0.63	5.6%	4.5%

EXHIBIT 14.3.
Internet Penetration (% population) Selected countries listed by number of users. Usually the countries that are least developed have the lowest Internet penetration. But even there, the Internet is growing.

Source: Internet Live Stats: Internet Users by Country http://www.internetlivestats.com/internet-users-by-country/

Overall, the data show that the accessibility problems of the Internet are increasingly out of the way. There is still a problem with government interference and Internet censorship in some countries but this will always be an "unknown" and hopefully recede over time.

Language Barrier

A second basic question is the potential language barrier. Communications require that you speak the same language. Not everyone speaks English, or feel comfortable doing business in a foreign language. Fortunately, this barrier can be overcome with some effort. Websites offer a choice of languages, and company subsidiaries will have their own sites and chat or Twitter in their own language. As companies expand into foreign markets, they also hire native managers and employees who can manage the necessary functions.

As firms develop multilingual websites and economic growth takes place, the Internet competency rises and English language capability is likely to rise as well. Even if Internet users prefer their own native language, the prevalence of English on the Internet has made many users more proficient in English. In due time, the same might happen with the Chinese language, as China's influence on the web expands.

Payment Systems

A third question is how to establish a reliable payment system that offers acceptable options for customers. Reliance on only strong currency (say, the U.S. dollar, the euro, or the Chinese yuan) might be feasible given their convertibility, but for most markets it will be necessary to offer prices in the local currency. How can a firm convert and bring home the payment, and how should credit worthiness be assessed?

With the global expansion of both Visa and MasterCard, payments problems have become considerably eased. In fact, the importance of credit cards in digital commerce can hardly be overstated. They make it possible to complete sales transactions at home and across borders without the need for credit checks, bank letters of credit and costly financial intermediaries (although there are usually currency-exchange charges imposed by the sponsoring bank for foreign transactions). As a seller the firm essentially gets paid (or at least gets assured of payment) before the product has to be shipped.

But credit cards are not available for everybody, and in addition the issuers charge pretty high fees. Furthermore, currency convertibility is a continuing problem, and even when hard currency is used, and the big banks have made money transfer between countries and currencies a very expensive business. Paying a euro invoice with a dollar Visa card can cost an extra 3.9 percent of the amount for just the exchange. Fortunately, this has spawned innovations in payment systems that now begin to challenge established big players, especially traditional banks.

For example, PayPal, the online payment system, opened for international transactions in 2002, simplifying the process and reducing costs. By establishing an account with PayPal, a free service backed by a credit card, one can now send money to a number of countries in dollars, and the recipient can withdraw the funds in the local currency. Where a regular bank transfer can cost as much as 4 percent, PayPal will charge only about 0.5 percent (assuming the recipient will be willing to sign up for a PayPal account as well, also free).

PayPal was a pioneer in creating a digital wallet and the anti-fraud device of CAPTCHAS, letters that only a human eye can decipher. This has helped the company set the pace in digital payments. Today, PayPal has 152 million active registered accounts and is available in 203 markets.[14] It has competitors, and especially the new Alibaba pay system, Alipay, promises to be a formidable competitor with its large base in China. In fact, in China as in the Scandinavian countries, mobile payments, using smart phones, have increasingly become the standard method of payment. Cash is not acceptable, while credit cards are only grudgingly tolerated.

According to one observer, "the economics of a digital bank will give it a vast competitive edge over a traditional incumbent." Within a few years, "more than two-thirds of banking customers in Europe are likely to be 'self-directed' and highly adapted to the online world."[15]

Another threat against traditional payment systems comes from Bitcoin, a digital currency that refuses to go away. Replacing actual money, **Bitcoin** is virtual currency that can serve as payment in the digital world in much the same way as paying an airline ticket with frequent-flier points. With smartphone payments now possible against a credit or store card, a Bitcoin future might not be so far away, although as of 2017, no cryptocurrency has been officially recognized by a government as an acceptable currency.

Financial Fraud

Credit card fraud, theft committed using a credit card or debit card as a fraudulent source of funds in a transaction to obtain goods without paying, or to obtain unauthorized funds from an account, is still an issue for worldwide commerce. But in this case, e-commerce is not alone. As stores have turned to scanners and credit card payments, in-store credit card fraud is also at risk. The 2013 hacking of the Target stores and its customers' credit cards, and the similar 2014 Home Depot problems show that even the largest stores can run into fraud problems.

In 2015, a hacking ring stole up to $1 billion from banks around the world in what would be one of the biggest banking breaches ever involving more than 100 banks in 30 countries.[16] In 2016 SWIFT (Society for Worldwide Interbank Financial Telecommunications) reported that its system was hacked, affecting over a dozen banks with a Bangladeshi Bank losing $81 million. So although one would have to assume that there are some people who do not use Internet shopping because of the financial risk, these risks are not limited to e-commerce.

Hackers, persons who use computers to gain unauthorized access to data, continue to be an ongoing problem. One illustration of the difficulties involved is the attack on Target. The big discount department store had about 40 million customers' credit and debit card numbers stolen by hackers during the Thanksgiving season 2013. The company established an advisory council with five outside experts to help the company develop high protective **firewalls,** special software hurdles—similar to passwords—to a computer system or network that are designed to block unauthorized access. The experts also helped develop the software that established close integration of digital marketing with the established store network. Such integration, called an **Omni-channel** approach, seeks to provide the customer with a seamless shopping experience whether the customer is shopping online from a desktop or mobile device, by telephone, or in a brick-and-mortar store.[17]

Internationally, the fact that credit card use leaves a traceable path does keep some consumers from using them. In China in particular (and also in Russia and some other countries) where government surveillance is a threat, consumers often prefer to pay through other less easily traced intermediaries. Alibaba's AliPay system of an electronic wallet offers one alternative. Even more careful consumers follow another path. They place the order online, having it shipped to an intermediary—which could be a local convenience store or similar outlet close to the buyer's residence—and then the buyer can pick up the merchandise and pay cash at pickup. Similar systems are in place in many other countries, including Japan. Cumbersome, but safer.

Fraud is a huge global problem in payments and given the history so far, it seems possible that the pirates and hackers will multiply and perhaps stay ahead of the pursuit forever. On this, only the future will tell.

Counterfeits

Counterfeits are still going to be a problem, however. For many products digital commerce has proved to be a boon to counterfeit producers. Since there is no way to really touch or experience the products, counterfeits have infiltrated many of the e-commerce sites, especially resale sites such as eBay. Although the companies—and the brand owners—make dedicated efforts to keep fake products and brands out, the proliferation is wide.

The range of products affected is wide—from over-the-counter drugs and personal-care products, to apparel and accessories, women's bags and glasses, to consumer electronics and computer software and industrial components and parts. Since China is one big source of counterfeits, its government has been prodded to enforce anti-pirating international agreements. Showing some goodwill effort, in January 2015 the government chastised the large e-commerce platform Alibaba for selling fake goods. Jack Ma, the founder of Alibaba, promised improvement, pronouncing counterfeits a "cancer" jeopardizing all e-commerce.[18] In 2017 Alibaba filed suit against two merchants on one of its e-commerce platforms for hosting fake items. It's the first time Alibaba—or any e-commerce site in China—has taken legal action against its sellers and comes amid increasing criticism of the company's alleged inability to tackle counterfeits. The U.S. Office of the Trade Representative added Alibaba's Taobao website to its "notorious markets" list. According to news reports, Alibaba has 2,000 permanent staff and 5,000 volunteers to help find counterfeit goods.

Brands are copied and sometimes altered to suggest a well-known competitor. In China, for example, you can find Haiyatt (for Hyatt) and Marvelot (for Marriott) hotels as well as a fake "Peninsula" hotel. Management claim to be paying tribute to the global brands, but are also happy to service any misled or careless web customers.[19]

Unfortunately, international digital commerce has spawned a huge market for counterfeit products and brands—giving e-commerce a bad name among some and potentially keeping customers away.

Political and Regulatory Threats

There are other political and regulatory threats as well. The biggest may be the political pressures toward censorship and blocking Internet access. In the big China market as in Russia these are clearly risks. Not only limiting access for potential customers, but also limiting access for marketers that somehow cross some invisible lines, regulatory or political. Even search engines such as Google have encountered problems. To limit their exposure, companies will likely keep options in traditional channels open, and also limit their dependence on these markets.

THE RISE OF SOCIAL MEDIA

Social media involves electronic communication through which users create online networks to share information, ideas, photos, and videos. At their roots, social media are not commercial, but they have gradually become infiltrated by commercial interests.

Many companies now have a prominent presence on social media sites. In fact, the reason social media figure in marketing at all is that these media have become the "new" means of communication with communities at large and potential customers (and even selling to consumers, although in a soft-sell way). When companies emphasize the *sustainability* and *corporate social responsibility* their communications necessarily involve a larger set of **stakeholders** than just customers.

Corporate social responsibility involves the continuing commitment by business to look beyond its make-a-profit objective and contribute to the economic development of all the stakeholders, by improving the community and society at large. For such audiences, the non-commercial aspects of social media become very attractive. While advertising means "tooting your own horn," companies can use social media to become community advisers, partners, and even leaders.

Digital global marketing involves social media not only because of the need for a **triple bottom line** (social, environmental, and financial goals), but also because the fast growth of social media vehicles in so many countries around the world.

EXHIBIT 14.4.
Selected social media icons

Social Media Platforms

The many options in social media make it a more complex tool to understand and manage. The social media tools include Facebook, Twitter, Tumblr, Pinterest, YouTube, and LinkedIn (see Exhibit 14.4).

Here is a short description of what these social media tools do (in order from the upper left hand icon):

Twitter is the social networking and microblogging site that allows users to send 140-character posts and real-time updates. It is used by thought leaders and B2B and B2C businesses.

YouTube allows users to upload and share video clips across the Internet through websites, mobile devices, blogs, and email. Users consist of both individuals and B2B and B2C businesses.

Facebook is the world's largest peer-to-peer online social networking website that connects people and businesses with friends and those of like interests. Great for B2B and B2C businesses with their own presence.

LinkedIn is the largest global professional networking website. It allows members to create business contacts, search for jobs, find potential clients, and create groups based on like interests.

Pinterest is where users go to collect stuff online that they want to "pin" on a board. This tool is useful for individuals and B2C businesses.

Flickr is a photo management and sharing network gallery that enables users to upload once and then send to any device, any screen, any friend, or any follower.

ShareThis is a sharing platform allowing users to share web and social content. This tool is important for many websites.

Social Feed. "Feed" is a RSS (Rich Site Summary) family of web feed formats used to publish frequently updated works—such as blogs, news headlines, audio, and video—in a standardized format.

Tumblr is a microblogging platform and social networking website owned by Yahoo! Inc. The service allows users to post multimedia and other content to a short-form blog.

Instagram is a way to share photos. It's akin to taking a picture or video and then share via Facebook, Twitter, and more.

People in many countries around the world have their own favorite social media platforms. Exhibit 14.5 shows a few.

Many existing and new entrepreneurs are capable of setting up a social media platform in a new country because of the low entry barriers. For example, most language differences are easily accommodated—Twitter allows users to send their tweets in 55 languages, including Chinese, Farsi, Arabic, Slovak, and Japanese. Also, exiting a country is not very difficult, since the actual investment is usually quite low compared to a brick-and-mortar business.

Social Media as Marketing Tools

To use social media for marketing purposes, it is important to recognize the business model of the platform owners.

EXHIBIT 14.5.
Ten social media platforms around the world

NETLOG™	Networking site, professional and personal, big in Europe and Middle East
ВКонтакте	Facebook clone, with biggest market share in Russia
ibibo i build · i bond	Indian, suffering as Facebook dominates
mixi	Japanese, the most popular networking site
CYWORLD	South Korea, networking site, hit by Facebook entry
orkut	A Google discussion platform, popular in Brazil with large share
TARINGA!	Argentina's social networking platform, large throughout Latin America
新浪微博 Sina Weibo	Microblogging a la Twitter; a third of China's users
renren	China's version of Facebook; estimated 160 million users
badOo	One of the top social networking sites in Europe

Membership in a social media vehicle is typically free.

By attracting a large number of sign-ups, the platform can establish itself as a place to reach many people. For marketing purposes, the more important figure is not the number of members, but the number of active users, usually defined as those who access the site and log in at least once in a month. Many active users mean the site can attract advertisers. Such advertising is often the main means by which the creators of the site can "monetize" their investment in the software. The profiles created by the users can be used to craft targeted ad pitches more precisely (although privacy protection can be a contentious issue in these sites).

Most social networking sites did not allow advertising in the build-up stages, and may not even allow it today. Even Facebook did not allow advertising in the beginning. Marketers, however, saw the benefit of signing up early, and many became early users of social media. Their typical strategy was to become valued contributors (and listeners) to whatever discussion, comments and interactions occurred, sometimes not necessarily divulging their commercial interests. They also started to provide content, information about technology, products, and services which enhanced the value of the platform (there was also the hope that some of this content would go viral—see box, "How social media are viral").[20]

BOX: How Social Media are Viral

Social media can help ideas and news **go viral**, that is, diffuse as an epidemic among a community or culture. The spreading is done via the links that the various sites have—the followers on Twitter who re-tweet messages, the friends on Facebook who pass on gossip, news, and information, and so on.

However, the virus can also spread in other ways. There are dedicated websites (such as BuzzFeed and Upworthy) that search the web to find the most noteworthy postings, and then uploads these to its own site or to other sites such as Instagram, the popular photo-sharing service.

There are also new web entrepreneurs known as **virologists** who go one further, and test out different ways of headlining and presenting interesting web postings. Spartz, Inc. out of Chicago is one. The same news item that caught the attention of BuzzFeed from Twitter, say, could be reformatted, jazzed up with additional material and a new headline, then re-posting it. Such sites can work very quickly, try different versions of framing the same news item and then upload it on several other sites using the most click-generating headline.[21]

Companies that do marketing through social media attempt to provide relevant and timely content. Whether or not such content goes viral depends partly on what these aggressive third-party "virologists" will do with the material. Yes, companies can upload the viral "embryos," trying to reach relevant stakeholders, including customers. But for getting the virus to spread, the most important "customers" may be the BuzzFeed and Upworthy middlemen and the republishing by the virologists.[22]

There are social media networking sites that do not accept advertising. For example, **WhatsApp** is a popular site (1.2 billion users worldwide in 2017) that instead of ads charges a dollar a year for access. WhatsApp does not collect personal information like your name, gender, address, or age. Once delivered, messages are deleted from WhatsApp's servers. The WhatsApp mantra is "No ads, no games, no gimmicks." This lean and successful operation, not surprisingly perhaps, was acquired by Facebook in 2014. In 2017 it was blocked in China by its Firewall in order to prohibit the showing of videos of internal unrest in the country.

There are two main ways marketers use social media:

- One way is as an advertising platform to reach a certain market segment.
- A second way is to create buzz and goodwill toward the brand by posting information and videos about corporate good deeds—whether about sustainable operations, CSR, or simply using the site as a way of creating excitement and engagement with the brand (see box, "Sustainability in Social Media").

A good example of using social media as an advertising platform is the NIKE and adidas efforts in the 2014 World Cup. The official sponsor of the Cup was adidas, but NIKE also was prominently featured through sponsored athletes.

Throughout the World Cup, adidas campaigned continuously in social media. According to Origamilogic.com, over the tournament period:

- adidas published more than 2 times more Facebook posts, 3 times more Twitter tweets, and 1.5 times more YouTube videos than NIKE.
- adidas received 3 times more views and likes on YouTube, compared to NIKE.
- adidas experienced 2.4 times more retweets on Twitter than NIKE.

However, NIKE also did score importantly. Its "Last Game" video, released right before the start of the Cup, garnered over 64 million views. The video, with recognizable soccer stars as game characters, was heavily promoted on NIKE's social channels and in television ads. The level of engagement was significantly higher than other posts although adidas did have one commercial, "The Dream," that did well with over 38 million views.

The outcome was deemed a draw. The lesson is that the advantages of a sponsorship can be offset by a very strong guerilla effort in social media.

BOX: Sustainability in Social Media

Many companies use social media to convey their efforts in sustainable operations. The feel-good stories do not necessarily make for great or engaging copy, so the story telling often resort to cartoon characters and fun dialogue to illustrate the efforts. Such characters also travel easily around the globe—the M&M red and green candy characters seem to be well known in many countries.

There are several booklets on how to effectively tell sustainability stories in social media.[23] The most common advice is to dramatize a personal story of tragedy and success, and playing down the role of corporate involvement. It is still difficult for many to align sustainability with the corporate profit motive.

Some sustainability examples in social media:

- M&M uses its cartoon characters to convey parent company Mars' sustainable cocoa initiatives.[24]
- Cheerios' Spoonfuls of Stories campaign, a long-running collaboration with Simon & Schuster and First Book aimed at childhood reading, utilizes the breakfast cereal brand's Facebook page to gain recognition. Cheerios has also been attacked for some of its postings.[25]
- Wal-Mart has created a green products and services Pinterest page to convey its environmental actions.
- Ford's team-up with YouTube action sports star Devin Super Tramp to show how much a Ford Focus can do on one tank of gas.
- Vestas' Act of Facts initiative uses Google Maps and an illustrated pamphlet to help people respond to negatives about wind turbines.

Many companies do good things, and they try to tell people about it. It is just that on social media, the main focus is on "me and my friends," so users have to be entertained. And their ire can get aroused very easily.

Although the social media effort is at the *upper-funnel level* today (a matter of awareness and buzz about the brand) their sites often feature links to their corporate website showcasing new products and services (the *lower-funnel* parts). Facebook technology experts are today busy creating metrics that can identify the exact *click-through rate* measuring how many actually click on ads and the value creation of an ad on its page.[26]

Thus today, the link between social media and e-commerce is increasingly strong. For global marketers, given the deep penetration of so many social media platforms in foreign countries, this inexpensive, fast, and relatively

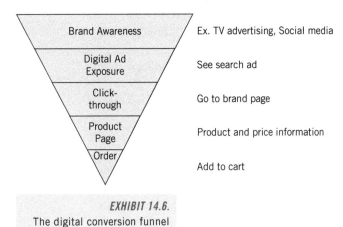

Brand Awareness — Ex. TV advertising, Social media

Digital Ad Exposure — See search ad

Click-through — Go to brand page

Product Page — Product and price information

Order — Add to cart

EXHIBIT 14.6.
The digital conversion funnel

unobtrusive promotional tool is increasingly attractive as a marketing platform for a large number of businesses.

The Conversion Funnel

But an advantage in digital advertising is the ability to track the actions of the user, including clicks for more information, clicks on other links, and so on. This makes it possible to compute **conversion rates,** the percentage of users who takes a desired action (in the end, the percentage of website visitors who buys something on the site).

A recent study on Facebook tested the effectiveness of online advertising for Samsung's Galaxy. One percent of the Facebook visitors were kept as a control group, without advertising, while other visitors were randomly presented with alternative ads. The groups' CTR rates were then compared. It was possible to identify those ads that resulted in greater click-through. However, there is a difference between click-throughs and conversion. The research so far shows that CTRs (click-through rates) are not strong predictors of purchases, but that it can be used for awareness and brand building.[27]

However, there is a difference between click-throughs and conversion. The research shows that the CTR's (click-through-rates) are not strong predictors of purchases, but that can be used for awareness and brand building. This difference between "sales lift" versus "brand lift" is common in advertising generally. The so-called **Hierarchy of Effects** model suggests that advertising should aim for communication objectives—knowledge, attitudes, and so on—and should not be expected to generate purchases without more promotional support. In digital advertising the hierarchy is often portrayed as a "funnel" with an upper and lower part (see Exhibit 14.6).

The upper part basically involves the creation of awareness of the brand, while the lower part of the funnel involves conversion and sales. Traditional media like TV is responsible for driving awareness (upper funnel) and digital media (search and display) are more about driving lower-funnel activities. The click-through rates at each step, accessing the product pages, and subsequent ordering show the *conversion rates*. The funnel gradually narrows as fewer and fewer customers remain for the next step. The conversion rates are key analytical metrics that allow alternative digital advertising options to be tested.

Mobile Commerce

With the rapid penetration of Internet-capable smartphones and tablets around the world, social media and e-commerce have turned mobile. The ability to access social platforms and e-commerce websites from handheld devices is particularly attractive in emerging markets, where the retail infrastructure is underdeveloped. Mobile commerce represents the idea that the consumer is always reachable wherever he or she is, or, for the individual, that you are empowered to be in touch with others, play games, and able to go shopping whenever or wherever you are. Mobile access has been particularly important

EXHIBIT 14.7.
A passenger on the phone in a rickshaw taxi in the center of Varanasi, a city in India. Because of the unreliability of electricity in many areas, cell phones with solar phone chargers are a popular product in India and other emerging countries.

Copyright © 2015 by Shutterstock/pjhpix.

in emerging markets where smartphones dominate PCs and tablets (see box, "India goes mobile").

Introducing mobile capability can involve a significant investment for the firm. In the global context, this is doubly so, since the local sites need to be designed with the local language, culture, and expectations in mind. It is one thing for PepsiCo to design the English-language sites for Doritos chips, and then also design a site for the Latin-American market, the Chinese market, and the Japan market. Some features travel well—cartoon characters, for example—but what should boost engagement in the brand in each market will not typically be the same.

EMERGING BUYER BEHAVIOR

As several observers have pointed out, digital marketing is often a matter of being "discovered" by the potential consumer browsing the web. Traditional marketing involves finding the customer—in digital the tables are turned. This thinking is particularly apt in social media, where the individual is typically not shopping. As new vehicles and platforms crop up, consumers change quickly, and marketers have to understand what their customers might be doing now—and where? Four examples of emerging behaviors are discussed here.

Search Behavior

Since search is such a fundamental channel for reaching the online consumer, understanding search behavior is important. Researchers are starting to unravel some of the more common search patterns that consumers follow on Google, but some of that knowledge might soon be outdated.

In the West, it is common to link search to keywords. Google's dominant search machine is set up to optimize a search by linking keywords to websites, ads, products, and brands.

Two things seem ready to change that.

- **Voice-based search**. One is the increasing role of voice recognition and the possibility that search will take place from voice commands. The Siri application on the iPhone is one example of this shift, freeing the user from the keyboard.
- **Image-based search**. The second change might be the use of visual imagery in search. Touching the icon was a revolutionary innovation when it came. Something similar might be happening to search. One reason is linguistics and the rising importance of China. The Chinese language lends itself much more to search by visual imagery, since the logograms (or *hanzi*) are really pictures. Already Google Image Search, Yahoo Image Search, and PicSearch offer image searching similar to word searching.

In the future, consumers everywhere might be freed from the keyboard. Just talking to a Siri-lookalike, and touching the screen.

Social Media Behavior

Many people have now progressed beyond the commonly available social media sites. Several factors have combined to limit the attractiveness of the open forums:

- Government crackdown is one thing.
- Then privacy concerns and reports of abusive comments and threats have also soured the social media land.
- Having the older generations start participating has lowered the attractiveness of sites for the younger segments.
- And then it is the recognition that what you might have posted can come back to haunt you—as you apply for a job or get engaged or just get profiled forever as a 14-year-old. The changes underway in Europe about the right to "scrub" information about yourself will perhaps change this trend.

The result is that very recently several alternative and more protected and limited networks have cropped up in several different countries. So-called **messaging apps,** third-party apps that enable messages to be sent and received and used in lieu of the carrier's app, because more limited and controllable access such as WhatsApp, WeChat, and KakaoTalk have become preferred to Facebook. WhatsApp was bought by Facebook in 2014 and was one of the most popular messaging app in the UK downloaded on half the country's iPhones, with more than

1.2 billion (as of 2017) monthly active users globally.[29] That makes it bigger with even more active users than Twitter, which counts 317 million. WhatsApp is on more than 95 percent of all smartphones in Spain. About 90 percent of the population of Brazil used messaging apps, three-quarters of Russians, and half of Britons. However, the UK prime minister in 2015 proposed banning WhatsApp, iMessage, and Snapchat in the UK since their high level of encrypted communication cannot be read by the UK's security services. While this legislative move is sure to face serious challenges from civil liberties groups, there is some uncertainty.[30] It is not just the Chinese government that sees control of the Internet as an important government activity.

The pioneer users and early adopters of these apps are typically under 25. According to industry observers, the reason the young people around the world are starting to avoid the better known media like Facebook is that their parents are now on them. Facebook has gained over a billion monthly active users by attracting the older generation—now the kids want to be left alone again.[31]

With people living ever longer, the consolation for the established sites is that the elderly is a growing segment. Problem is, they might not be spending as much money.

Music Listening

Since music is supposedly without a language barrier, the music business should be naturally global. In the "old" days, everybody loved the Beatles and Michael Jackson, kind of thing. However, as it turns out, today's sales figures show that each country has its own music culture, and that the music business is multi-domestic with preferences varying more by country than many would expect. For example, the data in Exhibit 14.8 show from where the top 10 artists in different countries hail.

Judging from Exhibit 14.8 the music and artists we hear are mostly our own and those that reflect our own culture. But even if the top acts are local, the labels they sign up for are mainly global who localize their stables. The producers of recorded music are still major global companies. The old labels such as RCA Victor, EMI, Decca, and Columbia/ Sony distributed their music worldwide. They had licensed affiliates across the globe. For example, the Beatle's Parlophone discs from the UK were licensed to Capitol in the United States (with, unfortunately, often inferior pressings). Today, their local affiliates mainly work with local talent—global localization.

There still however are a few examples of local music that becomes a global sensation:

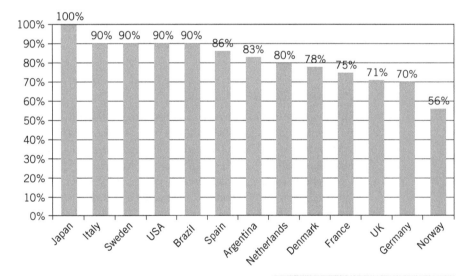

EXHIBIT 14.8.
Top artists are local. Percent of local acts in the national top 10 albums of 2013 (by artist nationality)[32]

Source: International Federation of the Phonographic Industry.

1. Wiz Khalifa, "See You Again" feat. Charlie Puth (2015) 2.9 billion views worldwide (American sung in English)
2. PSY, "Gangnam Style" (2012) 2.9 billion views worldwide (South Korean sung in Korean)
3. Luis Fonsi feat. Daddy Yankee, "Despacito" (2017) 2.5 billion views worldwide (Puerto Rican sung in Spanish)

It takes at least 2 billion views worldwide for a song to even break into the top 10.

Today, the technology of the Internet has changed the music business in fundamental ways. First iPod and iTunes virtually obliterated sales of the record albums, the compact discs, and the record stores. Now music comes "streaming." With music streaming from the cloud, more and more consumers around the world are listening on their PC or tablets or their smartphones. Music is mobile and available to us everywhere—extending further the visions behind Sony's Walkman of 1979 and the Apple's 2001 iPod, but now streaming and weightless.

Predictably, streaming music has become a global business. Not because the market itself is necessarily global—as Exhibit 14.8 shows—but because the technology can be scaled up and finance favors large size. Firms with a larger market share have an advantage in negotiating the necessary contracts with the labels, the artists, and their agents. There are some small network effects—that is, music streaming stations that are more popular might attract more people—but since music is basically a solitary consumption, what matters more is the selection of music. Larger firms have simply greater assortments of music acts. They can better afford the licensing fees that the best acts demand. Streaming access is expected to severely dampen demand for downloads and album sales (one reason the Beatles the highest selling group of all time, was not available for streaming until the end of 2015. The UK singer Adele is 21th on the bestselling list in 2017 if only physical media such as CDs are counted, but jumps to number 1 if streaming sales are added in.) But not all countries have said goodbye to the CDs of the first digital wave (see box, "Japan's counter-trend").

Streaming music really got started by Apple and iTunes, with Apple convincing the music labels to allow separately priced (basically $1) downloads of single tracks from albums. This allowed iPod to feature a customized and mobile playlist of favorite tracks. Today, the Cloud can house these lists, making your favorite music basically available all the time.

BOX: Japan's Counter-Trend[33]

As in so many other instances, Japan does things differently. Although in the forefront of progressive technology, Japanese music-lovers still cling to the CD format over streaming music.

According to data, about 85 percent of music sales in Japan are CDs. Customers still prefer collecting discs and albums that they can touch and store rather than the virtual and invisible music of streaming. One might think this is because a special Japanese penchant for keeping things near and close—think "Hello Kitty"—or some perception that CDs offers more fidelity and control. Also playing a role may be the fact that music copyrights laws in Japan are obscure and fragmented, making the necessary licensing deals with the big labels difficult for streaming start-ups. But another reason is that CDs have developed imaginative tactics to remain viable.

CD albums feature elaborate packaging, featuring artist photos, text, and memorabilia. The popularity of large girl and boy groups with as many as 20 singers and dancers has helped make album photos particularly effective in enhancing the listening experience. One popular girl group called AKB48 offered CDs containing tickets for access to live events, leading the biggest fans to buy multiple copies of an album.

Record stores still do good business in Japan. Tower Records still has 85 outlets, doing $500 million in business a year (although controlled by NTT DoCoMo, the largest telecom company in Japan). The stores attract customers by creating events, offering merchandise, free sample CDs, with groups performing for fans and autographing CDs.[34]

There is also online radio streaming, which allows individuals to listen to music either for free or for a small fee. Avoiding the $1 fee charged by iTunes by offering a free basic package, these services have grown fast worldwide. To ward off competition, in 2017 Apple announced new and improved streaming services with a subscription fee of $10 per month ($5 for students).[35]

Streaming online radio follows one of two different models:

- *Radio*. Members sign up for either free or paid monthly subscriptions. The site allows the listener to specify preferred types of music, which will then be streamed shuffle-style from a radio playlist. If free, advertising will be introduced at certain intervals. If paid, there is no advertising. Examples include Pandora from the United States which now offers Globalpandora.[36]
- *On demand*. Members can specify their favorite artists and focus on a personalized playlist for just one artist. Sign up for premium membership or free. If free, there will be advertising and some limits on specifying the playlist. Examples include Spotify from Sweden and Dreezer from France. Globally, Dreezer was in 182 countries and entered the United States in 2014, while Spotify was in 57 countries, including the United States, with plans to expand further into Asia.[37] A number of existing companies have expanded their business models and entered the personalized radio market, such as Grooveshark (entered 2007), iHeartRadio (entered 2008), Mog.com, TuneIn, AccuRadio, and Rhapsody.

Podcasting, which is a technology started by Apple in the early 2000s, allows a user to download their favorite program to a portable device and listen to it while offline. It is an alternative to streaming programs and while not experiencing much growth, 17 percent of U.S. adults claim to have listened to a podcast in 2015.[38] Listeners who have spent the time to download a program may be more attentive while they are listening to their favorite podcast shows and thus more attractive to potential advertisers.

The digital global expansion in online radio has not taken place via acquisitions of local start-ups but instead by foreign direct investments by the leading brands. Access to financing has allowed larger firms to establish their technology abroad and hire the necessary local management who understand the local tastes. One obstacle has been the need to negotiate the required licensing fees from local acts and recording labels, a time-consuming and expensive effort which has limited also local startups. Spotify, one leading company, based a recent global expansion on its acquisition of the Led Zeppelin back catalogue after a year of negotiations.[39]

Music streaming is a good example of how a basically multi-domestic market can still be dominated by global players who understand how to be locally responsive.

Game Playing

One example of the new kind of buying behavior that has come with digital is the emphasis on playing games, or gaming for short. It has become popular worldwide, and has also spread from young people to older demographics.

The early computer games pioneered by Atari and Nintendo and followed by Sony's Playstation and Microsoft's Xbox have now migrated to the Internet. Player consoles still sell, but an increasing number of gamers access the games on the web. The emergence 3G and 4G smartphones has further moved gaming online, enabling mobile access. A whole generation—the millennials have grown up with these games and some continue to play them whenever and wherever. These game players can be found all around the world (see Exhibit 14.9).

The gaming segment now trends upward toward the 18- to 35-year-olds and further, and is also getting traction among the elderly (the Nintendo Wii is one example). These people are multi-tasking, so attention spans are

EXHIBIT 14.9.
Comic-Con millennials at The Crocus Center on October 4, 2014, in Moscow, Russia. Comic-Con is the biggest and most prominent conference event for international gamers. Millennials refer to individuals around the world born between 1981 and 1999, a global generation that started with Nintendo, then Playstation and the Xbox, and later the online video games.

Copyright © 2014 by Bigstock/magicinfoto.

short. They favor word-of-mouth (WOM) and recommendations of friends in their social network. And they are present around the world, but especially among the new Asian consumers.

According to Newzoo.com, there are 2.2 billion gamers across the globe generating $108.9 billion in game revenues in 2017. Asia-Pacific is by far the largest region, with China expected to generate $27.5 billion, or one-quarter of all revenues in 2017. Nearly half of Internet users across the S.E. Asian region play online games every week.[40] What's more, nearly half of Malaysian gamers, for example, search online to learn more about a product or brand they first saw advertised in a game. Games have become an advertising medium of competitive online games on the Internet, with teams from different countries participating. There are even events where players and interested onlookers gather to watch actual combats between teams in big theaters. As of 2014, massive **open-platform multi-player games** were played to large audiences around the world. For example, one of the biggest e-sports leagues, Electronic Sports League (ESL), had 73,000 attendees at a four-day tournament in Katowice, Poland, in March 2014.[41] In 2016 ESL teamed up with Indian competitor NODWIN to bring E-Sports and electronic gaming to India.

Companies make use of the gaming instincts. Many promotions today include gaming characteristics to increase enjoyment and engagement. Shopkick.com, the "get your kicks" points app mentioned previously, is one example. In another example, Citibank launched a credit card aimed at 21- to 35-year-old Singaporeans by incorporating gaming features designed to let them personalize their experiences. Users could gain points by checking in at specific locations, such as restaurants or stores, and "sharing" or "liking" deals on Facebook. They could also vote for a particular experience or location and win a special deal of the month from winning establishments. Referring a friend can net $20 plus the friend gets a free cabin-size luggage.[42]

A more elaborate illustration of a gaming promotion comes from Volkswagen. In 2011, Volkswagen Group organized a contest in emerging countries to help the company develop an electric "people's car" (the German name means just that). Inviting young talented designers in China, Russia, and India to compete, participants were given an easy-to-use design tool and allowed to post their designs online. Site visitors voted for their favorites, with results continuously tracked online so that everybody could see how the competing designs were faring. The crowd-sourcing campaign received more than 260,000 ideas from 30 million people.[43] The three winning designs were given awards, and VW then developed a concept car based on the many ideas submitted and unveiled the car—an MPV that seats seven people—at the 2013 Shanghai Auto Show. A commercial showcased how the people's ideas integrated into the innovative features of the People's Car.[44] Volkswagen introduced its first all-electric car, the e-Golf in late 2014, incorporating many of the suggested ideas and selling for about $27,000 U.S.

Such contests are actually not that new as a promotional idea. But they have reached new heights with the increased sophistication of digital video games and the emergence of "the millennials" as a recognized market.

DIGITAL MARKET RESEARCH

Market research is one area where the digital impact has been particularly revolutionary. The traditional market surveys to assess demand potential in foreign markets are now largely based on online questionnaires and interviews, carried out via specialized survey vendors such as SurveyMonkey, QuestionPro, and FluidSurveys. As the Internet has spread into more countries and penetrated further in each, such research on foreign markets is inexpensive and very fast.

To realize how market research for digital marketing is really different, it is useful to go through some typical components of market research.

- *Market potential.* How does one assess whether a country market shows strong potential for a given product or service? One of the simplest ways is to track how often some relevant keywords appear in searches. If the company sells swim suits, for example, it is easy enough to check Google for the number of times "swimming" or "beach" or "ocean-side" have been searched for. Google is not the only search engine, of course, but it has great international reach and offers extensive service help. Here is from their website: "*We have offices in more than 60 countries, maintain more than 180 Internet domains, and serve more than half of our results to people living outside the United States. We offer Google's search interface in more than 130 languages.*"[45] To assist in judging the results from a search check, Google offers benchmark statistics for the specific country, so one can judge whether the frequencies found represent a viable market.
- *Brand image.* For brand image social media tend to be most useful. Simple queries online to ask people's reactions to a band name can be useful, and short surveys can be placed on various survey engine sites such as SurveyMonkey, Qualtrix, or Zoomerang. But for more in-depth and unvarnished truths, it is better to ask for a compilation of comments about the brand from so-called **crawler** web services such as Beewolve, PromptCloud, or Ortelio. A crawler is a program that visits websites and reads their pages and other information in order to find keywords and create entries for an index list that can be searched. A crawler is also known as a "spider" or a "bot." These services collect brand-relevant comments on social media sites, and provide a compilation of positive and negative comments that reflect the brand image in a particular community. When needed, translation from another language can also be obtained.

    If one wants to listen in on the conversation to really hear what is going on, a new service trumpets that it can offer real-time visualizations, like our patented Bubble Stream, show you who's talking, what they are saying, and where the conversations are happening.[46] Slightly ominous, perhaps, evoking images of George Orwell's Big Brother.
- *Qualitative research.* Qualitative research typically involves face-to-face interviews with individual respondents, and is therefore not as common in international market research. But digital access offers solutions also here.

    In one imaginative effort to demonstrate what is possible, a group of researchers set out to do one-day qualitative research in seven different countries.[47] The study involved snack-food consumption, and the target population was mothers of children age 6 to 10. The countries chosen were Australia, Brazil, Germany, India, Russia, the UK, and the U.S., countries with widely different Internet penetration, from India's 12.6 percent to Germany's 82.3 percent.

The research tools used were different in each country:

1. *Mobile geo-location design (Australia).* Members of a consumer panel were contacted when their smartphone was near a store selling snack foods, and, if agreed, answered on-the-spot questions over the phone about their shopping.
2. *Live mobile ethnography (UK).* This tool involved mobile streaming technology that enabled live video interviews with smartphone users through a wireless Internet connection. The verbal responses were supported by video from the respondents' homes, showing snack-food storage and uses.
3. *Mobile journaling (Brazil).* An application for iOS and Android operating systems was downloaded by respondents. The app allowed the researcher to send task assignments, such as filming a child eating a snack. The respondents could upload pictures, video, and text from the smartphone to the researcher's online platform.
4. *Online blogging (India).* In India, where Internet penetration is lower and bandwidth sometimes low, the researchers used online blogging. The blog format enabled respondents to provide question answers in free-form text using their own language.
5. *Online bulletin boards (Russia).* In Russia, online bulletin boards were used to recruit respondents and initiate online discussions. This made for a good environment to engage in iterations and get responses to help revise a contemplated product design change.
6. *Social media webcam interview (Germany).* Germany has more than 38 million Facebook subscribers, making Facebook a natural choice. With the webcam recording, researchers could see facial expressions and body language, approximating an in-depth interview, useful for a final product-design evaluation.

In some ways the lack of personal encounters in these settings might be an advantage since the more impersonal Internet connections can relax respondents' inhibitions and lead to more truthful answers.

Digital marketing research is not just online surveys and focus groups. It uses all the new technology and devices to cull information from all the social media and e-commerce interactions—and consumers around the world seem happy to participate.[48]

DIGITAL MARKETING STRATEGY

For the global marketer, digital B2C strategy is necessarily different from traditional marketing.

The most important change is that the digital marketing strategy has to start with the recognition that the standard distinctions between in-store, home, and work buying occasions are blurred. With digital access, especially mobile, the consumers can buy products and services in almost any situation and at any time. They are always potentially in-the-market, not necessarily something they cherish as individuals.

The Consumer Journey

Because of the unlimited access, it has become common for marketers to define consumer demand in terms of a continuous **consumer journey.** The consumer journey is the total sum of experiences that consumers go through when interacting with your company and brand. One useful visual representation of the journey is the circle

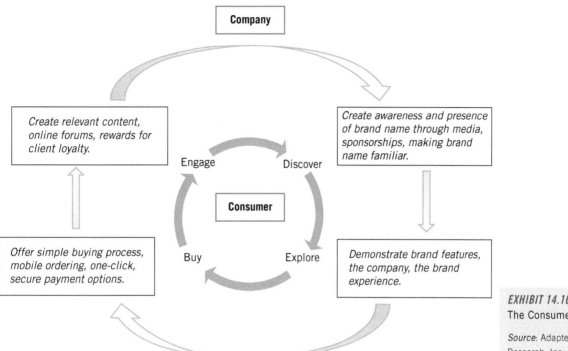

EXHIBIT 14.10.
The Consumer Journey.

Source: Adapted from Forrester Research, Inc.

used by Forrester, the online research company.[49] Exhibit 14.10 shows the basic components of the journey and how company actions differ along the journey:

The diagram shows the duality of the company-customer relationship in digital marketing. Because the consumer is always reachable, so should the company be.

With the consumer journey perspective, the several **touch-points** where the global marketer can offer information, advice and influential content can be identified:

Phase 1. *Discover:* This is where the awareness and recognition of the brand occurs, whether through traditional or digital media. Sponsorships of events, cause marketing, and other promotional activities help at this stage to create a presence. The brand and its logo should become familiar symbols. The marketer needs to be present in web communities where target consumers are; sponsor social content; link to search keywords; use SEO (search engine optimization); offer brand-related content; and emphasize user experiences.[50]

Phase 2. *Explore:* More brand-focused, in this phase the consumer is more interested, ready to learn more about a brand's features and the company behind it, including the sustainability and CSR efforts of the corporation. The marketer can communicate the brand experience through video and rich brand/product content, consumer reviews, and ratings.

Phase 3: *Buy:* To help the actual purchase, create a simple buying process, order, and fulfillment with one-click, immediate order feedback. The marketer might offer personalized help via chat; support cross-channel shopping; and provide secure and convenient payment options.

Phase 4: *Engage:* Consumers are always in the market. With all of this information available, marketers need to shift their mindset to think in terms of conversations continuing rather than short campaigns. To be in the conversation set, company information should be relevant, new, and interesting. Gaming is one digital strategy to create consumer engagement. Online forums for

EXHIBIT 14.11.
The original Levi's label—
another iconic image.

BOX: Levi's Commuter Campaign

Engagement has become a key watchword in social media marketing for a good reason. Since much of social media has nothing much to do with brand promotion and product sales, the marketers have looked for a metric that shows the effectiveness of a social media campaign. What do you get in return for your social media spend? The answer is engagement.

Engagement means basically mental involvement with the brand. In social media it has become more tactile and hands-on—it often means doing something with or to the brand. Actually, Levi's has traditionally not worried all that much about engagement, since in overseas markets old and worn original jeans have sometimes fetched huge markups on eBay and similar sites. More than that, its original brand tag (see Exhibit 14.11) has been a popular add-on in Asia, where it has been common to simply stitch on the brand label of your choice on your own, a sure sign of "engagement."

But today even a company like Levi's needs to use social media to create engagement. Its social media "Commuter" campaign is a good illustration of how a social media campaign can work. Together with its media agency, Levi's established a creative partnership with VSCO, a Cam photo-editing creator. Levi's wanted to target a creative class of young adults, and had narrowed this segment down to those who commute by bike regardless of the weather or hour of day.

First, Levi's created a series of documentary-style films for the Levi's YouTube channel, shot by 20 pro photographers. The brand then invited its fans to join the pro photographers in sharing photos of their commute. The idea was that using photography of and by bikers, engagement would be high.

Each photographer captured and shared their own Commuter photo stories both on their Instagram account and VSCO Grid. VSCO then curated a custom Levi's Grid that showcased stories from collaborating photographers in each city and the best submissions from consumers participating with the campaign.

Two measures were used to measure the effectiveness. *Total Engagements* (Likes + Comments on a post) was the number one metric. But participants to a campaign have varying numbers of followers, which directly impacts the total engagements they'll receive. For this reason, Levi's also included the *Engagement Rate* (total engagement/author's following).
Results:

- Levi's received 240,000 total engagements.
- Levi's saw a 22 percent increase in average engagement rate compared to the preceding year's campaign.

It is clear that engagement is valuable, but it is still at the *upper funnel*. How to get to the *lower funnel* and actual sales is less clear. One study that tried to provide an answer showed that engagement leads to *more usage*. Facebook users may be highly engaged, and use the site often and long, even though they may not be particularly satisfied with Facebook.[51]

As the study authors concluded, customer satisfaction may still be a better predictor of choice than engagement.[52]

customer service and user advice; encourage user feedback and reviews; rewards for client loyalty and involvement; exclusive services for fans; and creating specific digital content (for an example, see box, "Levi's Commuter Campaign").

BUILDING DIGITAL CAPABILITIES

In many ways today's need to "go digital" resembles the earlier need to "go global." Going global was once touted as an "imperative," today going digital has the same urgency. Just as going global required careful preparation by the company, so does going digital.

With digital, global is often thrust upon the company. Foreign buyers see the company website and want to order, or presence on Facebook catches the interest of prospects who want to have more information. But even if the first foreign business arrives at random, it is important to get organized and plan out a proper strategy. If not, there will soon be foreign entrepreneurs eager to fill the gap and pre-empt the market opportunity, or, even worse, copycats who will potentially ruin a good brand name.

In-House vs Outsourcing

It is unlikely that the typical large multinational company has senior managers with skill and experience in digital global marketing. According to industry observers, digital marketing is sufficiently new and developing so quickly that most companies will not be ready for digital marketing.[53] Many companies will simply have to hire new personnel and create an almost free-standing unit responsible for digital.

For most companies, it is a major commitment to establish a whole new separate unit for digital marketing. Johnson & Johnson, the global pharmaceutical company, is one corporation that has established an in-house digital unit. According to Gail Horwood, the company's vice president and head of digital strategy, one problem is the lack of talent to staff the unit.[54] Apparently most digital know-how is concentrated in the big metropolitan areas of the world, from Hong Kong and Singapore to Los Angeles, New York, and London—including, of course, San Francisco and Silicon Valley.

Fortunately, there is a large number of independent entrepreneurs that enable outsourcing of the digital functions. One example is Coca-Cola which has a large staff for digital and social media but still outsources special tasks. For the "Open Happiness" campaign [...], the search advertising portion was handled by a separate agency, iCrossing Global. According to their website, iCrossing was responsible for the SEO (search engine optimization) portion of the campaign. Here is how iCrossing defined its brief:

"From a video of Coke's beloved (and mischievous) polar bears on YouTube to a microsite that lets you bottle your laugh to the official brand sites for each of their brands, the amount of online content for Coca-Cola is huge. Multiply that content by more than 200 countries and it's just plain astonishing. To successfully optimize all that mind-boggling content for maximum online visibility, we established a global SEO governance team that matches up with Coca-Cola's multi-tiered business model."[55]

In plain English, this means that iCrossing was tasked to make sure that the appropriate links were established between relevant search keywords used by consumers and what Coca-Cola has available online. This is the essential definition of **search engine optimization (SEO).** This optimization part means that the links should use key words to rank as high as possible among search results and should show, if possible, without an advertising fee. Such a task is not really one for average marketing person but for a mathematician or computer specialist.

Coordination

There is still naturally a need for integration between the digital and traditional marketing units. For any one market, say China, advertising on television should logically be coordinated with online advertising. Sponsorship in a large event such as the Olympics should be leveraged in stores, online, on television, on-site merchandise, and client parties. These things have to be coordinated very systematically and implemented carefully, not easy since the concepts and tools differ greatly. Furthermore, timing differs greatly.

While digital involves virtually immediate response and adjustment, traditional promotions need more planning. One helpful device is to agree on one spokesperson for all the brand communications, as Nike did in Beijing 2008. Unfortunately, the sponsored athlete, China's hurdle star Liu Xiang, was injured during the games and did not make it to the final. The planned promotional footage and media placement had to be reduced at some substantial cost, while the digital media could be adjusted much more quickly.[56]

Especially in global marketing, outsourcing the digital marketing campaigns in different markets makes lot of sense, since local conditions vary considerably. Also, the cultural and political and economic differences in online usage can be more readily adapted to with local sourcing. There are still issues with managing different digital teams across countries, not an easy task. [...] One positive aspect is the ease of international communication—for digital marketing teams to communicate with each other across borders should not be much of a problem. Digital marketing communication is typically one-to-one without necessarily being face-to-face.

SUMMARY

In this chapter we have surveyed the new model of digital global marketing. We first discussed the obstacles to digital global marketing, showing that many of them are resolved. We then covered social media at length, discussing several of the new networking sites available in digital to reach customers everywhere. We also traced the changing consumer behavior induced by the new media, and how marketing research is done in digital marketing. This led into a discussion of the adaptation necessary in marketing strategy, introducing the notion of the consumer journey.

The chapter also covered what capabilities companies need to develop for digital global marketing. In many ways "going digital" is similar to "going global," requiring the development of new skills and competencies. As for strategies, the standard "campaign thinking" of traditional marketing has to give way to a more continuous effort in real time, with a "content" and "conversation" mindset. Digital promotion should offer information and "content" rather than persuasive arguments pro and con. With the consumer always "on," it becomes important for the brand to be accepted as a useful partner and one that engages the consumer imagination.

In the end it should perhaps be emphasized that the digital "revolution" has not yet penetrated very deeply in the big picture. Also, it is important to remember that not all product categories lend themselves easily to digital marketing. E-commerce seems natural to consumer packaged goods, helped by strong brands which simplify choices. Expensive durable products may be more in need of tactile information—Apple's success with its stores speaks to this—and buying a car online would certainly test delivery capability (although some dealers already deliver cars bought online).

Retailing is one of the industries most affected by the new digital consumer and what has come to be called e-tailing. But retailers do fight back, showing that they have options. The trick is to embrace the new technology, and use it to make the store a finer place to come to—or to order online from. With retailing getting increasingly globalized, digital global marketing will likely be ubiquitous in the future and further disrupt some existing business models in the process—but also revitalize others.

KEY TERMS

big data
Bitcoin
consumer journey
content provision
credit card fraud
early adopters
engagement
entry and exit barriers
e-services
e-wallet
firewalls
first-mover advantages
gaming
hackers
image-based search
Internet penetration
in-the-market
keywords
lock-in
lower funnel
Marketing 2.0
messaging apps
multi-domestic

music streaming
network effects
newsfeeds
non-bank intermediaries
omni-channel
online games
online radio
open-platform multi-person games
optimization
profiles
search engine optimization (SEO)
search pattern
social media
stakeholders
sticky
sustainability
touch-points
triple bottom line
upper funnel
virologists
voice-based search
well-established routines
WhatsApp

DISCUSSION QUESTIONS

1. What are the reasons for the growth of online shopping among young women? Among young men? Are the reasons the same? Why do you think the elderly have taken to online shopping? Are the reasons the same as for the young people?

2. What are the reasons emerging markets seem to have caught on to online shopping faster than more advanced market? What kind of established stores will still survive the online attack? Explain your reasoning.

3. What is the "Consumer Journey?" What is "engagement?" What is marketing "automation?" Give examples. Why do companies like automation? Why are consumers accepting and even happy about marketing automation?

4. Why is mobile marketing becoming so important? Will mobile marketing via smartphones and tablets make PCs outdated? What will be the role remaining for the laptop?

5. Assume you have been asked to advise a company about its digital promotional strategy. What would you suggest if the product involved fashionable apparel for young women? For young men? For your mother's age group? For your father's age group? What are the differences, if any?

TEAM CHALLENGE PROJECTS

1. As social media and social marketing expand worldwide, measuring their effectiveness continues to be a problem. Understanding effectiveness can help determine how much money to invest in this promotion area. Team 1: Orkut is one of the largest social network sites in India. What criteria will you use to measure its effectiveness? Team 2: How would you measure the effectiveness of Facebook in the U.S.? What criteria will you use?

2. Digital literacy and readiness are the ability of a population to find, understand, and use digital information and e-commerce systems. Digital rankings and readiness vary widely from country to country.

Digital Economy Rankings and Readiness (Out of 10)						
Ranking	Country	2016 Score		Ranking	Country	2016 Score
1	Korea (Rep.)	8.84		43	Russia	6.95
2	Iceland	8.83		63	Brazil	5.99
3	Denmark	8.74		81	China	5.19
4	Switzerland	8.68		88	S.Africa	5.03
5	United Kingdom	8.57		138	India	2.5
6	Hong Kong, China	8.46				
7	Sweden	8.45		169	Ethiopia	1.51
8	Netherlands	8.43		170	Congo (Dem. Rep.)	1.5
9	Norway	8.42		171	Burundi	1.42
10	Japan	8.37		172	South Sudan	1.42

Source: UN ICT Development Index.

Team 1: Describe what is important in your marketing plan and for each of the 4Ps for countries that are at the top of the list. Team 2: Describe what is important in your marketing plan and for each of the 4Ps for countries that are at the bottom of the list.

3. Team 1: Look at the international website of five countries for Mercedes Benz. What changes is Mercedes Benz making for each country and what is staying the same? Explain why. Do the sites tend to be globalized or localized? Team 2: Look at the international website of five countries for Nivea, a German skin care product. What changes is Nivea making for each country and what is staying the same? Explain why. Do the sites tend to be globalized or localized?

SELECTED REFERENCES

"2015 State of Marketing," *Salesforce Marketing Cloud*, 2015.
Afsar, Vala, "4 Must-Have Digital Marketing Core Competencies," *Huffington Post,* April 27, 2014.
Anderson, Mae, "Hackers Steal Up To $1 Billion from Banks," Huffington Post, February 15, 2015.
Baeb, Eddie, "Target Forms New Digital Advisory Council," *A Bulls Eye View*, May 28, 2014.
Balram, Tarun, "India's 243 Million Internet Users and the Mobile E-Commerce Revolution," *Forbes,* July 7, 2014.

Beech, Hannah, "The Other Side of the Great Firewall," *Time,* June 22, 2015, pp. 48–51.

Blanchard, Ben, "Beijing official says Chinese have no need for blocked websites," *Reuters,* March 25, 2015.

Boykoff, Pamela, "Japan won't give up CD obsession," *CNN Money,* Aug. 19, 2013.

Bruich, Sean, "Building Insights Off the Largest 'Mobile Panel' in History," *Marketing Science Institute,* Dec. 4, 2012.

Bryson, Jim, "7 Days, 7 Countries, 7 Ways," *Marketing Insights,* July/August 2014.

Calder, Bobby J., Mathew S. Isaac, and Edward C. Malthouse, "Taking the Customer's Point-of-View: Engagement or Satisfaction?" *MSI Report,* 2013, 13–102.

Cogan, Elizabeth, "Measuring Online Advertising Effectiveness," *Stratabeat,* June 11, 2013.

de la Merced, Michael J., "Chinese Agency Softens Criticism of Alibaba on Sales of Fake Goods," *The New York Times,* January 31, 2015, B3.

Downes, Larry, "Lessons from Uber: Why Innovation And Regulation Don't Mix," *Forbes,* February 6, 2013.

"Drinking Global, Thinking Local," *iCrossing,* 2015.

Eddy, Melissa, "An Uber Service Is Banned in Germany Again," *The New York Times,* Technology, March 18, 2015.

Fu, Rocky, "Baidu World 2014: Search Trend, Mobile Solution and BaiduEye," *China Internet Watch,* September 3, 2014.

Gibbs, Samuel and Stuart Dredge, "Led Zeppelin comes to Spotify along with free music streaming for mobiles," *The Guardian,* December 11, 2013.

"Global Internet penetration rate from 2009 to 2015, by region," *Statista,* 2015.

Goel, Vindy, "Facebook Sales Beat Forecasts, but Expenses Increase Even Faster," *The New York Times,* January 29, 2015, B3.

Goyette, Braden, "Cheerios Commercial Featuring Mixed Race Family Gets Racist Backlash (VIDEO)" *Huffington Press Business,* May 11, 2013.

Griffiths, James, "China blocks thousands more websites as 'Great Firewall' targets cloud services," *South China Morning Post,* November 18, 2014.

Guynn, Jessica and Ryan Faughnder, "Some teens aren't liking Facebook as much as older users," *Los Angeles Times,* May 30, 2012.

Hiltzik, Michael, "Anthem is warning consumers about its huge data breach," *The Los Angeles Times,* March 6, 2015.

Horwood, Gail, "Developing a global digital strategy," *McKinsey Insights & Publications,* October 2014.

Houghton, Bruce, "Spotify Plans Global Expansion, Says Top Exec," *Hypebot,* July 21, 2014.

Isaac, Mike, "Square Expands Its Reach into Small-Business Services," *The New York Times,* March 9, 2015, B1.

Issac, Mike and Michael de la Merced, "Why Apps for Messaging Are Trending," *The New York Times,* Jan. 26, 2015, B1, 6.

"Internet Users by Country 2014," *Internet Live Statistics,* 2015.

Jacobs, Jeff, Pallav Jain, and Kushan Surana, "Is sports sponsorship worth it?" *McKinsey & Company,* June 2014.

Kemp, Mary Beth, "CMOs Must Connect the Dots of the Online Brand," CMO & Marketing Leadership Professionals, *Forrester,* July 27, 2010.

Kumar, V., Xi (Alan) Zhang, and Anita Luo (*2014*) Modeling Customer Opt-In and Opt-Out in a Permission-Based Marketing Context. *Journal of Marketing Research,* August 2014, Vol. 51, No. 4, pp. 403–419.

Lange, Chris, "Market Verdict: Home Depot Hack Not as Bad as Target Hack (So Far)," *24/7 Wall Street Newsletter,* September 4, 2014.

Larson, Christina, "In China, It's Meet Me at Tmall," *Bloomberg Business,* September 11, 2014.

"Levi's: Commuter Fall 2014," *Creativity*, 2014.

"List of Countries by Internet Usage (2014)," *Internet Live Statistics*, 2015.

Manyika, James, Jacques Bughin, Susan Lund, Olivia Nottebohm, David Poulter, Sebastian Jauch and Sree Ramaswamy, "Global flows in a digital age," *McKinsey Global Institute,* April 2014.

Marantz, Andrew, "The Virologist," *The New Yorker*, January 5, 2015, 20–26.

McDuling, John, "Spotify's relentless global expansion will include Japan, eventually," *Quartz*, August 12, 2014.

Olanrewaju, 'Tunde, "The rise of the digital bank," *Financial Times*, October 25, 2013.

Olson, Parmy, "Teenagers say goodbye to Facebook and hello to messenger apps," *The Observer*, November 9, 2013.

Ovide, Shira and and Evelyn Rusli, "Microsoft Gets 'Minecraft'—Not the Founders," *The Wall Street Journal*, September 15, 2014.

"Quarterly Retail E-Commerce Sales, 1st Quarter 2015," *U.S. Census Bureau News*, May 15, 2015.

Reuters, "German case on Uber sedan service referred to European court," *Reuters Business*, May 18, 2017.

Ryan, Marco, Andy Sleigh, Kai Wee Soh and Zed Li, "Why gamification is serious business," *Accenture Outlook,* No. 1, 2013.

Scott, Mark and Melissa Eddy, "German Court Bans Uber Service Nationwide," *The New York Times*, September 3, 2014, B3.

"Share of the Internet economy in the gross domestic product in G-20 countries in 2016," *Statista*, 2015.

"Share of U.S. population that have listened to an audio podcast in the last month," *Statista*, 2015.

Sisario, Ben, "CD-Loving Japan Resists Move to Online Music," *The New York Times*, September 16, 2014, p. A1.

Smith, Ethan and Daisuke Wakabayaschi, "Apple, Feeling Heat From Spotify, to Offer Streaming Music Service," *The Wall Street Journal*, June 1, 2015.

Snelling, Dave, "Shock as WhatsApp, iMessage and Snapchat face UK ban," *Daily Star*, January 14, 2015.

Timmons, Heather, "How the New York Times is eluding censors in China," *Quartz*, April 5, 2015.

Toubia, Olivier and Andrew T. Stephen, "Intrinsic vs. Image-Related Utility in Social Media: Why Do People Contribute Content to Twitter?" *Marketing Science,* Volume 32 Issue 3, May-June, 2013.

"U.S. E-Commerce Sales as Percent of Retail Sales Chart," *YCharts Quarterly E-Commerce Reports*, April, 2015.

"Volkswagen China: Building the People's Car," *Pixomondo*, 2014.

Weed, Julie, "Welcome to the Haiyatt. In China, It's Not the Hotel It Sounds Like," *The New York Times*, April 29, 2014, B1.

Wingfield, Nick, "In E-Sports, Video Gamers Draw Real Crowds and Big Money," *The New York Times*, August 31, 2014, A1.

Woetzel, Jonathan, Gordon Orr, Alan Lau, Yougang Chen, Michael Chui, Elsie Chang, Jeongmin Seong, and Autumn Qiu, "China's digital transformation," *McKinsey Global Institute*, July 2014.

"World Internet Usage and Population Statistics," *Internet World Statistics*, December 31, 2014.

Xie, Lijia (Karen), "Marketing on the Move: Understanding the Impact of Mobile on Consumer Behavior," *Conference Summary*. Philadelphia, PA.: Marketing Science Institute, February 27–28, 2012.

Yeomans, Matthew, "How to tell sustainability stories on social media," *The Guardian*, Feb. 17, 2014.

ENDNOTES

1. See Scot and Eddy, 2014.
2. See Reuters, 2017.
3. See "Quarterly Retail E-Commerce Sales, 1st Quarter 2015" and "U.S. E-Commerce Sales as Percent of Retail Sales Chart," 2015.

4. See "Share of the Internet economy in the gross domestc product in G-20 countries in 2016," 2015.

5. See Manyika et al., 2014

6. See "List of Countries by Internet Usage (2014)," 2015.

7. See Manyika et al., 2014.

8. See Larson, 2014.

9. From Beech, 2015.

10. See Grifths, 2014.

11. See Timmons, 2015; Blanchard, 2015.

12. See "World Internet Usage and Populaton Statistics," 2014.

13. See Woetzel et al., 2014; Blanchard, 2015.

14. See Paypal Corporate website.

15. See Olanrewaju, 2013.

16. See Anderson, 2015; Lange, 2014.

17. See Baeb, 2014.

18. See de la Merced, 2015.

19. See Weed, 2014.

20. See Xie, 2012.

21. See Toubia and Stephen, 2013.

22. See Marantz, 2015; Isaac, 2015.

23. From Yeomans, 2014.

24. See Facebook Social Media Solutons website.

25. See Goyete, 2013.

26. See Goel, 2015.

27. See Bruich, 2012 and Cogan, 2013

28. See Balram, 2014.

29. Olson, 2013; Isaac and de la Merced, 2015.

30. See Snelling, 2015.

31. See Guynn, Jessica and Ryan Faughnder, 2012.

32. Source: Internatonal Federation of the Phonographic Industry (IFPI).

33. Sources: Boykof, 2013; Sisario, 2014.

34. See Sisario, 2014.

35. See Smith and Wakabayashi, 2015.

36. See McDuling, 2014.

37. See Houghton, 2014.

38. See "Share of U.S. populaton that have listened to an audio podcast in the last month," 2015.

39. See Gibbs and Dredge, 2013.

40. See Ovide and Rusli, 2014.

41. See Wingfeld, 2014.

42. See Citbank Singapore corporate website.

43. See "Volkswagen China: Building the People's Car," 2014.

44. See "Volkswagen China: Building the People's Car," 2014.

45. See Google Corporate website.

46. See Nuvi Corporate website.

47. See Bryson, 2014.

48. See Kumar et al., 2014.
49. See Kemp, 2010.
50. See Jacobs, Jain, and Surana, 2014.
51. See Calder, Isaac, and Malthouse, 2013.
52. See "Levi's: Commuter Fall 2014," 2014.
53. See Afsar, 2014.
54. See Horwood, 2014.
55. See "Drinking Global, Thinking Local," 2015.
56. See Jacobs, Jain, and Surana, 2014.

ABSTRACT

Hyundai experienced consistently improving consumer satisfaction ratings for the period 2001 through 2008. When U.S. auto sales fell to a 27-year low in January 2009, Hyundai registered 14 percent revenue growth versus the previous year, with a nearly 2 percent gain in market share for the brand.

Hyundai (D) concludes the four-part Hyundai case study.

HYUNDAI (D)

In 2008 the value of the Hyundai brand increased to nearly $5 billion, moving the company to 72nd on the list of the most valuable brands in the world, 12 places above where the brand stood in 2005.

The unprecedented warranty offered by Hyundai in 2000 continued to pay dividends. Not only did it build confidence among customers, but, due to decreasing costs of fulfilling the warranty, it was an even more effective marketing investment than initially believed.

The Hyundai 2007 ad campaign, "Think About It," featured ads that did not mention Hyundai by name but posed questions such as:

"Shouldn't a car have more airbags than cup holders?"

"Are car companies committed to quality, or to the phrase 'committed to quality'?"

In 2007 Hyundai introduced the $46,000 Veracruz to compete directly with the Lexus RX350 in the United States. In a drive-off contest between the Veracruz and the Lexus, according to one automotive reporter, "most of us left the event wondering why any consumer would pay [$11,000] more for the Lexus RX350."[1]

The Veracruz was followed in 2008 by the Genesis (high-$30,000 price range) to go against BMW models. Genesis won the North American Car of the Year award at the 2009 Detroit auto show.

In the period 2001–2008, Hyundai invested more than $200 million in design and testing facilities in North America. During this period, approximately 100 of their 500 designers worked in the United States and in Europe where they designed Hyunda models specifically to meet the needs of U.S. and European customers.

---

[1] *This case was prepared by Don Sexton, Professor of Marketing, Director, Center for International Business Education and Research, Columbia Business School. This case was sponsored by the Chazen Institute and the Columbia University Center for International Business Education and Research (CIBER).*

Hyundai's $25 million design center in California played a key role in developing the Santa Fe sport utility vehicle and the HCD6 concept vehicle.

Hyundai aired three advertisements during the 2009 Super Bowl and purchased time during the Academy Awards after General Motors and Ford canceled. Their ads introduced the Hyundai Assurance: finance or lease a new Hyundai and, if you lose your income during the coming year, you can return the car with no impact on your credit rating.

In January 2009, U.S. automobile sales fell to a 27-year low. Hyundai registered a 14 percent increase over sales in January 2008 with strong sales from the Sonata and Santa Fe crossover, giving it a 4.4 percent market share versus 2.6 percent in 2008.

DISCUSSION QUESTIONS

1. What did Hyundai do to improve its brand image?
2. What must Hyundai do going forward?

REFERENCES

Bloom, J. "Super Bowl Winner: Hyundai's Big Marketing Idea," *Advertising Age,* February 2, 2009.

Brown, W. "Hyundai's Mission Possible: Beat the Luxury Brands," *The Washington Post*, April 1, 2007.

Cato, J. "Hyundai Changing Strategy," *The Globe and Mail (Canada)*, October 26, 2006.

Cato, J. "Hyundai Is Betting That Two New Models Can Upgrade Its Image," *The Globe and Mail (Canada)*, April 10, 2008.

He-suk, C. "Hyundai Kia's U.S. Market Share Rises," *The Korea Herald,* March 5, 2009.

Jackson, K. "Hyundai Hits the Ground Running," *Automotive* News, February 9, 2009.

Jackson, K. "New Hyundai Ads Try to Shed Low-End Image," *Automotive* News, September 17, 2007.

Kiley, D. "Hyundai Still Gets No Respect," *Business Week*, May 21, 2007.

Kiley, D, Ilwahn, M. and Rowley, I. "Hyundai Floors It in the U.S.," *Business* Week, February 23, 2009.

So-hyun, K. "Hyundai Moves Closer to European Motorists," *Korea Times*, February 13, 2007.

So-hyun, K. "Hyundai-Kia Brand Value Rapidly Soaring," *The Korea Herald*, September 28, 2006.

ENDNOTE

1. Warren Brown, "Hyundai's Mission Possible: Beat the Luxury Brands," *The Washington Post*, April 1, 2007.

"OUR SECRET RECIPE FOR SUCCESS WAS TO bring the best of L'Oréal innovation to every country. Our mission is 'beauty for all' and I went about it through a process I call 'universalization.' It is at the core of our strategy," said L'Oréal global CEO, Jean-Paul Agon on a visit to India in January 2015. Universalization in the words of Agon is articulated in the statement: "We respect the differences among our consumers around the world. People don't have the same skin or hair. The traditional concepts of beauty change as you travel the world. Climates differ. We have global brands, but we need to adapt them to local needs." L'Oréal began entering emerging markets around the world in 1991 and by 1997—when Agon was made managing director of Asia zone—it was already operating in India.

L'ORÉAL IN INDIA: BACKGROUND

India is geographically a vast country with the second largest population in the world of 1.25 billion people. It is an emerging market economy with vast potential for consumer products. Beauty and personal care products, including cosmetics and toiletries, are one of the fastest-growing retail segments in India. The burgeoning Indian cosmetics market offers promising opportunities for both domestic and foreign companies. The Indian cosmetic market, which was traditionally a stronghold of a few major domestic players like Lakme and Ponds, has seen a lot of foreign entrants to the market during the last two decades. Among these foreign entrants is L'Oréal.

L'Oréal is an international company set up in 1909 in Paris by young chemist Eugène Schueller. It operates in six geographic zones around the world in 130 countries with the mission of beauty for all. Through its four divisions, it offers 28 international brands. Global revenue of L'Oréal is €22.53 billion with net profit of €4.91 billion in 2014. It has been operating in India as L'Oréal India as a private limited company since 1994 and is among its fastest growing subsidiaries around the world. In India, L'Oréal India operates in four businesses of consumer products, luxury products, professional products, and active cosmetics. The product lines are hair care, coloring, skin care, make-up, and perfume. Its major brands in consumer products are L'Oréal Paris, Garnier, and Maybelline New York. In luxury products it has Kiehl's, Lancôme, Ralph Lauren, Giorgio Armani, and Diesel. It also offers professional products such as Matrix and Cheryl's cosmeceuticals and active cosmetics like Vichy.

Jean-Christophe Letellier joined L'Oréal India in 2013 as the country manager and is now managing director. Dinesh Dayal played a key role in establishing L'Oréal India in 1994 and was appointed chief operating officer and director of external affairs. The other members of the executive team are Mohit James, director of human resources; Satyaki Ghosh, director of consumer products; and Aseem Kaushik, director of professional products. L'Oréal employs about 1500 people in India. It

[1] This case was written by Dr. Azhar Kazmi, Visiting Professor of Management at King Fahd University of Petroleum & Minerals, Dhahran, Saudi Arabia and Dr. Adela Kazmi, Lecturer in Management at Sophia College, Ajmer, India. It is intended for class discussion and not to illustrate effective or ineffective handling of a managerial or administrative situation.

has its headquarters at Mumbai, four regional offices across India, a factory in Pune, research and innovation centre at Mumbai, and advance research centre at Bengaluru.

GROWING DEMAND FOR COSMETICS IN INDIA

India has had a long history of using henna, perfumes, kohl, and flower fragrances. Indians have traditionally been using natural ingredients to make cosmetics and toiletries. Historical evidence shows that the ideas of self-beautification and use of cosmetics, both by women and men, in ancient India were prevalent. The deep understanding of the use of cosmetics in Indian history is evidenced in the cosmetic practices interwoven with seasons, daily rituals, longevity, health, and happiness. The concept of cosmetics in India has been products not just to enhance beauty or conceal ugliness but to ensure nutrition, health and well-being.

According to estimates by market research agencies, including Euromonitor, the market size and forecast for India was about U.S.$10.36 billion in 2014 expected to grow to U.S.$13.48 billion by 2018. Seen in comparison to the size of market in USA at U.S.$79.5 billion in 2018, the Indian market seems to be quite small. Even comparing it to China—that is likely to have a market size of U.S.$65 billion or Brazil at U.S.$59 billion in 2018—the Indian market is small and is nearly equal to that in Russia where the market is declining. The per-capita consumption of beauty and personal products in India is estimated to be quite low at U.S.$8.2 in 2014 and likely to grow to U.S.$10.1 by 2018. The highest consumption is in Brazil which, by 2018, is likely at be at U.S.$283.4 per person followed by that in USA at U.S.$242.2. China with its huge population has nearly five times more consumption per person as compared to that in India. India permits entry of imported cosmetics and they have had a major impact on the Indian market. Imports of cosmetics and toiletries products have been growing in recent years at a healthy pace.

The small market size, low per-capita consumption, and increasing imports in India are all indicators of the growing market for beauty and personal care products in India.

WHAT FACTORS DRIVE DEMAND FOR COSMETICS?

There are a number of factors that are seen as driving the demand for cosmetics and toiletries in India. Among these are: the emergence of a young urban elite population with increasing disposable income in cities; the rise of the aspirational class in rural and semi-urban areas that want to share the fruits of economic development; and an increase in the number of working women. There are also significant factors such as changing lifestyles of Indians, increased affordability of lifestyle-oriented and luxury products, desire to experiment with brands and products, penetration of satellite television, freer imports, and increasing appetite for Western goods. Indians have also experienced greater product choice and availability, rising awareness of products and brands, and the emergence of e-commerce in recent years. The growth of Indian film industry and fashion industry and crowning of many Indian women at international beauty pageants has also proved to be beneficial to the prospects of cosmetics and toiletries industry in India. Indian consumers tend to look toward Indian as well as international brands as lifestyle-enhancement products. Foreign products have enhanced growth of the Indian market by attracting aspirational consumers and most Indians generally perceive foreign brands as being of superior quality.

COMPETITION IN THE INDIAN COSMETICS INDUSTRY

In India, the cosmetics and toiletries industry could be broadly divided into the organized and unorganized sectors. The organized sector has three kinds of firms: multinational firms such as Hindustan Unilever, P&G, Colgate-Palmolive, L'Oréal, Revlon, Estee Lauder, Amway, and Avon. The second category is of large Indian firms, several of them international companies, such as Dabur, Godrej, Marico, Emami, Himalaya Herbals, Bajaj Corp, and Jyothi Labs. The third category of firms is micro, small, and medium-sized companies of which there were estimated to be more than 65,000 registered and unregistered units in 2011. The multinational companies, such as L'Oréal, compete with other multinational companies and large Indian companies in the Indian cosmetics market.

The potential size and the growth of sales of cosmetics and toiletries in Indian markets has encouraged more domestic companies to invest in growth and has attracted a large number of foreign companies into India. These companies, mostly from developed economies, face stagnation in their own markets and look to markets in developing and emerging economies such as China and India to fuel their continued growth. The Indian market, for instance, is experiencing double the growth that is seen in U.S. and Europe.

There is a large number of Indian and foreign companies vying for a share in the growing market. Competition is intense in view of the fact that the cosmetic and toiletries market is an open market and imports are allowed freely into India. Indigenous products have been doing well in the market against stiff competition from foreign products despite the latter being perceived as having better quality. Global brands face tough competition from long-entrenched domestic companies who have intimate knowledge of the local markets and decades of customer loyalty. But foreign companies are learning fast and responding with competitive moves of offering smaller packs, adopting natural, herbal, and Ayurveda formulations, setting up research and development centres, and generally trying to understanding the discerning Indian customer and her preferences and capacity and willingness to pay. "Ayurveda" literally means "science of life" and the term refers to the traditional Indian healing system based on herbal medicines and treatment, and yoga and dieting.

It is evident that, with intense focus on urban markets, the competitive arena is already crowded. Moving into the suburban and rural areas requires companies to hone their sales and distribution skills, speak to their customers in a language and idiom they understand, and make them identify brands and logos.

L'Oréal is believed to be placed at third position in Indian urban markets behind Hindustan Unilever and Colgate-Palmolive. With acquisition of Cheryl's Cosmeceuticals in 2013 it already is the leader in the professional products segment in India. It does not seem to have a plan to move into the burgeoning rural market believing that it does not have relevant products for such markets. However, it keeps its options open by acquiring Indian companies to enter herbal and Ayurveda segments through acquisitions, joint ventures, and partnerships.

THE INDIAN COSMETICS CONSUMER

Multinational companies, such as L'Oréal, face the major challenge of understanding the Indian customer. She is very different from the type of customers they cater to elsewhere in the world especially in the markets in Europe and U.S.

Consumers, especially among the growing number of working women in metros, like to pamper themselves and spend more on beauty and personal care products. Increasingly, it is not just women who are interested in buying cosmetics but there is a growing market for male grooming products. Indian men have a very different attitude to using cosmetics than their foreign counterparts. For instance, they are not ashamed of using their sisters' or wives' face cream or trying out their hair colouring. Demand is rising not just in the metropolitan cities but in smaller cities and towns. The consumption patterns are also undergoing change as earlier girls in schools and colleges did not wear make-up, but now they start early. This segment is growing but most companies seem to be focusing on the core segment of working women in metros aged between 21 and 28. Women in smaller towns use more of colour cosmetics after they get married; otherwise, it is occasion-based usage in India. Customers in these markets are price-sensitive, aware of the ill effects of chemical-based cosmetics and thus prefer natural and Ayurveda products.

How the products are used by Indian consumers also differs in some cases. For instance, oiling hair is a phenomenon unique to India. In many countries, nourishment is all about anti-dryness, while in India it is also about strength and beauty. L'Oréal was quick to latch on to this understanding and launched a shampoo brand, 6 Oil Nourish, based on oils for dry hair. The marketing personnel of L'Oréal realized it was a struggle to get people in their Paris headquarters to understand this launch since they could not understand how Indians like to use hair oil.

Indians have traditionally been perceived to be savers than spenders. Yet, there is a subtle change in behaviour affecting the spending pattern of consumers indicating that there is greater willingness to loosen the purse strings and start living for today than saving for tomorrow. This trend suits companies such as L'Oréal as they usually cater to the premium segment of the market.

L'Oreal Target Market in India

Copyright © by Azhar Kazmi. Reprinted with permission.

The likely areas for growth include colour cosmetics, fragrances, specialized skin care and hair care products, professional salon items, and makeup cosmetic products. In the skin care segment, the Indian consumer faces specific skin problems and looks for expertise in solving them. She also aspires to use international premium skin care brands. The shampoo segment is seeing consumers moving beyond basic hair washing to specific hair needs such as hair loss and baldness. The hair oil segment traditionally has had nearly half of consumption coming from purchase of loose hair oil which is perceived as having association with nutrition. There is growing awareness of better quality in packaged hair oil.

MARKETING COSMETICS IN INDIA

Positioning and branding is important in cosmetics and toiletries marketing. Association with foreign companies' names may make the Indian customers perceive them as better quality. Herbal content or Ayurveda base may attract many types of customers who are interested in cosmetics that have no side effects. In addition, the plethora of cosmetics products in the market makes it imperative for the positioning to be clear and focused. Positioning for premium segment of cosmetics is aimed at product differentiation. The success of Hindustan Unilever's Fair & Lovely cream serves to show the importance of positioning as it is marketed as a "change of destiny" product that makes the women transform in many ways and not just skin deep. L'Oréal's tagline of "because you're worth it" gives a hint of its positioning as making its customer feel valued and good about herself. L'Oréal's exclusive focus has enabled it to make more targeted investment in research, innovation, and advertising growing to be a formidable force in the industry. In colour cosmetics, L'Oréal is the leading provider while it has made strong strides in skin care through a number of launches based on cutting-edge technology.

Pricing is a sensitive issue in Indian cosmetic and toiletries industry owing to several unique factors. There is an impression that the Indian customers want the best but are not always willing to pay for the best. This may not really be true for the younger customer yet, generally, the Indian customers are indeed price-sensitive. The large number of foreign companies has had to grapple with the issue of appropriate pricing for their products. Normally they responded by bringing down the prices to cater to the preferences and budgets of the Indian consumer. Cosmetic and skin care packaged products manufacturers are targeting the masses with value brands cheaper by 20-30 percent from their existing lineup of brands. Companies such as L'Oréal known for their premium products have had to widen their product portfolios to include value products. Several companies have adopted the mode of offering smaller pack sizes to make them more affordable and this tactic has enabled those companies to capture market share. Hindustan Lever and Revlon were the first to introduce small pack sizes. Developing innovative pricing strategies is also very important, as India is a very price-sensitive market. L'Oréal attempted innovative pricing through offering Garnier Black Naturals in 2014 as upgrade from powder hair dye. For a single application the pricing was half-a-dollar. This product was positioned as a bridge product to motivate consumer to move up the consumption ladder toward higher-priced products gradually.

Distribution plays a key role in cosmetics and toiletries as they are included within the broad area of fast-moving consumer goods having repeat purchases. There are several distribution formats that have developed over the years. Broadly, the distributors fall into two groups of store-based retailing and non-store retailing. Among the store-based retailers are the grocery retailers and non-grocery retailers. Grocery retailers are of a large variety among them discounters, small grocery retailers, supermarkets, and hypermarkets. Non-grocery retailers are pharmacies, beauty specialists, department stores, variety stores, and mass merchandisers. Non-store retailing is done through direct selling, e-commerce or e-tailing, and home-shopping.

Google India's "Women & Web study," released in 2013, revealed that 60 million Indian women were online with 24 million of them accessing the web every day. These women seem to be increasingly searching for skin care and hair care among other things, with almost a quarter of these queries originating from mobile phones. L'Oréal was one of the most popular brands that women were searching on the Internet. This shows the significance of using online channels of selling and marketing communication for cosmetics companies such as L'Oréal.

Marketing communications play an extremely important role in cosmetics and toiletries industry. Factors such as rapid growth of the industry in recent years, increasing range of cosmetics products, entry of foreign companies, tougher competition, and emergence of satellite television and Internet has made marketing communication critical. Indian consumer is constantly exposed to advertisements and information of new cosmetics and personal care products.

L'Oréal India has retained the advertising agency Maxus India for all its media business including print, radio, and television, except digital. The focus of cosmetics brands in India is on women of today creating campaigns that try to catch attention for top-of-mind reference. For doing this, the companies are going all out on the digital space. Digital media has also become a platform for cosmetics brands to launch new products and create awareness about them. L'Oréal created a special app for the Cannes Film Festival. Women from across India had to pass stages of a contest—from dressing up and posting pictures of themselves on the "red carpet" to get a feel of being on the actual red carpet of one of the most celebrated international film festivals. L'Oréal relies on endorsements from popular Indian film actors such as Aishwarya Rai, Sonam Kapoor, Freida Pinto, and Katrina Kaif to publicize its products.

There are instances where misleading advertisements that make exaggerated claims about the capability and performance of the product have been created. Advertisements for fairness creams, which make up a large chunk of skin cream segment in India, have particularly been accused of depicting people with dark skin as being inferior to those who are fair. L'Oréal has had its share of complaints with regulatory authorities for instance in the case of its Total Repair 5 Shampoo advertisements not being backed up by data and test reports of efficacy.

Market segmentation mostly uses price as the basis creating premium and mass segments. The premium segment is a smaller, niche market with high-quality, better-packaged and higher-priced products. The mass segment is a high-volume and low-price segment that is aimed to attract first-time users among lower and middle classes who aspire to use cosmetics but cannot afford the highly priced ones. Multinational companies such as L'Oréal tend to rely on the premium segment more than the mass segment that is the preserve of local companies in the small and medium sector.

Globally, L'Oréal operates strict brand segmentation across its portfolio to retain its exclusive brand identity. For instance, for each of its brands L'Oréal maintains distinct retailing channels to keep its brand image intact. Its premium ranges Lancôme and Yves Saint Laurent are marketed through department stores while the mid- and lower-tier mass brands L'Oréal Paris and Garnier share the same retailing space but the distinctions are made on the basis of price and product offerings. L'Oréal also sells its premium-range formulations under L'Oréal Paris reserving it for urban consumers using Garnier to penetrate low-income consumers in emerging markets such as India. For premium and mid-tier brands, it launched more targeted products whereas for mass brands such as Garnier the focus has been on multi-functionality.

TAMING THE INDIAN MARKET THE HARD WAY

It has been an uphill task for foreign companies such L'Oréal to crack the Indian market and understand the Indian consumer. Among the approaches it has adopted is to target salons and hairdressers and encourage them to espouse L'Oréal products. It has set up 50 academies across India where it trains 150,000 hairdressers annually in the art of colouring, styling, perming, straightening—all using its own products. The academy offers a diploma in hairdressing. This approach has resulted in benefits for the small salons and individual hairdressers too in a highly unorganized Indian market. To L'Oréal it has brought loyal customers and hard-earned success where earlier attempts by companies such as Schwarzkopf of Germany with global brands did not succeed. Across India, it is common to find L'Oréal as the brand of choice for hair colour with the hair colour segment contributing to nearly 20 percent to L'Oréal's sale in India.

Another aspect of L'Oréal marketing strategy in India is to rely on research and innovation (R & I). This is necessary as Indian markets are very different from other markets that L'Oréal operates in. L'Oréal started focusing on R & I quite early and had a small R&I centre at its manufacturing facility in Pune. In 2013, it commissioned a larger R&I centre in Mumbai and in 2014 it launched a phyto-chemistry laboratory for basic research in Bangalore. Letellier, the CEO says that "Our only chance to be big in India is to invent new products, new categories. R&I is at the heart of our strategy here." Most R & I efforts aim to study the Indian preferences for cosmetics and translate them into products that are successful in the competitive markets. Examples of efforts include experimenting with different dye formulations on Indian hair, trying out myriad hair colour options suited to the Indian hair, and creating hair oils and facial creams for use in hot and humid climate. The phytochemistry laboratory is involved in trying out different traditional products such as henna to increase their efficacy and learning the use of Ayurveda ingredients in new formulations.

FUTURE PROSPECTS IN INDIAN COSMETICS MARKETS

A growing industry such as the cosmetics and toiletries industry in India offers exciting prospects but poses daunting challenges too. There are various challenges both to the domestic as well as foreign companies operating in India. These range from rising intensity of competition to regulation and safety requirements to be met.

Competition intensity has been on the rise making cosmetics companies respond in various ways. Domestic companies compete to protect their turf. Foreign companies compete to first gain a beach-head, venture into the market, and then hold on to their market share in the face of onslaughts from both domestic and foreign players. At present, the foreign companies such as Hindustan Unilever and Colgate-Palmolive are in the lead. They continue to leverage on their brand name, reach into the markets, and wide product portfolio. There are frequent launches of their international brands into the Indian market catering to customers willing to adopt or switch to pricey products due to their rising aspirations and disposable income. However, high import duties and packaging cost are still keeping many foreign companies away from the Indian markets. In addition, the price-conscious consumer remains an enigma as well as an irritant to the foreign companies. Domestic companies like Dabur whose product differentiation is based on natural and herbal products continue to hold their sway over the market.

To the foreign companies, understanding of Indian consumer behavior has been a lesson in un-learning many of the conventions and practices they are used to in their home markets. For instance, skin whitening is a unique feature of the skin care segment in Indian markets. To this companies have been adding other features such as skin brightening and spot reduction to enhance the acceptability of their products.

The widening of market segmentation to include men's grooming products is a welcome development for most foreign and Indian companies. It has helped them to widen their product portfolios and add to their sales revenue. Indian men are increasingly taking to the use of body sprays, perfumes, and other cosmetics and toiletries. Marketing communication including advertising also nudges the men to go forward and enjoy the benefits of making themselves more handsome and appealing. With rising demand from men, the Indian market is getting enlarged and many companies are coming out with cosmetic products, especially skin care products, for men. The challenge in this gender-based segment lies in catering to the specific demands of men and boys in the suburban and rural areas.

The role of modern retailing formats to sales of cosmetics and toiletries is significant. Increasing expansion of retail chains, rising footfall, more shelf space to personal care products, and Internet retailing all add up to better prospects for the cosmetics and toiletries industry. The challenge lies in adapting company's distribution channels and other marketing variables to the emerging scenario. By end-2013, L'Oréal was present in 700,000 stores, and planned to add 50,000 stores every year on an average to reach one million outlets by 2015. The company wants to dominate the urban market in which there are estimated about two million relevant stores in India. The L'Oréal's brand "The Body Shop" is doing quite well in India with good growth potential in e-commerce.

India not only has a burgeoning market for cosmetics and toiletries but is also a major hub for exports of personal care products to many countries in West Asia and Southeast Asia. The major countries to which India exports are Bangladesh, China, France, Germany, Malaysia, Nepal, Pakistan, Saudi Arabia, Singapore, South Africa, Turkey, UAE, and USA. Export of herbal and Ayurveda products also has demand in Europe and the U.S. Non-resident Indians, making up the world's second-largest diaspora, constitute a big market for Indian cosmetics and toiletries firms in some regions of the world. There is potential for L'Oréal to develop products in India and find markets for them outside. The launch of Dark and Lovely Amla Legend is a case in point where this six-pack hair relaxer and hair care product has been enthusiastically received in markets in South Africa and Kenya.

Overall, cosmetics and toiletries industry in India, which has witnessed a strong growth in the last few years, has emerged as one of the markets holding immense growth potential. New product launches catering to consumers' growing requirements will fuel growth in the industry, for which the future outlook seems exceptionally bright. Indian cosmetics and toiletries industry holds promising growth prospects for both existing and new players. Consumers are increasingly shifting toward "natural" and "herbal" cosmetic products as they are associated with bio-active ingredients and safe for human skin. Women are spending more on cosmetics as they are actively earning and spending money on grooming themselves. Men are joining enthusiastically in making themselves more presentable. Besides, rural India is also showing its willingness to look attractive. It is for the cosmetics and toiletries industry to take up the challenges and cater to the demand.

L'Oréal has prepared a blueprint to make India amongst its top five global markets in terms of revenue in 10 years. Its strategy in India includes localizing products, pushing distribution, and looking at cutting-edge India-specific innovations in its goal to reach a turnover of Indian rupees 7,000 crore (U.S.$1132 million) by 2020. On the anvil are plans to change from an urban-centric, premium products company to a mass products company in a bid to enhance the customer base from 40 million to 150 million consumers in India by 2020. L'Oréal has performed well in Indian markets owing to its focused strategies and segmented portfolio enabling it to cater to diverse customer groups. However, competitive intensity in Indian cosmetic markets is high and is increasing.

DISCUSSION QUESTIONS

1. What actions would L'Oréal need to take in order to improve its competitive positioning with respect to well-entrenched rivals such as Hindustan Unilever and Colgate-Palmolive?
2. Globally, L'Oreal does better than these rivals. But could it do better than them in India?
3. What else could L'Oréal do to localize its products and services to suit customer tastes and preferences in India?
4. Companies like Hindustan Unilever, owing to their long association with India, are perceived more as Indian companies. How could L'Oréal make itself more an Indian company providing products and services to Indians rather than a foreign company selling on its global brand name?

REFERENCES AND NOTES

Dibeyendu Ganguly, "L'Oréal builds Indian business painstakingly; now ready for the big leap," *The Economic Times*, February 28, 2014. Accessed February 8, 2015 at http://articles.economictimes. indiatimes.com/2014-02-28/news/47740340_1_l-oreal-india-jean-christophe-letellier-hair-colour.

ET Bureau, "Our mission is 'beauty for all', says L'Oréal global CEO Jean-Paul," *The Economic Times*, January 30, 2015. Accessed February 12, 2015 at http://economictimes.indiatimes.com/articleshow/46053691.cms?utm_source=contentofinterest&utm_medium=text&utm_campaign=cppst.

Euromonitor, *L'Oréal Company Profile – SWOT Analysis*, December 2012. Accessed February 8, 2015 at http://www.euromonitor.com/medialibrary/PDF/LOreal-Company-Profile-SWOT-Analysis.pdf.

Fourth All-India Survey of Micro, Small and Medium Enterprises 2006–2007, Ministry of Micro, Small and Medium Enterprises, Government of India. Accessed February 16, 2015 at http://164.100.44.182/iip/Censuses/censuses.htm.

"India's cosmetics industry may treble by 2020," *The Times of India*, December 24, 2013. Accessed February 10, 2015 at http://timesofindia.indiatimes.com/life-style/beauty/Indias-cosmetics-industry-may-treble-by-2020/articleshow/27844855.cms.

Official websites of L'Oréal Global http://www.loreal.com/default.aspx; and L'Oréal India at http://www.loreal.co.in/. Accessed February 2, 2015.

Sapna Agarwal, "L'Oreal India plans to take mass market route in growth efforts," Live Mint, December 3, 2013. Accessed February 6, 2015 at http://www.livemint.com/Companies/pPi8sRESJKWJ1NyMvJIOqI/LOreal-India-plans-to-take-mass-market-route-in-growth-effo.html?utm_source=copy.

Viveat Susan Pinto, "Our turnover will cross Rs 2,000 crore by year-end: Jean-Christophe Letellier," *Business Standard*, June 30, 2014. Accessed February 10, 2015 at http://www.business-standard.com/article/companies/our-turnover-will-cross-rs-2-000-cr-by-year-end-jean-christophe-letellier-114063000048_1.html.

AS PLANS FOR 2010 WERE BEING PREPARED, the leadership team of Teknosa, market leader in consumer electronics retailing in Turkey, was again at a juncture (Teknosa (A) describes the store chain in more detail). Attacks by foreign and local competitors had been rather aggressive and every one was declaring growth objectives. Pricing pressures had become even harder to cope with, also putting a strain on profitability. Instalment buying had come to Turkey in 2004. This had a big-bang effect in Turkey and retail sales skyrocketed. Consumers could purchase big-ticket items and pay for them in so many months through equal installments, allowing them to enjoy using the products right away. Postponed purchase intentions were revitalized, fueling retail sales.

The market was expected to resume growth again after the relative shrinkage due to the global economic crisis during 2008–09. Mr. Haluk Dinçer and Mr. Mehmet Nane (President of the Board and General Manager of Teknosa, respectively) had to decide the best strategy to follow. What course of action should be taken in order to protect Teknosa's leadership position in the market and continue its growth? Could Teknosa count on a certain store loyalty, or would that evaporate as new chains entered? Would price be less of an issue now that instalment buying had been instituted? The strategy adopted would clearly have to be guided by a better understanding of the consumers in the market.

THE TECHNOLOGY CONSUMER IN TURKEY

The transformation of retailing had been welcomed by Turkish consumers who flooded into the new stores as they opened. In fact, going to a mall became a family or social event. In a shopping mall, families and individuals could eat, entertain themselves, enjoy the lively environment, and rest and shop as they like and they could find all stores lined up next to each other in a comfortable environment.

Technology Consumer Profile

The profile of the technology consumer in Turkey slightly deviated from the general population statistics. The technology consumer was predominantly male, while the female proportion had been rising over the years, especially after the expansion of the product portfolios in the TSS channel to include major and small domestic appliances. Overall, the technology consumer was relatively more educated, urban, in his/her early thirties, bachelor or newly married. The socio-economic status of

[1] This is the second part of an abbreviated version of a case prepared by Dr. Cüneyt Evirgen with the assistance of Yüksel Kaplancık both at Sabanci University, Istanbul, Turkey. Dr. Evirgen was also a Member of the Board at Teknosa starting in 2005. The author would also like to thank Teknosa top management and Jones Lang LaSalle, Turkey for their support during data collection for the case. The case is intended as a basis for class discussion and not to serve as an endorsement, source of primary data or as an illustration for good or bad practice. Not to be reproduced or quoted without permission.

the technology consumer reflected the urban Turkish population indicating that the target group covered all strata of the population (See Exhibit 1).

Since the purchasing power of these consumers were correlated with their disposable income, demand for all price levels and types of products existed in the market.

The price sensitivity of consumers was relatively higher in white goods (home appliances) compared to the brown goods (high-end consumer electronics products such as LCD panel TVs or smartphones). The aspirational nature of technology products was a big driver of sales in consumer electronics retailers as people from all income levels visited the stores.

While sales of white goods were mostly driven by the replacement need, sales of IT products, panel TVs (plasma or LCD), and digital cameras were driven by their low penetration levels in Turkey. Cellular phones was a case of its own as Turkey had one of the highest cellular-phone usage rates in the world and cellular-phone ownership was almost 100 percent in urban households.

Consumer Purchasing Behavior

The technology consumer in Turkey made his/her buying decision on his/her own or jointly and was influenced by others in the family or others depending on the product category. Family members influencing the purchase decision also tended to vary based on the product category. Decisions regarding products for general household usage (e.g., TV, white goods, audio systems) were jointly made by the family members whereas 75 percent of cellular phones were purchased individually. Word of mouth and recommendations by relatives and close friends played a significant role on cellular-phone purchase decisions.

Children were particularly influential on computer, computer accessories, and game console purchase decisions, whereas female spouses heavily influenced white goods and small domestic appliance purchases. Technology consumers preferred to shop around and gather information about the products on their own during their store visits, but as the technical sophistication of the products increased (e.g., LCD TV, audio systems, laptops), so did the tendency to get consultancy and advice from a sales consultant in the store.

Among factors influencing purchase decision were desire to own better technology, recommendations by friends/relatives/colleagues, information and service given by the sales staff, web search, and sales promotions. However, the relative importance of these factors also significantly varied across different regions of Turkey.

For white goods, the primary reason for purchase was replacement of an existing product due to malfunctioning or getting old. In consumer electronics, by contrast, the desire to own the latest technology was a stronger motive. In purchases of game consoles, computers as well as cellular phones and recommendations by friends and relatives was another significant motive.

The primary reason for not making a purchase from a consumer electronics retailer visited was more price-related. Other reasons for not making a purchase were related to payment options offered, product not being in stock, product demonstration limitations, products on sales promotion not being available, and lack of product knowledge of the sales staff. These barriers pointed to the main challenges faced by all consumer electronics retailers.

Technology appeared to be a high-involvement product category for the Turkish consumers. The majority of technology consumers (77 percent) in Turkey were interested in using the latest technology, but were also involved in a search process (19 percent; see Exhibit 2 for figures regarding behavioral changes of Turkish consumers' regarding use of technology across the 2007–2009 periods).

The top five attributes that had the most impact on consumer electronics retailer brand equity were availability of wide variety of products, leadership, offering best shopping experience, good prices, and sales staff-related attributes. Other leading attributes included quality of products, trustability, wide distribution of stores, after sales service, responsiveness to customer need, and recommendations by others.

TEKNOSA MARKETING

Close to the Customer

A significant marketing initiative by Teknosa had been the establishment of Teknosa Academy. This was a training hub for Teknosa, particularly for the sales staff to manage retail staff turnover, continued organic growth, and changing and evolving product portfolio that demanded continuous product knowledge updating of the sales staff. The objective was to ensure that consumers were met by knowledgeable, service-oriented, professional sales staff at the stores who contribute to a rewarding and memorable shopping experience at Teknosa stores. The Academy also offered operational and procedural trainings and had an exclusive store training support group that was in the field providing on-site support to the stores. The trainings included in-class sessions, e-learning tools, model-store experience, capability-building workshops, etc.

In line with its customer-oriented business approach, Teknosa strongly emphasized to be close to the consumers and to listen to them. In order to keep up with the changing needs of the consumers and be aligned with their expectations, the marketing research budget was always kept large enough. In addition to running a series of consumer research studies on a continuous basis, a number of ad hoc research projects were carried out annually. This enabled Teknosa to be on top of consumers' needs and expectations and their evaluations of Teknosa as well as keeping track of competition and market situation.

Customer Loyalty

Teknosa Asist was introduced as the hub of after sales service at Teknosa. This service located in each store in its sub-branded format was set up to handle all after-sales service needs of the consumers. If a consumer had a need for after sales support (such as repair, return, installment, product usage, etc.) all s/he had to do was to visit the Teknosa Assist service counter and staff there responded to that need, facilitating the whole process for the consumer.

During the 2005-2010 periods, Teknosa also launched two other consumer initiatives one of which was Teknosa Guarantee. This was a service that offered extended warranty coverage for merchandise bought from Teknosa at an incremental cost for periods beyond the standard warranty offered by the brand manufacturers. The second was a consumer loyalty program, namely Teknosa Card that rewarded Teknosa consumers for their repeat business. The program also allowed development of personalized communication and special offers for Teknosa consumers.

Marketing Communications

The marketing communication program for Teknosa was multi-faceted. On one side, investments were made on brand-development communication to ascertain the value proposition of the Teknosa brand and increase its brand equity. On the other side, various campaigns were planned and executed to support and incentivize sales.

TV and radio commercials, print ads, sale promotion campaigns, social media, outdoor media, PR activities, and sponsorships were all used as alternative vehicles to support both the brand equity and sales at Teknosa. Among the sponsorships, some major initiatives were sports-related where Teknosa was the technology sponsor for the Turkish national football team, Turkish national basketball team, and the 2010 World Basketball Championship held in Turkey. Additionally, its Technology for Women sponsorship supported training programs offered for free to Turkish women particularly in less developed cities of Turkey to become computer-literate. The Technology for History program supported digitization of historical documents and archives in Turkey. Teknosa was also typically the technology sponsor for major conferences targeting the retail industry in Turkey. Additionally, working with youth-oriented celebrities or celebrity sponsorships were also used as part of the marketing communication campaigns.

Brand Image of Teknosa

Surveys among technology consumers in Turkey showed that Teknosa was leading among all brand attributes but that competitors were challenging Teknosa across different dimensions (see Exhibit 3). Leading brand attributes of Teknosa as perceived by consumers were being Turkish, leader, wide geographic spread of stores, trustable, best-quality products, and offering a wide variety of products all together. Teknosa consumers in particular noted trust, fair prices, wide variety of products and models, good payment conditions, and proximity to home or work as the leading reasons to shop from Teknosa rather than other retailers.

On the other hand, consumers visiting a Teknosa store, but leaving without making a purchase underlined high price as the main reason for not making a purchase. In fact, although industry experts noted Teknosa to be the price maker in the market, consumers perceived Teknosa to be at a premium price point. Real-time store price comparison studies carried out in the market with competitors validated the experts' opinion; however, consumers' perception was the contrary. Teknosa did not offer any private-label products and all products sold were well-known global brands.

Ongoing consumer surveys showed that customer loyalty as well as customer satisfaction indices of Teknosa had been increasing since 2006. However, while Teknosa was the most preferred consumer electronics retailer in the TSS channel, main competitors such as MediaMarkt and ElectroWorld were also steadily improving their scores on those dimensions as well.

In fact, all TSS retailers were heavily investing in media that could be tracked through syndicated media expenditure reports (see Exhibit 4). Sales-promotion communication was the strongest element in the communication mix of all competitors of Teknosa. In addition responding to all of these moves through its counterattacks, Teknosa also invested in brand building and development communication.

HOW TO STAY ON TOP?

As Teknosa expanded, it became the major retail outlet for consumer electronics product brands in Turkey. If a new product introduced in Turkey was not sold in Teknosa, its penetration success rate was seriously endangered. Hence, Teknosa became the retail channel preferred by the brand manufacturers as well. The result was that Teknosa was able to establish strong relationships with product suppliers in Turkey and run joint promotions and get their support on various initiatives.

The period 2005–2010 had been a continuous organic growth period for Teknosa. The company had 244 stores in 65 cities and 36 small towns across Turkey by the end of 2009. Moreover, market leadership was strengthened every year as Teknosa continued to gain market share year after year and grew faster than the market. Even in 2009, when the total market shrank by about 12 percent, Teknosa grew by 17 percent. Despite the growth of Teknosa, however, competitive pressure was significantly building up in the market with the entry of international consumer electronics retailers in Turkey with aggressive investment and growth objectives of their own.

DISCUSSION QUESTIONS

1. How would you describe Teknosa's market strengths and weaknesses?
2. What differentiates Teknosa from competition?
3. To what extent do you think there is some store loyalty that Teknosa can rely on?
4. What would you recommend for Teknosa?
5. The figures on store image in Exhibit 3 show that Teknosa is rated higher on virtually all features. The closest competitor is Media Mart.

   A factor analysis of the 17 image items showed two dimensions. The major one was "Leadership" (with high weights for "Trustable" and "Has wide store network" and "Good after-sales service"). A second axis was "Price," where "Has Good Prices," "Offers good payment options," and "Turkish" were highly weighted. On this axis "Sells the best quality and brands" had a slightly negative weight.

   Construct a two-axes positioning graph, and try to place the seven stores on that graph (use squares or triangles for the stores, and write the name inside). What does the graph reveal about what stores compete most?

6. Using the data on consumers in Exhibit 2, try to place the each of the five segments as a circle in the positioning graph from question 4. Make the circle roughly proportional to the size of the segment in Exhibit 2. Where is the main market? Which stores seem best positioned? Does this graph explain the preference results displayed in Exhibit 5?

EXHIBITS

Exhibit 1
Technology Consumer Profile

Gender		
	Female	31%
	Male	69%
Socioeconomic status*		
	AB	14%
	C1	30%
	C2	31%
	DE	25%
Education		
	University gradutate or above	15%
	High school graduate	38%
	Secondary school graduate	20%
	Primary school graduate	26%
	Uneducated	1%

Source: Teknosa research
*Socioeconomic status groups are defined based on the education level and occupation of people and is one of the standard segmentation variables used by in consumer marketing research studies. AB group typically represents the highest strata in terms of purchasing power while E group typically represents the lowest segment.

Exhibit 2

How do Turkish Consumers Define Themselves in Terms of Their Use of Technology

	2007	2008	2009
I always buy and use the latest technology as soon as it comes out	11%	13%	11%
I am not one of those who immediately purchase the latest technology, but I definitely begin to use it before many people do so	23%	16%	17%
I like using the latest technology, but only after a good investigation	48%	49%	49%
I would prefer using an established technology rather than trying out the latest	13%	17%	19%
I begin to use a technology only when it becomes the standard and widely available and no alternative is left	5%	6%	4%

Source: Teknosa (2009).

Exhibit 3

Brand Image for Retailers in the TSS Channel (2007) (top box scores)

	Teknosa	MediaMarkt	Electroworld	Darty	Vatan	Bimeks	Gold
Trustable	23%	9%	9%	3%	8%	6%	8%
Leader	23%	12%	6%	3%	9%	6%	5%
Good after sales service	19%	12%	4%	4%	8%	7%	6%
Recommended by others	19%	12%	4%	4%	8%	7%	6%
Cares for customer satisfaction	20%	12%	3%	4%	8%	7%	7%
Good sales service	20%	12%	4%	4%	7%	7%	5%
Understands consumers and caters to their needs	19%	14%	6%	5%	8%	6%	6%
Consumers feel close to	19%	11%	7%	4%	8%	6%	5%
Has wide store network	23%	12%	5%	4%	7%	5%	6%
Where best consumer experience is offered	21%	11%	6%	4%	8%	6%	6%
Has wide variety of electronics and technology products	29%	14%	9%	3%	11%	8%	8%
Offers the best products	25%	15%	7%	4%	8%	7%	7%
Sells best quality products and brands	23%	9%	9%	3%	8%	6%	8%
Has effective sales promotions and campaigns	19%	15%	7%	3%	8%	6%	5%
Has good prices	15%	15%	5%	3%	7%	6%	5%
Offers good payment options	20%	14%	5%	6%	10%	7%	7%
Turkish	20%	6%	5%	6%	21%	7%	9%

Source: Teknosa (2007).

Note: Bimeks, Gold and Vatan are Turkish retailers. MediaMarkt is part of Metro Group, Germany; ElectroWorld is part of the Dixons Group, UK; Darty is part of the Kesa Group, France.

Exhibit 4

**Approximate Media Expenses of TSS Channel
Retailers: 2007–2009**

(million TL)	2007	2008	2009
Teknosa	10.1	11.7	9.1
Media Markt	0.8	2.7	9.1
Electro World	1.8	1.6	4.1
Darty	0.8	2.3	2.0
Vatan	9.4	9.9	7.6
Bimeks	13.0	13.8	9.8
Gold	10.3	5.6	3.6

Source: Teknosa (2009).

Exhibit 5

**Most Preferred Retailer for Electronics and
Technology Products**

	2007	2008	2009
Teknosa	39%	38%	29%
Arcelik	30%	33%	31%
Vatan	6%	8%	6%
Gold	6%	4%	3%
Mediamarkt		1%	2%
Electroworld		1%	2%

Source: Teknosa (2009).

DEBBAS HOLDING SA IS A LEBANESE MULTINATIONAL company that has successfully established a global presence in manufacturing, selling, and installing completely integrated lighting systems. With over 2000 employees, $300 million in sales and operations in 17 countries, Debbas has now become a major player in its industry, competing with European and American heavyweights.

Some observers have viewed Middle East multinationals as "Arabian Knights," powered by the wealth of Gulf-sovereign wealth funds. However, as the Debbas case shows, there is more than mere financial muscle that can drive the success of emerging multinationals. It requires as some say managerial and leadership "concepts, connections, and competence."

Company logo

Source: Debbas.

COMPANY BACKGROUND

The development of the Debbas Group demonstrates that emerging multinationals from emerging markets is actually not a new phenomenon. César Debbas founded the company in 1910. He came from a family of artisans who originally moved from Syria to Beirut at the end of the 19th century. A visit to the Paris Exposition Universelle in 1900 introduced him to the new technology of electric lighting that was transforming European life, but was still largely absent from the Orient.

On his return to Lebanon, he set up his own electrical store in Beirut, which concentrated on providing lighting equipment at a time when main electricity was just beginning to become available. However, César was not just a trader, his artisan instincts enabled him to master the art of installation and eventually manufacturing electrical equipment. By the 1930s, his "Le Grand Magasin d'Electricité" was producing chandeliers as well as his own brand of long-lasting light bulb, the "Eternelle." Exports to neighboring countries in the region such as Jordan, Syria, Palestine, and Iraq quickly took off.

The company learned to cope with adversity, honed in response to Lebanon's history of political and economic turmoil. Its experiences during these disruptions led to a long-term commitment to its employees (many of whom have been with the company for multiple generations) and its belief in diversifying its markets. Thus, during the Civil War (1975–1990), not only did Debbas not lay off a

[1] *This case was prepared by Laurence Leigh, Professor at the Suliman S. Olayan School of Business, American University of Beirut. The case study was developed to be used as a basis for discussion in classroom. The case was developed in cooperation with Abdo Baaklini of Debbas Corporate Marketing team.*

single employee but it kept all its operations going through supplying products to its many customers elsewhere in the Middle East. When communications with Beirut became increasingly difficult, some design and engineering functions were even temporarily transferred to Debbas France, a satellite office opened in Paris.

The strength of family relationships is a cornerstone of many Mediterranean cultures and Lebanon is certainly no exception. In the case of Debbas, three generations have contributed to its ongoing stability and strength. The three sons of César Debbas, the pioneer, succeeded in complementing each other's talents in such a way that they could make individual contributions to the company's expansion without creating internal friction. Antoine, the eldest took over the commercial aspects of the business from his father in 1949. His brothers Robert and Fouad studied electrical engineering in London and Paris respectively and also joined the business. Indeed, their combination of skills and energy earned them the nickname "Les Frères Lumière." Fouad introduced new management processes and procedures into the growing organization, while Robert launched the contracting business. By 1967, the establishment of the factory in Dekwaneh, Lebanon, marked the transition of Debbas from a purely trading enterprise into a company capable of meeting the highest quality standards from its own resources.

From the 1950s onward, Debbas also obtained Middle East distribution rights for a wide range of electrical products such as Osram (light bulbs), Bega (light fixtures), and Bang and Olufsen (high-end audio-visual systems). However, Debbas continued to develop its core business of providing, installing, and maintaining sophisticated lighting systems throughout the region. The company's manufacturing operations expanded beyond Lebanon to support this activity with factories to produce panel boards, ceiling systems, and lighting fixtures established in the UAE, France, and China.

Like many successful family companies, Debbas faces the delicate balancing act imposed by wishing to maintain its family values and culture while at the same time growing increasingly global. Several members of the governing board are not immediate family members.

Debbas has offices in New York, Turkey, and Nigeria, as well as sales representation throughout the MENA (Middle East, North Africa) region. Its pre-eminence is illustrated by the company's role in providing both internal and external lighting systems for such high-profile buildings as the pilgrims' bridge leading to the Hajj sites in Mecca, the Kuwait Towers, the Rafiq Hariri International Airport in Beirut, and the Museum of Islamic Art in Qatar.

GOING GLOBAL

Debbas has a history of winning major lighting contracts outside the Middle East. For example, in Europe, the firm was responsible for lighting the Quai d'Orsay Museum and Stade de France in Paris, and the European Parliament Building in Brussels. But with its recent entry into India and China, Debbas can now be described as a truly global firm.

The company's "can-do" approach and flexibility was well-illustrated when the company prepared its bid to provide internal lighting for the construction of the New Delhi International Airport in 2010. Against fierce competition from major international firms, Debbas won the contract by agreeing to meet very demanding completion deadlines that the other bidders were not prepared to commit to.

Debbas' unique solution was to "think outside the box." To supply the many kilometers of LED lighting required, the company set up production equipment in tents on site. Craftsmen were recruited locally as well as being brought in from Debbas factories outside India. This way, the company managed to build and install both the lights and the customized ceiling fittings required in record time. Not only was the Indian client amazed by Debbas' successful completion of the job within the deadline, but its achievements led to contracts elsewhere in India including the planned new airport in Mumbai.

The newly built Indira Gandhi Airport in New Delhi, India.

Building on this outstanding success, the company's next step in Asia has been the establishment of a sales office in Shanghai and plans are being considered to establish a manufacturing facility in China as well.

MISSION AND VALUES

Debbas' mission statement is simple and clear: "We provide innovative turnkey solutions to help our clients realize today the spaces of tomorrow." The mission is supported by a set of values that have imbued its culture throughout its history. To make these clear to new recruits as the company expands these have been distilled into the following simple "IDEAL" mnemonic;

Innovate
Develop
Excel
Act Ethically
Learn

These are not just words, but guidelines for policy in relation to all company activities. For example, its commitment to Corporate Social Responsibility has led it to emphasize the most energy-efficient lighting solutions that are feasible. Normally this will involve maximum use of LED systems and, indeed, Debbas prides itself on refusing to implement energy-wasting solutions even if its clients propose them. Such a "green" approach also involves emphasizing conservation and recycling within its own manufacturing and office activities.

While "learning" may be one of Debbas' core values, the company also focuses on developing tools to disseminate its knowledge of the lighting industry. The "Debbas Academy" is an extensive training program designed to teach lighting in all its aspects. Based in the company's Beirut headquarters, the academy caters to Debbas team members as well as external parties. The Academy also offers custom-made programs in any location.

Another interesting demonstration of the company's customer-centric approach is the decision taken recently to form a subsidiary called WIP (for "Work in Progress"). WIP responds to the needs of architects and designers of smaller retail and residential spaces in Lebanon and elsewhere who are looking for original, innovative, and high-end lighting schemes. In order to specifically focus on these clients, who might otherwise have associated Debbas with major products requiring more standardized solutions, WIP has combined the talents of two young interior designers and an electrical engineer.

Although it is wholly owned by the Debbas Group, WIP is a separate design studio in order to offer a flexible and personalized service and is not required to recommend only Debbas products. Rather their team is always on the look-out for the latest innovations from producers in Italy and elsewhere. Such an "intrapreneurial" approach has not only generated a successful small business, but it also provides the Group with a window into the latest fashions and trends in the relationship between lighting, architecture, and interior design.

THE LEBANESE NETWORK

Another key ingredient in the Debbas' global expansion has been the network of contacts and culturally acclimated personnel available throughout the world by tapping into the resources offered by the Lebanese diaspora.

In the case of Lebanon, the size of the diaspora is remarkable. Compared to four million Lebanese living within the country, there are three times as many Lebanese living overseas. Successive waves of emigration from Lebanon have resulted from invasions, wars, and famine in their home country. Given the strong traditions of maintaining links with their extended families, each new group of emigrants were able to find relations who had already established themselves in distant locations in Europe or the Americas.

Unlike colonizing emigrants who could impose their own domestic culture, the Lebanese quickly learnt local languages and traditions in order to function successfully in commerce and the professions. Some argue that this is an inheritance from the Phoenician traders who operated throughout the Mediterranean and beyond during biblical times. Certainly Lebanese adaptability can be attributed to their origins in a multi-lingual, multi-confessional home country. Throughout its history,

Lebanon has had to absorb and adapt to invasions by armies or by refugees from outside (Greeks, Romans, Crusaders from all over Europe, Ottoman Turks, Armenians, French, Syrians, etc.).

Executives at Debbas are the first to recognize their debt to this "tribal" advantage. They are at ease operating in highly orthodox Muslim societies such as Saudi Arabia where Arabic is a required language. They are equally at ease doing business in French or English in Europe or the U.S. For example, when an important lighting design client recently moved from Germany to Colombia, the Colombian Lebanese community was approached to set up the necessary contacts. Even more significant, when Debbas planned its expansion into China, it was clear that they needed a Mandarin-speaking contact person to provide the necessary link with the head office. While company policy is that in all cases the "Country Manager" should be someone with strong Lebanese connections, a local should play a supporting role. A phone call to a Beirut University revealed that one of their recent graduates was a Lebanese who had studied Chinese culture and was fluent in Mandarin. A few months later, she was working for Debbas in Shanghai. The China country manager is French, with experience from Lebanon.

CONCLUSION

The first wave of successful multinationals came largely from Europe and the United States on the back of superior technology and a post-colonial world view. In many instances this was not accompanied by particular openness to the cultures of the countries in which they operated. The emergence of dynamic multinationals from emerging markets is much more a function of the ease with which the founders can adapt to different cultural environments and absorb new ideas. Countries such as Lebanon with a large and dynamic diaspora are ideally placed to do this. The journey of the Debbas Group from a back street Beirut lighting store to a multinational powerhouse in its industry illustrates the potential of this endowment. Emerging Market Multinational Companies (EMNCs) should therefore not necessarily view emigration of talented people from their home territory negatively, since their presence in overseas markets may provide an important resource that they can leverage to their advantage.

REFERENCES

Bell, J. (2009). "BRICOland brands: the rise of the new multinationals," *Journal of Business Strategy*, Vol. 30, No. 6, pp. 27–35.

Economist (2008), "The challengers—Emerging-market multinationals," Jan 12, p. 61.

Johansson, J.K., and Leigh, L. (2011). "The Rate of Penetration by Multinationals into Emerging Markets: evidence from BRIC," *Multinational Business Review*, No. 19. Vol. 3, pp. 272–289.

Kanter R., (1996), "Using Networking for Competitive Advantage: The Lippo Group of Indonesia and Hong Kong," *Strategy and Business*, No. 4, July 1, pp. 51–65.

Kotkin, J. (1992). *Tribes: How Race, Religion and Identity Determine Success in the New Global Economy*, Random House, New York, NY.

Parmentola, A. (2011), "The Internationalization Strategy of New Chinese Multinationals: Determinants and Evolution," *International Journal of Management,* Vol. 28, No. 1, pp. 369–386.

Singh, N. (2011), "Emerging Economy Multinationals: The Role of Business Groups," *Economics, Management and Financial Markets*, Vol. 6, No. 1, pp. 142–181.

DISCUSSION QUESTIONS

1. At this stage of Debbas expansion, how would you describe their strengths and weaknesses? Are these firm-specific (FSAs) or country-specific (CSAs)?

2. How would you characterize the expansion path followed by Debbas? Did they adhere to the "cultural distance" predictions? Is the expansion a waterfall or a sprinkler strategy? How did they gain the New Delhi airport contract?

3. What leadership qualities did César Debbas, the founder, display? Would these qualities be as effective in the typical professional Western company? In your judgment, how important in his success were the personal relationships in comparison to high-quality products and services? Explain your reasoning.

4. What were the advantages of the close family ties that seem to have been instrumental in Debbas' success? To what extent do you think such family ties can be detrimental?

ABSTRACT

The VW Group of Germany is facing a problem on two fronts in China. Its effort to use social media to introduce new models has backfired. A mistaken posting contrasting an aircraft disaster to its company's safety record has misfired, and the negative fallout has energized the Chinese population and domestic competitors. The company also faces political pressure from the governing communist party, displeased with the success of foreign automakers over domestic firms.

The case evaluates the record of the Volkswagen (VW) brand in the auto and truck manufacturing industry within the Chinese marketplace. It shows that the potential for VW's product line in China is great, but is jeopardized by regulation and political interference. As the traditional Chinese market is becoming highly competitive and maturing, what should Volkswagen Group's China strategy be in social media, and how can VW defend its position and embed itself more fully in the dragon?

THE CHINA REALITY TODAY

China's automotive market has the most growth potential in the world; per-capita car ownership is still remarkably low at 4.78 percent and is expected to grow significantly (Market analysis report, 2010). As of 2009, China became the world's largest automobile producer and market with annual sales of nearly 14 million vehicles significantly. In the first nine months of 2010, automobile production reached 13.08 million units, a 36.1 percent increase from a year ago. Significantly, industry growth has been primarily driven by rising domestic demand stemming from rising incomes, a growing middle class, and by supportive industry policies from the Chinese government.

Early on, China's growth markets were confined to the large metropolitan areas. With rapid modernization, however, midsized cities are now emerging as the new growth markets. More and more businesses are relocating and targeting midsize cities like Foshan, Changsha, and Wenzhou. As these cities are becoming more and more industrialized, salary level and housing price are growing rapidly, and the market growth rates are higher than in the mega cities.

The number of small-sized cities growth is the fastest among all the categories of administrative zones in China between 2005 and 2020. As mid-sized cities have the highest GDP growth rate, they will surpass, collectively, the size of mega cities in China in 2020.

China has several market opportunities for Volkswagen AG to become a competitive leader in the Chinese market. Having a full product line at the lower end for the new customers in midsized cities

---

[1] *This case was prepared by Masoud Kavoossi, Professor of International Business, School of Business, Howard University, Washington D.C., USA and Yuanyuan Li, MA in International Trade, College of Economics, Jinan University, Guangzhou, China, and Ph.D. student at the School of Business, Rutgers University, NJ., USA.*

will definitely be an advantage for the VW AG. That could mean revitalization for Volkswagen in the Chinese market. Looking from another angle, mega cities are becoming more and more crowded and saturated, and focusing on business in midsized cities would help the company avoid the fiercest competitive battles.

VOLKSWAGEN GROUP

Volkswagen AG is a German-based automobile manufacturer that operates in the auto and truck manufacturing industry. The company develops vehicles and components, and also produces and sells vehicles, in particular passenger cars and commercial vehicles. The automotive division is responsible for the development of vehicles and engines, the production and sale of passenger cars, commercial vehicles, trucks, and buses, and the genuine parts business.

The Group consists of 12 brands—luxury, passenger, and commercial: Volkswagen Passenger Cars, Lamborghini, Bugatti, SEAT, Bentley, Audi, Ducati, Porsche, Scania, MAN, Volkswagen Commercial Vehicles, and ŠKODA. Stemming from the largest carmaker in Europe, these brands come from seven different European countries. Martin Winterkorn serves as the Chairman of the Board of Management of Volkswagen AG while Ferdinand Piech is Chairman of the Supervisory Board of Volkswagen AG. Its major competitors are Ford Motor Company, General Motors Company, and Daimler AG.

Companies in the auto and truck manufacturing industry make passenger cars and light trucks. The profitability of companies in this industry depends on manufacturing efficiency, product quality, and effective marketing. Large companies have economies of scale in purchasing and marketing, whereas smaller companies compete by focusing on specialized markets. According to Market Line, the global automobile dealer industry generates more than $2 trillion in annual revenue. Leading countries for auto sales outside the mature markets of the U.S., Europe, and Japan include Brazil, Russia, India, and China (the BRIC nations), with China being by far the largest. The Chinese automotive market, based on unit sales, is larger than those of the three other BRIC nations combined.

Volkswagen is a global innovation leader. It has a strong technological record, such as developing vehicle designs and engineering (hybrid electric and pure electric engines, electric motors, and electric controls), upgrading productivity and quality (engines, transmissions, electronic control systems, and safety systems) and creating clean transportation technologies significantly (Market analysis report, 2010). Other competitors with similar technologies include domestic car manufacturers General Motors, Ford, and Honda (Young, 2013).

VOLKSWAGEN GROUP CHINA

In China, Volkswagen Group has two partnerships. The company entered early, in 1984, tying up with the Shanghai Auto Industry Corporation (SAIC). In 1990, a separate partnership was established with

First Auto Works (FAW), headquartered in Dalian, formerly known as Port Arthur, on the Liaodong Peninsula in northeast China. Joint ventures were the main form of cooperation and operation in China when Volkswagen entered China. The two partnerships helped VW to get quickly embedded into the surging China auto industry, and served well as the initial foundation of early successes.

VOLKSWAGEN Scirocco car at the BaiYun INT'L Auto-expo on April 28, 2012 in Guangzhou China.

Copyright © 2012 by Shutterstock/GuoZhongHua.

In emerging markets that are dominated by nonmarket forces, as China's is, there is an unavoidable relationship between a multinational's involvement in domestic political institutions and its market performance. The SAIC joint venture meant that Volkswagen was structurally locked into a relationship-based, cost-inefficient local supply network. The local Shanghai government and the price-insensitive institutional customers could guarantee a very generous margin for Volkswagen early on in the protected sector. That meant that the high production cost caused by subsidization of the local supply sector through inflated component prices was not a serious problem for Volkswagen. Rather, the inflated prices indicated that Volkswagen was supportive of the local development goals, helping to shore up the suppliers.

With the 2001 WTO membership, China reduced government-erected entry barriers. With the rapid increase in foreign auto manufacturers' interest in China, and the rise of price-sensitive individual customers, cost-inefficiency became a significant liability for Volkswagen. Furthermore, this problem of cost-inefficiency could not be easily and quickly resolved by VW alone. Although the Shanghai local partners could not offer any special treatment anymore, Volkswagen's former obligations to them continued. In the majority of cases, the VW assembly plant had a single supplier for each component in the local network, even though the original reciprocal relationships were no longer advantageous.

An added hindrance for Volkswagen in overcoming the structural lock-in concerned the increasing misalignment between the economic incentives for Volkswagen and the mixed incentives of the Shanghai government. In the early stage the two partners had focused on building basic manufacturing capabilities, so their incentives were largely in congruity. But now this was no longer the case. With rapid market liberalization and increased competition, Volkswagen needed to lower purchasing costs to improve the financial performance of the joint venture (JV). But the municipality of Shanghai had vested interests not only from the equity it held in the assembly JV, but also from parts supply firms that were part of the SAIC Group or located within the municipality. Moreover, SAIC had to maintain employment and social welfare benefits in the local parts supply sector. Therefore it was hard for Volkswagen to transform this local supplier network quickly enough through cost-cutting and downsizing.

With respect to downstream activities in the sales and distribution networks, Volkswagen was also locked into a hierarchical system that was originally designed for institutional users. Consequently, it could not get timely information about changing local consumer preferences, and the sales and service team were not adequately trained to serve private, rather than institutional, customers.

In fact, Volkswagen was deeply influenced by the old business model that once had made it so successful in China. The inability to shake off ingrained habits was at least partly responsible for the absence of new car models during the whole of the 1990s, and the failure of senior managers to realize the urgency of the challenges posed by the fast-changing competitive paradigm in the early 2000s. The deep downstream political involvement resulted in underdevelopment of market-based capabilities, including marketing competence and new product development. By comparison, latecomers such as GM, Honda, BMW, Mercedes Benz, Volvo, and Hyundai were not plagued by these political ties. They concentrated on the build-up of adapted China-based capabilities, such as private customer-oriented distribution system and car models, from the first days of their operations.

However, the 2008 financial crisis took a big bite out of the newcomers' China effort. Instead of investing further, many pulled back, eliminating planned investments in sales and distribution efforts. Even though the China auto market still grew rapidly, the intense competition made profits hard to come by. In this climate, VW's entrenched political ties turned a liability to an advantage. Finding it hard to extract itself from investments in China, VW management decided instead to move forward.

As other European volume carmakers sought to close factories and cut jobs, VW seized the initiative under its leader, Ferdinand Piech. He adopted an expansive world-domination strategy based on leading brands such as Audi and Porsche and also new marques such as Skoda from the Czech Republic. He managed to tame these semi-independent brands and get to grips with the global empire of factories, hiring new employees and firing underperforming executives. In 2012 Karl-Thomas Neumann was removed as head of VW's Chinese operations, supposedly for his disappointing performance, despite the juicy profits VW is making in China.

After finalizing its purchase of Porsche in 2012, Mr. Piech set the goal to be the world's largest carmaker in volume by 2018 ("VW Conquers the World," 2012). Its Group Strategy positions Volkswagen as the economic and environmental leader among global auto manufacturers by 2018 with four strategic goals:

- to use technologies and innovations to be the global leader in quality and customer service,
- to boost unit sales above 10 million vehicles annually,
- to increase before-tax return on sales at least 8 percent, and
- to be the top employer across multiple platforms.

Unique to Volkswagen is its ability to build its cars on a reduced number of platforms than its competitors allowing brand and style versatility while cutting manufacturing costs ("VW Conquers the World," 2012).

CURRENT SITUATION

In the world market today, Volkswagen AG is still expanding rapidly. Already dominating in Europe with its many brands, it is booming in China (see exhibits) and growing in America.

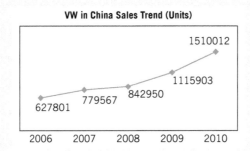

VW in China Sales Trend (Units)

Source: Volkswagen Group China (2010).

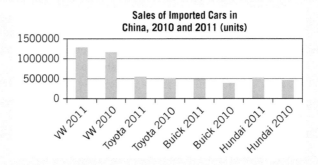

Sales of Imported Cars in China, 2010 and 2011 (units)

Source: Volkswagen Group China (2010).

China offers a big playing field for VW's future development. "We need to keep in mind that China is still quite poorer than Japan was at the time it started to penetrate the American market," said Barry J. Naughton, Sokwanlok chair of Chinese international affairs at the University of California at San Diego. "It might be that this is just a perfectly normal stage of development, and that we need to recalibrate our expectations." The auto market growth rate is above 30 percent since 2010.

However, these advances are not without consequences. China's energy security and foreign trade position are threatened as consumption is skyrocketing. Additionally, with the large population, congestion of roads and air pollution are causing environmental agencies to pressure the Chinese government for stronger regulations.

VW's new generation of all-electric and renewable-energy vehicles would have a golden opportunity in this market. However, as a foreign player in this highly regulated market, Volkswagen needs to be aware of not only current but also coming regulations and trends. How can Volkswagen maximize its competitive advantage in China?

Social Media Create Headaches

Just as things seemed to go swimmingly well for VW in China, on a sunny Saturday morning the German-based automaker's senior marketing executive woke up to find the following posting (in Chinese) on VW's Sina Weibo account:

"The rescue operation for the missing Malaysia Airlines MH370 plane is in full swing. Passenger safety is also a top priority at VW, AG, let's pray together for the 239 lives that were on board the plane. Bless them, and may a miracle occur."

Sina Weibo is China's answer to Facebook and Twitter, and with more than 500 million users it's a powerful marketing tool for companies doing business in China. The post, which the company says was up for about an hour before being removed, drew fire from Chinese social networkers who criticized the automaker for promoting its vehicles on the back of a disaster. The post was captured and reposted by numerous Sina Weibo account holders before being removed. Once a post goes viral, it's virtually impossible to remove it.

A VW spokesperson told the local *China Today* newspaper that the post originated from an outside agency the company uses to manage its digital communications. "We knew immediately this was inappropriate and wrong," said the spokesperson, who declined to name the agency in question. VW, which sells more cars in China than in EU, summoned representatives of the agency, the spokesman said. It asked for a report on the incident and ordered them to take corrective measures, he said. The damage was, however, already done.

The posting reemerged soon after it was removed VW site by hackers with additional incendiary comments to enrage the company's customers. Chinese "netizens" overcome the barriers of isolation and mutual distrust when they connect with like-minded individuals online. Agitated by crowds loyal to the emerging local brands of Cherry, Jill, and QQ, the posting quickly became an issue of national honor. Like several other foreign automakers in China, VW had already began to attract the attention of politicians in China who are concerned with foreign automakers profiting unduly. The posting added fuel to the fire.

VW has said it will rely heavily on social media and digital marketing as it unveils a wave of new products starting with the new second-generation mid-sized luxury crossover and its new all-electric vehicle. VW's PR mistake underscores the difficulties in managing digital marketing and the need to have experienced social media directors who know when something is inappropriate and risks raising ire against a brand. How should this be managed? Should they feature online ads on the website of Alibaba, the Chinese e-commerce giant, to soften the blow? Should they do a press conference? Who should be the public "fall guy," a German or a Chinese executive?

DISCUSSION QUESTIONS

- What is the competitive situation of Volkswagen in China?
- How did the political institutions in China affect VW's strategic decisions?
- Would you as the marketing manager of a domestic automaker stoke the ire against VW? Considering the reality of China's economy and institutional factors, what are the constraints on what you would do?
- What kind of plan for crisis management should VW establish? Can the political ties play a constructive role?
- Do a library search on the nature of Chinese automobile consumer. Does brand promotion play a role?

WORKS CITED

Auto dealers' industry profile in (2013). *First Research*. Retrieved from http://www.firstresearch.com/industry-research/Automobile-Dealers.html.

Auto manufacturing industry profile in (2013). *First Research*. Retrieved from http://www.firstresearch.com/industry-research/Automobile-Dealers.html.

Gan, L. (2003). Globalization of the automobile industry in China: dynamics and barriers in greening of the road transportation. *Energy policy, 31*(6), 537–551.

Forbes: Global 2000 Volkswagen. (2014). Retrieved from http://www.forbes.com/companies/volkswagen-group/.

Market analysis report: china's automotive industry in (2010). China: APCO Worldwide doi:www.export.gov.il/uploadfiles/03_2012/chinasautomotiveindustry.pdf.

Troush, S., 1999. China's Changing Oil Strategy and its Foreign Policy Implications. CNAPS Working Paper, Fall, The Brookings Institute Washington, DC.

Strategy. (n.d.). *Volkswagen Group*. Retrieved January 25, 2014, from http://www.volkswagenag.com/content/vwc.

Sun, P., Mellahi, K. and Thun, Eric, 2010, *The dynamic value of MNE political embeddedness: The case of the Chinese automobile industry*.

VW Conquers the World. (2012, July 7). *The Economist*. Retrieved January 26, 2014, from http://www.economist.com/node/21558269.

Volkswagen AGCompany Information. (n.d.). *Volkswagen AG*. Retrieved January 25, 2014, from http://www.hoovers.com/company-information/cs/company-profile.Volkswagen_AG.d73233d606131f3c.html.

Young, A. (2013, March 15). GM, Ford, VW dominate china's auto industry: Why can't Chinese companies like Saic, Dongfeng, Geely, and Gac make cars that people want to buy? *International Business Times*.

Case IV.6

Defendec: An Estonian hi-tech
start-up in the global defense
market[1]

"THINGS DO NOT JUST HAPPEN OVERNIGHT, IT takes time for technology to evolve. We want to be on top of the wave just before it becomes big," Jaanus Tamm, Defendec CEO.

Defendec is an innovative technology start-up focusing on smart dust technology development. Solutions based on this technology are designed for the security and military sectors but also for the infrastructure industry. Defendec was established in 2006 in Estonia, and in 2015 its products were used in over 20 countries of the world.

HOMELAND ESTONIA

Estonia, with a population of just 1.3 million people, is a small country in northeastern Europe. Estonia got re-independent from Soviet Union in 1991. Since 2004 Estonia is a member of EU and NATO and from 2008 NATO Cooperative Cyber Defence Centre is located there. Estonia has become also one of the leading countries as a digital society. In Estonia, where free Wi-Fi is stated as a human right, people are keen to use different e-services—for example, every citizen has an ID card, which can be used for giving signatures to electronic documents, making bank transfers, and voting by Internet on elections. Also, Estonia has e-government, e-business register, and e-tax register. All of this has given country the nickname e-stonia[1]. In 2014 the Republic of Estonia became the first country in the world offering e-residency. People from all over the world will have an opportunity to get a digital identity provided by the Estonian government—in order to get secure access to world-leading digital services from wherever you might be.[2]

These conditions have contributed Estonia becoming a hotbed of many successful start-ups. "Estonia may be tiny but in tech terms it's a giant."[3] It has been estimated that Estonia produced more start-ups than any other country in Europe per capita[4] and it has been named as "one of the next Silicon Valleys."[5] The best-known Estonian start-up is definitely Skype, which is now owned by Microsoft. Several others can be found like TransferWise (money transferring), NOW! Innovations (mobile parking), Fortumo (SMS payments), ZeroTurnaround (software development), Creative Mobile (video games), and Defendec (smart dust and security solutions). These are just some examples of globally attractive Estonian start-ups.

[1] This case was prepeared by ViireTäks, Ph.D. student, University of Tartu, Faculty of Economics and Business Administration, and Ph.D. Ermo Täks, Tallinn University of Technology, Faculty of Information Technology. The authors gratefully acknowledge the cooperation and assistance of Mr. Jaanus Tamm of Defendec Inc., and Ms. Heidi Kakko of Estonian Business Angels Network. The preparation of this case was supported by the project "The development of curricula of Tallinn University of Technology and University of Tartu in the field of innovation in cooperation with public and private sector organisations" (Project No 1.2.0402.09-0046). The case is for class use only.

FROM IDEA TO REALIZATION

Defendec's co-founders Jaanus Tamm and Tauri Tuubel's common business idea grew out from their previous business experience. When their previous company ceased to exist, they become employees again. *"After couple of years we started wondering about something big with potential to change the world. We started to follow technological trends in Internet to identify those with potential to revolutionize our lives as mobile phones once did. Then we found wireless sensor networks, an Internet of Things concept, which is going to change the world during next 10 ... 20 years,"* describes Jaanus[6] of the birth of their business idea.

Company logo

DEFENDEC®

So they started to develop *wireless sensor networks*. As soon as the business idea emerged, Jaanus and Tauri recognized a need for someone who had real relevant knowledge about technology. They found a computer scientist Jürgo Preden from Tallinn University of Technology, who became co-founder of the company. He had Ph.D. in IT and working experience in R&D from Europe and North America. He started to think how to turn this technology into applications, while Jaanus started to look for clients and Tauri started to define the product.[7]

Company, initially named Smartdust Solutions, was founded 2006. *"Our target was to find a market sector where superiority of smart dust would appear big enough outside of Estonia. The advantage of our technology appeared in areas where long distances make wiring expensive and there is a need to measure more than one parameter,"* told Jaanus.[8] Nevertheless the specific business idea was not identified immediately. Founders conducted a series of tests with sensor networks: measuring temperature and pressure of central heating pipelines, counting cars, testing ice sensors on roads, measuring vibrations in factories, and so forth.[9] Finally a solution was found with potential for bigger markets.

WHAT IS SMART DUST?

Smart dust "is a collection of microelectromechanical machines which incorporate sensors, processing capabilities, a power supply, and the ability to intercommunicate wirelessly with each other so as to form a single computing unit."[10] They are an autonomous monitoring system, allowing the encircling and monitoring of a defended area with the help of computers. For defence purposes, if the output signal is matched to the pattern of a human or a vehicle an alarm is triggered.

"These are like virtual eyes," says Jaanus. In essence we are talking about small cameras able to effectively defend very large areas.[11, 12] Detectors do have an ability to communicate independently, thus failure of one detector does not affect the capabilities of the full network. Radio-based connectivity

makes it less dependent from supporting infrastructure and easier to install them in hardly accessible areas like forests, jungle, mountain region, or desert. Defendec products do not fly in air, the hardware is compact, can be installed within minutes, and is easily hidden.

Starting in 2008 a promising marketing sector was found: border guard solutions. The first serious partner was Estonian Border Guard Board, willing to test the offered technology. A contract was signed in 2009, and in 2010 the company name was changed against Defendec to reflect the focus on security and the defence sector.

The competitive advantage of these products is the wireless connectivity and long battery lifetime. Defendec technology advantages:[13]

- Radio-based communication—provide a highly portable surveillance solution with minimum configuration requirements.
- Battery operates more than 400 days in one charging cycle.
- Up and running in minutes—the device can be installed in five minutes and it is operational right away—there are no further configuration requirements.
- Secure communications by using an elliptic curve cryptography approach developed in-house.
- Low nuisance-alarm rate. Only if the output signal is matched to the pattern of a human or a vehicle is an alarm triggered.
- Resistant to harsh weather conditions. Devices have proven to be suitable with extreme weather conditions and temperatures ranging from –42 up to +60 degrees in Celsius in real-life situations.
- Autonomous mode—the Detector automatically enters the autonomous mode in the field and no configuration is required.

Defendec has been awarded with several awards: most shining start-up in Tallinn, 2008, one of the five most promising European start-ups in European Venture Summit contest, Barcelona, 2010; in 2011, a honour from Estonian Boarder Guard Board for excellent partnership during build-up of border surveillance system and securing the border.

DEFENDEC PRODUCTS

In 2015 Defendec offers two different products: a border-guarding solution named Smartdec and a surveillance system for oil and gas producers named ReconEyez. In 2015 *Smartdec* had clients in Estonia, Ukraine, Romania, Albania, Monte-Negro, Bulgaria, but also in Mexico, Colombia, Kyrgyzstan, Tajikistan, and others. The proof of its value is the amount of smuggled goods and number of captured illegal immigrants in some of these border areas.

Defendec's second product is *ReconEyez*. It is similar to Smartdec, but is meant for infrastructure surveillance like oil or gas pipelines together with its warehouses and production sites. The solution allows reducing amount of thefts, terrorism incidents, and naturally or technologically originated catastrophes.

The potential market of this product is very big. Oil and gas thefts can reach up to 54 billion dollars yearly and involve about 36 percent of all environment-related crimes.[14] ReconEyez offers clients a service strategy for monthly rental of hard- and software which in some areas is the preferred solution.

Revenues for Defendec are growing year by year, doubling every year starting from 2013.

COMPETITION

The generic competition for Smartdec is offered by "blind" technologies, like seismic sensors, military unattended ground sensors, and the usual passive infrared sensors. Seismic sensors are mostly used in desert areas, plains, and inside fenced areas to detect movements. These have to be calibrated depending of the type of soil and have to be buried. In case there are a lot of roots from trees or seismic activity, these sensors can generate a lot of false alarms. The newest sensors can also follow groups of people and differentiate vehicles. Seismic sensors can also find out the direction of movement in monitored areas.

Potential competition for Smartdec consists of video surveillance, unmanned aerial vehicles (UAVs) and satellites. A major advantage of those is the huge monitoring area they can cover. UAVs are also capable of performing video tracking. At the same time these technologies do have other weaknesses, in particular high prices.

ReconEyez is a main competitor with video surveillance systems. It is effective only if suitable infrastructure exists. ReconEyez does not work in inaccessible regions with missing infrastructure.

Smartdec technology does not have cost-efficient alternatives in remote areas with harsh environment and lack of infrastructure.

Jaanus describes[15] competition as the following: *"Competitor does not always mean someone offering similar solutions. Competitors are those who go after same money on the same market. If client has a choice to buy our sensors or video surveillance cameras or radars, then our value offering should be better, containing more benefits."*

UAVs and satellites can in fact complement Smartdec technology in a way where Smartdec uncovers suspicious-activity hotspots and UAVs or satellites could be directed to the area, monitor, and take photos for later analysis.

GLOBALIZATION

Defendec has been a global company from the very beginning. *"From the first day we had access to all EU member state border guards and could negotiate directly with all of them,"* emphasizes Jaanus.[16] At the year 2015, has been projected 95 percent of turnover generated outside of Estonia.

Nevertheless Estonia was the first client and it is hugely important selling argument. *"Clients always ask whether our solution is in use in Estonia,"* says Jaanus.[17] The fact that the Defendec product is actively used in border of EU, NATO, and Russia is a strong selling argument. Because of this, Estonia as brand sells very well in Middle Asia, Europe, and Caucasus. In some countries more explanations are needed, because Eastern Europe's reputation is not good everywhere. In 2015 Southeast Asia was left aside, because it is extremely expensive to enter this market and Estonia lacks relations and competition advantage in this region.

During 2014, Defendec has started to cooperate more with its U.S. partners who finance several joint projects in foreign countries. Differently from previous entries, Defendec has started to incorporate a company in the U.S. A U.S.-Estonian company enables it to benefit from both countries' good advantages and offer high value to the customers.

ENTERING NEW MARKETS

"Choosing the target country a key role is played by local partners and presence of interested client. If one of those is missing- partner or client, we do not deal with this market," explains Jaanus.[18] Language barrier can be an obstacle in countries where the main language is neither English nor Russian. That is another reason why they need partners before entering the new market.

In 2011 the company probably made a mistake and globalized too quickly. Jaanus describes this as the following:[19] *"We did not plan our sales process well enough and if you do not have time and money to follow client needs, then it is just a waste of money to open too many sales processes. We opened too many negotiations in different countries and we did not have enough resources to proceed on all of these. In this sense we probably should have been more careful and been slower. If you deal with 40 countries at the same time, a choice has to be made during sales process follow-ups. If this is done right it might save a lot of time and money. Eventually we made these selections and solved the issue, but it took some time."*

Since then, preparations to enter new markets are done very carefully. It is preceded by information gathering about countries' cultures and habits and meeting with persons having done business there before. Also the background check is performed about decision-makers to market goods in the right way. A good example for such necessity is Jaanus' following experience with an important client:[20]

"I was selling my small sensors as usual, but meeting lasted only 5 minutes. Afterwards it was revealed, that this client loved big things—tanks, ships, airplanes. He just did not liked small things, such an interesting feature of the person. I did not know it then and as I tried to sell him small sensors it did not work out." Previous study of background helps to estimate the potency of the country and how complicated it is to make a business there. Also, it helps to estimate the probable length of the sales cycle.

Usually, two trips are made to estimate suitability of new markets. The company has developed a comprehensive sales process consisting of 36 steps, which is performed with suitable adjustments according to specific country needs and followed exactly.

MARKETING AND SALES

Marketing is done through fairs and direct sales. Defendec created finely targeted marketing efforts, mainly through personal contacts. Usually small events are preferred where direct sales can be performed.

Defendec's sales process has changed to an extent over the years. During the first years they believed that all the sales must be done by themselves and tried to avoid big resellers. There was a prejudice like *"we do not earn enough if we do not control fully all sales activities and it would be very easy to switch us out from this,"* shared Jaanus.[21] That way of marketing was very expensive and time-consuming. All the knowledge and experience had to be acquired by learning from their own mistakes. Although the emphasis on direct marketing still prevails, more attention is focused on system integrators with whom joint projects are developed. This presumes that one has a critical mass of references. References are important, but the peculiarity of defence sector is that not all of them can be used. *"We can use a name of the country where we have clients, but often we cannot use clients as a reference case study,"* concludes Jaanus.[22]

Sales in the defence sector are based on trust mostly. Defendec solutions are complex and border guarding is sensitive issue for countries, therefore the potential client wants to be absolutely sure about the quality of technology and credibility of seller. It is important also for Defendec to be sure whether client understands how technology works and whether it is consistent with client needs. This way later failures can be avoided. *"If there is a wish to sell, then B2B business is expecting your personal appearance and literally shake hands to close the deal—this is very important!"* explains Jaanus.[23] Social media is not useful for marketing in the defence sector. At the same time ordinary market surveys and consultants do not work well here because they offer too general information and insights that are insufficient for a successful business.

In case of companies that are selling products or services to other countries or to state institutions of other countries, the government can help. It is quite normal that top politicians do travel around and help to market their companies' products. It works especially well in cases where country policy and company activity is somehow connected. Naturally, it is expected for a company to do its work in the area of sale but the country can give some support and provide guarantees.

Another characteristic of defence sector is a very long sales cycle. It can take up to two years from the first meeting until the first contract is signed or even longer. Usually, it means a participation in the public procurement process.

FUTURE PLANS

In 2015 Defendec's solutions are in use in more than 20 countries. The company has offices spreading from Washington to Singapore, products have been sold in sum of more than 5,000,000 €, and in 2014 the company was profitable on first time.

Until 2011, the founders were able to operate based on their own capital. To open new perspectives, extra capital was needed, so they found investors from Spring Capital and WNB Projects. In 2011 Kredex (an Estonian financing institution) gave the first loan. In 2012 a venture capital institution named SmartCap invested in the company.

Defendec decided to spin-off all Internet of Things ideas and technology into a new start-up Thinnect, which will develop new platforms and applications for Internet of Things. Until 2013 Defendec developed also city light solution named Smart Cities in addition to security and defence solutions. Together with investors the management decided to separate anything that is not directly related to main business. So the Smart Cities formed the basis of the first Defendec spin-off Cityntel. There are thoughts on how the technology can be used in the challenging Afghanistan-Pakistan border, which is generally considered to be impossible to watch. Yet the resource is limited and the company has to make clear choices for the future.

The Defendec team has a lot of ideas to proceed with new *products*:

- Smart house solution, where data collected by different sensors can be used for heating or lighting.
- Smart road solutions and smart parking. It has been argued that up to 40 percent of driving in big cities involves finding a free parking slot. If a sensor network is able to detect free parking places and cars can make virtual queues, then it would be possible to reserve the parking slot and guide a car close to it.
- Smart garbage containers. Using Defendec technology it would be possible to monitor their fulfilment and make useful decisions regarding the logistics.
- Agriculture application, for example to estimate suitable seeding moments for cows.

There are also a lot of ideas about new *markets* for Defendec. Although Southeast Asia has lost its importance, it is still considered to be an attractive region. Target markets include Africa, whose potential is under investigation at the moment, and further plans are made based on resulting information.

From a business point of view the attention is more and more turned into developing relevant services. It might be desirable to expand the choice of services and hopefully more long-term contracts can be signed.

In general, business has gone well for Defendec. It is one of the few start-up companies offering concrete products for sale. Defendec has a lot of partners and big market potential in addition to innovative product lines. There are plenty of ideas to develop new products and entering new markets.

TABLE 1. Defendec timeline

Year	Event
2006	Establishment of Smartdust Solutions
2008	Investments from SpringCapital and WNB Project
2009	First Smartdec solution sales contract with Estonian Border Guard Board
2010	Renaming the company into Defendec
2010	5 positon in European Venture Summit Contest
2011	Kredex loan
2011	Honour from Estonian Police and Border Guard Board
2012	Market launch of ReconEyez
2012	Investment from Smart cap

Source: Defendec.

TABLE 2. Defendec sales and profit (€)

	2010[24]	2011[25]	2012[26]	2013[27]	2014[28]
Sales profit	205,880	340,449	658,309	1,010,046	2,100,000
EBITA	22,038	−596,665	−537,835	−799,933	600,000

Source: Defendec.

DISCUSSION QUESTIONS

1. What are Defendec's firm-specific advantages? What are the country-specific advantages?
2. What are the firm-specific difficulties in reaching new clients? What are the regional-specific difficulties in reaching new clients? How to minimize them?
3. What are the key factors in reaching new markets for Defendec?
4. Offer some ideas on how to make Defendec's marketing more effective. How would you design a marketing campaign for such a novel product? How would you differentiate the marketing of two products: Smartec and ReconEyez?
5. What kind of strategy would you recommend to Defendec—should they focus to develop new solutions or to expand to new markets?
6. Do you think the decision to focus only on the security and defence markets was a good one?

ENDNOTES

1. The e-Estonia website, https://e-estonia.com (accessed 17.03.2015).
2. Sikkut, S. 09.2014 "Become an Estonian e-resident," https://e-estonia.com/wp-content/uploads/2014/09/eResident_leaflet.pdf (accessed 16.03.2015).
3. Cassidy, N. 23.02.2014. Next Silicon Valleys: Small Estonia has big ideas, BBC News, http://www.bbc.com/news/technology-26275753 (accessed 09.03.2015).

4. Rooney, B. 14.07.2012. The Many Reasons Estonia Is a Tech Start-Up Nation, *The Wall street Journal*, http://online.wsj.com/news/articles/SB10001424052702303734204577464343888754210 (accessed 09.03.2015).

5. Cassidy, N. 23.02.2014. Next Silicon Valleys: Small Estonia has big ideas, BBC News, http://www.bbc.com/news/technology-26275753 (accessed 09.03.2015).

6. Tamm, J. An interview, saved 15.11.13 by Viire Täks.

7. Ibid.

8. Ibid.

9. Defendec: äri, mis raputab maailma. February 2011, Director, http://www.director.ee/defendec-ri-mis-raputab-maailma (accessed 09.03.2015).

10. Smart dust, Dictionary Of Engineering, http://www.dictionaryofengineering.com/definition/smart-dust.html, accessed 21.03.2015.

11. Arengufond investeeris targa tolmu tehnoloogiasse. 03.10.2012, Ärileht.ee, http://arileht.delfi.ee/news/uudised/arengufond-investeeris-targa-tolmu-tehnoloogiasse.d?id=65053002 (accessed 09.03.2015).

12. The homepage of Defendec Inc., http://defendec.com, (accessed 09.03.2015).

13. Oil Theft, *http://www.havocscope.com/tag/oil-theft/* (accessed 28.11.2013).

14. Tamm, J. An interview, saved 15.11.13 by Viire Täks.

15. Tamm, J. An interview, saved 15.11.13 by Viire Täks.

16. Ibid.

17. Ibid.

18. Ibid.

19. Tamm, J. An interview, saved 15.11.13 by Viire Täks.

20. Tamm, J. An interview, saved 06.03.15 by Viire Täks.

21. Ibid.

22. Ibid.

23. Annual report of Defendec 2011.

24. Ibid.

25. Annual report of Defendec 2013.

26. Ibid.

27. Tamm, J. An interview, saved 06.03.15 by Viire Täks.

ABSTRACT

In 1984 it would have taken a leap of faith to believe that Citibank could overcome its disadvantages in Japan to build a successful consumer banking business there. But by formulating and implementing an original strategy Citibank had a major impact on the retail financial services environment. Fast forward 25 years, and rumors began to circulate that the parent company in New York—now called Citigroup—wanted to get rid of its retail banking business in Japan because it was not profitable enough. This story deserves a happier ending, but the global banking climate may not permit a once-innovative strategy to ensure the survival of Citi's retail bank in Japan.

ACT ONE—CITIBANK ENTERS CONSUMER BANKING IN JAPAN

The Japanese Setting

Citibank, part of the huge American financial group Citicorp, was the largest foreign bank in Japan well before 1985. But given that foreign banks controlled barely 3 percent of Japan's banking assets in the mid-1980s that was not saying very much. Domestic retail banking in Japan was a profitable segment because of the rapid growth of Japan's economy and the solicitous protection the banking industry received from the Ministry of Finance. As of 1984, none of the foreign banks had targeted this market because of the daunting opposition they expected from the domestic industry and Japan's bureaucrats. As a result, they were small players there. Citibank, however, was a pioneer among large global banks. It adapted its worldwide consumer banking expansion plan when it launched into the potentially lucrative retail banking sector of Japan.

Citibank's Competitive Disadvantages in the Japanese Market

Citibank did not yet register on Japan's retail banking radar, so the first thing it had to do was to initiate a number of niche strategies to make a dent in local consumer consciousness. Segmentation was necessary, but which segment to target? Product differentiation could provide the competitive advantage the bank sought, so in Japan's strictly controlled market the real question was, "What features would make enough of a difference to lure Japanese consumers away from their customary domestic banks?" These and other problems were tackled and solved by Citi's multinational staff that

---

[1] *This case was prepared by Kenneth A. Grossberg, Professor at Waseda Business School, Waseda University, Tokyo, Japan. He was Citibank's chief strategist in the Asia-Pacific region at the time of the case. © 2015 by Kenneth Alan Grossberg. All rights reserved.*

Kenneth A. Grossberg, "Citibank: Success and Failure in Japan." Copyright © 2015 by Kenneth A. Grossberg. Reprinted with permission.

included Japanese managers. The starting point was, appropriately, market research, in order to find the chinks in Japan's banking armor.

Citibank's global logo

Japan's financial regulators hated disorderly markets the way nature abhors a vacuum. It had long been the custom in Japan to cartelize industries such as banking, essentially eliminating competition. This allowed the participating institutions to block any single competitor from obtaining a commanding market share, and ensured that all the players would get a piece of the pie. All banks of a given group, such as the major city banks (then 13, but today greatly reduced through government-sanctioned mergers) operated in concert. All were required by the Ministry of Finance to pay the same interest rates on yen-deposit products. All were required to observe a code of competitive behavior determined by their respective bank cartel's association. To break ranks and offer competitive products would create conflict with both regulators and their industry peers.

In 1985, even the smallest city bank had 41 branches in Tokyo, and the largest at the time—Dai-Ichi Kangyo—had 145. In addition, they also commanded a vast network of over 12,000 integrated ATMs which provided convenient access for their customers (see Exhibit 1) and armies of service staff to cosset retail customers the moment they stepped into a branch.

EXHIBIT 1. Branches and CD/ATM Networks of Japanese City Banks (1985)

Bank	Number of CD/ATMS	Branches in Tokyo
Dai-Ichi Kangyo Bank	1401	145
Fuji	1201	132
Taiyo Kobe	1191	99
Mitsubishi	1186	123
Sumitomo	1152	78
Sanwa	1083	66
Tokai	1053	47
Mitsui	1017	96
Saitama	753	54
Kyowa	752	82
Daiwa	715	42
Hokkaido Takushoku	623	41
Bank of Tokyo	76	19

Citibank, on the other hand, had in 1985 only two branches in Tokyo, and one each in Yokohama, Kobe, Osaka, and Nagoya, all major cities. As yet Citi had installed no ATMs and its personnel were not accustomed to dealing with small individual depositors and were not trained in customer service. Checking accounts, so popular in the U.S., were almost unknown. Instead, bills were paid in cash or via direct debit from one's bank account. To be able to direct debit, the Japanese bank had to have a relationship with the company to be paid, be it the telephone company or some other public utility. It also helped to be the bank into which the customer's employer directly deposited that person's paycheck, which gave that bank "first dibs" on that customer's cash. This system encouraged Japanese banks to cultivate long-term relationships, which instilled customer loyalty by stressing traditional Japanese service (called *omotenashi* in Japanese). Coincidentally, this system managed to exclude foreign banks from the large pool of cheap retail yen deposits.

The Customer Is the Loser

Citibank considered the cartelized system in Japan to be bad for the customer and for competition. When all banks were forced to offer the same products, at the same fixed interest rates, with strict advertising and media guidelines applied to all players, the retail customer was likely to be the loser. The postwar Japanese banking system used ordinary consumers to subsidize the cheap lending rates then made available to corporate and institutional clients. Japanese banks were at the time paying just .25 percent annual interest on savings accounts (less than the inflation rate of 1–2 percent). In the mid-1980s interest rates on customer accounts outside of Japan were quite a bit higher than that.

The Ministry of Finance (MOF) was a professional bureaucracy that stressed how much safer Japanese banks were than those in the U.S. and Europe. The average Japanese customer, having been conditioned to accept that Japanese banks were safer than foreign ones, would not be easy for Citibank to persuade that a small foreign institution could meet their needs better than the cartel member banks.

Citibank's SWOT Situational Analysis

By 1985, Citibank had been active in Japan in one form or another for eighty years, but it had always been a corporate, wholesale-oriented bank with very low visibility among the Japanese general public. In Japan's cash-oriented society the lack of branches and ATMs, meant that few Japanese companies would be willing to direct deposit their employees' salaries at Citi. It was obvious that Citibank had many hurdles to overcome if it was to succeed at building a retail franchise in Japan.

But Citibank also possessed some formidable resources to bring to the challenge. As one of the few truly global banking organizations, Citi had developed retail banking businesses in "exotic" markets as different from each other as Indonesia and Italy. And it had the strength to pursue a long-term strategy in Japan. Citi had been a pioneer in applying strategic marketing principles to banking, and it was an innovator in developing the hardware and software that all retail banks eventually came to employ, such as the ATM and the money-management account that linked all of a customer's accounts for easy management. As the largest foreign bank in Japan, Citi's words and deeds carried greater weight than their minuscule market share warranted—and they could use this to their advantage. The key lay in assembling all these elements to maximize Citi's competitive advantage in Japan's consumer banking marketplace.

The Plan

The strategy which Citibank developed in 1985 rested on three pillars:

- Augment
- Build from scratch
- Buy

Augment meant to strengthen the assets Citi already had in Japan, such as its branch network and a wholly owned finance company called Citicorp Credit K.K. (CCKK for short). *Build from scratch* referred to expanding the scope of consumer financial services beyond what already existed, such as installing ATMs and launching a new yen-denominated credit card. *Buy* meant attempting a quantum leap into the retail market by acquiring a Japanese bank.

Superficially, from the perspective of rapid market entry and penetration, the "buy" strategy seemed to be the most cost- and time-effective approach, and it was the first plan adopted. However, the closed and uniquely structured Japanese market made this assumption incorrect. Three years later Citibank finally admitted that buying a Japanese bank would not happen and so the "augment" and "build from scratch" were the only viable options. Together they gradually became the two pillars of a competitive thrust that enabled Citi to differentiate itself from Japanese banks and gain market share.

Citibank's Japan Strategy

The Basis for Differentiation.

In 1985 the average Japanese household had an income of 5.65 million yen (about $31,000 at the contemporary exchange rate of 180 yen to the dollar), savings of 6.92 million yen ($38,000), and debt of 2.5 million yen ($14,000). An estimated one million households had annual incomes of at least 10 million yen ($55,000), with average savings of 29 million yen ($161,000). Even before the yen began its historic climb, Japan already enjoyed more than $17,000 in personal financial assets per capita vs. almost $26,000 for the United States. During the late 1980s, due to continued economic expansion and the 50 percent appreciation in the value of the yen against the dollar after the Plaza Accords of 1985, these figures increased rapidly.

After researching the market Citibank decided to focus on affluent, "cosmopolitan" Japanese who were investment-oriented about their savings and liquid assets. To establish relationships with such individuals, Citi decided to differentiate both its products and its service from those of Japanese banks. This strategy had four components.

1. **Offer higher yield on foreign currency deposits.** Since there were no rules prohibiting a bank from setting its own interest rates for foreign currency deposits, Citibank decided to use that loophole to leverage its strength in this area. When it launched its first sales campaign for time deposits in U.S. dollars, the response was very strong, especially since the rate offered was about twice what a yen time deposit of the same term was then paying. In the spring of 1988 Citi upped the ante by launching an innovative multicurrency deposit product, and 1,200 accounts were opened in only 12 days. On average, 1,400 new customer relationships were formed each month.

2. **Advertise the yield advantage aggressively.** Japanese banks avoided using aggressive tactics or comparative advertising and adhered to the conservative guidelines set by the various banking associations. Citibank decided to challenge this practice by placing ads in newspapers and selected magazines, emphasizing the high interest rate being offered on its U.S. dollar time deposit. The response from the public was favorable, and though Japanese bankers and Ministry of Finance bureaucrats were not pleased, they did not go so far as to prohibit the ads. They did require the bank to add a warning to the effect that currency fluctuations could affect the ultimate return on foreign currency instruments.

3. **Introduce a different kind of banking service in Japan.** Traditional service in Japanese banks stressed courtesy and comfort, but not speed. That is why Japan's bank lobbies are furnished to this day with comfortable seating and supplied with reading matter for the waiting

customer, not unlike in a doctor's office. Waiting was very much a part of the experience. Citibank introduced banking by telephone for its retail customers—a radical departure in Japan in 1985. This helped Citi compensate for its inability to compete with its Japanese rivals in terms of bank branches and ATMs at many different locations.

4. **Appeal to sophisticated and cosmopolitan tastes.** Citibank realized that only a minority of Japanese would want to use a foreign "international" bank. The focus was therefore on a niche that included businesspeople who had overseas dealings and well-to-do individuals with considerable liquid assets who would have occasion to travel abroad and be comfortable dealing with an American institution.

Market Segmentation

Japanese banks in 1985 were not segmenting their market by customer type. Nor, as we have seen, did they differentiate their product and service offerings. Instead they served all Japanese with the same courtesy and the same sofas and magazines, and all banks offered savings accounts with the same anemic interest rate. Citibank knew that its real opportunity lay in appealing to selected segments of the Japan market that would respond favorably to its higher interest rates and unique products and services.

Professionals and Entrepreneurs

Doctors, dentists, and other professionals, as well as business owners, tend to have substantial liquid assets available for investment—and they don't like to waste time waiting in line. Citibank appealed to them by stressing its higher-yielding deposit products and the greater convenience of banking by phone.

Managerial Class Company Executives.

Among the higher-ranking salary men in large Japanese corporations a small segment had overseas living and working experience. They were accustomed to seeking out the best returns on their money, and were considered by Citi to be prime targets.

Professional Women.

Citibank saw that Japanese women in business and the professions were subjected to handicaps and prejudicial treatment. They could be attracted to Citi and become loyal clients based on the bank's American image and mystique. In fact, those women were highly yield-sensitive and somewhat more open to new products than males, as was revealed in focus-group research carried out in Tokyo in 1985 and 1986.

Expatriates.

Although the main thrust of Citibank's strategy was to penetrate the Japanese market and become "native," the foreigners (primarily Americans) working for large corporations in Japan provided the bank with a stable core of deposits with relatively high average balances. While Citi did not construct its strategy to cater to this segment, the *gaijin* were essentially a captive market. They had nowhere else to go for the kind of service they were accustomed to, such as checking accounts and efficient banking by phone. They also appreciated the easy transfer of funds between Japan and their overseas bank.

Implementation Success

It took three years to implement the strategy before it bore fruit, but then Citibank succeeded where no foreign bank ever had before. A majority of its retail customers were Japanese, and they banked with Citi despite the fact that by 1989 it still could boast only six branches. In 1987 Citibank successfully negotiated permission for its customers to use Tokyo's largest ATM network at the time, that of the Dai-Ichi Kangyo Bank.[1] This greatly improved convenience for their retail customers to make cash withdrawals all over the city. Distribution improved still more when Citi was allowed to link up with the 13 Japanese city banks' online cash dispenser network, called BANCS. With fewer than 20 ATMS of its own, Citibank was able to give its retail customers access to 20,000 cash dispensers at 3000 city bank branches throughout Japan.

As for product innovation, Citibank's strategy of offering high-interest deposit products to meet the customer need for nontraditional savings and investment options evolved into a unique, foreign currency integrated account called Multimoney. Positioning of Multimoney as a high-yield investment vehicle involved not only foreign currency and yen deposits, but gold, and a credit line secured by the deposits as well. This bundling, plus the convenience of banking by phone and an integrated statement—another innovation in Japan—was instrumental in growing the customer base from 8000 in 1985 to over 100,000 by 1989, a four-year compound growth rate greater than 85 percent. Admittedly, this was still a drop in the bucket. Tokyo and Osaka alone represented about four million households at the time with an average of $250,000 worth of financial assets. Nevertheless, the strategy was designed to secure a profitable niche for Citibank, and it looked like a very promising beginning.

Four years into the 1985 market launch, Citi boasted seven branches spread throughout Japan, with three more in the planning stage, including the relocation of its older branches to better locations. Word of mouth and direct-response ads in newspapers and magazines that offered toll-free telephone numbers and encouraged prospects to call had a positive effect on awareness of Citi. The direct response channel accounted for some 10,000 inquiries per month, and almost 10 percent of all transactions were being done over the phone. Citibank planned to extend its reach beyond Tokyo to areas where it did not yet have branches.

Citibank's consumer bank staff more than doubled from less than 200 full-time employees in 1985 to almost 500 by the end of the decade. Still, staff development remained an important need because of the competition for the best and most experienced banking professionals. Its niche strategy worked reasonably well during the first five years of its implementation, but there was concern that, as Japan's banks deregulated and learned how to segment their own market, Citi would remain a foreign interloper vulnerable to cannibalization by the more aggressive city banks. It was feared that, as in other industries, Japanese in banking would also learn fast and become formidable competitors even within the niche that Citibank tried to make its own.

Citibank knew that it would have to integrate and cross-sell the various retail businesses it had launched in Japan, including credit cards, consumer finance, and investment products. But this type of effective coordination went against traditional Citibank/Citicorp culture where business units were encouraged to compete with each other for the same target customers' business instead of creating synergies by cooperating with each other. So the question as to what market share they would be able to seize over the long run remained unanswered.

ACT TWO—CITIBANK DECIDES TO SELL ITS RETAIL FRANCHISE IN JAPAN

Citibank Japan: Retail Banking in 2014

As it turned out, Citibank continued to grow its retail franchise throughout the 1990s even after the bubble burst and Japanese economic growth came to a screeching halt. Branches and customer relationships were added under the guidance of an experienced Japanese executive, Masamoto Yashiro, who was brought over in 1989 from Esso Seikyu K.K., a Japanese securities firm. During the decade he was at the helm, Citi's consumer business in Japan expanded. In 1999 he left Citibank to Shinsei Bank where he promptly tried to recreate a strategy very similar to the one that had worked so well for Citibank.[2] But in 2008 he returned as Chairman and CEO of Citibank Japan. Under his leadership Citibank enhanced its position as the leading non-Japanese bank operating in the local market, particularly within the fiercely contentious retail sector, competing directly with the best of the Japanese houses. By the end of 2014 Citibank Japan could boast 32 branches throughout Japan and approximately 740,000 customer accounts. It had more than 1,500 employees.

The 2008 financial crisis hit Citigroup hard. The bank decided to pull its retail banking business out of eleven countries, including Costa Rica, the Czech Republic, Egypt, El Salvador, Guam, Guatemala, Hungary, Japan, Nicaragua, Panama, and Peru, as well as a consumer banking business in Korea. The ostensible reason was the bank's ongoing struggle to reduce its expenses.[3] On Christmas Day 2014 Citibank and Sumitomo Mitsui Banking Corporation issued a joint communique spelling out their sales agreement, slated to be consummated by October 2015.[4]

Forgetting Basic Marketing

What nobody seemed to notice was that Japan was the only one of the 11 countries that constituted a major first-world consumer banking market. Furthermore, Citibank had a century-long heritage in the country which it seemed to be willing to jettison for the sake of its short-term bottom line. Other units of Citibank in Japan had run afoul of Japan's financial regulators and its private banking business was forced to close down. But the retail banking business was untouched by the problems of these other units.

Citibank seemed to have forgotten the lessons from its own success in Japan. Its initial success in the late 1980s and early 1990s can be traced to the fact that it did not just blindly reproduce what the large Japanese banks did but instead it introduced a new hybrid. In fact, even as it was negotiating to sell its retail banking business to SMBC, it remained the one retail bank in Japan where it was relatively easy to transfer funds into and out of the country.

Citibank was in effect abandoning its customer base, who, while not as profitable as Citi had hoped they would be, was still a remarkably uniformly affluent cohort of customers for an institution that was not doing private banking. Despite the reassurance offered that Citibank's current retail banking account holders would suffer no decline or elimination of service after the handover, many of the bank's customers remained skeptical. After all, it was because of the parochial and bureaucratic nature of Japanese retail banking that they had opened their accounts with Citibank in the first place.

In part Citi had been worn down by the hostile oversight of Japan's financial bureaucrats and in part they were simply still trying to recover from the enormous losses incurred in the global financial crisis and its aftermath of 2008–2009. Still, one could easily speculate that before the decade was out the chief Citi decision makers back in New York would come to regret the hasty sale of such a long-standing franchise in such a rich and highly developed banking market.

DISCUSSION QUESTIONS

1. What are the entry barriers faced by Citibank in Japan? Often entry barriers can be over-come by joint ventures or FDI—how feasible are those options here?
2. Use the case to illustrate how protective barriers often mean that domestic companies are not very competitive against global competitors.
3. Discuss how consumers tend to be the ones to lose with protectionism. Are there any benefits here? Why might Japanese consumers not welcome a foreign bank offering new products and services?
4. Use the case to discuss how banking loyalty depends more on locking in and "stickiness" factors than emotional ties the bank. Why could this barrier hurt new foreign companies more than new domestic companies.
5. What actions could Citibank have taken to improve their retail business in Japan instead of selling it?

ENDNOTES

1. In 2000 DKB merged with Fuji Bank and the Industrial Bank of Japan to form the Mizuho Financial Group.
2. Yashiro's goal at Shinsei Bank was to earn the same 120 to 160 basis-point return on assets that the best-managed banks in the West earned, versus 30 in Japan. To get there, he strengthened Shinsei's consumer banking side by setting up telephone banking and offering mutual funds from Fidelity Investments and Goldman, Sachs & Co. And he initiated online banking for Shinsei. Brian Bremner, "The Japanese Banker Who Can Say No: Shinsei's Masamoto Yashiro is raising hackles in Tokyo," *BusinessweekOnline* (October 23, 2000).
3. David Henry and Anil D'Silva, "Citi pulls out of consumer banking in 11 countries, profit jumps," Thomson Reuters, 2014.
4. "Sumitomo Mitsui Banking Corporation and Citi reach agreement on acquisition of Citibank Japan's retail banking business," joint declaration by SMBC, SMBC Trust Bank Ltd. and Citibank Japan Ltd., Dec. 25, 2014.

TATA, A LEADING INDIAN CORPORATION, IS A giant conglomerate of 96 operating companies across a range of sectors, notably steels, automotive, chemicals, outsourcing and IT consultancy, communications, and luxury hotels. Its automobile arm, TATA Motors, was one of the companies within the larger group. With the opening up of the Indian economy in 1991, the TATA group was transformed into one of the most dominant and successful global corporations from an emerging market. The leader of this transformation, Ratan Tata, stepped down in 2012. By that time, the TATA group was a $100 billion global corporation operating in over 80 countries.

The TATA group's growth had come from spending over $20 billion in acquisitions of well-known global brands, often creating headline news. In particular, the daring 2008 takeover by TATA Motors of the UK's loss-making luxury car manufacturer, the Jaguar Land Rover (JLR) Group, had the press abuzz. It became Ratan Tata's crowning success at the helm.

GOVERNMENT SUPPORT

A major success factor for giant conglomerates like TATA has been in its management of the Government-Industry linkage, so vital in transition and emerging economies. The TATA group is known to have government support in India and leveraged this financially and politically in acquiring JLR. It was also able to capitalize on the long-standing ties between India and England. Independence in 1947 severed the colonial domination, but the long-standing familiarity between the two countries facilitates business negotiations and mutually acceptable arrangements.

TATA Motors bought JLR using Singapore as the base for funds syndicated by a consortium led by the State Bank of India and using a SPV (Special Purpose Vehicle) set up there. Funds came from Royal Bank of Scotland, the Governments of India and Singapore, HSBC, CITIBANK, other Indian State-owned financial houses, and Singapore's sovereign fund, TEMASEK.

Analysts argued that with a price tag of $2.3 billion TATA Motors overpaid for Jaguar Land Rover. It is true that JLR needed more cash injection from TATA and continued to lose money for another two years. Sales dropped to just under 72,000 units in 2009. The company was already saddled with a $3 billion debt and suffered losses of almost $468 million in 2009. Jaguar Land Rover was responsible for over $100 million of this loss. Newspaper reports indicated that JLR would need to close at least one of its plants in the UK. But TATA motors continued to invest money in Jaguar Land Rover amid a global downturn in the sales of luxury car brands. It finally succeeded in transforming the acquisition into a business that generated over $5.82 billion in 2012, with profits of over $533 million.

---

[1] *This case was prepared by Suresh George and Neil Pyper at Coventry Business School, Coventry University.*

HISTORY OF JAGUAR LAND ROVER

Historically separate car brands, Jaguar and Land Rover were part of Ford's premier automotive group (PAG) when acquired by TATA motors.

Jaguar was founded by William Lyons in 1922 to build motorcycle sidecars. The Swallow Sidecar Company later started building automobiles and moved to Coventry, switching its name to Jaguar after the Second World War. It produced premium saloons and sports cars, including the legendary XK120. Adding to Jaguar's reputation was its motorsport success in the 1950s, winning the Le Mans 24 Hours race twice with a C-type—in 1951 and again in 1953—and then with a D-type in 1955, 1956, and 1957. In 1961, the company launched what became perhaps the most iconic sports cars of all time, the E-type (see photo). In 1968 it merged with BMC (British Motor Corporation), which later became part of British Leyland and included Rover.

The Jaguar E-type

A succession of mergers followed until in 1989, the Ford Motor Company acquired Jaguar Cars for $2.5 billion. Ford was forced to sell Jaguar Land Rover in 2008 amid continued losses and to focus on its core U.S. business.

Today, Jaguar sells over 55,000 cars across four models; the XF, XJ, XK, and the R series. Sixty-six percent of total sales comes from the XF series followed by 11 percent from the XK series. Its main markets are in the UK, China, North America, and the rest of Europe.

The Land Rover was created in 1948 by the Rover Company. A series of takeovers and mergers followed through the next three decades, culminating in the formation of the Rover Group in 1986 and the takeover of its brands by BMW in 1984. Ford acquired Land Rover in 2000 for $2.96 billion and added both Jaguar and Land Rover Brands to its Premier Automotive Group until the 2008 sale to TATA motors.

Land Rover sells over 157,000 units across seven models; The Range Rover Evoque is the top seller (36 percent of total sales), followed by Range Rover Sport (19 percent), Freelander 2 (17 percent), Discovery (15 percent), Range Rover (9 percent), and the Defender (5 percent). Sales are predominantly from China (22 percent) and Europe (21 percent), the UK (17 percent), and North America (15 percent).

Declining sales of both brands continued until the Jaguar XK coupe, launched in 2006 (while still owned by Ford), began reviving interest in Jaguar cars. The model built on an aluminum chassis had a new design and styling that delivered on performance too! A two-door coupe was soon added and by 2008, the new successful XF model had arrived. The launch of the Range Rover Evoque in July 2011, a compact sport utility vehicle, redefined Jaguar Land Rover as a luxury brand that could compete with Mercedes, BMW, and Audi. The Range Rover Evoque or the "new Land Rover," as customers would now refer it, was designed to appeal to young, female, and new customers and sold 81,000 units in just nine months, contributing heavily to the profitability of JLR. Seventy-five percent of total sales are exports to 170 countries earning over $2 billion in revenue, with over 36,451 units sold in China alone.

TATA'S GROWTH STRATEGY

The TATA Motor's first moves focused on cost cutting and investments in new models. Cost competitiveness was improved, production was streamlined, and over 3000 jobs were cut in the company by 2009. Over $2 billion was invested into research and development activities and by 2010 a $12 billion investment project over the next five years was announced.

One of the main issues that had dogged Jaguar Land Rover was a lack of new models and new engines that could appeal to a broader segment. To solve this, TATA turned to low-cost centers in emerging regions like India and China. These regions provide the manufacturer with access to low-cost workers whose skills could be upgraded with training. They also provide a growing market for new products and brands, including luxury brands. With the rise in per-capita income in recent years these markets provide a vast opportunity at both ends of the market.

Most emerging markets like India and China have large and growing population segments at lower end of the market. Because of the extreme income inequality, they also have strong and growing demand within luxury segments, including luxury cars. In the case of China, the company saw a threefold growth in sales of Jaguar Cars. Using celebrity spokesperson Victoria Beckham, TATA also managed to sell $128,000 limited editions of the Evoque to affluent Chinese customers.

At a lower price point, the company also announced a joint venture agreement with the Chinese manufacturer Cherry Automobile to build vehicles for the Chinese market and an engine manufacturing plant for new models. JLR had tried several JVs before getting government approval for the JV with Cherry, another instance of drawing on favorable political treatment.

In India, TATA opened an assembly plant in Pune, India, where completely knocked down Freelander2 models were manufactured. This was planned as the hub for sourcing low-cost components for JLR's global supply chain. It was also intended to avoid Indian tariffs on fully imported cars—which can be as high as 100 percent. The Jaguar XF was also expected to be assembled in India following a government decision to raise import duties on luxury cars. Currently, India buys around 2000 cars a year and is expected to be another high-demand market.

TATA was considering a similar entry strategy for Brazil, where high tariffs had discouraged sales of its cars. Brazil was projected to be a growth market and to soon surpass Japan in automobile sales.

CHALLENGES TO SUSTAINED GROWTH

For Jaguar Land Rover, the future looks stable if new models generate the same levels of interest as the Evoque and new XK sportster in emerging markets. However, the last quarter sales of 2012 have been disappointing with total sales declining by 4 percent in September 2012. The slowing down of the Indian and Chinese markets in 2012 have also added an uncertainty to the stability of JLR's parent company, Tata Motors. Tata Motors currently depends on the company to provide more than 70 percent of its total global revenue and almost 90 percent of its profits.

Today, as sales of Jaguar Cars increase, it still contributes only 16 percent of total sales at the group. The rest comes from the Land Rover; the Evoque alone created over 1000 new jobs at the Halewood plant. In a continued economic downturn, sales of luxury SUV brands could be affected and impact cross subsidization of Jaguar Cars, reversing gains that have been made.

Scale is another issue. Jaguar Land Rover sells only about 305,000 cars as compared to 1.7 million units sold by BMW or 1.3 million units by Audi. Although Jaguar Land Rover is self-sufficient in generating cash, most of its profits are going into building of competences that are present with many its competitors. Will this be sustainable in a future amid declining sales? It is also a late mover into many emerging regions where competitors have entrenched positions.

A further shift of manufacturing into India and China could cause resentment and labor disruption in the UK, where most of its supply-chain cluster and technology cluster are located.

The continued dependence on emerging markets might turn out to be a risky proposition when these economies slow down. In addition, the continued recession in its traditional home markets of the Euro Zone and North America would dampen sales.

The development of new models and entry into newer markets or segments could potentially extend Jaguar Land Rover's success for years to come. But the rising cost of rubber and steel and other critical raw materials could cut into the profitability of the company as it prepares to compete on price in many segments in the market.

CASE QUESTIONS

1. Given India's growing domestic economy, why would TATA Motors not just focus on its home market?
2. What is the rationale behind acquiring well-known global brands?
3. What are the challenges for TATA Motors in managing the global brands? Is there an advantage for TATA in buying a British luxury brand?
4. Given the opportunities and threats listed at the end of the case, what would you recommend for TATA Motors as the next growth strategy?

Index

A

absolute advantage 41
acquisition 251
adaptation 330
adequate service 369
advanced countries 94
affluenza 21
agent 237
air express 418
Anglo-Saxon common law 130
anti-corruption laws 128
antidumping fines 138
arbitrage 395
artificial barriers 252
attitude scaling 217
augmented service 360

B

B24b 22
backroom operations 361
back translation 215
barter 391
basic service package 360
benefit segmentation 267
Big Data 219
bill of lading 239
Bitcoin 474
body language 149
B-O-P marketing 22
born global 333
bottom of the pyramid 22
brand equity 339
brand extensions 341
brand hierarchy 341
brand mis-fit 339
brand portfolio 341
brands 337
brand value 340
Build-Up Method 223

business regulations 131
business risk 120
buzz 20

C

CAGE 26
carbon footprints 104
cartel 387
causal marketing research 221
cause marketing 456
chasm, the 31
click-through rate 450
cluster analysis 267
communist 119
comparative advantage 41
compensation deals 393
competitive advantage 38
Confucian dynamics 151
consumer journey 488
consumer tourism 395
conversion rates 480
co-opetition 248
copyright and trademarks 100
copyrights 135
core benefit 158
core service 359
corporate social responsibility (CSR) 95
corruption 127
cost-insurance-freight (CIF) 244
cost-per-thousand (CPM) 449
cost-plus pricing 380
counterfeits 136
counter-purchases 393
countertrade 380
countervailing duties 138
country identification 206
country-of-origin (COO) effect 44
country-specific advantage (CSA) 42
credit card fraud 474
critical incident 368

cross-promotion 454
cultural adaptation 297
culture 147

D

damage control 457
Delphi method 224
demand characteristics 216
demographics 263
demonstration effect 383
descriptive market research 215
desired service 369
devaluation 378
developing countries 94
diamond of national advantage 43
diffusion process 30
digital advertising 439
direct exporting 236
direct observation 221
dispute resolution 134
dissipation of FSAs 252
distribution access 254
distribution alliance 248
diversification strategy 272
diversity 149
"Doing Business" reports 139
"dual channel" distribution 429
dumping 138

E

early adopters 483
ease of doing business 132
e-commerce 19
economic freedom 122
economic growth 92
economies of scale 338
educated elite 133
embargo 117
emerging countries 99
engagement 478
enlarged market potential 105
entry barriers 252

e-procurement 417
ethnocentric pricing 399
evoked set 279
e-wallet 475
exchange rate fluctuations 379
expected service 369
experience curve pricing 381
exploratory research 214
export 96
exporting 236
export license 243
export management company (EMC) 236
expropriation 124
extrapolation 224

F

fair trade 101
fair trade minimum price 388
family-owned companies 120
fast fashion 415
FDI in wholly owned manufacturing 249
final selection 210
fire-walls 475
firm-specific advantage (FSA) 42
first-mover advantages 32
FOB 239
focus group 214
focus strategy 272
forecasting by analogy 223
foreign direct investment (FDI) 125, 249
foreign sales subsidiary 252
forward contract 386
franchising 246, 369
free market capitalism 120
frontline operations 361
full-service wholesalers 410
functional analysis 391

G

gaming 485
gap model 368
gatekeeper 253

M

macro segmentation 267
manufacturing alliance 248
market potential 208
market segmentation 30
market share forecasts 226
masculine versus feminine 150
mass customization 331
media selection 449
mega-cities 89
mega-ports 419
message translation 448
messaging apps 482
micro-segmentation 267
mobile media 439
modes of entry 235
modular design 331
moment of truth 368
multicultural 147
multi-domestic 483
multi-domestic advertising 445
multi-domestic market 277
music streaming 484

N

national security 121
nation branding 47
natural barriers 252
new trade theory 44
non-bank intermediaries 474
nontariff barriers 254
non-verbal communication 149

O

offset deals 394
omni-channel 429, 475
online games 486
online radio 485
on-site promotions 444
open-platform multi-player games 486
opportunities 95

optimization 489
original equipment manufacturing (OEM) 247
outsourcing 104

P

parallel distribution 430
parallel imports 395
patent registration 135
patents 135
pattern standardization 442
peer groups 265
penetration price 379
perceived service 369
perceived value pricing 381
perceptual maps 274
perishability 358
PESTEL 83
planned command system 119
point-of-purchase (p-o-p) promotions 450
political risk 105
political risk analysis 125
polycentric pricing 397
population 88
Porter's Five Forces Model 54
preferential treatment 100
preliminary screening 206
premium price differential 381
press releases 455
price corridors 396
price discrimination 387
price elasticity 382
price escalation 240
price-quality relationship 395
primary data 212
private ownership 120
privatization 124
product buy-backs 394
product life cycle (PLC) 30
product line pricing 398
product placement 455
product positioning 30, 274
product space 274
profiles 478

prototype advertising 442
publicity 454
public utilities 121
Purchasing Power Parity (PPP) 91

Q

questionnaire 215

R

R&D alliance 248
real GDP 93
Regional Economic Communities (RECs) 105
regionalization 25
regional products 327
reservation prices 381
resource allocation 121
reverse dumping 138
roll-on-roll-off (RORO) 420
Roman law 130
royalties 246

S

sales forecast 224
salesman as a person 155
salesmanship 461
sales subsidiary 237
sampling frames 218
sanctions 126
scale equivalence 216
scope economies 328
search and destroy 137
search engine optimization (SEO) 491
search pattern 482
secondary data 212
secondary data sources 138
segmentation criteria 263
service delivery system 361
service quality 368
service satisfaction 368
servicescape 366
service standardization 361
shared manufacturing 248

silent languages 149
skimming price 379
social-democratic hybrid 122
social media 476
sponsorship 453
sprinkler strategy 272
stakeholders 476
strategic alliance (SA) 248
subsidies 99
supply chain management 416
surveys 215
sustainability 476
sustainable development 96
swap 386

T

target research 336
tariff barriers 254
test marketing 336
The International Court 131
third-country prices 138
tit-for-tat 126
title 243
touch-points 489
trade barriers 99
trade bloc 104
trade credit 240
trade deficits 99
trade fairs 241
trade negotiations 134
trade promotions 450
trade survey 220
trading companies 236
transferability 49
transfer prices 379
Triad 26
triple bottom line 96, 476
TRIPS (Trade-Related Aspects of Intellectual Property Rights) 100
trust 149
two-stage segmentation 267
type A negotiator 154
type B negotiator 154

U

uncertainty avoidance 150
uniform positioning 277
unrepresentative sample 214
upper funnel 479
usage experience 21

V

value-based segmentation 264
vertical integration 411
virologists 478
voice-based search 482

W

waterfall strategy 272
web advertisements 440
well-established routines 471
WhatsApp 478
wholly owned manufacturing subsidiary 236
World Trade Organization (WTO) 99

Z

zone of tolerance 369

CPSIA information can be obtained
at www.ICGtesting.com
Printed in the USA
BVHW012346161221
624229BV00001B/1